# Human Resource Development

4th Edition

**Jon M. Werner**
*University of Wisconsin-Whitewater*

**Randy L. DeSimone**
*Rhode Island College*

THOMSON
™
SOUTH-WESTERN

Australia · Canada · Mexico · Singapore · Spain · United Kingdom · United States

# Human Resource Development, 4e

### Jon M. Werner and Randy L. DeSimone

**VP/Editorial Director:**
Jack W. Calhoun

**VP/Editor-in-Chief:**
Dave Shaut

**Acquisitions Editor:**
Joe Sabatino

**Developmental Editor:**
Leslie Kauffman

**Marketing Manager:**
Jacque Carrillo

**Production Editor:**
Amy McGuire

**Manager of Technology, Editorial:**
Vicky True

**Technology Project Editor:**
Kristen Meere

**Web Coordinator:**
Karen Schaffer

**Sr. Manufacturing Coordinator:**
Doug Wilke

**Production House:**
Rozi Harris,
Interactive Composition Corp.

**Printer:**
R. R. Donnelley
Crawfordsville Manufacturing
Division

**Art Director:**
Tippy McIntosh

**Cover and Internal Designer:**
Joseph Pagliaro Design

**Cover Image:**
PhotoDisc

For permission to use material from
this text or product, submit a request
online at http://www.
thomsonrights.com.

For more information contact:
Thomson Higher Education
5191 Natorp Boulevard
Mason, Ohio, 45040
USA
Or you can visit our Internet site at:
http://www.swlearning.com

ASIA (including India)
Thomson Learning
5 Shenton Way
#01-01 UIC Building
Singapore 068808

CANADA
Thomson Nelson
1120 Birchmount Road
Toronto, Ontario
Canada M1K 5G4

AUSTRALIA/NEW ZEALAND
Thomson Learning Australia
102 Dodds Street
Southbank, Victoria 3006
Australia

UK/EUROPE/MIDDLE EAST/AFRICA
Thomson Learning
High Holborn House
50-51 Bedford Road
London WC1R 4LR
United Kingdom

LATIN AMERICA
Thomson Learning
Seneca, 53
Colonia Polanco
11560 Mexico
D. F. Mexico

SPAIN (includes Portugal)
Thomson Paraninfo
Calle Magallanes, 25
28015 Madrid, Spain

*For Barbara and Taina*

---

"Pass on what you heard from me . . . to reliable leaders who are competent to teach others." (II Timothy 2:2; *Message* translation)

# PREFACE

Employee skills and motivation are critical for organizational success. This has always been true, yet the pace and volume of modern change is drawing increased attention to the ways that human resource development (HRD) activities can be used to ensure that organization members have what it takes to successfully meet their challenges. While there is solid evidence that HRD works, it is not a "magic bullet." The challenges many organizations face are complex, and new dimensions, such as globalization and an increasingly diverse workforce, make it more difficult to ensure HRD efforts will succeed. Unless those responsible for training and development make informed choices about the content and methods of delivering the developmental experience, the results of many HRD efforts will fail to meet expectations.

Fortunately, there is a growing base of theory, research, and practical experience to support HRD efforts. We wrote this book to help students, HRD professionals, and managers at all levels take advantage of this knowledge and experience. We firmly believe that if they do so, they will increase their effectiveness, along with that of individuals with whom they work and the organizations of which they are a part.

*INTENDED AUDIENCE.* We wrote *Human Resource Development* to serve primarily as a comprehensive text for undergraduate and graduate courses in business, management, public administration, educational administration, and other fields that prepare individuals to train and develop other people. As such, the book:

- covers the entire field of HRD (as defined by two different competency studies by the American Society for Training and Development), from orientation and skills training, to career development and organizational development.
- provides a clear understanding of the concepts, processes, and practices that form the basis of successful HRD.
- shows how concepts and theory can and have been put into practice in a variety of organizations.
- focuses on the shared role of line management and human resource specialists in HRD.
- reflects the current state of the field, blending real-world practices and up-to-date research.

In addition to being an appropriate text for academic courses, this book is an excellent resource for HRD professionals. It can serve as a comprehensive introduction for managers and supervisors who have had limited (or no) course work or experience with HRD. Not only can they become better trainers and developers, they will become more informed consumers of the HRD efforts offered by their organizations.

*PEDAGOGICAL FEATURES.* We have included a number of pedagogical aids in the text to enhance student learning and interest. These aids include:

- *Learning objectives* and *opening questions* at the beginning of each chapter.
- An *opening case* in each chapter that places the contents of the chapter into a meaningful context.
- *Illustrations, examples,* and *boxed inserts* throughout the book to help readers better assimilate the information.
- A *return to the opening case* to provide closure and show how the chapter contents may be used to address the issues in the case.
- A list of *key terms and concepts* at the end of each chapter.
- *End-of-chapter discussion questions* to stimulate thought and provide students with an opportunity to discuss and apply the information in the chapter.
- *Exercises* have been included in every chapter to provide further experience with applying materials from the text, or to see how the materials relate to a real-world setting.
- A *glossary* of key terms and concepts is included at the end of the book.

Numerous examples from organizations, along with perspectives offered by organization leaders and HRD professionals, are used to reinforce concepts and demonstrate the importance of effective HRD to organizational success.

*NEW TO THE FOURTH EDITION.* The fourth edition of this book has been updated to reflect the thinking on HRD theory and practice that has taken place since 2001. Information from over 300 new sources has been added. Some examples of areas that have been added to the third edition are:

- An emphasis on the HRD roles and competencies identified in the 2004 ASTD competency study (Chapter 1).
- Updated discussion of the influences on employee behavior to include recent research (Chapter 2).
- An increased emphasis on individual learning styles and preferences, along with an exercise and link to an online questionnaire that readers can use to measure their learning preferences (Chapter 3).
- Revised discussions of organizational, task, and person analyses to emphasize key issues at each level of analysis, and (we hope) to assist readers in seeing the "forest through the trees" concerning how to conduct needs assessment (Chapter 4).
- Updated information concerning the use of particular training topics, methods, and media used to deliver training (Chapter 5).
- Updated coverage of major methods of providing HRD programs, with expanded emphasis on computer and Internet-based training, and a new exercise on designing e-learning materials (Chapter 6).

■ Condensed discussion of HRD evaluation models; a strong emphasis remains on the use of return on investment (ROI) and utility estimates for communicating HRD effectiveness. An integrative case has been added to tie together the concepts from Chapters 4 through 7 (Chapter 7).

■ Condensed coverage of stage models of socialization, with expanded discussion of ways to effectively use technology in orientation programs (Chapter 8).

■ Updated information on all aspects of skills and technical training, and a new exercise for students to measure the effectiveness of a class project team (Chapter 9).

■ An expanded focus on both coaching and performance management, and how these two topics should complement one another (Chapter 10).

■ Updated research on the need for, and effectiveness of, employee counseling and worksite health promotion programs to address such issues as alcohol and drug abuse, stress, hypertension, and fitness (Chapter 11).

■ Updated discussion of the shifts occurring in career development, including the changing employment relationship, new models of career development, team-based career development, and the individual's responsibility in career development (Chapter 12).

■ Discussion of recent thinking about the nature of managerial work, strategic management development, global management development, competency-based management education, and new practices in leadership development, including transformational leadership and experience-based approaches (Chapter 13).

■ Updated discussion of the concept of high performance work systems, as well as a new exercise applying force field analysis to a relevant current issue (Chapter 14).

■ A strong focus on the need for diversity training, as well as an expanded discussion of ways organizations can go beyond training to effectively managing diversity to serve the needs of all employees (Chapter 15).

We have worked hard to maintain the elements that made the previous editions a useful and meaningful resource to students and practitioners, including clear writing, a comprehensive approach to HRD, a strong research base, and a balance between theory, research, and practice. To promote ease of reading, yet still provide easy access to the reference materials, all citations are included as endnotes in each respective chapter.

We welcome questions, comments, and suggestions from users and potential adopters of this book. You can reach Jon Werner at the Department of Management, University of Wisconsin–Whitewater, Whitewater, WI 53190, by telephone at (262) 472-2007, or by e-mail at wernerj@uww.edu. You can reach Randy DeSimone at the Department of Management & Technology, Rhode Island College, 600 Mt. Pleasant Avenue, Providence, RI 02908, by telephone at (401) 456-8036, or by e-mail at rdesimone@ric.edu.

*ANCILLARIES.* A number of excellent supplements have been developed to accompany the fourth edition.

- **Instructor's Manual with Test Bank (0-324-31576-7).** The Instructor's Manual (IM) contains chapter outlines, sample syllabi, and follow-up materials for the opening cases and many of the exercises in the text. An all-new test bank, prepared by Richard Wagner of the University of Wisconsin–Whitewater, is available in both paper and computerized forms. The test bank has been greatly expanded and now contains numerous objective questions and short-answer essay questions for each chapter.

- **Lecture Presentation Software.** For each chapter we have prepared a computerized slide program using Microsoft® PowerPoint®. The slide show is designed to be used as a supplement in class lectures. Each chapter includes session objectives, key points, and selected chapter figures and tables, and presents the complete chapter as a dynamic lecture guide. The PowerPoint® slides were created by Wells Doty of Clemson University.

- **Instructor's Resource CD-ROM (0-324-31577-5).** Key instructor ancillaries (Instructor's Manual, test bank, ExamView, and PowerPoint® slides) are provided on CD-ROM, giving instructors the ultimate tool for customizing lectures and presentations.

- **Website.** A host of ancillary materials are available for students and instructors on the text website (http://werner.swlearning.com). For students, there are useful web links for each chapter, a glossary of key terms, plus other related materials. For faculty, there are outlines for each chapter, PowerPoint® slides available for each chapter, a test bank, follow-up information for the cases and many of the exercises in the text, plus other materials we hope will be helpful in using our text in the classroom. We hope you will bookmark this web page, and make use of the materials available there.

*ACKNOWLEDGMENTS.* We are impressed by and grateful to the talented and dedicated team put together by Thomson/South-Western. This was truly a virtual team effort — not a single piece of paper was transmitted in the entire process of creating the fourth edition. It was all electronic, and it worked great! We thank Joe Sabatino for his commitment to the project, and the South-Western leadership team for their support for a fourth edition of this book. We also thank Jacque Carillo for her superb marketing of the text. Leslie Kauffman and her staff at LEAP Publishing Services, Inc. deserve special thanks for expert guidance in revising the text for the fourth edition, and in obtaining all the needed permissions. That was huge! We are grateful to Amy McGuire for her skill in shepherding the completed manuscript through the production process. We thank Tippy McIntosh for the new look and text design for the fourth edition and Kristen Meere and Karen Schaffer for their assistance with the web links and technology features related to the text. We also thank Rozi Harris and her team at Interactive Composition Corporation for their expertise in turning drafts into page proofs. We thank Melissa Messina for copyediting, Susan Swanson for proofreading, and Lynn Grimes for revising the indexes. Experts all! Many, many thanks to all of you.

Jon Werner thanks his wife, Barbara, and his children, Hans, Noelle, and Abigail, for their love and forbearance during the latest revision process. What a year this has been for all of us! To my wife: you are the best — for me! To my children: as each of you develops into unique and delightful young people, I want to express again how much you mean to me. Never forget: Ich liebe Euch! I thank my mother, Dorothy, for her sacrificial love and support throughout my life. What a model you were of a successful career professional and loving mother. I thank mentors such as Ken Wexley, John Hollenbeck, and Dan Ilgen for shaping my academic career, as well as my uncle, Robert Davis, whose guidance and insights have meant so much to me. I am grateful for the encouragement I have received from my department colleagues, especially my HR colleagues: Peggy Anderson, Marcia Pulich, and Dick Wagner. I am also grateful for the support provided by my department chair, Yezdi Godiwalla, and my dean, Christine Clements. I thank Dick Wagner and Roger Yin for their valuable assistance with particular topics in the text, and Ruthann Guendert for her work on the project.

Randy DeSimone thanks his colleagues at Rhode Island College for their enthusiasm for this project. In particular, I thank I. Atilla Dicle, Crist Costa, and Halil Copur, who each served as department chairperson during the development of this book, for their support, especially by way of sympathetic class scheduling and arranging released time from teaching. My department's student assistants, Jen Richard and Beth Winsor, earned thanks for their help in doing some of the clerical tasks that were a part of producing a manuscript.

Randy DeSimone thanks his family and friends for their support. In particular, I thank my mother and father, Mary and Carmen DeSimone, for their continued love and support, and for their pride in the work that I have done. Thanks especially to my mother, who not only read the book, but put it to use in her work and encouraged her colleagues to do the same. How many management authors can say that? I am also grateful for the encouragement I have received from my brothers and sisters, aunts and uncles, and my wife's mother and sister. Thanks are due to John Fiore, Marjorie Roemer, Meg Carroll, and David Blanchette for their support, friendship, and wisdom during the writing process. Above all, I thank my wife and best friend, Taina, for her unwavering love, wisdom, and bedrock support. Thank you, Taina.

Both Jon and Randy would like to express our enduring gratitude to David M. Harris, our coauthor on previous editions of the book. Although no longer with us, David was instrumental in creating the kind of book you see before you. Even though it was the third edition that was "In Memorium" to David, we continue to lift up his memory with thankfulness for what he did to create the first edition of the book.

The publisher and the authors wish to acknowledge the following reviewers for providing extremely valuable input and suggestions on the development of this edition:

Sally Dresdow, University of Wisconsin–Green Bay
Selina A. Griswold, University of Toledo
Christine M. Hagan, University of Miami
Linda Seifert, Pittsburg State University
Vicki Spivey, Southeastern Technical College
Ernest R. Wren III, Columbia College

# Brief Contents

# CONTENTS

# CONTENTS

CHAPTER 5
## DESIGNING EFFECTIVE HRD PROGRAMS

## PART 3
## HUMAN RESOURCE DEVELOPMENT APPLICATIONS

## CHAPTER 8

# CONTENTS

## CHAPTER 14
## ORGANIZATION DEVELOPMENT AND CHANGE

## CHAPTER 15
## HRD AND DIVERSITY: DIVERSITY TRAINING AND BEYOND 612

# PART

# FOUNDATIONS OF HUMAN RESOURCE DEVELOPMENT

# 1

# INTRODUCTION TO HUMAN RESOURCE DEVELOPMENT

## Learning Objectives

*After reading this chapter, you should be able to:*

1. Define human resource development (HRD).

2. Relate the major historical events leading up to the establishment of HRD as a profession.

3. Distinguish between HRD and human resource management (HRM).

4. Identify and describe each of the major HRD functions.

5. Describe how HRD can be linked to the goals and strategies of the organization.

6. Recognize the various roles and competencies of an HRD professional.

7. Cite some of the contemporary challenges facing HRD professionals.

8. Identify the major phases of the training and HRD process.

■

## OPENING CASE

TRW Inc. has been a major global manufacturer of automotive and aerospace products. In December 2002, it was acquired by Northrop Grumman Corporation, which then sold the automotive business to the Blackstone Group in February 2003. TRW Automotive then became a publicly traded company in February 2004. Air bags, antilock brakes, and seat belt systems are among their leading products. One of the challenges that both the former TRW Inc. and the present TRW Automotive have faced is the fact that over half of their employees are not U.S. employees. TRW executives recognized that there was a need for more company leaders with global expertise. They wanted executives with expertise concerning issues in more than one country. They also wanted leaders who could help promote a "seamless" organization, that is, an organization that had fewer boundaries between functions, business units—and countries.

TRW had already established an executive development program that it called the Business Leadership Program (BLP). This program was aimed at developing the top 1 percent of "promotable" employees. The BLP addressed issues such as global strategy, leadership style and behavior, culture, and organization capabilities. The program used various techniques during the formal training portion, including lectures, discussion, individual projects, case studies, and team-building interaction. There was also an "action learning" module, where trainees worked on individual or team projects based on actual issues that the company was currently facing. Approximately thirty-five people at a time went through the BLP process.

An assessment made by TRW senior managers was that, in general, TRW management did not have the level of global competency that was required to manage their increasingly global corporation. In particular, the company's succession planning process had identified a sufficient gap between the global skills required and those possessed by their top managers. This led them to refocus their leadership program, which they renamed the Global Leadership Program (GLP). This was also connected to their performance appraisal, professional development, and succession management processes.

*Questions: If you were part of the leadership development team at TRW, what types of global or international issues would you like to see emphasized in the new GLP? What types of training methods do you think might be appropriate for training top managers and executives?*

*Why? Are there other things that you would include in addition to formal training (e.g., projects, mentoring, overseas assignments)? Finally, do you think it is necessary for a global leader to have the capacity to work outside of his or her normal comfort zone? Why or why not?*

SOURCE: Neary, D. B., & O'Grady, D. A. (2000). The role of training in developing global leaders: A case study at TRW Inc. *Human Resource Management, 39*(2/3), 185–193; Neary, D. B. (2002). Creating a company-wide, on-line, performance management system: A case study at TRW Inc. *Human Resource Management, 41*(4), 491–498.

## INTRODUCTION

Have you ever:

- *trained a new employee to do his or her job (either formally or informally)?*
- *taught another person how to use a new technology, for example, how to conduct an effective PowerPoint® presentation, or set up a wireless Internet connection?*
- *attended an orientation session for new employees?*
- *taken part in a company-sponsored training program, for example, diversity training, sexual harassment awareness and prevention, or career development?*
- *gone through an experiential training experience, such as a "ropes" course or other outdoor learning experience?*
- *completed some type of career planning project or assessment, for example, a vocational interest inventory?*
- *participated in an organization-wide change effort, for example, your organization was seeking to change its culture and move toward a flatter, more team-oriented structure?*

If you said "yes" to any of the previous questions, you've been involved in some form of "human resource development." It is often said that an organization is only as good as its people. Organizations of all types and sizes, including schools, retail stores, government agencies, restaurants, and manufacturers have at least one thing in common: they must employ competent and motivated workers. This need has become even stronger as organizations grapple with the challenges presented by a fast-paced, highly dynamic, and increasingly global economy. To compete and thrive, many organizations are including employee education, training, and development as an essential part of their organizational strategy. As much as 26 percent of the increase in U.S. production capacity between 1929 and 1982 has been attributed to education and training efforts.[1] In 2002, U.S. organizations identified as "training investment leaders" spent an average of 4.1 percent of their payroll on employee training and development, and averaged 62 hours of training per employee.[2] Human resource managers in large organizations ranked training and development as the most important functional area they had to deal with. This was followed in descending order by recruiting and selection, productivity and quality, succession planning, employee job satisfaction, compensation, globalization, and diversity.[3] In February 2004, Alan Greenspan, chairman of the U.S. Federal Reserve Board, stated that a "critical aspect of wealth creation in the United States, and doubtless globally, is the level of knowledge and skill of the population. Today, the knowledge required to run the economy, which is far more complex than in the past, is both deeper and broader than ever before. We need to ensure that education in the United States, formal or otherwise, is supplying skills adequate for the effective functioning of our economy."[4]

**Human resource development (HRD)** can be defined as a set of systematic and planned activities designed by an organization to provide its members with the opportunities to learn necessary skills to meet current and future job demands. *Learning* is at the core of all HRD efforts (and will be the central focus of Chapter 3). HRD activities should begin when an employee joins an organization and continue throughout his or her career, regardless of whether that employee is an executive or a worker on an assembly line. HRD programs must respond to job changes and integrate the long-term plans and strategies of the organization to ensure the efficient and effective use of resources.

This chapter provides a brief history of the significant events contributing to contemporary thought within the HRD field. We briefly discuss human resource management and HRD structure, functions, roles, competencies, and process. We also discuss certification and education for HRD professionals. We then describe several critical challenges facing HRD professionals. Finally, we present a systems or process framework that can guide HRD efforts.

## THE EVOLUTION OF HUMAN RESOURCE DEVELOPMENT

Although the term *human resource development* has only been in common use since the 1980s, the concept has been around a lot longer than that. To understand its modern definition, it is helpful to briefly recount the history of this field.

### EARLY APPRENTICESHIP TRAINING PROGRAMS

The origins of HRD can be traced to **apprenticeship training** programs in the eighteenth century. During this time, small shops operated by skilled artisans produced virtually all household goods, such as furniture, clothing, and shoes. To meet a growing demand for their products, craft shop owners had to employ additional workers. Without vocational or technical schools, the shopkeepers had to educate and train their own workers. For little or no wages, these trainees, or apprentices, learned the craft of their master, usually working in the shop for several years until they became proficient in their trade. Not limited to the skilled trades, the apprenticeship model was also followed in the training of physicians, educators, and attorneys. Even as late as the 1920s, a person apprenticing in a law office could practice law after passing a state-supervised exam.[5]

Apprentices who mastered all the necessary skills were considered "yeomen," and could leave their master and establish their own craft shops; however, most remained with their masters because they could not afford to buy the tools and equipment needed to start their own craft shops. To address a growing number of yeomen, master craftsmen formed a network of private "franchises" so they could regulate such things as product quality, wages, hours, and apprentice testing procedures.[6] These craft guilds grew to become powerful political and social forces within their communities, making it even more difficult for yeomen to establish independent craft shops. By forming separate guilds called "yeomanries," the yeomen counterbalanced the powerful **craft guilds** and created a collective voice in negotiating higher wages and better working conditions.[7] Yeomanries were the forerunners of modern labor unions.

## EARLY VOCATIONAL EDUCATION PROGRAMS

In 1809, a man named DeWitt Clinton founded the first recognized privately funded vocational school, also referred to as a manual school, in New York City.[8] The purpose of the manual school was to provide occupational training to unskilled young people who were unemployed or had criminal records. Manual schools grew in popularity, particularly in the midwestern states, because they were a public solution to a social problem: what to do with "misdirected" youths. Regardless of their intent, these early forms of occupational training established a prototype for vocational education.

In 1917, Congress passed the Smith-Hughes Act, which recognized the value of vocational education by granting funds (initially $7 million annually) targeted for state programs in agricultural trades, home economics, industry, and teacher training.[9] Today, vocational instruction is an important part of each state's public education system. In fact, given the current concerns about a "skills gap" (especially for technical skills), vocational education has become even more critical.

## EARLY FACTORY SCHOOLS

With the advent of the Industrial Revolution during the late 1800s, machines began to replace the hand tools of the artisans. "Scientific" management principles recognized the significant role of machines in better and more efficient production systems. Specifically, semiskilled workers using machines could produce more than the skilled workers in small craft shops. This marked the beginning of factories as we know them today.

Factories made it possible to increase production by using machines and unskilled workers, but they also created a significant demand for the engineers, machinists, and skilled mechanics needed to design, build, and repair the machines. Fueled by the rapid increase in the number of factories, the demand for skilled workers soon outstripped the supply of vocational school graduates. To meet this demand, factories created mechanical and machinist training programs, which were referred to as "factory schools."[10]

The first documented factory school, in 1872, was located at Hoe and Company, a New York manufacturer of printing presses. This was soon followed by

Westinghouse in 1888, General Electric and Baldwin Locomotive in 1901, International Harvester in 1907, and then Ford, Western Electric, Goodyear, and National Cash Register.[11] Factory school programs differed from early apprenticeship programs in that they tended to be shorter in duration and had a narrower focus on the skills needed to do a particular job.

## EARLY TRAINING PROGRAMS FOR SEMISKILLED AND UNSKILLED WORKERS

Although both apprenticeship programs and factory schools provided training for skilled workers, very few companies during this time offered training programs for unskilled or semiskilled workers. This changed after two significant historical events. The first was the introduction of the Model T by Henry Ford in 1913. The Model T was the first car to be mass-produced using an assembly line, in which production required only the training of semiskilled workers to perform several tasks.

The new assembly lines cut production costs significantly and Ford lowered its prices, making the Model T affordable to a much larger segment of the public. With the increased demand for the Model T, Ford had to design more assembly lines, and this provided more training opportunities. Most of the other automobile manufacturers who entered the market used assembly line processes, resulting in a proliferation of semiskilled training programs.

Another significant historical event was the outbreak of World War I. To meet the huge demand for military equipment, many factories that produced nonmilitary goods had to retool their machinery and retrain their workers, including the semiskilled. For instance, the U.S. Shipping Board was responsible for coordinating the training of shipbuilders to build warships. To facilitate the training process, Charles Allen, director of training, instituted a four-step instructional method referred to as "show, tell, do, check" for all of the training programs offered by the Shipping Board.[12] This technique was later named job instruction training (JIT) and is still in use today for training many workers on the job.

## THE HUMAN RELATIONS MOVEMENT

One of the undesirable by-products of the factory system was the frequent abuse of unskilled workers, including children, who were often subjected to unhealthy working conditions, long hours, and low pay. The appalling conditions spurred a national anti-factory campaign. Led by Mary Parker Follett and Lillian Gilbreth, the campaign gave rise to the "**human relations**" movement advocating more humane working conditions. Among other things, the human relations movement provided a more complex and realistic understanding of workers as people instead of merely "cogs" in a factory machine.

The human relations movement highlighted the importance of human behavior on the job. This was also addressed by Chester Barnard, the president of New Jersey Bell Telephone, in his influential 1938 book *The Functions of the Executive*.[13] Barnard described the organization as a social structure integrating traditional management and behavioral science applications.

The movement continued into the 1940s, with World War II as a backdrop. Abraham Maslow published his theory on human needs, stating that people can be motivated by both economic and noneconomic incentives.[14] He proposed that human needs are arranged in terms of lesser to greater potency (strength), and distinguished between lower order (basic survival) and higher order (psychological) needs. Theories like Maslow's serve to reinforce the notion that the varied needs and desires of workers can become important sources of motivation in the workplace.

## THE ESTABLISHMENT OF THE TRAINING PROFESSION

With the outbreak of World War II, the industrial sector was once again asked to re-tool its factories to support the war effort. As with World War I, this initiative led to the establishment of new training programs within larger organizations and unions. The federal government established the Training Within Industry (TWI) Service to coordinate training programs across defense-related industries. TWI also trained company instructors to teach their programs at each plant. By the end of the war, the TWI had trained over 23,000 instructors, awarding over 2 million certificates to supervisors from 16,000 plants, unions, and services.[15]

Many defense-related companies established their own training departments with instructors trained by TWI. These departments designed, organized, and coordinated training across the organization. In 1942, the American Society for Training Directors (ASTD) was formed to establish some standards within this emerging profession.[16] At the time, the requirements for full membership in ASTD included a college or university degree plus two years of experience in training or a related field, or five years of experience in training. A person working in a training function or attending college qualified for associate membership.

## EMERGENCE OF HUMAN RESOURCE DEVELOPMENT

During the 1960s and 1970s, professional trainers realized that their role extended beyond the training classroom. The move toward employee involvement in many organizations required trainers to coach and counsel employees. Training and development (T&D) competencies therefore expanded to include interpersonal skills such as coaching, group process facilitation, and problem solving. This additional emphasis on employee development inspired the ASTD to rename itself as the **American Society for Training and Development (ASTD)**.

The 1980s saw even greater changes affecting the T&D field. At several ASTD national conferences held in the late 1970s and early 1980s, discussions centered on this rapidly expanding profession. As a result, ASTD approved the term *human resource development* to encompass this growth and change. Influential books by individuals such as Leonard and Zeace Nadler appeared in the late 1980s and early 1990s, and these helped to clarify and define the HRD field.[17] Further, in the 1990s and up to today, efforts were made to strengthen the *strategic* role of HRD, that is, how HRD links to and supports the goals and objectives of the organization.[18]

There was also an emphasis within ASTD (and elsewhere) on *performance improvement* as the particular goal of most training and HRD efforts, and on viewing organizations as **high performance work systems.**[19] In 2004, ASTD had approximately 70,000 members in over 100 countries, and remains the leading professional organization for HRD professionals.[20] Recent emphases in HRD (and within ASTD) will be discussed more fully in the following section, but first it would be helpful to discuss the relationship between human resource management and HRD.

## THE RELATIONSHIP BETWEEN HUMAN RESOURCE MANAGEMENT AND HRD/TRAINING

In some organizations, training is a stand-alone function or department. In most organizations, however, training or human resource development is part of a larger human resource management department. **Human resource management (HRM)** can be defined as the effective selection and utilization of employees to best achieve the goals and strategies of the organization, as well as the goals and needs of employees. An important point to stress is that the responsibility for HRM is (or, at least, should be) *shared* by human resource specialists and line management. How the HRM function is carried out varies from organization to organization. Some organizations have a centralized HRM department with highly specialized staff, but in other organizations, the HRM function is decentralized and conducted throughout the organization.

The most comprehensive way to present the HRM function is to examine the activities carried out by a larger department, such as the HRM division headed by a vice president depicted in Figure 1-1. HRM can be divided into primary and secondary functions. *Primary functions* are directly involved with obtaining, maintaining, and developing employees. *Secondary functions* either provide support for general management activities or are involved in determining or changing the structure of the organization. These functions are detailed below.

**FIGURE 1-1**     **ORGANIZATIONAL CHART OF A LARGE HRM DIVISION**

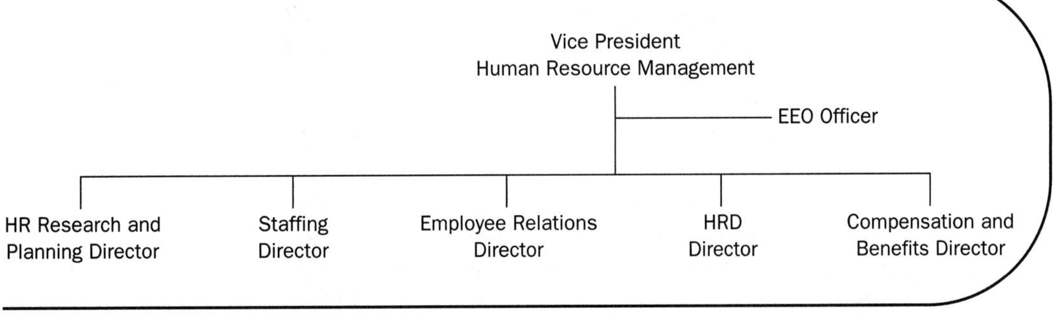

Vice President
Human Resource Management

— EEO Officer

HR Research and Planning Director

Staffing Director

Employee Relations Director

HRD Director

Compensation and Benefits Director

## PRIMARY HRM FUNCTIONS

- **Human resource planning** activities are used to predict how changes in management strategy will affect future human resource needs. These activities are critically important with the rapid changes in external market demands. HR planners must continually chart the course of the organization and its plans, programs, and actions.

- **Equal employment opportunity** activities are intended to satisfy both the legal and moral responsibilities of the organization through the prevention of discriminatory policies, procedures, and practices. This includes decisions affecting hiring, training, appraising, and compensating employees.

- **Staffing (recruitment and selection)** activities are designed for the timely identification of potential applicants for current and future openings and for assessing and evaluating applicants in order to make selection and placement decisions.

- **Compensation and benefits** administration is responsible for establishing and maintaining an equitable internal wage structure, a competitive benefits package, as well as incentives tied to individual, team, or organizational performance.

- **Employee (labor) relations** activities include developing a communications system through which employees can address their problems and grievances. In a unionized organization, labor relations will include the development of working relations with each labor union, as well as contract negotiations and administration.

- **Health, safety, and security** activities seek to promote a safe and healthy work environment. This can include actions such as safety training, employee assistance programs, and health and wellness programs.

- **Human resource development** activities are intended to ensure that organizational members have the skills or competencies to meet current and future job demands. This last point, quite obviously, is the focus of this book.

## SECONDARY HRM FUNCTIONS

Other functions that may be shared by HRM units include the following:

- **Organization/job design** activities are concerned with interdepartmental relations and the organization and definition of jobs.

- **Performance management and performance appraisal systems** are used for establishing and maintaining accountability throughout the organization.

- **Research and information systems** (including Human Resource Information Systems) are necessary to make enlightened human resource decisions.

## LINE VERSUS STAFF AUTHORITY

One of the primary components of an organization's structure is the authority delegated to a manager or unit to make decisions and utilize resources. *Line authority* is given to managers and organizational units that are directly responsible for the production of goods and services. *Staff authority* is given to organizational units that advise and consult line units. Traditionally, HRM functional units, including HRD, have staff authority. In general, line authority supersedes staff authority in matters pertaining to the production of goods and services. For example, suppose several trainees miss training sessions because their supervisor assigned them to duties away from the job site. Can the HRD manager or trainer intervene and force the supervisor to reassign these employees so that they can meet their training responsibilities? The short answer is no. The long answer is that HRD managers and staff must exert as much influence as possible to ensure that organizational members have the competencies to meet current and future job demands. At times this may require some type of intervention (such as organization development) to achieve a greater amount of understanding across the organization of the values and goals of HRD programs and processes.

# HUMAN RESOURCE DEVELOPMENT FUNCTIONS

Human resource development, as we discussed, can be a stand-alone function, or it can be one of the primary functions within the HRM department. An ASTD-sponsored study by Pat McLagan sought to identify the HRD roles and competencies needed for an effective HRD function.[21] This ASTD study documented a shift from the more traditional training and development topics to a function that included career development and organization development issues as well. The study depicted the relationship between HRM and HRD functions as a "human resource wheel." The original HR wheel from McLagan identified three primary HRD functions: (1) training and development, (2) organization development, and (3) career development. We will now discuss these functions in greater detail.

### TRAINING AND DEVELOPMENT (T&D)

**Training and development (T&D)** focus on changing or improving the knowledge, skills, and attitudes of individuals. *Training typically involves providing employees the knowledge and skills needed to do a particular task or job, though attitude change may also be attempted* (e.g., in sexual harassment training). *Developmental activities, in contrast, have a longer-term focus on preparing for future work responsibilities, while also increasing the capacities of employees to perform their current jobs.*

T&D activities begin when a new employee enters the organization, usually in the form of employee orientation and skills training. **Employee orientation** is the process by which new employees learn important organizational values and norms, establish working relationships, and learn how to function within their jobs. The HRD staff and the hiring supervisor generally share the responsibility for designing the orientation process, conducting general orientation sessions, and beginning the initial skills training. **Skills and technical training** programs then narrow in scope to teach the new employee a particular skill or area of knowledge.

Once new employees have become proficient in their jobs, HRD activities should focus more on developmental activities—specifically, coaching and counseling. In the **coaching** process, individuals are encouraged to accept responsibility for their actions, to address any work-related problems, and to achieve and sustain superior levels of performance. Coaching involves treating employees as partners in achieving both personal and organizational goals. **Counseling** techniques are used to help employees deal with personal problems that may interfere with the achievement of these goals. Counseling programs may address such issues as substance abuse, stress management, smoking cessation, or fitness, nutrition, and weight control.

HRD professionals are also responsible for coordinating **management training and development** programs to ensure that managers and supervisors have the knowledge and skills necessary to be effective in their positions. These programs may include supervisory training, job rotation, seminars, or college and university courses.

## ORGANIZATION DEVELOPMENT

**Organization development** (OD) is defined as the process of enhancing the effectiveness of an organization and the well-being of its members through planned interventions that apply behavioral science concepts.[22] OD emphasizes both macro and micro organizational changes: macro changes are intended to ultimately improve the effectiveness of the organization, whereas micro changes are directed at individuals, small groups, and teams. For example, many organizations have sought to improve organizational effectiveness by introducing employee involvement programs that require fundamental changes in work expectations, reward systems, and reporting procedures.

The role of the HRD professional involved in an OD intervention is to function as a *change agent*. Facilitating change often requires consulting with and advising line managers on strategies that can be used to effect the desired change. The HRD professional may also become directly involved in carrying out the intervention strategy, such as facilitating a meeting of the employees responsible for planning and implementing the actual change process.

## CAREER DEVELOPMENT

**Career development** is "an ongoing process by which individuals progress through a series of stages, each of which is characterized by a relatively unique set of issues, themes, and tasks."[23] Career development involves two distinct processes: career planning and career management. **Career planning** involves activities performed by an individual, often with the assistance of counselors and others, to assess his or her skills and abilities in order to establish a realistic career plan. **Career management** involves taking the necessary steps to achieve that plan, and generally focuses more on what the organization can do to foster employee career development. There is a strong relationship between career development and T&D activities. Career plans can be implemented, at least in part, through an organization's training programs.

## THE "NEW LEARNING AND PERFORMANCE WHEEL"

Recently, ASTD sponsored another study of trends affecting HRD, as well as skills or competencies that are required of HRD professionals.[24] As part of this study, Paul Bernthal and his colleagues developed a new learning and performance wheel (see Figure 1-2). Several things should be noted about this wheel. First, as

**FIGURE 1-2**   **LEARNING AND PERFORMANCE WHEEL**

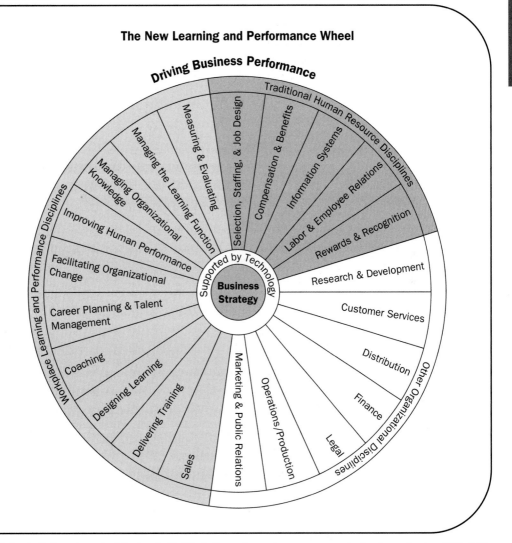

SOURCE: Davis, P., Naughton, J., & Rothwell, W. (2004). New roles and new competencies for the profession. *T&D, 58*(4), April, 26–36. Copyright © April 2004 from T+D by Davis, P., Naughton, J., & Rothwell, W. Reprinted with permission of American Society for Training & Development.

described below, business strategy should be at the hub or center of all HRD efforts. Second, the upper right spokes depict traditional human resource management functions, as presented earlier in this chapter. Third, the lower right spokes portray how other organizational disciplines, such as sales, production, and finance, also are major drivers of organizational performance. Finally, and most importantly for our purposes, the left side of the diagram depicts an expanded view of human resource development. You can still see the core functions of training and development, career management, and managing organizational change and development, as presented by McLagan. However, there is an increased emphasis on learning and performance rather than primarily on training and development. Indeed, functions such as managing organizational change and managing organizational knowledge are considerably broader than what has traditionally been viewed as the domain of HRD. We think this expanded wheel provides an excellent picture of what HRD is, as well as how it fits with other organizational functions. Next, we expand upon the notion of business strategy as the "hub" of the wheel, discussing the critical (though often underdeveloped) linkage between strategic management and HRD.

## STRATEGIC MANAGEMENT AND HRD

Strategic management involves a set of managerial decisions and actions that are intended to provide a competitively superior fit with the external environment and enhance the long-run performance of the organization.[25] It involves several distinct processes, including strategy formulation, strategy implementation, and control. At the formulation level, top management must first assess the viability of the current mission, objectives, strategies, policies, programs, technology, workforce, and other resources. Then, they must monitor and assess different aspects of the external environment that may pose a threat or offer potential opportunities. Finally, in light of these assessments, management must identify strategic factors (for example, mission, technology, or product mix) that need to be changed or updated.

The past two decades have seen increasing interest, research, and action concerning strategic human resource management.[26] The emphasis has been on more fully integrating HRM with the strategic needs of the organization. To do this, two types of fit or alignment are necessary. First, as just described, *external alignment* is necessary between the strategic plans of the organization and the external environment that it faces. Second, *internal alignment* is necessary within the organization. That is, the strategy of the organization must be aligned with the mission, goals, beliefs, and values that characterize the organization.[27] Further, there needs to be alignment among the various subsystems that make up the organization. Some areas that need to be addressed include:

- management practices—how employees are managed and treated (e.g., how much do employees participate in decision making?)
- organizational structure—how the organization is structured (e.g., how "flat" is the organization's managerial hierarchy?)

- human resource systems—how employees are selected, trained, compensated, appraised, and so on (e.g., how closely is pay linked to individual, team, or organizational performance measures?)

- other work practices and systems (e.g., to what extent is technology or information systems used to facilitate the work process?)

The value of this approach lies in looking at the organization as an entire system. All of the parts of an organization must work together as a whole to reach the goals of the organization. Some of the desired outcomes of such a high performance work system are increased productivity, quality, flexibility, and shorter cycle times, as well as increased customer and employee satisfaction and quality of work life.[28] As one example, Federal Express uses several different practices that foster high performance. Much of their employee training is conducted via interactive video instruction. A pay-for-knowledge system has been implemented that rewards employees who have completed the video training and passed job knowledge tests. A performance management system is in place that allows employees to track service performance, and an elaborate information system is used to monitor the progress of each item in the FedEx system. All of this is complemented by a survey feedback process that allows employees to "grade" their manager's leadership skills, as well as provide suggested solutions for any problems they encounter. As you can see, it is the effective synergy of everything working together that defines high performance work systems.[29]

A current challenge (or opportunity) for HRD professionals is to play a more strategic role in the functioning of their organization. Progress has been made in moving toward a more "strategically integrated HRD."[30] In particular, HRD executives and professionals should demonstrate the strategic capability of HRD in three primary ways: (1) directly participating in their organization's strategic management process, (2) providing education and training to line managers in the concepts and methods of strategic management and planning, and (3) providing training to all employees that is aligned with the goals and strategies of the organization.[31]

First, HRD executives should contribute information, ideas, and recommendations during strategy formulation and ensure that the organization's HRD strategy is consistent with the overall strategy. The HRD strategy should offer answers to the following questions: Are the organization's HRD objectives, strategies, policies, and programs clearly stated? Are all HRD activities consistent with the organization's mission, objectives, policies, and internal and external environment? How well is the HRD function performing in terms of improving the fit between the individual employee and the job? Are appropriate concepts and techniques being used to evaluate and improve corporate performance? Tom Kelly, director of worldwide training for Cisco Systems in San Jose, California, states that there have been dramatic changes in the HRD field since 1999. He adds, "This is our chance to actually achieve strategic partnerships within the organization."[32]

A second strategic role for HRD professionals is to provide education and training programs that support effective strategic management. Training in strategic management concepts and methods help line managers develop a global perspective that is essential for managing in today's highly competitive environment.

These issues are offered as part of the organization's management development program. According to a survey of HRD professionals by *Training* magazine, approximately 50 percent of organizations provide training in strategic planning.[33] Management education efforts (such as university programs, which will be discussed in Chapter 13) also place a heavy emphasis on strategic management issues. Increasingly, separate courses (or portions of courses) are emphasizing strategic HR issues and how these relate to organizational strategies and outcomes.

Finally, HRD professionals must ensure that all training efforts are clearly linked to the goals and strategies of the organization. Although this may seem obvious, unfortunately, it is not uncommon for the link between training programs and organizational strategy to be far from clear. As an extreme example, a medical products manufacturer, Becton-Dickinson, went through a major restructuring in 1983, in response to a downturn in its business. Before that, the company had offered a large number of training and education opportunities, particularly to its managers. After restructuring, these education and training programs were completely eliminated.[34] Some have argued that the reason why training is frequently the first thing to be cut or reduced in times of financial stress is that top executives fail to see a link between training and the bottom line.[35] In contrast, IBM has set up a Human Resource Service Center in Raleigh, North Carolina. The goal was to provide information and high quality service to over 500,000 active and retired IBM employees. An array of technology is in place to assist Service Center employees. This includes a website within the organization's intranet (called HR INFO), a call tracking system, and an HR Information System, which employees and managers can use to view and retrieve HR-related information, as well as process certain HR transactions (salary changes, address changes, etc.). However, the key factor in the success of this effort has been training. According to Bob Gonzales and colleagues, "Training Customer Service Representatives well [was] critical to the Center's success because they are the initial point of contact with the customer."[36] Service representatives are carefully selected, and then put through three weeks of intensive training, including lectures, role playing, and partnering with an experienced employee. Refresher training is provided throughout the employee's career, as well as additional training whenever new programs are offered. This example suggests how training can be linked to the strategic goals and strategies of the organization (in this case, a shift to a centralized HR Service Center). As we will discuss in Chapter 7, HRD professionals are increasingly expected to demonstrate that their efforts are contributing to the viability and financial success of their organization. The growing emphasis on strategic HRD is part of this movement to build a stronger business case for HRD programs and interventions.[37] This fully supports the placement of business strategy at the center of the learning and performance wheel, as presented by Bernthal et al. (Fig. 1-2).

## THE SUPERVISOR'S ROLE IN HRD

Supervisors play a critical role in implementing many HRD programs and processes. As we emphasize throughout this book, many organizations rely on line supervisors to implement HRD programs and processes such as orientation, training, coaching,

**FIGURE 1-3**

## ORGANIZATIONAL CHART OF A LARGE HRD DEPARTMENT

and career development. Especially in smaller organizations, there may be no "training department" (or even an HR department), so most HRD effort falls upon supervisors and managers.

## ORGANIZATIONAL STRUCTURE OF THE HRD FUNCTION

The HRD function, like HRM, should be designed to support the organization's strategy. Using the chart from Figure 1-1, Figure 1-3 further delineates how the HRD function might be organized within an HRM department. Alternatively, Figure 1-4 depicts how the HRD function might be organized in a multiregional sales organization. In this example, the training activities, except for management/executive development, are decentralized and other HRD activities are centralized.

## ROLES AND COMPETENCIES OF AN HRD PROFESSIONAL

An HRD professional must perform a wide variety of functional roles. A functional role is a specific set of tasks and expected outputs for a particular job, for example, classroom trainer or instructional designer. To carry out these various roles, HRD professionals need to possess many different skills or **competencies.** In their "Mapping the Future" study, Bernthal et al. described three areas of "foundational" competencies needed by all HRD professionals (see Figure 1-5).[38] Foundational competencies are depicted as falling into three areas: personal, interpersonal, and business/management. HRD professionals then make use of these foundational competencies as they develop particular areas of expertise. These areas of expertise

**FIGURE 1-4**     **ORGANIZATIONAL CHART OF AN HRD DEPARTMENT IN A MULTIREGIONAL SALES ORGANIZATION**

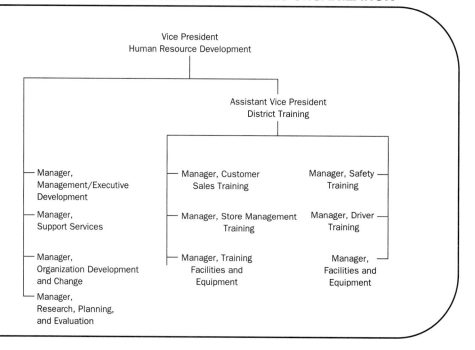

are shown in the middle of the pyramid (and correspond to the terms used to describe HRD in the learning and performance wheel shown in Figure 1-2). Finally, the top of the pyramid shows four key roles for HRD professionals: learning strategist, business partner, project manager, and professional specialist. The learning strategist is involved in the high-level decision making concerning how HRD initiatives will support the goals and strategies of the organization. The business partner works together with managers and others in determining how the HRD initiative will be implemented and evaluated. The project manager is involved with the day-to-day planning, funding, and monitoring of HRD initiatives, whereas the professional specialist adds his or her expertise in particular areas, for example, designing, developing, delivering, and evaluating the HRD initiative. HRD managers and executives are most likely to be involved with the learning strategist and business partner roles. Next, we will briefly discuss the roles played by two types of HRD professionals: the HRD executive/manager and the HRD practitioner.

## THE HRD EXECUTIVE/MANAGER

The HRD executive/manager has primary responsibility for all HRD activities. This person must integrate the HRD programs with the goals and strategies of the organization, and normally assumes a leadership role in the executive development program, if one exists. If the organization has both an HRM and an HRD executive, the HRD executive must work closely with the HRM executive as well. The HRD

**FIGURE 1-5**

# THE 2004 ASTD COMPETENCY MODEL

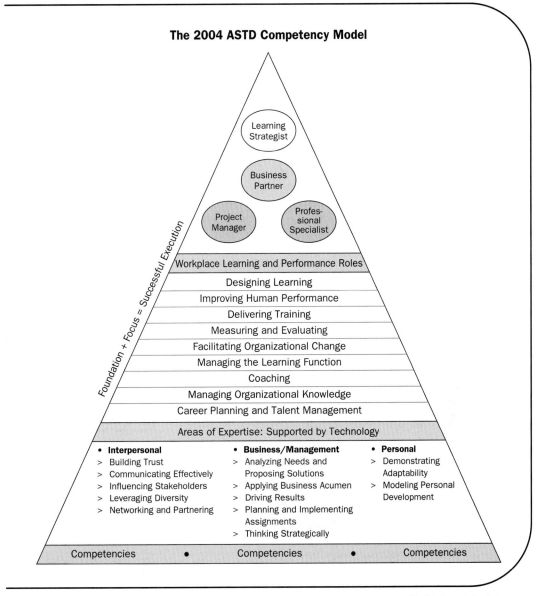

The 2004 ASTD Competency Model

SOURCE: K. Colteryahn & P. Davis (2004). Eight trends you need to know. *T&D, 58*(1), January, 28–36. Copyright © January 2004 from T+D by Colteryahn, K., & Davis, P. Reprinted with permission of American Society for Training & Development.

executive often serves as an adviser to the chief executive officer and other executives. The outputs of this role include long-range plans and strategies, policies, and budget allocation schedules.

One of the important tasks of the HRD executive is to promote the value of HRD as a means of ensuring that organizational members have the competencies to meet current and future job demands. If senior managers do not understand the value of HRD, it will be difficult for the HRD executive to get their commitment to HRD efforts and to justify the expenditure of funds during tough times. Historically, during financial difficulties, HRD programs (and HRM, in general) have been a major target of cost-cutting efforts. Unless the HRD executive establishes a clear relationship between HRD expenditures and organizational effectiveness (including profits), HRD programs will not receive the support they need. But how does an HRD executive who wants to offer a program on stress management, for example, compete with a line manager who wants to purchase a new piece of equipment? The answer is clear: the executive must demonstrate the benefit the organization receives by offering such a program. Evaluation data are vital to the HRD executive when presenting a case.

The role of the HRD executive has become more important and visible as organizations make the necessary transition to a global economy. The immediate challenge to HRD executives is to redefine a new role for HRD during this period of unprecedented change. According to Jack Bowsher, former director of education for IBM, when HRD executives "delve deeply into reengineering, quality improvement, and strategic planning, they grasp the link between workforce learning and performance on the one hand, and company performance and profitability on the other."[39] The HRD executive is in an excellent position to establish the credibility of HRD programs and processes as tools for managing in today's challenging business environment. A 2002 *Training* magazine survey found that average salaries for U.S. HRD executives ranged from $85,377 in central/plains states to $125,045 in the northeast.[40]

## OTHER HRD ROLES AND OUTPUTS FOR HRD PROFESSIONALS

As organizations have adjusted to environmental challenges, the roles played by HRD professionals have changed as well. According to McLagan, HRD professionals perform at least nine distinct roles, which are described below.[41] These roles are more likely to correspond to the job titles or job descriptions for professional positions in HRD.

The **HR strategic advisor** consults strategic decision makers on HRD issues that directly affect the articulation of organization strategies and performance goals. Outputs include HR strategic plans and strategic planning education and training programs.

The **HR systems designer and developer** assists HR management in the design and development of HR systems that affect organization performance. Outputs include HR program designs, intervention strategies, and implementation of HR programs.

The **organization change agent** advises management in the design and implementation of change strategies used in transforming organizations. The outputs include more efficient work teams, quality management, intervention strategies, implementation, and change reports.

The **organization design consultant** advises management on work systems design and the efficient use of human resources. Outputs include intervention strategies, alternative work designs, and implementation.

The **learning program specialist (or instructional designer)** identifies needs of the learner, develops and designs appropriate learning programs, and prepares materials and other learning aids. Outputs include program objectives, lesson plans, and intervention strategies.

The **instructor/facilitator** presents materials and leads and facilitates structured learning experiences. Outputs include the selection of appropriate instructional methods and techniques and the actual HRD program itself.

The **individual development and career counselor** assists individual employees in assessing their competencies and goals in order to develop a realistic career plan. Outputs include individual assessment sessions, workshop facilitation, and career guidance.

The **performance consultant (or coach)** advises line management on appropriate interventions designed to improve individual and group performance. Outputs include intervention strategies, coaching design, and implementation.

The **researcher** assesses HRD practices and programs using appropriate statistical procedures to determine their overall effectiveness and communicates the results to the organization. Outputs include research designs, research findings and recommendations, and reports.

A 1999 article on "hot jobs" in HRD focused on employees in four jobs where there was a high demand for HRD professionals.[42] Three of those jobs are found in the previous list: instructional designer (for a consulting firm), change agent (for a California city), and executive coach (working as a consultant to teach "soft" skills to executives). The fourth job, multimedia master, is not depicted in the list. This individual was trained in instructional technology and graphic design and is involved in designing online learning courses for an information technology firm in Arlington, Virginia. For more information on this particular position and individual, see the nearby box, "Master of Multimedia."

## CERTIFICATION AND EDUCATION FOR HRD PROFESSIONALS

One indication of the growth of the HRD field is the push for professional certification. According to a survey of over 1,500 trainers, approximately 60 percent expressed a preference for some form of certification.[43] This was probably based on an increasing desire to enhance the credibility of the HRD field. In response, ASTD is planning to pilot a certification program in 2005, based upon the competencies identified in its recent "Mapping the Future" study (Figure 1-5).[44]

For human resource management in general, there are two certification exams offered by the **Human Resource Certification Institute (HRCI)** (in conjunction with the Society for Human Resource Management). They are called the Professional in Human Resources (PHR) and Senior Professional in Human Resources (SPHR) exams. Both exams consist of 225 multiple-choice items that cover various HRM topics.[45] Fifteen percent of the PHR and 13 percent of the SPHR exam covers human resource development. To be certified, individuals must pass the test and have two years of HR exempt-level work experience. Students who pass the test, but lack the work experience, are certified once they have obtained the relevant work experience. As of December 2003, over 65,000 HR professionals have been certified with either the PHR or SPHR designations.[46]

## Master of Multimedia

Consider the following want ad: "Creator of award-winning training programs has immediate opening for dynamic individual in multimedia development department. Must have instructional design background and knowledge of Authorware or Dreamweaver. General business knowledge a plus." Although this may not have been exactly how this appeared in a newspaper, this captures the type of person that Centech Group in Arlington, Virginia, was seeking to hire. Centech designs training programs for other organizations and makes extensive use of the Internet and CD-ROMs for their programs. Therefore, they were looking for people with strong computer skills, especially knowledge of HTML and graphic design.

For example, Kevin Schmohl earned a master's degree in instructional technology from Bloomsburg University in Bloomsburg, Pennsylvania. Prior to that, he had worked in public relations and advertising. He was considered a "hot commodity" because of his knowledge of HTML, as well as software programs such as ToolBook, Quest, Designer's Edge, Authorware, and Director. However, what really set him apart was his ability to know when to use web-based training and when not to. "Until we get a totally computerized generation, we will always need some form of stand-up training," he says. As Kim Kiser writes, "Just because a company can put training on the Web doesn't mean employees will find those courses interesting or, for that matter, learn anything from them." What is most critical is to find course designers who understand training and instructional design issues, as well as the technological issues involved. Such people must "speak the language of both the training and information systems departments," says Kiser.

David Brinkerhoff, a recruiter of HRD professionals, finds that some of his most difficult searches have been for people like Schmohl who possess the necessary computer skills, and also understand how to get their message across to various audiences. "It's a very unique combination," Brinkerhoff says. "Those people are worth their weight in gold, if they can deliver what they say."

When Schmohl interviewed at Centech after graduation, he was offered a position as an instructional technologist for $46,500. When he got home later that day, there was a message from Centech saying they wanted him so badly, they were increasing their offer by $2,000.

SOURCE: Adapted from Kiser, K. (1999). Hot jobs, *Training*, 32.

Over the past fifteen years, the HRD profession has become better connected to and involved with the academic community. Three developments illustrate this relationship: (1) The *Human Resource Development Quarterly,* a research journal focusing on HRD issues has been published since 1990. (2) ASTD changed its governance structure to include a Professor's Network and an Academic Relations Committee. (3) Another organization has been formed, the Academy of Human Resource Development, to further advance scholarly research concerning human resource development issues.

HRD programs at colleges and universities are most often found in one of three academic departments: business/management, psychology, and education. The Academy of Human Resource Development lists HRD programs (and links) on its website.[47] The content and philosophy of these programs tend to reflect the founding professors.[48] Certain schools of business (or management) offer majors or minors in HRD, with courses in training and development, organization development, and career development. The SHRM Foundation has recently published a directory of graduate HR programs, and placed this on the SHRM website.[49] Some psychology departments offer degree programs and courses in industrial and organizational psychology and personnel psychology with specific courses in HRD. In addition to HRD classes, schools of education may also offer degrees and courses in fields related to HRD, such as educational technology, curriculum development, adult education, and organization development.

Another way HRD professionals can keep current is to examine the practices of leading organizations. ASTD has established a Benchmarking Forum for the purpose of identifying and learning about "best practices" among member organizations so that they can be adopted by other organizations. The benchmarking process involves a questionnaire that "helps to define the focus, criteria, and context for practices, and provides information about the incidents that led to adopting the practices."[50] The best practices organizations are selected at a biannual meeting of ASTD and members of the Benchmarking Forum. These organizations and a description of their practices are published in ASTD reports and highlighted in the professional journal *T&D* (formerly *Training & Development*).

## CHALLENGES TO ORGANIZATIONS AND TO HRD PROFESSIONALS

Many challenges face organizations as a new century unfolds before us. The recent ASTD-sponsored study mentioned earlier presented eight emerging workplace trends that impact HRD.[51] These trends are depicted in Figure 1-6. Along the same lines, Michael Hitt and his colleagues have identified increasing globalization and the technological revolution (in particular, the Internet) as two primary factors that make for a new competitive landscape.[52] They suggest a number of actions that organizations can take to address the uncertainty and turbulence in the external environment. These actions include developing employee skills, effectively using new technology, developing new organizational structures, and building cultures that foster learning and innovation. These obviously have a great deal to do with human resource development. We will add to and build upon their list to present five challenges currently facing the field of HRD. These challenges include (1) increasing workforce diversity, (2) competing in a global economy, (3) eliminating the skills gap, (4) meeting the need for lifelong individual learning, and (5) facilitating organizational learning. Each of these challenges and their potential impact on HRD will be briefly discussed in the following sections and further amplified in later chapters.

### INCREASING WORKFORCE DIVERSITY

The workforce has become increasingly more diverse, and this trend toward diversity will continue.[53] This includes increasing diversity along racial, ethnic, and gender lines, as well as an increasing percentage of the workforce that is over age 55.[54]

**FIGURE 1-6**                                    **EMERGING WORKPLACE TRENDS**

1. **Drastic times, drastic measures:** Uncertain economic conditions force organizations to reconsider how they can grow and be profitable.
2. **Blurred lines—life or work?** New organizational structures are changing the nature of work for employees and HRD professionals.
3. **Small world and shrinking:** Global communication technology is changing the way people connect and communicate.
4. **New faces, new expectations:** Diversity in the workplace continues to rise.
5. **Work be nimble, work be quick:** The accelerated pace of change requires more adaptable employees and nimbler organizations.
6. **Security alert!** Concerns about security and about the ability of governments to provide protection have increased individual anxiety levels worldwide.
7. **Life and work in the e-lane:** Technology, especially the Internet, is transforming the way people work and live.
8. **A higher ethical bar:** Ethical lapses at the highest levels in large organizations have shaken employees' loyalty, trust, and sense of security.

SOURCE: Davis, P., Naughton, J., & Rothwell, W. (2004). New roles and new competencies for the profession. *T&D, 58*(4), April, 26–36. Copyright © April 2004 from T+D by Davis, P., Naughton, J., & Rothwell, W. Reprinted with permission of American Society for Training & Development.

Effectively managing diversity has been identified as one of five distinguishing features of organizations that make it onto *Fortune* magazine's list of "100 Best Companies."[55] Diversity issues have several implications for HRD professionals. First, organizations need to address racial, ethnic, and other prejudices that may persist, as well as cultural insensitivity and language differences (this will be discussed in more detail in Chapter 15). Second, with the increasing numbers of women in the workforce, organizations should continue to provide developmental opportunities that will prepare women for advancement into the senior ranks and provide safeguards against sexual harassment. Third, the aging of the workforce highlights the importance of creating HRD programs that recognize and address the learning-related needs of both younger and older workers (this will be discussed in Chapter 3).

### COMPETING IN A GLOBAL ECONOMY

As U.S. companies compete in a global economy, many are introducing new technologies that require more educated and trained workers. In fact, in the United States today, over one-half of all jobs require education beyond high school. Thus, successful organizations must hire employees with the knowledge to compete in an increasingly sophisticated market. Competing in the global economy requires more than educating and training workers to meet new challenges. In addition to retraining the workforce, successful companies will institute quality improvement processes and introduce change efforts (for example, high involvement programs). The workforce must learn to be culturally sensitive to communicate and conduct business among different cultures and in other countries. Developing managers to be global leaders has been identified as a major challenge for organizations in this decade.[56] Developing globally competent managers will be discussed in more detail in Chapter 13. Additionally, employers are learning and implementing new ways of managing their employees. Approaches to managing change will be discussed in Chapter 14.

## ELIMINATING THE SKILLS GAP

As we discussed, for companies to compete successfully in a global economy, they must hire *educated* workers; however, at least in the United States, portions of the public education system are in need of considerable reform. Almost 30 percent of today's high school students fail to graduate, and employers must confront the fact that many young adults entering the workforce are unable to meet current job requirements. Even though the United States has one of the highest standards of living in the world, the Upjohn Institute for Employment Research reports that between 25 and 40 percent of hourly employees have some basic skills deficiency.[57]

This skills gap poses serious consequences for American companies. For example, how can trainees learn how to operate new equipment if they cannot read and comprehend operating manuals? Furthermore, how can new employees be taught to manipulate computer-controlled machines if they do not understand basic math? Obviously, the business community has a vested interest in education reform. There are some encouraging signs, however. For example, the Los Angeles public school system is offering a guarantee to employers, stating that if any high school graduate is found to be deficient in basic skills, such as computation and writing, the school system will retrain the graduate at no cost to the employer.

Other industrialized nations have made systematic changes in order to bridge the skills gap. For example, Japan and Germany, two of the United States' biggest competitors, have educational systems that do a better job of teaching students the basic skills needed by most employers. Among other things, Germany emphasizes vocational education and school-to-work transition programs, so that school-age children can begin apprenticeship programs as part of their formal education. These and other approaches will be discussed in more detail in Chapter 9.

## THE NEED FOR LIFELONG LEARNING

Given the rapid changes that all organizations face, it is clear that employees must continue the learning process throughout their careers in order to meet these challenges. This need for lifelong learning will require organizations to make an ongoing investment in HRD. Lifelong learning can mean different things to different employees. For example, for semiskilled workers, it may involve more rudimentary skills training to help them to build their competencies. To professional employees, this learning may mean taking advantage of continuing education opportunities.

This is particularly important for certified professionals who are required to complete a certain number of continuing education courses to maintain their certification. To managers, lifelong learning may include attending management seminars that address new management approaches.

The challenge to HRD professionals is to provide a full range of learning opportunities for all kinds of employees. One way that organizations are meeting this challenge is by establishing multimedia learning centers (sometimes on the organization's intranet). These centers offer a variety of instructional technologies that can be matched to each trainee's unique learning needs. Individual assessments can determine deficiencies or gaps in employees' performance capabilities, while also pointing out their preferred learning styles. For instance, self-motivated employees found to be deficient in arithmetic might be trained in an interactive video program allowing them to set their own pace. A multimedia learning center could also provide teleconferencing facilities for technical and professional employees to participate in a seminar that is being conducted thousands of miles away. These and other different approaches to learning will be discussed in future chapters. What is clear, however, is that whether they use multimedia or other training approaches, organizations must find a way to provide lifelong learning opportunities to all of their employees.

### FACILITATING ORGANIZATIONAL LEARNING

Organization development scholars such as Chris Argyris, Richard Beckhard, and Peter Senge, author of the book *The Fifth Discipline*, have recognized that if organizations are going to make fundamental changes, they must be able to learn, adapt, and change.[58] A survey of HRD executives reported that 94 percent of the respondents felt that it is important for an organization to become a **learning organization.**[59] Chapter 14 includes a discussion of how macrolevel organization transformation approaches can be used to help an organization adopt the principles of a learning organization.

Although such principles emphasize the organizational level, they also have implications at the group and individual levels. One challenge for HRD professionals is to facilitate the transition of traditional training programs to an emphasis on learning principles and tactics, on how learning relates to performance, and more importantly, on the relationship between learning and fundamental change.[60] To do this, HRD professionals must develop a solid understanding of learning theory and be able to devise learning tools that enhance **individual development.** These concepts and tools will be discussed in more detail in Chapters 3, 9, and 12.

### A FRAMEWORK FOR THE HRD PROCESS

HRD programs and interventions can be used to address a wide range of issues and problems in an organization. They are used to orient and socialize new employees into the organization, provide skills and knowledge, and help individuals and groups become more effective. To ensure that these goals are achieved, care must be taken when designing and delivering HRD programs.

Designing HRD interventions involves a process, which includes a four-step sequence: needs assessment, design, implementation, and evaluation. For ease of memory, this can be referred to as the "A DImE" framework (assess, design, implement, and evaluate). In this book, we will use this four-phase process approach to describe HRD efforts: needs assessment, design, implementation, and evaluation (see Figure 1-7).[61]

## NEEDS ASSESSMENT PHASE

HRD interventions are used to address some need or "gap" within the organization. A need can be either a current deficiency, such as poor employee performance, or a new challenge that demands a change in the way the organization operates (new

**FIGURE 1-7**

**TRAINING AND HRD PROCESS MODEL**

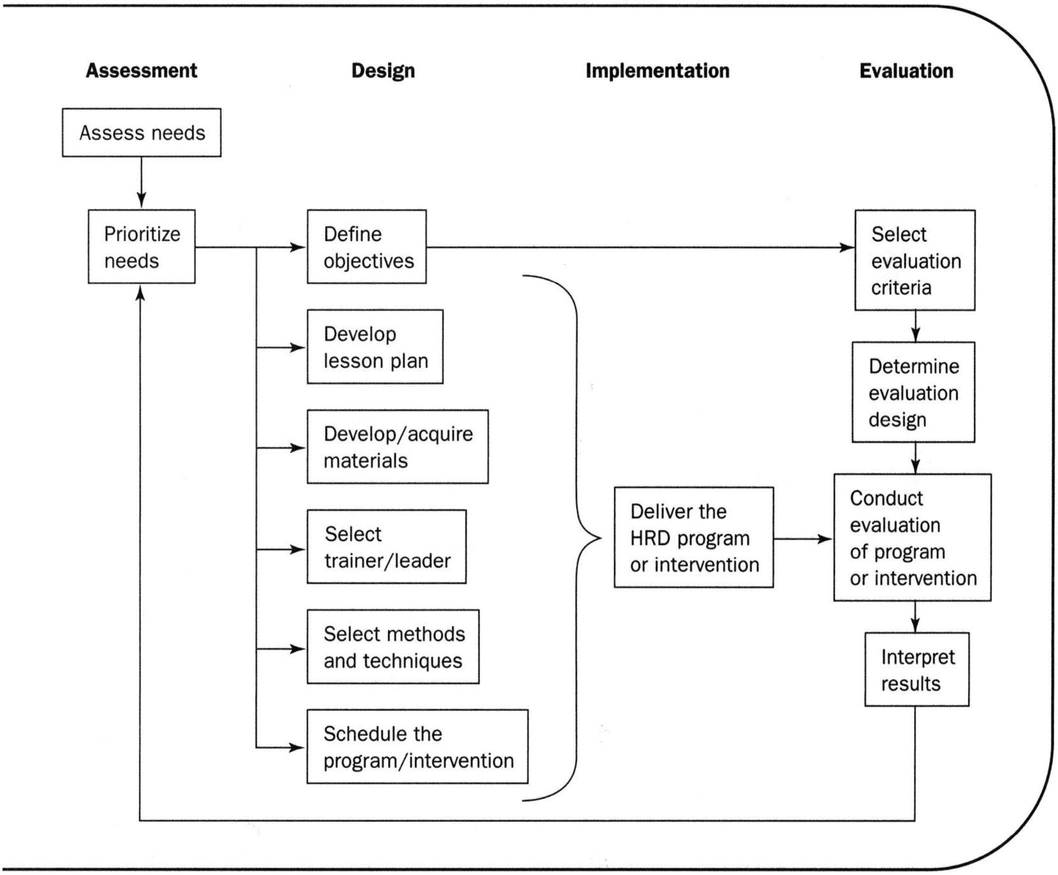

| Assessment | Design | Implementation | Evaluation |
| --- | --- | --- | --- |

Assess needs → Prioritize needs

Define objectives → Select evaluation criteria → Determine evaluation design

Develop lesson plan

Develop/acquire materials

Select trainer/leader

Select methods and techniques

Schedule the program/intervention

Deliver the HRD program or intervention → Conduct evaluation of program or intervention → Interpret results

legislation or increased competition). For example, in 1997, when the extent of sexual harassment and sexist behavior in the U.S. Army became clear, the Army added one week to its eight-week basic training for new recruits to provide training in the values that the Army felt were necessary to end this behavior and ensure that its mission will be fulfilled.

Identifying needs involves examining the organization, its environment, job tasks, and employee performance. This information can be used to:

- establish priorities for expending HRD efforts
- define specific training and HRD objectives
- establish evaluation criteria

## DESIGN PHASE

The second phase of the training and HRD process involves designing the HRD program or intervention. If the intervention involves some type of training or development program, the following activities are typically carried out during this phase:

- selecting the specific objectives of the program
- developing an appropriate lesson plan for the program
- developing or acquiring the appropriate materials for the trainees to use
- determining who will deliver the program
- selecting the most appropriate method or methods to conduct the program
- scheduling the program

Once the assessment phase has been completed, it is important to translate the issues identified in that phase into clear objectives for HRD programs. This should also facilitate the development of clear lesson plans concerning what should be done in the HRD program. Selecting the proper person to deliver the HRD program is also an important decision, and it can be difficult, depending on the resources available. If the organization employs a group of full-time HRD professionals, the choice will depend largely on the expertise and work schedules of those professionals. However, if the organization does not have an HRD staff, it will have to rely on other people, including managers, supervisors, coworkers, or outside consultants. Using such individuals raises a host of issues, including their willingness, ability, and availability to train, as well as cost issues.

The design phase also involves selecting and developing the content of the program. This means choosing the most appropriate setting for the program (e.g., on the job, in a classroom, online, or some combination), the techniques used to facilitate learning (such as lecture, discussion, role play, simulation), and the materials to be used in delivering the program (such as workbooks, job aids, web-based or web-enhanced materials, films, videos, Microsoft® PowerPoint® presentations, etc.). Inherent in these decisions is the issue of whether to develop the program in-house or purchase it (or parts of it) from an outside vendor.

Scheduling the program may not be as easy as it appears. Issues to be resolved include lead time to notify potential participants, program length and location, covering participants' regular job duties, and potential conflicts (such as vacations, busy periods, and facility availability).

The needs assessment may also reveal that training is not the ideal solution for the issues or problems facing the organization. It may be that some management practice needs to be changed, or that changes need to be made in another human resource practice (such as staffing or compensation). It may also be the case that a different type of HRD intervention is called for besides training, for example, a change in the organization of work, or a change in the focus on total quality or process reengineering. Such HRD interventions would not require a "lesson plan." However, other design issues occur with career management and organizational development interventions (and these will be discussed in later chapters of the text).

## IMPLEMENTATION PHASE

The goal of the assessment and design phases is to implement effective HRD programs or interventions. This means that the program or intervention must be delivered or implemented, using the most appropriate means or methods (as determined in the design phase). Delivering any HRD program generally presents numerous challenges, such as executing the program as planned, creating an environment that enhances learning, and resolving problems that may arise (missing equipment, conflicts between participants, etc.).

## EVALUATION PHASE

Program evaluation is the final phase in the training and HRD process. This is where the effectiveness of the HRD intervention is measured. This is an important but often underemphasized activity. Careful evaluation provides information on participants' reaction to the program, how much they learned, whether they use what they learned back on the job, and whether the program improved the organization's effectiveness. HRD professionals are increasingly being asked to provide evidence of the success of their efforts using a variety of "hard" and "soft" measures, that is, both bottom line impact, as well as employee reaction.[62] This information allows managers to make better decisions about various aspects of the HRD effort, such as:

- continuing to use a particular technique or vendor in future programs
- offering a particular program in the future
- budgeting and resource allocation
- using some other HR or managerial approach (like employee selection or changing work rules) to solve the problem

It is important that HRD professionals provide evidence that HRD programs improve individual and organizational effectiveness. Armed with this information, HRD managers can better compete with managers from other areas of the organization when discussing the effectiveness of their actions and competing for organizational resources.

## ORGANIZATION OF THE TEXT

The text is organized into three parts: foundation, framework, and applications. The picture we would convey is that of building a new home or other structure. First, Part 1 of the book, which includes Chapters 1 through 3, presents *foundational* material. Part 1 is meant to ensure that the reader has a strong base of foundational concepts before exploring the HRD process and the various ways that HRD is practiced in organizations. As you have just seen, Chapter 1 presents an overview of HRD, including its three major areas of emphasis: training and development, career development, and organizational development. Because all HRD efforts involve trying to bring about changes in learning and behavior, it is important for you to understand why people in the workplace behave the way they do and how people learn. These issues are the focus of Chapters 2 and 3. Chapter 2 explores the major factors that affect workplace behavior, and Chapter 3 focuses on how people learn, the factors that affect learning, and ways to maximize learning.

Part 2 of the book includes Chapters 4 through 7. In these chapters, we describe the HRD and training process, focusing on the activities described earlier, namely needs assessment, design and implementation, and evaluation. These chapters are anchored in the *framework* shown in Figure 1-7, and provide the "heart" or main "story line" of the book. Chapter 4 details the importance of assessing the need for HRD and the approaches that can be used to perform a needs assessment. Chapter 5 focuses on designing HRD interventions based on the information obtained from the needs assessment. Activities discussed in this chapter include establishing program objectives and content, selecting the trainer, HRD methods and media, and the practical issues involved in delivering the program. Chapter 6 emphasizes implementation issues, and highlights the different types of training methods that are available to deliver training content, especially the increasing use of technology to deliver HRD programs. Chapter 7 completes our discussion of the HRD process by explaining the importance of evaluating HRD efforts and ways that evaluation can be done to ensure that decisions made about HRD programs are based on meaningful and accurate information.

The remainder of the book, Part 3, focuses on particular topic areas within human resource development, that is, HRD *applications*. Chapters 8 through 12 focus more on individual-level employee development issues, from orientation to career development. Chapter 8 discusses the socialization process, its importance to employee and organizational effectiveness, and how orientation programs can be used to facilitate successful socialization. Chapter 9 describes skills training programs, including ways to ensure that employees possess the specific skills (such as literacy, technological, and interpersonal skills) that they need to perform effectively and contribute to the organization's success. Chapter 10 discusses the importance of coaching as an employee development process and explains how supervisors and line managers can successfully fulfill their critical coaching responsibilities. Chapter 11 provides an overview of employee counseling as a way to help employees overcome personal and other problems (such as substance abuse or stress) to remain effective in the workplace. Finally, Chapter 12 focuses on career development as a way to ensure organization members can be prepared to meet their own and the organization's needs over the course of their working lives.

The final three chapters in the book focus on more macro issues in HRD. Chapter 13 discusses how individuals can be developed to fulfill the multifaceted challenge of becoming effective managers. Chapter 14 explores how HRD can be used to prepare organizations for change, including ways to diagnose organizational problems and how to create and implement intervention strategies to improve individual, group, and organizational effectiveness. Chapter 15 closes the book with a discussion of the challenges organizations face as the workforce becomes increasingly diverse, and the role HRD can play in meeting these challenges and achieving the goal of full participation by all members of the organization.

We think you will find this to be an exciting and dynamic field. Everyone working in an organization of any size is impacted by human resource development. Whether you currently work in the field, some day hope to do so, or simply want to learn more about HRD, you will be impacted by the topics discussed in this book. Our hope is that you will study and learn the content of this book, enjoy the process (really!), and then apply what you learn to your own work experiences. The concepts and models in this book can make you a more effective employee, manager, or trainer/HRD professional. The text before you (along with the materials available on the South-Western website) are our part. Your professor or instructor will add her or his part. But the last piece of the equation is yours—what will you put into and get out of your study of the field of human resource development? Enjoy the journey!

## RETURN TO OPENING CASE

TRW faced a number of challenging issues as it restructured its leadership training to form the Global Leadership Program. Many of the issues it faced have been mentioned in this chapter. Your instructor has additional information concerning what was done at TRW to develop greater global competence among its top managers.

## SUMMARY

This chapter traced several historical events that contributed to the establishment of human resource development. Early training programs (such as apprenticeships) focused on skilled training. At the turn of the 20th century, more emphasis was placed on training semiskilled workers. Training departments as we know them today were introduced in many large companies during World War II. The establishment of the professional trainer led to the formation of a professional society (ASTD). This culminated in the 1980s when ASTD, in partnership with the academic community, officially recognized the professional designation of *human resource development*.

HRD, as part of a larger human resource management system, includes training and development, career development, and organization development programs and processes. HRD managers and staff must establish working relationships with line managers to coordinate HRD programs and processes throughout the organization. To be effective, HRD professionals must possess a number of competencies and must be able to serve in a number of roles. These roles will help the HRD professional meet the challenges facing organizations in this new century. These challenges include increasing workforce diversity, competing in a global economy, eliminating the skills gap, meeting the need for lifelong learning, and becoming a learning organization. The systems or HRD process framework (A DImE—assess, design, implement, evaluate) was presented as the major framework for promoting effective HRD efforts. The remainder of the book expands upon the concepts introduced in this chapter.

## KEY TERMS AND CONCEPTS

apprenticeship training
ASTD
career development
career management
career planning
coaching
competencies
counseling
craft guilds
employee orientation
high performance work system
human relations
Human Resource Certification
  Institute (HRCI)
human resource development
  (HRD)
human resource management
  (HRM)
HR strategic advisor
HR systems designer and
  developer

individual development
individual development and
  career counselor
instructor/facilitator
learning organization
learning program specialist
  (or instructional designer)
management training and
  development
organization change agent
organization design consultant
organization development
performance consultant
  (or coach)
researcher
skills and technical training
training and development
  (T&D)

## QUESTIONS FOR DISCUSSION

1. Do supervisors have HRD responsibilities? If so, how do they coordinate these with HRD professionals?

2. In your opinion, what HRD skills or competencies does an HRD manager need? How are these skills and competencies learned?

3. What qualities do you think an HRD professional must possess to be effective in an organization of approximately 1,000 employees? How might your answer be different for an organization with 10,000 employees? Support your answers.

4. Briefly describe an HRD effort in a familiar organization. Was it successful? If so, why? If not, what contributed to its failure?

5. A manager states that "HRD must become more strategic." What does this statement mean, and what can HRD professionals do to practice "strategic HRD?"

6. Which challenges to HRD professionals discussed in this chapter will directly affect your present or future working environment? What additional challenges do you foresee affecting HRD?

## EXERCISE: INTERVIEW AN HRD PROFESSIONAL

Conduct an informational interview with an HRD professional. This could be someone working in the areas of training and development, career development, or organizational development. Some of the questions you might ask include (1) what do they do in their job? (2) what has changed in their job over the past five to ten years? and (3) where do they see the HRD field going in the next five to ten years? Your instructor will give you guidelines as to the appropriate length and format for the written document you turn in for this assignment.

Visit http://werner.swlearning.com for links to informative websites for this chapter.

## REFERENCES

1. Carnevale, A. P., & Gainer, L. J. (1989). *The learning enterprise.* Alexandria, VA: The American Society for Training and Development and Washington, DC: Government Printing Office.

2. The American Society for Training and Development (ASTD) (2003). *State of the industry report.* Alexandria, VA: Author.

3. Langbert, M. (2000). Professors, managers, and human resource education. *Human Resource Management, 39,* 65–78.

4. Greenspan, A. (2004). The critical role of education in the nation's economy. Remarks at the Greater Omaha Chamber of Commerce 2004 Annual Meeting, Omaha, Nebraska, February 20. Retrieved September 4, 2004, from http://www.federalreserve.gov/boarddocs/speeches/2004/200402202/default.htm

5. Steinmetz, C. S. (1976). The history of training. In R. L. Craig (Ed.), *Training and development handbook* (pp. 1–14). New York: McGraw-Hill.

6. Hodges, H. G., & Ziegler, R. J. (1963). *Managing the industrial concern.* Boston: Houghton Mifflin.

7. Miller, V. A. (1987). The history of training. In R. L. Craig (Ed.), *Training and development handbook* (pp. 3–18). New York: McGraw-Hill.

8. Nadler, L., & Nadler, Z. (1989). *Developing human resources.* San Francisco: Jossey-Bass.

9. Steinmetz 1976, *supra* note 4.

10. Pace, R. W., Smith, P. C., & Mills, G. E. (1991). *Human resource development.* Englewood Cliffs, NJ: Prentice Hall.

11. Steinmetz (1976), *supra* note 5.

12. Miller (1987), *supra* note 7.

13. Barnard, C. (1938). *The functions of the executive.* Cambridge, MA: Harvard University Press.

14. Maslow, A. H. (1943). A theory of human behavior. *Psychological Review, 50,* 370–396.

15. Miller (1987), *supra* note 7.

16. Nadler & Nadler (1989), *supra* note 8.

17. Nadler & Nadler (1989), *supra* note 8; Nadler, L. (Ed.). (1990). *The handbook of human resource development* (2nd ed.). New York: Wiley.

18. Gilley, J. W., & Maycunich, A. (1998). *Strategically integrated HRD: Partnering to maximize organizational performance.* Reading, MA: Perseus Books; Grieves, J. (2003). *Strategic human resource development.* Thousand Oaks, CA: Sage; Yorks, L. (2005). *Strategic human resource development.* Mason, OH: South-Western.

19. Parry, S. B. (2000). *Training for results: Key tools and techniques to sharpen trainers' skills.* Alexandria, VA: The American Society for Training and Development; Van Buren, M. E., & Werner, J. M. (1996). High performance work systems. *Business & Economic Review, 43–1,* 15–23; Willmore, J. (2004). The future of performance. *T&D, 58*(8), 26–31.

20. The American Society for Training and Development (2004). *About ASTD.* Retrieved September 4, 2004, from http://www.astd.org/ASTD/About_ASTD

21. McLagan, P. A. (1989). Models for HRD practice. *Training and Development Journal, 41*(9), 49–59.

22. Beckhard, R. (1969). *Organization development: Strategies and models.* Reading, MA: Addison-Wesley; Alderfer, C. P. (1977). Organization development. *Annual Review of Psychology, 28,* 197–223; Beer, M., & Walton, E. (1990). Developing the competitive organization: Interventions and strategies. *American Psychologist, 45,* 154–161.

23. Greenhaus, J. H. (1987). *Career management* (p. 9). Hinsdale, IL: Dryden Press.

24. Bernthal, P. R., Colteryahn, K., Davis, P., Naughton, J., Rothwell, W. J., & Wellins, R. (2004). *Mapping the future: Shaping new workplace learning and performance competencies.* Alexandria, VA: The American Society for Training and Development.

25. Wheelen, T. L., & Hunger, J. D. (1986). *Strategic management and business policy* (2nd ed.). Reading, MA: Addison-Wesley; Daft, R. L. (1995). *Understanding management.* Fort Worth, TX: Dryden Press.

26. Dyer, L. (1984). Studying strategy in human resource management: An approach and an agenda. *Industrial Relations, 23*(2), 156–169; Schuler, R. S. (1992). Strategic human resources management: Linking the people with the strategic needs of the business. *Organizational Dynamics, 21,* 18–32; Ulrich, D. (1997). *Human resource champions.* Boston: Harvard Business School Press; Bamberger, P., & Meshoulam, I. (2000). *Human resource strategy: Formulation, implementation, and impact.* Thousand Oaks, CA: Sage.

27. Van Buren & Werner (1996), *supra* note 19.

28. *Ibid.*

29. *Ibid.*

30. Gilley & Maycunich (1998), *supra* note 18; Rothwell, W. J., & Kazanas, H. C. (2004). *The strategic development of talent* (2nd ed.). Amherst, MA: HRD Press; Littlefield, D., & Welch, J. (1996, April 4). Trainers focus on a more strategic role. *People Management, 2*, 11–12.

31. Torraco, R. J., & Swanson R. A. (1995). The strategic roles of human resource development. *Human Resource Planning, 18*(4), 10–29.

32. Ellis, K., & Gale, S. F. (2001). A seat at the table. *Training, 38*(3), March, 90–97.

33. Industry Report. (1996). Who's learning what? *Training, 33*(10), 55–66.

34. Williamson, A. D. (1995). *Becton-Dickinson (C): Human resource function.* Boston: Harvard Business School, Case 9-491-154.

35. Watad, M., & Ospina, S. (1999). Integrated managerial training: A program for strategic management development. *Public Personnel Management, 28*, 185–196.

36. Gonzales, B., Ellis, Y. M., Riffel, P. J., & Yager, D. (1999). Training at IBM's human resource center: Linking people, technology, and HR processes. *Human Resource Management, 38*, 135–142.

37. Phillips, J. J. (1996). How much is the training worth? *Training & Development, 50*(4), 20–24.

38. Bernthal et al. (2004), *supra* note 24.

39. Sorohan, E. G. (1995). Basic skills training on the rise. *Training & Development, 49*(5), 12–13; Gonzales et al. (1999), *supra* note 36.

40. Schettler, J. (2002). Withering heights: 21st annual salary survey. *Training, 39*(11), 36–48.

41. McLagan, P. (1996). Great ideas revisited. *Training & Development, 50*(1), 60–65.

42. Kiser, K. (1999). Hot jobs. *Training*, August, 28–35.

43. Lee, C. (1986). Certification for trainers: Thumbs up. *Training, 23*(11), 56–64.

44. Bernthal et al. (2004), *supra* note 24; Rothwell, W., & Wellins, R. (2004). Mapping your future: Putting new competencies to work for you. *T&D, 58*(5), 94–101.

45. HRCI PHR & SPHR Certification Handbook. Accessed on October 7, 2004 at: http://www.hrci.org/handbook/phrsphr_2004.pdf

46. HR Certification Institute (HRCI) (2004). *Certification count, by area.* Retrieved August 30, 2004, from http://www.hrci.org/directory/stats.html

47. http://www.ahrd.org/ahrd/

48. Gerber, B. (1987). HRD degrees. *Training, 24*(7), 49.

49. http://www.shrm.org/foundation/directory/

50. Overmeyer-Day, L., & Benson, G. (1996). Training success stories. *Training & Development, 50*(6), 24–29.

51. Bernthal et al. (2004), *supra* note 24; Colteryahn, K., & Davis, P. (2004). Eight trends you need to know. *T&D, 58*(1), 28–36.

52. Hitt, M. A., Keats, B. W., & DeMarie, S. M. (1998). Navigating in the new competitive landscape: Building strategic flexibility and competitive advantage in the 21st century. *Academy of Management Executive, 12,* 22–42.

53. Judy, R. W., & D'Amico, C. (1997). *Workforce 2020: Work and workers in the 21st century.* Indianapolis, IN: Hudson Institute.

54. *Ibid.*

55. Joyce, K. (2003). Lessons for employers from *Fortune's* "100 Best." *Business Horizons, 46*(2), 77–84.

56. Black, J. S., & Gregersen, H. B. (2000). High impact training: Forging leaders for the global frontier. *Human Resource Management, 39*(2/3), 173-184; Dotlich, D. L., & Noel, J. L. (1998). *Action learning: How the world's top companies are re-creating their leaders and themselves.* San Francisco: Jossey-Bass.

57. Sorohan, E. G. (1995). High performance skill survey. *Training & Development, 49*(5), 9–10.

58. Senge, P. M. (1990). *The fifth discipline: The art & practice of the learning organization.* New York: Doubleday.

59. Gephart, M. A., Marsick, V. J., Van Buren, M. E., & Spiro, M. S. (1996). Learning organizations come alive. *Training & Development, 50*(12), 35–45.

60. Argyris, C. (1994). The future of workplace learning and performance. *Training & Development, 48*(5), S36–S47.

61. Goldstein, I. L. (1974). *Training: Program development and evaluation.* Monterey, CA: Brooks/Cole.

62. Goldwasser, D. (2001). Beyond ROI. *Training, 38*(1), 82–87.

# INFLUENCES ON EMPLOYEE BEHAVIOR

## Learning Objectives

*After reading this chapter, you should be able to:*

1. Identify the major external and internal factors that influence employee behavior.

2. Describe two primary types of outcomes that may result from behavior and tell how they may influence future behavior.

3. State how a supervisor's leadership and expectations for employees can affect their behavior.

4. Recognize the impact that coworkers and the organization itself have on employee behavior.

5. Define motivation and describe the main approaches to understanding motivation at work.

6. Discuss how knowledge, skill, ability, and attitudes influence employee behavior.

**OPENING CASE**

United Technologies Corporation (UTC) is a Fortune 100 conglomerate with headquarters in Hartford, Connecticut. In 2003, it had a worldwide workforce of over 200,000 employees.[1] Some of its major subsidiaries include Pratt & Whitney (jet engines), Carrier (air-conditioning systems), Otis (elevators), Hamilton Sundstrand (aerospace and industrial equipment), Sikorsky (helicopters), and the recently acquired Chubb security group. Since 1990, it has undergone several major reductions of its U.S. workforce, with a substantial increase in its workforce outside the United States. George David, CEO of UTC, stated, "We and others create jobs overseas fundamentally for market access, to extend our global market leadership and thereby to make our company stronger and to assure employment at home." Later, he stated that "we cannot guarantee anyone a job, but we are nonetheless obliged to provide employees reasonable opportunities to reestablish themselves, ideally on more favorable conditions, in the event of job loss." One of the commitments made by UTC was to provide tuition reimbursement for undergraduate or graduate courses taken by their employees.[2]

The Pratt & Whitney subsidiary has been hit hard by the overall decline in the world aerospace markets. It has approximately 31,000 employees worldwide, with roughly 40 percent of these employees working in Connecticut. In 2000, Pratt & Whitney announced the elimination of up to 1,700 jobs, primarily in Connecticut. This is in addition to the 3,500 jobs cut since 1998 as part of its restructuring.[3] An obvious challenge in the midst of such changes is the maintenance of employee skills and morale.

*Questions: What happens to employee training and development efforts in the midst of a downsizing of this magnitude? Will employees take advantage of such a tuition reimbursement program during restructuring? What happens to employees who are laid off at the time they are taking college classes? Can Pratt & Whitney (and UTC) maintain their commitment to tuition reimbursement in such an environment?*

[1]SOURCES: Hoover's on-line (2004). Retrieved September 6, 2004, from http://www.hoovers.com/pratt-&-whitney/—ID__99062—/free-co-factsheet.xhtml

[2]George David (1995). Remarks on restructuring. National Press Club, December 14, 1995, http://www.utc.com/company/ARCHIVE/gdavid2.htm

[3]Pratt & Whitney to reduce manufacturing workforce, http://www.pratt-whitney.com/news/2000/0121.html

# INTRODUCTION

Have you ever wondered:

- *why a coworker behaves the way he or she does?*
- *why people so often live up (or down) to the expectations that others have for them?*
- *why managers seem to develop relationships of different quality with different subordinates?*

- *why some work teams develop more trust and cohesiveness than others?*
- *how motivation influences employee behavior?*
- *whether there are some general frameworks or models that can help in understanding the various influences on employee behavior?*

The overarching goal of Human Resources Development interventions is to assist employees *and* organizations in attaining their goals. HRD professionals can help employees meet their personal goals by providing programs and interventions that promote individual development, for example, career development activities, mentoring, and formal training and educational opportunities. Concerning organizational goals, the ultimate objective of most, if not all, HRD programs is to *improve organizational performance.* HRD efforts are certainly not the only contributors to organizational performance; however, they are increasingly recognized as a critical component of organizational success.[1] Further, a major focus of most HRD interventions is an effort to *change employee behavior.* That is, the hope is that providing employees with the skills and behaviors they need to perform successfully should lead to the greatest accomplishment of both employee and organizational goals. Thus, the field of HRD has always had a strong focus on employee behavior. However, to change any behavior, we must first understand the factors that cause employees to behave the way that they do. Armed with this knowledge, we can more accurately diagnose performance problems, understand what makes effective performance possible, and design HRD programs to foster the behavior we want.

Identifying the causes of employee behavior is no easy task. The factors contributing to any behavior are numerous, complex, and difficult to ascertain. Yet, however difficult this may be, a thorough understanding of employee behavior and its causes is critical for any HRD program to be effective. The purpose of this chapter is to introduce readers to the major factors influencing employee behavior and their implications for HRD. Students with backgrounds in organizational behavior or applied psychology will find that this chapter provides an important review and an opportunity to relate these issues to topics within HRD.

## MODEL OF EMPLOYEE BEHAVIOR

The model of employee behavior shown in Figure 2-1 presents what we consider to be the key factors affecting employee behavior and their corresponding relationships. It includes two main categories: (1) *external forces* — that is, those found in the *external environment* (outside the organization), as well as in the *work environment* (inside the organization), including leadership, aspects of the organization itself, coworkers, and the outcomes of performance (such as praise); and (2) *internal forces* — that is, those within the employee, including motivation, attitudes, and KSAs (knowledge, skills, and abilities). The model assumes that external and internal forces interact or combine to produce a given behavior, and that employee behavior has a direct relationship to the personal and organizational outcomes that are obtained. Although it may be possible in some cases to trace the cause of a behavior to one or two dominant forces, we believe that overall patterns of behavior can best be explained by the combination of many factors.

FIGURE 2-1

# MODEL OF EMPLOYEE BEHAVIOR

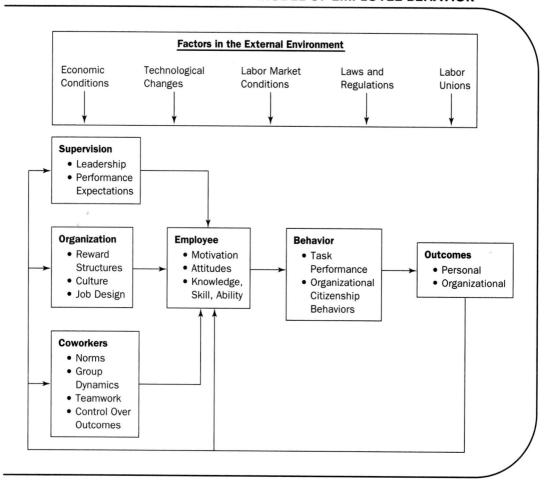

The model is relatively simple for purposes of clarity and relevance to HRD. Our goal is not to cover all possible causes for employee behavior, but to include only those most critical to designing, delivering, and using HRD programs. Additional relevant concepts will be presented in later chapters. The remainder of this chapter will focus on the elements contained within the model.

## MAJOR CATEGORIES OF EMPLOYEE BEHAVIOR

If HRD efforts are primarily intended to change employee behavior, then it is useful to first ask what types of behavior they are intended to change. Recent research strongly suggests that individual performance is multidimensional.[2] Although many different aspects or dimensions of individual performance have been identified, one vital distinction is between those behaviors that are central to performing one's job (often called *task performance*), and other behaviors that are less central yet still valuable for the effective functioning of the team, department, or organization as a whole.[3] Many training efforts focus on the first group of behaviors, namely those relating to performing the critical tasks associated with a given job. But the second category of behaviors is also important. Behaviors in this category have been given different labels (such as organizational citizenship behaviors or contextual performance).[4] A central aspect of such behaviors (we term them *organizational citizenship behaviors*) is that in the aggregate, they contribute to organizational effectiveness.[5] For example, HRD efforts to inculcate a culture of innovation and initiative taking would be focusing more on this second category of behaviors. Similarly, team-building efforts that promote cooperation and teamwork emphasize such citizenship behaviors. Alternately, coaching or mentoring efforts often seek to promote behaviors that are helpful to the organization as a whole, yet are not "enforceable requirements" of a given job.[6] The motivational issues discussed later in this chapter are particularly critical in determining the extent to which employees engage in behaviors that are "above and beyond" their formal job requirements. As Daniel Katz wrote many years ago, "An organization which depends solely upon its blueprints of prescribed behavior is a very fragile social system."[7] As we present a "systems" perspective on human resource development, we begin our discussion by highlighting these two critical aspects of individual employee behavior. Next, we describe the major factors that influence such behavior.

## EXTERNAL INFLUENCES ON EMPLOYEE BEHAVIOR

### FACTORS IN THE EXTERNAL ENVIRONMENT

Influences from outside the organization, that is, the external environment, clearly influence employee behavior. Factors from the *external environment* include the general state of the economy (e.g., the rate of inflation, level of unemployment); the various governmental laws, regulations, and regulatory agencies; what other organizations or competitors are doing; plus the many global and technological issues mentioned in Chapter 1. Our model in Figure 2-1 depicts these as general forces that influence the organization and all parts within it.[8] Even organizations with strong internal work environments and high levels of employee behaviors can be negatively impacted by external factors such as a downturn in the economy or a sudden technological change. External forces often lead organizations to reduce their workforce. **Downsizing** refers to voluntary actions on the part of organizations to reduce the overall size of their workforce, generally to reduce costs.[9] A huge number of companies have reduced their workforce over the past twenty-five years, including AT&T, Boeing, DuPont, IBM, Xerox, and United Technologies (the organization highlighted in the Opening Case). Despite the widespread nature of downsizing, there is little solid evidence concerning its effectiveness as a business practice.[10] A study by Wayne Cascio of companies that downsized more than 3 percent in a given year between 1980–1990 found no improvement in financial or stock performance as a result of downsizing.[11] An ASTD survey found that downsized organizations reported lower organizational performance, lower quality products or services, and lower employee satisfaction compared to organizations that had not downsized.[12]

For organizations to ensure their future success, they must maintain their investment in their workforce, even when they are restructuring or downsizing.[13] This includes training the "survivors" of downsizing on how to carry out their responsibilities after downsizing has occurred,[14] but can also include decisions to retrain rather than lay off employees. For example, Digital Equipment, Eastman Kodak, Hallmark, Pacific Bell, and Raychem all have been cited for their efforts to retrain workers who would otherwise be laid off.[15] The ASTD study cited earlier found that organizations did best when they emphasized both organizational and individual performance. In particular, three individual-level practices were more common in companies designated as "high performance work systems," namely coaching and mentoring, individual development, and multirater feedback. Further, companies with the most extensive high performance work systems were nearly three times less likely to cut their workforces than were companies with less extensive usage of such practices.[16] It should be clear from this brief discussion that downsizing has enormous implications for human resource development, and conversely, that HRD efforts can have a significant impact on the effectiveness of organizational downsizing. A leading HRD scholar, Warner Burke, has argued that HRD professionals should play a more active role in challenging or redirecting corporate downsizing efforts.[17]

## FACTORS IN THE WORK ENVIRONMENT

In addition to factors in the external environment, there are also factors within the organization that influence employee behavior. We emphasize four sets of forces within the *work environment* that affect employee behavior: outcomes, the supervisor, characteristics of the organization itself, and coworkers. Table 2-1 presents a list of these forces and some of the issues found in each.

*OUTCOMES.* **Outcomes** occur as a result of a given employee behavior. Outcomes can be personal or organizational in nature. *Personal outcomes* are those that have value to the individual, such as pay, recognition, and emotions. *Organizational outcomes* are things valued by the organization, such as teamwork, productivity, and product quality. These outcomes are what the organization would ultimately hope to achieve by the collective efforts of all organizational members. The word *value* in this context should not imply that outcomes are always positive or desirable. Behavior can also result in outcomes that employees fear or dislike. Embarrassment, disciplinary actions, transfers, loss of pay or privileges, and ostracism are all possible unpleasant outcomes of employee behavior.

Figure 2-1 presents these outcomes as following from employee behaviors. Although there are clearly other factors that influence individual and organizational outcomes, we have limited our discussion to those things that influence employee behaviors, and the subsequent influence that these behaviors have on personal and organizational outcomes. However, it is also important to note the likely influence that organizational outcomes have on employee behaviors (this is actually the reverse of the ordering presented in Figure 2-1). For example, several of the

**TABLE 2-1**  **INFLUENCES ON EMPLOYEE BEHAVIOR**

### FROM THE WORK ENVIRONMENT

| Factor | Issues |
| --- | --- |
| Outcomes | Types |
| | Effect on Motivation |
| Supervision | Leadership |
| | Performance Expectations |
| Organization | Reward Structure |
| | Organizational Culture |
| | Job Design |
| Coworkers | Norms |
| | Group Dynamics |
| | Teamwork |
| | Control of Outcomes |

motivation theories presented later in the chapter propose that *employee percep-tions* of outcomes are important determinants of behavior. Here are two examples:

1. **Expectancy theory** states that people will perform behaviors that they perceive will bring valued outcomes. If employees fulfill certain obligations to the organization but do not receive promised outcomes (such as promotions or pay raises), they may reduce their expectations about the link between their performance and the desired outcomes and thus choose to behave differently. Further, if outcomes are not as rewarding as anticipated, the employees may revise their judgments about the value of that outcome and perform different behaviors.[18]

2. **Equity theory** states that outcomes are evaluated by comparing them to the outcomes received by others. If employees perceive an inequity, they may change their performance or cognitions, or both, to reduce the inequity. In addition, outcomes can serve as a form of feedback to employees. Bonuses and recognition, for example, let employees know if they have performed appropriately and if their performance is valued by the organization.[19]

Consider for a moment why outcomes and outcome perceptions are so important to HRD. If employees do not believe that attending a training program will lead to valued outcomes, they may choose not to attend the program, or may devote little effort to learning and using the skills being taught. If an employee perceives that company training will require increased individual effort with no greater personal outcomes than what other employees receive, the training may be seen as unfair. As a result, the employee may resist participating in the program.

It is often the outcomes of performance (such as embarrassment or a poor evaluation) that serve as attention getters, convincing an employee that training or development is needed. For example, if a nurse who treats patients rudely never experiences any unpleasant outcomes as a result (such as complaints to the supervisor or disciplinary actions), it is unlikely that the nurse will perceive any need to change this behavior. Similarly, if college professors who have not kept current in their field continue to receive support and recognition for their work in the classroom, they may perceive that their behavior is acceptable and see no reason to attend professional seminars or engage in other developmental actions.

Thus, it is important that managers remain aware of the outcomes of their subordinates' performance, as well as how their subordinates view these outcomes. This knowledge can be useful in detecting needs for training, motivating employees to participate in training, and in ensuring that what employees learn in training is applied to their jobs.

*SUPERVISION AND LEADERSHIP.* The immediate supervisor plays an important role in the employee's work life, delegating tasks and responsibilities, setting expectations, evaluating performance, and providing (or failing to provide) feedback, rewards, and discipline. Even with the shift toward greater use of teams, including more self-directed work teams, supervisors continue to play a critical role in the success of most organizations.[20] Although the influences supervisors have on subordinates are numerous and sometimes complex, two factors deserve comment: self-fulfilling prophecy and leadership.

Research on **self-fulfilling prophecy,** or the Pygmalion effect, has shown how the expectations a supervisor establishes can influence a subordinate's behavior. First demonstrated in classroom settings, self-fulfilling prophecy states that expectations of performance can become reality because people strive to behave consistently with their perceptions of reality. If supervisors (or trainers) expect good performance, their behavior may aid and encourage their subordinates (or trainees) to raise their own self-expectations, increase their efforts, and ultimately perform well. The opposite would happen if supervisors or trainers expected poor performance.[21] Dov Eden and his colleagues have demonstrated in a variety of work settings that raising managers' performance expectations leads to higher levels of performance in their employees.[22] The implications for supervisors and HRD professionals who conduct training programs are clear: all must be aware of their own expectations and what they communicate to others, while taking advantage of the benefits resulting from high but realistic expectations. This effect has also been demonstrated recently concerning *team member* expectations for new members.[23] In addition, supervisory expectations play a key role in the coaching process, which will be discussed in greater detail in Chapter 10.

The supervisor's approach to leadership can influence employee performance as well. **Leadership** is the use of noncoercive influence to direct and coordinate the activities of a group toward accomplishing a goal.[24] There are almost as many definitions of leadership and theories about it as there are leadership researchers! Two examples serve to demonstrate the effect a supervisor's leadership may have on employee behavior.

First, Robert House argued in his path-goal theory that a leader's role is to identify goals and clarify the paths employees may take to reach these goals.[25] If this is done effectively (according to the theory, by applying one of four possible leader styles, depending on employee characteristics and environmental factors), then motivation, job satisfaction, and employee performance are all predicted to increase. Subsequent research has provided support for the theory's predictions regarding job satisfaction.[26]

Second, George Graen's Leader-Member-Exchange (or LMX) model of leadership (earlier called the vertical-dyad linkage approach) observes that supervisors tend to develop different quality relationships with different subordinates.[27] In early research, this was depicted in terms of two extremes, that is, those employees with high quality relationships with the supervisor (the "in-group"), and those with low quality relationships (the less favored "out-group"). In-group members have relationships with their supervisors characterized by respect, liking, mutual trust, and influence; the opposite is true of relationships for out-group members. In-group members tend to have higher performance and satisfaction than out-group members, lower turnover, and more positive career outcomes.[28] More recent writing on LMX has focused on improving the leadership exchange relationship managers have with *all* employees. As Graen and Uhl-Bien write, the emphasis is now placed "not on how managers discriminate among their people but rather on how they may work with each person on a one-on-one basis to develop a partnership with each of them."[29] Supervisors should work to develop effective dyadic relationships with each employee under their supervision.

These and other leadership theories highlight the effect the immediate supervisor has on employee behavior. Subordinates look to their managers for cues about appropriate and inappropriate behavior. If a manager or supervisor speaks and behaves in ways that indicate training and development are unimportant, employees will likely have little enthusiasm for these activities. Alternatively, if managers and supervisors take these activities seriously and reward employees for learning and using new skills, techniques, and attitudes, HRD efforts will be more effective, and ultimately the employee, manager, and organization will benefit. Leadership is also a key aspect of management development. Many organizations use management development programs (discussed in Chapter 13) as a way to improve the leadership skills of managerial employees.

In organizations that use teams as the primary way to accomplish tasks, some of the influences supervisors ordinarily control can be controlled by team members or the team leader (if one exists), or by both. There is evidence that the differential quality of exchange relationship among team members can influence team cohesiveness, satisfaction with coworkers, and general job satisfaction.[30] Although the dynamics of a self-managed team are more complex than the traditional supervisor-subordinate relationship, the impact of expectations and leadership will likely be similar. More will be said about teams in Chapter 14.

*THE ORGANIZATION.* The organization itself can influence employee behavior through its reward structure, culture, and job design. **Reward structure** focuses on

- the *types* of rewards an organization uses (material, social);

- how rewards are *distributed* (e.g., equally to all, relative to each individual's contribution, or on the basis of need); and
- the *criteria* for reward distribution (results, behavior, or nonperformance issues, such as seniority or tenure).[31]

Further, **rewards** include not only tangible things, such as financial bonuses and plaques, but also intangible things, such as recognition and acceptance. Reward systems should ideally provide the outcomes desired by members of the organization. Similar to our previous discussion of "outcomes," motivation theories can serve as the foundation for organizational reward systems as well. That is, motivation theories can help to explain why reward systems sometimes fail. As both expectancy and reinforcement theory predict, employees tend to do things for which they are rewarded. If management does not carefully design and implement the reward system, then it may unintentionally reinforce undesirable behavior in employees (such as lack of initiative, acceptance of the status quo, and low participation rates in HRD programs). Also, when reward systems are perceived too strongly as "control mechanisms," this can serve to reduce employee motivation and performance.[32]

Therefore, it is important for supervisors and HRD professionals to understand what the organization's reward system is intended to do, how it is put into practice, and how employees respond to it. Some performance problems may be solved simply by adjusting the reward system. It must also be understood that a major reason why many employees become involved in HRD programs is to obtain valued rewards, such as promotions, pay increases, and more desirable work assignments. As mentioned earlier, some organizations choose to highlight the linkages between desired rewards and HRD as a way to pique employee interest in them. Rewards and their effective distribution can also be a topic of training, particularly in management development programs. In some instances, access to HRD programs can be used as a reward, or access may be perceived to be a reward.

An organization's culture can also have a strong effect on individual behavior. **Organizational culture** is a set of values, beliefs, norms, and patterns of behavior that are shared by organization members and that guide their behavior.[33] Individuals who understand an organization's culture are better able to accurately interpret organizational events, know what is expected of them, and behave in appropriate ways in new or unfamiliar situations. Organizations that have a strong culture try to perpetuate that culture by selecting individuals who already share the culture (as Southwest Airlines does in its efforts to recruit people who have a "fun," team-oriented attitude) and by socializing new members so that they accept these norms and values.

Two examples can illustrate the impact of organizational culture on individual behavior. If an organization firmly embraces the idea of continuous improvement as the way to ensure high levels of quality (as in total quality management efforts), employees should be motivated to find ways to improve quality, engage in HRD programs to improve their knowledge and skills, and focus their efforts on satisfying customer needs and expectations. Similarly, in organizations committed to diversity (where individuals from all cultural backgrounds are viewed and treated as full organizational members and participate fully within the organization), employees will behave in ways that encourage acceptance and the active participation of all members in achieving the organization's goals. One clear implication of organizational culture for HRD is that HRD can be a means through which an organization's culture is perpetuated or changed, and HRD can also be influenced by the organization's culture (in terms of HRD content, importance, and acceptance).

**Job design** is the development and alteration of the components of a job (such as the tasks one performs, and the scope of one's responsibilities) to improve productivity and the quality of the employee's work life. As proposed by Richard Hackman and Greg Oldham, when jobs contain factors that satisfy employees' personal growth needs or provides elements that generate feelings of responsibility, meaningfulness, and knowledge of results, employees will be more satisfied and more productive. Job design has received considerable attention and research support.[34] The implication of job design for HRD is twofold. First, the way an organization chooses to construct its jobs can affect an employee's behavior and attitudes. Second, to improve an employee's performance and attitudes (or reduce stress), the focus can be on altering the job rather than the employee. Job design will receive more attention in our discussion of organizational development in Chapter 14.

*COWORKERS AND TEAMS.* Coworkers, and especially team members, can exert a strong influence on an employee's behavior in at least three ways. First, coworkers control some of the outcomes valued by an employee, and may use those outcomes to influence the employee's behavior. For example, if an employee behaves in a way coworkers value, they may reward or reinforce that behavior by offering friendship and recognition. Similarly, coworkers may choose to react to behavior they disapprove of by withholding desired outcomes or punishing the employee through insults, ostracism, or threats. This is especially true in team situations, where members hold each other accountable for behaviors and performance, and where access to rewards is based on team performance.

Second, **norms,** or informal rules for appropriate behavior established within work groups, can serve as guidelines for appropriate behavior, if the employee chooses to comply.[35] Norms send a clear message about what behavior is expected and may lead employees to behave in ways that differ from typical patterns.

Third, because HRD programs are often administered to groups of employees and employees must perform newly learned behaviors in group settings, HRD professionals need to understand the effect of group dynamics on behavior. **Group dynamics** influence the way an employee may behave when interacting in a group. Dynamics such as groupthink and social loafing show that the performance of individuals within groups can differ from their behavior alone.[36] **Groupthink** occurs when group members are primarily concerned with unanimity, making poor decisions by failing to realistically assess alternatives. **Social loafing** is the tendency for group members to reduce their effort as the size of the group increases. The implication of dynamics such as social loafing and groupthink is that consideration must be given to how employees will behave when they are in group settings. Care should be taken when designing and implementing HRD programs to ensure that group dynamics do not undermine the learning process. **Teamwork** both amplifies the importance of coworkers' influences on individual behavior and brings other dynamics to the forefront. Two teamwork issues are trust and cohesiveness. **Trust** has to do with expectations that another person (or group of people) will act benevolently toward you. There is a certain vulnerability or riskiness to trust, in that the other party may not fulfill your expectations. Yet, research has demonstrated strong links between interpersonal trust and employee performance (including citizenship behaviors), problem solving, and cooperation.[37] **Cohesiveness** is the members' sense of togetherness and willingness to remain as part of the group. Given team members' high level of interdependence, they must trust one another and feel a sense of cohesiveness if the team is to work together and be successful.

Similarly, group and team dynamics should be taken into account when planning actions designed to ensure that what is learned is transferred back to the job. Managers and team leaders can monitor potentially destructive dynamics, as well as the level of trust and cohesiveness, and act to address them to maximize the chances that what employees learn in training and development activities will be used. Involving coworkers and team members in the learning process, as participants or trainers, can increase their acceptance of newly learned skills and the likelihood that they'll use them on the job. Likewise, managers should pay attention to employee attitudes toward training and toward using new methods and skills.

## MOTIVATION: A FUNDAMENTAL INTERNAL INFLUENCE ON EMPLOYEE BEHAVIOR

**Motivation** is one of the most basic elements of human behavior. Motivational theories attempt to explain how effort is generated and channeled. Terry Mitchell synthesized many definitions of work motivation as "the psychological processes that cause the arousal, direction, and persistence of voluntary actions that are goal directed."[38]

This definition makes several important points. First, work motivation pertains to the causes of *voluntary* behavior — the nature of nearly all behaviors performed in the workplace. Even in situations where employees feel they do not have a choice, their behavior reflects their consideration of the perceived consequences of their actions.

Second, motivation focuses on several processes affecting behavior:

- **Energizing** — The generation or mobilization of effort
- **Direction** — Applying effort to one behavior over another
- **Persistence** — Continuing (or ceasing) to perform a behavior

Third, motivation at work is usually seen as an individual phenomenon because all people have unique needs, desires, attitudes, and goals.[39] Most motivational theories recognize these differences, and often include components that describe how they affect the motivational process.

Understanding motivation is critical to HRD. The success of many HRD programs and processes depends in part on whether the individual is motivated to participate, learn, and use what is learned to improve performance. The reason a person chooses to attend a training class, but then fails to use the skills learned in training back on

**TABLE 2-2**

## APPROACHES TO EXPLAINING MOTIVATION

| Approach | Theories |
|---|---|
| **Need Based** | Maslow's Need Hierarchy Theory |
| Underlying needs, such as the needs for safety or power, drive motivation. | Alderfer's Existence, Relatedness, and Growth (ERG) Theory |
| | Herzberg's Two-Factor Theory |
| **Cognitive Process** | Expectancy Theory |
| Motivation is a process controlled by conscious thoughts, beliefs, and judgments. | Goal-Setting Theory |
| | Social Learning Theory |
| | Equity Theory |
| **Noncognitive** | Reinforcement Theory |
| Motivation is explained as an interaction between behavior and external events without appealing to internal thoughts or needs. | |

the job may be rooted in motivation. Programs designed with an eye toward motivation can explicitly address these issues. In addition, motivation theories are useful in diagnosing the cause of performance problems and often serve as the basis for designing or choosing HRD programs to remedy those problems.

Theories of work motivation abound. Although some theories share common processes and constructs,[40] there is no single, inclusive, and widely accepted explanation of work motivation.[41] In general, approaches to explaining motivation can be grouped into the three categories displayed in Table 2-2: need-based, cognitive, and noncognitive. After we present various prominent motivational theories, we will use a diagnostic model of motivation to synthesize these various theories.[42]

## NEED-BASED THEORIES OF MOTIVATION

Several motivational theories are rooted in the concept of needs. **Needs** are deficiency states or imbalances, either physiological or psychological, that energize and direct behavior. Henry Murray proposed that humans experience a large number of needs, such as aggression, affiliation, autonomy, and achievement.[43] Although needs are internal states, they can be influenced by forces in the environment. The opening case, for example, suggests that forces in the global economy and the potential for layoffs within an organization may heighten an employee's need for security, thereby reducing motivation to learn or engage in educational opportunities.

**FIGURE 2-2**  **THE NEED ACTIVATION-NEED SATISFACTION PROCESS**

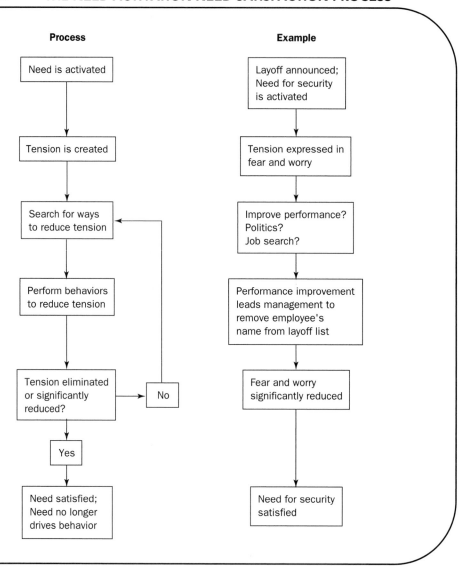

Needs are said to drive behavior through the combination of need activation and need satisfaction, a process depicted in Figure 2-2. A need becomes activated when a person lacks something necessary for maintaining psychological or physiological equilibrium. The activated need is felt as tension. The tension may be a recognizable feeling such as loneliness, or it may be more general, such as anxiety. Because tension is unpleasant, the person will look for ways to reduce the tension by eliminating the deficiency that is causing it. That person will continue to perform different behaviors until one is found that effectively reduces the tension and, thus, satisfies that need. Only activated needs can be motivational, because only an activated need produces the tension the person is motivated to eliminate. Once the need is satisfied, the tension is gone and the need is no longer felt.

Two widely cited need-based theories of motivation, Maslow's need hierarchy theory[44] and Alderfer's existence, relatedness, and growth (ERG) theory,[45] suggest that needs are arranged in a hierarchy. They propose that needs emerge in a particular pattern, in which certain groups of needs (those important to physical survival) emerge first and must be satisfied before other needs (psychological and social needs like affiliation and esteem) can emerge and affect behavior. Once the currently activated needs are satisfied, the next most powerful group of needs are felt and thus will drive behavior.

Maslow's need hierarchy lists five categories or levels of needs: physiological, safety and security, love, status and esteem, and self-actualization. Alderfer's ERG theory reduces Maslow's hierarchy to three levels of needs: existence, relatedness, and growth. More important, ERG theory proposes that if a person becomes frustrated trying to satisfy the currently activated needs, this frustration will cause previously satisfied needs to be activated and drive behavior.

Another widely discussed need-based theory is Herzberg's *two-factor theory*.[46] Herzberg claimed that people have two sets of basic needs, one focusing on survival and another focusing on personal growth. He argued that factors in the workplace that satisfy survival needs, or *hygiene factors,* cannot provide job satisfaction — they only prevent dissatisfaction. Alternatively, *motivator factors,* which satisfy the growth needs, can create feelings of job satisfaction, but their absence will not necessarily lead to dissatisfaction. Following the two-factor theory, workers can be motivated by ensuring that hygiene factors are present, thereby preventing dissatisfaction, and then adding motivator factors to create job satisfaction. This strategy is referred to as **job enrichment.**

Need-hierarchy theories have been popular with managers and students in part because they are easy to understand and are intuitively appealing. They seem to make sense. Unfortunately, need theories are difficult to rigorously test, in that they require measuring internal states that people find difficult to accurately identify and explain. Although most of the studies of Maslow's theory have failed to support it, much of this research has not been conducted properly.[47] Some research has been conducted to test the ERG theory, but there is insufficient evidence to support or reject the theory.[48] Needs exist, but a generalizable hierarchy explaining the relationships among them is not yet available.

Similar problems exist with two-factor theory. Herzberg's initial studies supported the notion that there are two separate sets of factors that affect job satisfaction differently.[49] However, other researchers could not replicate these results using other methods. The theory became embroiled in controversy.[50] Although there is some support for job enrichment as a way to motivate employees, the validity of the two-factor theory remains unclear.

So although need-based theories of motivation provide some insight into one category of possible forces that drive behavior, they have proven difficult to test and apply and are insufficient as an explanation of motivation. Even so, HRD programs based on need-based theories, such as job enrichment and achievement motivation training, have been used in organizations with some success.

## COGNITIVE PROCESS THEORIES OF MOTIVATION

Few of us would deny that our conscious thoughts play a role in how we behave. A second group of motivation theories, called cognitive process theories, recognizes this and argues that motivation is based on a person's thoughts and beliefs (or cognitions). These theories are sometimes referred to as process theories because they attempt to explain the sequence of thoughts and decisions that energize, direct, and control behavior.

Cognitive motivation theories have direct relevance to HRD. Most HRD programs include attempts to change employee behavior by influencing their thoughts, beliefs, and attitudes. Learning, which lies at the heart of HRD, is often seen as a cognitive process (learning will be discussed in Chapter 3). We can do a better job of designing and implementing HRD programs if we understand how employees' thoughts and beliefs affect their behavior. In the following section, we briefly review four cognitive theories of motivation: expectancy theory, goal-setting theory, social learning theory, and equity theory. Each theory has relevance for the practice of HRD.

*EXPECTANCY THEORY. Expectancy theory,* first proposed by Victor Vroom, assumes that motivation is a conscious choice process.[51] According to this theory, people choose to put their effort into activities that they believe they can perform and that will produce desired outcomes. Expectancy theory argues that decisions about which activities to engage in are based on the combination of three sets of beliefs: expectancy, instrumentality, and valence.

**Expectancy** beliefs represent the individual's judgment about whether applying (or increasing) effort to a task will result in its successful accomplishment. Stated another way, people with high expectancy believe that increased effort will lead to better performance, but people with low expectancy do not believe that their efforts, no matter how great, will affect their performance. All other things being equal, people should engage in tasks for which they have high expectancy beliefs.

The second belief, called **instrumentality,** is a judgment about the connection the individual perceives (if any) between task performance and possible outcomes. Making instrumentality judgments is like asking the question, "If I perform this task successfully, is it likely to get me something I want (or something I don't want)?" Instrumentality ranges from strongly positive (the individual is certain that performing a task will lead to a particular outcome), through zero (the individual is certain there is no relationship between performing the task and the occurrence of a particular outcome), to strongly negative (the individual is certain that performing a certain task will prevent a particular outcome from occurring).

The third belief important to expectancy theory is called **valence.** Valence refers to the value the person places on a particular outcome. Valence judgments range from strongly positive (for highly valued outcomes), through zero (for outcomes the person doesn't care about), to strongly negative (for outcomes the person finds aversive).

Expectancy theory states that employees will make these three sets of judgments when deciding which behaviors and tasks to engage in. Specifically, the theory predicts that employees will choose to put effort into behaviors they

**FIGURE 2-3**     **A GRAPHIC REPRESENTATION OF EXPECTANCY THEORY**

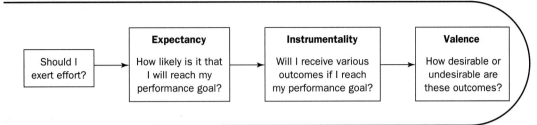

- believe they can perform successfully (high expectancy) and
- believe are connected (high instrumentality) to outcomes they desire (high valence) or
- believe will prevent (negative instrumentality) outcomes they want to avoid (negative valence).

Figure 2-3 graphically depicts this process. For example, suppose the manager of a bus company tries to motivate bus drivers to drive more safely by offering safe drivers additional vacation days. Whether this will motivate a driver to drive more safely depends on whether

1. the driver thinks he or she can improve his or her safety record to the level desired by the manager (expectancy),
2. the driver believes the manager will give more vacation days if his or her safety record is improved to the desired level (instrumentality), and
3. the driver values having more vacation days (valence).

Do people behave in the way expectancy theory predicts? Empirical studies testing the theory have shown support for its predictions.[52] However, methodological problems in some of these studies may have led to underestimates of the theory's predictive ability.[53] Expectancy theory may seem complex, and more research is needed to understand whether the theory accurately represents the behavioral choices we make.[54] Expectancy theory is, however, clearly relevant to HRD. It offers a way to diagnose performance problems and then suggests how these problems can be overcome. In addition, expectancy theory has implications for the design and effectiveness of HRD programs. For example, according to expectancy theory, employees will not be motivated to attend HRD programs and try to learn from them unless they believe

1. their efforts will result in learning the new skills or information presented in the program,
2. attending the program and learning new skills will increase their job performance, and
3. doing so will help them obtain desired outcomes or prevent unwanted outcomes.

Viewing employee behavior from an expectancy theory perspective, supervisors and HRD professionals can design and market programs in ways to ensure that employees make the appropriate judgments and as a result will be motivated to attend, learn, and apply what they have learned back on the job. Some ways to do this include offering incentives such as holding HRD programs in attractive locations, offering paid time off from work to attend, designing a program that is interesting and enjoyable, providing proof that the program is effective, and making success in the program a prerequisite for promotion and other desirable outcomes.

*GOAL-SETTING THEORY.* A second cognitive theory of motivation is **goal-setting theory.** Goal-setting theory states that performance goals play a key role in motivation. The theory proposes that goals can mobilize employee effort, direct their attention, increase their persistence, and affect the strategies they will use to accomplish a task.[55] Goals influence the individual's intentions, which are defined as the "cognitive representations of goals to which the person is committed."[56] This commitment will continue to direct employee behavior until the goal is achieved, or until a decision is made to change or reject the goal.

Goal setting is probably the best-supported theory of work motivation, and one of the best-supported theories in management overall.[57] Research convincingly shows that goals that are specific, difficult, and accepted by employees will lead to higher levels of performance than easy, vague goals (such as "do your best"), or no goals at all. This research also demonstrates that the presence of feedback enhances the effectiveness of goal setting.[58]

Further research is needed to understand how and under what conditions goal setting works best.[59] For example, a study on the effectiveness of assertiveness training gave "assigned" goals to half the trainees at the end of the training program. These trainees were told to use the key points taught in training in two settings per week for four weeks. Checklists were provided to assist these trainees in tracking their goal attainment. Interestingly, trainees who had been assigned goals liked the training significantly less right after training than those in the no goal-setting condition. However, in a follow-up session four weeks later, reactions from trainees in the goal-setting condition had improved. More importantly, they could reproduce from memory a significantly larger portion of the training content than could the trainees without assigned goals, and they also demonstrated more assertive behaviors in a role-playing experience than could the no goal trainees. A basic point of this research is that adding a goal-setting condition to an already effective training program made it more effective.[60]

Goal setting has become an integral part of many HRD programs, particularly in helping participants understand the desired result of each program and to motivate them to achieve these results. Goals can then be discussed with their supervisors back on the job to ensure that the employees use what they have learned during the HRD program to improve their performance. For example, a key component of the career development process is setting career goals.[61] According to goal-setting theory, an employee who establishes career goals is more likely to advance his or her career, especially if the goals are specific, challenging, and accompanied by regular feedback on progress toward the goals. Career development programs should

**FIGURE 2-4**

## A MODEL OF THE RELATIONSHIP BETWEEN SELF-EFFICACY AND PERFORMANCE

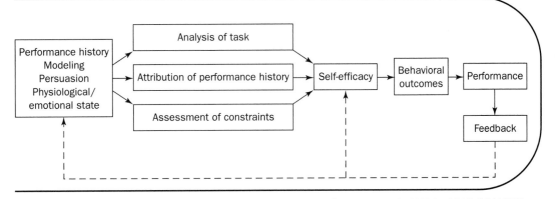

SOURCE: ACADEMY OF MANAGEMENT REVIEW by Gist, M. E., Mitchell, T. R. Copyright 2005 by ACAD OF MGMT. Reproduced with permission of ACAD OF MGMT in the format Textbook via Copyright Clearance Center.

ensure that employees set such goals and help employees and the organization establish mechanisms for regular feedback.

*SOCIAL LEARNING THEORY.* Albert Bandura developed a third cognitive theory of motivation, which is **social learning theory.**[62] Bandura proposes that outcome and self-efficacy expectations affect individual performance (see Figure 2-4). An **outcome expectation** (similar to instrumentality in expectancy theory) is a person's belief that performing a given behavior will lead to a given outcome. **Self-efficacy** can be defined as "people's judgments of their capabilities to organize and execute courses of action required to attain designated types of performances. It is concerned not with the skills one has but with judgments of what one can do with whatever skills one possesses."[63] A shorthand way of looking at self-efficacy is that it is a person's judgment of the likelihood that he or she can successfully perform a particular task or activity. Self-efficacy beliefs are malleable and can be influenced by one's accomplishments, observations of others, verbal persuasion, and physiological states.[64]

The major prediction of the social learning theory is that a person's self-efficacy expectations will determine

1. whether a behavior will be performed,
2. how much effort will be spent, and
3. how long the person will continue to perform the behavior.

Bandura argues that people who have high self-efficacy for a particular task will focus their attention on the challenges of the situation and use greater effort in mastering them, thus increasing the chances of successful task performance. Conversely, people who have low self-efficacy for a particular task will focus their thoughts on obstacles and shortcomings, and as a result, reduce their chances of successful task performance. Research shows that self-efficacy is strongly related to task performance.[65] Furthermore, research has also shown that self-efficacy can predict performance in training programs.[66] Clearly, self-efficacy has direct relevance for success in HRD. If employees have low self-efficacy expectations, it is unlikely that they will attempt to improve performance. If they do try to improve performance, they will not put forth the same effort as persons with high self-efficacy. Therefore, trainers and supervisors should behave in ways that increase the trainees' judgments of their self-efficacy.

Of particular relevance to HRD, social learning theory also proposes that most behavior is learned by observing others, a process called *modeling*. Research suggests that through observing the behavior and its consequences in others, individuals can learn new behaviors and make decisions about whether to perform a particular behavior themselves. Modeling has also been applied to HRD with great success in a training approach known as **behavior modeling.**[67] In behavior modeling training, the trainee is told the components of the behavior to be learned (for instance, firing a poor performer) and shown a film or videotape in which an actor (the model) demonstrates how to perform the behavior. Then the trainee practices the behavior with feedback from others and finally receives social reinforcement for performing the behavior.

*EQUITY THEORY.* A fourth cognitive theory of motivation, called *equity theory,* suggests that motivation is strongly influenced by the desire to be treated fairly and by people's perceptions about whether they have been treated fairly. As a theory of work motivation, it is based on three assumptions:

1. People develop beliefs about what is fair for them to receive in exchange for the contributions that they make to the organization.
2. People determine fairness by comparing their relevant returns and contributions to those of others.
3. People who believe they have been treated unfairly (called inequity) will experience tension, and they will be motivated to find ways to reduce it.[68]

Equity theory predicts that employees who believe they are being treated fairly (a judgment called equity) will be motivated to continue their present performance and behavior patterns, whereas employees who believe they are victims of inequity will search for ways to reduce their feelings of unfairness. There are at least five ways in which individuals reduce their feelings of inequity:

1. cognitively *distorting* views of contributions or rewards ("She must be smarter than I thought.")
2. influencing *the perceived rival to change* his or her contributions or rewards (e.g., convincing the person to be less productive)
3. *changing* one's own contributions or rewards (either working harder or contributing less)
4. *comparing* oneself to a different person
5. *leaving* the situation (requesting a transfer or quitting)[69]

**FIGURE 2-5**

### A GRAPHIC REPRESENTATION OF EQUITY THEORY

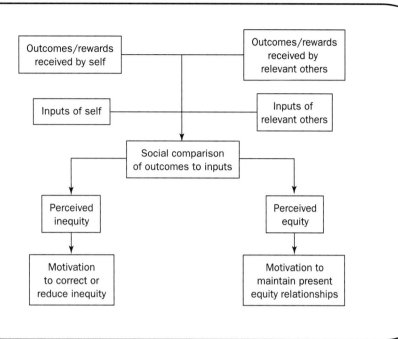

Typically, people choose the way to reduce inequity that appears to be the least costly to them.[70] Figure 2-5 depicts this process.

Are the predictions made by equity theory supported by research? In general, there is support for the predictions made about what people do when they believe they are underrewarded.[71] There is less support for predictions about what people do when they believe they are overrewarded.[72]

Equity theory has clear implications for HRD, particularly in understanding how employees perceive HRD programs and their response to them. In some organizations, participation in HRD programs is used (or perceived) as a reward for good performance or punishment for poor performance. Also, the decisions concerning which employees will be included in HRD programs are not without consequences. Equity theory suggests, for example, that employees who consider themselves unjustly left out of an HRD program (such as a management development seminar) will experience inequity. As a result, those employees may attempt to reduce the inequity by lowering their job performance or becoming less committed to the organization. Employees may even leave the organization for someplace where they feel their talents will be more appreciated. To prevent this from occurring, managers should make the selection criteria for attending HRD programs clear and provide employees with feedback so they can see that participation judgments are made fairly.

Equity theory can also help us determine whether employees will use the skills or knowledge they have learned back on the job. For example, if the employees view the application of their new skills or knowledge as an input in their exchange with the employer, they may expect the organization to provide them with certain outcomes in return. If the employees see other employees who lack the newly acquired skills receiving the same outcomes as themselves, they may choose not to use the new skills on the job as a way to restore a feeling of equity.

## REINFORCEMENT THEORY: A NONCOGNITIVE THEORY OF MOTIVATION

The last motivation theory we will discuss, **reinforcement theory,** is rooted in behaviorism, which attempts to explain behavior without referring to unobservable internal forces such as needs or thoughts.[73] Behaviorists seek to explain behavior by focusing only on things that can be directly observed: the behavior itself and environmental events that precede and follow the behavior. In short, reinforcement theory argues that behavior is a function of its consequences. This is based on the **law of effect,** which states that behavior that is followed by a pleasurable consequence will occur more frequently (a process called reinforcement), and behavior that is followed by an aversive consequence will occur less frequently.[74] According to reinforcement theory, a manager or trainer can control an employee's behavior by controlling the consequences that follow the employee's behavior.

Reinforcement theory can be applied using a set of techniques known as **behavior modification.** Behavior modification suggests four choices for controlling an employee's behavior:

1. **Positive reinforcement** refers to increasing the frequency of a behavior by following the behavior with a pleasurable consequence.

2. **Negative reinforcement** increases the frequency of a behavior by removing something aversive after the behavior is performed.

3. **Extinction** seeks to decrease the frequency of a behavior by removing the consequence that is reinforcing it.

4. **Punishment** seeks to decrease the frequency of a behavior by introducing an aversive consequence immediately after the behavior.

In addition to the type of consequence that follows a behavior, the way that consequences are paired with behaviors, called a schedule of reinforcement, is an important part of how behavior modification can be effectively applied.

Reinforcement theory has received strong support in a large body of research and has helped increase our understanding of work-related behavior.[75] Reinforcement theory has also had a strong influence on HRD. Methods of instruction, such as programmed instruction and some approaches to computer-based training, draw heavily from reinforcement theory (this will be discussed more in Chapter 6). Trainers and managers can also motivate employees to learn and use what they have learned back on the job by using behavior modification techniques.[76] Although a strict behaviorist would reject any emphasis on thoughts or needs (i.e., all the methods covered earlier), we feel that such an approach is too narrow, and that an effective HRD professional should consider a more holistic or integrated approach to motivation.

## SUMMARY OF MOTIVATION

As we have seen, there are many approaches to explaining and understanding motivation.[77] Each theory we have discussed enhances our understanding of employee behavior and has at least some research support (with the strongest support going to goal setting, reinforcement theory, social learning theory, and expectancy theory). In addition, each approach offers valuable insight into the design and implementation of HRD programs.

This brief discussion of different approaches to work motivation is not exhaustive and does not explain the complexity and interrelationships among theories. Some theories, such as expectancy theory and reinforcement theory, make many similar predictions.[78] In addition, researchers have attempted to integrate several theories into a larger, more inclusive model (for example, the Porter-Lawler model, which combines expectancy and equity theories). One attempt to synthesize multiple motivational models was proposed by John Wagner and John Hollenbeck.[79] Their model can be seen in Figure 2-6. In this model, four employee outcomes are of particular interest (these are the rectangles in the center of the model): employee

**FIGURE 2-6**

### THE WAGNER-HOLLENBECK MODEL OF MOTIVATION AND PERFORMANCE

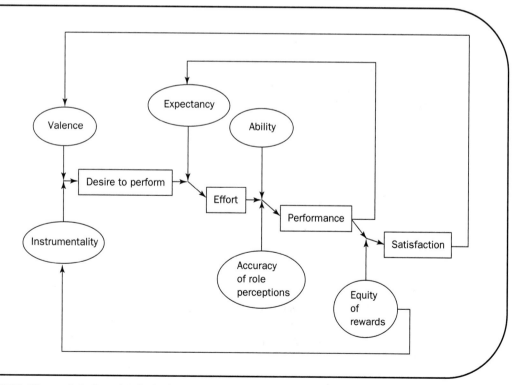

SOURCE : Wagner, J. A., III, and Hollenbeck, J. R. (1995). *Management of Organizational Behavior* (2nd ed.). Englewood Cliffs, NJ: Prentice-Hall.

desire to perform, the effort they put forth, their performance, and their satisfaction. Expectancy theory is used as the overarching framework to depict influences on employee motivation and performance. However, the other theories described earlier also are used to increase our understanding of how this process unfolds.

For example, valence, instrumentality, and expectancy were described previously in our discussion of expectancy theory. However, the various need theories can assist us in understanding *valences,* that is, what it is that people value or want. Similarly, both reinforcement theory and social learning theory can provide guidance in understanding what employees believe will lead to the attainment of what they want, that is, their *instrumentality* beliefs. The various forms of reinforcement, as well as the vicarious learning via modeling (suggested by social learning theory) lead to such instrumentality beliefs. These combine to produce a given desire to perform on the part of employees. As suggested by expectancy theory, this then interacts with *expectancy* (the judgment that one's efforts will lead to a successful outcome) to produce a high level of effort. Effort, in turn, must be accompanied by a sufficient level of ability (described later), as well as accurate role perceptions. Goal-setting theory is useful here in providing guidance to employees concerning what needs to be done, at what performance level, and who has responsibility for doing it. When effort, ability, and accurate role perceptions are all present, then high levels of individual performance are predicted to occur. The final variable in this model, satisfaction, is predicted to follow from performance, as well as from a perception that rewards have been given out fairly. Equity theory provides a helpful framework for understanding employees' perceptions of the equity of rewards. Finally, the model portrays return arrows back to valence, instrumentality, and expectancy. This is meant to portray the dynamic nature of employee motivation and performance, that is, motivation and performance can change over time. A highly motivated person can lose motivation when valence, instrumentality, or expectancy decline. On the other hand, when one of the aspects of this model is improved or increased, then higher levels of motivation, performance, and satisfaction are predicted to occur. We view this model as a useful diagnostic tool to understand employee motivation, as it very effectively synthesizes and summarizes our discussion of the various motivational theories.

We hope that this discussion encourages the reader to appreciate both the importance of motivation in determining employee behavior as well as the richness of potential applications that motivation theories have for HRD. We hope you share our conviction that motivation is a foundational topic for HRD. For an interesting motivational challenge faced by corporate trainers many years ago, see the nearby box, "An HRD Classic: 'On the Effectiveness of Not Holding a Formal Training Course.'"

## OTHER INTERNAL FACTORS THAT INFLUENCE EMPLOYEE BEHAVIOR

Internal factors, in addition to motivation, that influence employee behavior include attitudes and knowledge, skills, and abilities (KSAs). Each of these factors is discussed in the following sections.

## An HRD Classic: "On the Effectiveness of Not Holding a Formal Training Course"

Have you ever wondered if maybe training *isn't* the answer to an organization's performance problems? Industrial psychologists Paul Thayer and William McGehee faced this question many years ago when they worked for Fieldcrest Mills in North Carolina. The plants were unionized, and the managers were urging McGehee, the training director at the time, to hold training courses for the supervisors on the contents of the company's contract with the union. It seems that the union stewards (who spoke on behalf of the employees in the various plants) knew the contract in great detail, and were frequently challenging the authority of the supervisors to assign jobs, discipline employees, or conduct other supervisory responsibilities. Thayer and McGehee write that a supervisor's request "that a loom fixer fill in for an operator for a brief time, for example, might be challenged by an unsupported reference to certain clauses in the union contract. Stewards capitalized on [supervisor] ignorance. Many managers suspected that stewards frequently ran bluffs just for sport" (p. 455).

Although these trainers felt they could provide competent instruction, they were concerned that a course on the contract would not be well received by the supervisors. Their concern was that the stewards' actions were more frustrating to the managers than they were to the supervisors, and that an "essential condition for learning was missing," namely motivation. Their suggestion was that, before conducting training, some baseline data should be collected to see what the supervisors already knew and avoid covering unnecessary materials. Because each supervisor could make use of a pocket edition of the contract on the job, the test should be open book.

As an incentive, the company president agreed to host a steak dinner for the supervisor with the best score on the test. That individual's manager would also be invited. While preparations were being made for the supervisors to take the test, suggestions were made among the managers that certain supervisors would do better than others. This led quickly to bets "being placed at all levels among plants, from [supervisor] to manager" (p. 456). A very difficult, "hair-splitting" exam was prepared, and then delivered to all mills on the same morning. Supervisors began taking the exam "before work, during breaks, at lunch, after work, at home, etc." (p. 456). Thayer and McGehee comment that Thayer's phone did not stop ringing for a week, with supervisors claiming that there were two, three, or even four correct answers to various questions.

Within a week, all exams were turned in, and all were perfect or near perfect. Two weeks later, the president hosted a steak dinner for 75 supervisors and their managers. Thayer and McGehee raise the question of whether supervisors learned something from this "nontraining course." Throughout the course of the dinner, "Thayer was surrounded by indignant [supervisors] who quoted sections of the contract verbatim to support contentions as to the unfairness of certain exam questions" (p. 456). Perhaps just as interesting was that the pressure from the mill managers to provide such a training course for supervisors "disappeared." They ask, "Essential learning conditions must exist. Do we look at those conditions first before — or instead of — building a course?" (p. 456). In the context of this chapter, it is evident that proper *motivation* for training was lacking among the supervisors.

However, a rather ingenious manipulation of incentives (an informal part of the reward system) led to significant changes in how the supervisors treated the union contract. Despite the passage of fifty years, there is a lesson in this classic note for current HRD professionals.

SOURCE: Thayer, P. W., & McGehee, W. (1977). Comments: On the effectiveness of not holding a formal training course. *Personnel Psychology, 30*, 455–456.

## ATTITUDES

**Attitudes** are the second major internal influence depicted in our model of work behavior (refer again to Figure 2-1 on page 40. Attitudes add to our understanding of employee behavior by showing another way that thoughts can influence behavior. Many HRD interventions, including training evaluation, management development, and organizational development, either focus on modifying employee attitudes or use attitudes as a central component. For example, one common way HRD programs are evaluated is by means of assessing employee attitudes toward the program and its content.

What is an attitude? An attitude "represents a person's general feeling of favorableness or unfavorableness toward some stimulus object."[80] Attitudes are always held with respect to a particular object — whether the object is a person, place, event, or idea — and indicate one's feelings or affect toward that object. Attitudes also tend to be stable over time and are difficult to change.[81]

Of particular interest to HRD is the relationship between attitudes and behavior. Although common sense tells us that attitudes often cause behavior, the reality is more complex. If attitudes did directly affect our behavior, without any other intervening factors, our behavior should be consistent with those attitudes. Unfortunately, this is not always the case. Attitudes can be used to predict behavior, but the predictions are at best only moderately accurate. Researchers attempting to prove a direct relationship between attitudes and behavior have experienced considerable frustration.

Research conducted over the past thirty years suggests that the relationship between attitudes and behavior is not simple or direct. One widely discussed model that explains this relationship is the **behavioral intentions model**.[82] This model states that it is the *combination* of attitudes with perceived social pressure to behave in a given way (called subjective norms) that influences an individual's intentions. These intentions, in turn, more directly influence behavior (see Figure 2-7). When attitudes and subjective norms conflict, the stronger of the two plays the dominant role in determining what the individual's intentions will be. According to the behavioral intentions model, then, attitudes appear to affect behavior only to the extent that they influence one's intentions.

One example of how the behavioral intentions model of attitudes can inform HRD practice is when measuring a program's effectiveness (see Chapter 7). Relying solely on measuring attitudes to determine whether employees will apply what they have learned in an HRD program will likely produce only moderately accurate results. The behavioral intentions model suggests that it may be more useful to measure

| FIGURE 2-7 | **A GRAPHIC REPRESENTATION OF THE BEHAVIORAL INTENTIONS MODEL** |

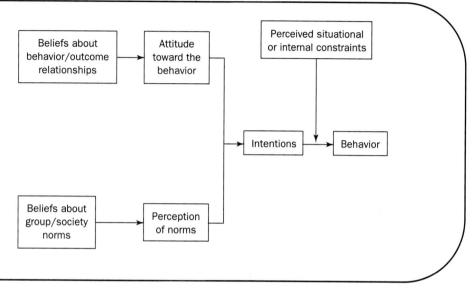

SOURCE: From *Organizational Behavior 5th edition* by Hellriegel/Slocum/Woodman. © 1989. Reprinted with permission of South-Western, a division of Thomson Learning: www.thomsonrights.com. Fax 800 730-2215.

trainees' intentions to use what they have learned, because intentions incorporate attitudes and more directly influence behavior. Although this is no substitute for assessing an actual change in job behavior, the behavioral intentions model implies that intentions, rather than attitudes alone, may be a better indicator of program effectiveness.

Attitudes are an important factor in HRD programs. Ray Noe proposed that two types of attitudes, reaction to skills assessment feedback and career/job attitudes, can have a direct effect on the motivation to learn.[83] An empirical test of the model suggested that these factors do in fact influence motivation and learning in a training program.[84] We believe that explicitly considering and understanding the effects that trainees' attitudes can have on training effectiveness, as suggested here, is a promising avenue of research — one that will likely yield new insights into ways HRD programs can be made more effective.

## KNOWLEDGE, SKILLS, AND ABILITIES (KSAs)

The third and final internal factor included in our model of employee behavior (Figure 2-1) is the employee's knowledge, skills, and abilities (KSAs). It is clear that KSAs have a significant impact on employee performance. All other things being equal, if employees lack the KSAs to perform a task or behavior, they will likely fail. Almost all HRD programs focus on improving or renewing the KSAs of employees.

Despite the ubiquitous nature of KSAs, these factors can be difficult to define with precision. Definitions differ according to the person defining them. Edwin Fleishman, a leading researcher of human abilities, defines **abilities** as general capacities related to the performance of a set of tasks.[85] Abilities develop over time through the interaction of heredity and experience, and are long-lasting. **Skills** are similar to abilities, but differ in that they combine abilities with capabilities that are developed as a result of training and experience.[86] Skills are often categorized as psychomotor activities, whereas abilities tend to be more cognitive, and skills are typically measured in terms of the ease and precision evident in the performance of some task.[87] Finally, **knowledge** is defined as an understanding of factors or principles related to a particular subject.

Over 100 different types of abilities have been identified, including general intelligence, verbal comprehension, numerical ability, and inductive reasoning.[88] Some types of abilities, like general strength, have even been partitioned into subcategories (including explosive, dynamic, and static abilities).[89] Researchers have developed taxonomies to describe the abilities needed to perform particular tasks. Taxonomies help HRD professionals to select and assign employees to training, choose appropriate learning strategies for individuals of differing skill levels, and specify training needs and content when designing training programs. Fleishman and colleagues have developed one such taxonomy that has been applied to HRD.[90] We will discuss needs assessment in Chapter 4.

It should be clear from the preceding discussion that motivation, attitudes, and ability are critical to explaining employee behavior and to understanding and applying HRD. It is the combination of these influences with the external influences described earlier that affect employee behavior.

### RETURN TO OPENING CASE

Pratt & Whitney and UTC established an Employee Scholars Program that pays 100 percent of the costs of tuition and books for employees pursuing college courses at any accredited educational institution. According to the UTC website, "Employees can obtain a degree in any field, whether or not it's job-related. Be it a bachelor's degree in art or a graduate degree in physics, students can receive up to 50 percent of the total credit hours for all courses taken in an academic period as paid time off for studying, to a maximum of three hours per week. UTC further rewards its employee scholars when they graduate. U.S.-based employees who complete a bachelor's or graduate degree are awarded $10,000 in UTC stock. Those who receive an associate's degree are awarded $5,000 worth, and another $5,000 if they go on to complete a bachelor's[1] As of 2003, over 13,500 UTC employees had received college degrees through this program.[2] Your instructor has additional information about what happened to Pratt & Whitney, UTC, and their Employee Scholars Program after the restructuring in 2000.

[1]Employee Scholars Program (2004). Retrieved September 6, 2004, from http://www.utc.com/careers/esp/index.htm

[2]2003 Annual Report, United Technologies Corporation. Retrieved September 6, 2004, from http://www.utc.com/annual_reports/2003/review/page8.htm

## SUMMARY

Because HRD interventions are attempts to change employee behavior, it is important to understand the factors that influence employee behavior. This chapter presented a number of such factors that have direct relevance to HRD, using a simple model of employee behavior to guide the discussion. The model contains two sets of factors that interact to influence employee behavior: (1) external factors, which include factors in the external environment (economic, governmental, and competitive issues), as well as those in the work environment (e.g., outcomes, the supervisor, the organization, and coworkers), and (2) internal factors, which include motivation, ability, and attitudes.

Outcomes — the results of performing a behavior in a particular way — are an external influence on employee behavior. Both personal outcomes (relevant to the individual, like pay or recognition) and organizational outcomes (relevant to the organization, like productivity or profits) can be used to diagnose and motivate employees to attend, learn, and apply what they have learned in HRD programs. Theories of motivation, such as equity theory, expectancy theory, and reinforcement theory, attempt to explain whether and how outcomes affect employee behavior.

Supervisors, through their leadership and expectations, also influence employee behavior. A supervisor can use leadership (noncoercive influence) to affect a subordinate's performance, attitudes, and motivation. According to the leader-member exchange theory, employees who are treated by their supervisor with trust, respect, and friendship are more satisfied and perform better than those who are not. Research on self-fulfilling prophecy has shown that a supervisor's expectations of an employee can affect the way the supervisor interacts with the employee, with the employee's performance tending to live up or down to those expectations.

Two additional factors in the work environment that influence employee behavior are coworkers and the organization itself. Coworkers provide influence through group norms, group dynamics, and teamwork, and by controlling valued outcomes. The organization can also affect employee behavior in several ways, including its culture, reward structure, and the way it designs the employee's job.

One of the key internal factors that influence employee behavior is motivation. Motivation is defined as the psychological processes that energizes, directs, and leads to the persistence of voluntary behavior. Theories of motivation use different sources to explain behavior, including needs (Maslow's need hierarchy, Alderfer's ERG theory, and Herzberg's two-factor theory), cognitions (expectancy theory, goal-setting theory, social learning theory, and equity theory), and the consequences of behavior (reinforcement theory). Each of these theories has implications for developing and conducting HRD programs. The Wagner-Hollenbeck model of motivation and performance was presented as a useful means of combining the various theories to diagnose motivational and performance issues.

Attitudes and the employee's knowledge, skills, and abilities (KSAs) are also important internal factors of behavior. Without ability (the capability one has to perform a set of tasks), a person will be unable to perform a given behavior, regardless of motivation. Attitudes, which are made up of beliefs, feelings, and behavioral tendencies, affect behavior indirectly through intentions. According to the behavior intentions model, attitudes combine with the perception of social pressure to form intentions, which in turn directly affect behavior. Research has shown that both employee attitudes and ability play a role in the effectiveness of HRD programs.

HRD professionals and managers are in the business of understanding and influencing employee behavior. As the sampling of concepts and theories in this chapter shows, there are many possible explanations for employee behavior, though fewer unequivocal facts. The techniques discussed in the chapters that follow draw upon the foundations laid by researchers of work motivation and behavior. Obviously, applying these theories to a given situation requires judgment and modifications. In this sense, designing and delivering HRD interventions is an art as well as a science.

## KEY TERMS AND CONCEPTS

| | |
|---|---|
| abilities | leadership |
| attitudes | motivation |
| behavioral intentions model | needs |
| behavior modeling | norms |
| behavior modification | organizational culture |
| cohesiveness | outcome expectation |
| downsizing | outcomes |
| equity theory | reinforcement theory |
| expectancy | rewards |
| expectancy theory | reward structure |
| goal-setting theory | self-efficacy |
| group dynamics | self-fulfilling prophecy |
| groupthink | skills |
| instrumentality | social learning theory |
| job design | social loafing |
| job enrichment | teamwork |
| knowledge | trust |
| law of effect | valence |

## QUESTIONS FOR DISCUSSION

1. Describe at least three ways that factors in the external environment influence employee behavior. If you were an HRD professional involved with an action team that was charged with evaluating the likely success of a proposed downsizing of your organization, what factors would you want to consider in making this recommendation? That is, based on what you know of HRD to this point, how can HRD professionals impact the likely success or failure of this action?

2. Select a familiar problem that you have encountered in the workplace. Use the model of employee behavior presented in this chapter to seek to explain why this problem exists. Be specific.

3. Suppose that you are the recruitment manager for a medium-sized bank. One of your best recruiters appears to be unmotivated lately. The number of recruits the recruiter brings in is normally above the average for effective performance but has fallen below the standard for the past two weeks. What might expectancy theory suggest is causing the drop in the employee's performance? What might equity theory suggest? Based on your knowledge of equity and expectancy theories, develop two recommendations for helping to improve the recruiter's performance.

4. Suppose you are the HRD manager for a large electric/utility company. The quarterly report shows a 25 percent decrease in participation in management development programs over the same quarter last year. The number of managers employed by the company has not changed, and the company's profits have remained stable. You already hold these programs in desirable locations off-site (conference centers) and participating in these programs counts toward the employees' annual performance evaluation. Using your knowledge of motivation theory, suggest three possible reasons that could explain why participation rates are down. If, after investigation, those reasons turned out to be the true causes, what might you be able to do to improve participation rates?

5. Compare and contrast the need-based and cognitive-based approaches to understanding motivation.

6. The HRD manager for a chicken processing plant has come to you for advice. Even though all employees in the plant recently completed a safety training program, the accident rate has not improved. In particular, the manager has found that employees are not wearing safety gear (goggles, shoes with nonskid soles, etc.) consistently and are not following safe procedures. Using your knowledge of attitudes and supervisory expectations, develop two possible reasons to explain the employees' behavior. If your hypotheses are true, how could the HRD manager improve the situation?

7. Why do people with low self-efficacy perform more poorly in training programs than those with high self-efficacy?

8. Briefly describe three ways that coworkers can affect an employee's behavior at work.

9. Recall a time at work or school when you found it difficult to motivate yourself to complete a required task (like start a report or study for an exam). Using two different motivation theories, explain why this lack of motivation may have occurred.

## EXERCISE: INCREASING EMPLOYEE MOTIVATION

Assume that you have been asked to design a portion of the orientation program that your organization is using for new employees. How might the three concepts from expectancy theory (expectancies, instrumentality, and valence; see Figure 2-3) be used to increase the motivation of these new employees? That is, what activities or discussions might be conducted that would increase the likelihood that employees will exert high levels of effort toward achieving work-related goals?

Visit http://werner.swlearning.com for links to informative websites for this chapter.

## REFERENCES

1. Willmore, J. (2004). The future of performance. *T&D, 58*(8), 27–31; Ellis, K., & Gale, S. F. (2001). A seat at the table. *Training, 38*(3), March, 90–97.

2. Campbell, J. P., McCloy, R. A., Oppler, S. H., & Sager, C. E. (1993). A theory of performance. In N. Schmitt & W. C. Borman (Eds.), *Personnel selection in organizations* (pp. 35–70). San Francisco: Jossey-Bass; Werner, J. M. (2000). Implications of OCB and contextual performance for human resource management. *Human Resource Management Review, 10*, 3–24; Becker, T. E., & Kernan, M. C. (2003). Matching commitment to supervisors and organizations to in-role and extra-role performance. *Human Performance, 16*(4), 327–348.

3. Murphy, K. R., & Shiarella, A. H. (1997). Implications of the multidimensional nature of job performance for the validity of selection tests: Multivariate frameworks for studying test validity. *Personnel Psychology, 50*, 823–854.

4. Organ, D. W. (1988). *Organizational citizenship behavior: The Good Soldier syndrome.* Lexington, MA: Lexington Books; Tompson, H. B., & Werner, J. M. (1997). The impact of role conflict/facilitation on core and discretionary behaviors: Testing a mediated model. *Journal of Management, 23*, 583–601; Borman, W. C., & Motowidlo, S. J. (1993). Expanding the criterion domain to include elements of contextual performance. In N. Schmitt & W. C. Borman (Eds.), *Personnel selection in organizations* (pp. 71–98). San Francisco: Jossey-Bass.

5. Organ, D. W. (1997). Organizational citizenship behavior: It's construct clean-up time, *Human Performance, 10*(2), 85–97.

6. *Ibid;* Werner (2000), *supra* note 2.

7. Katz, D. (1964). The motivational basis of organizational behavior. *Behavioral Science, 9,* 131–133.

8. Heneman, H. G., III, Schwab, D., Fossum, J., & Dyer, L. (1989). *Personnel/human resource management* (4th ed.). Homewood, IL: Irwin.

9. Nelson, D. L., & Burke, R. J. (1998). Lessons learned. *Canadian Journal of Administrative Sciences, 15,* 372–381.

10. Mishra, K. E., Spreitzer, G. M., & Mishra, A. K. (1998). Preserving employee morale during downsizing. *Sloan Management Review, 39,* Winter, 83–95.

11. Cascio, W. F. (1998). Learning from outcomes: Financial experiences of 311 firms that have downsized. In M. K. Gowing, J. D. Kraft, & J. C. Quick (Eds.), *The new organizational reality: Downsizing, restructuring, and revitalization* (pp. 55–70). Washington, DC: American Psychological Association.

12. Bassi, L. J., & Van Buren, M. E. (1997). Sustaining high performance in bad times. *Training & Development, 51,* 32–41.

13. Nelson & Burke (1998), *supra* note 9.

14. Mishra et al. (1998), *supra* note 10.

15. Allan, P. (1997). Minimizing employee layoffs while downsizing: Employer practices that work. *International Journal of Manpower, 18,* 576–596.

16. Bassi & Van Buren (1997), *supra* note 12.

17. Burke, W. W. (1997). The new agenda for organization development. *Organizational Dynamics, 26,* Summer, 7–20.

18. Mitchell, T. R. (1974). Expectancy models of satisfaction, occupational preference, and effort: A theoretical, methodological, and empirical appraisal. *Psychological Bulletin, 81,* 1053–1077.

19. Campbell, J. P., & Pritchard, R. D. (1976). Motivation theory in industrial and organizational psychology. In M. D. Dunnette (Ed.), *Handbook of industrial and organizational psychology* (63–130). Chicago: Rand McNally.

20. Mohrman, S. A., Cohen, S. G., & Mohrman, A. M., Jr. (1995). *Designing team-based organizations: New forms for knowledge work.* San Francisco: Jossey-Bass.

21. Eden, D. (1984). Self-fulfilling prophecy as a management tool: Harnessing Pygmalion. *Academy of Management Review, 9,* 64–73.

22. Eden, D., & Ravid, G. (1982). Pygmalion versus self-expectancy: Effects of instructor and self-expectancy on trainee performance. *Organizational Behavior and Human Performance, 30,* 351–364; Eden, D., & Shani, A. B. (1982). Pygmalion goes to boot camp: Expectancy, leadership, and trainee performance. *Journal of Applied Psychology, 67,* 194–199.

23. Chen, G., & Klimoski, R. J. (2003). The impact of expectations on newcomer performance in teams as mediated by work characteristics, social exchanges, and empowerment. *Academy of Management Journal, 46*(5), 591–607.

24. Jago, A. G. (1982). Leadership: Perspectives in theory and research. *Management Science, 22,* 315–336.

25. House, R. J. (1971). A path-goal theory of leader effectiveness. *Administrative Science Quarterly, 16,* 321–338.

26. Al-Gattan, A. A. (1985). Test of the path-goal theory of leadership in the multinational domain. *Group and Organizational Studies, 10,* 425–429; Schriesheim, C., & DeNisi, A. (1981). Task dimensions as moderators of the effects of instrumental leadership: A two-sample replicated test of path goal leadership theory. *Journal of Applied Psychology, 66,* 587–589.

27. Davis, W. D., & Gardner, W. L. (2004). Perceptions of politics and organizational cynicism: An attributional and leader–member exchange perspective. *Leadership Quarterly, 15*(4), 439–465; Graen, G. B., & Uhl-Bien, M. (1995). Relationship-based approach to leadership: Development of Leader-Member Exchange (LMX) theory of leadership over 25 years: Applying a multi-level multi-domain perspective. *Leadership Quarterly, 6,* 219–247; Dansereau, F., Graen, G. B., & Haga, W. (1975). A vertical dyad linkage approach to leadership in formal organizations. *Organizational Behavior and Human Performance, 13,* 46–78.

28. Vecchio, R. P., & Godbell, B. C. (1984). The vertical dyed linkage model of leadership: Problems and prospects. *Organizational Behavior and Human Performance, 34,* 5–20; Ferris, G. R. (1985). Role of leadership in the employee withdrawal process: A constructive replication. *Journal of Applied Psychology, 70,* 777–781; Wakabayashi, M., & Graen, G. B. (1984). The Japanese career progress study: A 7-year follow-up. *Journal of Applied Psychology, 69,* 603–614.

29. Graen & Uhl-Bien (1995), *supra* note 27, p. 229.

30. Murphy, S. M., Wayne, S. J., Liden, R. C., & Erdogan, B. (2003). Understanding social loafing: The role of justice perceptions and exchange relationships. *Human Relations, 56*(1), 61–84; Seers, A., Petty, M. M., & Cashman, J. F. (1995). Team-member exchange under team and traditional management: A naturally occurring quasi-experiment. *Group and Organization Management, 20,* 18–38.

31. Pearce, J. L., & Peters, R. H. (1985). A contradictory norms view of employer-employee exchange. *Journal of Management, 11,* 19–30; Von Glinow, M. A. (1985). Reward strategies for attracting, evaluating, and retaining professionals. *Human Resource Management, 24*(2), 191–206.

32. Deci, E. L., & Porac, J. (1978). Cognitive evaluation theory and the study of human motivation. In M. R. Lepper & D. Greene (Eds.), *The hidden costs of rewards.* Hillsdale, NJ: Erlbaum.

33. Schein, E. H. (1985). *Organizational culture and leadership.* San Francisco: Jossey-Bass.

34. Hackman, J. R., & Oldham, G. R. (1980). *Work redesign.* Reading, MA: Addison-Wesley; Loher, B. T., Noe, R. A., Moeller, N. L., & Fitzgerald, M. P. (1985). A meta-analysis of the relation of job characteristics to job satisfaction. *Journal of Applied Psychology, 70,* 280–289.

35. Feldman, D. C. (1984). The development and enforcement of norms. *Academy of Management Review, 9,* 47–53.

36. Janis, I. (1982). *Groupthink* (2nd ed.). Boston: Houghton Mifflin; Latane, B., Williams, K., & Harkins, S. (1979). Many hands make light the work: The causes and consequences of social loafing. *Journal of Personality and Social Psychology, 37,* 822–832.

37. For a review, see Whitener, E. M., Brodt, S. E., Korsgaard, M. A., & Werner, J. M. (1998). Managers as initiators of trust: An exchange relationship framework for understanding managerial trustworthy behavior. *Academy of Management Review, 23,* 513–530.

38. Mitchell, T. R. (1982). Motivation: New directions for theory, research, and practice. *Academy of Management Review, 7,* 80–88.

39. *Ibid.*

40. Evans, M. G. (1986) Organizational behavior: The central role of motivation. *Journal of Management, 12,* 203–222; Ilgen, D. R., & Klein, H. J. (1988). Individual motivation and performance: Cognitive influences on effort and choice. In J. P. Campbell & R. J. Campbell (Eds.), *Productivity in organizations.* San Francisco: Jossey-Bass.

41. Katzell, R. A., & Thompson, D. E. (1990). Work motivation: Theory and practice. *American Psychologist, 45,* 144–153; Pinder, C. C. (1984). *Work motivation: Theory, issues, and applications.* Glenview, IL: Scott, Foresman.

42. Wagner, J. A., III, & Hollenbeck, J. R. (1995). *Management of organizational behavior* (2nd ed.). Englewood Cliffs, NJ: Prentice Hall.

43. Murray, H. (1938). *Explorations in personality.* New York: Oxford University Press.

44. Maslow, A. H. (1943). A theory of human behavior. *Psychological Review, 50,* 370–396; Maslow, A. H. (1954). *Motivation and personality.* New York: Harper & Row; Maslow, A. H. (1968). *Toward a psychology of being* (2nd ed.). New York: Van Nostrand Reinhold.

45. Alderfer, C. P. (1969). An empirical test of a new theory of human needs. *Organizational Behavior and Human Performance, 4,* 143–175; Alderfer, C. P. (1972). *Existence, relatedness, and growth.* New York: Free Press.

46. Herzberg, F. H. (1966). *Work and the nature of man.* Cleveland, OH: World Publishing.

47. Wahba, M. A., & Bridwell, L. G. (1976). Maslow reconsidered: A review of research on the need hierarchy. *Organizational Behavior and Human Performance, 15,* 121–140; Mitchell, V. F., & Moudgill, P. (1976). Measurement of Maslow's need hierarchy. *Organizational Behavior and Human Performance, 16,* 334–349.

48. Alderfer (1972), *supra* note 45.

49. Herzberg, F. H., Mausner, B., & Snyderman, B. B. (1959). *The motivation to work.* New York: Wiley.

50. See Pinder, C. C. (1984). *Work motivation: Theory, issues, and applications.* Glenview, IL: Scott, Foresman; and Caston, R. J., & Braito, R. (1985). A specification issue in job satisfaction research. *Sociological Perspectives,* April, 175–197.

51. Vroom, V. H. (1964). *Work and motivation.* New York: Wiley.

52. Mitchell (1974). s*upra* note 18; Wanous, J. P., Keon, T. L., & Latack, J. C. (1983). Expectancy theory and occupational/organizational choice: A review and test. *Organizational Behavior and Human Performance, 32,* 66–86.

53. Behling, O., & Starke, F. A. (1973). The postulates of expectancy theory. *Academy of Management Journal, 16,* 373–388; Mitchell (1974), s*upra* note 18; Van Eerde, W., & Thierry, H. (1996). Vroom's expectancy models and work-related criteria: A meta-analysis. *Journal of Applied Psychology, 81,* 575–586.

54. For a summary, see Landy, F. J., & Becker, L. J. (1987). Motivational theory reconsidered. In L. Cummings & B. Staw (Eds.), *Research in organizational behavior* (Vol. 9). Greenwich, CT: JAI Press; and Kanfer, R. (1990). Motivation theory and industrial and organizational psychology. In M. D. Dunnette & L. M. Hough (Eds.), *Handbook of industrial and organizational psychology* (2nd ed., Vol. 1, pp. 75–170). Palo Alto, CA: Consulting Psychologists Press.

55. Locke, E. A. (1968). Toward a theory of task motivation and incentives. *Organizational Behavior and Human Performance, 3,* 157–189; Locke, E. A., Shaw, K. N., Saari, L. M., & Latham, G. P. (1981). Goal setting and task performance: 1969–1980. *Psychological Bulletin, 90,* 125–152.

56. Katzell, R. A., & Thompson, D. E. (1990). Work motivation: Theory and practice. *American Psychologist, 45,* 144–153.

57. Locke, E. A., & Latham, G. P. (2004). What should we do about motivation theory? Six recommendations for the 21st Century. *Academy of Management Review, 29,* 388–403; Pinder, C. C. (1984), s*upra* note 41; Miner, J. B. (1984). The validity and usefulness of theories in an emerging organizational science. *Academy of Management Review, 9,* 296–306.

58. Locke et al. (1981), s*upra* note 55; Mento, A. J., Steele, R. P., & Karren, R. J. (1987). A meta–analytic study of the effects of goal setting on task performance: 1966–1984. *Organizational Behavior and Human Performance, 39,* 52–83.

59. Wexley, K. N., & Baldwin, T. T. (1986). Posttraining strategies for facilitating positive transfer: An empirical exploration. *Academy of Management Journal, 29,* 503–520.

60. Werner, J. M., O'Leary-Kelly, A. M., Baldwin, T. T., & Wexley, K. N. (1994). Augmenting behavior-modeling training: Testing the effects of pre- and post-training interventions. *Human Resource Development Quarterly. 5,* 169–183. See also Wexley & Baldwin (1986), s*upra* note 59.

61. Greenhaus, J. H. (1987). *Career management.* Hinsdale, IL: Dryden Press.

62 Bandura, A. (1977). *Social learning theory.* Englewood Cliffs, NJ: Prentice Hall.

63. Bandura, A. (1986). *Social foundations of thought and action* (p. 391). Englewood Cliffs, NJ: Prentice Hall.

64. Bandura, A. (1977). Self-efficacy: Toward a unifying theory of behavior change. *Psychological Bulletin, 84,* 122–147.

65. Bandura, A., & Cervone, D. (1983). Self-evaluation and self-efficacy mechanisms governing the motivational effects of goal systems. *Journal of Personality and Social Psychology, 45,* 1017–1028; Bandura, A., & Cervone, D. (1987). Differential engagement of self-reactive influences in cognitive motivation. *Organizational Behavior and Human Decision Processes, 38,* 92–113; Brief, A. P., & Hollenbeck, J. R. (1985). An exploratory study of self-regulating activities and their effects on job performance. *Journal of Occupational Behavior, 6,* 197–208; Frayne, C. A., & Latham, G. P. (1987). The application of social learning theory to employee self-management of attendance. *Journal of Applied Psychology, 72,* 387–392; Locke, E. A.,

Frederick, E., Lee, C., & Bobko, P. (1984). Effects of self-efficacy, goals, and task strategies on task performance. *Journal of Applied Psychology, 69,* 241–251. A more detailed discussion of the implications of self-efficacy for work behavior is provided by Gist, M. E. (1987). Self-efficacy: Implications for organizational behavior and human resource management. *Academy of Management Review, 12,* 472–485; and Gist, M. E., & Mitchell, T. R. (1992). Self-efficacy: A theoretical analysis of its determinants and malleability. *Academy of Management Journal, 17,* 183–211.

66. Gist, M. E., Schwoerer, C., & Rosen, B. (1989). Effects of alternative training methods on self-efficacy and performance in computer software training. *Journal of Applied Psychology, 74,* 884–891; Gist, M. E., Stevens, C. K., & Bavetta, A. G. (1991). Effects of self-efficacy and post-training interventions, on the acquisition and maintenance of complex interpersonal skills. *Personnel Psychology, 44,* 884–891; Mathieu, J. E., Martineau, J. W., & Tannenbaum, S. I. (1993). Individual and situational influences on the development of self-efficacy: Implications for training effectiveness. *Personnel Psychology, 46,* 125–147; Tannenbaum, S. I., Mathieu, J., Salas, E, & Cannon-Bowers, J. (1991). Meeting trainees' expectations: The influence of training fulfillment on the development of commitment, self-efficacy, and motivation. *Journal of Applied Psychology, 76,* 759–769.

67. Baldwin, T. T. (1992). Effects of alternative modeling strategies on outcomes of interpersonal-skills training. *Journal of Applied Psychology, 77,* 147–154; Decker, P. J., & Nathan, B. R. (1985). *Behavior modeling training: Principles and applications.* New York: Praeger; Goldstein, A. P., & Sorcher, M. (1974). *Changing supervisor behavior.* Elmsford, NY: Pergamon Press.

68. Adams, J. S. (1963). Toward an understanding of inequity. *Journal of Abnormal and Social Psychology, 67,* 422–436; Carrell, M. R., & Dittrich, J. E. (1978). Equity theory: The recent literature, methodological considerations, and new directions. *Academy of Management Review, 3,* 202–210.

69. Campbell, J. P., & Pritchard, R. D. (1976). Motivation theory in industrial and organizational psychology. In M. D. Dunnette (Ed.), *Handbook of industrial and organizational psychology* (63–130). Chicago: Rand McNally.

70. *Ibid.*

71. *Ibid;* Pinder (1984), *supra* note 41.

72. Mowday, R. T. (1979). Equity theory predictions of behavior in organizations. In R. D. Steers & L. W. Porter (Eds.), *Motivation and work behavior* (2nd ed.). New York: McGraw-Hill; Huseman, R. C., Hatfield, J. D., & Miles, E. W. (1987). A new perspective on equity theory: The equity sensitivity construct. *Academy of Management Review, 12,* 222–234.

73. Skinner, B. F. (1953). *Science and human behavior.* New York: Macmillan; Skinner, B. F. (1974). *About behaviorism.* New York: Knopf; Watson, J. B. (1913). Psychology as the behaviorist views it. *Psychology Review, 20,* 158–177.

74. Thorndike, E. L. (1913). *The psychology of learning: Educational psychology* (Vol. 2). New York: Teachers College Press.

75. See Campbell, J. P. (1971). Personnel training and development. *Annual Review of Psychology, 22,* 565–602.

76. A more complete discussion of how reinforcement theory has been applied to HRD can be found in Latham, G. P. (1989). Behavioral approaches to the training and learning process. In I. L. Goldstein & Associates (Eds.), *Training and development in organizations* (pp. 256–295). San Francisco: Jossey-Bass.

77. Steers, R. M., Mowday, R. T., & Shapiro, D. L. (2004). The future of work motivation theory. *Academy of Management Review, 29,* 379–387.

78. Vecchio, R. P. (1991). *Organizational behavior* (2nd ed.). Hinsdale, IL: Dryden Press.

79. Wagner & Hollenbeck (1995), *supra* note 42, p. 172.

80. Fishbein, M., & Ajzen, I. (1975). *Belief attitude, intention, and behavior* (p. 216). Reading, MA: Addison-Wesley.

81. Staw, B. M., & Ross, J. (1985). Stability in the midst of change: A dispositional approach to job attitudes. *Journal of Applied Psychology, 70,* 469–480.

82. Ajzen, I., & Fishbein, M. (1977). Attitude-behavior relations: A theoretical analysis and review of empirical research. *Psychological Bulletin, 84,* 888–918; Ajzen, I., & Fishbein, M. (1980). *Understanding attitudes and predicting social behavior.* Englewood Cliffs, NJ: Prentice Hall; Fishbein, M., & Ajzen, I. (1975). *Belief attitude, intention, and behavior.* Reading, MA: Addison-Wesley.

83. Noe, R. A. (1986). Trainee's attributes and attitudes: Neglected influences on training effectiveness. *Academy of Management Review, 11,* 736–749.

84. Noe, R. A., & Schmitt, N. (1986). The influence of trainee attitudes on training effectiveness: Test of a model. *Personnel Psychology, 39,* 497–523.

85. Fleishman, E. A. (1972). On the relation between abilities, learning, and human performance. *American Psychologist, 27,* 1017–1032.

86. Dunnette, M. D. (1976). Aptitudes, abilities, and skills. In M. D. Dunnette (Ed.), *The handbook of industrial and organizational psychology* (pp. 473–520). Chicago: Rand McNally.

87. Goldstein, I. L. (1991). Training in work organizations. In M. D. Dunnette & L. M. Hough (Eds.), *The handbook of industrial and organizational psychology* (2nd ed., Vol. 2, pp. 507–619). Palo Alto, CA: Consulting Psychologists Press.

88. See Guilford, J. P. (1967). *The nature of human intelligence.* New York: McGraw-Hill; Dunnette (1976), *supra* note 86; Fleishman, E. A. (1975). Toward a taxonomy of human performance. *American Psychologist, 30,* 1127–1149.

89. Fleishman, E. A., & Mumford, M. D. (1988). The ability requirement scales. In S. Gael (Ed.), *The job analysts handbook for business, government, and industry.* New York: Wiley.

90. *Ibid;* see also Fleishman, E. A. (1967). Development of a behavior taxonomy for describing human tasks: A correlational-experimental approach. *Journal of Applied Psychology, 51,* 1–10; Fleishman, E. A. (1972). On the relation between abilities, learning, and human performance. *American Psychologist, 27,* 1017–1032; Fleishman, E. A., & Quaintance, M. K. (1984). *Taxonomies of human performance: The description of human tasks.* Orlando, FL: Academic Press.

**3**

# LEARNING AND HRD

## Learning Objectives

*After reading this chapter, you should be able to:*

1. Define learning and list at least three learning principles.

2. Describe the three broad categories of issues that should be considered to maximize learning.

3. Identify and discuss several personal characteristics (such as ability, personality) that affect trainee learning.

4. Identify and discuss the training design issues that can be used to maximize learning.

5. Identify and discuss the factors that affect the transfer of training, and how these can be used to maximize learning.

6. Discuss how various individual differences affect the learning process.

7. Discuss the value of adult learning theory to HRD interventions.

8. Describe the role that learning styles, learning strategies, and perceptual preferences play in learning.

9. Cite recent perspectives from instructional and cognitive psychology that have importance for HRD.

■

## OPENING CASE

Until recently, one of the hallmarks of the utility industry in the United States has been its stability. Gas and electric companies have been highly regulated, and generally must go through a lengthy government approval process before they can increase the rates they charge for their services. However, over the past decade or more, the prospects of deregulation have promised (threatened?) substantial changes in how utility companies do business. All the recent headlines and turmoil surrounding the collapse of Enron Corporation have added tremendous instability to this industry.[1] Today, we remain in a kind of an in-between period, where there are both regulated and unregulated portions of the energy industry. Often, regulated utilities are branching out into unregulated areas, in an effort to deal with the challenges they expect to face in an increasingly deregulated industry.

Wisconsin Public Service Corporation (WPSC) is a regulated electric and natural gas utility serving northeastern and central Wisconsin. With headquarters in Green Bay, WPSC serves over 400,000 customers in twenty counties and has approximately 2,500 employees. Because of the expected changes brought about by deregulation, "We are entering a time when we will be offering a lot more products and services, not just electricity and gas," says Kathy Now, a WPSC learning systems leader. "And we are looking at training as a way to retool our employees and get them ready for the transition so the company can take advantage of all these new opportunities that now exist" (p. 43).[2]

Since 1996, Wisconsin Public Service has operated what it calls Learning Centers at multiple locations. Four central issues had to be addressed as these centers were established:

1. What should be the primary areas of learning, that is, what skills, knowledge, or attitudes did employees need to develop further?

2. What types of training media would be used to make these resources available to employees, for example, print, video, computer, classroom training?

3. Who should be involved in providing the training and educational assistance to employees, that is, should this be done by WPSC staff, by outside providers, or some combination of the two?

4. What could be done to ensure that employees had the time and opportunity to take advantage of

these Learning Centers, once they were operating?

*If you were part of the learning team tasked with opening the Learning Centers at WPSC, what recommendations would you make?*

[1]SOURCES: Wilcox, J. (2004). 2003: The year that was. *Power Economics, 8*(1), 13–15; O'Leary, C. (2003). Utilities: Back to the basics. *Investment Dealers' Digest, 69*(39), 9–10.

[2]Cited in D. P. McMurrer, M. E. Van Buren, & W. H. Woodwell, Jr. (2000). Making the commitment. *Training & Development 54*, 41–48.

## INTRODUCTION

"Quiz"—Do you agree or disagree with the following statements?

■ *For learning to take place, the most important variable to consider is whether the individual learner has sufficient ability to learn what is being taught.*

■ *In general, people learn best and remember the most when they can spread out the time spent learning new material.*

■ *Learning something to the point of "overlearning" is generally a waste of time, and should be avoided.*

■ *If training has been effective, then it really doesn't matter whether there is support in the work environment or not.*

■ *Trainers should always seek to match the type of training delivery methods to the characteristics of the individuals being trained.*

■ *Adult learners typically respond best to a lecture-style approach to training.*

[We encourage you to look for the answers to these questions as you read through this chapter.]

Learning is a vital aspect of all HRD efforts.[1] Whether you are training a carpenter's apprentice to use a power saw, conducting a workshop to teach managers how to use discipline more effectively, trying to get meatpackers to understand and follow new safety procedures, or promoting career development among your employees, your goal is to change behavior, knowledge, or attitudes *through learning.* Supervisors and HRD professionals who understand the learning process and how to create an environment that facilitates learning can design and implement more effective HRD interventions. In fact, with the recent growth of corporate universities and other learning centers, there is a new position within the top leadership of many large organizations, namely, *chief learning officer.* This is more than a renaming of the training director's position. Such an individual must emphasize both individual and organizational (strategic) objectives, and be able to make effective use of different forms of learning delivery (not just a classroom approach).[2]

The purpose of this chapter is to define learning and present the learning-related issues important to HRD. The topics we will cover include the relationship between learning and instruction, maximizing learning, and the importance of recognizing and dealing with various individual differences in the learning process.

## LEARNING AND INSTRUCTION

**Learning** is defined as a relatively permanent change in behavior, cognition, or affect that occurs as a result of one's interaction with the environment. Several aspects of this definition are important. First, the focus of learning is *change,* either by acquiring something new (like skill in conducting meetings) or modifying something that already exists (like a soldier becoming more accurate in shooting a rifle). Second, the change must be *long lasting* before we can say learning has really occurred. If an administrative assistant can recall the commands needed to create a macro operation in a word processing program on the second day of a training course but cannot remember them four days later back on the job, learning has not occurred. Third, the focus of learning can include *behavior, cognitions, affect,* or any combination of the three. Learning outcomes can be skill based (climbing a utility pole), cognitive (procedures for applying for a research grant), or affective (becoming more safety conscious). Finally, learning results from an *individual's interaction with the environment.* Learning does not include behavior changes attributable to physical maturation or a temporary condition (such as fatigue or drugs).

Researchers have studied learning from a variety of perspectives, such as behaviorism and cognitivism, using both humans and animals in their experiments. Two main approaches have been used. One approach is to study how people learn simple tasks, such as identifying symbols or associating pairs of meaningless syllables (such as *bix, rik,* and *moc*). The goal of this line of research is to identify basic principles that apply to learning any kind of content. The other approach focuses on how people learn complex tasks, including school subjects such as reading and math. Although some researchers who use this approach seek generalizable principles, many believe that learning cannot be separated from what is being learned, and therefore different principles may apply to different learning outcomes.[3]

### THE SEARCH FOR BASIC LEARNING PRINCIPLES

Concerning this first approach, research over the past 100 years has yielded a number of principles thought to govern learning. The cornerstone of learning theory is the concept of association.[4] **Association** is the process by which two cognitions become paired together (e.g., "dozen" and "twelve items"), so that thinking about one evokes thoughts about the other.[5] Three principles that influence the learning of associations include:

1. **Contiguity** Objects that are experienced together tend to become associated with each other.[6] For example, learning vocabulary in a foreign language usually involves pairing a new word with an object or picture of an object (like the German word *Katze* and a picture of a cat).

2. **The Law of Effect** As discussed in Chapter 2, the law of effect states that a behavior followed by a pleasurable consequence is likely to be repeated.[7] For example, when a superior compliments a police officer who values recognition for the way he or she handled a difficult arrest, the officer associates the

compliment with the arrest method and will likely use that method to make difficult arrests in the future.

3. **Practice** Repeating the events in an association will increase the strength of the association. For example, the more times someone rappels down a cliff or wall, the more adept he or she becomes at rappelling. But practice alone is not enough to guarantee a strong association. The effect of practice is strengthened with reinforcement, such as receiving a pleasurable consequence.[8]

An alternative to the association view of learning was offered by a group of researchers known as Gestalt psychologists. These researchers proposed that learning does not occur by trial and error or by associating facts and ideas, but rather happens suddenly in the form of an insight (sometimes called an epiphany or an "a-ha!" experience).[9] Insight is seen as a sudden reconceptualization of one's experiences that results in a new idea or in discovering the solution to a problem. For example, learning to solve a puzzle may occur in the form of a series of sudden flashes in which new ideas bring one closer and closer to solving the puzzle.

"Sudden insight" as a mechanism for learning has been questioned. Some critics seek to explain "insight" by stating that people simply transfer what they have learned in one set of situations to another setting.[10] If this is true, then insight may not be a particularly useful model for how people learn. That is, although considerable learning may indeed occur through sudden insights, knowledge of this may not be very helpful in designing effective learning experiences. Many of the behaviors of interest to HRD program designers (such as learning a new set of regulations or procedures) are likely to be learned in other, probably more structured ways. On the other hand, proponents of experiential learning (such as David Kolb, whose views on learning styles are presented later in this chapter) argue that many experiential exercises and simulations do a good job of promoting insight or "a-ha!" experiences. Thus, as we will discuss further in Chapters 5 and 6, the value of this approach to learning may depend upon the particular objectives to be obtained, as well as the particular HRD methods employed.

## LIMITS OF LEARNING PRINCIPLES IN IMPROVING TRAINING DESIGN

Unfortunately, when it comes to improving training design, these general principles are not as helpful as one might expect. Much of the research that demonstrated these principles was conducted in tightly controlled laboratory settings using artificial tasks, which limit the applicability of the findings to many "real-world" training settings.

Robert Gagné convincingly demonstrated the limited benefit of learning principles to increase training effectiveness in a landmark article, "Military Training and Principles of Learning."[11] Gagné showed that practice and reinforcement failed to improve performance of three representative military tasks: gunnery (a motor skill), turning on a radar set (a procedural task), and diagnosing malfunctions in complex electronic equipment (troubleshooting). Rather than relying on the prevailing learning principles, Gagné argued that training could be improved by using three principles:

1. **Task Analysis** Any task can be analyzed into a set of distinct component tasks.

2. **Component Task Achievement** Each component task must be fully achieved before the entire task may be performed correctly.

3. **Task Sequencing** The learning situation should be arranged so that each of the component tasks is learned in the appropriate order before the total task is attempted.[12]

## THE IMPACT OF INSTRUCTIONAL AND COGNITIVE PSYCHOLOGY ON LEARNING RESEARCH

Beginning in the 1960s, the field of **instructional psychology** developed, and it has since become an active field of theory and research on how the learning environment may be structured to maximize learning. Whereas traditional learning theorists focused on describing what happens in learning situations, instructional theorists focus on what must be done *before* learning can take place.[13] Robert Glaser characterized instructional psychology as "focusing on the acquisition of human competence" (p. 299) with the following four components:

1. describe the *learning goal* to be obtained

2. analyze the *initial state* of the learner (what the learner knows or can perform prior to learning)

3. identify the *conditions* (instructional techniques, procedures, and materials) that allow the learner to gain competence

4. *assess and monitor* the learning process to determine progress and whether alternative techniques should be used[14]

Since the 1970s, instructional psychology (and much of psychology in general) has been heavily influenced by developments in *cognitive psychology*, adopting the language, methods, and models that portray humans as information processors.[15] A major goal of cognitive psychology is to develop models and theories that explain how people function. These methodologies and theories can help create an "integrated understanding of how cognitive processes produce intelligent behavior," such as learning.[16] One of the foundational ideas of cognitive psychology is that of **cognitive architecture,** which is defined as "a fixed system of mechanisms that underlies and produces cognitive behavior."[17] The structures described by a cognitive architecture will determine in part how humans process information and come to learn and understand the world around them.

Two main views of cognitive architectures have dominated the field, each of which focuses at a different level of analysis. *Symbolic architectures* rely heavily on the notion that humans process information in the form of symbols and language (e.g., schema that are stored in memory structures, such as long-term memory). This approach draws many of its ideas from computer science. On the other hand, *connectionist architectures* are focused on the way information is processed on the neural level (e.g., information exists within interconnected groups or neurons and is processed by the spread of activation or inhibition among the groups) and draws its ideas from brain research and neurobiology.[18] A basic distinction is between viewing information processing using a computer metaphor (the symbolic approach) versus using a brain metaphor (the connectionist approach).

Although symbolic and connectionist architectures specify different structures and have different assumptions about how humans process information, they should not be seen as mutually exclusive. It is likely that information processing occurs at both levels, and that phenomena that are not explained by one approach may be explained by the other.[19] Therefore, both views can provide useful ideas about learning and how we can create situations that increase the chances learning will occur. One implication for HRD is that HRD interventions should be based on the cognitive architecture that best explains how a particular task or skill operates and is learned. Relying on an inappropriate architecture may lead to poorer performance both during the HRD intervention and back on the job.[20]

Various reviews of research in instructional psychology,[21] cognitive psychology,[22] and adult learning[23] provide a good place for the reader to investigate the developments in these fields, and how they will shape HRD and training methods in the future. Instructional psychology and cognitive psychology hold promise for maximizing learning from HRD programs. As the nature of work continues to shift from manual skill to more complex mental processes, the findings from these fields will help pave the way for effective HRD efforts in the future. Researchers William Howell and Nancy Cooke have shown how information processing models and instructional psychology concepts can be applied to training.[24] We will consider some of these applications at the end of this chapter.

## MAXIMIZING LEARNING

Our definition of learning makes it clear that people acquire and develop skills, knowledge, and change behavior as a result of an interaction between forces within the learner and in the environment. In this section of the chapter, we present factors that have been shown to affect learning and discuss their outcomes. We discuss three primary areas as we emphasize ways to maximize learning, namely trainee characteristics, training design, and the transfer of training (see Table 3-1).

### TRAINEE CHARACTERISTICS

A learner or trainee's personal characteristics will influence how he or she learns new tasks and new information. Three such characteristics are trainability, personality, and attitudes.

*TRAINABILITY.* **Trainability** focuses on the trainee's readiness to learn and combines the trainee's level of ability and motivation with his or her perceptions of the work environment.[25] A simple formula to convey this is:

Trainability = $f$ (Motivation $\times$ Ability $\times$ Perceptions of the Work Environment)

**TABLE 3-1**

## ISSUES INVOLVED IN MAXIMIZING LEARNING

### Trainee Characteristics

Trainability
  Motivation
  Ability
  Perception of the work environment
Personality and attitudes

### Training Design

Conditions of practice
  Active practice
  Massed versus spaced practice sessions
  Whole versus part learning
  Overlearning
  Knowledge of results (feedback)
  Task sequencing
Retention of what is learned
  Meaningfulness of material
  Degree of original learning
  Interference

### Transfer of Training

Identical elements
General principles
Stimulus variability
Support in the work environment
  Opportunity to perform
  Transfer-of-training climate

This formula illustrates that a trainee must have both the motivation and the ability to learn; if either is lacking, learning will not occur. The equation also shows that a very high level of one cannot completely overcome a very low level of the other.[26] In addition, if employees perceive little support in the work environment for learning new knowledge or skills, they will be less likely to learn and use them.[27] Thus, it is important to note that trainability is not just a function of the individual trainee, but also of the work environment in which the learner will be asked to use what was presented in the HRD intervention.

Trainability is extremely important in HRD. Placing employees in programs they are not motivated to attend or are not prepared to do well in wastes time and resources. Trainees with less ability take longer to learn, which can increase the length of the training period and the expense involved in conducting training. In fact, it is possible that such trainees may never learn to the levels desired by the organization.

To illustrate this, suppose a service technician for an office equipment company is in a training program designed to teach selling skills for the equipment being serviced. Selling requires skills in oral communication and interpersonal relations. If the technician lacks either skill, it is likely that learning to sell effectively will be difficult. The technician may want to learn and try hard to do so, but this low level of ability will hinder learning. Similarly, if the technician has excellent communication skills but sees selling as unpleasant or distasteful, or does not think learning to sell will help to achieve his or her own personal goals, no effort may be made to learn the sales skills. A number of studies have shown the clear links between ability and learning.[28] The same is true for motivation,[29] as well as for perceptions of the work environment.[30]

Over the past several years, researchers have studied the notion of *pretraining motivation*.[31] Findings of recent research include:

■ The *way trainees perceive training* (e.g., as remedial versus advanced, or as an unpleasant task versus an opportunity) affects levels of learning, perceptions of efficacy, anxiety, and perceptions of fairness.[32]

■ The *way in which individuals view their own ability* (as a fixed entity or an acquirable skill) affects anxiety level, efficacy perceptions, and the learning of declarative (factual) knowledge.[33]

■ *Experiencing negative events on the job prior to training* can *increase* trainees' motivation to learn and their performance in training.[34]

■ A number of *other factors have been found to increase individuals' motivation to participate in and learn from training*. Factors investigated include involvement in decisions about training, perceptions that participation in training will lead to benefits (e.g., increased job performance and career advancement opportunities), and perceptions of support,[35] or lack of obstacles to use what has been learned in the work environment.[36]

■ *Characteristics of the organization* (e.g., policies and guidelines regarding training participation) have been linked to participation in developmental activities.[37]

These findings are useful in that they suggest ways in which organizations can increase the motivation to participate in and learn from HRD interventions. For example, to ensure that trainees perceive the value of what is being presented, they must see training as an opportunity, as a way to address a need they have, and as a way to achieve valued outcomes. Further, trainees must perceive the organization and their immediate work environment as supporting participation in training and in using what has been learned. However, for an interesting study of the potential *downfall* of allowing trainees some choice in what training they receive, see the boxed insert nearby entitled, "The Perils of Participation."

## "The Perils of Participation"

Picture the following: you've agreed to attend a two-hour, skill-based training session. When you enter the room, packets are handed out that list four choices for possible training topics for this session. One of the topics is "performance appraisal and feedback." You either select this topic as your most preferred option — or you don't. The question is: will your pretraining motivation and posttraining learning be any different depending upon whether you received your top choice or whether you didn't? Further, would results differ for other trainees who were given no choice, that is, they were told when they entered the room that they would be taking part in a training session on performance appraisal and feedback?

Researchers at Indiana University addressed these questions. Through a pretest of other similar trainees, they discovered that performance appraisal was rated as average among trainee preferences for potential training content. Through a clever manipulation, some trainees saw other options on their sheet (besides appraisal), which the results from the pretest suggested most trainees would view more favorably than performance appraisal (hence, trainees would be less likely to select appraisal as their preferred training topic). Other trainees received packets where all the other options had been rated considerably lower than appraisal (making it more likely that appraisal would be selected as the preferred training choice). Through a true majority vote (no deception here), the performance appraisal topic was always selected as the "choice" for training content.

What the researchers found was that pretraining motivation was highest for those who received the training of their choice, and lowest for those who didn't (the mean for those given no choice was in between). As far as learning the material taught in training, those in the "choice-received" condition learned more than those in the "choice-not received" condition. Somewhat surprisingly, however, learning was greatest for those who had been given no choice concerning training content.

Given the natural expectation that providing trainees some choice would be a "good thing," this study raises the question of whether there may be potential risks in allowing choices in a training context. That is, it may not be practically or physically possible for every trainee to receive the training of his or her choice. If that is the case, then there could indeed be some "perils of participation." Not receiving one's choice of training topics could result in lower training motivation and worse outcomes than having been provided no choice at all. Trainee motivation is such a vital aspect of trainability (in this study, trainee cognitive ability was measured and statistically "controlled," so as to emphasize the effects of the three choice manipulations on pretraining motivation). Although choice and participation *are* generally "good things" in a training context, this project demonstrates the potential dangers of raising trainee expectations and then not meeting them. The same training program resulted in different learning and motivational outcomes, depending upon how it was presented to trainees. That's rather thought provoking, don't you think?

From Timothy T. Baldwin, Richard J. Magjuka, & Brian T. Loher (1991), "The perils of participation: Effects of choice of training on trainee motivation and learning," *Personnel Psychology, 44*, 51–66.

An experiment on the impact of ability and prior job knowledge on learning found that general cognitive ability (i.e., intelligence) had a direct impact on the acquisition of job knowledge, but prior job knowledge had almost no effect on the acquisition of subsequent job knowledge.[38] This finding suggests that cognitive ability rather than prior job knowledge should be used to select trainees into programs designed to teach complex tasks.

Trainability testing is one approach that can be used to ensure that trainees have both the motivation and the ability to learn. This approach focuses on measuring the motivation and relevant abilities of candidates for training and selecting for training only those who show a sufficient level of trainability. For example, some military researchers developed a questionnaire that measured motivational and personality factors to predict success in combat training. The questionnaire measured such things as independence, sociability, and motivation to serve in a combat unit. The combination of questionnaire responses and other predictors was strongly related to training success.[39]

Another approach to trainee testing is to allow candidates to complete part of the training program and use their performance on that section as a predictor of how well they will perform during the remainder of training. For example, Arthur Siegel described a method called miniature training and evaluation testing, in which U.S. Navy recruits were trained on a sample of important tasks and tested on their ability to perform these tasks. Using eleven training and evaluation modules, the approach yielded better predictions of success for several jobs than the test normally conducted by the Navy.[40] In a manufacturing setting, auto manufacturer BMW took a similar approach when it opened its first U.S. manufacturing facility in Greer, South Carolina. To lure the company to South Carolina, state government officials offered generous tax incentives. The state also agreed to create training facilities to BMW's specifications, and worked with BMW to recruit and train potential BMW employees. Once trainees completed their training, BMW selected only those they wanted to hire to be among the initial 1,500 associates in its new plant. BMW stated that it was looking for associates with a strong commitment to quality and teamwork, and this procedure allowed the company to select the very best among those who had completed the rigorous training program administered by the state's technical college system. The quality and success of the cars made at this plant (including the Z3 roadster), as well as subsequent expansions of the plant and workforce, indicate that this "train, and then select" strategy was successful.[41] Similarly, from the research literature, a meta-analysis of research studies examining the use of work sample tests of trainability concluded that such tests predict success in training and job performance for untrained job applicants.[42] Trainability testing has also been effective in predicting the training success of older workers.[43]

*PERSONALITY AND ATTITUDES.* Although not explicitly mentioned in the definition of trainability, a trainee's personality and attitudes can also have an effect on learning (see Chapter 2). Ray Noe suggested that an employee's attitudes toward career exploration and job involvement impact learning and its applications to the job.[44] Other research has shown that job involvement, expectations for training, and trainee confidence are all related to success in training.[45]

**Personality** is the stable set of personal characteristics that account for consistent patterns of behavior. Personality traits that are related to employee learning include locus of control, the need for achievement,[46] activity, independence, and sociability.[47] Murray Barrick and Michael Mount reported the results of a meta-analysis showing that two personality dimensions — extraversion and openness to experience — are valid predictors of success in training.[48] Joseph Martocchio and Jane Webster found that an individual's level of *cognitive playfulness* (which is in part the spontaneity, imagination, and exploratory approach a person brings to task performance and learning) affects learning, mood, and satisfaction with training.[49] They also found that individuals with low levels of cognitive playfulness were affected more by positive feedback than individuals with higher levels of cognitive playfulness. As further research is conducted on the impact of personality characteristics on success in training, it may be useful to include measures of relevant traits in the selection process before trainees are sent to expensive or lengthy training and other HRD programs.

To summarize, assessing employee's relevant abilities, motivation, and personality prior to HRD programs can be important in maximizing the chances that learning will occur. This approach to maximizing learning fits with Glaser's notion that knowing the initial state of the learner is an important part of effective training.[50]

## TRAINING DESIGN

**Training design** involves adapting the learning environment to maximize learning. Training design issues include (1) the conditions of practice that influence learning and (2) the factors that impact retention of what is learned.

Although much of the research on this topic was conducted before 1970, new research in instructional psychology has revived interest. Although the information presented in the following sections can be helpful in designing an effective training program, not all the findings will work in all situations. Recall Gagné's arguments cited earlier about traditional learning principles.[51] There is no substitute for conducting a thorough task analysis and clearly specifying what is to be learned (task analysis will be discussed in Chapter 4).

*CONDITIONS OF PRACTICE.* At least six issues have been studied that relate to practice and learning. They include active practice, massed versus spaced practice sessions, whole versus part learning, overlearning, knowledge of results, and task sequencing.

**Active practice** suggests that learners should be given an opportunity to repeatedly perform the task or use the knowledge being learned. For example, if a paramedic is learning how to operate the "jaws of life" (to extract passengers from vehicles damaged in accidents), the training sessions should include multiple opportunities for the paramedic to operate the "jaws."

Researchers have also been interested in whether **mental practice,** the "cognitive rehearsal of a task in the absence of overt physical movement," can improve task performance.[52] Although early research on the topic yielded mixed results, a meta-analysis of many studies concluded that mental practice is effective for both cognitive and physical tasks (though more so for cognitive tasks). This study also showed that the effect of mental practice on performance decreases as the time interval between practice and performance increases.[53] These findings suggest that trainees should be encouraged to mentally rehearse the tasks they are learning to perform outside of the training environment as one way to enhance their performance.

*Massed versus spaced practice sessions* concern whether to conduct the training in one session or divide it into segments separated by some period of time. For example, is it better to study for an exam over a period of several days (spaced practice) or in one cram session (massed practice)? In general, information and skills can be learned either way, but spaced practice sessions with a reasonable rest period between them lead to better performance and longer retention of what is learned than a massed practice session.[54] For difficult, complex tasks, an initial massed session followed by spaced practice sessions has led to improved performance.[55]

Using a massed rather than a spaced practice session is often a matter of practicality winning out over science. Time and resource constraints may influence organizational decision makers to schedule a single training session, even though a series of spaced sessions would be more effective. However, HRD professionals should realize that under these conditions retention may suffer. It may be necessary to schedule follow-up sessions to boost retention. Further, the effectiveness of the approach used to motivate trainees during training may be affected by whether massed or spaced sessions are used. One research study found that trainees who were assigned specific, difficult goals in massed practice performed more poorly than those simply told to "do your best," whereas those in spaced sessions who were assigned specific, difficult goals performed slightly better than those told to "do your best."[56]

*Whole versus part learning* concerns the size of the unit to be learned, that is, should trainees practice an entire task (or study certain material as a whole), or should the task or material be learned in separate parts or chunks? Gagné argued that procedural material (material organized into a series of steps) should be analyzed and divided into subunits, with the trainees mastering each subunit before performing the entire procedure.[57]

Actually, the answer to which method is most effective appears to depend on the nature of the task to be learned. When the subtasks are relatively easy to perform and are well organized (interrelated), the *whole method* is superior. Otherwise, the *part method* has proven to be more effective.[58] For example, operating a chain saw involves adding fuel, holding it properly, starting it, making various cuts, and turning it off. Given that these subtasks are interrelated, it makes sense that they be learned together. The task of supervising others, however, includes subtasks such as scheduling, evaluating employee performance, disciplining, planning, and delegating work. These subtasks are less closely related and would best be learned by focusing on each subtask separately. To teach someone how to drive a stick shift automobile, which approach would you use?

**Overlearning** is defined as practice beyond the point at which the material or task is mastered.[59] For example, an instructor teaching cardiopulmonary resuscitation (CPR) in a first-aid course would be using overlearning if trainees were required to repeatedly practice the CPR procedure even after they had successfully "revived" the training dummy.

The rationale for overlearning is threefold. First, overlearning may improve performance in a variety of different situations. By developing stronger associations between the parts of a task or unit of knowledge, it is less likely that situational changes will interfere with learning.[60] Second, overlearning provides additional practice in using the skill or knowledge when there is little opportunity for doing so in the job setting.[61] For example, overlearning the procedure to handle an engine flameout would be useful in pilot training because pilots don't often face this situation when flying. Third, overlearning should make what is learned more "automatic," thereby improving performance in stressful or emergency situations.[62] For instance, U.S. and coalition soldiers in the Persian Gulf War repeatedly practiced their maneuvers and tasks (including setup and firing procedures for Patriot missile batteries, troop movements, and use of chemical warfare gear), so that when the orders came to attack, these tasks would be second nature to the soldiers and they could perform them quickly and correctly.

Research indicates that overlearning does, in fact, increase retention of what is learned.[63] Quite obviously, its major drawback is that overlearning can increase the time and expense of training.

*Knowledge of results,* or *feedback,* provides objective information regarding the adequacy of one's performance, and it can come from observers, the performer, or the task itself. A sizable body of research suggests that feedback enhances learning and retention.[64] Trainers and educators generally agree that feedback improves learning. However, a recent meta-analysis of research on feedback interventions found that feedback actually *decreased* performance in one-third of the studies examined.[65] Avraham Kluger and Angelo DeNisi theorized that this had to do with the *level of control* individuals go through when learning and performing tasks. They argued that individuals proceed through three hierarchical levels of control (task learning, task motivation, and metatasks or self-regulatory actions), and that feedback changes the individual's locus of attention to a particular level of control. They suggested that the effectiveness of feedback decreases as the individual moves through the levels from task learning to task motivation to metatasks. Kluger and DeNisi's theory supports the use of feedback during skill and knowledge acquisition, but suggests that feedback will be less effective (and may even harm performance) as individuals perform back on the job.

Other researchers suggest that feedback is both *informational* — when it helps learners determine whether they've performed something correctly, and *motivational* — when it is valued by the learner or indicates valued outcomes.[66] The effectiveness of feedback also seems to depend on how it is provided, especially in regard to timing and specificity. To ensure that the learner clearly understands the relationship between the feedback and the behavior, it should be provided as soon as possible after the behavior occurs.[67] Further, the attributions individuals make about feedback (whether it is attributed to factors within or outside of the trainee's control) can affect efficacy beliefs, with feedback attributed to factors within the trainee's control increasing perceptions of efficacy.[68] In addition, recall the research cited earlier that found that the impact of feedback may be moderated by elements of the individual's personality (i.e., cognitive playfulness).[69]

Finally, *task sequencing* suggests that tasks and knowledge can be learned more effectively if what is to be learned is divided into subtasks that are arranged and taught in an appropriate sequence.[70] Gagné and colleagues provide guidelines for how task sequencing can help in learning intellectual skills, motor skills, and attitudes.[71] The success of an intelligent medical diagnosis-tutoring program called GUIDON supports this approach,[72] as does the research of Philip Decker and others on behavior modeling training.[73] However, more research is needed before definitive conclusions are reached about the effectiveness of task sequencing.

To summarize, research on the various conditions of practice offers some practical guidelines for designing more effective HRD interventions. In general, overlearning, feedback, and practice sessions spaced over time all tend to increase learning.

## RETENTION OF WHAT IS LEARNED

The goal of training goes beyond ensuring that the trainee learns the task or material being presented. It is equally important that newly learned material is *retained*. Three additional issues that influence retention are the meaningfulness of material, the degree of original learning, and interference.

The **meaningfulness of material** is the extent to which it is rich in associations for the individual learner. For example, a new way of soldering circuits might be quite significant to an electronics enthusiast, yet absolutely meaningless to a professional athlete or a hair stylist.

Simply put, the more meaningful factual material is, the easier it is to learn and remember.[74] Thus, training should be designed to be more meaningful to employees to encourage learning retention. Overviews of topics at the beginning of training sessions can help trainees understand the course content as a whole. Using examples and terminology familiar to trainees and mnemonic devices (such as creating a word out of the first letters of items in a list) also increase meaningfulness by providing more associations.[75] Textbook writers (us included) often seek to use this principle when introducing and presenting the material in each chapter.

The **degree of original learning** also influences learning retention. The more effectively that information is initially learned, the more likely it will be retained — after all, you can't retain something you never had to begin with. Though this is not surprising, it does reinforce the research on overlearning, massed versus spaced practice, and whole versus part learning as ways to ensure initial learning.

**Interference** can also affect the extent to which learning is retained. Interference can be of two types.[76] First, material or skills learned *before* the training session can inhibit recall of the newly learned material. For example, an accountant who is an expert on the New York tax code may have difficulty remembering recent instruction regarding the tax code and procedures for Florida. The accountant's prior knowledge is so well learned that he or she may automatically follow New York procedures when helping a client who must file in Florida.

Second, information learned *after* a training session may also interfere with retention. For example, a firefighter trained to operate the power ladder on the city's older fire trucks may have difficulty retaining that knowledge if a different sequence of steps must be learned for the same operation on a newer fire truck.

Both types of interference are similar in that the learner is required to make different responses to the same situation. The more responses one learns, the greater the chances are for interference in learning to occur.

## TRANSFER OF TRAINING

**Transfer of training** is a recurring theme in HRD literature. A main goal of HRD is to ensure that employees perform their jobs effectively. In addition to learning and retaining new material, employees must also use it on the job to improve performance. The transfer of training to the job situation is critically important to the success of HRD efforts.

Transfer can take different forms. *Positive transfer* occurs when job performance is improved as a result of training. *Zero transfer* occurs when there is no change in job performance as a result of training. *Negative transfer* occurs when job performance is worse as a result of training. Negative transfer may seem unlikely, but recall the detrimental effect interference can have on learning and performance. Tennis players, for example, may find that their tennis shots become less accurate after learning how to play racquetball. Although the two sports seem similar, an accurate tennis shot requires a locked wrist, yet racquetball players use their wrists during the swing. Therefore, the player's tennis stroke may become more "wristy" after learning racquetball, leading to less accurate shots in tennis.

Another distinction that should be made is between "near transfer" and "far transfer." *Near transfer* has to do with the ability to directly apply on the job what has been learned in training, with little adjustment or modification, whereas *far transfer* has to do with expanding upon or using what was learned in training in new or creative ways.[77] Other writers have referred to this as a distinction between skill reproduction and skill generalization.[78] For example, in a study of assertiveness training, a negative relationship was observed between near and far transfer, that is, trainees who had done well during training in demonstrating their mastery of the training content did less well in a "surprise" test of their ability to demonstrate transfer outside of training, and vice versa.[79] It obviously depends upon the context whether an organization is more concerned with near transfer, far transfer, or both, though in most cases, far transfer is the best indicator that training has been successful.

Timothy Baldwin and Kevin Ford developed a model of the training transfer process (see Figure 3-1).[80] The model suggests that training inputs — including trainee characteristics, training design, and the work environment — affect learning, retention, and transfer, with trainee characteristics and the work environment affecting transfer directly. However, Baldwin and Ford were critical of the lack of a strong theoretical framework and the limited number of research studies in this area, as this limits our ability to generalize the findings from studies of transfer of training to organizational settings. Despite these concerns, these principles and the results of recent research offer many ideas for maximizing training transfer. These include the use of identical elements, general principles, stimulus variability, and the degree of support for transfer in the work environment.

*IDENTICAL ELEMENTS.* The principle of **identical elements,** first proposed by Thorndike and Woodworth in 1901, suggests that the more similar the training and the performance situations are in terms of the stimuli present and responses required, the more likely it is that training transfer will occur.[81] For example, if customer service representatives are expected to handle complaints from angry,

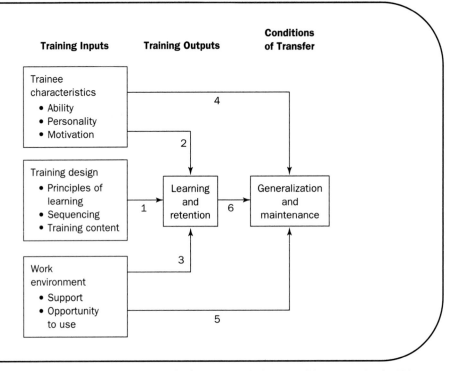

**FIGURE 3-1**

**BALDWIN & FORD'S (1988) TRANSFER OF TRAINING MODEL**

SOURCE: From "Transfer of training: A review and directions for future research" by T. T. Baldwin & J. K. Ford, 1988, *Personnel Psychology, 41,* p. 65. Reprinted by permission.

impatient customers, practice with such customers (possibly by using role playing) can improve the transfer of training. But if the only examples used in training are customers who are polite, reasonable, and patient, training transfer to the job is less likely.

Similarity has two dimensions: physical and psychological fidelity. **Physical fidelity** is the extent to which the conditions of the training program, such as equipment, tasks, and surroundings, are the same as in the performance situation. Building a highly realistic airline cockpit simulator, with the same controls, appearance, and physical sensations as experienced in true flight, would be an attempt to achieve a high level of physical fidelity. **Psychological fidelity** is the extent to which trainees attach similar meanings to both the training and performance situations. Psychological fidelity would be encouraged in a learning experience that imposes time limits on training tasks that are similar to those back on the job. Although there is some evidence that psychological fidelity is more important to training transfer than is physical fidelity,[82] Baldwin and Ford argue that more research is needed to support this claim.

The principle of identical elements is particularly relevant to simulation training, such as case studies, business games, or role plays. However, increasing fidelity often involves increasing complexity and costs, which can strain HRD budgets. So, once again, there are frequently trade-offs between what is desired and what can actually be carried out in terms of fidelity and identical elements.

*GENERAL PRINCIPLES.* Rather than focusing on identical elements, the *general principles theory* suggests that learning the fundamental elements of a task will ensure transfer from training. This was demonstrated in a project that taught trainees to accurately hit an underwater target by learning the principle of refraction of light.[83] Because light bends when crossing the air-water boundary, the target is not exactly where it visually appears to be. Understanding this principle allowed trainees to correctly judge where the target really was and adjust their aim accordingly.

However, it is often difficult to identify and include in training those principles that maximize positive transfer. It is still not clear whether training programs that apply the general principles theory will result in skilled performance on specific tasks.[84]

*STIMULUS VARIABILITY.* Transfer can be enhanced when training contains a variety of stimuli, such as using multiple examples of a concept or involving the trainee in several different practice situations.[85] For example, stimulus variability is increased when clothier trainees are required to practice making buttonholes in a variety of fabrics, rather than in only one or two types of fabric. Stimulus variability has been found to increase training transfer.[86]

*SUPPORT IN THE WORK ENVIRONMENT.* The extent to which trainees perceive support for using newly learned behavior or knowledge on the job affects transfer of training. For example, if a supervisor who is trying to become more participative is ridiculed by peers and receives the cold shoulder from subordinates, it is unlikely that this person will continue to use these skills.

*Supervisory support* is an important aspect of work environment support. Supervisory support is a multidimensional concept. Components such as encouragement to attend training, goal setting, reinforcement, and behavior modeling have all been shown to increase transfer.[87]

Support at the *organizational level* is also important. Janice Rouiller and Irwin Goldstein studied employee perceptions of the **transfer of training climate,** which is defined as "those situations and consequences which either inhibit or help to facilitate the transfer of what has been learned in training into the job situation."[88] Climate perceptions affected learning and behavior back on the job. Bruce Tracey, Scott Tannenbaum, and Michael Kavanagh investigated the effect of both transfer of training climate and the presence of a **continuous-learning work environment** (where "organizational members share perceptions and expectations that learning is an important part of everyday work life" p. 241) on employee behavior after training. They found that the presence of both transfer of training climate and a continuous-learning work environment affected behavior after training. This research suggests that the organizational climate should be examined to determine the supportiveness of the work environment during needs assessment, and that areas found wanting should be modified to increase the chances training will transfer back to the workplace. Also, organizations that promote a continuous-learning environment stand a better chance of having what is learned transfer back to the job.[89]

Robert Marx proposed a model of improving training transfer based on counseling techniques used to prevent relapse by substance abusers. The approach teaches trainees and supervisors to anticipate and prevent regressions to old behavior patterns. By developing strategies to cope with and overcome foreseen obstacles, the trainee will feel a greater sense of control and self-efficacy, thereby reducing the chances of relapse.[90] A field study of research scientists who went through a coaching skills training program found that the relapse prevention tactics had the greatest effect when individual scientists also reported a strong transfer climate in their department. However, by themselves, the relapse prevention strategies had a small and statistically nonsignificant impact on each of the three outcome measures used in this study.[91]

Overall, supervisory support can increase transfer by clarifying the manager's and trainee's expectations prior to training, and by making managers aware of their role in the transfer process so they can develop ways to encourage transfer.[92]

The **opportunity to perform** what has been learned back on the job is an important element of the work environment. Work by Kevin Ford and colleagues is useful here. They define the opportunity to perform as "the extent to which a trainee is provided with or actively obtains work experiences relevant to tasks for which he or she was trained."[93] The opportunity to perform is influenced by both the organization and the individual. Ford et al. investigated the effects of three groups of variables (organizational level, work level, and individual characteristics) on the opportunity to perform. They found that subjects did have different opportunities to perform trained tasks on the job and that the variables that most influenced their opportunities to perform included the supervisors' attitudes toward training, work group support, and the trainees' self-efficacy and cognitive ability.

A recent study by Lim and Johnson asked trainees to list reasons for the lack of transfer from an organizational training program. The number one reason cited for low transfer (listed by over 64 percent of trainees!) was "lack of opportunity to apply on the job."[94] More research is needed to specify the factors that influence the opportunity to perform. However, it is clear that an effective HRD strategy should include ensuring that trainees have opportunities to use their new skills and knowledge if real organizational benefit is expected from HRD interventions.

Research on transfer of training offers a number of suggestions for designing training and HRD programs, eight of which are listed in Table 3-2. We view these as some practical "take away" or lessons to be learned from our discussion of training transfer.

## INDIVIDUAL DIFFERENCES IN THE LEARNING PROCESS

As discussed earlier, trainee characteristics play a role in the learning, retention, and transfer of skills and factual material. We now identify three additional factors that account for differences in individual learning processes: namely, different rates of trainee progress, interactions between attributes and treatment, and the training of adults and older workers.

| TABLE 3-2 | SUGGESTIONS FOR INCREASING THE CHANCES TRAINING WILL TRANSFER BACK TO THE JOB |

1. Develop (and follow) clearly stated learning objectives for the training.
2. Maximize the similarity between the training situation and the job situation.
3. Provide ample opportunity during training to practice the task.
4. Use a variety of situations and examples, including both positive and negative models of the intended behavior.
5. Identify and label important features of a task.
6. Make sure trainees understand general principles.
7. Provide support back in the work environment, including clear goals, checklists, measurement, feedback, and rewards for using the new behaviors on the job.
8. Provide ample opportunity to perform what is learned back on the job.

SOURCES: "Transfer of training: A review and directions for future research" by T. T. Baldwin & J. K. Ford, 1988, *Personnel Psychology, 41*, 63–103; "Effects of alternative modeling strategies on outcomes of interpersonal skills training" by T. T. Baldwin, 1992, *Journal of Applied Psychology, 77*, 147–154; "Augmenting behavior-modeling training: Testing the effects of pre- and post-training interventions" by J. M. Werner, A. M. O'Leary-Kelly, T. T. Baldwin, & K. N. Wexley, 1994, *Human Resource Development Quarterly, 5*, 169–183; *The transfer of learning* by H. C. Ellis, 1965, New York: Macmillan; J. K. Ford, M. A. Quiñones, D. J. Sego, & J. S. Sorra, 1992, "Factors affecting the opportunity to perform trained tasks on the job," *Personnel Psychology, 45*, 511–527; "How to ensure transfer of training" by P. L. Garavaglia, 1993, *Training & Development, 47*(10), 63–68.

## RATE OF PROGRESS

People learn at different rates. Some people progress more quickly than others, and individual learners may even progress at different rates during the same training program. For example, a new employee learning how to operate a punch press may show little progress at first, making many mistakes, and then suddenly master the procedure and quickly progress to competence.

A useful way to show rates of learning is by drawing **learning curves.** A learning curve is plotted on a graph with learning proficiency indicated vertically on the y-axis and elapsed time indicated horizontally on the x-axis. Five types of learning curves are shown in Figure 3-2.

The learning curve for Trainee 1 shows a fast rate of learning, taking little time to achieve high performance. The curve for Trainee 2 shows a slower rate of learning, with training ending at a lower level of final performance than for Trainee 1. Trainee 3 reaches a moderate level of performance quickly but then makes little further progress despite continued practice. This contrasts to the progress of Trainee 4, who learns slowly at first but steadily improves to a high level of performance. Finally, the S-shaped learning curve for Trainee 5 shows rapid progress at first, followed by a period of little progress during the middle of training, and then rapid progress in the latter part of training.

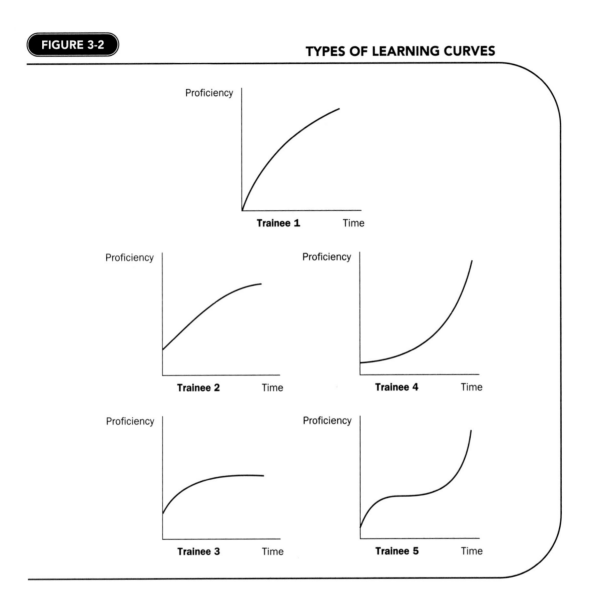

**FIGURE 3-2** TYPES OF LEARNING CURVES

Learning curves can provide useful feedback to both trainers and trainees. For instance, if a trainer notices a plateau (the flat part of a curve indicating no progress is being made), a different approach, encouragement, or some other intervention may be needed for the trainee to improve. When implementing a new HRD program, plotting learning curves can be used as a baseline for communicating expectations of progress to future trainees and trainers, and as aids in scheduling and planning future sessions.

## ATTRIBUTE-TREATMENT INTERACTION (ATI)

Interest in the effect of trainee intelligence on learning has led some researchers to hypothesize that the effectiveness of training methods may be influenced by various trainee characteristics. Stated simply, some methods of training may be better suited to certain types of people. Thus, research on attribute-treatment interactions (ATI) has sought to develop training systems that can be adapted to differences between individual learners.[95]

Two variables that have received considerable attention in ATI research are cognitive ability and motivation. The expectancy theory of motivation (discussed in Chapter 2) suggests that when motivation is low, both high- and low-ability individuals will perform at low levels, but when motivation is high, differences in performance can be expected between high- and low-ability individuals.[96] To date, research has found little conclusive evidence of an interaction between motivation and ability. Jeff Terborg argued that the mixed evidence regarding the existence of a motivation-ability ATI may be due to differences in complexity of the tasks studied. Terborg suggested that tasks of moderate difficulty would be the place where ATIs would most likely occur.[97]

An illustration of a well-developed ATI theory is the **cognitive resource allocation theory** proposed by Ruth Kanfer and Philip Ackerman.[98] Their theory uses an information processing perspective to explain the existence of a cognitive ability-motivation ATI for both skill acquisition and task performance of moderately difficult tasks. We will discuss this theory in some detail to illustrate the ATI approach, and to also give the reader a sense of the contributions being made to HRD by cognitive psychology.

Cognitive resource allocation theory is based on several propositions, which are explained below.[99]

1. The attentional demands made by a task will determine the contribution of both ability and motivation to task performance.

2. The attentional demands required to acquire a skill change during the skill acquisition process. Skill acquisition occurs in three phases: *declarative knowledge* (forming a mental representation of the task), *knowledge compilation* (integration of cognitive and motor processes needed to perform a task), and *procedural knowledge* (knowing how to perform cognitive processes and being able to perform the task "automatically," with little attention).[100] Attentional demands are highest during the declarative knowledge phase, but are reduced significantly during knowledge compilation and proceduralization.

3. Cognitive ability is related to the amount of attentional resources an individual has: the higher the level of cognitive ability (e.g., general intelligence), the more attentional resources the individual has. For example, research shows that intelligence predicts performance best during the declarative knowledge phase (when attentional demands are high) and predicts performance less well during the procedural knowledge phase (when attentional demands are low).

4. Motivational processes place a limit on the amount of cognitive resources available (e.g., attention) that an individual will apply to a task (e.g., the more motivation, the more available attention the individual will apply to the task). In addition, *motivational processes* that determine how the individual allocated cognitive resources (e.g., self-regulation, goal setting) require cognitive resources themselves, thereby using resources that could be used to learn or perform the task. Therefore, to the extent that motivational processes use cognitive resources that can only be taken from the resources needed to perform the task, task performance will be hindered rather than facilitated by the motivational attempt.

Cognitive resource allocation theory predicts that:

1. Individuals with higher levels of cognitive ability will perform better than those with lower levels of cognitive ability during the declarative knowledge phase (because they have more attentional resources available), but that this differential will decrease as the knowledge becomes proceduralized (because attentional demands are reduced during this phase).

2. Motivational efforts will reduce performance during the declarative knowledge phase (because they use part of the limited attentional resources available to learn the task), but enhance performance during the compilation and proceduralization phases (because attentional demands of these phases are less, freeing up resources for motivational processes), especially for low-ability individuals.

3. The negative impact of using attentional resources for motivation during the declarative knowledge phase will have less of an impact on high-cognitive-ability individuals (because they have a greater amount of resources to draw upon).

The research conducted to date generally supports these predictions.[101] It appears as though ability and self-efficacy are better predictors of performance in the early stages of skill acquisition, whereas motivation is a better predictor of performance during later stages. Perhaps the most direct implication of this research is that motivational efforts may be best saved until later phases of training for moderately complex tasks when they are less likely to harm performance and more likely to lead to higher levels of performance. Further research of this type will help us to better understand those attributes that influence training design effectiveness in organizational settings.

## TRAINING ADULT AND OLDER WORKERS

Given the graying of the workforce and the rate at which jobs have been changing, some theorists have questioned whether training older workers requires a different approach than training younger people. This subject has been approached from several directions, including adult learning theory and gerontology.

*ADULT LEARNING THEORY.* Researchers such as Malcolm Knowles noted that many principles of learning and instructional methods were developed with and for children, and argued that teaching adults requires using a different set of techniques.[102] **Pedagogy** (PED a go gee) is the term traditionally used for instructional methodology, and this has most often emphasized educating children and teenagers through high school. Knowles proposed an adult-oriented approach to learning that he called **andragogy** (AN dra go gee). Table 3-3 lists important differences between a pedagogical and an andragogical approach to learning.

Andragogy is based on four assumptions about differences between adults and children:

1. Adults are *self-directed.*

2. Adults have acquired a large amount of *knowledge and experience* that can be tapped as a resource for learning.

3. Adults show a greater *readiness to learn tasks that are relevant* to the roles they have assumed in life.

4. Adults are *motivated to learn* in order to solve problems or address needs, and they *expect to immediately apply* what they learn to these problems and needs.[103]

Andragogical instructional techniques are designed with these factors in mind. These techniques include joint planning, self-diagnosis, formulation of learning objectives, a collaborative teaching process, and involvement of students in the evaluation of success.[104] Two examples illustrate how this approach has been applied. First, an andragogical approach was used to teach writing to adults. The program used fifteen strategies including the following:

- Consider the audience (for instance, conduct a needs assessment).
- Remember that adults need to be self-determining.
- Use peer collaboration.
- Include assessment to enhance course content.
- Find clear applications for writing.
- Rely on students' experiences.
- Include students in evaluating writing.[105]

A second example comes from an article discussing the differences between "how learners learn" and "how trainers teach." Shari Caudron spells out a number of differences between traditional (student) and nontraditional (adult) learners.[106] These ideas are presented in Table 3-4 and may generate some discussion among class members.

Although andragogy has intuitive appeal, there are also some major concerns. Critics argue that separating the learning process into two stages — child and adult learning — makes little sense. Rather, they see learning as a continuous process.[107] In addition, other significant problems and weaknesses of the andragogical approach have been noted. Some of the issues raised include the rigidity of the paradigm, the extent to which learners are either children or adults in their approach

**TABLE 3-3**

## COMPARING PEDAGOGY AND ANDRAGOGY
## ON SEVEN ISSUES

| Characteristic | Pedagogy | Andragogy |
|---|---|---|
| Structure | Based on aging process | Flexible, open, broad |
| | Rigid format | Responsive |
| | Subject/curriculum-centered | Interdisciplinary |
| | Rules, procedures, laws | Developmental |
| Atmosphere | Authority-oriented | Relaxed, trusting, mutually respectful |
| | Formal, low trust | Informal, warm |
| | Competitive | Collaborative, supportive |
| | Win-lose | Win-win |
| Leadership | Teacher dominant | Innovative, creative |
| | High task, low relationship | High task, high relationship |
| | Controlling | Interdependent, mature |
| | Does not value experience | relationship |
| | Assumes student immaturity | Mentoring, modeling |
| | and dependency | Experiential |
| | Low risk | High risk |
| Planning | Administration and teacher | Administration, faculty, and |
| | Emphasizes rationale, legal | students |
| | mechanisms | Mutual assessment |
| | Policies, plans, and decisions | Collaborative needs assessment |
| | Highly political | Mutual negotiation |
| | | Problem centered |
| Motivation | External rewards and | Internal incentives (curiosity) |
| | punishments | Self-directed |
| | | Learning contracts |
| Communication | One-way downward | Two-way |
| | Transmittal techniques | Mutually respectful |
| | Feelings repressed | Feelings expressed |
| | | Supportive |
| Evaluation | Teacher | Criterion-based |
| | Norm-referenced (curve) | Objective and subjective |
| | Grades | Jointly chosen standards by |
| | Subjective | students, peers, and teachers |

SOURCE: From "Adult learning and organizations," by N. Dailey, 1984, *Training and Development Journal, 38,* pp. 66, 68. Adapted by permission. Copyright © November 1984 from Training & Development Journal by Dailey, N. Adapted with permission of American Society for Training & Development.

**TABLE 3-4**

## SOME PROPOSED DIFFERENCES BETWEEN "TRADITIONAL" AND "NONTRADITIONAL" LEARNERS

| TRADITIONAL | NONTRADITIONAL |
|---|---|
| 1. Need motivation; not always sure why they are in training. | Highly motivated; want to learn. |
| 2. Raise few questions; often have little real-world experience to connect to the training content | Raise many questions in class and seek opportunities to analyze training content in terms of own experiences; Need to connect class materials to real-world experiences. |
| 3. Developed a tolerance for bureaucracy. | Have a low tolerance for bureaucracy. |
| 4. Resist participation; expect to be told what to do and how to do it. | Want to participate. Dislike being talked at; value discussions and projects. |
| 5. More future-oriented. Don't expect to immediately apply what they learn in training. | Concerned with immediate problems and their solutions. |
| 6. Major focus on good grades. | Primarily interested in content and its relevance to career and personal life. |
| 7. Tend to be idealistic. | Tend to be practical. |
| 8. Have a restricted worldview. | Have considerable knowledge to bring to training. |
| 9. Want to know "the answer," and tend to see things one way. | Look at problems as having several possible alternatives worth evaluating. |
| 10. Impatient; want things to happen "overnight." | Have patience with the world; understand that change takes time. |
| 11. Likely to accept information that they are given. | Can and will verify information given in training. |
| 12. Have few specific expectations. | Often have preconceived expectations of training that the instructor should try to identify if possible. If the training isn't what participants expected, they are likely to consider it to be a failure. |

SOURCE: Adapted from "Learners speak out" by Shari Caudron, 2000, *Training and Development, 54*(4), pp. 52–58. Adapted by permission. Copyright © April 2000 from Training & Development by Caudron, S. Adapted with permission of American Society for Training & Development.

to learning, the approach's lack of recognition of the differences among adult learners, and the reluctance of many HRD professionals to criticize the approach because it presents a socially desirable view of adults as learners.[108]

Although Knowles moderated some of his original claims, he continued to argue that andragogical techniques can be used to teach both adults and more traditional school-aged students.[109] Indeed, many of the recent trends in elementary and secondary education (e.g., group learning, writing based on students' experiences) seem remarkably similar to Knowles' suggestions for adult learning.

What seems necessary at this point is to move beyond andragogy by offering a more complex (and more realistic) view of adults as learners. As several recent reviews make clear, a significant amount of progress has been made recently in understanding adult learning.[110] For example, Sharan Merriam and Rosemary Caffarella present andragogy as *one* approach to adult learning, and present other approaches as well. In a different vein, John Newstrom and Mark Lengnick-Hall developed a contingency model that assumes that "adult learners are a heterogeneous group requiring different approaches to training and development depending on individual differences across important characteristics."[111] Based on this approach, trainee differences should be actively considered in designing HRD programs, leading to programs adapted to fit the characteristics of the participants. Newstrom and Lengnick-Hall propose assessing groups on ten dimensions, including attention span, self-confidence, and locus of control (see Table 3-5). This very much supports our emphasis on individual differences in this chapter.

**TABLE 3-5**

## A CONTINGENCY APPROACH TO ADULT LEARNING: DIMENSIONS FOR ASSESSING THE TRAINEE

1. **Instrumentality** Degree to which the trainee is concerned with the immediate applicability of the concepts and skills being taught.
2. **Skepticism** Degree to which the trainee exhibits a questioning attitude and demands logic, evidence, and examples.
3. **Resistance to Change** Degree to which the trainee fears the process of moving to the unknown, or the personal effects of that process.
4. **Attention Span** Length of time the trainee can focus attention before substantial attentiveness is diminished.
5. **Expectation Level** Level of quality (process) and quantity (content) that the trainee requires from the trainer or the training.
6. **Dominant Needs** Range of intrinsic and extrinsic individual needs that currently drive the trainee.
7. **Absorption Level** Pace at which the trainee expects and can accept new information.
8. **Topical Interest** Degree to which the trainee can be expected to have personal (job-relevant) interest in the topic.
9. **Self-confidence** Degree of trainee's independence and positive self-regard, thus requiring high or low levels of feedback, reinforcement, and success experiences.
10. **Locus of control** Degree to which the trainee perceives that training can be implemented successfully back on the job with or without organizational support.

SOURCE: From "One size does not fit all" by J. W. Newstrom & M. L. Lengnick-Hall, 1991, *Training and Development Journal, 45*(6), p. 46. Adapted by permission. Copyright © June 1991 from Training & Development by Newstrom, J. W., & Lengnick-Hall, M. L. Adapted with permission of American Society for Training & Development.

This contingency approach to adult learning shares some similarities with the notion of ATIs discussed earlier, but as with andragogy, research has yet to determine its superiority to other adult learning approaches. As Merriam and Caffarella state in concluding their discussion of various theories of adult learning, "The process of model and theory building does . . . stimulate inquiry and reflection, all of which may eventually provide some of the answers to our questions about adult learning."[112]

GERONTOLOGY. A second approach to the question of whether older adults need to be trained differently is rooted in gerontology and industrial gerontology. **Gerontology** is the scientific study of old age and aging. Recent research suggests some differences between older and younger adults in certain learning situations. For example, several studies have reported that older trainees performed worse on tests of declarative knowledge in computer training, although it is not clear whether these results are due to ability or motivation.[113] Also, in an open learning situation (i.e., self-directed participation in training activities such as use of videos, computer-based training, or interactive video), older trainees exhibited lower learning scores (i.e., ratings of learning by a tutor) than did younger trainees.[114] However, research is increasingly challenging the common stereotypes concerning older adults' ability to learn.[115] A consistent finding is that, although older adults can take longer to learn new knowledge and skills and tend to make more errors during learning, they can and do attain performance levels equal to those achieved by younger adults. In addition, individual expertise can be maintained throughout one's lifetime.

Five principles can be used for the effective training and development of older adults:

1. Older workers can and do develop.
2. Supervisors need to realize that they may consciously or unconsciously exclude older workers from training opportunities because of unwarranted negative attitudes.
3. For a training program to be effective for older workers, attention must be paid to motivation, structure, familiarity, organization, and time.
4. The organizational climate must reward entry into training and transfer of skills back to the job.
5. Training must be considered within an integrated career perspective.[116]

With respect to motivation, older adults may need more encouragement to attend training programs because of the negative attitudes others have about their ability to learn. Because older adults tend to take longer to reach proficiency, sufficient time should be scheduled to allow them to do so. And, because older adults may have a fear of failure or competition and may feel alienated in traditional training settings, active participation in the training program should be encouraged.[117] For a thoughtful discussion of the progress made in educating older adults since the 1960s, as well as the challenges still to be faced by the swelling numbers of such individuals, see a review by Ronald Manheimer.[118]

## LEARNING STRATEGIES AND STYLES

Another perspective on the learning process and how to maximize learning examines what people do when they learn. Learning styles and strategies can be important in determining learning outcomes. In this section, we briefly relate a sampling of ideas from the research studies regarding this aspect of learning.

### KOLB'S LEARNING STYLES

David Kolb, a leading theorist on experiential learning, argues that the learning process is not the same for all people. Because of the complex nature of the learning process, there are opportunities for individual differences and preferences to emerge. A **learning style** represents how individual choices made during the learning process affect what information is selected and how it is processed. Kolb illustrates the notion of learning styles by observing how people learn to play pool:

> Some people just step up and hit the ball without bothering to look very carefully at where their shot went unless it went in the pocket. Others seem to go through a great deal of analysis and measurement but seem a bit hesitant on the execution. Thus, there seem to be distinctive styles or strategies for learning and playing the game.[119]

Differences in learning styles can explain why some individuals are more comfortable and successful with some training approaches (e.g., role playing, lectures, and videotapes) than others. Similarly, learning style differences among trainers can also contribute to their preferences for certain training approaches over others.

Kolb theorizes that an individual's learning style is based on that person's preferred modes of learning. A **mode of learning** is the individual's orientation toward gathering and processing information during learning. Kolb proposed four basic modes of experiential learning:

1. **Concrete Experience (CE)** An intuitive preference for learning through direct experience, emphasizing interpersonal relations and *feeling* as opposed to thinking. For example, someone using this mode to learn about job politics would personally use various political tactics in different group situations to get a sense of how each one feels, while also gauging others' responses during each interaction.

2. **Abstract Conceptualization (AC)** A preference for learning by *thinking* about an issue in theoretical terms. For example, a person using this mode to learn about job politics would analyze political tactics and their implications, perhaps consulting or constructing a model that includes abstract representations of the components of political activities.

3. **Reflective Observation (RO)** A preference to learn by *watching* and examining different points of view to achieve an understanding. For example, people using the RO mode to learn about job politics would most likely observe others involved in political activities and reflect on what they've seen from a variety of perspectives.

4. **Active Experimentation (AE)** A preference for learning something by actually *doing* it and judging its practical value. For example, someone using this mode to learn about job politics might experiment with various political tactics, determining their effectiveness by the amount of influence they had on other people.

Kolb argues that an individual's learning style often combines two modes of learning, such as abstract conceptualization and active experimentation (thinking and doing). Each learning style emphasizes some learning abilities and deemphasizes others. Based on his own work and the work of earlier theorists (including Lewin, Dewey, and Piaget), Kolb identified four learning styles:

1. **Divergent** A combination of concrete experience and reflective observation (*feeling and watching*), emphasizing imagination, an awareness of values, and the ability to generate alternative courses of action.

2. **Assimilation** A combination of abstract conceptualization and reflective observation (*thinking and watching*) that stresses inductive reasoning, the integration of disparate observations into an explanation, and the creation of theoretical models.

3. **Convergent** A combination of abstract conceptualization and active experimentation (*thinking and doing*), with a focus on problem solving, decision making, and the practical application of ideas.

4. **Accommodative** A combination of concrete experience and active experimentation (*feeling and doing*), this style is usually demonstrated by accomplishment, executing plans, and involvement in new experiences.

Kolb theorizes that learning styles are developed as a result of life experiences, as well as hereditary influences. He notes that although individuals may have a dominant learning style, they may use other styles in particular situations. To help individuals identify their learning style, Kolb developed a questionnaire called the *Learning Style Inventory (LSI)*. The LSI, currently marketed by the Hay Group (Hay Resources Direct), assesses an individual's orientation toward the four modes of the learning process (CE, RO, AC, and AE).[120] Scores also reflect the individual's tendencies toward abstractness over concreteness and action over reflection.

Kolb's theory and the LSI can help HRD professionals, supervisors, and employees identify and appreciate different approaches to learning. As a result, interventions can be tailored to individual learner preferences in both traditional HRD programs and especially in those using computerized instruction. For example, a team at the University of Colorado at Colorado Springs developed a computer-based tutoring system that assesses an individual's learning style, using Kolb's theory, and adjusts its presentation accordingly.[121]

## LEARNING STRATEGIES

Similar to Kolb's modes of learning, **learning strategies** represent the "behavior and thoughts a learner engages in during learning."[122] Learning strategies are the techniques learners use to rehearse, elaborate, organize, and/or comprehend new material as well as to influence self-motivation and feelings. Learning strategies can be grouped into various categories (examples of each are listed in parentheses):

1. **rehearsal strategies** (e.g., repeating items in a list; underlining text in an article; copying notes)
2. **elaboration strategies** (e.g., forming a mental image; taking notes, paraphrasing, or summarizing new material)
3. **organizational strategies** (e.g., grouping or ordering information to be learned; outlining an article; creating a hierarchy of material)
4. **comprehension monitoring strategies** (e.g., self-questioning)
5. **affective strategies** (increasing alertness; relaxation; finding ways to reduce test anxiety)[123]

HRD efforts have applied learning strategies in learning-to-learn programs, which seek to provide learners with the skills necessary to learn effectively in *any* learning situation. Given the dynamic nature of organizations and the environment, as described in Chapter 1, there is now a greater pressure on individuals to learn throughout their lives. Learning-to-learn programs are aimed at enhancing the learning process and making individuals more independent. The programs emphasize selecting those learning strategies needed to cope effectively with the nature of the material and the demands of the learning situation. Clearly, if employees can acquire and become skilled in applying a variety of learning strategies, they will likely benefit more from both formal learning opportunities (such as training programs) as well as informal ones (such as a problem-solving meeting).

## PERCEPTUAL PREFERENCES

Just as individuals have preferences about the types of information they seek out in learning situations and how they process it, they also have preferences for the sensory channels they use to acquire information.[124] For example, someone who asks you for directions may request that you write the directions out, draw a map, explain them verbally, or use some combination of the three (it's tempting to enter into the popular debate about whether some people *ever* stop to ask for directions — but we probably don't want to go there, do we?).

Wayne James and Michael Galbraith propose seven primary perceptual preferences:

1. **print** (reading and writing)
2. **visual** (such as graphs and charts)
3. **aural** (auditory, i.e., listening)
4. **interactive** (discussing, asking questions)
5. **tactile/manipulative** (hands-on approaches, such as touching)
6. **kinesthetic/psychomotor** (role playing, physical activities)
7. **olfactory** (association of ideas with smell or taste)[125]

Recently, Neil Fleming developed the VARK questionnaire, which he described as a scale measuring one's "preference for taking in and putting out information in a learning context."[126] This questionnaire is available online (see Exercise 2 at the end of this chapter). The four preferences measured by this scale are visual (V), aural (A), read/write (R), and kinesthetic (K). These preferences correspond to items 1, 2, 3, and 6 in the list above from James and Galbraith. In his research to date, Fleming has found no differences in preferences between males and females. Differences have emerged between students (who have a greater preference for the kinesthetic) and teachers/professors (who have a greater preference for reading and writing).

Other research suggests that the majority of adults have a preference for visual material. Females are more likely than males to assimilate information from all available sources, whereas males tend to focus on fewer information sources.[127] Further, similar to Fleming's findings concerning differences between students and teachers, it has been argued that people who grew up watching more television and movies and playing interactive computer games may have different perceptual preferences than previous generations, and may need to be trained in different ways.[128]

Perceptual preferences imply that trainers should, if possible, tailor their material and techniques to match trainee preferences. For example, a study of advanced safety training for truck drivers focused on individuals with aural versus kinesthetic preferences. Training was provided either by lecture (with visuals) or by a hands-on, simulation approach. Trainees with auditory preferences learned substantially more when taught via lecture, whereas those with kinesthetic preferences learned substantially more when taught via the hands-on approach. The reverse was also true, that is, when preferences and training method were mismatched, training achievement and trainee attitudes were significantly lower.[129] Another implication of the research on perceptual preferences is that it would be desirable to train learners to increase their learning efficiencies by taking advantage of multiple perceptual channels.

## RECENT DEVELOPMENTS IN INSTRUCTIONAL AND COGNITIVE PSYCHOLOGY

As we discussed earlier, instructional psychology focuses on identifying instructional principles and techniques that maximize learning. Progress in this field — in particular, the four areas that we will now present — should yield applications that make HRD efforts more effective. We feel it is useful to give the reader a sense of the types of research currently underway.

### THE ACT*/ACT-R APPROACH TO LEARNING PROCEDURAL SKILLS

John Anderson and his colleagues at Carnegie-Mellon University have developed instructional computer programs that have been effective in teaching students how to perform complex procedural skills, such as solving algebraic equations and programming using the computer language LISP.[130] The underlying theory is called

ACT* *theory,* which assumes that the learning process is the same regardless of the material being learned. ACT* theory focuses on the changes that occur as a learner proceeds from knowing what to do (called **declarative knowledge**) to knowing how to do it (**procedural knowledge**).[131]

Progressing from declarative to procedural knowledge is important to successful performance. For example, a person who understands the steps involved in making an effective sales presentation may not actually be able to do so. It is one thing to learn what must be done, and another thing to actually accomplish it.

An instructional technique called *model tracing* is used in developing a computer-tutoring program. This approach starts with the assumption that there is an ideal way to solve problems in the content area being learned. This is identified, along with the types of mistakes that are commonly made. A learning model is then developed that contains all the correct and incorrect rules for performing the task, and includes a set of assumptions about how a student's knowledge changes after each step in the process.

Through problem solving, trainees learn by doing. The tutoring program helps learners identify problems and corrects their errors immediately. The tutor reduces the burden placed on a learner's memory by displaying the goals to be reached and helping to fill in some of the details. The tutor in effect guides the student through the learning process.

The ACT* approach features an intelligent computer-assisted instruction program. One example of a company using this approach is the Campbell Soup Company, which has a computer-based Cooker Maintenance Advisor.[132] Campbell's food-processing plants use a huge cooker to sterilize processed food. Cooker breakdowns are expensive because they disrupt all other operations in the plant. Because cookers are such complex systems, it is not easy to train engineers and mechanics to install, operate, and maintain them. When the engineer who knew the system best was nearing retirement, the company developed an intelligent tutoring software program that captured much of the knowledge he had acquired over forty-four years on the job.

The Cooker Maintenance Advisor is an interactive system that uses a question-and-answer format. Engineers and maintenance technicians use the system in training and as an aid when on the job. Use of the Cooker Maintenance Advisor has resulted in both cost and time savings, and employees throughout the company can benefit from the expert's advice and experience.

Anderson has outlined a newer iteration of ACT*, which he referred to as ACT-R (R for rational). ACT-R contains revisions to the theory that have come from continued research and technical developments in the simulation models used to test the theory. Although ACT-R shares many of the same assumptions and basic predictions of ACT*, some concepts and processes have been modified to reflect new findings about how declarative knowledge becomes procedural knowledge, and how humans continue to fine-tune the procedural knowledge they have gained.[133]

The ACT*/ACT-R approach focuses on the acquisition of procedural skills. Given that many of the skills used in organizations today are procedural in nature (e.g., the proper way to use a piece of equipment), this technique holds promise, especially as computer-assisted HRD training programs are developed.

## LEARNING TO REGULATE ONE'S OWN BEHAVIOR

What is it that makes experts able to perform more quickly and at higher levels than novices? Research suggests that experts develop *self-regulation and control strategies* through experience. These strategies enable them to monitor their performance by quickly checking their work, accurately judging how difficult a problem is, allocating their time, assessing progress, and predicting the results of their efforts.[134]

The development of expertise is an important goal of HRD, and one way to reach this goal is to teach trainees these self-regulatory and control skills. For example, a reading comprehension program was developed based on a technique called reciprocal teaching, in which students learn strategies they can use to monitor their own performance. By individually applying learning techniques such as questioning, clarifying, summarizing, and predicting, with the teacher serving as a coach, the group shares responsibility for its own learning.[135]

Although this research has been conducted using schoolchildren, such an approach should also be effective in organizational training. HRD approaches such as behavior modeling (which will be discussed in Chapter 12) already use components of this strategy. For example, when trainees in a behavior modeling session practice the behaviors they are learning, they often receive feedback and coaching from one another on the adequacy of their performance and on ways it can be improved.[136] Similar programs have been developed to improve general problem-solving and thinking skills as a way to improve learning.[137] However, a review of such techniques called for additional research on their effectiveness.[138]

## EXPERT AND EXCEPTIONAL PERFORMANCE

Recent research has addressed the topic of expert or exceptional performance. What factors lead to the acquisition and production of human performance at the highest level? Perhaps the most significant finding is that "counter to the common belief that expert performance reflects innate abilities and capacities, recent research in different domains of expertise has shown that expert performance is predominantly mediated by acquired complex skills and physiological adaptations."[139]

**Expert performance** is defined as "consistently superior performance on a specified set of representative tasks for a domain."[140] Defining expert performance in this way captures the idea that experts can reliably display their high performance levels on demand, which makes it possible to study it under laboratory conditions, allowing careful observation and firm conclusions. Expertise in a wide range of domains has been studied, including chess, medical diagnosis, auditing, athletic performance, music, typing, bridge, and physics. Literature reviews have reported the following findings:

- Exceptional abilities and performance are *acquired primarily under optimal environmental conditions*. A superior level of innate ability is not a sufficient (or even necessary) condition for expert-level performance. For example, IQ is only weakly related to performance among experts in chess and music.

- Exceptional performance is *acquired through deliberate practice,* done consistently over a period of a decade or longer. **Deliberate practice** is "an effortful activity motivated by the goal of improving performance" and provides the best opportunity for learning and skill acquisition.[141] Deliberate practice is often performed under the guidance of a master teacher or coach using methods and techniques developed over a long period. For example, many marveled when U.S. cyclist Lance Armstrong won the Tour de France six consecutive times from 1999–2004, especially because he had been diagnosed with cancer in 1996. However, what is less well known is his almost single-minded commitment to intensive, daily practice. His ascents up mountains such as Mount Hautacam are attributed to both his conditioning and his motivation to win.[142]

- To perform deliberate practice daily over a period long enough to attain the highest levels of performance requires sustaining *a very high level of motivation,* especially given that practice in and of itself is not inherently pleasurable.

- Over time, *deliberate practice leads to anatomical and physiological adaptations* that contribute to high levels of performance. This is especially true for children and adolescents, whose bodies are developing at the same time extreme demands are being made upon them by deliberate practice activities.

- Given the demands that deliberate practice places on a person, it is estimated that over the long period that is needed to achieve elite performance *the maximum amount of practice time that a person can tolerate is four 1-hour sessions per day, separated by periods of rest.* Experts structure their lives to be able to do this, often sleeping more (in the form of naps) than amateurs and novices do.

- Although it has been widely believed that expert performance is highly automaticized (done without conscious awareness), research has shown that *expert performance is facilitated by planning, reasoning, and anticipation.* For example, a tennis player begins to prepare to return a serve before the server hits the ball, moving and anticipating the flight of the ball from the movement of the server's arm and toss of the ball.

- Experts are generally expert *in a limited performance domain.*

- The *age at which an individual can attain peak performance levels varies based on the domain of expertise* but most often occurs in the twenties, thirties, or forties. Differences in the age at which an individual begins practice and the amount of time spent weekly in practice produce significant differences in performance and total practice time.[143]

It is not realistic to expect performance at the highest human levels from all employees in all kinds of work (and this would be impossible, given the definition of exceptional performance among humans). Nevertheless, effective organizational performance does demand very high levels of performance in key positions by key members. The study of exceptional performance offers many insights into how such performance is acquired and can be maintained. It can also offer ideas for how higher levels of performance can be reached.

One implication for HRD has to do with the opportunity to engage in deliberate practice in the workplace. Although normal working conditions provide some opportunities for learning and improvement, these opportunities are not ideal and are unlikely by themselves to lead to high levels of performance. One explanation for this is that the factors that influence performance in the workplace (e.g., reliable production at a given level, motivated by external social and monetary rewards) are significantly different from the factors that encourage deliberate practice.[144] Therefore, provision has to be made for deliberate practice to occur on a regular basis if exceptional performance is expected to develop and be maintained. A second implication from this research concerns task analysis and the development of training methods. For example, studying "expert performers and their master teachers and coaches offers a nearly untapped reservoir of knowledge about optimal training and specific training that has been accumulated in many domains for a long time."[145]

## GAGNÉ'S THEORY OF INSTRUCTION

The Gagné (or Gagné-Briggs) theory of instruction focuses on the kinds of things people learn and how they learn them.[146] The theory argues that different learning outcomes are learned in different ways; in other words, there is not one best way to learn everything. The two main components of the theory are a taxonomy of learning outcomes (what is being learned) and the techniques needed to teach them. Gagné proposed that human performance could be divided into five categories, each of which requires a different set of conditions for maximizing learning, retention, and transfer. The categories are:

1. **Verbal information,** or declarative knowledge, involves the ability to state or declare something, such as a fact or an idea. Reciting the Bill of Rights or the provisions of the Americans with Disabilities Act are examples of verbal information.

2. **Intellectual skills,** sometimes called procedural knowledge, are the rules, concepts, and procedures that we follow to accomplish tasks. Intellectual skills may be simple or complex. English grammar is an example of an intellectual skill.

3. **Cognitive strategies,** or strategic knowledge, are the skills used to control learning, thinking, and remembering. Cognitive strategies allow us to determine what procedural knowledge and verbal information we need to perform a task. For example, an IRS representative uses a cognitive strategy when selecting the auditing approach to take for a particular tax audit.

4. **Attitudes** are internal states of mind that can influence which of several behaviors we may choose (recall our discussion in Chapter 2). Attitudes are not learned simply by hearing facts from others. For instance, is it likely that your attitude toward nuclear power is going to change just because someone tells you it is good or bad? Something additional, such as reinforcement or

**TABLE 3-6**

| Instructional Event | Type of Capability | |
| --- | --- | --- |
| | Verbal Information | Intellectual Skill |
| 1. Gaining Attention | Introduce stimulus change; variations in sensory mode (same for all) | |
| 2. Informing learner of objective | Indicate the kind of verbal question to be answered | Provide description and example of the expected performance |
| 3. Stimulating recall of prerequisites | Stimulate recall of context of organized information | Stimulate recall of relevant rules and concepts |
| 4. Presenting the stimulus material | Present information in propositional form | Present examples of rules and concepts |
| 5. Providing learning guidance | Provide verbal links to a larger meaningful context | Provide verbal cues for proper combining/ sequencing of rules or concepts |
| 6. Eliciting the performance | Ask for information in learner's own words (paraphrase) | Ask learner to apply rules or concepts to new examples |
| 7. Providing feedback | Confirm correctness of statement of information | Confirm correctness of rule or concept application |
| 8. Assessing performance | Learner restates information in paraphrased form | Learner demonstrates application of rules or concepts |
| 9. Enhancing retention and transfer of information | Provide verbal links to additional areas of information | Provide spaced reviews including a variety of examples |

SOURCE: From Principles of Instructional Design 4th edition by GAGNE/WAGER. © 1992. Reprinted with permission of Wadsworth, a division of Thomson Learning: www.thomsonrights.com. Fax 800 730-2215.

    personal experience regarding the object of the attitude, is needed for learning to occur. Even so, attitudes are often highly resistant to change.

5. **Motor skills** involve using our bodies to manipulate something. Writing, icing a cake, and balancing a tray of dishes are examples of motor skills. Motor skills are learned by practicing the movement, and in doing so the quality of the movement should improve.

## INSTRUCTIONAL EVENTS AND THE CONDITIONS OF LEARNING THEY IMPLY FOR FIVE TYPES OF LEARNED CAPABILITIES

| Type of Capability | | |
|---|---|---|
| Cognitive Strategy | Attitude | Motor Skill |
| Clarify the general nature of the solution expected | Provide example of the desired choice of action | Provide a demonstration of expected performance |
| Stimulate recall of task strategies and associated intellectual skills | Stimulate recall of relevant information, skills, and human model identification | Stimulate recall of sub-routine and part-skills |
| Present novel problems | Present human model, demonstrating choice of personal action | Provide external stimuli for performance, including tools or implements |
| Provide prompts and hints to novel solutions | Provide for observation of model's choice of action, and of reinforcement received by model | Provide practice with feedback on performance achievement |
| Ask for problem solution | Ask learner to indicate choices of action in real or simulated situations | Ask for execution of the performance |
| Confirm originality of problem solution | Provide direct or vicarious reinforcement of action choice | Provide feedback on degree of accuracy and timing of performance |
| Learner originates a novel solution | Learner makes desired choice of personal action in real or simulated situation | Learner executes performance of total skill |
| Provide occasions for a variety of novel problem solutions | Provide additional varied situations for selected choice of action | Learner continues skill practice |

According to Gagné, these five categories are important because

> they differ, first as human performances, second, because the requirements for their learning are different despite the pervasiveness of such general conditions as contiguity and reinforcement, and third because the effects of learning, the continued learning, appear also to differ from each other.[147]

Gagné and his colleagues argue that successful performance on any given task requires learning in one or more of these categories. Research continues concerning which techniques are best suited to teaching each kind of outcome. Table 3-6 presents a summary of this work. The events listed in the left-hand column of the table are the nine steps, or instructional events, that should be used in instructional design. Corresponding entries in the table list the actions that should be taken to implement each of these steps for each of the five categories of learning outcomes. Gagné's theory provides a rich source of ideas for HRD professionals looking for ways to enhance the effectiveness of their training programs. It has been cited as a "training classic" that helped "to turn the free-form art of instruction into something more reliable" (p. 32).[148]

### RETURN TO OPENING CASE

Since 1997, the American Society for Training and Development (ASTD) has conducted a Benchmarking Service on employer-provided training. In the 2000 ASTD *State of the Industry Report*, the Wisconsin Public Service Corporation (WPSC) was honored as among the top ten "Training Investment Leaders" among medium-sized organizations (500–4,999 employees). For all organizations in the survey, the average number of employees receiving training in the previous year was 76 percent. For organizations identified as Training Investment Leaders, this average rose to 96 percent. At WPSC, the figure was 100 percent. The average number of hours spent in training per employee was nearly fifty-four hours, which is over 80 percent higher than the average for all organizations surveyed. Your instructor has other information concerning this organization and the questions that were raised in the Opening Case.

D. P. McMurrer, M. E. Van Buren, & W. H. Woodwell, Jr. (2000). Making the commitment. *Training & Development 54*, 45.

### SUMMARY

Understanding the learning process and how learning can be maximized are critical issues in designing and implementing HRD programs. Learning is a relatively permanent change in behavior or cognitions that occurs as a result of one's interaction with the environment. Traditional research on the learning process identified three principles of learning: contiguity, the law of effect, and practice. Although these principles enhance our understanding of the learning process, they are not sufficient for designing programs that maximize learning.

Trainee characteristics play a significant role in the learning process. Three trainee characteristics that affect the extent to which trainees learn are trainability, personality, and attitudes. Trainability is a combination of motivation, ability, and the work environment. The higher the level of trainability, the more likely it is that trainees will learn. Several personality traits, such as locus of control and the trainee's attitudes, have also been shown to affect learning.

Knowledge of training design issues — in particular, the conditions of practice — should also be used to maximize learning. These conditions include active practice, massed versus spaced practice sessions, whole versus part learning, overlearning, knowledge of results, and task sequencing. In general, trainee learning is improved by overlearning, feedback, and practice sessions spaced over time, with sufficient rest periods between them.

The information or skills an employee learns are of little value to the organization if the employee does not retain or use them back on the job. Retention of what is learned is influenced by such factors as the meaningfulness of material, the degree of original learning, and interference. Factors that affect learning transfer to the work situation include identical elements, general principles, stimulus variability, and support in the work environment.

Obviously, not all trainees are alike. Individual differences among trainees affect the learning process. First of all, different people learn at different rates, a fact that should be considered in designing training programs. Second, people with different characteristics (such as intelligence levels) may learn best using different training approaches. And third, contrary to many stereotypes, older adults can learn as well as younger adults, but they do learn differently. Finally, recent research in instructional psychology demonstrates significant promise for the future of HRD. Research on the ACT*/ACT-R approach, reciprocal teaching, expert performance, and Gagné's theory of instruction suggest creative ways to design training approaches that maximize learning. As we said at the start of this chapter, learning is a vital aspect of all HRD efforts.

Now that you've read the chapter, have any of your answers to the true-false questions we posed on p. 76 changed? Dare we ask if learning has taken place? For our answers to these questions, visit the website for this book (http://werner. swlearning.com).

## KEY TERMS AND CONCEPTS

active practice
andragogy
association
cognitive architecture
cognitive resource allocation
    theory
component task achievement
contiguity
continuous-learning work
    environment
declarative knowledge
degree of original learning
deliberate practice
expert performance
gerontology
identical elements
instructional psychology
interference
law of effect
learning

learning curve
learning strategy
learning style
meaningfulness of material
mental practice
mode of learning
opportunity to perform
overlearning
pedagogy
personality
physical fidelity
practice
procedural knowledge
psychological fidelity
task analysis
task sequencing
trainability
training design
transfer of training
transfer of training climate

## QUESTIONS FOR DISCUSSION

1. Compare and contrast the pedagogical and andragogical approaches to instruction. Suppose the president of a local hospital asks you to design a program to increase employee awareness of sexual harassment and train participants in ways to deal with harassment complaints. Which principles (from either approach) do you feel might be useful? Support your choices.

2. Explain the role that trainability plays in the effectiveness of an HRD program or intervention. Briefly describe the options available to assess the trainability of employees.

3. Robert Gagné and others have argued that traditional principles of learning (such as contiguity and association) are not sufficient for designing effective training programs. State the reasoning behind this argument. What does research in instructional psychology and cognitive psychology offer as a resolution to these problems? Do you agree with this solution? Support your answer.

4. Few HRD professionals would disagree that practice plays an important role in learning and retention. Using your knowledge of the conditions of practice, what sort of practice do you think would be most effective for training mechanics in a new installation procedure for automobile air-conditioners? How about for training new supervisors to comply with the U.S. Americans with Disabilities Act?

5. Identify and discuss the factors that can affect whether training transfers back to the job. Which two factors do you feel are the most important to ensure transfer? Support your choices.

6. A common stereotype about older workers is that they find learning difficult. Does research from the field of gerontology support or disprove this stereotype? Explain. What two findings or recommendations do you feel supervisors should follow to ensure effective training experiences for older workers?

7. Research by David Kolb and others suggests that individuals have different learning styles. How would a manager who has a convergent learning style and a manager who has a divergent learning style differ in their approach to learning? Suppose you are going to conduct training sessions designed to teach managers how to give feedback to subordinates. These two managers are scheduled to participate. What might you do (if anything), to handle their style differences to ensure that both of them learn the material you present?

8. Learning strategies are used by learners to rehearse, organize, elaborate, and comprehend new material. From the learning strategies discussed in this chapter, select two that you have used. For each one, identify how you applied it and how it helped you learn more effectively.

9. Supervisors and coworkers are often asked to serve as trainers. Although they may be experts on the material they are teaching others, many times they are novices when it comes to understanding how others learn. Based

on the material presented in this chapter, what three things do you think supervisors and coworkers who train others should know about learning? Describe each one, and explain why you feel it is important.

## EXERCISE 1: LEARNING STYLES

Review the material on learning styles presented earlier (from David Kolb). In your opinion, which of the four learning styles best describes you? Have a friend or someone close to you look over this material and see what learning style *they* think you have (hopefully, there is agreement between the two of you). Finally, discuss your individual learning styles with a small group of students (e.g., in the class). What sorts of implications are there for group work when group members have different learning styles? How might this carry over to the workplace?

## EXERCISE 2: VARK QUESTIONNAIRE

You are encouraged to take the VARK questionnaire concerning your preferences for taking in information. It is available at http://www.vark-learn.com/english/index.asp

As an additional assignment (if requested by your instructor), work with others in your class on a "mini training design project." Specifically, take the four preferences emphasized in the VARK questionnaire (visual, aural, reading/writing, and kinesthetic) and make specific recommendations for how training can be designed to maximize learning for individuals with each of these different preferences. For example, what type of learning experiences would best serve a visual learner? An aural learner (one who learns best by listening)? Someone who learns best by reading and writing? Someone who learns best by doing, that is, by physical activity? What are the implications of your recommendations for effective training program design?

---

Visit *http://werner.swlearning.com* for links to informative websites for this chapter.

---

## REFERENCES

1. Clarke, N. (2004). HRD and the challenges of assessing learning in the workplace. *International Journal of Training & Development, 8*(2), 140–156.

2. Baldwin, T. T., & Danielson, C. (1998, September–October). Executive briefing: Management development. *Business Horizons*, 2–4; Short, D. C., Bing, J. W., & Kehrhahn, M. T. (2003). Will human resource development survive? *Human Resource Development Quarterly, 14*(3), 239–243.

3. Gagné, R. M., & Glaser, R. (1987). Foundations in learning research. In R. M. Gagné (Ed.), *Instructional technology: Foundations.* Hillsdale, NJ: Erlbaum.

4. *Ibid.*

5. Anderson, J. R., & Bower, G. H. (1973). *Human associative memory.* Washington, DC: Winston.

6. James, W. (1890). *Principles of psychology.* New York: Holt, Rinehart and Winston.

7. Thorndike, E. L. (1913). *The psychology of learning: Educational psychology* (Vol. 2). New York: Teachers College Press.

8. Gagné & Glaser (1987), *supra* note 3.

9. Kohler, W. (1927). *The mentality of apes.* New York: Harcourt Brace Jovanovich; Wertheimer, M. (1959). *Productive thinking.* New York: Harper & Row.

10. Gagné, R. M. (1985). *The conditions of learning and theory of instruction* (4th ed.). New York: Holt, Rinehart and Winston.

11. Gagné, R. M. (1962). Military training and principles of learning. *American Psychologist, 17,* 83–91.

12. *Ibid.*

13. Bruner, J. S. (1966). *Toward a theory of instruction.* New York: Norton.

14. Glaser, R. (1982). Instructional psychology: Past, present, and future. *American Psychologist, 37,* 292–305.

15. Resnick, L. B. (1981). Instructional psychology. *Annual Review of Psychology, 32,* 659–704.

16. Lord, R. M., & Maher, K. J. (1991). Cognitive theory in industrial and organizational psychology. In M. D. Dunnette & L. M. Hough (Eds.), *Handbook of industrial and organizational psychology* (2nd ed., Vol. 2, pp. 1–62). Palo Alto, CA: Consulting Psychologists Press, p. 4.

17. Newell, A., Rosenbloom, P. S., & Laird, J. E. (1989). Symbolic architectures for cognition. In M. Posner (Ed.), *Foundations of cognitive science* (pp. 93–131). Cambridge, MA: MIT Press, p. 93.

18. Lord & Maher (1991), *supra* note 16.

19. *Ibid.*

20. *Ibid.*

21. Gagné, R. M., & Dick, W. (1983). Instructional psychology. *Annual Review of Psychology, 34,* 261–295; Glaser, R., & Bassok, M. (1989). Learning theory and the study of instruction. *Annual Review of Psychology, 40,* 631–666; Pintrich, P. R., Cross, D. R., Kozma, R. B., & McKeachie, W. J. (1986). Instructional psychology. *Annual Review of Psychology, 37,* 611–651.

22. Ericsson, K. A., & Lehman, A. C. (1996). Expert and exceptional performance: Evidence of maximal adaptation to task constraints. *Annual Review of Psychology, 47,* 273–305; Healy, A. F., & McNamara, D. S. (1996). Verbal learning and memory: Does the modal model still work? *Annual Review of Psychology, 47,* 143–172; Lord & Maher (1991), *supra* note 16; VanLehn, K. (1996). Cognitive skill acquisition. *Annual Review of Psychology, 47,* 513–539; Weiss, H. M. (1990). Learning theory and industrial and organizational psychology. In M. D. Dunnette & L. M. Hough (Eds.), *Handbook of industrial and organizational psychology* (2nd ed., Vol. l, pp. 171–221). Palo Alto, CA: Consulting Psychologists Press.

23. Reardon, M. (1998/1999). The brain. *Adult Learning 10*(2), 10–17; Merriam, S. B., & Caffarella, R. S. (1999). *Learning in adulthood: A comprehensive guide* (2nd ed.). San Francisco: Jossey-Bass.

24. Howell, W. C., & Cooke, N. J. (1989). Training the human information processor: A review of cognitive models. In I. L. Goldstein and associates, *Training and development in organizations* (pp. 121–182). San Francisco: Jossey-Bass.

25. Maier, N. R. F. (1973). *Psychology in industrial organizations* (4th ed.). Boston: Houghton Mifflin; Noe, R. A. (1986). Trainee's attributes and attitudes: Neglected influences on training effectiveness. *Academy of Management Review, 11,* 736–749.

26. Maier (1973), *supra* note 25.

27. Noe (1986), *supra* note 25.

28. Downs, S. (1970). Predicting training potential. *Personnel Management, 2,* 26–28; Gordon, L. V. (1955). Time in training as a criterion of success in radio code. *Journal of Applied Psychology, 39,* 311–313; Gordon, M. E., & Klieman, L. S. (1976). The predication of trainability using a work sample test and an aptitude test: A direct comparison. *Personnel Psychology, 29,* 243–253; McGehee, W. (1948). Cutting training waste. *Personnel Psychology, 1,* 331–340; Neel, R. G., & Dunn, R. E. (1960). Predicting success in supervisory training programs by the use of psychological tests. *Journal of Applied Psychology, 44,* 358–360; Taylor, C. W. (1952). Pretesting saves training costs. *Personnel Psychology, 5,* 213–239; Taylor, R. K., & Tajen, C. (1948). Selection for training: Tabulating equipment operators. *Personnel Psychology, 1,* 341–348.

29. Eden, D., & Ravid, G. (1982). Pygmalion versus self-expectancy: Effects of instructor and self-expectancy on trainee performance. *Organizational Behavior and Human Performance, 30,* 351–364; Eden, D., & Shani, A. B. (1982). Pygmalion goes to boot camp: Expectancy, leadership, and trainee performance. *Journal of Applied Psychology, 67,* 194–199; Hicks, W. D., & Klimoski, R. J. (1987). Entry into training programs and its effects on training outcomes: A field experiment. *Academy of Management Journal, 30,* 542–552; Komaki, J., Heinzemann, A. T., & Lawson, L. (1980). Effects of training and feedback: Component analysis of a behavioral safety program. *Journal of Applied Psychology, 65,* 261–270; Reber, R. A., & Wallin, J. A. (1984). The effects of training, goal setting, and knowledge of results on safe behavior: A component analysis. *Academy of Management Journal, 27,* 544–560; Wexley, K. N., & Baldwin, T. T. (1986). Posttraining strategies for facilitating positive transfer: An empirical exploration. *Academy of Management Journal, 29,* 503–520.

30. Peters, L. H., O'Connor, E. J., & Eulberg, J. R. (1985). Situational constraints: Sources, consequences, and future considerations. In G. Ferris & K. Rowland (Eds.), *Research in Personnel and Human Resource Management* (Vol. 3, pp. 79–114). Stamford, CT: JAI Press.

31. Werner, J. M., O'Leary-Kelly, A. M., Baldwin, T. T., & Wexley, K. N. (1994). Augmenting behavior-modeling training: Testing the effects of pre- and post-training interventions. *Human Resource Development Quarterly, 5,* 169–183.

32. Martocchio, J. J. (1992). Microcomputer usage as an opportunity: The influence of context in employee training. *Personnel Psychology, 45,* 529–552; Quiñones, M. A. (1995). Pretraining context effect: Training assignment as feedback. *Journal of Applied Psychology, 80,* 226–238.

33. Martocchio, J. J. (1994). Effects of ability on anxiety, self-efficacy, and learning in training. *Journal of Applied Psychology, 79,* 819–825.

34. Smith-Jentsch, K. A., Jentsch, F. G., Payne, S. C., & Salas, E. (1996). Can pretraining experiences explain individual differences in learning? *Journal of Applied Psychology, 81,* 110–116.

35. Clark, C. S., Dobbins, G. H., & Ladd, R. T. (1993). Exploratory field study of training motivation. *Group & Organization Management, 18,* 292–307; Noe, R. A., & Wilk, S. L. (1993). Investigation of the factors that influence employees' participation in development activities. *Journal of Applied Psychology, 78,* 291–302.

36. Mathieu, J. E., Tannenbaum, S. I., & Salas, E. (1992). The influences of individual and situational characteristics on measures of training effectiveness. *Academy of Management Journal, 35,* 828–847.

37. Maurer, T. J., & Tarulli, B. A. (1994). Investigation of perceived environment, perceived outcome, and person variables in relationship to voluntary development activity by employees. *Journal of Applied Psychology, 79,* 3–14.

38. Ree, M. J., Carretta, T. R., & Teachout, M. S. (1995). Role of ability and prior job knowledge in complex training performance. *Journal of Applied Psychology, 80,* 721–730.

39. Tubiana, J. H., & Ben-Shakhar, G. (1982). An objective group questionnaire as a substitute for a personal interview in the prediction of success in military training in Israel. *Personnel Psychology, 35,* 349–357.

40. Siegel, A. I. (1983). The miniature job training and evaluation approach: Additional findings. *Personnel Psychology, 36,* 41–56.

41. Kinzer, A. (1995). BMW Manufacturing Corp. and South Carolina: An exciting partnership. *South Carolina Business, 15,* 26–29; BMW plant in US (1995, March/April). *Presidents & Prime Ministers 4*(2), 23–31; Panke: Quality, training are keys at S.C. plant (1999, Nov. 22). *Automotive News 74*(5849), 26; BMW weighs another expansion of U.S. plant (2000, Jan. 17). *Automotive News, 74*(5857), 22.

42. Robertson, I., & Downs, S. (1979). Learning and prediction of performance: Development of trainability testing in the United Kingdom. *Journal of Applied Psychology, 64,* 42–50.

43. *Ibid.*

44. Noe (1986), *supra* note 25.

45. Noe, R. A., & Schmitt, N. (1986). The influence of trainee attitudes on training effectiveness: Test of a model. *Personnel Psychology, 39,* 497–523; Maurer & Tarulli (1994), *supra* note 37; Ryman, D. H., & Biersner, R. J. (1975). Attitudes predictive of driving training success. *Personnel Psychology, 28,* 181–188.

46. Baumgartel, H., Reynolds, M., & Pathan, R. (1984). How personality and organizational-climate variables moderate the effectiveness of management development programmes: A review and some recent research findings. *Management and Labour Studies, 9,* 1–16.

47. Tubiana & Ben-Shakhar (1982), *supra* note 39.

48. Barrick, M. R., & Mount, M. K. (1991). The big-five personality dimensions and job performance: A meta-analysis. *Personnel Psychology, 44,* 1–26.

49. Martocchio, J. J., & Webster, J. (1992). Effects of feedback and cognitive playfulness on performance in microcomputer software training. *Personnel Psychology, 45,* 553–578.

50. Glaser, R. (1984). Education and thinking: The role of knowledge. *American Psychologist, 39,* 93–104.

51. Gagné (1962), *supra* note 11.

52. Driskell, J. E, Copper, C., & Moran, A. (1994). Does mental practice enhance performance? *Journal of Applied Psychology, 79,* 481–492, p. 481.

53. *Ibid.*

54. Briggs, G. E., & Naylor, J. C. (1962). The relative efficiency of several training methods as a function of transfer task complexity. *Journal of Experimental Psychology, 64,* 505–512; Naylor, J. C., & Briggs, G. E. (1963). The effect of task complexity and task organization on the relative efficiency of part and whole training methods. *Journal of Experimental Psychology, 65,* 217–224.

55. Holding, D. H. (1965). *Principles of training.* London: Pergamon Press.

56. Kanfer, R., Ackerman, P. L., Murtha, T. C., Dugdale, B., & Nelson, L. (1994). Goal setting, conditions of practice, and task performance: A resource allocation perspective. *Journal of Applied Psychology, 79,* 826–835.

57. Gagné (1962), *supra* note 11.

58. Blum, M. L., & Naylor, J. C. (1968). *Industrial psychology.* New York: Harper & Row; Naylor & Briggs (1963), *supra* note 54.

59. McGehee, W., & Thayer, P. W. (1961). *Training in business and industry.* New York: Wiley.

60. *Ibid.*

61. Goldstein, I. L. (1986). *Training in organizations: Needs assessment, development, and evaluation* (2nd ed.). Pacific Grove, CA: Brooks-Cole.

62. Fitts, P. M. (1965). Factors in complex skill training. In R. Glaser (Ed.), *Training research in education.* New York: Wiley.

63. Atwater, S. K. (1953). Proactive inhibition and associative facilitation as affected by degree of prior learning. *Journal of Experimental Psychology, 46,* 400–404; Hagman, J. D., & Rose, A. M. (1983). Retention of military tasks: A review. *Human Factors, 25,* 199–213; Mandler, G. (1954). Transfer of training as a function of response overlearning. *Journal of Experimental Psychology, 47,* 411–417; Schendel, J. D., & Hagman, J. D. (1982). On sustaining procedural skills over a prolonged retention interval. *Journal of Applied Psychology, 67,* 605–610.

64. Thorndike, E. L. (1927). The law of effect. *American Journal of Psychology, 39,* 212–222; Komaki, Heinzemann, & Lawson (1980), *supra* note 29; Wexley, K. N., & Thornton, C. L. (1972). Effect of verbal feedback of test results upon learning. *Journal of Educational Research, 66,* 119–121.

65. Kluger, A. N., & DeNisi, A. (1996). The effects of feedback interventions on performance: A historical review, a meta-analysis, and a preliminary feedback intervention theory. *Psychological Bulletin, 119,* 254–284.

66. Ilgen, D. R., Fisher, C. D., & Taylor, M. S. (1979). Consequences of individual feedback on behavior in organizations. *Journal of Applied Psychology, 64,* 349–371.

67. Wexley & Thornton (1972), *supra* note 64.

68. Martocchio, J. J., & Dulebohn, J. (1994). Performance feedback effects in training: The role of perceived controllability. *Personnel Psychology, 47,* 357–353.

69. Martocchio & Webster (1992), *supra* note 49; for a more complete discussion of feedback and how it affects performance, see Taylor, M. S., Fisher, C. D., & Ilgen, D. R. (1984). Individuals' reactions to performance feedback in organizations: A control theory perspective. In K. M. Rowland and G. R. Ferris (Eds.), *Research in personnel and human resource management* (Vol. 2). Greenwich, CT: JAI Press; and Kluger & DeNisi (1996), *supra* note 65.

70. Gagné (1962), *supra* note 11.

71. Gagné, R. M., Wagner, W. W., Golas, K., & Keller, J. M. (2005). *Principles of instructional design* (5th ed.). Belmont, CA: Wadsworth.

72. Clancey, W. J. (1984). Teaching classification problem solving. *Proceedings of the Cognitive Science Society Conference.* Boulder, CO, 44–46.

73. Decker, P. J. (1980). Effects of symbolic coding and rehearsal in behavior modeling training. *Journal of Applied Psychology, 65,* 627–634; Decker, P. J. (1982). The enhancement of behavior modeling training of supervisory skills by the inclusion of retention processes. *Personnel Psychology, 32,* 323–332.

74. McGehee & Thayer (1961), *supra* note 59.

75. Wexley, K. N., & Latham, G. P. (1991). *Developing and training human resource in organizations* (2nd ed.). New York: HarperCollins.

76. Bourne, L. E., & Ekstrand, B. R. (1973). *Psychology: Its principles and meanings.* Hinsdale, IL: Dryden Press.

77. Garavaglia, P. (1995, December). *Transfer of training: Making training stick*, INFO-LINE, No. 9512. Alexandria, VA: American Society for Training and Development.

78. Simon, S. J., & Werner, J. M. (1996). Computer training through behavior modeling, self-paced, and instructional approaches: A field experiment. *Journal of Applied Psychology, 81*, 648–659; Baldwin, T. T. (1992). Effects of alternative modeling strategies on outcomes of interpersonal skills training. *Journal of Applied Psychology, 77*, 147–154.

79. Baldwin (1992), *supra* note 78.

80. Baldwin, T. T., & Ford, J. K. (1988). Transfer of training: A review and directions for future research. *Personnel Psychology, 41*, 63–103.

81. Thorndike, E. L., & Woodworth, R. S. (1901). (I) The influence of improvement in one mental function on the efficiency of other functions. (II) The estimation of magnitudes. (III) Functions involving attention, observation, and discrimination. *Psychological Review, 8*, 247–261, 384–395, 553–564.

82. Berkowitz, D., & Donnerstein, E. (1982). External validity is more than skin deep: Some answers to criticisms of laboratory experiments. *American Psychologist, 37*, 245–257.

83. Hendrikson, G., & Schroeder, W. (1941). Transfer of training to hit a submerged target. *Journal of Educational Psychology, 32*, 206–213.

84. Goldstein (1986), *supra* note 61.

85. Ellis, H. C. (1965). *The transfer of learning.* New York: Macmillan; Kazdin, A. E. (1975). *Behavior modification in applied settings.* Homewood, IL: Dorsey Press.

86. Baldwin, T. T. (1987, August). *The effect of negative models on learning and transfer from behavior modeling: A test of stimulus variability.* Presented at the 47th annual meeting of the Academy of Management, New Orleans, LA; Shore, B., & Sechrest, L. (1975). Concept attainment as a function of positive instances presented. *Journal of Educational Psychology, 52*, 303–307.

87. Baumgartel et al. (1984), *supra* note 46; Huczynski, A. A., & Lewis, J. W. (1980). An empirical study into the learning transfer process in management training. *Journal of Management Studies, 17*, 227–240; Sims, H., & Manz, C. C. (1982). Modeling influences on employee behavior. *Personnel Journal, 61*(1), 45–51; Wexley, K. N., & Baldwin, T. T. (1986). Management development. *Journal of Management, 12*, 277–294.

88. Rouiller, J. Z., & Goldstein, I. L. (1993). The relationship between organizational transfer climate and positive transfer of training. *Human Resource Development Quarterly, 4*, 377–390, p. 379.

89. Tracey, J. B., Tannenbaum, S. I., and Kavanagh, M. J. (1995). Applying trained skills on the job: The importance of the work environment. *Journal of Applied Psychology, 80*, 239–252.

90. Marx, R. D. (1982). Relapse prevention for managerial training: A model for maintenance of behavioral change. *Academy of Management Review, 7*, 433–441.

91. Burke, L. A., & Baldwin, T. T. (1999). Workforce training transfer: A study of the effect of relapse prevention training and transfer climate. *Human Resource Management, 38*, 227–242.

92. Leifer, M. S., & Newstrom, J. W. (1980). Solving the transfer of training problem. *Training and Development Journal, 34*(8), 42–46; Michalak, D. F. (1981). The neglected half of training. *Training and Development Journal, 35*(5), 22–28.

93. Ford, J. K., Quiñones, M. A., Sego, D. J., and Sorra, J. S. (1992). Factors affecting the opportunity to perform trained tasks on the job. *Personnel Psychology, 45,* 511–527, p. 512.

94. Lim, D. H., & Johnson, S. D. (2002). Trainee perceptions of factors that influence learning transfer. *International Journal of Training and Development, 6*(1), 36–48.

95. Cronbach, L. J. (1967). How can instruction be adapted to individual differences? In R. M. Gagné (Ed.), *Learning and individual differences.* Columbus, OH: Charles E. Merrill; Cronbach, L. J., & Snow, R. E. (1977). *Aptitudes and instructional methods.* New York: Irvington.

96. Vroom, V. H. (1964). *Work and motivation.* New York: Wiley.

97. Terborg, J. R. (1977). Validation and extension of an individual differences model of work performance. *Organizational Behavior and Human Performance, 18,* 188–216.

98. For example, Kanfer, R., & Ackerman, P. L. (1989). Motivation and cognitive abilities: An integrative/aptitude-treatment interaction approach to skill acquisition. *Journal of Applied Psychology, 74,* 657–690; Kanfer, R. (1990). Motivation theory and industrial and organizational psychology. In M. D. Dunnette & L. M. Hough (Eds.), *Handbook of industrial and organizational psychology* (2nd ed., Vol. 1, pp. 75–170). Palo Alto, CA: Consulting Psychologists Press.

99. Unless otherwise noted, the ideas presented in this section are drawn from Kanfer and Ackerman (1989) and Kanfer (1990), both *supra* note 98.

100. Anderson, J. R. (1993). Problem solving and learning. *American Psychologist, 48,* 35–44.

101. Kanfer & Ackerman (1989), *supra* note 98; Kanfer et al. (1994), *supra* note 56; Mitchell, T. R., Hopper, H., Daniels, D., George-Falvy, J., & James, L. R. (1994). Predicting self-efficacy and performance during skill acquisition. *Journal of Applied Psychology, 79,* 506–517; see also reviews by Kanfer (1990), *supra* note 98; Ackerman, P. L. (1992). Predicting individual differences in complex skill acquisition: Dynamics of ability determinants. *Journal of Applied Psychology, 77,* 598–614; Ackerman, P. L., & Humphreys, L. G. (1992). Individual differences theory in industrial and organizational psychology. In M. D. Dunnette & L. M. Hough (Eds.), *Handbook of industrial and organizational psychology* (2nd ed., Vol. 1, pp. 223–282). Palo Alto, CA: Consulting Psychologists Press. DeShon, R. P., Brown, K. G., & Greenis, J. L. (1996). Does self-regulation require cognitive resources? Evaluation of resource allocation models of goal setting. *Journal of Applied Psychology, 81,* 595–608, questioned the idea that self-regulatory processes **necessarily** use attentional resources that could otherwise be devoted to task performance.

102. Knowles, M. S. (1970). *The modern practice of adult education: Andragogy versus pedagogy.* New York: Association Press.

103. *Ibid.*

104. Knowles, M. S., & Associates, (1984). *Andragogy in action: Applying modern principles of adult learning.* San Francisco: Jossey-Bass.

105. Sommer, R. F. (1989). *Teaching writing to adults: Strategies and concepts for improving learner performance.* San Francisco: Jossey-Bass.

106. Caudron, S. (2000). Learners speak out. *Training and Development, 54,* 52–58.

107. Davenport, J., & Davenport, J. A. (1985). A chronology and analysis of the andragogy debate. *Adult Education, 35,* 152–159.

108. Newstrom, J. W., & Lengnick-Hall, M. L. (1991). One size does not fit all. *Training and Development Journal, 45*(6), 43–48.

109. Knowles (1970), *supra* note 102; Knowles & Associates (1984), *supra* note 104.

110. Merriam & Caffarella (1999), *supra* note 23; Kuchinke, K. P. (1999). Adult development toward what end? A philosophical analysis of the concept as reflected in the research, theory, and practice of Human Resource Development. *Adult Education Quarterly, 49,* Summer, 148–162; Sleezer, C. M. (2004). The contribution of adult learning theory to human resource development (HRD). *Advances in Developing Human Resources, 6*(2), 125–128.

111. Newstrom & Lengnick-Hall (1991), *supra* note 108, p. 46.

112. Merriam & Caffarella (1999), *supra* note 23, p. 287.

113. Elias, P. K., Elias, M. F., & Robbins, M. A. (1987). Acquisition of word-processing skills by younger, middle-age, and older adults. *Psychology and Aging, 2,* 340–348; Martocchio (1994) *supra* note 33; Webster, J., & Martocchio, J. J. (1993). Turning work into play: Implications for microcomputer software training. *Journal of Management, 19,* 127–146.

114. Warr, P., & Bunce, D. (1995). Trainee characteristics and the outcomes of open learning. *Personnel Psychology, 48,* 348–374.

115. Sterns, H. L., & Doverspike, D. (1988). Training and developing the older worker: Implications for human resource management. In H. Dennis (Ed.), *Fourteen steps to managing an aging workforce.* New York: Lexington; Sterns, H. L., & Doverspike, D. (1989). Aging and the training and learning process. In I. L. Goldstein and Associates, *Training and development in organizations* (pp. 292–332). San Francisco: Jossey-Bass; Sterns, H. L. (1986). Training and retraining adult and older adult workers. In J. E. Birren, P. K. Robinson, & J. E. Livingston (Eds.), *Age, health, and employment.* Englewood Cliffs, NJ: Prentice Hall.

116. Sterns & Doverspike (1988), *supra* note 115, p. 108.

117. *Ibid.*

118. Manheimer, R. J. (1998). The promise and politics of older adult education. *Research on Aging, 20*(4), 391–414.

119. Kolb, D. A. (1984). *Experiential learning.* Englewood Cliffs, NJ: Prentice Hall, p. 66.

120. Kolb, D. A. (2004). Kolb learning style inventory. Retrieved September 8, 2004, from http://www.hayresourcesdirect.haygroup.com/Learning_Self-Development/ Assessments_Surveys/Learning_Style_Inventory/Overview.asp

121. Eurich, N. P. (1990). *The learning industry: Education for adult workers.* Lawrenceville, NJ: Princeton University Press.

122. Weinstein, C., & Mayer, R. (1986). The teaching of learning strategies. In M. Wittrock (Ed.), *Handbook of research on teaching* (3rd ed., p. 315). New York: Macmillan.

123. *Ibid.*

124. *Ibid.*

125. James, W., & Galbraith, M. W. (1985). Perceptual learning styles: Implications and techniques for the practitioner. *Lifelong Learning,* January, 20–23.

126. Fleming, N. (2001). VARK: A guide to learning styles. Retrieved September 8, 2004, from http://www.vark-learn.com/english/page.asp?p = faq#What%20is%20VARK

127. Darley, W. K., & Smith, R. E. (1995). Gender differences in information processing strategies: An empirical test of the selectivity model in advertising response. *Journal of Advertising, 24,* 41–56; Meyers-Levy, J. (1989). Gender differences in information processing: A selectivity interpretation. In P. Cafferata & A. M. Tybout (Eds.), *Cognitive and affective responses to advertising.* Lexington, MA: Lexington.

128. Caudron, S. (1997). Can Generation Xers be trained? *Training & Development, 51*, 20–24; Zemke, R., Raines, C., & Filipczak, B. (1999). Generation gaps in the classroom. *Training,* November, 48–54.

129. Dunn, R., & Ingham, J. (1995). Effects of matching and mismatching corporate employees' perceptual preferences and instructional strategies on training achievement and attitudes. *Journal of Applied Business Research, 11*(3), Summer, 30–37.

130. Lewis, M. W., Milson, R., & Anderson, J. R. (1988). Designing and intelligent authoring system for high school mathematics ICAI: The teacher apprentice project. In G. Kearsley (Ed.), *Artificial intelligence and instruction: applications and methods.* New York: Addison-Wesley; Anderson, J. R., Farrell, R., & Sauers, R. (1984). Learning to program in LISP. *Cognitive Science, 8*, 87–129.

131. Anderson, J. R. (1983). *The architecture of cognition.* Cambridge, MA: Harvard University Press; Anderson (1993), *supra* note 100.

132. Eurich (1990), *supra* note 121.

133. The reader is referred to Anderson, J. R. (1993). *Rules of the mind.* Hillsdale, NJ: Erlbaum, for a detailed discussion of the improvements and implications contained in ACT-R.

134. Brown, A. L. (1978). Knowing when, where, and how to remember: A problem of metacognition. In R. Glaser (Ed.), *Advances in instructional psychology* (Vol. 1). Hillsdale, NJ: Erlbaum; Chi, M.T.H., Glaser, R., & Rees, E. (1982). Expertise in problem solving. In R. J. Sternberg (Ed.), *Advances in the psychology of human intelligence* (Vol. 1). Hillsdale, NJ: Erlbaum; Larkin, J. H., McDermott, J., Simon, D. P., & Simon, H. A. (1980). Models of competence in solving physics problems. *Cognitive Science, 4*, 317–345; Miyake, N., & Norman, D. A. (1979). To ask a question one must know enough to know what is known. *Journal of Verbal Learning and Verbal Behavior, 18*, 357–364; Simon, D. P., & Simon, H. A. (1978). Individual differences in solving physics problems. In R. S. Siegler (Ed.), *Children's thinking: What develops?* Hillsdale, NJ: Erlbaum.

135. Brown, A. L., & Palinscar, A. S. (1984). Reciprocal teaching of comprehension fostering and monitoring activities. *Cognitive Instruction, 1*(2), 175–177; Brown, A. L., & Palinscar, A. S. (1988). Guided, cooperative learning and individual knowledge acquisition. In L. B. Resnick (Ed.), *Knowing, learning and instruction: Essays in honor of Robert Glaser.* Hillsdale, NJ: Erlbaum.

136. Werner, O'Leary-Kelly, Baldwin & Wexley (1994), *supra* note 31.

137. Nickerson, R. S., Perkins, D. N., & Smith, E. E. (1985). *The teaching of thinking.* Hillsdale, NJ: Erlbaum; Sternberg, R. J. (1986). *Intelligence applied.* San Diego, CA: Harcourt Brace Jovanovich.

138. Glaser & Bassok (1989), *supra* note 21.

139. Ericsson, K. A., & Charness, N. (1994). Expert performance: Its structure and acquisition. *American Psychologist, 49*, 725–747.

140. Ericsson & Lehman (1996), *supra* note 22, p. 277.

141. Ericsson & Charness (1994), *supra* note 139, p. 738.

142. Thomsen, I. (2000, July 24). Heavenly ascent: Making a molehill out of a mountain, Lance Armstrong surged toward his second Tour de France win. *Sports Illustrated, 93*(4), pp. 40–48; Abt, S. (2000, July 24). Tall in the saddle, Armstrong triumphs. *New York Times*, D1.; Montoya, M. (2004, August 25). Yellow fever. *Times-Picayune*, p. 1.

143. Ericsson & Charness (1994), *supra* note 139; Ericsson & Lehman (1996), *supra* note 22.

144. Ericsson, K. A., Krampe, R. T., & Tesch-Romer, C. (1993). The role of deliberate practice in the acquisition of expert performance. *Psychological Review, 100,* 363–406.

145. Ericsson & Charness (1994), *supra* note 139, p. 745.

146. Gagné et al. (2005), *supra* note 71; Gagné, R. M. (1972). Domains of learning. *Interchange, 3,* 1–8; Gagné, R. M. (1984). Learning outcomes and their effects: Useful categories of human performance. *American Psychologist, 39,* 377–385; Gagné, R. M., & Briggs, L. J. (1979). *Principles of instructional design* (2nd ed.). New York: Holt, Rinehart and Winston.

147. Gagné (1984), *supra* note 146, p. 384.

148. Zemke, R. (1999). Toward a science of training. *Training, 36*(7), July, 32–36.

# PART 2

# FRAMEWORK FOR HUMAN RESOURCE DEVELOPMENT

**4**

# ASSESSING **HRD** NEEDS

## Learning Objectives

*After reading this chapter, you should be able to:*

1. Discuss the purpose and advantages of conducting a needs assessment.

2. State the purpose of conducting a strategic/ organizational analysis, and describe the four issues it is intended to address.

3. Discuss the five steps that can be used to conduct a task analysis.

4. Conduct a task analysis for a job of your choosing.

5. Explain the importance of identifying individual performance deficiencies and developmental needs in planning and developing training and HRD programs.

6. Discuss the pros and cons of using multiple sources to collect data for person analysis.

7. Explain the importance of prioritizing training and HRD needs.

## OPENING CASE

HRD programs can be key components when an organization seeks to revitalize itself and change its organizational culture. For instance, Cathay Pacific Airways is an international airline based in Hong Kong that serves over eighty-five destinations on five continents. In 2003, Cathay Pacific carried over 10 million passengers, and also maintained a considerable cargo operation. Worldwide, approximately 14,000 people work for the airline. A survey in the 1990s revealed that travelers felt that Cathay Pacific service was good, but not as warm and friendly as customers desired. Some even described the service as "robotic." This led to a reexamination of how the company recruited, trained, and managed its employees.

One major change that Cathay Pacific made was in its in-flight training department. In the past, trainers devised and followed careful lesson plans. This was intended to provide a set standard of service on all flights. However, to increase customer retention, especially among business travelers, Cathay Pacific decided that something more was needed.

*Questions: Assume you are a training manager at this airline. First, how would you go about designing a needs assessment for the airline? What methods would you use to design training that emphasized exceptional customer service? Second, what type(s) of training would you recommend for flight attendants, if the new goal was to provide exceptional customer service? How might the training programs themselves have to change in order to promote innovation and collaboration among flight attendants, as well as from the trainers?*

## INTRODUCTION

How would you rate the following statements as reasons for adopting a new management development program?

- *"Look at all the big companies that are using this program. It's got to be right for us."*
- *"We're going to get Professor X to do our program. Everybody's talking about how great she is."*
- *"We asked managers to list the topics they wanted in the program. About a third responded, and we've included everything they suggested."*
- *"Purchasing just asked for management training in two weeks. Here's a firm that will do it."*
- *"A consulting firm tells us they've been successfully running this program for years."*
- *"A consulting firm tells us that, if we spend a lot of time and money, they will tailor their program to our environment."*

Hopefully, you are looking at the previous list with some suspicion. Stated another way, can you see anything wrong with starting a new training program for any of the reasons listed? The scary thing (to us, at least) is that these types of sentiments were expressed by HRD professionals (many years ago, thankfully).[1] Scarier still is how easy it is for managers and HRD professionals even today to engage in such behaviors, that is, using a training program because of a follow-the-leader mindset, or because of "star gazing," or with a "burger-and-fries-to-go" mentality.[2] Engaging in training or any other form of HRD intervention for any of these reasons is most *unlikely* to lead to improved individual, team, or organizational performance.

Ultimately, the goal of HRD is to improve an organization's effectiveness by:

1. solving current problems (like an increase in customer complaints)
2. preventing anticipated problems (such as a shortage of skilled technicians)
3. including as participants those individuals and units that can benefit most

In short, HRD is effective if it successfully addresses some organizational need (as illustrated by Cathay Pacific's experience described in the opening case). How are those needs identified? The answer is through conducting *needs assessments*.

As discussed in Chapter 1, HRD interventions should be designed and conducted using a four-phase approach: needs assessment, design, implementation, and evaluation (see Figure 4-1). The framework laid out in Figure 4-1 is often described as the instructional systems design (ISD) approach.[3] The purpose of this chapter is to discuss the first phase of this approach, namely needs assessment, and how various assessment efforts are used to then design, implement, and evaluate HRD programs and activities.

## DEFINITION AND PURPOSES OF NEEDS ASSESSMENT

**Needs assessment** is a process by which an organization's HRD needs are identified and articulated. It is the starting point of the HRD and training process. A needs assessment can identify:

- an organization's goals and its effectiveness in reaching these goals
- discrepancies or gaps between employees' skills and the skills required for effective current job performance
- discrepancies (gaps) between current skills and the skills needed to perform the job successfully in the future
- the conditions under which the HRD activity will occur

With this information, HRD professionals learn where and what kinds of programs or interventions are needed, who needs to be included in them, and whether there are currently any roadblocks to their effectiveness. Criteria can then be established to guide the evaluation process. It is obvious, then, that needs analysis is *critical* for an effective HRD effort.

However, despite its importance, many organizations do not perform a needs analysis as frequently or as thoroughly as they might. If anything, the competitive pressures currently facing organizations have made it more difficult than ever to

**FIGURE 4-1**　　　　　**TRAINING AND HRD PROCESS MODEL**

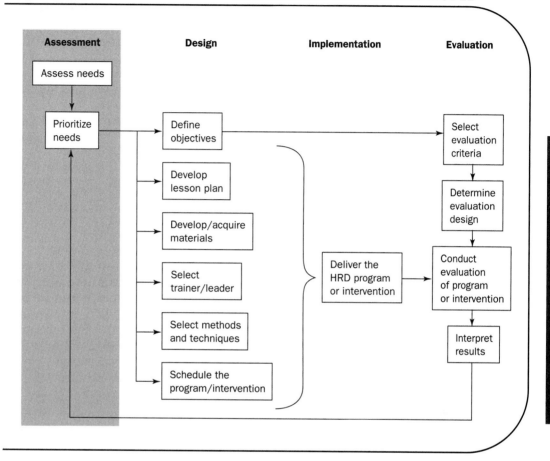

carry out a needs assessment.[4] Needs assessments are not conducted for a number of reasons, such as:

1. **A needs assessment can be a difficult, time-consuming process.** A complete needs analysis involves measuring a variety of factors at multiple levels of the organization.

2. **Action is valued over research.** Managers often decide to use their limited resources to develop, acquire, and deliver HRD programs rather than to do something they see as a preliminary activity.

3. **Incorrect assumptions are made that a needs assessment is unnecessary because available information already specifies what an organization's needs are.** As indicated earlier, factors such as fads, demands from senior managers, and the temptation to copy the HRD programs of widely admired organizations or competitors often lead to such conclusions.

4. **There is a lack of support for needs assessment.** This can be caused by a lack of bottom-line justification, or by the HRD professional's inability to sell needs assessment to management. Documenting the assessment and its benefits, and using analogies from respected fields (e.g., medical diagnosis, engineering scoping) are two ways to build support for doing needs assessment.[5]

These factors should be considered when promoting needs assessment. Although it is possible to improve the organization's effectiveness without accurate needs assessment information, the results are by no means guaranteed. If the limited resources available are spent on programs that don't solve the organization's problems (or help it take advantage of opportunities), the effort is a failure and the resources are wasted. Plus, the original problems still demand solutions.

Before discussing different approaches to needs analysis, it is useful to examine what is meant by the term "need."

## WHAT IS A TRAINING OR HRD NEED?

In this context, the concept of *need* typically refers to a discrepancy or *gap* between what an organization expects to happen and what actually occurs.[6] For example, a discrepancy exists if a shipping supervisor has been charged to maintain an average turnaround time of twenty-four hours for shipping customer orders, and it is actually taking his or her department an average of thirty-six hours. A similar inconsistency is demonstrated when a police officer is expected to use minimum force to apprehend suspects, but the department receives documented complaints that the officer has used excessive force with suspects. These discrepancies may become the foundation of a training or HRD need.

Identified needs in this sense focus on correcting substandard performance. In some cases, an HRD intervention such as coaching or skills training may be necessary to correct the discrepancy. However, sometimes another HRM strategy (such as improving compensation or changing staffing practices), or another management action (like replacing machinery or negotiating new work rules with the union) may be more appropriate solutions. It is important to stress that not every need identified can or should be addressed by training or even by other, broader HRD efforts such as team building or organizational development.

Robert Brinkerhoff has argued that focusing *only on* performance deficiency in needs analysis is too restrictive and proposed other ways of looking at training needs.[7] These include diagnostic and analytic needs. **Diagnostic needs** focus on the factors that lead to effective performance and *prevent* performance problems, rather than emphasizing existing problems. Diagnostic needs are identified by studying the different factors that may impact performance. The goal is to determine how effective performance is obtained. **Analytic needs** identify new, better ways to perform tasks. These needs are generally discovered by intuition, insight, or expert consideration. We would add another type of need, namely compliance. **Compliance needs** are those needs that are mandated by law. This most often deals with mandated training programs, such as safety training or food handling. It is important to recognize that some HRD interventions are driven primarily by legal mandate, as this can affect how the intervention is perceived, as well as how it is conducted.

This discussion of needs is meant to reinforce the notion that HRD should be *proactive* and future oriented. Addressing needs from an analytic or diagnostic perspective is proactive in its emphasis on preventing problems and enhancing performance and productivity, a notion that is consistent with continuous improvement, such as the recent focus on total quality management and learning organizations. This focus contrasts with a *reactive* approach in which performance discrepancies only (or compliance needs alone) are the basis for training and HRD. Clearly, organizations are better served if HRD efforts consider different types of needs, focusing on ways to maintain effective performance and make it even better, as well as fixing what is done poorly.

Roger Kaufman provides some timely advice concerning why HRD professionals should "bother with" needs assessment. He frames this in terms of potentially hazardous shortcuts and why they should be avoided (see Table 4-1).[8] A critical concern of Kaufman and others (such as Dana Gaines Robinson and James Robinson) is that HRD professionals must always maintain a focus on organizational performance.[9] Loriann Roberson, Carol Kulik, and Molly Pepper provide an excellent recent example of how needs assessment can be used to enhance the effectiveness of diversity training programs.[10]

**TABLE 4-1**     **TRAPS TO AVOID WHEN DOING NEEDS ASSESSMENT**

| Potential Trap | Why This Should be Avoided |
| --- | --- |
| Focus *only on* individual performance deficiencies. | This can lead to fixing problems that don't impact group or organizational performance. |
| Start with a training needs assessment. | There is no need for a needs assessment if you already know that training is the answer! |
| Just send out questionnaires asking people what they need. | Trainee input can be good, yet such open-ended questioning can encourage suggestions that are not tied to organizational results. |
| Use soft data only. | Opinions need to be linked to performance and consequences. |
| Use hard data only. | Performance data is often collected on what is easy to measure, missing other critical information in the process. |

SOURCE: From R. Kaufman. (1997). Needs assessment basics. In R. Kaufman, S. Thiagarajan, & P. MacGillis (Eds.), *The guidebook for performance improvement* (pp. 107–129). San Francisco: Pfeiffer/Jossey-Bass.

| | |
|---|---|
| **TABLE 4-2** | **LEVELS OF NEEDS ASSESSMENT** |

| Level | What Is Measured |
|---|---|
| Strategic/Organizational | Where is training needed and in what conditions will the training be conducted? |
| Task | What must be done to perform the job effectively? |
| Person | Who should be trained? What kind of training do they need? |

## LEVELS OF NEEDS ANALYSIS

Needs can exist at any of at least three levels, considering the organization, the job/task, and the individual. To ensure an effective HRD effort, needs must be measured on each level. As a result, three types of assessments must be conducted: organizational analysis, task analysis, and person analysis.[11] Each level of assessment measures different aspects of the organization (see Table 4-2). **Strategic/ organizational analysis** suggests where in the organization training is needed and under what conditions it will occur. **Task analysis** explains what must be done to perform a job or complete a process successfully. **Person analysis** reveals who needs to be trained, and what kind of training they need.

# STRATEGIC/ORGANIZATIONAL ANALYSIS

Needs assessment at the organization level is usually conducted by performing an organizational analysis. Organizational analysis is a process used to better understand the characteristics of the organization to determine where training and HRD efforts are needed and the conditions within which they will be conducted. Kavita Gupta has referred to this type of analysis as a strategic analysis.[12] For example, some years ago, Scott Paper purchased a food service operation that suffered from low employee morale. An extensive needs assessment process resulted in the food service division implementing a succession planning and management development program. Within four years, product defects dropped dramatically, on-time delivery rates increased to 98 percent, and plant capacity was increased by 35 percent. The point to stress here is that the organizational analysis they conducted (as part of the overall needs assessment) provided the impetus for a successful HRD effort, as well as the content of the actual development program.[13]

## COMPONENTS OF A STRATEGIC/ORGANIZATIONAL NEEDS ANALYSIS

This type of analysis requires a broad or "whole system" view of the organization and what it is trying to accomplish. The organizational characteristics studied may include goals and objectives, reward systems, planning systems, delegation and control systems, and communication systems. According to Irwin Goldstein, an organizational analysis should identify:

1. organizational goals
2. organizational resources
3. organizational climate
4. environmental constraints[14]

Each of these factors provides important information for planning and developing HRD programs and is described further in the following sections.

*ORGANIZATIONAL GOALS.* Understanding the organization's goals and strategy provides a starting point in identifying the effectiveness of the organization. Areas where the organization is meeting its goals probably don't require training efforts, but should be monitored to ensure that opportunities for improvement and potential problems are identified early. Effective areas can be used as models, and as a source of ideas for how things can be done more effectively in other areas. Areas where goals are not being met should be examined further and targeted for HRD or other appropriate HR or management efforts.

*ORGANIZATIONAL RESOURCES.* An awareness of the organization's resources is particularly useful in establishing HRD needs. Obviously, the amount of money available is an important determinant of HRD efforts. In addition, knowledge of resources such as facilities, materials on hand, and the expertise within the organization also influence how HRD is conducted. Resource availability can dictate some of the options to be considered when designing and implementing HRD programs and can influence the priorities given to HRD needs. For example, if there are no classroom or conference room facilities within the organization, the scheduling and location of an HRD program that requires such facilities can become very difficult and expensive. In this case, it may be necessary to use an off-site location, such as a conference center or hotel, or to schedule the program in the company cafeteria after working hours.

*ORGANIZATIONAL CLIMATE.* The climate within the organization is an important factor in HRD success. If the climate is not conducive to HRD, designing and implementing a program will be difficult. For example, if managers and employees do not trust one another, employees may not participate fully and freely in a training program. Similarly, if problems exist between senior and middle management, as has happened in many organizations during restructuring, middle managers may resist or not fully cooperate in the training effort, seriously reducing training effectiveness. As discussed in Chapter 3, research shows that an organization's transfer of training climate affects whether employees use the skills they acquire in HRD programs back on the job.[15]

*ENVIRONMENTAL CONSTRAINTS.* Environmental constraints include legal, social, political, and economic issues faced by the organization. Demand for certain types of HRD programs can be affected by these constraints. For example, in 1998, the

Supreme Court decided two significant cases concerning sexual harassment.[16] Unfortunately, in both cases, supervisory training concerning sexual harassment was inadequate or nonexistent.[17] In fiscal year 2003, the U.S. Equal Employment Opportunity Commission received over 13,500 complaints of sexual harassment, and won monetary awards of $50 million dollars for cases resolved.[18] We discuss sexual harassment further in the final chapter, and will highlight other legal issues in relevant chapters throughout the book. Suffice it to say that legal issues play an important role in HRD.

Knowledge of legal issues can ensure that the HRD effort is in compliance and will not itself be a source of problems. For example, equal employment opportunity goals should be considered when determining how people will be assigned to a training program, especially if the program is a prerequisite for entry into a particular job. Similarly, economic issues, such as increased competition, can also have an impact on HRD programs. If an organization decides to reduce staff as a part of a cost-cutting program, training may be necessary to ensure that the employees who remain will be able to perform the tasks that were performed by the laid-off workers.

## ADVANTAGES OF CONDUCTING A STRATEGIC/ORGANIZATIONAL ANALYSIS

As discussed earlier, an organizational analysis reveals where HRD is needed and the organizational and environmental conditions that may affect the HRD effort. Knowledge of these issues ensures that all HRD programs are tied to the organization's strategy and mission, which is crucial to its success. Communicating the link between HRD activities and the organization's strategic plan to operating managers and employees makes the importance of HRD programs clear. This may also generate support for HRD efforts and increase the motivation of those being trained.[19]

One way to establish this connection is to link organizational analysis with the strategic planning process, especially because much of the same information is obtained in both procedures. The strategic plan can be a valuable source of information for organizational analysis, whereas HRD efforts can become a major component of carrying out the strategic plan. For example, if an insurance company decides as part of its strategic plan to expand the services it offers to clients (e.g., pension management), it is likely that the current employees will require training in the new service area to ensure successful implementation of the plan. Carnevale, Gainer, and Villet provide a list of questions that can be used to assess strategic issues.[20] A sampling of these questions is provided in Table 4-3.

## METHODS OF STRATEGIC/ORGANIZATIONAL ANALYSIS

Strategic/organizational analysis methods depend on the particular organization. A list of data sources is available for determining training and HRD needs (see Table 4-4).[21] The list includes the following: human resource inventories (formerly known as manpower inventories), skills inventories, organizational climate measures, and efficiency indexes. Some of these sources, such as efficiency indexes,

| TABLE 4-3 | QUESTIONS TO ASK TO OBTAIN STRATEGIC INFORMATION IN AN ORGANIZATION ANALYSIS |

**Broad Strategic Issues**

1. Is the organization's industry evolving or stable? What do the growth trends of competitors look like? Who are the main foreign and domestic competitors, and what is the organization's main advantage over these competitors?

2. Why has the organization been successful in the past?

3. What new technology does the organization plan to use? If new technology is being planned, when will it become available?

4. Are innovations anticipated that could change the competitive playing field?

5. What new management philosophies or procedures will be instituted by the organization? When?

6. Are there any regulatory issues, current, pending, or anticipated, that could influence strategic considerations?

7. What functional strategies will be employed by the various divisions or operating units to effect the overarching strategy? Why? How?

**Human Resource Issues**

1. What are the current strengths and weaknesses of the workforce?

2. What changes, if any, must occur in the job(s), organizational culture, and skill levels of the workforce?

3. Is the organization's overall strategy likely to result in layoffs and turnover? How much is anticipated?

4. If applicable, how will union contracts be affected? What is the strategic role of the union?

5. What HRM policies should be reviewed in light of the organization's current strategic effort?

6. What are the training and HRD implications of the overarching strategy? How could training/HRD help the organization reach any or all of its strategic goals?

7. What kind of specific training and HRD interventions are needed? Does the organization have in-house capability to implement the necessary programs? Are there outside experts who can assist? Who are they?

8. How has training and HRD been regarded: By the workforce in the past? By management? How credible are the programs, trainers, and other HRD professionals?

9. What delivery mechanisms are the most cost-effective and practical for each program?

10. What kind of HRD evaluation process is currently being used? Does it provide information on return on investment (ROI)? If not, would such a process contribute to the strategic management of the organization?

11. Is there a formal procedure to ascertain if current training/HRD is appropriate in light of new strategies, or, alternatively, to identify training needs that will be dictated by new strategies?

12. Do HRM functions other than training and HRD need to be reviewed? Should they be modified?

SOURCE: From A. P. Carnevale, L. J. Gainer, & J. Villet (1991). *Training in America* (pp. 203–205). San Francisco: Jossey-Bass. Reprinted with permission of John Wiley & Sons, Inc.

PART 2: FRAMEWORK FOR HUMAN RESOURCE DEVELOPMENT

**TABLE 4-4**

## SOURCES OF DATA FOR ORGANIZATIONAL NEEDS ANALYSIS

| Data Source Recommended | HRD/Training Need Implications |
|---|---|
| 1. Organizational Goals and Objectives | Where HRD or training emphasis can and should be placed. These provide normative standards of both direction and expected impact, which can highlight deviations from objectives and performance problems. |
| 2. Human Resource (Manpower) Inventory | Where HRD/training is needed to fill gaps caused by retirement, turnover, age, etc. This provides an important demographic database regarding possible scope of training needs. |
| 3. Skills Inventory | Number of employees in each skill group, knowledge and skill levels, training time per job, etc. This provides an estimate of the magnitude of the specific needs for HRD/training. Useful in cost-benefit analysis of HRD projects. |
| 4. Organizational Climate Indexes | These "quality of working life" indicators at the organization level may help focus on problems that have HRD/training components. |
| Labor-Management data — strikes, lockouts, etc. Grievances Turnover Absenteeism Suggestions Productivity Accidents Short-term sickness Observation of employee behavior | All of these items related to either work participation or productivity are useful both in discrepancy analysis and in helping management set a value on the behaviors it wishes improved once HRD or training have been established as relevant solutions. |
| Attitude surveys | Good for locating discrepancies between organizational expectations and perceived results. |
| Customer complaints | Valuable feedback; look especially for patterns and repeat complaints. |
| 5. Analysis of Efficiency Indexes Costs of labor Costs of materials Quality of product Equipment utilization Costs of distribution Waste Downtime Late deliveries Repairs | Cost accounting concepts may represent ratio between actual performance and desired or standard performance. |

*continued*

**TABLE 4-4**                                              **CONTINUED**

| Data Source Recommended | HRD/Training Need Implications |
| --- | --- |
| 6. Changes in System or Subsystem | New or changed equipment may present HRD or training problems. |
| 7. Management Requests or Management Interrogation | One of most common techniques of HRD/training needs determination. |
| 8. Exit Interviews | Often information not otherwise available can be obtained in these. Problem areas and supervisory training needs especially. |
| 9. MBO or Work Planning and Review Systems | Provides performance review, potential review, and long-term business objectives. Provides actual performance data on a recurring basis so that baseline measurements may be known and subsequent improvement or deterioration of performance can be identified and analyzed. |

SOURCE: ACADEMY OF MANAGEMENT REVIEW by M. L. Moore, P. Dutton. Copyright 2005 by ACAD OF MGMT. Reproduced with permission of ACAD OF MGMT in the format Textbook via Copyright Clearance Center.

are continuously monitored by many organizations as part of the normal control procedures and the data are readily available. Ferdinand Tesoro and Jack Tootson of Dell Computers provide some excellent guidance for using existing organizational measures as the basis for training and performance improvement efforts.[22] Other sources, such as organizational climate, may require the administration of an employee survey. Such surveys can be designed by the organization or purchased commercially. For example, the Institute for Social Research at the University of Michigan markets two instruments — Survey of Organizations and Michigan Organizational Assessment Questionnaire — that are supported by substantial reliability and validity data.[23]

Goldstein provides a list of questions to ask during an organizational analysis:

1. Are there any unspecified organizational goals that should be translated into training objectives or criteria?

2. Are the various levels in the organization committed to the training objectives?

3. Have the various levels or participating units in the organization been involved with developing the program, starting with the assessment of the desired end results of training?

4. Are key individuals in the organization ready to accept the behavior of the trainees, and also to serve as models of the appropriate behavior?

5. Will trainees be rewarded on the job for the appropriate learned behavior?

6. Is training being used to overcome organizational problems or conflicts that actually require *other* types of solutions?

7. Is top management willing to commit the necessary resources to maintain the organization and work flow while individuals are being trained?[24]

As we have suggested, organizational analysis can be a critical component of an effective HRD effort. Although it would be optimal to conduct a complete organizational analysis on a regular basis, resource and time limitations often make this difficult. At the very least, HRD managers and professionals should continuously monitor the organization's environment, goals, and effectiveness by taking advantage of information already collected by the organization (what Ron Zemke refers to as sifting through "found data").[25] This responsibility is increasingly expected of *all* managers and supervisors (and many employees), as the environment becomes increasingly more turbulent and competition more fierce.

The municipal government for Los Angeles County recently completed a customized needs assessment process for its human resource managers.[26] An analysis of external and internal challenges (i.e., an organizational analysis) led county leaders to seek a more active "strategic partner" role for their human resources professionals.[27] Before conducting strategic HRM training, a thorough needs assessment was conducted. The emphasis was on the important skills or competencies HR professionals should possess. Comparisons were then made concerning the extent to which HR professionals currently possessed these strategic competencies. Competencies rated as most important included understanding customers and the organizational environment, as well as high levels of business ethics and communication skills. Comparing the gaps between what was most important and what was viewed as the current state of preparedness provided the rationale for what should be emphasized in training. For example, the ability to "see the big picture in decision making" was viewed as very important, yet was rated much lower in current preparedness. This became of one of the "imperatives" for the strategic HR training conducted by Los Angeles County. We see this as an excellent example of how strategic/organizational analysis can lead to tailored training and HRD programs that fit the needs of the organization. We next discuss the second level of needs assessment, namely task analysis.

## TASK ANALYSIS

*Task analysis* (sometimes called operations analysis) is a systematic collection of data about a specific job or group of jobs to determine what an employee should be taught to achieve optimal performance.[28] Results of a task analysis typically include the appropriate standards of performance, how tasks should be performed to meet these standards, and the knowledge, skills, abilities, and other characteristics (KSAOs) that employees need to possess in order to meet the standards.

Table 4-5 lists a variety of data sources available for a task analysis, including job descriptions, observing the job, asking questions about the job, and reviewing literature about the job.[29]

**TABLE 4-5** — **SOURCES OF DATA FOR TASK NEEDS ANALYSIS**

| Technique for Obtaining Job Data | HRD/Training Need Implications |
|---|---|
| 1. Job Descriptions | Outlines the job in terms of typical duties and responsibilities but is not meant to be all-inclusive. Helps define performance discrepancies. |
| 2. Job Specifications or Task Analysis | List specified tasks required for each job. More specific than job descriptions. Specifications may extend to judgments of knowledge, skills, and other attributes required of job incumbents. |
| 3. Performance Standards | Objectives of the tasks of job and standards by which they are judged. This may include baseline data as well. |
| 4. Perform the Job | Most effective way of determining specific tasks but has serious limitations the higher the level of the job in that performance requirements typically have longer gaps between performance and resulting outcomes. |
| 5. Observe Job-Work Sampling | |
| 6. Review Literature Concerning the Job<br>    Research in other industries<br>    Professional journals<br>    Documents<br>    Government sources<br>    Ph.D. and master's theses | Possibly useful in comparison analyses of job structures but far removed from either unique aspects of the job structure within any *specific* organization or specific performance requirements. |
| 7. Ask Questions About the Job<br>    Of the job holder<br>    Of the supervisor<br>    Of higher management | |
| 8. Training Committees or Conferences | Inputs from several viewpoints can often reveal training needs or HRD/training desires. |
| 9. Analysis of Operating Problems<br>    Downtime reports<br>    Waste<br>    Repairs<br>    Late deliveries<br>    Quality control | Indications of task interference, environmental factors, etc. |
| 10. Card Sort | "How to" statements sorted by training importance. |

SOURCE: ACADEMY OF MANAGEMENT REVIEW by M. L. Moore, P. Dutton. Copyright 2005 by ACAD OF MGMT. Reproduced with permission of ACAD OF MGMT in the format Textbook via Copyright Clearance Center.

Although there is general agreement about the purpose of task analysis, there are differing views of how it should be accomplished. We combine the approaches used by others into the following five-step process: [30]

1. Develop an overall job description.
2. Identify the task.
    a. Describe what should be done in the task.
    b. Describe what is actually done in the task.
3. Describe KSAOs needed to perform the job.
4. Identify areas that can benefit from training.
5. Prioritize areas that can benefit from training.

We expand upon these steps in our subsequent discussion.

## THE TASK ANALYSIS PROCESS

*STEP 1: OVERALL JOB DESCRIPTION.* The first step in the process is to develop an overall description of the job or jobs being analyzed. A **job description** is a narrative statement of the major activities involved in performing the job and the conditions under which these activities are performed. In some organizations, job descriptions are readily available and are updated regularly, so that they accurately reflect the job as it is performed. If this is the case, the HRD professional should obtain and review the description. Without up-to-date job descriptions, however, it may be necessary to conduct a job analysis.

A **job analysis** is a systematic study of a job to identify its major components. The job analysis process (described in detail by Gael and Gatewood and Field) generally involves observing the job being performed; asking job incumbents and supervisors questions about the job, tasks, working conditions, and KSAOs; examining the outcomes of the job; and reviewing relevant literature about the job.[31] Sometimes, the *task* portion of the job analysis is referred to as the job description, whereas the *KSAO* portion is called the **job specification;** however, both task and KSAO portions are generally included in written job descriptions.

Even if a current job description is already available, it is valuable to observe the job as it is performed — a sort of reality test that can give the HRD professional a clearer idea about the tasks and the conditions employees face.

*STEP 2: TASK IDENTIFICATION.* **Task identification** focuses on the behaviors performed within the job. In task identification, the following information about the job is determined and clearly described:

- the major tasks within the job
- how each task should be performed (i.e., performance standards)
- the variability of performance (how the tasks are actually performed in day-to-day operations)

Both performance standards and performance variability are critical to an effective needs analysis. Although the standards describe *what should be done*, information about the variability of performance shows *what is done*. This allows the HRD professional to identify discrepancies that should be remedied and what the trainees should be able to do at the conclusion of training. Both of these are important in developing training objectives.

Five methods for task identification include:

1. stimulus-response-feedback

2. time sampling

3. critical incident technique

4. job inventories

5. job-duty-task method

The **stimulus-response-feedback method** breaks down each task into three components.[32] The first component is the stimulus, or cue, that lets an employee know it is time to perform a particular behavior. The second component is the response or behavior that the employee is to perform. The third component is the feedback the employee receives about how well the behavior was performed. For example, when a buzzer (the stimulus) signals that French fries are done cooking, a fast-food worker should respond by lifting the basket of fries out of the cooking oil and hanging it on a rack to drain (the behavior). Whether the basket stays in place or falls is the feedback on how well the behavior was performed. As another example, for a teacher involved in giving students career guidance, the stimulus would be the "need to respond to student's academic goals" and the appropriate response would be "provide a list of career options to students."[33]

This task identification method results in a list of the cues, behaviors, and feedback that make up each task involved in the job. It is well suited for jobs with relatively simple tasks that can be directly observed, whether by a supervisor, the job incumbent, or a trained analyst.[34]

**Time sampling,** the second task identification method, involves having a trained observer watch and note the nature and frequency of an employee's activities. By observing at random intervals over a period of time, a clearer picture of the job is understood and recorded.

The **critical incident technique (CIT)** developed by John Flanagan can also be used for task identification.[35] The CIT involves having individuals who are familiar with the job record incidents of particularly effective and ineffective behavior that they have seen on the job over a period of time (like one year). This can be done by individuals or in groups. For each incident, the observer is asked to describe the circumstances and the specific behaviors involved, and suggest reasons why the behavior was effective or ineffective. The CIT results in an understanding of what is considered both good and poor performance.

A **job inventory questionnaire** is a fourth approach to task identification. A questionnaire is developed by asking people familiar with the job to identify all of its tasks. This list is then given to supervisors and job incumbents to evaluate each task in terms of its importance and the time spent performing it. This method

FIGURE 4-2 **APPLYING THE JOB-DUTY-TASK METHOD OF TASK ANALYSIS TO THE JOB OF HRD PROFESSIONAL**

Job title: HRD Professional

Specific duty: Task Analysis

| Tasks | Subtasks | Knowledge and Skills Required |
|-------|----------|-------------------------------|
| 1. List tasks | 1. Observe behavior | List four characteristics of behavior<br>Classify behavior |
| | 2. Select verb | Knowledge of action verbs<br>Grammatical skills |
| | 3. Record behavior | State so understood by others<br>Record neatly |
| 2. List subtasks | 1. Observe behavior | List all remaining acts<br>Classify behavior |
| | 2. Select verb | State correctly<br>Grammatical skills |
| | 3. Record behavior | Neat and understood by others |
| 3. List knowledge | 1. State what must be known | Classify all information |
| | 2. Determine complexity of skill | Determine if a skill represents a series of acts that must be learned in a sequence |

SOURCE: From G. E. Mills, R. W. Pace, & B. D. Peterson (1988). *Analysis in human resource training and organizational development* (p. 57). Reading, MA: Addison-Wesley. Reprinted by permission.

allows for input from many people and gives numerical information about each task that can be used to compute indexes and be analyzed with statistics.

Finally, the fifth approach is the **job-duty-task method.** In this method, the job is divided into its subparts, providing a comprehensive list that identifies the job title; each of its duties (and the tasks and subtasks that make up that duty); and, finally, the knowledge, skills, abilities, or other characteristics (KSAOs) required to perform each subtask. An example of the results of a job-duty-task analysis is shown in Figure 4-2.

Each of these five methods uses job experts (i.e., incumbents or supervisors) or trained observers to provide and evaluate job information. To obtain a more complete view of the job, it is desirable to use more than one method. This, of course, depends upon the nature of the job being studied and the time and resources available. Methods that involve a range of organization members (supervisors, managers, and employees), such as the CIT and task inventory, have the advantage of building commitment and accountability to the overall HRD effort.[36] This can help facilitate the progress of the HRD intervention down the line.

It is vital that all task statements are evaluated in terms of their importance for job performance, the frequency with which the tasks are performed, and how difficult it is to become proficient at the tasks.[37] Armed with this information, the next step in the task analysis process is to identify the characteristics it takes to perform the tasks.

*STEP 3: IDENTIFY WHAT IT TAKES TO DO THE JOB.* Successful task performance requires that employees possess the KSAOs to perform the task. The HRD professional must specify the KSAOs because it is these competencies (reviewed in Table 4-6) that employees must develop or acquire during the training program.

As noted earlier, a thorough job analysis will contain this information in the job specification section. If this information is not available or is not current, the HRD professional can determine these factors by questioning supervisors, job incumbents, and other experts and by reviewing relevant literature. Clear KSAO statements should be written and then evaluated as to their importance to job performance, learning difficulty, and the opportunity to acquire them on the job.[38]

Information on KSAOs required to perform a job is valuable in determining the focus of an HRD program. Some KSAOs, such as oral and written communication skills or knowledge of safety procedures, are necessary for effective performance in many jobs. If this is the case, it may be possible to develop and conduct an HRD program that can be offered to employees in a wide range of jobs.

*STEP 4: IDENTIFY THE AREAS THAT CAN MOST BENEFIT FROM TRAINING OR HRD.* In this step, the focus is on determining which tasks and capabilities should be included in HRD programs. Both ratings of *tasks* as well as ratings of *KSAOs* should be examined. Task ratings should be studied concerning their importance, time spent, and the ease of acquisition. KSAO ratings should be studied for their importance, the difficulty of learning, and opportunity to acquire them on the job. The tasks and KSAOs receiving the highest ratings should be considered the primary candidates for inclusion in HRD programs.

Care must be taken to balance the concerns raised by these ratings. For example, a high rating on time spent and ease of learning may indicate that a particular task should be included in training. However, if that same task is also rated low in importance to successful job performance, it may not be worth the time and effort involved in training (or perhaps less expensive training methods can be used). It is

PART 2: FRAMEWORK FOR HUMAN RESOURCE DEVELOPMENT

**TABLE 4-6**     **DEFINITIONS OF KNOWLEDGE, SKILL, ABILITY, AND OTHER CHARACTERISTICS (KSAOS)**

| | |
|---|---|
| Knowledge | An understanding of a body of information, usually of a factual or procedural nature, that makes for successful performance of a task. |
| Skill | An individual's level of proficiency or competency in performing a specific task. Level of competency is usually expressed in numerical terms. |
| Ability | A more general, enduring trait or capability an individual possesses when he or she first begins to perform a task, e.g., the power to perform a physical or mental function. |
| Other Characteristics | Includes personality, interests, and attitudes. |

SOURCE: From *Human Resource Selection*, 5th edition by Gatewood/Field. Copyright 2001. Reprinted with permission of South-Western, a division of Thomson Learning: www.thomsonrights.com. Fax 800-730-2215

also important to remember that not all problems are appropriately dealt with through HRD programs. Other HR or management approaches may be better suited for particular issues and situations.

*STEP 5: PRIORITIZE TRAINING NEEDS.* At the end of Step 4, it should be clear which tasks and KSAOs could benefit from training. These tasks and KSAOs should be prioritized to determine which ones should be addressed first. Again, inspection of the ratings provided in Steps 2 and 3 can facilitate the prioritization process (more will be said about prioritizing training needs at the end of this chapter).

## AN EXAMPLE OF A TASK ANALYSIS: TEXAS INSTRUMENTS

A task analysis performed to develop a train-the-trainer program at Texas Instruments Corporation (TI) provides a good illustration of the ideas included in our discussion of the task analysis process.[39] The training staff at TI needed to determine training needs and deliver an inexpensive program to quickly train expert engineers to instruct new engineers. Consultants began the process by meeting with branch managers, department heads, and employees from five TI branches to determine the following information:

- the mission of the department
- perceived training needs
- current and previous efforts in staff development
- the roles, responsibilities, and team arrangements within the different branches

This organizational analysis identified the significant issues involved, and the training team then used this information in persuading top managers to commit to a five-step approach to task analysis:

1. List typical tasks.
2. Survey staff.
3. Observe the classroom.
4. Conduct structured interviews.
5. Prepare and present a final report.

The *list of tasks* was developed by examining literature on training delivery, including company technical reports and the American Society for Training and Development's *Models for Excellence* study. TI managers reviewed the initial list of tasks, added several tasks, and reworded other task statements. The list was then organized into five areas of responsibility and given to employees to review and supplement. This step ensured that all the professionals had input into defining their jobs from their perspectives, and it resulted in a 117-item list of tasks that trainers would typically be expected to perform.

For the *staff survey*, all members of the department received a questionnaire listing the tasks and asking them to rate each task according to (1) its importance to their job and (2) their interest in receiving more training related to that task. Each item was given a mean rating score on importance and interest. The results were examined to determine whether differences existed for the five branches (they did not).

*Classroom observations* of experienced and new TI trainers were conducted to provide additional information on instructional delivery. Teams of observers viewed instructors for one hour and met with each instructor to provide feedback. Individuals from each branch participated in *structured interviews* to maintain consistency between the survey findings and the classroom observations. This allowed the training team to gather more information about each branch and to "validate" the data gathered earlier. The interview results were consistent with data from the other sources.

The final step was preparation of the *final report*. This consisted of examining the results and developing an executive summary outlining strengths and recommendations for training in each of the five areas of the task list, along with data for each data collection method.

The needs analysis was described as a success because it allowed input and participation at all levels, ensuring cooperation and comprehensiveness.[40] As a result, the training team was able to identify and rank training needs based on sound information rather than relying on intuition alone.

This example reinforces several important points about task analysis:

1. Input from managers, supervisors, and employees can ensure support for needs analysis and pave the way for support for training.

2. Multiple methods not only provide unique information but also enable the analyst to confirm findings and identify and resolve discrepancies.

3. Ratings of tasks allow for quantitative analysis of which tasks may benefit from training and which should be addressed.

4. Viewing needs from a broad perspective, rather than focusing only on performance deficiencies, results in a better understanding of training needs and can build support for training programs.

## A UNIQUE TASK ANALYSIS APPROACH AT BOEING

The ASTD Benchmarking Forum recognized Boeing Corporation for its task analysis approach involving engineers who were being trained to use computer-aided drafting and computer-aided manufacturing (CAD-CAM) software.[41] The approach involved assessing expert CAD-CAM users' thinking processes for solving problems, dealing with uncertainty, and minimizing risks. The analysis was performed by using a system called the Knowledge Analysis and Design Support (KADS), a technique originally designed to build automated knowledge-based systems (recall our discussion of expert performance in Chapter 3). Once the expert thinking processes were identified, the HRD analysts worked with course developers, and together they were able to define CAD-CAM learning objectives and training course curricula.

## SUMMARY OF TASK ANALYSIS

Task analysis focuses on the job, rather than on the individual doing the job. Information from task analysis and organizational analysis gives a clear picture of the organization and the jobs that are performed within it, and knowledge of the two provides a sound foundation for planning and developing HRD efforts. Respected scholar Richard Swanson has written a book entitled *Analysis for Improving Performance*.[42] In his book, Swanson covers task analysis similar to the way we have previously discussed it. He also extends his discussion to provide extensive comments about three other forms of analysis: procedural task analysis, systems task analysis, and knowledge task analysis. With the many changes in the nature of jobs and organizations taking place today, we expect that task analysis will have to adapt to meet these demands. We recommend Swanson's work to the reader interested in pursuing these ideas in further detail. We also urge the interested reader to consider completing the "Conducting a Task Analysis" exercise at the end of this chapter.

Two final questions remain: Who needs training? and What kind of training do they need? The answers to these questions can be found in person analysis.

## PERSON ANALYSIS

*Person analysis* is directed at determining the training needs of the individual employee. The focus is typically on how well each employee is performing key job tasks, but this process may identify a wide range of both common and unique HRD needs. Someone who can observe the employee's performance on a regular basis is in the best position to conduct a person analysis. Traditionally, person analysis has involved an employee and that employee's immediate supervisor. Depending on the nature of an individual's work, that employee's peers, customers, and subordinates may also be in a position to provide information that can be used to identify person-level needs. In fact, an evaluation approach called **360-degree performance appraisal** uses as many of these sources as possible to get a complete picture of an employee's performance. This approach will be discussed later in this chapter.

Immediate supervisors play a particularly important role in person analysis. Not only are they in a position to observe employee performance, but it is also their responsibility to do so. Also, access to HRD programs in many organizations requires the supervisor's nomination and support. Many methods of person assessment require an effective supervisor to implement them properly.

The sources for person analysis data include performance evaluation, direct observation, tests, questionnaires, and critical incidents as sources of information available for person assessment (see Table 4-7).[43] In addition, for individuals recently hired into an organization, the information collected as part of the selection process can also be used to determine any developmental needs that the individual has.

**TABLE 4-7**

# DATA SOURCES AVAILABLE FOR PERSON NEEDS ASSESSMENT

| Technique or Data Obtained | HRD/Training Need Implications |
|---|---|
| 1. Performance Data or Appraisals as Indicators of Problems or Weaknesses<br>　Productivity<br>　Absenteeism or tardiness<br>　Accidents<br>　Short-term sickness<br>　Grievances<br>　Waste<br>　Late deliveries<br>　Product quality<br>　Downtime<br>　Repairs<br>　Equipment utilization<br>　Customer complaints | Include weaknesses and areas of improvement as well as strong points. Easy to analyze and quantify for purposes of determining subjects and kinds of training needed. These data can be used to *identify* performance discrepancies. |
| 2. Observation Work Sampling | More subjective technique but provides both employee behavior and results of the behavior. |
| 3. Interviews | Individual is only one who knows what he (she) believes he (she) needs to learn. Involvement in need analysis can also motivate employees to make an effort to learn. |
| 4. Questionnaires | Same approach as the interview. Easily tailored to specific characteristics of the organization. May produce bias through the necessity of prestructured categories. |
| 5. Tests<br>　Job knowledge<br>　Skills<br>　Achievement | Can be tailor-made or standardized. Care must be taken so that they measure job-related qualities. |
| 6. Attitude Surveys | Useful in determining morale, motivation, or satisfaction of each employee. |
| 7. Checklists or Training Progress Charts | Up-to-date listing of each employee's skills. Indicates future training requirements for each job. |
| 8. Rating Scales | Care must be taken to ensure relevant, reliable, and objective employee ratings. |
| 9. Critical Incidents | Observed actions that are critical to the successful or unsuccessful performance of the job. |
| 10. Diaries | Individual employee records details of his (her) job. |

*continued*

**TABLE 4-7**                                                                                              **CONTINUED**

| Technique or Data Obtained | HRD/Training Need Implications |
| --- | --- |
| 11. Devised Situations<br>    Role play<br>    Case study<br>    Conference leadership<br>    Training sessions<br>    Business games<br>    In-baskets | Certain knowledge, skills, and attitudes are demonstrated in these techniques. |
| 12. Diagnostic Rating | Checklists are factor analyzed to yield diagnostic ratings. |
| 13. Assessment Centers | Combination of several of the above techniques into an intensive assessment program. |
| 14. Coaching | Similar to interview one-to-one. |
| 15. MBO or Work Planning and Review Systems | Provides actual performance data on a recurring basis related to organizational (and individually or group-negotiated standards) so that baseline measurements may be known and subsequent improvement or deterioration of performance may be identified and analyzed. This performance review and potential review is keyed to larger organization goals and objectives. |

SOURCE: ACADEMY OF MANAGEMENT REVIEW by M. L. Moore, P. Dutton. Copyright 2005 by ACAD OF MGMT. Reproduced with permission of ACAD OF MGMT in the format Textbook via Copyright Clearance Center.

## COMPONENTS OF PERSON ANALYSIS

In whatever manner the data for person analysis is collected, an effective person analysis should consist of two components: summary person analysis and diagnostic person analysis.[44] *Summary person analysis* involves determining the overall success of individual employee performance. *Diagnostic person analysis* tries to discover the reasons for an employee's performance. Effective performers may be the source for ideas on how to improve employee performance, whereas analysis of ineffective performers can identify what interventions (HRD or otherwise) are needed to improve performance. Table 4-8 lists and describes these two components of person analysis.

Recall from our discussion of needs that current performance deficiencies make up only one type of need. Therefore, an effective person analysis should identify *future* developmental needs as well.

**TABLE 4-8** **COMPONENTS OF THE PERSON ANALYSIS PROCESS**

**Summary Person Analysis**

A global analysis; it is an overall evaluation of an individual employee's performance; a classification of an individual as a successful versus unsuccessful performer.

**Diagnostic Person Analysis**

Determine *why* results of individual employee's behavior occur; determine how individual's knowledge, skills, abilities, and other characteristics (KSAOs), effort, and environmental factors combine to yield the summary person analysis.

Together, the summary and diagnostic person analyses combine to determine *who* is performing successfully/unsuccessfully and *why* the individual is performing successfully/unsuccessfully. This is the Person Analysis.

SOURCE: From G. R. Herbert & D. Doverspike (1990). Performance appraisal in the training needs analysis process: A review and critique. *Public Personnel Management, 19*(3), 255. Reprinted by permission.

### PERFORMANCE APPRAISAL IN THE PERSON ANALYSIS PROCESS

Performance appraisal can be a valuable tool for collecting person analysis data.[45] However, although it may be tempting to think that performance appraisal by itself can be the sole source of person analysis information, this view is shortsighted. In reality, using performance appraisal in needs analysis requires a manager to "have access to a variety of different pieces of information and make a number of complex decisions."[46] A model of performance appraisal in the person analysis process begins with the following steps (see Figure 4-3):

1. Perform or have access to a complete, accurate performance appraisal.
2. Identify discrepancies between the employee's behavior and/or traits and those required for effective performance.
3. Identify the source of the discrepancies.
4. Select the intervention appropriate to resolve the discrepancies.[47]

Two steps in this process bear further comment. First, one should not assume that performance appraisal information is necessarily complete or accurate. Many performance appraisals are flawed by either poor appraisal processes or errors committed during the appraisal.[48] Examination of an organization's appraisal process and practices can help assess the quality of the appraisal. Second, there are a variety of possible sources for a performance or skill discrepancy. Recalling our discussion of employee behavior in Chapter 2, the cause could be either within the employee (like motivation or attitudes) or in the environment (such as a lack of support, outdated equipment, or obstructive work rules). Therefore, identifying the source of the discrepancies will likely involve integrating information from organizational analysis, task or job analysis, and any individual skill or ability testing completed by the employee.[49]

**FIGURE 4-3**

**A MODEL OF PERFORMANCE APPRAISAL IN THE PERSON ANALYSIS PROCESS**

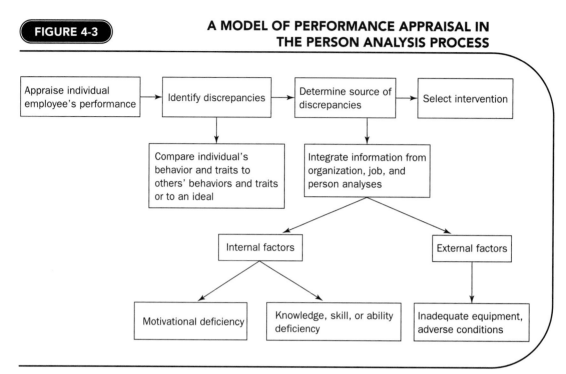

SOURCE: From G. R. Herbert & D. Doverspike (1990). Performance appraisal in the training needs analysis process: A review and critique. *Public Personnel Management, 19*(3), 254. Reprinted by permission.

Unfortunately, conditions for conducting performance appraisal and person analysis are often less than ideal, with many potential problems, such as:

1. There can be enormous costs and complexity when considered at an organization-wide level.

2. The ability of the manager to make accurate judgments is questionable given evidence of rating errors and biases in making causal attributions.

3. The rating system must include *all* areas of required performance that can be identified.

4. Intentions to use performance appraisal data for needs analysis must be specified *before* the system is developed, operationalized, and implemented.

5. Raters must be motivated to make accurate performance ratings.

6. The manager or training professional must be able to match deficiencies identified to specific remedial activities.[50]

The discussion so far has assumed that an employee's superior will be conducting the performance appraisal. This is most often the case, and in fact, a survey of employee preferences for different rating sources revealed that employees most preferred to be rated by their supervisor.[51] However, employees and supervisors alike express intense dissatisfaction with their existing ("top-down") performance appraisal systems.[52] So, rather than relying strictly on supervisors to conduct appraisals, peers, subordinates, and customers may also be in a position to effectively observe and evaluate an employee's performance. David Dell, from the Conference Board, argues that "flattening the organizational structure and moving toward a cross-functional work environment means that a top-down performance appraisal is no longer appropriate."[53]

The practice of using multiple sources to gather performance information, called *360-degree performance appraisal* (or performance evaluation), has become more widespread in organizations. Edwards and Ewen reported that almost 90 percent of Fortune 1000 companies use some form of multisource appraisals for developmental feedback, among other purposes.[54] This approach encourages feedback from "key constituencies representing the full circle of relevant viewpoints, subordinates, peers, supervisors, customers, and suppliers who may be internal or external to the organization, and self-ratings."[55]

The main advantage of using peer, subordinate, and customer input in performance appraisal is that these individuals observe the employee from different perspectives, which allows them to add information that other sources cannot. For instance, coworkers may be in a better position to evaluate employees on the "citizenship" or "teamwork" behaviors than are most supervisors, because they typically have more day-to-day contact with the employee than does his or her supervisor.[56] At the same time, coworkers' reviews offer an opportunity to obtain verification or confirmation of observations made by other sources. Furthermore, involving peers and subordinates in appraising a manager's performance and assessing a manager's developmental needs has two other potential benefits: it may make these individuals feel that their input matters, and it may create a more supportive work environment in which managers can apply their new skills and knowledge.[57]

Research investigating multisource feedback is not at a point that permits many firm conclusions. It has been suggested that peer and self-ratings will be more lenient than supervisory ratings, especially if the ratings are performed for administrative purposes,[58] and there is some evidence to suggest this may be true.[59] Researchers are also investigating the possible impact of individual differences (e.g., in race, rater ability, job knowledge) on ratings from various sources,[60] as well as the extent to which the employee/manager being rated will accept ratings from nonsupervisory sources.[61]

One important question is, To what extent do performance ratings from various sources agree? Lack of agreement among sources is not necessarily bad. To the extent that the lack of agreement between different sources represents *true* differences observed by those sources (e.g., subordinates observe and rate behavior that has not been seen by a supervisor), lack of agreement is a positive thing. However, to the extent that the lack of agreement is due to rater error and other biases unique to each source, lack of agreement is a sign of potential problems and poor information. Two meta-analyses offer some information on the extent of agreement, but not directly on the underlying causes. One study analyzed research on the agreement of self-supervisor, self-peer, and peer-supervisor ratings and found that the average correlation of ratings between these sources varied.[62] Peer-supervisor ratings had the highest amount of agreement ($r = 0.62$), whereas correlations between self and peer ratings ($r = 0.36$) and between self and supervisor ratings ($r = 0.35$) were lower. A second study meta-analyzed research on the reliability of supervisory and peer performance ratings and found that supervisory ratings had higher interrater reliability than peer ratings.[63]

From a needs assessment perspective, one potentially limiting factor of much of the performance appraisal literature is that it has frequently focused on ratings done for administrative purposes. However, survey research suggests that employees are much more positive toward peer and upward appraisals when ratings are made for *developmental purposes* rather than administrative purposes.[64] For example, peers may be reluctant to honestly evaluate each other's performance if the ratings will be used to make pay or layoff decisions, but may be more willing to do so if the ratings are only used for developmental purposes.

Overall, multiple source performance appraisal has potential both for needs assessment and as a tool for enhancing individual performance. Clearly, organizations are using it. We believe that HRD practitioners should use multiple source performance appraisal information as *one element* of person analysis, but that they should do so with caution (recall the concerns we raised about performance appraisal earlier in this section). It is important to verify any information gathered and to monitor the research being done on the properties of multisource performance data to be sure the quality of the information gained is high enough to accurately identify HRD needs.

## DEVELOPMENTAL NEEDS

Person analysis data are also used to define developmental needs, which can be identified during the periodic performance evaluation. The primary use of developmental data is for maintaining and increasing the knowledge, skills, and abilities of each employee. However, the information can also be important to career development by preparing the employee for future job responsibilities, which we will discuss in Chapter 12.

A skills inventory can also help determine a person's need for training. This assesses employees' KSAOs by examining their education, training, experience, certification, performance reviews, and recommendations. Many organizations today use a *human resource information system (HRIS)* to compile this information for easy retrieval. Although this type of information is traditionally used to assess the readiness of individuals to take on higher levels of responsibility (a promotion), it can also be used for training needs assessment. Some organizations analyze this information to determine the best strategy for developing their human resources. For instance, if the organization is contemplating changes that require new skills, the skills inventory may provide necessary information for devising new training or other HRD programs.

## THE EMPLOYEE AS A SOURCE OF NEEDS ASSESSMENT INFORMATION

Another source of information for training needs is the employee himself or herself. Two studies provide some useful information regarding the accuracy of employees' self-ratings of training needs.[65]

McEnery and McEnery compared self- and supervisory ratings of training needs for 200 managers and professionals.[66] They found that although self-ratings were more lenient than supervisory ratings, self-ratings exhibited less halo error (that is, allowing an overall impression to guide the ratings rather than evaluating each item separately). They also found that the two sources of ratings were not significantly related and that self-ratings discriminated among aspects of performance *more than* supervisory ratings did. They concluded that self-ratings of training needs may be a useful, valid part of a needs assessment process. Ford and Noe found that managerial level, function, and attitude toward training usefulness all had a small but significant effect on self-ratings of training needs, concluding that more research is needed to examine this issue.[67]

Taken together, these studies suggest that although self-ratings of training needs may be a useful part of a needs assessment, HRD professionals would be wise to use multiple sources of needs assessment information to ensure validity.

### THE "BENCHMARKS" SPECIALIZED PERSON ANALYSIS INSTRUMENT

One option in collecting person analysis data is to design an instrument that can be used for a specific population of interest (for instance, clerical workers or supervisors). This can be especially useful if the organization's HRD strategy targets a category of employees for development. The Center for Creative Leadership has developed Benchmarks, a specialized person analysis instrument used to identify the development needs of *managers*.[68]

Research conducted at the Center for Creative Leadership on how executives develop, learn, and change over their careers provided the impetus for Benchmarks.[69] This research identified key developmental events, the lessons learned from these events, and reasons why executives succeeded or did not succeed.[70] The Benchmarks instrument is divided into two sections. Section 1 focuses on the lessons executives have learned from key developmental events, and contains sixteen scales (e.g., resourcefulness, team orientation, and self-awareness). Section 2 is based on the flaws that lead to an executive's derailment, and contains six scales (e.g., lack of follow-through, overdependence).[71]

A supervisor evaluates the manager using the Benchmarks instrument, resulting in a profile of the manager's strengths and weaknesses that can be used to plan the manager's future development. Research on the validity and psychometric properties of Benchmarks has been encouraging, and ongoing efforts to refine this instrument should make this a valuable tool for making management development efforts more systematic.[72] Efforts like Benchmarks can only improve the effectiveness of HRD by providing an accurate, meaningful base for making program and participant decisions.

## PRIORITIZING HRD NEEDS

Assuming that a needs assessment reveals multiple needs, management and the HRD staff must prioritize these needs. As in any organizational function, limited resources are usually available for the HRD effort. Decisions must be made about what resources — including facilities, equipment, materials, skilled personnel, travel, and consultant fees — will be used in HRD. A central question to ask in this process is, What are the potential gains or return on investment from various options? The projected impact on organizational performance must always be kept in mind when prioritizing HRD needs.[73]

## PARTICIPATION IN THE PRIORITIZATION PROCESS

The prioritizing of HRD needs works best when individuals throughout the organization are involved. Because HRD programs are intended to serve a specific area or areas of the organization, representatives from those areas should have input in this decision. Some HRD departments regularly solicit ideas from employees, and this information can be used to refine and improve ongoing programs, as well to gauge the demand for future programs. With this input, there is a greater likelihood that more employees will perceive the HRD programs as being relevant to the organization and to themselves. By involving others in critical HRD decisions, there is a greater likelihood that more people in the organization will support the total HRD effort.

## THE HRD ADVISORY COMMITTEE

One way to continuously reflect the needs of employees and assist in prioritizing needs is to establish an HRD advisory committee. The role of this committee is to meet regularly and review needs assessment and evaluation data and offer advice on the type and content of HRD programs to be offered. The advisory committee should be composed of members from a cross-section of the organization. This provides different perspectives on HRD needs and can create a broader level of support from all parts of the organization. The organization should also recognize those employees who volunteer their time to serve on advisory and other committees. This includes the recognition that meeting time may take employees away from their normal job responsibilities.

An example of this comes from a General Motors plant in Lansing, Michigan. A press operation (called the blanker area) was selected for study, as this area was experiencing major changes in technology, and was not meeting company goals for production level or cost. A needs analysis team was formed, consisting of three training specialists (one from the United Auto Workers union), a supervisor, plus two hourly employees. This team identified symptoms and likely causes of the problems in this area, planned, collected, and analyzed data concerning these issues, and then reported their results back to the leaders and employees in this area. Nine solutions were ultimately recommended, consisting of both training solutions (e.g., train all production workers in statistical process control, or SPC) and nontraining solutions (e.g., color code the dies for each press). The solution that had the greatest impact was training the workers in SPC. These courses were already available by in-house trainers, so the cost was minimal. As stated by the two hourly workers on the team, "The results were improved quality and a 30 percent reduction in scrap rate. The value was a savings of $502,825 in the first year. The benefits were the financial savings and workers' pride of ownership for the improvements."[74] This is certainly a positive example of how a number of the things recommended in this chapter were utilized to rectify a performance problem in a large organization.

## THE HRD PROCESS MODEL DEBATE

As we have discussed, a thorough needs assessment establishes the foundation for an HRD or training program. Next, we turn our attention to how HRD programs are designed (Chapter 5) and implemented (Chapter 6), and to how such programs can be evaluated to determine their effectiveness (Chapter 7).

Before closing this chapter, we add a cautionary note. This chapter and book are based on the instructional systems design or "A DImE" model depicted in Figure 4-1. This model (or some variation of it) has been the dominant model in human resource development since the 1970s.[75] Recently, this approach has been strongly criticized.[76] We summarize these criticisms in the boxed insert nearby, "The Attack on ISD." This article generated a very vehement reader response, including eleven letters that the editors of *Training* magazine published under the label "The Counterattack of ISD."[77] There is obviously much to consider in these criticisms and the counterresponses. There are times when it simply isn't feasible to do a "full-blown" needs assessment, as laid out in this chapter. The Zemke article referenced above provides some helpful guidance here.[78] Further, Darin Hartley has written a book entitled *Job Analysis at the Speed of Reality* that provides a model of quick, yet thorough task analysis.[79] Finally, consultant Jack Asgar offers the following questions to assist trainers in identifying important issues, even when it may not be possible to conduct all of the analyses described in this chapter:

- What are the operating problems? (*Don't ask*, What is the training need?)
- Did human behavior cause or contribute to the operating problem? If yes, describe the present behavior and the desired performance.
- Could the employees perform correctly if they had to? Have they performed the task correctly lately?
- Is the employees' manager currently requiring the desired performance from employees? If not, what assurance do you have that the new behavior will be reinforced on the job after training has been completed?
- What evidence shows that the present performance is a problem? What would be some observable signs that the problem has been solved (e.g., observing employees using particular skills)?
- What other issues might be contributing to this operating problem?
- Based on this analysis, is training needed? If yes, what skills should be learned?
- If training is needed, will managers commit themselves to active involvement in the training process before, during, and after the training?[80]

## The Attack on ISD

Well-known leaders in the HRD field have raised some serious issues concerning the systems model and instructional systems design (ISD) approach that has dominated the field of human resource development over the past three-plus decades. Four main charges or complaints are raised concerning the model:

1. the model is too slow and clumsy to meet today's training needs

2. there's no "there" there (hang on, we'll explain this one)

3. used as directed, it produces bad results

4. it clings to the wrong world view

Concerning the first charge, the argument is that the whole process of needs assessment takes too long for a "speed-maddened world." When training is called for in 90 days, and HRD professionals say they need that much time at a minimum *just to do the needs assessment,* the potential for trouble is evident. The biggest problem is argued to be the bureaucratic systems that sometimes develop in training departments, which can produce slow and cumbersome responses to managers' requests for quick action. Fred Nickols, of the Educational Testing Service, says, "ISD takes too long, it costs too much, and by the time you're through, the opportunity you were trying to exploit through training has passed you by."

Second, the ISD model is a "process" model, meaning that it focuses on the process by which effective training can take place. As such, it can be an orderly way to organize instruction to produce consistent results. The problems come when emphasis gets placed on whether all the steps in the process are getting done, versus on solving the problem that training was designed to address. The ultimate goal of training should be to accomplish something of value "out there," i.e., in the organization. The question should be asked, "How do you know when you've developed good training?" Nickols suggests that, if the only thing you can say is, "It's good training because it was developed using the following process," then your product probably isn't worth much.

The third charge against the ISD model is that, even if it is used as intended, it produces "bad" (as in narrow or incomplete) solutions. The primary focus has been on achieving narrowly worded behavioral or cognitive objectives. Attitudes and emotions are often ignored or minimized. Diane Gayeski, of OmniCom Associates, says that "the executives I work with are more concerned with developing a creative and resilient work force than with having employees memorize and play out some predetermined set of steps. We inadvertently may be creating 'disabled' learners when we spoon-feed them instructions in an effort to achieve homogeneous outcomes: You know, 'Upon completion of course, everyone will have learned to behave in exactly the same way.'"

The last point is that the ISD model works best when jobs are well defined, and HRD professionals can spell out exactly what the trainee should know or do after completion of training. Nickols calls this "prefigured" work, where the job is clearly laid out. In contrast, an increasing amount of work is "configured," meaning that it is *not* clear ahead of time what a person is supposed to do. With the ISD model, a performance gap is typically viewed as the difference between expected and obtained results for a well-defined job. According to Nickols, when work is configured, "you encounter a problem whenever you have to figure out what to do next. The core skill becomes problem solving."

SOURCE: Gordon, J., & Zemke, R. (2000). The attack on ISD. *Training, 37*(4), 42–53.

We close by reminding you of our comments at the start of this chapter concerning "why bother?" Many things can go wrong when needs assessment efforts are missing or inadequate. As Jack Bowsher, former director of training for IBM, wrote in response to the "Attack" article in *Training* magazine, "People who want to throw training together over the weekend are as professional as architects who want to construct buildings without a blueprint to speed up the project. There are a lot of unqualified people in every profession who take shortcuts. I would not want my job to depend on 'quick and easy' courses."[81]

## RETURN TO OPENING CASE

In 1996, Cathay Pacific unveiled a new motto and business philosophy, "Service straight from the heart." A retraining of its trainers was emphasized. In addition, each trainer conducted an individualized research project relating to the airline's customer service effort. In 1999, Cathay Pacific was named the Best Long-Haul Airline for Business by *Conde Nast Traveller's,* based on surveys taken in the United Kingdom. In that same year, it was also named as one of the ten best international airlines by the U.S.-based *Beyond Borders* magazine, despite flying to only five North American cities at the time (in 2004, it flew to twenty-eight North American cities).[1] In June, 2004, the airline was named among the top six Most Admired Asian Brands by *Asiamoney* magazine.[2] Your instructor has additional information on what Cathay Pacific did with regards to its in-flight training efforts.

[1]SOURCES: http://www.cathay-usa.com/News/press/230999.stm. Accessed September 23, 1999.

[2]Don't make promises you can't keep. (2004, June). *Asiamoney, 15*(5), pp. 44–46.

## SUMMARY

In this chapter, we focused on the needs assessment phase of the HRD process model (design, implementation, and evaluation will be emphasized in the following chapters). Needs assessment should be performed on three levels: organization, task, and person. The *strategic/organizational level* asks the questions, Where in the organization is there a need for training/HRD? Under what conditions will it be conducted? and How is training/HRD linked to and supporting team or organizational performance? Strategic/organizational analysis focuses on the organization's goals and its effectiveness in achieving those goals, organizational resources, the climate for training, and any environmental constraints. The purpose of organizational analysis is to understand what the organization is trying to accomplish, where HRD efforts may be needed to enhance effectiveness, and what potential roadblocks exist.

The *task analysis level* asks the question, What tasks and KSAOs should be included in training? This analysis involves five steps: (1) describing the job, (2) identifying the tasks within the job, (3) identifying the KSAOs needed to perform the job, (4) identifying areas that can benefit from training, and (5) prioritizing the areas that can benefit from training.

The *person analysis level* asks these questions, Who needs to be trained? and What for? Individual performance deficiencies and developmental needs can be used to suggest the content of the training program. This information can also serve to identify which employees should participate in the HRD programs.

Because of limited HRD resources, it is necessary to prioritize training needs. This ensures that resources have the greatest impact on organizational goals. Whenever possible, numerous individuals should be encouraged to participate in prioritizing needs.

## KEY TERMS AND CONCEPTS

| | |
|---|---|
| analytic needs | needs assessment |
| compliance needs | person analysis |
| critical incident technique (CIT) | stimulus-response-feedback method |
| diagnostic needs | strategic/organizational analysis |
| job analysis | task analysis |
| job description | task identification |
| job-duty-task method | 360-degree performance appraisal |
| job inventory questionnaire | time sampling |
| job specification | |

## QUESTIONS FOR DISCUSSION

1. Why is needs assessment information critical to the development and delivery of an effective HRD program?

2. What is the relationship between organizational needs analysis and strategic planning? How can tying HRD programs to an organization's strategic plan make it easier to justify requests for resources to develop and deliver HRD programs?

3. Suppose you have been asked to perform a task analysis for the job of dispatcher in a city police department. Which method(s) of task analysis do you think would be most appropriate for analyzing this job? Support your choice(s).

4. Briefly describe the pros and cons of using performance appraisal information when conducting a person needs analysis. Do you think that HRD professionals should use performance appraisals to enhance the value of the information obtained from a person analysis? Support your answer.

5. One important source of person needs assessment information is the potential trainees' own opinions about their developmental needs. What are the advantages and disadvantages of relying on such self-report information as part of a person needs assessment?

6. Why should HRD needs, once identified, be prioritized? What are the benefits, if any, of obtaining the participation of a variety of organization members in the prioritization process?

7. Why is needs assessment so often *not* performed in many organizations? How could an HRD professional encourage a reluctant manager or executive to approve the time and resources necessary for a needs assessment before selecting and implementing an HRD program?

8. What is your response to "The attack on ISD" (presented in the boxed insert)? If you were an HRD professional seeking to conduct a needs assessment, how would you respond to each of these issues?

## EXERCISE: CONDUCTING A TASK ANALYSIS

Working alone or in groups, select a job that is familiar to you (e.g., secretary, server, cashier), and conduct a task analysis for this job. Reviewing the materials in the chapter, which method or methods make the most sense for analyzing this job? Why? What are the major tasks or responsibilities that you identified for this job? What knowledge, skill, ability, or other characteristics are needed to perform each of these major tasks? If requested to by your instructor, write out your findings in the form of a job description (including a job specification).

Visit http://werner.swlearning.com for links to informative websites for this chapter.

## REFERENCES

1. Mitchell, W. S., Jr. (1984). Wanted: Professional management training needs analysis. *Training and Development Journal, 38*(10), 68.

2. *Ibid.*

3. Gordon, J., & Zemke, R. (2000). The attack on ISD, *Training, 37*(4), April, 42–53.

4. *Ibid*; Zemke, R. (1998). How to do a needs assessment when you think you don't have time, *Training, 35*(3), March, 38–44.

5. Rossett, A. (1990). Overcoming obstacles to needs assessment. *Training, 36*(3), 36, 38–40.

6. Dubois, D., & Rothwell, W. (2004). Competency-based or a traditional approach to training? *T&D, 58*(4), 46–57.

7. Brinkerhoff, R. O. (1986). Expanding needs analysis. *Training and Development Journal, 40*(2), 64–65.

8. Kaufman, R. (1997). Needs assessment basics. In R. Kaufman, S. Thiagarajan, & P. MacGillis (Eds.), *The guidebook for performance improvement* (pp. 107–129). San Francisco: Pfeiffer/Jossey-Bass.

9. Robinson, D. G., & Robinson, J. C. (1998). *Moving from training to performance.* San Francisco: Berrett-Koehler.

10. Roberson, L., Kulik, C. T., & Pepper, M. B. (2003). Using needs assessment to resolve controversies in diversity training design. *Group & Organization Management, 28*(1), 148–174;

Ford, R. L. (2004). Needs assessment helps ensure effective diversity training. *Public Relations Tactics, 11*(7), July, 6.

11. McGehee, W., & Thayer, P. W. (1961). *Training in business and industry*. New York: Wiley.

12. Gupta, K. (1999). *A practical guide to needs assessment*. San Francisco: Jossey-Bass/Pfeiffer.

13. Sahl, R. J. (1992). Succession planning drives plant turnaround. *Personnel Journal, 71*(9), 67–70.

14. Goldstein, I. L. (1986). *Training in organizations: Needs assessment, development, and evaluation* (2nd ed.). Pacific Grove, CA: Brooks-Cole.

15. Rouiller, J. Z., & Goldstein, I. L. (1993). The relationship between organizational transfer climate and positive transfer of training. *Human Resource Development Quarterly, 4*, 377–390; Tracey J. B., Tannenbaum, S. I., & Kavanagh, M. J. (1995). Applying trained skills on the job: The importance of the work environment. *Journal of Applied Psychology, 80*, 239–252.

16. Belton, R. (1998). Employment law: A review of the 1997 term decisions of the Supreme Court, *Employee Rights and Employment Policy Journal, 2*(2), 267–315 (quotation from p. 270).

17. Burlington Industries, Inc. v. Ellerth, 118 S. Ct. 2257 (1998); Faragher v. City of Boca Raton, 118 S. Ct. 2275 (1998).

18. Equal Employment Opportunity Commission (2004). Retrieved September 13, 2004, from http://eeoc.gov/stats/harass.html

19. Robinson & Robinson (1998), *supra* note 9.

20. Carnevale, A. P., Gainer, L. J., & Villet, J. (1991). *Training in America: The organization and strategic role of training*. San Francisco: Jossey-Bass.

21. Moore, M. L., & Dutton, P. (1978). Training needs analysis: Review and critique. *Academy of Management Review, 3*,532–545.

22. Tesoro, F., & Tootson, J. (2000). *Implementing global performance measurement systems: A cookbook approach*. San Francisco: Jossey-Bass/Pfeiffer.

23. Huse, E. F., & Cummings, T. G. (1985). *Organization development and change* (3rd ed.). Mason, OH: Thomson/South-Western.

24. Goldstein, I. L. (1986). *Training in organizations: Needs assessment, development and evaluation* (2nd ed., p. 36). Pacific Grove, CA: Brooks-Cole; Goldstein, I. L., Macey, W. H., & Prien, E. P. (1981). Needs assessment approaching for training development. In H. Meltzer & W. R. Nord (Eds.), *Making organizations more humane and productive: A handbook for practitioners*. New York: Wiley-Interscience.

25. Zemke (1998), *supra* note 4.

26. Gorman, P., McDonald, B., Moore, R., Glassman, A., Takeuchi, L., & Henry, M. J. (2003). Custom needs assessment for strategic HR training: The Los Angeles County experience. *Public Personnel Management, 32*(4), 475–495.

27. Ulrich, D. (1997). *Human resource champions*. Boston, MA: Harvard Business School Press.

28. Moore, M. L., & Dutton, P. (1978). Training needs analysis: Review and critique. *Academy of Management Review, 3*, 532–545.

29. *Ibid.*

30. Campbell, J. P. (1988). Training design for performance improvement. In J. P. Campbell & R. J. Campbell (Eds.), *Productivity in organizations*. San Francisco: Jossey-Bass; Goldstein, I. L.

(1993). *Training in organizations: Needs assessment, development, and evaluation* (3rd ed.). Pacific Grove, CA: Brooks-Cole; Goldstein, I. L., Macey, W. H., & Prien, E. P. (1981). Needs assessment approaching for training development. In H. Meltzer & W. R. Nord (Eds.), *Making organizations more human and productive: A handbook for practitioners.* New York: Wiley-Interscience; McGehee, W., & Thayer, P. W. (1961). *Training in business and industry.* New York: Wiley; Wexley, K. N., & Latham, G. P. (1991). *Developing and training human resource in organizations* (2nd ed.). Glenview, IL: Scott, Foresman.

31. Gael, S. (Ed.). (1988). *The job analysis handbook for business, industry and government* (Vols. I & II). New York: Wiley; Gatewood, R. D., & Field, H. J. (2001). *Human resource selection* (5th ed.). Mason, OH: Thomson/South-Western.

32. Miller, R. B. (1962). Task description and analysis. In R. M. Gagne (Ed.), *Psychological principles in systems development.* New York: Holt, Rinehart and Winston.

33. Deterline, W. A. (1968). *Instructional technology workshop.* Palo Alto, CA: Programmed Teaching; Mills, G.E., Pace, R. W., & Peterson, B. D. (1988). *Analysis in human resource training and organizational development.* Reading, MA: Addison-Wesley.

34. Wexley & Latham (1991), *supra* note 30.

35. Flanagan, J. C. (1954). The critical incident method. *Psychological Bulletin, 51,* 327–358.

36. Campbell (1988), *supra* note 30; Cureton, J. H., Newton, A. F., & Tesolowski, D. G. (1986). Finding out what managers need. *Training and Development Journal, 40*(5), 106–107.

37. Goldstein, Macey, & Prien (1981), *supra* note 30.

38. *Ibid.*

39. Wircenski, J. L., Sullivan, R. L., & Moore, P. (1989). Assessing training needs at Texas Instruments. *Training and Development Journal, 43*(4), 61–63.

40. *Ibid.*

41. Overmyer-Day, L., & Benson, G. (1996). Training success stories. *Training & Development, 50*(6), 24–29.

42. Swanson, R. A. (1994). *Analysis for improving performance.* San Francisco: Berrett-Koehler.

43. Moore, M. L., & Dutton, P. (1978). Training needs analysis: Review and critique. *Academy of Management Review, 3,* 532–545.

44. McGehee, W., & Thayer, P. W. (1961). *Training in business and industry.* New York: Wiley.

45. Gray, G. R., & Hall, M. E. (1997). Training practices in state government agencies. *Public Personnel Management, 26*(2), 187–202.

46. Herbert, G. R., & Doverspike, D. (1990). Performance appraisal in the training needs analysis process: A review and critique. *Public Personnel Management, 19*(3), 253–270, p. 253.

47. *Ibid.*

48. Werner, J. M. (1994). Dimensions that make a difference: Examining the impact of in-role and extrarole behaviors on supervisory ratings. *Journal of Applied Psychology, 79,* 98–107.

49. Herbert & Doverspike (1990), *supra* note 46.

50. *Ibid,* p. 255.

51. Gosselin, A., Werner, J. M., & Hallé, N. (1997). Ratee preferences concerning performance management and appraisal. *Human Resource Development Quarterly, 8,* 315–333.

52. HR execs dissatisfied with their performance appraisal systems. (2000). *HR Focus, 77*(1), January, 2.

53. *Ibid.*

54. Edwards, M. R., & Ewen, A. J. (1996). *360 degree feedback.* New York: American Management Association.

55. London, M., & Smither, J. W. (1995). Can multi-source feedback change perceptions of goal accomplishment self-evaluation, and performance-related outcomes? Theory-based applications and directions for research. *Personnel Psychology, 48,* 803–804.

56. Werner, J. M. (2000). Implications of OCB and contextual performance for human resource management. *Human Resource Management Review, 10,* 3–24.

57. Cardy, R. L., & Dobbins, G. H. (1994). *Performance appraisal: Alternative perspectives.* Mason, OH: Thomson/South-Western.

58. Murphy, K. R., & Cleveland, J. N. (1991). *Performance appraisal.* Boston: Allyn and Bacon.

59. Harris, M. M., & Schaubroeck, J. (1988). A meta-analysis of self-manager, self-peer, and peer-manager ratings. *Personnel Psychology, 41,* 43–62.

60. Borman, W. C., White, L. A., & Dorsey, D. W. (1995). Effects of rate task performance and interpersonal factors on supervisor performance ratings. *Journal of Applied Psychology, 80,* 168–177; London, M., & Smither, J. W. (1995). Can multi-source feedback change perceptions of goal accomplishment self-evaluation, and performance-related outcomes? Theory-based applications and directions for research. *Personnel Psychology, 48,* 803–839; Maurer, T. J., & Tarulli, B. A. (1996). Acceptance of peer/upward performance appraisal systems: Role, work context factors, and beliefs about managers' developmental capacity. *Human Resource Management, 35*(2), 217–241; Mount, M. K., Sytsma, M. R., Hazucha, J. F., & Holt, K. E. (1997). Rater-ratee race effect in developmental performance ratings of managers. *Personnel Psychology, 50,* 51–70.

61. Maurer, T. J., & Tarulli, B. A. (1996). Acceptance of peer/upward performance appraisal systems: Role, work context factors, and beliefs about managers' developmental capacity. *Human Resource Management, 35*(2), 217–241; Gosselin et al. (1997), *supra* note 51.

62. Harris & Schaubroeck (1988), *supra* note 59.

63. Viswesvaran, C., Ones, D. S., & Schmidt, F. L. (1996). Comparative analysis of the reliability of job performance ratings, *Journal of Applied Psychology, 81,* 557–560.

64. Bettenhausen, K. L., & Fedor, D. B. (1997). Peer and upward appraisals. *Group & Organization Management, 22*(2), 236–263.

65. Ford, J. K., & Noe, R. A. (1987). Self-assessed training needs: The effects of attitude toward training, managerial level, and function. *Personnel Psychology, 40,* 39–53; McEnery, J., & McEnery, J. M. (1987). Self-rating in management training needs assessment: A neglected opportunity? *Journal of Occupational Psychology, 60,* 49–60.

66. McEnery & McEnery (1987), *supra* note 65.

67. Ford & Noe (1987), *supra* note 65.

68. McCauley, C. D., Lombardo, M. M., & Usher, C. J. (1989). Diagnosing management development needs: An instrument based on how managers develop. *Journal of Management, 15,* 389–403.

69. McCall, M. W., Jr., Lombardo, M. M., & Morrison, A. M. (1988). *The lessons of experience: How successful executives develop on the job.* Lexington, MA: Lexington Books.

70. Lindsey, E. H., Homes, V., & McCall, M. W. (1987). *Key events in executives' lives* (Technical Report No. 32). Greensboro, NC: Center for Creative Leadership; McCall, M. W., & Lombardo, M. M. (1983, February). What makes a top executive? *Psychology Today,* pp. 26–31.

71. McCauley, Lombardo, & Usher (1989), *supra* note 68.

72. *Ibid.*

73. Robinson & Robinson (1998), *supra* note 9.

74. Finison, K., & Szedlak, F. (1997). General Motors does a needs analysis. *Training & Development, 51*(5), 103–104.

75. Dubois & Rothwell (2004), *supra* note 6.

76. Gordon & Zemke (2000), *supra* note 3.

77. Letters: The counterattack of ISD (2000). *Training, 37*(6), June, 18–23.

78. Zemke (1998), *supra* note 4.

79. Hartley, D. E. (1999). *Job analysis at the speed of reality.* Amherst, MA: HRD Press; see also Hartley, D. E. (2004). Job analysis at the speed of reality. *T&D, 58*(9), September, 20–22.

80. Speedy needs assessment (1998). *Training, 35(7),* July, 13.

81. Bowsher, J. E. (2000). Letters: The counterattack of ISD. *Training, 37*(6), June, 21.

**5**

# DESIGNING EFFECTIVE HRD PROGRAMS

## Learning Objectives

*After reading this chapter, you should be able to:*

1. Write training objectives for a specific program or HRD intervention that contain all three qualities for useful objectives (described by Robert Mager).

2. Identify several sources outside one's own organization where HRD programs could be obtained.

3. Compare the relative merits of developing an HRD program in-house versus purchasing it from an outside source.

4. List the activities involved in employer-designed HRD programs.

5. Compare various types of training materials and describe how they are prepared.

6. Point out some of the constraints to scheduling HRD programs, and suggest ways of dealing with them.

■

## OPENING CASE

Rockwell Collins is a manufacturer of electronic controls and communications devices. The company is headquartered in Cedar Rapids, Iowa, and employs over 14,000 employees. Almost half of these employees work in Cedar Rapids, with other large operations in California, Florida, Texas, and Mexico. Rockwell Collins also has subsidiaries in Europe and Australia, as well as service locations around the world. In 2001, it was spun off from Rockwell International to become a publicly traded company.

Rockwell Collins has long maintained a strong commitment to employee training and development. However, until 1998, all Rockwell Collins training was being conducted via classroom instruction. Twelve in-house trainers provided much of this training. One difficulty was that most of the employees who worked outside of Cedar Rapids had very limited access to training. In that same year, 28 percent of those who signed up for training within the company did not attend that training, citing work demands in a majority of the cases as the reason for canceling. In an effort to provide more training to a greater number of employees, the Learning and Development group at Rockwell Collins considered making increased use of outside training vendors, as well as changing the types of methods used to deliver training.

*Questions: If you were manager of learning and development at Rockwell Collins, where would you start in your efforts to improve the availability and effectiveness of company-sponsored training efforts? What suggestions would you have concerning how training is designed and provided? Further, what suggestions do you have concerning who should provide the training (i.e., in-house trainers versus outside vendors)? Finally, how would you seek to "sell" your recommendations to top management?*

## INTRODUCTION

Once needs assessment has been done, an HRD professional faces a number of important questions, such as:

■ *Is this an issue that can and should be addressed by a training or HRD intervention?*

■ *If so, how do I translate the results of the needs assessment into a specific training or HRD intervention?*

- *If training is necessary, how do we handle the "make" or "buy" decision, that is, do we create the training program in-house, or purchase it from an outside vendor?*
- *Who will be an effective trainer (or trainers) for this particular training or development project?*
- *What is the best way to organize the program or intervention?*
- *How should training methods and materials be selected or prepared?*
- *Are there particular scheduling issues that should be considered in preparing for training?*

The purpose of this chapter is to discuss the second phase of the HRD process: designing training and HRD interventions. Recent discussions of training program design issues have addressed such diverse populations as firefighters, credit managers, and insurance underwriters.[1] At this point, an organization following effective HRD practices will have completed Phase I of the training and HRD process — needs assessment — and will have data that indicate:

1. where the training or HRD program is needed
2. what kind of training or HRD program is needed
3. who needs to be trained
4. the conditions under which training will occur

In addition, the needs identified will have been prioritized so that senior management and the HRD staff know which programs or issues require attention and resources.

We recognize that in some cases the availability of needs assessment data may be limited. Although HRD practitioners may feel that it will be difficult to design effective training programs, sometimes they must improvise and make the best of such suboptimal situations. At the same time, every effort should be made to persuade management of the importance of conducting needs analysis and prioritizing HRD needs, as time and resources allow.

Armed with needs assessment data, the focus now turns to designing an effective HRD program. The key activities involved in designing an HRD program are:

1. setting objectives
2. selecting the trainer or vendor
3. developing a lesson plan
4. selecting program methods and techniques
5. preparing materials
6. scheduling the program

Figure 5-1 shows where these activities fit within the training and HRD process model. It is important to stress at the outset that program design can be a lengthy process. HRD professionals must simultaneously accomplish several other critical tasks throughout the design process. These responsibilities are presented in the boxed insert nearby. Although the focus of this chapter is on more pragmatic concerns

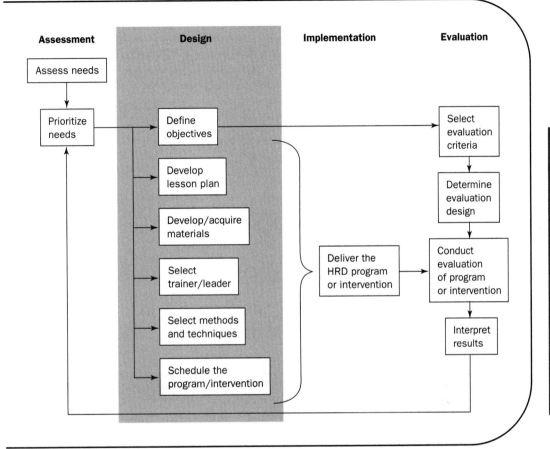

**FIGURE 5-1**  **TRAINING AND HRD PROCESS MODEL**

**Assessment**

Assess needs

Prioritize needs

**Design**

Define objectives

Develop lesson plan

Develop/acquire materials

Select trainer/leader

Select methods and techniques

Schedule the program/intervention

**Implementation**

Deliver the HRD program or intervention

**Evaluation**

Select evaluation criteria

Determine evaluation design

Conduct evaluation of program or intervention

Interpret results

PART 2: FRAMEWORK FOR HUMAN RESOURCE DEVELOPMENT

relating to the six points mentioned earlier (and described in more detail in the following sections), the "big picture" responsibilities described by Ronald Sims are vital to the success of any program that results from such design efforts. Readers are well advised to keep these overarching responsibilities in mind as they design new HRD initiatives.

Assuming that an important need for training has been identified, the manager or HRD professional must then translate that need into a set of objectives. Objectives define what participants will be expected to learn or do as a result of participating in the HRD program or intervention. However, some managers and HRD professionals may be tempted to make a decision about whether to design the program internally or purchase the program or its key parts, that is, contract a consultant to serve as a trainer, buy program materials, and so on, *before* establishing objectives. In outside purchases, the organization typically uses the objectives developed by the vendor rather than defining its own. However, the chances of success are far greater if the organization identifies the HRD objectives first, before deciding whether to design or purchase the program. How can HRD professionals or top

## Seven Overarching Responsibilities of HRD Professionals When Designing HRD Programs

Management professor Ronald Sims argues that training and development initiatives must emphasize "pivotal" employee competencies (or KSAOs, as we've described them in Chapter 4). To do this, HRD professionals must engage in a number of significant actions, including the following:

1. Identify the kinds and levels of KSAOs that employees need to attain high levels of performance and to achieve organizational results.

2. Develop and maintain organizational structures, conditions, and climates that are conducive to learning.

3. Generate and provide the necessary resources to conduct a program design.

4. Identify and provide access to off-the-job as well as on-the-job learning resources.

5. Provide individual assistance and feedback on various dimensions of individual performance.

6. Serve as role models and mentors to trainees and the organization in the pursuit of mastery of "pivotal" KSAOs.

7. Develop efficient learning processes that take into account individual learning styles, abilities, and work and life circumstances.

These types of responsibilities (especially points 2 and 3) cannot be completed without active support and involvement from top management. However, with the increasing focus on high performance from all organizations and employees, HRD professionals must ensure that every HRD initiative serves to meet the organization's strategic goals and objectives. The previous activities must be carried out at the same time that other design issues are being addressed.

SOURCE: From *Reinventing Training and Development*, by Ronald R. Sims. Copyright 1998 by Quorum Books. Reproduced with permission of Greenwood Publishing Groups, Inc., Westport, CT.

managers know what to buy when they haven't clearly defined what they want the program to accomplish?

Statements of HRD needs are often not detailed enough to be used as specific program outcomes. Rather, they state the problem at hand, and ideally, include a diagnosis of the problem's causes. Objectives, in contrast, should state the *outcome* the program is intended to produce, including the specific performance expected, the conditions under which it will be performed, and the criteria to be used to judge whether the objective has been achieved.

## DEFINING THE OBJECTIVES OF THE HRD INTERVENTION

Defining the objectives for the training or HRD program is one of the first things an HRD professional should do — after completing the needs assessment.[2] Robert Mager defines an objective as a "description of a performance you want learners to be able to exhibit before you consider them competent."[3] As such, HRD or **training program objectives** describe the intent and the desired result of the HRD program. The results can be achieved in many ways (such as lectures, role play, and coaching), but this is not specified in the objective. Rather, objectives are used as the *basis* for determining which methods should be used to achieve the specified outcome.

As we have stated, objectives are essential to a successful training or HRD program. In addition to forming the basis for selecting the program content and methods, objectives are used by the organization to evaluate the program's success, and they also help participants to focus their own attention and efforts during the program.[4] In short, objectives tell you where the program is going and how to know when you have reached your desired target. The measurement and evaluation issues that we will cover in Chapter 7 are predicated on defining clear objectives in the design phase; without these, learning is less likely to occur, and evaluation less likely to succeed. For example, a recent study measured the impact of training on company performance among a sample of Chinese manufacturing organizations.[5] Training effectiveness was measured in terms of perceived achievement of training objectives, as well as by comparing training expenditures to company productivity.

Needs assessment data are useful for defining program objectives because they identify the deficiencies or challenges to be addressed. For example, suppose the needs assessment data from a brokerage firm showed that many brokers were insensitive to clients' fears and concerns about the future. A training program could be designed that would increase the brokers' sensitivity to and support for their clients. The objectives of this program will be determined by the specific deficiencies, client preferences, concerns, and other factors identified in the needs assessment.

Mager states that useful objectives include three critical aspects or qualities, that is, they should describe (1) the performance the learners (trainees) should be able to do, (2) the conditions under which they must do it, and (3) the criteria (how well they must do it) used in judging its success (see Table 5-1).[6]

**TABLE 5-1**         **THE QUALITIES OF USEFUL OBJECTIVES**

| | |
|---|---|
| **Performance** | An objective always says what a learner is expected to be able to do and/or produce to be considered competent; the objective sometimes describes the product or result of the doing. Example: "Write a product profile for a proposed new product." |
| **Conditions** | An objective describes the important conditions (if any) under which the performance is to occur. Example, "Given all available engineering data regarding a proposed product, trainee will write a product profile." |
| **Criteria** | Wherever possible, an objective identifies the criteria of acceptable performance by describing how well the learner must perform in order to be considered acceptable. Example: "The product profile must describe all of the commercial characteristics of the product that are appropriate for its introduction to the market, including descriptions of at least three major product uses." |

SOURCE: From *Preparing Instructional Objectives* (3rd ed., pp. 46–47, 55) by R. F. Mager, Copyright 1997, The Center for Effective Performance, Inc., 1100 Johnson Ferry Road, Suite 150, Atlanta, GA 30342. www.cepworldwide.com 800-558-4237. Reprinted with permission. All rights reserved. No portion of these materials may be reproduced in any manner without the express written consent from The Center for Effective Performance, Inc.

Some examples of program objectives include the following:

- Given a packing list, the trainee will correctly identify (by circling) all items on the list that have not been included in the shipment.
- Given standard hospital equipment, the trainee will draw 10 cc of blood from a patient's arm in not more than two tries (using any member of the class).
- Using the information found on a completed loan application, identify (in writing) whether a client meets the bank's criteria for an acceptable auto loan candidate.
- After completion of training, the trainee will accurately identify and describe all major points in the organization's antidiscrimination policy.

Program objectives that lack clear statements concerning performance, conditions, and criteria are often ambiguous and can cause those who interpret the objectives differently to feel frustrated and come into conflict with one another. Two ways to ensure that objectives are clear are to choose words carefully and have the objectives reviewed by others (such as managers and potential participants). If a reviewer is confused, the objectives should be revised.

Writing objectives for behaviors that can be directly observed by others (like giving a patient an injection or performing the Heimlich maneuver to aid a choking victim) can be easier than writing objectives for behaviors that are unobservable (like judging whether a painting is of high quality or determining whether the use of deadly force is warranted). When dealing with broad or "unobservable" objectives, it is necessary to specify observable behaviors that indicate whether an unobservable outcome has been achieved.[7] Thus, an objective for judging whether a painting is of high quality can be written as "to be able to judge whether a painting is of high quality by orally listing the characteristics the painting possesses that indicate its quality."

In many cases, simply presenting trainees with objectives for learning or performance may be enough to elicit the desired behavior.[8] That is, sometimes people do not meet performance expectations because they were never clearly told what the expectations were or how they were supposed to meet them. Clear objectives provide this information and represent the organization's expectations, which can play a key role in shaping employee performance.

Writing objectives is a challenging but essential aspect of effective HRD. Table 5-2 provides a list of the main issues that are essential to consider when writing useful program objectives. Some questions to ask when writing objectives include:

- Is your main intent stated (concerning what you want the trainee to do)?
- Have you described all of the conditions that will influence trainee performance?
- Have you described how well the trainee must perform for his or her performance to be considered acceptable?[9]

It is remarkably easy to write objectives for training or educational courses that contain phrases with little or no meaning (Mager calls these "gibberish" objectives).[10]

| TABLE 5-2 | GUIDELINES FOR DEVELOPING USEFUL OBJECTIVES |

1. An objective is a collection of words, symbols, pictures and/or diagrams describing what you intend for trainees to achieve.
2. An objective will communicate your intent to the degree that you describe: what the learner will be **doing** when demonstrating achievement or mastery of the objective, the important conditions of the doing, and the criteria by which achievement will be judged.
3. To prepare a useful objective, continue to modify a draft until these questions are answered:

   ■ What do I want trainees to be able to do?
   ■ What are the important conditions or constraints under which I want them to perform?
   ■ How well must trainees perform for me to be satisfied?

4. Write a separate statement for each important outcome or intent; write as many as you need to communicate your intents.
5. If you give your written objectives to your trainees, you may not have to do much else. Why? Because often employees are already able to do what you are asking them to do and will be happy to demonstrate their ability, now that they know what is expected of them.

SOURCE: From *Preparing Instructional Objectives* (3rd ed., pp. 46–47, 55) by R. F. Mager, Copyright 1997, The Center for Effective Performance, Inc., 1100 Johnson Ferry Road, Suite 150, Atlanta, GA 30342. www.cepworldwide.com 800-558-4237. Reprinted with permission. All rights reserved. No portion of these materials may be reproduced in any manner without the express written consent from The Center for Effective Performance, Inc.

PART 2: FRAMEWORK FOR HUMAN RESOURCE DEVELOPMENT

For example, after reading this textbook, we might wish for you to "demonstrate a thorough comprehension of the systems or process model of training" (presented in Figure 5-1, among other places). Although this may be fine as an overarching goal, can you see the weaknesses here if this is presented as an objective? (Hint: if not, go back to Tables 5-1 and 5-2 for guidance). An effective behavioral objective will spell out clearly what is expected of the learner/trainee. In the previous example, what does it mean to "demonstrate a thorough comprehension of . . .? This fuzzy statement needs to be clarified to be of real value as a learning objective.

As another example, of the following two statements, which do you think is the better (as in more specific) objective?

1. In at least two computer languages, be able to write and test a program to calculate arithmetic means.

2. Discuss and illustrate principles and techniques of computer programming.[11]

Our choice (and Mager's) is Statement 1, as it describes an intended outcome, that is, something the learner is expected to be able to do. The second statement is more like a training program or course description. It is not clear concerning precisely what the learner would do to demonstrate competence in this area. As this is such a critical HRD topic, we include two exercises at the end of the chapter for individual or group practice in writing clear objectives.

Several comments are in order before leaving this topic. First, behavioral objectives have served HRD professionals extremely well for the past forty-plus years, as they put the focus squarely on what the trainee is expected to *do* at the completion of training. Without this, it is very easy to get lost in muddled or "mushy" training that doesn't end up producing much in the way of tangible results. However, as noted in Chapter 4, an increasing number of HRD interventions deal with changing attitudes and emotions, for example, managing diversity, or increasing the "emotional intelligence" of employees. As Leonard and Zeace Nadler remind us, efforts to change attitudes are often the most controversial of all training or learning endeavors.[12] Although not impossible, it is much harder to write specific behavioral objectives for interventions dealing with attitudes or emotions. The reader is advised that writing good objectives becomes more difficult as one moves from knowledge- and skill-based training to training intended to change attitudes and emotions.

Further, Danny Langdon has promoted the idea of moving beyond objectives to what he terms developing "proformas."[13] A key point Langdon makes is that objectives can fail to make clear all of the issues going on *in the organization* that can influence individual performance. His approach suggests six issues that should be emphasized: inputs, process, outputs, consequences, conditions, and feedback. Langdon highlights issues taking place during the process of training, as well as the ongoing feedback that is received from various parties interested in training. This approach emphasizes that training and trainee behaviors must be seen as taking place within a dynamic organizational context. Further work along these lines is encouraged. Developing a proforma does not take the place of writing objectives, yet it does provide considerably more detail about how training and issues within the organization *interact* to produce (or fail to produce) desired organizational outcomes. Although we covered these issues when discussing strategic/organizational analysis in Chapter 4, we agree with Langdon that these same issues need to be considered when formulating program objectives.

## THE "MAKE VERSUS BUY" DECISION: CREATING OR PURCHASING HRD PROGRAMS

After a manager or HRD professional has identified the program objectives, a series of decisions must be made regarding the development and delivery of the program. One of those decisions is whether to design the program internally, purchase it (or portions of it) from an outside vendor, or use some combination of the two.[14] Many services are available through outside vendors or consultants, including:

- assisting with conducting needs assessment
- guiding internal staff to design or implement a program
- designing a program specifically for the organization
- providing supplemental training materials (exercises, workbooks, computer software, videos)

■ presenting a previously designed program
■ conducting a train-the-trainer program to improve the instructional skills of internal content experts[15]

There are many sources of HRD programs, materials, and advice, and their number continues to grow. Many consulting firms, educational institutions, professional societies, trade unions, publishing houses, governmental agencies, and nonprofit community-based organizations offer training programs and information to interested organizations. The American Society for Training and Development, as well as *T&D* and *Training* magazines, are useful places to begin a search for external training providers.

Table 5-3 lists a number of factors that should be considered when making a purchase decision. For example, suppose a small manufacturer desires to computerize its billing operation. Given the nature of the training needed, it is likely that the firm's management would contract with an outside vendor because (1) the firm would probably not have the expertise to design the program in-house, (2) management would not likely have the time to design the program, and (3) it is not likely that the firm has an HRD department or full-time HRD professional. In general, when the number of people needing the HRD intervention is small, it is more

PART 2: FRAMEWORK FOR HUMAN RESOURCE DEVELOPMENT

**TABLE 5-3**  **FACTORS TO CONSIDER BEFORE PURCHASING AN HRD PROGRAM**

| | |
|---|---|
| Expertise | When an organization lacks specialized KSAOs needed to design and implement an HRD program. |
| Timeliness | When it is timelier to hire an outside agency to facilitate the process. |
| Number of Trainees | Generally, the larger the number of trainees the greater the likelihood the organization would be willing to design the program itself. Thus, for just a few trainees the HRD department would send them to an outside training agency. |
| Subject Matter | If the subject matter is sensitive or proprietary the HRD department would conduct the program in-house using employees as trainers. |
| Cost | The HRD department always considers cost, but only in concert with other factors. |
| Size of HRD | The size of the HRD department is important for assessing the capacity to design, conduct, and/or implement skills training as opposed to using an outside agency. |
| "X" Factor | Some other extraneous conditions that would make it preferable that an outside agency be used to conduct the skills training. |

SOURCE: From P. Carnevale, L. J. Gainer, J. Villet, & S. L. Holland (1990). *Training Partnerships: Linking Employers and Providers* (p. 6). Alexandria, VA: American Society for Training and Development.

likely that the project will be outsourced. That is, those needing the intervention may be sent outside the organization for the program. This could come in the form of the organization providing the resources for professional development or tuition reimbursement.

Other factors that may influence an organization's decisions include personal contacts or past experience with an outside vendor, geographical proximity to the vendor, local economic conditions, and the presence of government incentives to conduct training.[16]

Once an organization decides to purchase a program or part of a program from an outside source, a vendor must be chosen. One rational way to do this is to determine the match between the vendor's product or capability with the organization's needs and objectives. The criteria for these decisions vary among organizations, but in general they include:

1. **cost:** price relative to program content and quality
2. **credentials:** including certificates, degrees, and other documentation of the vendor's expertise
3. **background:** number of years in business and experience in the particular content area
4. **experience:** vendor's prior clients, success with those clients, references
5. **philosophy:** comparison of the vendor's philosophy to that of the organization
6. **delivery method:** training methods and techniques used
7. **content:** topics included in program or materials
8. **actual product:** including appearance, samples, or whether a pilot program is available
9. **results:** expected outcomes
10. **support:** especially in terms of implementation and follow-up
11. **request for proposal (RFP):** the match between a vendor's offer and the requirement spelled out in the organization's request for a proposal[17]

Some of these factors will carry greater weight with particular managers. For example, some managers want to work only with the "best" providers, so they may weigh the vendor's experience and client list more heavily. Other managers may be swayed by "star power," as evidenced by the vendor's identity as a leading expert (such as management professor Dave Ulrich for training concerning strategic human resource management) or the presence of a movie or TV star in the vendor's films and videos (actor John Cleese appears in a series of widely used training films).

A recent study of outsourcing in the training area provides some interesting data.[18] Training managers were polled concerning their use of outside vendors for training and development. They reported spending about 25 percent of their budgets on outsourced training. The most frequent topics conducted by vendors were management development (27 percent), technical training (23 percent), and computer training (14 percent). Although overall satisfaction with the outsourced training was fairly high, only 29 percent reported that they had saved money as a result of outsourcing. Developing trust and maintaining strong communications with vendors were cited as major factors leading to the successful outsourcing of training. Gainey and Klaas argue that it is better to outsource in order to "acquire expertise and enhance the overall design and delivery of training," rather than primarily as a means to cut costs.[19]

In summary, outside training vendors offer organizations a wide choice of options in designing and developing training and HRD programs. These programs represent viable options when organizations have a small HRD function and a small number of trainees and when program content has no proprietary value. Even large organizations that have well-respected training functions make regular use of outside vendors for a variety of HRD programs. When organizations, large or small, elect to go outside to purchase training services and programs, they should, of course, first conduct a needs assessment so that they can make an informed decision.

## SELECTING THE TRAINER

Once the organization has made a decision to design its own training program, or has purchased a program that it will run, a trainer must be selected, provided that the instructional format will include one (we will discuss online options in Chapter 6). Selecting a trainer can be fairly easy when an organization has a large, multifaceted training staff with the competencies and subject matter expertise to train in high demand areas. **Training competency** involves the knowledge and varied skills needed to design and implement a training program. Effective trainers must be able to communicate their knowledge clearly, use various instructional techniques, have good interpersonal skills, and have the ability to motivate others to learn.

*Subject matter expertise* refers to the mastery of the subject matter. However, subject-matter expertise alone does not guarantee that an individual will be an effective trainer — many experts (including some college professors, we are sad to say) make poor trainers. Ideally, then, a **subject matter expert (SME)** should have the ability to train others. Individuals who lack the ability to design and implement effective training programs may rely too heavily on a single method of instruction that may be inappropriate to the subject matter (such as using a lecture format only to train employees in CPR and other first-aid techniques), or they may lack the interpersonal skills to effectively interact with or motivate participants. For example, an ASTD study found that training was most effective when trainers possessed an advanced level of expertise as instructors and facilitators.[20] However, in a later survey, 165 technical trainers (and ASTD members) rated their proficiency in various instructor/facilitator competencies as "intermediate," on average.[21]

Alternately, trainers who lack subject matter expertise may rely too heavily on a textbook or other training materials and not be able to explain important concepts and/or how these are applied to the job. In addition to contracting with an outside vendor, less qualified trainers can be aided through:

1. *teaming* skilled trainers with in-house subject matter experts to form an instructional team[22]

2. *using a training technique that does not require a human trainer,* such as computer-aided or online instruction programs (these options will be discussed in the next chapter)

3. *train-the-trainer programs,* which involve identifying in-house content experts who lack training skills and training them to become effective trainers

## TRAIN-THE-TRAINER PROGRAMS

The purpose of **train-the-trainer programs** is to provide subject matter experts (SMEs) with the necessary instructional knowledge and skills to design and implement a training program. Train-the-trainer programs are available through local professional associations, colleges, and consultants. These programs range from instruction in a single training technique (e.g., behavior modeling) to a comprehensive program on how to design a training program. The latter would present several training methods and techniques with an emphasis on how each can be used to maximize learning in different situations. Some training providers, such as Development Dimensions International (DDI), conduct train-the-trainer programs in which their client's employees become certified by the consulting firm to present their programs to the organization.

Some organizations design their own train-the-trainer programs, which can be desirable when there is a constant demand for skilled or technical trainers, or when employers want to emphasize a particular training technique. These programs should focus on many of the issues discussed in this chapter, including:

1. developing trainee objectives and lesson plans

2. selecting and preparing training materials

3. selecting and using training aids (e.g., Microsoft® PowerPoint® slides, videos, overhead projectors)

4. selecting and using different training methods and techniques

When it is not possible to design a train-the-trainer program, some organizations have developed training manuals that include these various components of the design and implementation process. Manuals can be valuable when there are insufficient numbers of SMEs to warrant a train-the-training program or when the potential trainers are in different geographical areas. For example, the Training Center of Alexander Consulting Group in Massachusetts relied on subject matter experts to provide the majority of their technical and financial training. These individuals had the expertise to teach the necessary courses, but were often lacking in the skills necessary to design and implement effective training courses. The organization created a self-directed Instructor's Guide. This guide provided information and techniques to conduct needs assessment, translate this information into course objectives and course content, and then select appropriate instructional techniques and visual aids. After the subject matter experts completed this self-directed training, trainee reactions were very positive. Further, 90 percent of all SMEs indicated that they found the Instructor's Guide to have been invaluable in preparing them to be a trainer.[23]

Overall, the selection of the trainer is an important decision for any HRD effort. Obviously, even a competently designed program that has the potential to address a significant organizational need can be a failure if an incompetent, unmotivated, or disinterested trainer delivers it. An ideal trainer would be someone with the requisite competencies as a trainer, as well as peer recognition for his or her subject matter expertise. If the trainer does not have the necessary subject matter expertise, then it is imperative that this individual should work together with a subject matter expert in the design phase, so that an effective matching of training content with training design and delivery can take place.[24] Recent efforts have developed train-the-trainer programs to train peers or coworkers to conduct health and safety training.[25] As one example, the American Nurses Association offers a course for nurse-trainers entitled "Protecting Nurses from Blood Borne Hazards in the Workplace." After completing this workshop, nurse-trainers are expected to conduct workshops on this topic in their own workplaces.[26]

## PREPARING A LESSON PLAN

Program objectives are necessary for pinpointing desired outcomes of a training or HRD program, but these statements alone are insufficient for determining the content of the training program, as well as the training methods, techniques, and materials. To translate program objectives into an executable training session, the development of a **lesson plan** is recommended.

A lesson plan is a trainer's guide for the actual delivery of the training content. Creating a lesson plan requires the trainer to determine in advance what is to be covered and how much time to devote to each part of the session. Gilley and Eggland suggest that a lesson plan should specify:

- content to be covered
- sequencing of activities
- selection or design of training media
- selection or development of experiential exercises, or both
- timing and planning of each activity
- selection of the method of instruction to be used
- number and type of evaluation items to be used[27]

Some organizations have program designers whose responsibilities may include defining training objectives and developing lesson plans. Individuals with educational backgrounds in instructional design (especially from colleges of education) are often hired for such positions. The kind of assistance that program designers can provide is particularly important for subject matter experts who have limited training skills. Some organizations include a section on lesson planning in their train-the-trainer programs. For example, an organization called New Environment Inc. has created a five-day train-the-trainer program concerning hazardous waste operations and emergency response (HAZWOPER) training. This program includes

FIGURE 5-2

**A GENERAL LESSON PLAN TEMPLATE**

Program title:

Objectives of this lesson:

Preparation required:

1. Physical environment

2. Equipment and materials

3. Instructor

4. Trainee(s)

| Time | Major Topics | Instructor Activity | Trainee Activity | Instructional Strategies Intended to Be Achieved |
|------|------|------|------|------|

SOURCE: From Nadler, L., & Nadler, Z. (1994). *Designing training programs: The critical events model* (2nd ed., p. 145). Houston, TX: Gulf Publishing.

providing videos and complete lesson plans that trainers can use when implementing this training back in their own organizations.[28]

To assist trainers, we suggest using a standardized lesson plan form. Figure 5-2 presents a general form recommended by Nadler and Nadler. As an alternative, Figure 5-3 presents a condensed version of a completed lesson plan for an experiential team-building training program. As can be seen in this example, the lesson plan serves as a blueprint for conducting the whole weekend training program.

First Citizens Bank of Raleigh recently initiated online lesson plans for the majority of its training of new branch employees.[29] According to a bank executive, the new courseware provides a more flexible and efficient approach to training than past classroom efforts (because employees are spread over 300-plus branches, it would have taken a year to train employees using classroom training alone). As another example, CrossTec Corporation has developed software called NetOp School v. 3.0 that can be used by teachers or trainers using networked classrooms.[30] One feature included in this package is a tool that allows the instructor to create interactive lesson plans for each session.

PART 2: FRAMEWORK FOR HUMAN RESOURCE DEVELOPMENT

**FIGURE 5-3**

## A SAMPLE COMPLETED LESSON PLAN
## EXPERIENTIAL TEAM BUILDING RETREAT
### (RICHARD J. WAGNER, TRAINER)

| TIME | ACTIVITY |
|---|---|
| **Friday Night** | |
| 6–7:30 p.m. | DINNER |
| 7:30–9:00 p.m. | Program introduction and completion of prequestionnaires. |
| | Initial experiential activity — Silent birthday line-up. Have the group members line up in order of their birthdays (month and day only) without talking. |
| | Discussion of what happened during the activity and how the group handled the issues it encountered. Presentation of Kolb's experiential learning model (activity, review/discussion, theory development, and generalization), and how this will be used to develop teamwork during the weekend. |
| | Discussion of the plan for the weekend and some of the goals for the retreat. |
| **Saturday** | |
| 7–8 a.m. | BREAKFAST |
| 8–9 a.m. | Brainstorming session on group goals for the retreat using a flip chart to record the issues. Seek to uncover some of the problems that the group encounters at work, and generate an initial discussion of how working as a team can help deal with these issues. |
| | Experiential activity — The Marble Pass. Direct the group to move a marble from a starting point to a barrel 40 feet away and then get the marbles into a barrel using a series of 2- to 3-foot-long plastic pipes. The participants may not move the marble backward, and they must work as a group to get this done. |
| 9–10 AM | Discussion of how the group members accomplished the task, what problems they encountered, and how they solved these problems. A critical issue will be the discussion of how their problem-solving skills might relate to problems encountered at work, and what they can do to anticipate and solve some of these problems. |
| 10–10:30 a.m. | BREAK |
| 10:30–12:00 p.m. | Experiential activities, working in two groups. |
| | Blind Polygon. Group members are blindfolded and directed to form a square using a rope. |

*continued*

**FIGURE 5-3**                                                                    **CONTINUED**

| TIME | ACTIVITY |
|---|---|
| 10:30–12:00 p.m. | Group Juggle. Group members pass a ball around a circle in a pattern, first establishing the pattern, then seeking speed, and then using more than one ball.<br><br>All Aboard. Everyone has to stand on a 2-by-2 platform at the same time.<br><br>Have the groups try each of the activities and do their own planning for subsequent activities. |
| 12–1 p.m. | LUNCH |
| 1–2 p.m. | Discussion of the morning activities and what needs to be done to make the afternoon successful. |
| 2–3:30 p.m. | Experiential activities, working in two groups.<br><br>Trolleys. Sort of group skiing, with about six people on the skis at the same time. The group must move everyone about 40 feet using these trolleys.<br><br>Hot Stuff. Using only some ropes and other provided equipment, the group must transfer water from one can to another in the center of a 10-foot circle without going into the circle. |
| 3:30–4 p.m. | BREAK |
| 4–5 p.m. | Review and discussion of the concept of teamwork and how the activities of the day have helped show the group members how effective teams work. |
| 5–7 p.m. | DINNER |
| AFTER DINNER ACTIVITY | NASA Moon Survival, an indoor activity. |
| **Sunday Morning** | |
| 8–9 a.m. | BREAKFAST |
| 9–10 a.m. | Review and discussion of the NASA Moon Survival activity, focusing on how the activity was accomplished using the concepts of teamwork reviewed during the program. |
| 10–12 p.m. | Final discussion of teamwork, focusing on specific issues of the organization. The trainer will facilitate this discussion, but the VP will be the leader in developing the issues. |

To this point, we have discussed selecting the trainer and then preparing the lesson plan. This is a logical sequence, particularly when the trainer is also the one preparing the lesson plan. But sometimes the HRD intervention (including the general lesson plans) is designed before the trainers are selected. This would be most likely to occur in large organizations. Even here, though, the trainer should modify or adapt the general lesson plan to fit each situation in which he or she is asked to present the HRD program.

## SELECTING TRAINING METHODS AND MEDIA

Up to this point we have discussed some preliminary steps involved in the design and implementation of a training program. The next step in the training process is to select the appropriate **training methods.** A 2003 survey conducted by *Training* magazine revealed that, contrary to popular belief, classroom programs were still the most popular instructional method (see Table 5-4). The survey indicated that 91 percent of organizations use the classroom format "always" or "often" to deliver at least some of their training.[31] There has been considerable recent growth in web-based self-study programs and work-based performance support programs. More general public seminars continue to remain popular as well. Data concerning training media usage are reported in Table 5-4. Workbooks and manuals continue to be most widely used, though there has been a substantial recent increase in the use of the Internet/company intranets and CD-ROM/DVDs to provide training. The types of training most frequently offered can be seen in Table 5-5. Computer applications, orientation, management development, technical training, communication skills, and sexual harassment were the topics most frequently offered. Of relevance to this chapter, 74 percent of organizations reported frequent use of train-the-trainer programs.

An ASTD survey revealed that, in 2002, organizations surveyed reported using instructor-led classroom training for 72 percent of their training, with 19 percent of training being delivered via learning technologies such as computer-based training, multimedia, CD-ROMs, and company intranets. For organizations identified as training investment leaders, the figures for delivery via classroom versus learning technologies were 62 percent and 29 percent, respectively.[32]

One way of classifying training is by the degree of activity expected or required of trainees. On one end, the lecture method and videotapes are generally the least active (or most passive) form of training. At the other extreme, highly experiential methods such as outdoor training, role-playing exercises, games, and simulations demand the greatest amount of activity or action from trainees. Other approaches such as computer-based instruction or videoconferencing fall somewhere in between.

Training approaches can also be grouped into two broad categories: on-the-job methods, which typically occur in the employee's normal work setting, and classroom methods, which typically take place away from the job (such as in a conference room or lecture hall). This categorization is not definitive, however, because some training methods have multiple applications. **Computer-based training (CBT),** for example, can be implemented using a computer at an employee's desk or workstation, in a company classroom, or even at an employee's home. We will discuss many

| TABLE 5-4 | PERCENT OF ORGANIZATIONS MAKING FREQUENT USE OF VARIOUS TRAINING METHODS AND MEDIA[1] |

| Methods | Percent |
| --- | --- |
| Instructor-led Classroom Programs | 91 |
| Self-Study, Web-based | 44 |
| Job-based Performance Support | 44 |
| Public Seminars | 42 |
| Case Studies | 40 |
| Role Plays | 35 |
| Games or Simulations, Non-computer-based | 25 |
| Self-Study, Non-computer-based | 23 |
| Virtual Classroom, with Instructor | 21 |
| Games or Simulations, Computer-based | 10 |
| Experiential Programs | 6 |
| Virtual Reality Programs | 3 |
| **Media** | |
| Workbooks/Manuals | 79 |
| Internet/Intranet/Extranet | 63 |
| CD-ROM/DVD/Diskettes | 55 |
| Videotapes | 52 |
| Teleconferencing | 24 |
| Videoconferencing | 23 |
| Satellite/Broadcast TV | 12 |
| Audiocassettes | 4 |

SOURCE: From 2003 Industry Report (2003). *Training, 40*(9), 21–38.

[1]Respondents were asked the extent to which they used these methods "always," "often," "seldom," or "never." The figures shown here are for those who reported using each method "always" or "often."

of the particular training methods in greater detail in Chapter 6 (under the topic of implementing training). This placement of training methods in the implementation chapter was primarily driven by our desire to have more space in that chapter to emphasize the various methods currently in use. However, we hope it is clear to you that the decision concerning which methods or media will be used must be made during the *design* phase of training.

With such an array of training methods and media available (as seen in Table 5-4), how does an HRD professional choose which approach is most appropriate for maximum learning? Several factors should be considered:

1. **The objectives of the program** This factor is paramount. As will be clear, some approaches are more appropriate for achieving particular objectives

**TABLE 5-5**

## MOST FREQUENT TYPES OF TRAINING OFFERED[1]

| Type | Percent |
|---|---|
| Computer Systems/Applications | 96 |
| New Hire Orientation | 96 |
| Management Development, Nonexecutive | 91 |
| Technical Training | 90 |
| Communication Skills | 89 |
| Sexual Harassment | 88 |
| Supervisory Skills | 88 |
| Leadership | 85 |
| New Equipment Operation | 85 |
| Performance Management/Appraisal | 85 |
| Team Building | 82 |
| Customer Service | 81 |
| Product Knowledge | 79 |
| Executive Development | 78 |
| Safety | 77 |
| Computer Programming | 76 |
| Personal Growth | 76 |
| Managing Change | 75 |
| Problem Solving/Decision Making | 75 |
| Time Management | 74 |
| Train-the-Trainer | 74 |
| Diversity/Cultural Awareness | 72 |
| Hiring/Interviewing | 71 |
| Strategic Planning | 69 |
| Customer Education | 68 |
| Quality/Process Improvement | 65 |
| Public Speaking/Presentation Skills | 62 |
| Basic Life/Work Skills | 61 |
| Ethics | 61 |
| Sales | 55 |
| Wellness | 54 |

SOURCE: 2003 Industry Report (2003). *Training, 40*(9), 21–38.

[1]Respondents were asked the extent to which they used these methods via classroom, via technology, via a blended approach, or do not provide. The figures shown here are for those who reported using any of the three means of providing training.

than others. For example, if the objective is to improve interpersonal skills, then more active approaches such as videotaping, role playing, or behavior modeling would be better choices than the lecture or computer-based training methods.

2. **Time and money available** In an ideal world, we would have all the time and money we need to accomplish our goals. Unfortunately, in many organizations, managers often ask the HRD department to design and implement programs quickly, while spending as little money as possible. Competing needs may also force HRD professionals to select certain approaches because of their low cost. For example, when designing a program to train mechanics to repair a complicated mechanical system, an interactive, computer-based program might be optimal, but because of its cost, the HRD professional may have to settle for a combination of traditional classes (using lecture, discussion, and reference books) and on-the-job training.

3. **Availability of other resources** Some methods require highly trained trainers and specialized equipment and facilities to be delivered effectively. Again, trade-offs are likely to be necessary by choosing alternative approaches with less demanding resources.

4. **Trainee characteristics and preferences** The issue here focuses on both trainee readiness and the diversity of the target population. Methods such as computer-based training require a fairly high level of literacy. If literacy or fluency is a problem, either a less reading- and writing-intensive method (such as videotape) may be used, or literacy training must be done first. Similarly, because individuals have different learning styles, some training methods may be more appropriate than others. For example, Ronald Sims argues that, in designing any program, trainers must pay particular attention to the principles of learning laid out in Chapter 3, and in particular to the learning styles described by David Kolb.[33]

In the end, the selection of training methods and media requires that program designers have knowledge of different HRD techniques, and then use sound judgment in their decision making. HRD professionals should investigate all available methods, and when in doubt, consult experienced colleagues, instructional designers, and consultants. For a useful application of these issues to the topic of customer service training, see a recent article by Frank Jossi.[34]

## PREPARING TRAINING MATERIALS

After the training methods have been selected, the next logical step is to prepare or purchase the training materials, depending upon whether the program is purchased or designed by the organization. If a training program is purchased from an outside vendor, training materials such as books, handouts, and videos will usually be part of the package. Programs designed in-house will require the preparation of materials. If the program is similar to past training programs, those materials may simply need to be modified to fit the current program.

Many kinds of training materials are used, but we will focus our discussion here on program announcements, syllabi or program outlines, training manuals, and textbooks.

## PROGRAM ANNOUNCEMENTS

Program announcements inform the target audience about the training program. The announcement should indicate the purpose of the program, when and where it will be held, and how the employee can qualify to participate in the program. Sufficient lead time should be given to employees so that they can adjust their schedules and process the necessary request forms. Typically, announcements are sent through supervisory channels, union stewards, company newsletters, an organization's intranet, or mailed individually to employees. Some organizations designate a bulletin board for announcing training opportunities or make use of electronic mail systems. Some organizations publish periodic bulletins to provide this information.

## PROGRAM OUTLINES

Program outlines (or course syllabi) are documents that communicate the content, goals, and expectations for the program. Typically provided at the beginning of the program, these include such things as course objectives, topical areas to be covered, materials or tools needed, requirements of each trainee, and a tentative schedule of events.

The program outline can be used to establish behavioral expectations including punctuality, attendance, work habits, class participation, and courtesy toward other trainees. Such expectations should be clearly explained. For example, it is important for trainees to be present at all sessions if training content is sequenced. The attendance policy should reflect this requirement and explain that any trainees who are absent may be required to begin a new program from the start.

## TRAINING MANUALS OR TEXTBOOKS

Most trainers rely on a training manual or textbook for the basic instructional material, readings, exercises, and self-tests. Some documents are organized into modules that make it easy to organize the training program into sessions. *Textbooks* provide a broad treatment of the subject, whereas training manuals are better known for their brevity and hands-on approach. Trainers who decide to use a textbook would normally contact the publisher and determine whether individual modules can be purchased separately, how useful other trainers found the item, and how easily the item can be customized to the needs of the organization.[35] In addition to these factors, the purchase price should be compared with the cost of producing a comparable training manual. For example, Thomson/South-Western has an active custom publishing operation (called TextChoice) that allows educators and trainers to select portions of their content as well as add original materials to create a customized textbook.[36]

**Training manuals** can be readily produced by an organization, particularly given the availability of desktop publishing software. The production cost would include staff time for curriculum design and writing, cost of equipment, and printing. The availability of desktop publishing software and laser printers makes it much easier to produce a high quality training manual in-house. Even so, unless there is a large demand for the manual, it is usually less expensive in the long run to purchase a commercially produced manual, if one is available.

Before leaving this topic, we address an issue seldom raised in textbooks. It is an infringement of copyright to use materials created by someone else without proper attribution or permission by the author or copyright holder. Unfortunately, this sort of "borrowing" of material from other sources is quite common in work settings, including among HRD professionals and educators. We are aware of a colleague who is both a professor and consultant. Once a student brought materials from his workplace to show the professor in class — only to find out that the materials had been developed by that professor for another client many years earlier! The student was unaware that his employer did not have permission to use this material. The lesson here is something a parent might say, that is, "Just because everyone is doing it doesn't make it right!" We urge readers to err on the side of caution when making use of material developed by others.

## SCHEDULING THE HRD PROGRAM

The task of scheduling a training or other HRD program may seem relatively straightforward when compared to other decisions made by the trainer, but this is definitely not the case. Organizations can be busy, hectic, and unpredictable environments, making scheduling HRD and other activities very difficult. The goal in scheduling an HRD program is to ensure that the participants (both trainer and learners) are available and have their attention focused on the learning task at hand. In this section, we will discuss some of the issues HRD professionals should consider when scheduling programs. Our discussion applies to scheduling programs that require participants to be in attendance at the time the program is delivered. In contrast, one of the main advantages of individually oriented delivery methods, such as CD-ROM or self-paced instruction, is that such approaches can be done whenever the participants have the time to do them.

### SCHEDULING DURING WORK HOURS

One popular option for program scheduling is to run the program during normal working hours. This timing both avoids outside conflicts (such as commuting, family, and personal obligations) and sends a message to employees that learning is an important part of their job. When scheduling a program during normal work hours, the HRD professional should consider factors such as the day of the week, time of day, peak work hours, staff meeting times, and travel requirements.

The *day of the week* becomes an issue because employees often favor some days for time off, such as Monday, Friday, and the days surrounding a holiday. Employees may wish to extend their weekends and holidays, so these days are often avoided (if possible) when scheduling training.

*Time of day* is another factor. Programs scheduled for the start of the workday may face a significant proportion of tardy or tired participants. Scheduling a program for the lunch hour may require building in time for employees to eat during the program, providing lunch, or requiring employees to eat before or after training. Midafternoon programs coincide with the time that many people's circadian rhythms are at a low point, resulting in sluggishness and shorter attention spans. To combat this, the program should include active participation, break periods, or the availability of light snacks and beverages (many trainees appreciate the availability of beverages that include caffeine!). In addition, employees attending programs scheduled close to quitting time may be distracted or have to leave early to attend to personal or family demands. Obviously, a program has to be scheduled sometime, but the wise trainer will note these issues and take steps to deal with them as best as possible.

In addition to day of the week and time of day, other working-hour constraints may be unique to particular organizational units or occupational groups. These include peak work hours, staff meeting times, and travel requirements. *Peak work hours* are the times of the day, week, month, or year that departments are the busiest and when scheduling a training program would cause a potential conflict. For example, scheduling a professional development program for accountants and auditors during tax season would prevent most potential participants from attending. Managers and supervisors should also be contacted before scheduling programs to determine if participants have any *staff meetings, travel requirements,* or any other special scheduling needs. This information will help the trainer to select the best times and develop contingency plans for any potential conflicts.

## SCHEDULING AFTER WORK HOURS

Sometimes, HRD programs are scheduled after work or during the weekend to avoid some of the organizational constraints previously discussed. This approach can create other problems. Extending the workday and workweek can cause a hardship for some employees, particularly those who have family obligations or other personal commitments. Even when employees know about a scheduled training program in advance, family problems could arise, causing some trainees to miss important training sessions. Another problem is fatigue. Employees may be physically tired from a day's work and may not be mentally alert. For example, in response to employee requests, a supervisory training program at the Electric Boat Division of General Dynamics was held between midnight and 2:00 a.m. for employees working the second shift (4:00 p.m. to midnight). The training program was poorly attended, however, and those who did attend experienced fatigue by the second hour of the class. As a result of this experience, the company suspended all future midnight training programs.

Even when after-work and weekend programs do not cause hardships, many employees are reluctant to give up their leisure time. In these situations, some organizations provide inducements, including overtime pay, compensatory time (equal time off), training as a qualification for promotion, and leisure activities to coincide with the training session (e.g., by conducting the training at a resort area).

## REGISTRATION AND ENROLLMENT ISSUES

One practical headache for many training programs is managing the registration process. It must be clear to participants and managers how one should register for training, who is responsible for logistical issues (e.g., travel arrangements, lodging, meals), and what people are to do if they need to cancel or reschedule their training. Fortunately, e-mail and organizational intranets have made this process much easier than it once was. Also, many of the popular Human Resource Information Systems currently available include training registration and tracking modules. Such computer programs and other uses of technology can be a tremendous help to busy HRD professionals as they manage the enrollment process for various HRD programs. One such program is called RegOnline, and it provides online registration for many types of events, including training programs.[37] Several pricing options are available for larger versus smaller programs.

## RETURN TO OPENING CASE

Since 1998, Rockwell Collins has done extensive work to overhaul its training efforts.[1] Cliff Purington was hired as manager of learning and development in September 1998 to "change the way the company delivered training to its 14,000 employees."[2] Your instructor has additional information describing what Rockwell Collins did, as well as some of the outcomes of its efforts.

[1]Purington, C., Butler, C., & Gale, S. F. (2003). *Built to learn: The true story of how Rockwell Collins became a true learning organization.* New York: AMACOM.

[2]Fister, S. (2000). Reinventing training at Rockwell Collins. *Training*, April, 64–70.

## SUMMARY

This chapter described several important activities related to the design of training and development programs. After an organization identifies a need for training, the next step is to decide whether to purchase the program from an outside vendor or design the program in-house. If the organization decides to stay in-house, the trainer must be selected. If there is a full-time trainer with content knowledge available, the decision will be an easy one. If not, then a content specialist may need to be identified and sent to a train-the-trainer program.

The trainer or program development team has the responsibility for developing training objectives that define the desired outcomes of the training program. This information should be translated into a lesson plan that provides a thorough guide for the training implementation. Well-written program objectives also help in selecting the appropriate training methods and media, and in evaluating program success. There are three primary training approaches: on-the-job training, classroom, and computer-based training. Each approach has a number of techniques appropriate for particular situations. The trainer needs to select the best combination of techniques that will maximize trainee learning. Once the trainer designs the program, the next step is to determine the best schedule while avoiding potential conflicts.

## KEY TERMS AND CONCEPTS

computer-based training (CBT)
lesson plan
subject matter expert (SME)
training competency

training manual
training methods
training program objectives
train-the-trainer programs

## QUESTIONS FOR DISCUSSION

1. What are the three essential features of an effective HRD or training program objective? Why is each one so important? Discuss training or classroom experiences that you have had where objectives either did or did not follow the recommendations made by Robert Mager and others.

2. Why are behavioral objectives and lesson plans important to effective HRD interventions? What role should objectives play in the design, implementation, and evaluation of HRD programs?

3. Describe the relative merits of using a trainee's coworkers as potential trainers. What should be done to ensure that a coworker is an effective trainer?

4. What are the advantages of designing an HRD program in-house versus purchasing programs from vendors?

5. What are the advantages of holding a training program on-site? Off-site?

6. How do you feel about attending training sessions or classes scheduled early in the morning? After lunch? What can a trainer do to maximize the chances that such a session will be effective?

## EXERCISE 1: OBJECTIVE WRITING FOR A DIVERSITY TRAINING PROGRAM

Evaluate the following statement as a program objective for a diversity training program. Individually or in small groups, rewrite this objective to conform more closely to the principles cited earlier concerning effective program objectives.

Develop a thorough understanding of the corporate culture of our organization, including our policies on harassment, ethnic and gender diversity, and equal access to individual counseling and promotion opportunities.[38]

## EXERCISE 2: OBJECTIVE WRITING FOR A TRAINING PROGRAM OF YOUR CHOICE

Individually or in small groups, write your own program objective(s) for a training program of your choice. Critique your objectives by comparing them to the principles described in Tables 5-1 and 5-2.

Visit *http://werner.swlearning.com* for links to informative websites for this chapter.

## REFERENCES

1. Buckman, J. M. (2004). Training methods. *Fire Engineering, 157*(4), April, 16–18; Bodimer, J. (2003). Keeping a staff motivated through training and development. *Business Credit, 105*(3), March, 15–17; Huling, E. (2002). Innovative training avoids "brain drain." *National Underwriter, 106*(42), October 21, 14.

2. Duguay, S. M., & Korbut, K. A. (2002). Designing a training program which delivers results quickly! *Industrial and Commercial Training, 34*(6), 223–228.

3. Mager, R. F. (1984). *Preparing instructional objectives* (2nd ed., p. 3). Belmont, CA: Pitman Learning.

4. *Ibid.*

5. Ng, Y. C., & Siu, N.N.Y.M. (2004). Training and enterprise performance in transition: Evidence from China. *International Journal of Human Resource Management, 15*(4/5), June/August, 878–894.

6. Mager, R. F. (1997). *Preparing instructional objectives* (3rd ed.). Atlanta: Center for Effective Performance.

7. *Ibid.*

8. *Ibid.*

9. *Ibid*, p. 166.

10. *Ibid*, p. 142.

11. *Ibid*, p. 25.

12. Nadler, L., & Nadler, Z. (1994). *Designing training programs: The critical events model* (2nd ed.). Houston, TX: Gulf Publishing.

13. Langdon, D. (1999). Objectives? Get over them. *Training & Development*, February, 54–58.

14. Sims, R. R. (1998). *Reinventing training and development*. Westport, CT: Quorum Books.

15. Carnevale, A. P., Gainer, L. J., Villet, J., & Holland, S. L. (1990). *Training partnerships: Linking employers and providers*. Alexandria, VA: American Society for Training and Development.

16. *Ibid.*

17. *Ibid.*

18. Gainey, T. W., & Klaas, B. S. (2002). Outsourcing the training function: Results from the field. *Human Resource Planning, 25*(1), 16–22; Gainey, T. W., & Klaas, B. S. (2003). The outsourcing of training and development: Factors impacting client satisfaction. *Journal of Management, 29*(2), 207–229.

19. Gainey & Klaas (2002), *ibid*, p. 22.

20. McLagan, P. (1989). *Models for excellence: The conclusions and recommendations of the ASTD training and development competency study.* Alexandria, VA: ASTD.

21. Williams, S. W. (1999). Improving technical training: The effectiveness of technical subject matter experts as trainers. In K. Peter Kuchinke (Ed.), *Academy of Human Resource Development: Vol. 1. 1999 Conference Proceedings* (pp. 588–595). Baton Rouge, LA: AHRD.

22. Building a winning team with subject matter experts (1997). *Spectrum Online.* Retrieved October 19, 2004 from http://cted.inel.gov/cted/spectrum/may_1997/gn-sme.html

23. Dumas, M. A., & Wile, D. E. (1992). The accidental trainer: Helping design instruction. *Personnel Journal*, June, 106–110.

24. Building a winning team with subject matter experts (1997), *supra* note 22.

25. McClellan, P., & Pater, R. (2004). The power of training trainers. *Occupational Health & Safety, 73*(7), July, 96–100.

26. Train-the-trainer workshops in full gear. (2003). *The American Nurse, 35*(2), March/April, 11.

27. Gilley, J. W., & Eggland, S. A. (1989). *Principles of human resource development.* Reading, MA: Addison-Wesley.

28. HAZWOPER Training (2004). *Occupational Health & Safety, 73*(5), May, 129.

29. Bills, S. (2004). N.C.'s First Citizens E-training. *American Banker, 169*(108), June 7, 18.

30. CrossTec Corporation (2004). Class management system. *TechDirections, 63*(10), May, 28; Retrieved September 18, 2004, from http://www.crossteccorp.com/netopschool/

31. 2003 Industry Report (2003). *Training, 40*(9), 21–38.

32. 2003 State of the Industry Report (2003). Alexandria, VA: American Society for Technical Development.

33. Sims (1998), *supra* note 14.

34. Jossi, F. (2003). Lesson plans. *HR Magazine, 48*(2), February, 72–76.

35. McCullough, R. C. (1987). To make or buy. *Training and Development Journal, 41*(1), 25–26.

36. Thomson Custom Publishing (2004). TextChoice. Retrieved September 20, 2004, from http://archive.thomson.com/pam/

37. RegOnline (2004). Retrieved September 17, 2004, from http://www.regonline.com/default.aspx

38. Mager, (1997), *supra* note 6. Adapted from p. 143.

# 6

# IMPLEMENTING HRD PROGRAMS

## Learning Objectives

*After reading this chapter, you should be able to:*

1. Describe three broad approaches to training delivery and the advantages and disadvantages of each approach.

2. Describe five primary categories of classroom training and the advantages and disadvantages of each one.

3. Describe the advantages and disadvantages of self-paced training approaches to training delivery.

4. Determine when various training techniques are more or less effective in different situations.

5. Develop expertise as a facilitator of a training topic or module.

6. Describe several ways that technology is being used to provide and improve HRD programs.

7. Develop greater expertise in effectively using technology to deliver training content.

8. Understand and explain the activities involved in implementing an HRD program.

■

## OPENING CASE

The company has four strategic initiatives: "driving global growth, attaining product leadership, continuously improving customer experience, and enhancing a winning culture." This company was quick to make use of the Internet to sell its computers. In 2004, the company reported over 1.4 billion page requests or "hits" on its direct sales web page — per quarter! Customer use of the Internet for support services is also extensive.

The company? Dell Inc. For many years, Dell experienced "hyper-growth," often adding 200 to 300 new employees per week. How could they train new employees and develop new managers amidst such rapid growth? Their major response was to create Dell Learning (formerly Dell University) as a major entity within the company.

*Questions: If you were in charge of Dell Learning, what types of training and learning opportunities would you emphasize? Are there particular methods you would expect to emphasize? Why? To what extent would you emphasize technology-based learning? How much control would you encourage or allow trainees in determining what training they receive? Would you seek to involve top management in the training process, and if so, how?*

## INTRODUCTION

As you begin this chapter, do you think the following statements are true or false?

■ *The best way to learn any new skill is to learn it on the job.*

■ *The lecture method is a very poor method to use for training purposes.*

■ *It is relatively easy to come up with questions to stimulate useful group discussion.*

■ *Generally, the more "bells and whistles" that you can put in a computer slide presentation, the better.*

■ *In most cases, when trainers have trainees discuss a case study, this is little more than a time filler or a chance for the trainer to take a break from lecturing.*

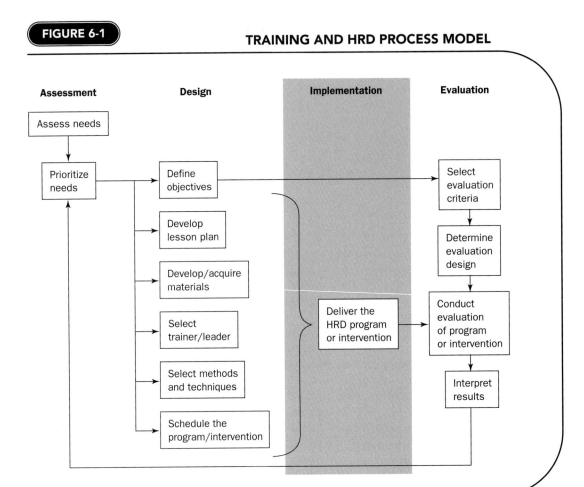

**FIGURE 6-1**

**TRAINING AND HRD PROCESS MODEL**

- *Computer-based training has become the dominant form of delivery method across a wide variety of HRD applications.*

*Note: our answers are at the end of the chapter.*

This chapter focuses on the third phase of the training process: implementing training and HRD programs. Both assessment and design issues should have been addressed by this point. Figure 6-1 shows where these activities fit within the training and HRD process model.

Proper delivery or implementation assumes that an important need for training has been identified and that program objectives have been spelled out. The program objectives should greatly influence the design issues described in Chapter 5, as well as the selection of training methods used to conduct or implement training. In this chapter, we will focus in more detail on the array of methods available for conducting training. Some of the most exciting developments in HRD concern the increased use of technology in program implementation. This can come in the form of technology replacing the traditional classroom delivery approach (e.g., online courses), or when technology is blended in or used along with other classroom approaches. Technological developments will be discussed toward the end of the chapter.

## TRAINING DELIVERY METHODS

Our discussion of learning in Chapter 3 covered differences between expert and novice levels of employee performance. Clearly, training is intended to increase the expertise of trainees in a particular area. When thinking about what training method (or methods) to use, it is useful to consider the *current level of expertise* that trainees possess. Figure 6-2 depicts a learning pyramid. At the bottom are learning prerequisites, that is, the basic skills or knowledge the learner needs to get started.[1] As the figure suggests, the novice learner may easily get confused or anxious, and therefore novice trainees generally require more guided or instruction-centered training methods. In contrast, as trainees' existing level of expertise increases, they become more creative and confident. Thus, the desired or ideal training methods are also likely to shift more toward exploratory or experiential methods. The middle arrow

**FIGURE 6-2**

### A LEARNING PYRAMID TO GUIDE IN THE SELECTION OF APPROPRIATE TRAINING METHODS

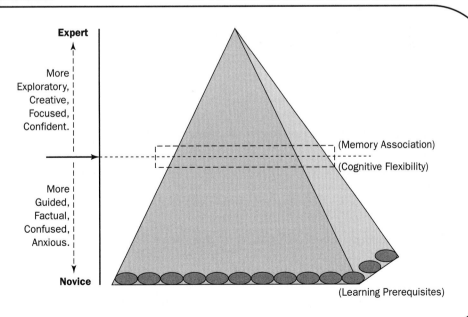

SOURCE: From L. R. Yin (2004). Learning pyramid. Accessed September 27, 2004, from http://www.yinnovate.com/learning-pyramid.html. Used by permission.

in Figure 6-2 depicts the point at which individual trainees are ready to shift from more guided to more exploratory learning approaches.[2]

Because experiential methods generally require more time to complete than instruction-centered approaches, they are not as commonly used to reach large numbers of individuals (hence, the pyramid shape of Figure 6-2). This figure is also consistent with the distinction made in Chapter 3 between declarative and procedural knowledge, that is, in most cases, an individual must first learn *what to do* (declarative knowledge) before he or she can learn *how to do it* (procedural knowledge). An effective training or HRD program should first identify where trainees are in terms of this pyramid, and then provide assistance for all trainees to "move up" toward an expert level of performance. In many situations, both guided and experiential approaches will be used, for example, when organizations combine the use of lecture, discussion, case studies, behavior modeling, role playing, and games or simulations. This combined approach is especially valuable when trainees have different learning styles and preferences. Methods of training delivery are described in the following sections. Our first point, though, is that the choice of training method should be guided by both the program objectives (discussed in Chapter 5), as well as an explicit consideration of the current level of trainee expertise.

Training methods can be classified by whether they take place on the job versus away from the employee's normal work setting. We will first discuss on-the-job methods, and then discuss classroom approaches, which typically take place away from the job (such as in a conference room or classroom). Yet a third category of training methods includes those that use a self-paced or individualized approach. For example, computer training can take place on the job (e.g., when an employee works at a computer at his or her desk), or in a computerized classroom. However, much of the recent growth of computer training has used a self-paced approach (e.g., CD-ROM, web-based, or distance learning) that may be done in a variety of different settings. Table 6-1 lists the on-the-job, classroom, and self-paced training methods that we will discuss in this chapter. Other training methods used for particular audiences (such as mentoring for management development) will be discussed in the appropriate chapters.

## ON-THE-JOB TRAINING (OJT) METHODS

**On-the-job training (OJT)** involves conducting training at a trainee's regular workstation (desk, machine, etc.). This is the most common form of training; most employees receive at least some training and coaching on the job. Virtually any type of one-on-one instruction between coworkers or between the employee and supervisor can be classified as OJT. On-the-job training has been promoted as a means for organizations to deal with the shortage of applicants who possess the skills needed to perform many current jobs, and as a means for organizations to deal with accelerating market cycles.[3] Unfortunately, much on-the-job training is conducted informally, without formal structure, planning, or careful thought. At the extreme, such informal efforts are caricatured with the picture of the busy supervisor telling the new hire to "go sit by Joe."[4] Yet, research indicates that informal OJT "leads to increased error rates, lower productivity, and decreased training efficiency."[5] Why do you suppose that might be?

| | TRAINING METHODS AND TECHNIQUES |
|---|---|

**TABLE 6-1**

**Methods** | **Techniques**
---|---
On-the-job training | Job instruction training
 | Job rotation
 | Coaching
 | Mentoring
Classroom | Lecture
 | Conference/Discussion
 | Audiovisual
 |    static media (e.g., handouts, books)
 |    dynamic media (e.g., DVD, video, film)
 |    telecommunication (e.g., satellite transmission, Internet)
 | Experiential techniques
 |    case study
 |    business games
 |    role play
 |    behavioral modeling
 | Computer-based training (classroom based)
 |    networked computer labs/classrooms
Self-paced | Paper-based training
 |    workbooks (e.g., programmed instruction)
 | Computer-based training (non-classroom-based)
 |    computer-aided instruction (e.g., multimedia CD-ROM)
 |    Internet/intranet
 |    intelligent computer-aided instruction

Structured OJT programs are generally conducted by an assigned trainer who is recognized, rewarded, and trained to provide appropriate instructional techniques. A survey of OJT practices found that (1) supervisors, coworkers, and to a lesser degree, HRD staff members conducted most of the structured OJT programs; (2) a majority of organizations provided train-the-trainer programs for these assigned OJT trainers (see Chapter 5); and (3) top management generally expressed support for structured OJT programs.[6] Formal OJT has two distinct advantages over classroom training. First, OJT facilitates the transfer of learning to the job because the trainee has an immediate opportunity to practice the work tasks on the job. Transfer of learning is enhanced because the learning environment is the same as the performance environment (see our discussion of physical fidelity in Chapter 3). Second, OJT reduces training costs because no training facilities are needed. For example, the Hard Rock Cafe conducts almost all of its training on the job. Supervisors conduct most training at the start of each new work shift. Job aids are used heavily, and these materials make extensive use of graphics and bullet points, rather than lengthy training manuals. Younger workers are reported to view this approach very favorably, and this is a major source of employees for this restaurant chain.[7]

There are, however, several limitations to OJT. First, the job site may have physical constraints, noise, and other distractions that could inhibit learning. Many of these cannot be changed because of the nature of the job. Second, using expensive equipment for training could result in costly damage or disruption of the production schedule. Third, using OJT while customers are present may inconvenience them and temporarily reduce the quality of service. Fourth, OJT involving heavy equipment or chemicals may threaten the safety of others who are working in close proximity. Precautions should be taken by the trainer to minimize the potential problems from these four areas.

In many cases, OJT is used in conjunction with off-the-job training. For example, KLM Royal Dutch Airlines uses classroom-based training to provide initial customer service training for new flight attendants. However, follow-up training is conducted on evaluation flights. Trainees are asked to demonstrate their service delivery skills on the evaluation flights in front of experienced flight attendants.[8] A study of best OJT practices in Great Britain found that OJT was much more likely to be successful when it was operated in a systematic fashion, when there was clear top management support, and when line managers were committed to it. Further, for complex jobs, OJT was more effective when classroom training, OJT, and computer-based training were used in combination.[9]

There are at least four identifiable OJT techniques, including job instruction training (JIT), job rotation, coaching, and mentoring. We will focus on JIT and job rotation now, and discuss coaching and mentoring in later chapters.

## JOB INSTRUCTION TRAINING (JIT)

**Job instruction training (JIT)** is defined as a sequence of instructional procedures used by the trainer to train employees while they work in their assigned job. It is a form of OJT. The content of a JIT program is distinguished by its simplicity. Table 6-2 details a simple four-step process that helps the trainer to prepare the worker, present the task, and allow practice time and follow-up. *Preparing the workers* is important because they need to know what to expect. Preparation may include providing employees with a training manual, handouts, or other job aids that can be used as references. *Presenting the task* should be carried out in such a way that the trainee understands and can replicate the task. Some trainers demonstrate the task before asking the trainee to repeat the process. *Practice time* is important for the trainee to master a particular set of skills. Finally, the trainer needs to conduct a follow-up as a way of ensuring that the trainee is making progress. During this follow-up session, the trainer should apply coaching techniques when appropriate.

For example, Cummins Engine Company combined the JIT-approach with the Japanese philosophy of continuous improvement, referred to as Kaizen, in a program the company called Just Do It training (JDIT). The JDIT approach begins with

**TABLE 6-2**                   **JOB INSTRUCTION TRAINING**

**Step 1: Prepare the Worker.**

a. Put trainee at ease.

b. Find out what trainee knows.

c. Motivate.

d. Set up the task.

**Step 2: Present the Task.**

a. Tell.

b. Show.

c. Explain.

d. Demonstrate.

**Step 3: Practice.**

a. Have trainee perform the task(s).

b. Have trainee explain the steps.

c. Give feedback on performance.

d. Reinforce correct behavior.

**Step 4: Follow up.**

a. Have trainee perform on his or her own.

b. Encourage questioning.

c. Check performance periodically.

d. Gradually taper off training.

SOURCE: From Wexley, K. N., & Latham, G. P. (2002). *Developing and training human resources in organizations*, 3e. Reprinted with permission of Pearson Education, Inc., Upper Saddle River, NJ.

instruction on basic principles and then moves to the job where a need for improvement has been identified. The improvement process follows five steps: (1) observe work processes in action and identify problems; (2) brainstorm possible improvements; (3) analyze each improvement option; (4) implement improvements; and (5) analyze results and make adjustments.[10] The role of the trainer in this approach is to guide the learners and help them to discover potential problems and find solutions on their own. The instructor can then provide feedback and reinforce learning.

The success of JIT depends on the ability of the trainer to adapt his or her own style to the training process. The trainer, particularly if this person is the trainee's coworker or supervisor, should have an opportunity to assess the trainee's needs before beginning the training. If the training material is too difficult or too easy, the OJT trainer should adjust the material or techniques to fit the needs of the trainee. Once the trainees have demonstrated that they can do the work, they should be allowed to work on their own. However, it is important for the trainer or supervisor to check back periodically to answer questions and make sure everything is going well. As Urbaniak puts it, "Above all, don't turn trainees loose and forget them."[11]

## JOB ROTATION

So far we have discussed techniques that are intended to develop job-related skills. **Job rotation** is similar in intent, but with this approach the trainee is generally expected to learn more by observing and doing than by receiving instruction. Rotation, as the term implies, involves a series of assignments to different positions or departments for a specified period. During this assignment, the trainee is supervised by a department employee, usually a supervisor, who is responsible for orienting, training, and evaluating the trainee. Throughout the training cycle, the trainee is expected to learn how each department functions, including some key roles, policies, and procedures. At the end of the cycle, the accumulated evaluations will be used to determine the preparedness of the trainee and if and where the person will be permanently assigned.

Job rotation is frequently used for first-level management training, particularly for new employees. When this technique is used, it is generally assumed that new managers need to develop a working knowledge of the organization before they can be successful managers. For example, the Tribune Company used formal job rotation programs for its information technology (IT) workers, with the goal of broadening their skills outside the IT area, thus preparing them for future promotions.[12] Job rotation has been used frequently as a means of career development for nurses as well.[13] A study of the Spanish chemical industry found that job rotation was positively related to measures of organizational learning.[14] Economists Sandra Black and Lisa Lynch argue that work practices such as job rotation help account for current increases in U.S. productivity.[15] A recent cover story in *HR Magazine* discussed how Human Resource professionals have often developed job rotation programs for finance, marketing, or operations professionals.[16] Yet, citing research data from Lawler, HR professionals have made little use of job rotation to develop themselves for higher level, "strategic" positions within their own organizations. Harvey Resnick of the Hay Group states, "It's akin to the shoemaker's children going barefoot."[17]

Two other forms of on-the-job training, coaching and mentoring, also involve one-on-one instruction. Coaching typically occurs between an employee and that person's supervisor and focuses on examining employee performance and taking actions to maintain effective performance and correct performance problems. In mentoring, a senior manager is paired with a more junior employee for the purpose of giving support, helping the employee learn the ropes, and preparing the employee for increasing responsibility. These techniques will be discussed in Chapters 10 and 12, respectively.

## CLASSROOM TRAINING APPROACHES

**Classroom training** approaches are conducted outside of the normal work setting. In this sense, a classroom can be any training space set away from the work site, such as the company cafeteria or a meeting room. Although many organizations capitalize on whatever usable space they have available to conduct training sessions, some larger organizations (including McDonald's, Motorola, Dunkin Donuts, and Pillsbury) maintain facilities that serve as freestanding training centers. These training centers are now increasingly referred to as corporate universities (McDonald's refers to its center as Hamburger U.), with curricula that include courses covering a wide range of skill and content areas. Dell Computer calls its area Dell Learning, to signify that it includes more than classroom training.

Conducting training away from the work setting has several advantages over on-the-job training. First, classroom settings permit the use of a variety of training techniques, such as video/DVD, lecture, discussion, role playing, and simulation. Second, the environment can be designed or controlled to minimize distractions and create a climate conducive to learning. Third, classroom settings can accommodate larger numbers of trainees than the typical on-the-job setting, allowing for more efficient delivery of training. On the other hand, two potential disadvantages of classroom methods, as a group, include increased costs (such as travel and the rental or purchase and maintenance of rooms and equipment) and dissimilarity to the job setting, making transfer of training more difficult.

Five primary categories of classroom training include:

1. lecture
2. discussion
3. audiovisual media
4. experiential methods
5. computer-based training (classroom-based)

## THE LECTURE APPROACH

The **lecture method** involves the oral presentation of information by a subject matter expert to a group of listeners. As we have noted, the lecture continues to be a popular training technique. One of the reasons the lecture method is so popular is that it is an efficient way of transmitting factual information to a large audience in a relatively short amount of time. When used in conjunction with visual aids, such as slides, charts, maps, and handouts, the lecture can be an effective way to facilitate the transfer of theories, concepts, procedures, and other factual material.

The lecture method has been widely criticized, particularly because it emphasizes one-way communication. It has been suggested that the lecture method perpetuates the traditional authority structure of organizations, thus promoting negative behavior (such as passivity and boredom), and it is poorly suited for facilitating transfer of training and individualizing training.[18] Similarly, although a skilled lecturer may effectively communicate conceptual knowledge to trainees who are prepared to receive it, the lecture has little value in facilitating attitudinal and behavioral changes.[19] Trainees must be motivated to learn because, when it is used alone, the lecture method does not elicit audience responses.

A related disadvantage of the lecture method is the lack of sharing of ideas among the trainees. Without dialogue, the trainees may not be able to put things into a common perspective that makes sense to them. Also, many people claim to dislike the lecture method. Training directors ranked the lecture method ninth out of nine training methods for acquisition of knowledge.[20] A separate survey reported only 17 percent of respondents (members of a regional ASTD chapter) believed the lecture was an effective training delivery method.[21]

Empirical research, however, does not support such a harsh judgment. For example, a meta-analysis found positive learning effects from the lecture method, both when used alone and when used in combination with other methods, such as discussion and role playing.[22] Role playing and lecture methods were found to be equally effective in a skills training course.[23] A comparison of dental education provided via lecture versus by means of an interactive multimedia courseware package found no significant differences in learning between the two approaches.[24] Finally, a meta-analysis of the effects of lecture, modeling, and active participation on the performance of older trainees found that all three methods had positive and statistically significant effects on learning and skill measures.[25] Could it be that people often don't like lectures, even though they can and do learn from them?

The results cited earlier suggest that further research is needed to identify the conditions under which the lecture method is effective as well as ways to improve its effectiveness.[26] At present, two points seem clear. First, interesting lectures promote greater learning than dull lectures. Trainers should make every effort to make their lectures as interesting as possible. Some experienced trainers have argued that younger workers (i.e., those under thirty) are especially likely to tune out lectures that they perceive to be uninteresting or irrelevant.[27] Second, there are advantages to supplementing the lecture with other methods (including discussion, video, and role playing), particularly when abstract or procedural material is to be presented. These combinations can increase two-way communication and facilitate greater interaction with the material.

## THE DISCUSSION METHOD

The **discussion method** involves the trainer in two-way communication with trainees, and the trainees in communication with each other. Because active participation is encouraged, the discussion method offers trainees an opportunity for feedback, clarification, and sharing points of view. Given this dynamic, the discussion technique can overcome some of the limitations of the straight lecture method. A common maxim for discussion facilitators is, "Never do for the group what it is doing for itself." However, the success of this method is dependent upon the ability of the trainer to initiate and manage class discussion by asking one or more of the following types of questions:

- *Direct questions* can be used to illustrate or produce a very narrow response (e.g., Who are the key players in this case?).
- *Reflective questions* can be used to mirror what someone else has said to make sure the message was received as intended (e.g., So are you saying that you think this manager failed to connect his actions to the goals and strategies of the organization?).

■ *Open-ended questions* can be used to challenge the trainees to increase their understanding of a specific topic (e.g., But if what this manager did was effective, why are there so many problems, as described at the end of the case?).

Managing discussion goes beyond questioning participants. The trainer must ensure that trainees are reinforced for their responses. The trainer must also act as a gatekeeper, giving everyone an opportunity to express their point of view and not letting the discussion be dominated by a few vocal participants. Managing discussion in large training classes (e.g., thirty or more trainees) can be difficult. Not only are the opportunities for an individual to participate reduced in a large group, some participants may feel intimidated and be reluctant to get involved. Dividing a large class into smaller discussion groups, which can then share their ideas with other groups, can increase the opportunity for discussion.

There are several limitations of the discussion method. First, a skilled facilitator is needed to manage the discussion process. Skill in facilitating a discussion is not something that one acquires quickly; skilled facilitators have generally practiced extensively and prepared thoroughly before leading a discussion. Second, sufficient time must be available for meaningful discussion to take place. Third, trainees need to have a common reference point for meaningful discussion to occur. Assigning reading material before the discussion session can help overcome this obstacle.

On balance, most trainers and trainees find a well-done discussion to be more interesting and energizing than a traditional lecture. Of course, adequate time, motivation, and resources must be available for this method to work effectively, but then, this is true of any method of delivering training.[28]

## AUDIOVISUAL MEDIA

Both the lecture and discussion methods are limited in their ability to adequately portray dynamic and complex events. **Audiovisual methods** take advantage of various media to illustrate or demonstrate the training material. Audiovisual media can bring complex events to life by showing and describing details that are often difficult to communicate in other ways. For purposes of this chapter, we categorize audiovisual methods into three groups: static media, dynamic media, and telecommunications.[29]

*STATIC MEDIA.* **Static media** typically involve fixed illustrations that use both words and images. This can include printed materials, slides, and overhead transparencies. *Printed materials*, such as handouts, charts, guides, reference books, and textbooks, allow trainees to keep the material, referring to it before, during, and after the training session (some issues involved in selecting and preparing printed materials were discussed in Chapter 5). *Slides* are often used in ways similar to printed materials, but by projecting a computer- or camera-generated image onto a screen, they can serve as a common focus for discussion. Slides can also be synchronized with audiotapes to form a standardized presentation. Such a setup can be delivered without using a skilled trainer; at a minimum, someone is needed to operate and monitor the equipment (slide projector and tape player). *Overhead* *transparencies* also allow the trainer to project printed materials or other images on a screen. Transparencies can be more flexible than slides because the trainer can also write on the transparency sheets, turning the screen into a sort of chalkboard. Table 6-3 provides some guidelines for the effective use of computer slides and transparencies to improve training presentations.

**TABLE 6-3**

## GUIDELINES FOR PRESENTATION SLIDES AND OVERHEAD TRANSPARENCIES

### Preparation

1. Present one major idea or concept on each slide or transparency.
2. Use a limited number of key words or phrases (e.g., fewer than six words per line and six lines per slide).
3. Make sure letters and graphics are large and legible (can they read it in the back of the room?).
4. Are your slides well designed?
5. Are your slides interesting? Use color, different type styles, graphics, and pictures (especially for visual learners).
6. Are your slides appropriate for the subject?
7. Do your slides add to the presentation?
8. Is current technology being appropriately utilized when making and using the slides?
9. If using Microsoft® PowerPoint® (or similar software), do the extras (sound, music, clip art, video clips, special graphics) add or detract from the presentation?
10. Ensure that the audiovisual or computer equipment is set up and used appropriately.

### Presentation

11. Have a clear outline for your presentation.
12. Look at the audience, not at the screen.
13. Ensure lighting and seating are appropriate for all to see both the presenter and the screen.
14. Emphasize information by pointing; however, do not point at the screen — point on the transparency, or use a mouse pointer on computer slides.
15. Avoid reading bullet points exactly as they appear on the slide or transparency.
16. Control the pace by progressive disclosure, for example, a cardboard sheet underneath a transparency allows you to see the whole transparency, yet only reveal the points to the audience as you are ready to discuss them.
17. Cover the projector (or make it blank) to emphasize an important verbal point.
18. Use two projectors for increased effect (e.g., when using multiple media).
19. Obtain group involvement by writing on a white board, blank transparency, or flip chart.

SOURCES: From Abram, S. (2004). PowerPoint: Devil in a red dress. *Information Outlook, 8*(3), March, 27–28; Eyre, M. (2000). The presenter's toolkit. *Management, 47*(6), July, 11–12; Beaver, H. D. (2000). Visual aids: How much is too much? *ABA Banking Journal, 92*(6), June, 80; Kupsch, J., & Graves, P. R. (1993). *How to create high impact business presentations.* Lincolnwood, IL: NTC Business Books; Ellis, S. K. (1988). How to survive a training assignment. Reading, MA: Addison-Wesley; Kearsley, G. (1984). *Training and technology* (p. 19). Reading, MA: Addison-Wesley.

The use of computer-generated slides (such as Microsoft® PowerPoint® presentations) has increased dramatically in recent years. Some go so far as to argue that "the ability to prepare a slide presentation has become an indispensable corporate survival skill."[30] However, major efforts to produce fancier and more elaborate slide presentations has also led to a backlash. For example, in April 2000, General Hugh Shelton, chairman of the U.S. Joint Chiefs of Staff, sent out an order to all U.S. military bases stating that all briefings should stick to the point and avoid unnecessary "bells and whistles" in their PowerPoint® presentations.[31] It seems that all the e-mailed briefings were using so much of the military's computer bandwidth that they were slowing down more critical communications between headquarters and the field! Hence, in Table 6-3, we stress (in point 9) that every aspect of a computer-generated slide show should add value to rather than detract from the overall presentation.[32] This is all the more important as such presentations are increasingly being given over the Internet (see the following section).[33]

*DYNAMIC MEDIA.* Techniques that present dynamic sequences of events are considered **dynamic media** and include compact discs (CDs), DVDs, diskettes, videotape, film, and audiocassettes. As of 2003, the category of CD-ROM/DVD/Diskettes has become the most commonly used form of dynamic media for training. A *Training* magazine survey found the following usage rates for various dynamic media: CD-ROM/DVD/diskettes (55 percent), videotapes (52 percent), teleconferencing (24 percent), videoconferencing (23 percent), satellite/broadcast TV (12 percent), and audiocassettes (4 percent).[34] Organizations as diverse as Taco Bell and New England Mutual Insurance are taking advantage of the ease with which videotaped training programs can be sent to employees around the country. There are literally thousands of commercially produced films, videos, and DVDs available to HRD professionals through film libraries, professional societies, and retail outlets. Many training vendors emphasize the sale or rental of training DVDs and videos. In addition, many organizations are able to produce their own videos at relatively low cost. For example, Southwest Airlines produced a nine-minute rap music video that introduces employees to work procedures and company operations, while at the same time conveying the team spirit and fun-oriented culture that typifies the company. The Travelers Insurance Company maintains a $20 million education center that produces videos and transmits satellite broadcasts of training programs throughout the company.[35] Entire training programs can be self-contained within a single film or video presentation.

An effective DVD or video takes advantage of the capabilities of the medium rather than simply reproducing a printed or static presentation. Unfortunately, many videos are indeed little more than reproductions of traditional lectures. Producing an effective training video is not as simple as owning the equipment and having the desire to be "the company's Steven Spielberg." Film and video development involves many activities, including design (like storyboarding), preproduction (including scheduling, casting, crew and equipment selection, prop and set preparation), shooting the film or video, postproduction (including editing and sound mixing), and distribution.[36] The inexperienced HRD professional would be wise to consult a trained professional to produce (or assist in producing) company films and videos.

Some HRD professionals argue that the baby boomers and later generations, who grew up watching films and television, may actually prefer this form of presentation. Yet, one potential limitation of this technique is that trainers may rely too much on the film or video, and focus too little on the training content. Such reliance can lead to complacency among trainees who view the films and videos as entertainment, rather than as opportunities to learn.

Videotape is also used as a visual aid for behavior modeling training by recording role plays and then asking group members to critique their experience while they watch the video. For example, a sales training program may include a videotaping segment, so that trainees can observe themselves performing an in-class exercise on how to close a sale. This approach also provides an opportunity for the trainer to reinforce desired behaviors. One potential limitation of this technique is that trainees may feel intimidated by the camera and may even resent the process. To offset this limitation, the trainer must be supportive and create a "safe" environment during the program.

TELECOMMUNICATIONS. The transmission of training programs to different locations via **telecommunications** has become increasingly feasible via satellite, cable, and fiberoptic networks. Linking several locations for instructional and conference purposes, known as *instructional television (ITV)*, or interactive television, allows entire courses to be televised. For example, colleges and universities are increasingly offering both bachelor's and master's degrees "delivered entirely by cable television and satellite."[37] The National Technological University (NTU) network offers interactive, satellite-transmitted continuing-education courses to professionals such as engineers and computer scientists in companies like IBM, General Electric, and Hewlett-Packard.[38] In 2002, NTU was purchased by Sylvan Learning Systems and is now part of its Laureate Education unit.[39]

Telecommunication technology also allows organizations to conduct conferences between remote locations. This technique, known as *teleconferencing*, or **videoconferencing,** is being used by organizations such as JCPenney, IBM, AT&T, Domino's Pizza, and Texas Instruments. JCPenney also sells this service to other organizations.[40] Colleges and universities are also taking advantage of teleconferencing to benefit both their students and corporate clients. Teleconferencing helps organizations to reduce trainer, travel, and facility costs, and it increases the availability of training to remote locations.[41] It is estimated that about 23 percent of organizations use video teleconferencing.[42] The North Carolina Office of Day Care Services conducted a study comparing the average cost of traditional classroom training with teleconferencing. It concluded that although teleconferencing cost more for curriculum and materials development, traditional classroom training cost more for trainer, travel, and delivery, but both methods are considered equally effective.[43] One issue that merits further research concerns the extent to which teleconferencing affects the interaction between the trainer and trainees.[44]

Computer conferencing is not as widely used as other training techniques. However, given the availability of personal computers linked into company intranets and public networks such as the Internet, this has changed dramatically since the mid-1990s (see our later discussion on intranet training). Also, whereas organizations commonly use communication networks primarily for business operations, they have an unlimited potential as training vehicles. It has been suggested that computer networks should be used to train adults nationwide, although the start-up cost of hardware and the low level of reading and writing skills may keep some low-income and other potential learners from benefiting from such a system.[45] The rapidly decreasing cost of videoconferencing systems has made this technology increasingly available, even to small- and medium-sized organizations.[46] For example, FedEx Kinko's has videoconferencing facilities available at over 150 U.S. locations, with costs as low as $225 per hour.[47]

Studies have consistently shown that audiovisual training methods like film, television, and videoconferencing are as effective, if not more effective, than other methods (primarily lecture).[48] Given the many choices available, HRD professionals must select the most appropriate audiovisual method for each particular HRD program. Kearsley made five recommendations concerning media selection:

1. Identify the media attributes required by the conditions, performance, or standards of each instructional objective.

2. Identify student characteristics that suggest or preclude particular media.

3. Identify characteristics of the learning environment that favor or preclude particular media.

4. Identify practical considerations that may determine which media are feasible.

5. Identify economic or organizational factors that may determine which media are feasible.[49]

This list includes both learning-related and practical considerations. Rothwell and Kazanas pose several further questions that can guide the proper selection of audiovisual methods:

1. How much time is available to plan and test instruction?

2. What equipment is available to use in designing or delivering instruction, or in doing both?

3. For what media can instructional designers prepare instruction? Do staff skills lend themselves to some media better than others?

4. How much is an organization willing to spend on the design and development of instruction?[50]

Readers who want to know more about these various audiovisual methods and how to select among them would do well to consult other sources.[51]

## EXPERIENTIAL METHODS

So far, we have discussed training methods that focus primarily on presentation of training content. In many of these methods, such as video and lecture, the learner is generally assumed to be a passive (or somewhat passive) recipient of information. Experiential learning advocates, such as David Kolb, argue that effective learning requires active engagement on the part of the learner. Keys and Wolfe summarize this point of view as follows:

> Experientialists believe that effective learning is an active experience that challenges the skills, knowledge, and beliefs of participants. This is accomplished by creating a contrived, yet realistic, environment that is both challenging and psychologically safe for the participant to investigate and to employ new concepts, skills, and behaviors. Experiential instructors recognize that learners bring to the learning environment a set of accumulated knowledge and learning methods that are simultaneously functional and/or dysfunctional depending on the learning situation. (p. 214)[52]

Experiential training methods commonly used in organizations include case studies, games and simulations, role playing, and behavior modeling. These methods fall more toward the exploratory side of the learning continuum presented in Figure 6-2. Each of these methods is described in the following sections.

*THE CASE STUDY METHOD.* The **case study method** helps trainees learn analytical and problem-solving skills by presenting a story (called a case) about people in an organization who are facing a problem or decision. Cases may be based on actual events involving real people in an organization, or they can be fictional. Case studies are typically included in college textbooks and courses in management, public administration, law, sociology, and similar subjects. They are increasingly available in video, DVD, and other media formats and not just on paper.

Although cases vary in complexity and detail, trainees should be given enough information to analyze the situation and recommend their own solutions. In solving the problem, trainees are generally required to use a rational problem-solving process that includes:

1. restating important facts
2. drawing inferences from the facts
3. stating the problem or problems
4. developing alternative solutions and then stating the consequences of each
5. determining and supporting a course of action

Cases can be studied by individuals or small groups, and the completed analysis and solutions are typically presented by the trainees to the rest of the class. According to a 2003 survey in *Training* magazine, the case study method is used in about 40 percent of organizations for employee and management training.[53]

Proponents of the case study method argue that this form of problem solving within a management setting offers illustrations of the concepts students are expected to learn and use, improves communication skills, and facilitates the linkage between theory and practice.[54] Proponents also claim that cases allow students to discuss, share, and debate the merits of different inferences, problems, and alternative courses of action. Such insight can help students to develop better analytical skills and improve their ability to integrate new information.[55]

The case study method also has vigorous critics who argue that it can cause groupthink, focuses too much on the past, limits the teaching role of the trainer, reduces the learner's ability to draw generalizations, reinforces passivity on the part of the learner, and promotes the quantity of interaction among students at the expense of the quality of interaction.[56] Andrews and Noel claim that cases often lack realistic complexity and a sense of immediacy, and inhibit development of the ability to collect and distill information.[57] In addition, trainees may get caught up in the details of the situation, at the expense of focusing on the larger issues and concepts they are trying to learn.

Argyris argues that case studies can undermine the learning process by not leading trainees to question assumptions and positions taken, and that the case study method may encourage trainees to be dependent on the instructor or facilitator.[58] He feels that trainers should create an atmosphere in which trainees are free to confront themselves and each other without defensiveness, to allow examination of whether the ideas they claim they believe in are consistent with their actions. Berger countered these criticisms by suggesting that Argyris did not adequately define the case method and that methodological flaws undermined his study.[59]

Although there appears to be plenty of rhetoric regarding the advantages and disadvantages of the case study method, there is not a large amount of empirical evaluation studies to help us determine the facts.[60] The few studies that do exist offer no clear trend from which to draw conclusions.

To overcome these limitations, the trainer should make expectations clear and provide guidance when needed. In addition, the trainer must effectively guide the discussion portion of the case study to ensure trainees have an opportunity to explore differing assumptions and positions they have taken and the rationale for what constitutes effective responses to the case. The point in discussing cases is not necessarily to find the "right" solution, but to be able to provide a reasoned and logical rationale for developing a course of action. Variations in the case method have also been proposed.[61] One such variation, called a living case, has trainees analyze a problem they and their organization are currently facing.[62]

Osigweh encourages potential users of the case study method to match factors such as:

- specific instructional objectives
- objectives of the case approach
- attributes of the particular incident or case (i.e., its content)
- characteristics of the learner
- instructional timing
- general prevailing environment (class size, course level, etc.)
- the teacher's own personal and instructional characteristics[63]

*BUSINESS GAMES AND SIMULATIONS.* Like the case method, **business games** are intended to develop or refine problem-solving and decision-making skills. However, this technique tends to focus primarily on business management decisions (such as maximizing profits). It is estimated that 25 percent of organizations use non-computer-based games or simulations, with 10 percent using computer-based games or simulations.[64]

One example is a business game titled Looking Glass, Inc., developed by the Center for Creative Leadership.[65] The game requires participants to role play decision makers in a fictitious glass manufacturing company and use realistic organizational data to make a variety of decisions. The three-day Looking Glass training program includes one day each for performing the simulation (in which participants operate the company), giving feedback, and practicing the skills emphasized during the feedback sessions.[66] Martin Marietta Inc. has used Looking Glass as a diagnostic and feedback tool in its executive development program.[67] The developers of Looking Glass have reported research that shows the activities of trainees in the simulation are similar to those of managers in the field,[68] and suggests that the program is effective, at least in the short term.[69]

Business games, particularly computer simulations of organizations and industries, are widely used in business schools. A review of sixty-one studies reported support for the effectiveness of business games in strategic management courses. Whether these results can be generalized to organizational settings remains an open question.[70]

Another type of simulation used in management development programs and assessment centers is the **in-basket exercise.** The goal of this technique is to assess the trainee's ability to establish priorities, plan, gather relevant information, and make decisions. The sequence of events involved in an in-basket exercise typically includes the following:

1. The trainees are told that they have been promoted to a management position that was suddenly vacated. They are given background information about the organization including personnel, relationships, policies, and union contracts.

2. The trainees then receive the contents of the manager's in-basket. This material includes documents such as telephone messages, notes, memos, letters, and reports.

3. The trainees are then asked to read, organize, prioritize, and make decisions regarding the issues presented by the in-basket material.

4. At the end of the decision period, the trainees' decisions are then evaluated by trained scorers.

The object of this technique is to force trainees to make decisions in the allotted time period. Because there is usually insufficient time to read each document and respond, the trainees must make quick and accurate decisions. The trainees are evaluated not only on the quality of their decisions but also on their ability to prioritize and to deal effectively with all the critical documents. Research on the in-basket technique has shown it to be successful in improving trainee effectiveness,[71] as well as in predicting future managerial effectiveness, either alone or in combination with other devices.[72]

One limitation of business games and simulations is that although they can be quite complex, these techniques often lack the realistic complexity and information present in real organizations. Factors such as organizational history and politics, social pressures, the risks and consequences of alternatives, and the organization's culture are difficult to replicate in a simulation.[73] This may undermine the extent to which what is learned in the game or simulation will transfer back to the job.

In addition, many games and simulations emphasize the use of quantitative analysis in making business decisions and underplay the importance of interpersonal issues in managerial effectiveness. It has also been argued that the popularity of simulation techniques is based more on circumstantial evidence than on rigorous evaluative research,[74] but because simulations are used in conjunction with other techniques, isolating their effect in research has been difficult.[75]

*ROLE PLAYING.* A popular training technique, **role playing** is reportedly used by 35 percent of organizations.[76] In the role-playing technique, trainees are presented with an organizational situation, assigned a role or character in the situation, and asked to act out the role with one or more other trainees. The role play should offer trainees an opportunity for self-discovery and learning. For example, a management development program could include a role-play situation emphasizing interpersonal conflict between a manager and a subordinate. Management trainees would have an opportunity to role-play both the manager and the subordinate role, in order to better understand some of the dynamics of this situation, as well as practice interpersonal skills. The value of this technique is enhanced by conducting a feedback session following the role play, in which trainees and the trainer critique the role player's performance. In many organizations, the role episode is videotaped, as discussed earlier, which allows for better feedback and self-observation.

Although self-discovery and opportunity to practice interpersonal skills are outcomes of role playing, this method does have some limitations. First, as discussed earlier, some trainees may feel intimidated by having to act out a character (and possibly be videotaped doing so). Trainers should take sufficient time in introducing the exercise, explaining the process in detail, and most of all, emphasizing how participation will help each trainee to better understand and apply different interpersonal skills.

A second limitation of the technique is the extent to which trainees are able to transfer this learning to their jobs. Some trainees may perceive role playing as artificial or as fun and games, but not as a legitimate learning tool. Trainees who do not take this technique seriously may interfere with other trainees' learning. The trainer must manage the process effectively and keep reinforcing the importance of participation.

*BEHAVIOR MODELING.* Social learning theory (see Chapter 2) suggests that many of our behavioral patterns are learned from observing others. This theory forms the basis for **behavior modeling.** In organizations, employees learn all kinds of behaviors (some work related and some not), from observing supervisors, managers, union leaders, and coworkers who serve as role models. Under normal conditions, role models can have a tremendous influence on individual behavior.

In this technique, trainees observe a model performing a target behavior correctly (usually on a video or DVD). This is followed by a discussion of the key components of the behavior, practicing the target behavior through role playing, and receiving feedback and reinforcement for the behavior they demonstrate. Behavior modeling is widely used for interpersonal skill training and is a common component of many management training programs.

Research has shown behavior modeling to be an effective training technique. It is described in greater detail in our discussion of management development (Chapter 12).[77]

*OUTDOOR EDUCATION.* Outdoor-based education, such as ropes courses, have generated considerable interest from employers and employees alike, with estimates of over $100 million spent annually on such efforts.[78] This can include work teams being involved with outdoor games, orienteering, or rafting. Frequently, such programs include either low ropes or high ropes elements. A low ropes course typically has limited physical risks, whereas high ropes courses typically have higher perceived risks. Low ropes courses can also be conducted indoors (for an example of such a program, refer to Figure 5-3, the example of a completed lesson plan). Both types of courses usually have a strong focus on group problem solving and team building. Though there is evidence that such courses can impact work team functioning and performance, overall, the empirical results to date have been mixed.[79] Those considering use of such programs should make sure that the programs match the objectives set out for training, and that follow-up evaluation is conducted. A recent article by Scott Williams and colleagues provides helpful guidance concerning how multiple outcomes can be measured to evaluate the success of outdoor training.[80] As Mark Weaver has stated, "Too often, the fun, engaging methodology has outweighed the transfer to workplace issues."[81] Given the current popularity of outdoor education, HRD professionals should ensure that proper assessment and evaluation are included in any such program that is offered.

## SELF-PACED/COMPUTER-BASED TRAINING MEDIA AND METHODS

As mentioned, **computer-based training (CBT)** can be conducted in either a classroom or an individual, self-paced format. Indeed, with the increased availability of networked computer labs, there can be an almost limitless interplay between instructor-led and individual-based computer training.[82] As such, we discuss computer-based training both as one of the five approaches to classroom training, as well as a major example of current self-paced training approaches. Before the 1980s, most self-paced training was paper based. For example, Fred Fiedler and colleagues developed culture assimilator training for Americans traveling to particular countries (such as India or Greece). Trainees read various vignettes about another culture, and then made choices concerning why they thought a particular action had been taken. Each response directed the trainee to a particular page in the workbook.[83]

Computers have had an enormous impact on the delivery of training in organizations.[84] Today, it is estimated that 55 percent of organizations use computer-based training (CBT) via CD-ROM in their training programs, with other multimedia-based efforts certainly pushing the number of computer-based training approaches much higher than this.[85] One of the biggest influences on the growth of CBT was the advent of microcomputers and the rapid increase in their capabilities. In the early days of CBT, one had to have access to terminals connected to a mainframe computer and software that was time-sharing with other business computing needs.[86] PCs are now present in virtually all organizations, and important advances in hardware and software are occurring at a dizzying pace.

The primary advantage CBT has over other methods of training is its interactivity.[87] The interaction between the learner and the computer in many CBT programs mirrors the one-on-one relationship between student and tutor: questions and responses can go back and forth, resulting in immediate feedback. Advanced forms of CBT, like intelligent computer-aided instruction, can even analyze the pattern of a student's responses and errors, draw conclusions, and tailor the lesson the learner receives accordingly. An additional advantage of technology-based training is that it is well suited to "on-demand learners," that is, trainees who need (and increasingly demand) greater control over when and how training is delivered.[88] Three approaches to CBT include computer-aided instruction (CAI), intranet training, and intelligent computer-assisted instruction (ICAI).

*COMPUTER-AIDED INSTRUCTION.* **Computer-aided instruction (CAI)** programs can range from electronic workbooks, using the drill-and-practice approach, to compact disc read-only memory (CD-ROM) presentations of a traditional training program. CAI software packages are available at relatively low cost for a wide range of material, from teaching basic skills such as reading and typing, to highly technical scientific, engineering, and machine maintenance topics. CAI programs are available not only as part of business software programs (like the tutorial programs that come with such word-processing packages as Microsoft® Word), but also through retail outlets, and some have become software bestsellers. Some organizations custom design software from scratch or modify existing programs to meet their unique needs. For example, Manpower's SKILLWARE program was originally developed by the company (the largest U.S. agency for temporary office workers) but is also used, either as is or with modifications, by some of Manpower's clients, including Xerox and Miller Brewing Company.[89]

Multimedia programs offer an improvement over the more traditional CAI programs because they provide more appealing visual and audio content. The multimedia platform can bring the course to life and make the learning experience more enjoyable. Because audio and video files are very large, most multimedia courses are stored and distributed on a CD-ROM disk. Many companies have replaced instructor-led courses with CD-ROMs. For example, AT&T replaced its three-day new-employee orientation program with a CD-ROM package that explains how the company is organized, the role and mission of each department, and how departments relate to each other.[90]

There are several advantages to CAI as compared to other training methods and techniques, especially considering the *interactive* nature of CAI. Based on the trainee's responses, the computer will present various levels of material until the trainee reaches mastery. A second advantage is CAI's *self-pacing* feature that allows trainees to control the speed of instruction and makes them self-sufficient learners.[91] A third advantage is the *logistics* of CAI that make it more accessible through an internal distribution system or downloaded from a central computer or over the Internet to remote sites to eliminate travel and per diem costs.[92] Finally,

CAI offers an *instructional management and reporting system* that automatically "tracks student progress and the allocation and use of instructional resources, including terminals, instructors, and classrooms."[93]

The effectiveness of CAI, like other training methods and techniques, can be measured by changes in productivity and profits. Reinhart reported that a four-hour CAI program, which trained sales representatives on selling a piece of computer software, resulted in additional revenues of $4.6 million for Xerox.[94] Another measure of effectiveness is a cost-benefit analysis that compares CAI to other techniques. A financial institution in New York, which was paying trainees while they waited for available classroom training programs, switched to CAI and realized enough savings to offset the cost of developing the CAI program.[95] Andersen Consulting realized significant savings in facilities, travel, and payroll costs when it replaced a required six-week instructor-led training program on basic business practices with a CD-ROM program.[96] Research has also shown that trainees using CAI take less time to learn the same amount of material as conventional methods, with no significant difference in test scores.[97] On the other hand, critics worry about the loss of personal interaction between a human trainer and the learner, and suggest that reliance on CBT may restrain the development of interpersonal skills.[98]

CD-ROMs can be purchased off the shelf for less than $100, but they are not particularly effective for material that has to be tailored to an organization's needs. An alternative to purchasing the program is to produce one in-house. Munger reported that it takes an average of about two to ten hours of development time to produce each hour of instruction at an average cost of $5,000 per hour of instruction.[99]

CAI may not always be the most appropriate training method. For instance, in training situations that emphasize interpersonal skill building, other techniques (like role playing) may be preferred. Also, traditional training methods might be more suitable for unmotivated trainees who may find it difficult to complete a CAI program without the assistance of a trainer.

*INTERNET- AND INTRANET-BASED TRAINING.* The Internet remains one of the fastest growing technological phenomena the world has ever seen. Today, tens of millions of computers are connected to one another via modems, telephone and cable lines, superconducting (ISDN) transmission lines, and the Internet.[100] **Intranets** are computer networks that use Internet and World Wide Web technology, software tools, and protocols for finding, managing, creating, and distributing information within one organization.[101] A 2000 survey found that 61 percent of U.S. workers said they would prefer to receive training via computers, the Internet, or television, yet only 26 percent said they actually received training in this manner.[102] Similarly, in the *2003 State of the Industry Report* published by ASTD, only 15 percent of training is currently being delivered using learning technologies (e.g., CBT, CD-ROM, and intranets).[103] Much technology-based training today is referred to as e-learning, for electronic learning, and most of this makes use of Internet or intranet technology and systems.[104] There is currently a growing body of research on web-based instruction.[105] Some recommended design principles for developing e-learning materials are provided in Table 6-4.

| TABLE 6-4 | DESIGN PRINCIPLES FOR E-LEARNING MATERIALS |

1. Select a realistic or authentic problem/scenario for the class or lesson. Generate questions for the scenario that students must answer by being as close as possible to a real situation.
2. Use as many different physical senses as possible (i.e., a rich learning environment) to accommodate different learning styles, preferences, and patterns.
3. Provide the simplest possible initial instructions to give learners basic skills to solve the problem or address the scenario.
4. Encourage learners to accomplish a simple yet complete task in the shortest possible period. Gradually increase the difficulty level for subsequent tasks.
5. When designing the printed or "flat" instructions (e.g., on the web page), if students have difficulty finding "where they are" from a verbal description alone, add related graphical icons and appropriate screen captures.
6. Identify where in the lesson learners tend to have problems, and then design and position anticipatory feedback near the spots where these problems tend to occur.
7. For learners who like to try new steps (exploratory learning), lessons should be flexible. However, for those who do not like to explore new things, more structured lessons or examples should be provided (guided learning). To accommodate different combinations of these preferences, both approaches should be coherently designed.

SOURCE: L. R. Yin (2004). Design principles for E-learning materials. Accessed September 25, 2004, from http://facstaff.uww.edu/yinl/elearn.html. See also http://ctl.sdsu.edu/effect_prac.htm for explanation of the instructional theories and concepts.

Personal computers with a TCP/IP networking protocol make it possible for individuals with different operating systems (such as Windows, Mac, and the various UNIX-based OSs), to communicate with each other, access information, transmit data, and download data. Current technology also creates a number of safeguards that can limit access to information and ensure privacy. Safeguards include firewalls, encryption, and passwords. Firewalls are "hardware or software that sit between the Internet and your company's private network to form a barrier between your organization and the outside world . . . and which keeps track of everyone who tries to access your site."[106] Encryption capability allows individuals to transmit messages through a deciphering mechanism that encodes data when transmitted and then decodes at the destination.

**Intranet-based training (IBT)** uses internal computer networks for training purposes.[107] Through their organization's intranet, HRD professionals can communicate with learners; conduct needs assessment and other administrative tasks; transmit course materials, training documents, and multimedia programs; and administer tests at any time and throughout the organization, whether an employee is in the United States or located overseas.[108] IBT is an especially powerful delivery system for international organizations that are spread out across the globe. IBT has most of the features of a multimedia CD-ROM program, plus the capability for users to communicate quickly. With current advances in real-time multimedia technology (e.g., Java, Shockware, and Virtual Reality Modeling Language), IBT is now fully interactive with sound, video, and 3-D imaging, and will compete with disk-based media like CD-ROMs as a primary means of providing training via technology. Companies like Ernst & Young rely heavily on IBT for distributing and updating their computer-based training.[109]

An innovative development with technology-based training was the development in 1996 of the LearnShare consortium. LearnShare, based in Toledo, Ohio, originally consisted of seventeen noncompeting organizations, including Owens Corning, 3M, General Motors, Motorola, Northwest Airlines, and Levi Strauss. These organizations agreed to share some of their existing training materials with one another, with a particular focus on building up their online training course offerings. In 1999, 103 programs were available for use by LearnShare member organizations.[110] In September 2004, the consortium included thirty-two member organizations employing over 2.5 million people.[111] This remains an intriguing model of collaborative online learning.

There are a number of limitations to IBT. Given the multimedia format, which uses large video and audio files, the primary limitation to date has been the network bandwidth — the size of a network's transmittal capacity.[112] However, with the rapid advances in technology (greater bandwidth, and improved abilities to compress data), this limitation is increasingly being overcome. Another limitation has been the use of multiple, potentially incompatible browser software configurations that determined which media types and HyperText Markup Language (HTML) format options were available.[113] Further, different authoring packages (i.e., the programs used to create the training content) have often been incompatible with one another. These limitations are also being overcome, as organizations adopt standard browser software packages, such as Microsoft® Internet Explorer or Netscape Communicator, which are capable of accessing format options and multimedia. Further, Microsoft Corporation developed a Learning Resource Interchange Toolkit that uses Extensible Markup Language, or XML. This software has the potential to serve as a universally accepted programming tool that would allow organizations to retrieve and use information from the Internet, regardless of what authoring package was used to create it.[114]

On the practical side, online learning has been criticized for pushing the time for learning to the employee's nonwork or off time. That is, the proposed benefit of "anytime, anywhere" learning can in fact mean that trainees are expected to do the training on their own, and often without compensation.[115] Also, many trainees find it difficult to complete self-paced training. This led to an ASTD/MASIE Center study of reasons why some trainees abandon technology-based training after only a few sessions.[116]

*INTELLIGENT COMPUTER-ASSISTED INSTRUCTION.* **Intelligent computer-assisted instruction (ICAI)** goes beyond CAI in terms of flexibility and the ability to qualitatively evaluate learner performance. Whereas a typical CAI program may allow the learner to select from among several levels of presentation (novice, intermediate, etc.), an ICAI program is able to discern the learner's capability from the learner's response patterns and by analyzing the learner's errors. The goal of ICAI systems is to provide learners with an electronic teacher's assistant that can

> patiently offer advice to individual learners, encourage learner practice and stimulate learners' curiosity through experimentation. This would potentially make the teacher more available for more creative endeavors, or for helping learners to overcome subtle or difficult problems beyond the capability of ICAI.[117]

Although the availability of ICAI programs is limited compared to that of CAI, the potential for ICAI is enormous. For example, DIAGNOSER is an Internet-based quiz program designed for the State of Washington. It allows high school physics students to take quizzes online and receive guided feedback concerning their answers while taking the quiz.[118] Other examples of ICAI programs are the LISP computer language tutor from Carnegie-Mellon University and the U.S. Navy's STEAMER program, which allows students to learn to operate and repair a ship's complex steam propulsion system.[119] Expert systems, like Campbell Soup's cooker maintenance program ALDO, which capture the knowledge and experience of experts in a particular field or content area, are also considered ICAI programs.

ICAI programs are based on advances in artificial intelligence, which involves "engineering some aspects of the human thought process" into a computer.[120] Artificial intelligence research is uncovering ways to improve ICAI programs' capability to use natural language to interact with the learner and to understand the learner (by tracking learner responses and learning from them). Given the rate of progress in computer hardware, software, artificial intelligence, and knowledge engineering (designing and organizing information and finding effective ways to present it), it would not be surprising to see ICAI programs become common in training and educational programs in the not-too-distant future.

## SOME FINAL ISSUES CONCERNING TRAINING PROGRAM IMPLEMENTATION

So, how should the choice of which method or methods to use to deliver training be made? Trainers should make this decision while simultaneously considering the objectives to be achieved, the resources available, and trainee characteristics and expertise (see Chapters 3 through 5). Although trends are clearly moving strongly in the direction of technology-based training, this may not be the best solution for every training situation. In this regard, we present to you an interesting response to the "e-learning bandwagon" (see the boxed insert nearby). Further, there is increasing discussion of **blended learning,** which is some combination of traditional (classroom based) and technology-enhanced training.[121] This has enormous implications for trainers and trainees alike, but holds considerable promise for providing advantages to both trainees and organizations beyond what can be obtained using any single delivery method by itself.[122]

## Long Live C-Learning

Recent surveys and indicators all point to the rapid and continuing growth of technology-based training. Such training can be more individualized than group- or classroom-based training, and is often touted as cheaper, given the reduced needs for trainees to travel to the training site, or even to be away from their workplace. However, as we have already pointed out, classroom training remains the dominant form of instructional delivery. Consultant James Farrell argues that there are, in fact, good reasons why classroom training (c-learning) remains popular. Face-to-face instruction has the greatest capacity for "information richness." Information richness has to do with the types of cues that are sent to the receiver of information, for example, when a trainee has the ability to observe the trainer's body language, voice inflection, and nonverbal cues, this can increase the accuracy of the communication that is received. As one moves away from face-to-face communication, such as with distance learning, computer-based learning, video- and print-based instruction, there is less capacity for rich communication. This may be fine for situations where the knowledge or skills to be taught are relatively straightforward. However, when the skills or procedures to be taught are completely new or different from what has been done in the past, these more complex situations may not be well suited for technology-based learning.

Farrell presents the following as a humorous (if extreme) example of where distance learning may not be ideal for attaining certain training objectives:

> You're in a hospital emergency room, and a nurse says you need immediate brain surgery. Two physicians are available, and you must choose. One has undergone traditional one-on-one training with an experienced surgeon. The other has been trained trough the hospital's revolutionary new distance learning program for brain surgeons, which included the completion of a 12-step CD-ROM course. Which surgeon do you want to operate on you? (p. 44).

Farrell argues that it is important to look at the information processing demands placed on learners. When such demands are high, more face-to-face (or classroom) interaction is likely going to be necessary. Although the newer learning technologies can have advantages concerning speed, flexibility, and cost, HRD professionals must make sure that they are appropriate for the given training situation. "Despite the rise in e-learning," Farrell concludes, "it appears that classroom training is here to stay" (p. 46). What do you think? How does this fit with the discussion of Figure 6-2 at the start of the chapter?

SOURCE: Farrell, J. N. (2000). Long live C-learning. *Training & Development*, 54(9), September, 43–46.

The primary responsibility for implementing the training program lies, of course, with the trainer. In Chapter 5, we discussed the preparation of training objectives and the lesson plan, as well as issues involved in determining the best schedule. In this chapter, we focused on the selection of training methods, techniques, and materials. Obviously, at some point, the trainer must pull all these issues together and put them into practice. Some final thoughts are presented toward this end.

## ARRANGING THE PHYSICAL ENVIRONMENT

An important implementation decision concerns arranging the physical environment. The environment is particularly important to on-the-job training because the trainee must feel comfortable enough to concentrate and learn. If the OJT area has a number of distractions (like noise and phone calls) that may interfere with the training process, for instance, the trainer must find ways to remove or minimize them. Interruptions are another common OJT distraction, particularly when the supervisor is the trainer. Interruptions can be avoided by setting aside certain times of the day or a special location for training that is free from distractions. Alternatively, the supervisor can arrange for someone who is not receiving training to handle calls and inquiries during the time established for training.

In a classroom setting, a number of factors should be considered when arranging the physical environment. These include the seating arrangement, comfort, and physical distractions. *Seating* is important because it establishes a spatial relationship between the trainer and the trainees. For example, a classroom with fixed seats in vertical rows limits what the trainer can do in that setting, but this arrangement may be preferred for the lecture technique because it focuses the participants on the lecturer. In a classroom with movable seats, however, the trainer can arrange the seats to facilitate the program objectives. Arranging the rows on angles (or a chevron shape) or in a semicircle allows the trainees to view each other during a class discussion. This arrangement can encourage interaction and feedback among the participants. In a large class, the seats can be arranged in small groups to facilitate group discussion.

The physical *comfort level* is also important for successful learning. Extremes in room temperature can inhibit learning. A warm, stuffy room can make participants feel tired. A room that is too cold can distract participants and reduce manual dexterity. One of the authors recalls participating in a management development seminar in a room so cold that trainees spent more time focusing on how uncomfortable they were (and consuming hot beverages) than dealing with the training content.

The third factor that should be considered when arranging the physical environment is the potential for *physical distractions*, such as noise, poor lighting, and physical barriers. Noise, including activity outside the classroom, can often be controlled by closing the door or placing a sign stating "Quiet: Training in session" outside the area. Inappropriate lighting can make it difficult for participants to take notes or read printed material or overheads, or it can render projected material unviewable. The trainer should inspect the room in advance if possible to determine whether any physical barriers, such as poles, fixed partitions, and the like, will interfere with the planned activities. If such problems exist, it may be possible to find a more suitable location.

Additional physical factors a trainer may want to consider include wall and floor coverings and colors (carpeted rooms are quieter), the type of chairs, the presence of glare, windows (a view may distract participants), acoustics, and the presence of electrical outlets to run necessary equipment.[123] Also, whenever possible, the screen for overheads or computer slides should be arranged in such a way that it does not block off simultaneous use of the white board or flip chart. Finally, computers and other technology should be tested and tried out *in advance* to ensure that they work as intended during the training program.

## GETTING STARTED

Having all the elements needed to implement an HRD intervention or program — a viable lesson plan, materials, audiovisual and/or computer equipment on hand, and the physical environment ready — the final step is to do it! It is important for the trainer to get the program off to a good start and maintain it. If there are to be multiple sessions, the first session sets the tone for the remainder of the program. As discussed, a trainer can establish clear expectations by preparing a course outline or syllabus that explains the purpose, objectives, topics, and requirements that establishes class norms for relevant issues (punctuality, participation, participant interaction, and so on). The course outline should be handed out and explained in detail during the first session and, if needed, restated and reinforced periodically throughout the training program.

In addition to establishing expectations, the trainer should try to determine each trainee's capacity and motivation to learn if this was not done before the session. One way to make this determination is to conduct an initial exercise or pretest to assess initial ability. This may be particularly important in one-on-one OJT sessions. Rather than assess participant motivation, it may be more beneficial to include activities that reinforce motivation. Such activities could include asking participants what they'd like to accomplish, illustrating the benefits of achieving the training objectives, explicitly addressing participants' fears or concerns, or having participants complete a learning contract.

Many training programs include some sort of ice-breaker exercise to help participants get to know each other and establish rapport with each other and the trainer. This is important for at least two reasons. First, a benefit of many HRD programs is the opportunity for participants to network and get to know their colleagues in other parts of the organization. Second, in HRD programs, as in any group setting, people generally seek social acceptance. For instance, in classes with one or two minority group members (ethnic, racial, gender, etc.), these individuals may feel socially isolated, which can affect their ability to perform effectively in that setting. It is important that the trainer be sensitive to the social needs of trainees and respond in ways that enhance their feelings of belonging. Finally, the trainer should make every effort to build a climate characterized by mutual respect and openness. This in turn will make it easier for trainees to seek help when they need it.

There are many skills involved in effectively running a group meeting and in teaching or facilitating learning. We encourage you to read about the subject and seek out opportunities to build platform and interpersonal skills. A good source for inexperienced trainers is the *Training and Development Yearbook* by Carolyn Nilson.[124] This yearbook includes reprints of articles, cases, and other materials concerning HRD. A final section, entitled "The trainer's almanac," includes a list of conferences, print resources, and a rating of training websites. Professional journals like *T&D* and *Training* also include frequent articles on effective training skills. In addition, becoming involved in a local ASTD chapter can be very beneficial. In this spirit, we close this chapter with a list of tips offered by several trainers to increase training effectiveness (see Table 6-5).[125]

**TABLE 6-5**                                    **TIPS FOR TRAINERS**

1. Overprepare — know your subject matter inside and out.
2. Your personal appearance (attire and grooming) should be both professional and appropriate to your audience.
3. Get the trainees' attention early (have a "grabber").
4. Your message(s) should be as concise and direct as possible.
5. Focus on the trainees' concerns rather than your own.
6. Ask some initial questions that the trainees can answer, and then continually work for interaction.
7. Listen and acknowledge ideas.
8. Create positive behavior through reinforcement, for example, praise people as they learn.
9. Direct questions back to people.
10. Put people at ease.
11. Ask for examples from the trainees' experience.
12. Share your experiences with the trainees.
13. Don't become a slide narrator, that is, don't let your slides become your presentation.
14. Admit to not knowing an answer — let trainees help you.
15. Avoid disputes and making right and wrong judgments.
16. Show that you enjoy instructing people. Have fun!
17. Spend additional time with trainees when necessary.
18. Express confidence in trainees.
19. Make notes, and follow up on them.
20. Use trainees' words when writing on the flip chart or board.
21. Summarize — provide learning points and closure to celebrate what trainees have learned.

SOURCES: From Harper, J. (2004). Presentation skills. *Industrial and Commercial Training, 36*(3), 125–127; Abernathy, D. J. (1999). Presentation tips from the pros. *Training & Development, 53*(10), 19–25; Fetteroll, E. C. (1985). 16 tips to increase your effectiveness. *Training & Development Journal, 39*(6), 68–70.

## RETURN TO OPENING CASE

Dell Learning has enjoyed the active support of Michael Dell, the founder and chairman of the company. It has used a variety of different means to promote training and learning within the corporation. Your instructor has additional information on Dell Learning and the questions raised in the opening case.

Taylor, C. (2003). Recession survivors. *T&D, 57*(10), October, 29–35; Coné, J. (2000). How Dell does it. *Training & Development, 54*(6), June, 58–70.

## SUMMARY

This chapter described several important activities related to the implementation or delivery of training and development programs. There are three primary training methods: OJT, classroom, and self-paced training (computer-based training can be either classroom based, self-paced, or both). Each method has a number of techniques appropriate for particular situations. The trainer needs to select the best combination of techniques that will maximize trainee learning. Once the trainer designs and schedules the program, the final step is the actual implementation of the program. This includes arranging the physical environment and getting started on a positive note.

Look again at the true-false questions we presented at the beginning of the chapter. We would categorize each of those questions as false. Although there may be *some* truth to each of them, in an absolute sense, we do not think they hold up as accurate statements. It is hoped that our discussion of each topic in this chapter has provided you with our rationale for this.

## KEY TERMS AND CONCEPTS

| | |
|---|---|
| audiovisual methods | intelligent computer-assisted instruction |
| behavior modeling | (ICAI) |
| blended learning | intranet-based training (IBT) |
| business games | intranets |
| case study method | job instruction training (JIT) |
| classroom training | job rotation |
| computer-aided instruction | lecture method |
| (CAI) | on-the-job training (OJT) |
| computer-based training (CBT) | role playing |
| discussion method | static media |
| dynamic media | telecommunications |
| in-basket exercise | videoconferencing |

## QUESTIONS FOR DISCUSSION

1. What experiences have you had with on-the-job training? What can make it function as effectively as possible?

2. Why do you suppose the five categories of classroom training are so popular in HRD? Identify two types of training programs a manager might *not* want to conduct in using a classroom format.

3. State and justify your opinion regarding the effectiveness of the lecture method. What can be done to ensure a lecture is effective?

4. Using a training topic (or module) of your choice, what audiovisual methods would be most appropriate in presenting this method to a group of trainees? Why did you pick the method or methods that you did?

5. In what circumstances would learning be promoted through use of the case study method or simulations?

6. What experiences have you had with role playing in training? Under what conditions might a role play be effective? Ineffective?

7. What sorts of skills and knowledge do you think computer-based training methods (such as computer-aided instruction) are well suited for? Poorly suited for?

8. What is blended learning? What do you think of this as an approach to training new professional employees?

9. Why is it important for trainers and trainees to establish a rapport with each other before a training session?

## EXERCISE 1: GENERATING QUESTIONS FOR DISCUSSION LEADING

Consider a training topic or module that you are interested in. Generate at least five questions that could be used to facilitate group or classroom discussion on this topic. Evaluate the extent to which each question is likely to stimulate useful discussion of this training topic.

## EXERCISE 2: DESIGNING E-LEARNING MATERIALS

Consider a training module that you are interested in. For this exercise, it should be a topic where you think trainees would benefit by having e-learning materials available. As one example, a goal of your module might be that trainees can independently post their own resumes on an online recruiting website (such as Monster.com). Using as many of the principles given in Table 6-4 as possible, generate web-based materials for this (or any other) topic. How would you evaluate the extent to which your materials do in fact assist trainees in learning this topic?

Visit http://werner.swlearning.com for links to informative websites for this chapter.

## REFERENCES

1. Gagné, R. M. (1985). *The conditions of learning and theory of instruction* (4th ed.). New York: Holt, Rinehart and Winston.

2. Yin, L. R. (2004). Learning pyramid. Retrieved September 27, 2004, from http://www.yinnovate.com/learning-pyramid.html

3. Scott, J. (1999). Employees get OJT. *Memphis Business Journal, 21*(1), May 7, 1–3; Salopek, J. J. (2004). Balancing work and learning. *T&D, 58*(7), 16–18.

4. Chase, N. (1997). OJT doesn't mean "sit by Joe." *Quality, 36*(November), 84.

5. Jacobs, R. L., & Jones, M. J. (1995). *Structured on-the-job training* (p. 19). San Francisco: Berrett-Koehler.

6. Rothwell, W. J., & Kazanas, H. C. (1994). *Improving on-the-job training.* San Francisco: Jossey-Bass.

7. Knight, J. (2000). The school of hard rocks. *Training,* August, 36–38.

8. Jacobs, R. L., & Jones, M. J. (1997). Teaching tools: When to use on-the-job training. *Security Management, 41*(9), 35–41.

9. Cannell, M. (1997). Practice makes perfect. *People Management, 3*(5), March 6, 26–31.

10. Taylor, D. L., & Ramsey, R. K. (1993). Empowering employees to "just do it." *Training & Development, 47*(5) 71–76.

11. Urbaniak, A. (2004). Training employees. *Supervision, 65*(2), February, 6–7.

12. Goff, L. (1999). Get promoted. *Computerworld, 33*(35), September 30, 54–55.

13. Järvi, M., & Uusitalo, T. (2004). Job rotation in nursing: A study of job rotation among nursing personnel from the literature and via a questionnaire. *Journal of Nursing Management, 12*(5), September, 337–347.

14. Gómez, P. J., Lorente, J.J.C., & Cabrera, R. V. (2004). Training practices and organizational learning capability. *Journal of European Industrial Training, 28*(2–4), 234–255.

15. Black, S. E., & Lynch, L. M. (2004). *Workplace practices and the new economy.* Federal Reserve Bank of San Francisco, Economic Letter, April 16, 2004-10. Retrieved September 24, 2004, from http://www.frbsf.org/publications/economics/letter/2004/el2004-10.html

16. Grossman, R. J. (2003). Putting HR in rotation. *HR Magazine, 48*(3), March, 50–57.

17. *Ibid*, p. 52.

18. Korman, A. K. (1971). *Industrial and organizational psychology.* Englewood Cliffs, NJ: Prentice Hall; Middendorf, J., & Kalish, A. (1996). The "change-up" in lectures. *TRC Newsletter, 8*(1), Fall. Retrieved September 24, 2004, from http://www.indiana.edu/~teaching/changeups.html

19. Bass, B. M., & Vaughn, J. A. (1966). *Training in industry.* Belmont, CA: Wadsworth.

20. Carroll, S. J., Paine, F. T., & Ivancevich, J. J. (1972). The relative effectiveness of training methods — Expert opinion and research. *Personnel Psychology, 25,* 495–510.

21. Cohen, D. J. (1990). What motivates trainees? *Training and Development Journal, 44*(11), 91–93.

22. Burke, M. J., & Day, R. R. (1986). A cumulative study of the effectiveness of managerial training. *Journal of Applied Psychology, 71,* 232–245.

23. Early, P. C. (1987). Intercultural training for managers: A comparison of documentary and interpersonal methods. *Academy of Management Journal, 30,* 685–698.

24. Aly, M., Elen, J., & Willems, G. (2004). Instructional multimedia program versus standard lecture: A comparison of two methods for teaching the undergraduate orthodontic curriculum. *European Journal of Dental Education, 8*(1), February, 43–46.

25. Callahan, J. S., Kiker, D. S., & Cross, T. (2003). Does method matter? A meta-analysis of the effects of training method on older learner training performance. *Journal of Management, 29*(5), 663–680.

26. Middendorf & Kalish (1996), *supra* note 18.

27. Zemke, R., Raines, C., & Filipczak, B. (1999). Generation gaps in the classroom. *Training*, November, 48–54.

28. Welty, W. M. (1989). Discussion method teaching: How to make it work. *Change*, July/August, 41–49.

29. Kearsley, G. (1984). *Training and technology*. Reading, MA: Addison-Wesley.

30. Nunberg, G. (1999, December 20). Slides rule: The trouble with PowerPoint. *Fortune*, pp. 330–331.

31. Jaffe, G. (2000, April 26). What's your point, Lieutenant? Just cut to the pie charts. *Wall Street Journal*, p. A1.

32. Abram, S. (2004). PowerPoint: Devil in a red dress. *Information Outlook, 8*(3), March, 27–28.

33. Branzburg, J. (2004). New and noteworthy presentation apps. *Technology & Learning, 24*(9), April, 9.

34. 2003 Industry Report. (2003). *Training, 40*(9), 21–38.

35. Eurich, N. P. (1990). *The learning industry: Education for adult workers.* Lawrenceville, NJ: Princeton University Press.

36. Kearsley (1984), *supra* note 29.

37. Watkins, B. T. (1991) 18 Universities join effort to offer bachelor degrees in management, entirely through cable television. *The Chronicle of Higher Education, 38*(5), A18–A19; James, M. L. (1997). Delivering the MBA via the Internet: Where do we begin? *Academy of Educational Leadership Journal*, 1, 41–46.

38. Stackel, L. (1988). National Technological University: Learning by satellite. In J. Casner-Lotto and Associates (Eds.), *Successful training strategies*. San Francisco: Jossey-Bass.

39. Arnone, M. (2002). Sylvan Learning Systems to acquire National Technological U. *Chronicle of Higher Education, 48*(30), April 5, A-29; For-profit champion rebrands (2004, June 11). *Times Higher Education Supplement, 1644*, p. IV.

40. Eurich (1990), *supra* note 35.

41. Lowenthal, J., & Jankowski, P. (1983). A checklist for selecting the right teleconferencing mode. *Training and Development Journal, 37*(12), 47–50; Bove, R. (1984). Reach out and train someone. *Training and Development Journal, 38*(7), 26.

42. Industry Report (2003), *supra* note 34.

43. Berdiansky, H. (1985). The invisible trainer. *Training and Development Journal, 39*(3), 60–63.

44. Wittock, M. (1986). *The handbook of research on teaching.* New York: Macmillan.

45. Eurich (1990), *supra* note 35.

46. Fister, S. (2000). Tech trends. *Training*, April, 30, 32.

47. FedExKinko's Videoconferencing (2004). Retrieved September 27, 2004, from http://www.fedex.com/us/customersupport/officeprint/faq/videoconf.html?link=4#topthree12

48. Schramm, W. (1962). Learning from instructional television. *Review of Educational Research, 32*, 156–167; Chu, G. C., & Schramm, W. (1967). *Learning from television: What the research says.* Washington, DC: National Association of Educational Broadcasters; Berdiansky, H. (1985). The invisible trainer. *Training and Development Journal, 39*(3), 60–63; Eurich (1990), *supra* note 35.

49. Kearsley (1984), *supra* note 29, p. 145.

50. Rothwell, W. J., & Kazanas, H. C. (1992). *Mastering the instructional design process* (pp. 190–191). San Francisco: Jossey-Bass.

51. Andres, H. P. (2004). Multimedia, information complexity and cognitive processing. *Information Resources Management Journal, 17*(1), 63–78; Hill, S., Hill, A., & Hampton, D. (2004). Videoconferencing in a hospital school: Removing barriers. *Journal of Audiovisual Media in Medicine, 27*(2), 58–61; Rothwell & Kazanas (1992), *supra* note 50; Romiszowski, A. J. (1988). *The selection and use of instructional media* (2nd ed.). New York: Nichols; Kearsley (1984), *supra* note 29.

52. Keys, B., & Wolfe, J. (1988). Management education and development: Current issues and emerging trends. *Journal of Management, 14,* 205–229, p. 214.

53. Industry Report (2003), *supra* note 34.

54. Osigweh, C.A.B. (1986–1987). The case approach in management training. *Organizational Behavior Teaching Review, 11*(4), 120–133.

55. Barnes, L. B., Christensen, C. R., & Hansen, A. J. (1994). *Teaching and the case method: Text, cases, and readings* (3rd ed.). Boston: Harvard Business School Press; Naumes, W., & Naumes, M. J. (1999). *The art and craft of case writing.* Thousand Oaks, CA: Sage; Wassermann, S. (1994). *Introduction to case method teaching: A guide to the galaxy.* New York: Teachers College Press.

56. Osigweh (1986–1987), *supra* note 54.

57. Andrews, E. S., & Noel, J. L. (1986). Adding life to the case study method. *Training and Development Journal, 40*(2), 28–29.

58. Argyris, C. (1980). Some limitations to the case method: Experiences in a management development program. *Academy of Management Review, 5,* 291–298.

59. Berger, M. A. (1983). In defense of the case method: A reply to Argyris. *Academy of Management Review, 8,* 329–333.

60. Garvin, D. A. (2004). *Participant-centered learning and the case method* (CD-ROM). Boston: Harvard Business School Press; Keys & Wolfe (1988), *supra* note 52; Osigweh (1986–1987), *supra* note 54.

61. Argyris, C. (1986). Skilled incompetence. *Harvard Business Review, 64*(5), 74–79.

62. Andrews & Noel (1986), *supra* note 57.

63. Osigweh (1986–1987), *supra* note 54, p. 131.

64. Industry Report (2003), *supra* note 34.

65. McCall, M. W., & Lombardo, M. M. (1982). Using simulation for leadership and management research: Through the looking glass. *Management Science, 28,* 533–549.

66. Kaplan, R. E., Lombardo, M. M., & Mazique, M. S. (1985). A mirror for managers: Using simulation to develop management teams. *Journal of Applied Behavioral Science, 21,* 241–253.

67. Thornton, G. C., & Cleveland, J. N. (1990). Developing managerial talent through simulation. *American Psychologist, 45,* 190–199.

68. McCall & Lombardo (1982), *supra* note 65.

69. Kaplan, Lombardo, & Mazique (1985), *supra* note 66.

70. Keys & Wolfe (1988), *supra* note 52.

71. Butler, J. L., & Keys, J. B. (1973). A comparative study of simulation and rational methods of supervisory training in human resource development. In T. B. Green & D. F. Ray (Eds.), *Academy of management proceedings* (pp. 302–305). Boston: Academy of Management.

72. Thornton, G. C., & Byham, W. C. (1982). *Assessment centers and managerial performance.* New York: Academic Press.

73. Thornton, G. C., & Cleveland, J. N. (1990). Developing managerial talent through simulation. *American Psychologist, 45,* 190–199.

74. Wexley, K. N., & Baldwin, T. T. (1986). Management development. *Journal of Management, 12,* 277–294.

75. Keys & Wolfe (1988), *supra* note 52.

76. Industry Report (2003), *supra* note 34.

77. Burke, M. J., & Day, R. R. (1986). A cumulative study of the effectiveness of managerial training. *Journal of Applied Psychology, 71,* 232–245; Werner, J. M., & Crampton, S. M. (1992). The impact of behavior modeling training on measures of learning, behavior, and results: A meta-analytic review. In M. Schnake (Ed.), *Proceedings.* San Antonio, TX: Southern Management Association, 279–284.

78. Weaver, M. (1999). Beyond the ropes: Guidelines for selecting experiential training. *Corporate University Review, 7*(1), January/February, 34–37.

79. *Ibid*; Meyer, J. P. (2003). Four territories of experience: A developmental action inquiry approach to outdoor-adventure experiential training. *Academy of Management Learning and Education, 2*(4), 352–363; Wagner, R. J., & Roland, C. C. (1996). Outdoor-based training: Research findings and recommendations for trainers. *Resources in Education,* June, 7–15.

80. Williams, S. D., Graham, T. S., & Baker, B. (2003). Evaluating outdoor experiential training for leadership and team building. *Journal of Management Development, 22*(1/2), 45–59.

81. Weaver (1999), *supra* note 78, p. 35.

82. Roschelle, J., Penuel, W. R., & Abrahamson, L. (2004). The networked classroom. *Educational Leadership, 61*(5), 50–54.

83. Fiedler, F. E., Mitchell, T., & Triandis, H. C. (1971). The culture assimilator: An approach to cross-cultural training. *Journal of Applied Psychology, 55,* 95–102; Cushner, K. H. (1987). Teaching cross-cultural psychology: Providing the missing link. *Teaching of Psychology, 14,* 220–224.

84. Marquardt, M. J., & Kearsley, G. (1999). *Technology-based learning: Maximizing human performance and corporate success.* Boca Raton, FL: St. Lucie Press.

85. Industry Report (2003), *supra* note 34.

86. Verser, T. G. (1989). An evaluation of eight personnel training methods for small business owners. *Journal of Organizational Change Management, 2*(3), 41–53.

87. Kearsley (1984), *supra* note 29.

88. Hartley, D. E. (2000). *On-demand learning: Training in the new millennium.* Amherst, MA: HRD Press; Hartley, D. E. (2004). The need for speed. *T&D, 58*(10), October, 22–23.

89. Hamburg, S. K. (1988). Manpower temporary services: Keeping ahead of the competition. In J. Casner-Lotto & Associates (Eds.), *Successful training strategies.* San Francisco: Jossey-Bass.

90. Caudron, S. (1996). Wake up to new learning. *Training & Development, 50*(5), 30–35.

PART 2: FRAMEWORK FOR HUMAN RESOURCE DEVELOPMENT

91. Ganger, R E. (1990). Computer-based training works. *Personnel Journal, 69*(9), 85–91.

92. Schwade, S. (1985). Is it time to consider computer-based training? *Personnel Administrator, 30*(2), 25–35.

93. Hillelsohn, M. J. (1984). How to think about CBT. *Training and Development Journal, 38*(1), 42–44, p. 43.

94. Reinhart, C. (1989). Developing CBT-The quality way. *Training and Development Journal, 43*(11), 85–89.

95. Ganger (1990), *supra* note 91.

96. Caudron (1996), *supra* note 90.

97. Wexley, K. N. (1984). Personnel training. *Annual Review of Psychology, 35,* 519–551.

98. Foegen, J. H. (1987). Too much negative training. *Business Horizons, 30*(5), 51–53.

99. Munger, P. D. (1996). A guide to high-tech training delivery: Part I. *Training & Development, 50*(12), 55–57.

100. Marquardt & Kearsley (1999), *supra* note 84.

101. Croft, B. (1996). The Intranet: Your newest training tool. *Personnel Journal, 75*(7), 27–28; Curtin, C. (1997). Getting off to a good start on intranets. *Training & Development, 51*(2), 42–46.

102. Workers praise Internet but bemoan lack of training. (2000). *Training, 37*(5), May, 26.

103. The 2003 State of the Industry Report (2003). Alexandria, VA: ASTD, p. 15.

104. Gascó, J. L, Llopis, J., & González, M. R. (2004). The use of information technology in training human resources: An e-learning case study. *Journal of European Industrial Training, 28*(5), 370–382; Totty, P. (2004). E-learning comes of age. *Credit Union Management, 70*(7), 55–56; Hartley, D. (2000). All aboard the e-learning train. *Training & Development, 54*(7), July, 37–42.

105. Long, L. K., & Smith, R. D. (2004). The role of web-based distance learning in HR development. *Journal of Management Development, 23*(3/4), 270–284; Tham, C. M., & Werner, J. M. (2004). Designing and evaluating E-learning in higher education: A review and recommendations. *Journal of Leadership and Organizational Studies, 11*(2), Fall, 15–25; Holley, D., Haynes, R. (2003). The "INCOTERMS" challenge: Using multi-media to engage learners. *Education & Training, 45*(7), 392–401.

106. Glener, D. (1996). The promise of Internet-based training. *Training & Development, 50*(9), September, 57–58.

107. Fichter, D. (2002). Intranets and E-learning: A perfect partnership. *Online, 26*(1), January/February, 68–71.

108. Kruse, K. (1997). Five levels of Internet-based training. *Training and Development, 51*(2), 60–61.

109. Cohen, S. (1997). Intranets uncovered. *Training & Development, 51*(2), February, 48–50.

110. Anfuso, D. (1999). Trainers prove many heads are better than one: A unique consortium is raising the training function's value. *Workforce, 78*(3), March, 60–65.

111. KnowledgeNet to sponsor and exhibit at annual Sharing@LearnShare conference on September 9, 2004. (2004, September 9). *Business Wire,* p. 1; Fortune 500 leaders headline LearnShare corporate training conference. Retrieved September 22, 2004, from http://www.learnshare.com/

112. Cohen (1997), *supra* note 109.

113. Curtin, C. (1997). Getting off to a good start on Intranets. *Training & Development, 51*(2), February, 42–46.

114. McCown, S. (2004). Databases flex their XML. *InfoWorld, 26*(17), April 26, 34–42; Dobbs, K. (2000). A step up for standards: Online learning gets compatible. *Training,* May, 36, 39.

115. Zielinski, D. (2000). The lie of online learning. *Training,* May, 38–40.

116. ASTD/MASIE Center. (2001). E-learning: If we build it, will they come? Retrieved September 27, 2004 from http://www.astd.org/NR/rdonlyres/9094AF2C-7B2F-41CE-9FEE-5D81D216B805/0/LearningTechnologyAcceptanceStudy.pdf; Zielenski, D. (2000). Can you keep learners online? *Training,* March, 64–75.

117. McCalla, G. I., & Greer, J. E. (1987). *The practical use of artificial intelligence in automated tutoring systems: Current status and impediments to progress.* Saskatoon, Canada: University of Saskatchewan, Department of Computational Science. Cited in N. P. Eurich (1990), *The learning industry: Education for adult workers.* Lawrenceville, NJ: Princeton University Press, p. 74.

118. Thissen-Roe, A., Hunt, E., & Minstrell, J. (2004). The DIAGNOSER project: Combining assessment and learning. *Behavior Research Methods, Instruments, & Computers, 36*(2), 234–240.

119. Eurich (1990), *supra* note 35.

120. *Ibid,* p. 71.

121. Zenger, J., & Uehlein, C. (2001). Why blended will win. *T&D, 55*(8), August, 55–60.

122. Derouin, R. E., Fritzsche, B. A., & Salas, E. (2004). Optimizing e-learning: Research-based guidelines for learner-controlled training. *Human Resource Management, 43*(2/3), 147–162; Johnson, G. (2003). Brewing the perfect blend. *Training, 40*(11), December, 30–34; Coppola, N. W., Hiltz, S. R., & Rotter, N. G. (2002). Becoming a virtual professor: Pedagogical roles and asynchronous learning networks. *Journal of Management Information Systems, 18*(4), 169–190; The next generation of corporate learning (2003). *T&D, 57*(6), June, 47.

123. Finkel, C. (1986). Pick a place, but not any place. *Training and Development Journal, 40*(2), February, 51–53.

124. Nilson, C. (2002). *Training & development yearbook 2002.* New York: Aspen Publishers.

125. Harper, J. (2004). Presentation skills. *Industrial and Commercial Training, 36*(3), 125–127; Abernathy, D. J. (1999). Presentation tips from the pros. *Training & Development, 53*(10), 19–25; Fetteroll, E. C. (1985). 16 tips to increase your effectiveness. *Training and Development Journal, 39*(6), June, 68–70.

# EVALUATING HRD PROGRAMS

## Learning Objectives

*After reading this chapter, you should be able to:*

1. Define *evaluation* and explain its role in HRD.

2. Compare different frameworks for HRD evaluation.

3. Discuss the various types of evaluation information available and compare the methods of data collection.

4. Explain the role of research design in HRD evaluation.

5. Describe the ethical issues involved in conducting HRD evaluation.

6. Identify and explain the choices available for translating evaluation results into dollar terms.

7. Calculate a utility estimate for a target organization.

## OPENING CASE

One day, Dave Palm, the director of training at LensCrafters, got a call suggesting that top executives were looking to improve the company's bottom line, and couldn't find enough tangible evidence that the company's training programs were producing a measurable return on the company's investment. Top management at this optical retailer understood that employee training was important, but they wanted to know what evidence was available to show that there was in fact a payoff to the organization from the money being spent on training. The phone conversation ended with a challenge, "What are you going to do about this?"

*Questions: If you were the director of training in this situation, what types of measures would you like to have available before you respond to top management? That is, what types of evidence do you think that management would find convincing that training was having a positive impact on the organization? Why did you pick the measures that you did? How would you go about collecting the data for the measures you have selected?*

SOURCE: Purcell, A. (2000). 20/20 ROI. *Training & Development*, 54(7), July, 28–33.

## INTRODUCTION

In this chapter, we'll deal with some of the following questions:

- *How do you evaluate training and HRD interventions?*
- *What measures can be used to evaluate training interventions?*
- *Is there one best model or framework to use to evaluate training?*
- *What important issues should be considered as one prepares to evaluate HRD interventions?*
- *What are the ethical issues involved in evaluating HRD interventions?*
- *To what extent can the value of HRD interventions be expressed in terms of costs and benefits, or dollars and cents?*

In the previous three chapters, we discussed how to identify HRD needs and then design and deliver a program or intervention to satisfy those needs. The training and HRD model (shown in Figure 7-1) illustrates how the evaluation phase relates to the needs assessment, design, and implementation phases in the HRD process.

In this chapter, we discuss the question: Was the HRD program effective? This is not an easy question, and it raises a number of concerns, such as:

- What is meant by effectiveness? Is it the same thing as efficiency?
- How is effectiveness measured?
- What is the purpose of determining effectiveness? That is, what decisions are made after a program is judged effective or ineffective?

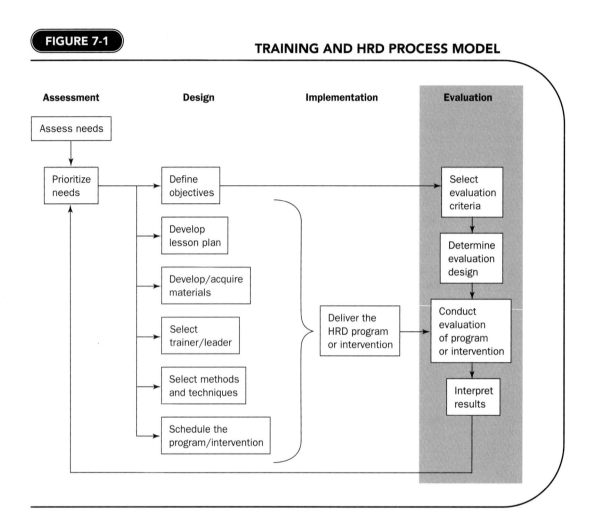

**FIGURE 7-1**

**TRAINING AND HRD PROCESS MODEL**

As we will see in this chapter, the answers to these questions are far from simple. The term *effectiveness* is relative. Typically, effectiveness is determined with respect to the achievement of a goal or a set of goals. HRD effectiveness must be determined with respect to the goals of the program or programs being examined. Therefore, it makes sense to ask the question of effectiveness more specifically. An HRD or training program can be effective in meeting some goals (like staying within budget or increasing a participant's skills) and be ineffective in meeting others (like improving customer satisfaction).

In this chapter, we will define HRD evaluation, describe its purposes and the options available for conducting an evaluation of training and other HRD interventions, and discuss how evaluation findings can be communicated.

## THE PURPOSE OF HRD EVALUATION

**HRD evaluation** is defined as "the systematic collection of descriptive and judgmental information necessary to make effective training decisions related to the selection, adoption, value, and modification of various instructional activities."[1] This definition makes several important points. First, when conducting an evaluation, both descriptive and judgmental information may be collected. Descriptive information provides a picture of what is happening or has happened, whereas judgmental information communicates some opinion or belief about what has happened. For example, the statement "25 percent of first-line supervisors attended a budgeting workshop in the last year" contains only descriptive information; it simply states the facts. Similarly, a statement that "20 percent fewer supervisors attended this workshop than in the previous 12 months" also contains descriptive information. However, the statement, "the turnout for the budgeting workshop over the last six months is disappointingly low compared to last year's turnout" provides judgmental information—someone's opinion based on the facts. Both descriptive and judgmental information are needed in an HRD evaluation. Some judgments are made by those involved in the program, while individuals not involved in the program make others.

Second, evaluation involves the systematic collection of information according to a predetermined plan to ensure that the information is appropriate and useful. Finally, evaluation is conducted to help managers, employees, and HRD professionals make informed decisions about particular programs and methods. For example, if part of a program is ineffective, it may need to be changed or discarded; if a certain program proves valuable, it may be replicated in other parts of the organization.

Evaluation can serve a number of purposes within the organization. According to Phillips, evaluation can help to

- determine whether a program is accomplishing its objectives
- identify the strengths and weaknesses of HRD programs, which can lead to changes, as needed
- determine the cost-benefit ratio of an HRD program
- decide who should participate in future HRD programs
- identify which participants benefited the most or least from the program
- gather data to assist in marketing future programs
- establish a database to assist management in making decisions[2]

Better and more informed decision making, then, is an important benefit of conducting an HRD evaluation. But there are other benefits as well. Zenger and Hargis identified three additional reasons for conducting HRD evaluations:

1. If HRD staff cannot substantiate its contribution to the organization, its funding and programs may be cut during the budgeting process, especially when the organization faces tough times.

2. Evaluation can build credibility with top managers and others in the organization.

3. Senior management often wants to know the benefits of HRD programs (see the Opening Case on LensCrafters).[3]

Building credibility is a key aspect of conducting an evaluation. After all, other functions performed within the organization are evaluated to determine their effectiveness. If the HRD department cannot demonstrate effectiveness, it may not be taken seriously within the organization. Thus, evaluation is a critical step in the HRD process. It is the only way one can know whether an HRD program has fulfilled its objectives.[4]

## HOW OFTEN ARE HRD PROGRAMS EVALUATED?

Given their importance, one might expect that HRD programs are regularly and carefully evaluated. Unfortunately, this is not the case. A survey of management training and education practices of U.S. companies found that while 92 percent of companies surveyed conduct some form of evaluation for company-sponsored training, 42 percent conduct no evaluation at all for the executive MBA programs they used.[5] In addition, the survey showed that the most commonly used form of evaluation was participant *reaction*, which as we will discuss, is useful for only a few of the decisions that must be made about HRD programs. More recent research has found the same thing.[6]

Such findings are not atypical. Many HRD researchers have lamented the lack of evaluation of HRD programs.[7] Many articles have been written about the importance of conducting evaluations, but more organizations pay lip service to evaluations than actually conduct them.

Why aren't evaluations done more frequently? There are several possibilities. First, conducting an evaluation is not an easy process. It requires time, resources, and expertise that the HRD staff may not have or may not be willing to expend. Second, many factors beyond the program itself (including the economy, equipment, policies and procedures, other HR efforts, and resource availability) can affect whether employee performance improves, thus making it difficult to evaluate the impact of training. Third, those associated with HRD programs may be afraid of criticism and program cuts if the evaluation shows that the program was not effective. Yet the fact is that HRD evaluations can and should be done in organizations to ensure effectiveness and accountability.[8] It is our belief that it is the ethical responsibility of HRD professionals to prove to the organization whether their programs are indeed beneficial.

## THE EVALUATION OF TRAINING AND HRD PROGRAMS PRIOR TO PURCHASE

As we discussed in Chapter 5, many HRD and training programs are purchased by organizations from third parties, such as consultants or vendors. Some practitioners believe that they fulfill their evaluation responsibility in their prepurchase decision. Their logic follows that they wouldn't buy a program they didn't think was going to work, so if they have made a wise purchasing decision (or evaluated the program before buying it), then it isn't necessary to conduct any postprogram evaluation.

Indeed, supervisors and HRD professionals should be wise consumers of programs and equipment used in their HRD efforts. However, it is equally important to judge the effectiveness of the program or device *after* it has been put into place. We have all made personal purchases that have not lived up to expectations, even after careful shopping, and it is unreasonable to assume that HRD and training purchases will be any different.

## CHANGING EVALUATION EMPHASES

Goldstein suggests that efforts at training evaluation have moved through the following four stages since the 1960s:

1. *Stage One* focuses on anecdotal reactions from trainers and program participants. Judging from the survey results cited earlier, it appears many organizations still operate at this level.[9]

2. *Stage Two* involves borrowing experimental methodology from academic laboratories to use for program evaluation. Organizational constraints (including time, resources, and the inability to randomly select participants or use control groups that receive no training) make application of these designs difficult, thus discouraging evaluation efforts.

3. *Stage Three* creatively matches the appropriate research methodology to existing organizational constraints, thus making program evaluation more practical and feasible.

4. *Stage Four* recognizes that the entire training and HRD process affects the organization, and shifts the focus of evaluation from postprogram results to the entire HRD process.[10]

It should be emphasized that it is possible to creatively apply sound research methods to HRD evaluation designs and have useful data for making decisions. Finding ways to perform effective evaluation serves all parties: the organization, the trainer or HRD professional, and the trainees. Before we discuss data collection and research design, however, we will examine several models and frameworks of evaluation.

## MODELS AND FRAMEWORKS OF EVALUATION

A model of evaluation outlines the criteria for and focus of the evaluation. Because an HRD program can be examined from a number of perspectives, it is important to specify which perspectives will be considered. Many different frameworks of HRD evaluation have been suggested.[11] The most widely used evaluation approach has been the framework laid out by Donald Kirkpatrick. We will discuss this first. While the different models and frameworks share some features, they also differ in important ways. The frameworks that we will discuss are presented in Table 7-1.

---

**TABLE 7-1**  **HRD EVALUATION MODELS/FRAMEWORKS**

| Model | Training Evaluation Criteria |
|---|---|
| 1. Kirkpatrick (1967, 1987, 1994) | Four levels: Reaction, Learning, Job Behavior, and Results. |
| 2. CIPP (Galvin, 1983) | Four levels: Context, Input, Process, and Product. |
| 3. Brinkerhoff (1987) | Six stages: Goal Setting, Program Design, Program Implementation, Immediate Outcomes, Intermediate or Usage Outcomes, and Impacts and Worth. |
| 4. Kraiger, Ford, & Salas (1993) | A classification scheme that specifies three categories of learning outcomes (cognitive, skill based, affective) suggested by the literature and proposes evaluation measures appropriate for each category of outcomes. |
| 5. Holton (1996) | Identifies five categories of variables and the relationships among them: Secondary Influences, Motivation Elements, Environmental Elements, Outcomes, Ability/Enabling Elements. |
| 6. Phillips (1996) | Five levels: Reaction and Planned Action, Learning, Applied Learning on the Job, Business Results, Return on Investment. |

## KIRKPATRICK'S EVALUATION FRAMEWORK

The most popular and influential framework for training evaluation was articulated by Kirkpatrick.[12] Kirkpatrick argues that training efforts can be evaluated according to four criteria: reaction, learning, job behavior, and results.

1. **Reaction (Level 1)** Did the trainees like the program and feel it was valuable? At this level, the focus is on the trainees' perceptions about the program and its effectiveness. This is useful information. Positive reactions to a training program may make it easier to encourage employees to attend future programs. But if trainees did not like the program or think they didn't learn anything (even if they did), they may discourage others from attending and may be reluctant to use the skills or knowledge obtained in the program. The main limitation of evaluating HRD programs at the reaction level is that this information cannot indicate whether the program met its objectives beyond ensuring participant satisfaction.

2. **Learning (Level 2)** Did the trainees learn what the HRD objectives said they should learn? This is an important criterion that an effective HRD program should satisfy. Measuring whether someone has learned something in

training may involve a quiz or test — clearly a different method from assessing the participants' reaction to the program.

3. **Job Behavior (Level 3)** Does the trainee use what was learned in training back on the job? This relates back to our discussion of training transfer in Chapter 3. This is also a critical measure of training success. We all know coworkers who have learned how to do something but choose not to. If learning does not transfer to the job, the training effort cannot have an impact on employee or organizational effectiveness. Measuring whether training has transferred to the job requires observation of the trainee's on-the-job behavior or viewing organizational records (e.g., reduced customer complaints, a reduction in scrap rate).

4. **Results (Level 4)** Has the training or HRD effort improved the organization's effectiveness? Is the organization more efficient, more profitable, or better able to serve its clients or customers as a result of the training program? Meeting this criterion is considered the "bottom line" as far as most managers are concerned. It is also the most challenging level to assess, given that many things beyond employee performance can affect organizational performance. Typically at this level, economic and operating data (such as sales or waste) are collected and analyzed.

Kirkpatrick's framework provides a useful way of looking at the possible consequences of training and reminds us that HRD efforts often have multiple objectives. Recently, Arthur and colleagues conducted a meta-analysis of 162 training evaluation studies. They found that the average or mean effect sizes ($d_t$) for training interventions (across all topics and methods used) were fairly large.[13] That is, effect sizes were as follows: 0.60 for reaction, 0.63 for learning, 0.62 for behavior, and 0.62 for results. Practically, we can assure you that effect sizes of this magnitude should lead to meaningful positive changes in most organizational settings, so this is a most encouraging finding. One interesting side note is that some of the strongest effects they found ($d_t = 1.93$) were for those few studies where it was mentioned that needs assessment at the organizational and person level had been completed before training (see Chapter 4). For a nice recent example of safety training for food service workers that was evaluated at multiple levels, see Sinclair et al.[14]

Unfortunately, one of the more enduring (and in our view, depressing) findings about HRD evaluation is the extent to which most organizations do *not* collect information on all four types of outcomes. For instance, in the 2003 ASTD *State of the Industry Report*, a survey of 276 organizations reported the following: 75 percent collected reaction measures, 41 percent collected learning measures, 21 percent collected behavior measures, and 11 percent collected results measures.[15] The subgroup of organizations that ASTD highlighted as "training investment leaders" reported higher usage on the latter three measures (72 percent, 59 percent, 33 percent, and 14 percent, respectively), but these numbers are still not terribly high.[16] This raises the question as to why usage rates are so low, particularly for behavior and results measures, as these provide organizations with vital, even invaluable information.

## OTHER FRAMEWORKS OR MODELS OF EVALUATION

Many discussions about HRD evaluation are organized around Kirkpatrick's four levels of criteria. However, Kirkpatrick's approach has also been the target of considerable criticism and modification. Some authors point out that the framework evaluates only what happens *after* training, as opposed to the entire training process.[17] A second criticism is that Kirkpatrick's framework would be better described as a *taxonomy* of outcomes, rather than a true model of training outcomes.[18] Kraiger, Ford, and Salas argue that Kirkpatrick's approach fails to specify what sorts of changes can be expected as a result of learning and what assessment techniques should be used to measure learning at each level.[19] Alliger and Janak question the validity of the assumptions that are implied by the framework (e.g., achieving the outcomes stated in higher levels of the model assumes achievement of outcomes at the lower levels).[20] They suggest that it "may never have been meant to be more than a first, global heuristic for training evaluation" (p. 339). Kirkpatrick responded to this criticism by stating that "I personally have never called my framework 'a model'" (p. 23), and "I don't care whether my work is called a model or a taxonomy as long as it helps to clarify the meaning of evaluation in simple terms and offers guidelines and suggestions on how to accomplish an evaluation" (pp. 23–24).[21]

Training researchers have expanded Kirkpatrick's ideas to encourage practitioners to do a more thorough job of evaluation. Several authors have suggested modifications to Kirkpatrick's four-level approach that keep the framework essentially intact. These include:

- expanding the reaction level to include assessing the participants' reaction to the training methods and efficiency[22]
- distinguishing between cognitive and affective reactions to training[23]
- splitting the reaction level to include assessing participants' perceptions of enjoyment, usefulness (utility), and the difficulty of the program[24]
- adding a fifth level (beyond results) to specifically address the organization's return on investment (ROI)[25]
- adding a fifth level (beyond results) to address the societal contribution and outcomes created by an HRD program[26]

Galvin, building on studies in the education field, suggested the CIPP (Context, Input, Process, Product) model.[27] In this model, evaluation focuses on measuring the *context* for training (needs analysis), *inputs* to training (examining the resources available for training, such as budgets and schedules), the *process* of conducting the training program (for feedback to the implementers), and the *product* or outcome of training (success in meeting program objectives). Galvin also reported survey results indicating that ASTD members preferred the CIPP model of evaluation to Kirkpatrick's framework. Warr et al. proposed a similar model.[28]

Brinkerhoff extends the training evaluation model to six stages. He suggests a cycle of overlapping steps, with problems identified in one step possibly caused by things occurring in previous steps. His stages or steps are:

1. Goal Setting: What is the need?
2. Program Design: What will work to meet the need?
3. Program Implementation: Is it working, with the focus on the implementation of the program?
4. Immediate Outcomes: Did participants learn?
5. Intermediate or Usage Outcomes: Are the participants using what they learned?
6. Impacts and Worth: Did it make a worthwhile difference to the organization?[29]

At least two attempts have been made to develop models that incorporate research and theory on learning outcomes and the variables that influence them. Kraiger, Ford, and Salas offered one such model.[30] Noting that learning outcomes can be of three types (i.e., cognitive, skill-based, and affective), they propose a classification scheme for evaluating learning outcomes in each of these three areas. This scheme (shown in Table 7-2) is quite specific, identifying the types of measures that can be used for learning outcomes in each category.

Holton suggests a complex model that has outcomes similar to Kirkpatrick's (i.e., learning, individual performance, and organizational results).[31] The model includes individual variables (e.g., motivation to learn, motivation to transfer, ability, job attitudes) and environmental variables (e.g., transfer climate, external events) that influence these outcomes.

## COMPARING EVALUATION FRAMEWORKS

As you might have noticed, all of the evaluation frameworks incorporate Kirkpatrick's levels of evaluation in one way or another, either as explicit steps in the model or as information collected within the steps. None are incompatible with the framework Kirkpatrick proposed.[32] The most dramatic extension beyond Kirkpatrick's ideas is the notion that HRD professionals should be concerned about the impact their programs have on constituencies *outside* of the organization.[33] Whether that sort of assessment should be routinely included in HRD evaluation would probably depend on how the individual and the management of the organization view their organization's social responsibility. Further, it is likely that those who feel strongly about social responsibility would consider and assess the societal impact of all of their activities, regardless of whether an evaluation model specifies that they should or not. For those who do not, inclusion of such a level is unlikely to lead them to change their point of view.

Some models differ from Kirkpatrick's in that they bring the earlier phases of the training process, needs assessment, design, and implementation, into the evaluation phase. For example, the first three stages of Brinkerhoff's model (goal setting, program design, and program implementation) explicitly include these activities.[34] Merging the rest of the training process into evaluation may improve Kirkpatrick's

| TABLE 7-2 | | A CLASSIFICATION SCHEME FOR LEARNING OUTCOMES FOR TRAINING EVALUATION | |
|---|---|---|---|

| Category | Learning Construct(s) | Focus of Measurement | Potential Training Evaluation Methods |
|---|---|---|---|
| **Cognitive** | | **Cognitive outcomes** | |
| Verbal knowledge | Declarative knowledge | Amount of knowledge Accuracy of recall Speed, accessibility of knowledge | Recognition and recall tests Power tests Speed tests |
| Knowledge organization | Mental models | Similarity to ideal Interrelationships of elements Hierarchical ordering | Free sorts Structural assessment (e.g., Pathfinder) |
| Cognitive strategies | Self-insight Metacognitive skills | Self-awareness Self-regulation | Probed protocol analysis Self-report Readiness for testing |
| **Skill based** | | **Skill-based outcomes** | |
| Compilation | Composition Proceduralization | Speed of performance Fluidity of performance Error rates Chunking Generalization Discrimination Strengthening | Targeted behavioral observation Hands-on testing Structured situational interviews |
| Automaticity | Automatic processing Tuning | Attentional requirements Available cognitive resources | Secondary task performance Interference problems Embedded measurement |
| **Affective** | | **Affective outcomes** | |
| Attitudinal | Targeted object (e.g., safety awareness) Attitude strength | Attitude direction Attitude strength Accessibility Centrality Conviction | Self-report measures |
| Motivation | Motivational disposition | Mastery versus performance orientations Appropriateness of orientation | Self-report measures |
| | Self-efficacy | Perceived performance capability | Self-report measures |
| | Goal setting | Level of goals Complexity of goal structures Goal commitment | Self-report measures Free recall measures Free sorts |

SOURCE: K. Kraiger, J. K. Ford, & E. Salas (1993). "Application of cognitive, skill-based, and affective theories of learning outcomes to new methods of training evaluation." *Journal of Applied Psychology, 78*, table 1, 323. Copyright © 1993 by the American Psychological Association. Adapted with permission.

approach, as there is some merit in helping managers, supervisors, and HRD professionals realize that evaluation is an ongoing activity, not one that should begin only after the training program has been implemented. Effective HRD involves many decisions, and having accurate, meaningful information available throughout the process can improve the decision-making process and enhance the overall effectiveness of HRD efforts.

Overall, we believe that the most serious shortcomings of Kirkpatrick's framework are (1) the lack of explicit causal relationships among the different levels, (2) the lack of specificity in dealing with different types of learning outcomes, and (3) the lack of direction concerning which measures are appropriate to assess which outcome measures. As we have shown in Chapter 3, much has been discovered about the learning process and learning outcomes. We agree with Alliger and Janak that Kirkpatrick's approach provides a useful starting point for HRD evaluation.[35] However, there does *not* appear to be an inherent hierarchy among the four levels, that is, that trainees must first like the training, then learn something, then perform the desired behaviors, and then produce positive results.[36]

For example, in a research project on enhancing the effectiveness of behavior modeling training, a reaction measure was collected immediately after training. Trainees who were told that they needed to use a checklist to track their progress for four weeks after training liked the training significantly *less* than did trainees told to "do their best" to use the principles taught in training. When the same reaction measure was given four week later, however, the trainees who had used the checklists were now more favorable about the training as a whole, whereas those in the "do your best" condition were less favorable toward the training. The means on this measure were now indistinguishable. Furthermore, the trainees who used the checklists demonstrated significantly more retention of the training material four weeks after training, and could demonstrate more of the key behaviors in a spontaneous role-play exercise than could the trainees who had not made use of the checklists.[37] Our point is simply that trainers should not assume positive (or negative) scores on one type of measure will *necessarily* translate into similar scores on measures of a different training outcome.

We believe that efforts to incorporate research and theory on learning and learning outcomes are the most useful additions to the training evaluation literature. Holton's model may prove to be useful, although it requires further development, refinement, and empirical testing.[38] It seems to us that Kraiger, Ford, and Salas's classification scheme represents the most promising new direction for training evaluation. It both addresses a specific need (offering conceptually based measurement suggestions to fit various types of learning) and can be used as a foundation on which to build a theory-based model of HRD evaluation. Finally, recent work on return on investment (ROI), pioneered by Jack Phillips, also represents a significant development in HRD evaluation.[39] We discuss ROI issues later in the chapter.

Despite all the criticism, Kirkpatrick's approach remains a useful way to categorize the criteria that an effective HRD program must satisfy. If possible, information assessing all four levels of criteria should be collected (depending on the questions being asked that prompt the evaluation study). It is also important to make informed decisions about all aspects of the HRD program. The proper techniques, including those we discussed in Chapters 4 through 6, along with those we will introduce in this chapter, can ensure that such information is available.

In its simplest form, evaluation should address the question of whether the training program achieved its objectives.[40] Basing training objectives on needs assessment information, and then evaluating those objectives, is the most parsimonious way of summarizing what training evaluation is all about.[41] The process framework we have emphasized in Chapters 4 through 7 provides a strong platform for systematically approaching HRD efforts (see Figure 7-1). *If* this framework is in place, and is used, then we think that evaluation efforts can focus on some combination of the following points (depending upon the situation). While this is only a modest expansion of Kirkpatrick, it highlights some aspects not fully captured by the "four levels."

1. reaction
   a. affective — How well did trainees like the training? (See the affective measures in Table 7-2.)
   b. perceived usefulness/utility — What was the perceived usefulness of this training?
2. learning — How much did trainees learn from the training? (See the cognitive measures in Table 7-2.)
3. behavior — What behavior change occurred as a result of training? (See the skill-based measures in Table 7-2.)
4. results
   a. What tangible outcomes or results occurred as a result of training?
   b. What was the return on investment (ROI) for this training? (See ROI and utility sections below.)
   c. What was the contribution of this training program to the community/larger society?

## DATA COLLECTION FOR HRD EVALUATION

By definition, any evaluation effort requires the collection of data to provide decision makers with facts and judgments upon which they can base their decisions. Three important aspects of providing information for HRD evaluation include data collection methods, types of data, and the use of self-report data.

### DATA COLLECTION METHODS

In Chapter 4, we listed data sources and collection methods that can be used to provide information for needs assessment. The same data collection methods and sources are available when conducting training evaluation. Table 7-3 lists some common methods for collecting evaluation data, including interviews, questionnaires, direct observation tests and simulations, and archival performance data. Additionally, recall the suggestions offered by Kraiger, Ford, and Salas concerning learning

| TABLE 7-3 | DATA COLLECTION METHODS FOR HRD EVALUATION |

| Method | Description |
| --- | --- |
| 1. Interview | Conversation with one or more individuals to assess their opinions, observations, and beliefs |
| 2. Questionnaire | A standardized set of questions intended to assess opinions, observations, and beliefs |
| 3. Direct Observation | Observing a task or set of tasks as they are performed and recording what is seen |
| 4. Tests and Simulations | Structured situation to assess an individual's knowledge or proficiency to perform some task or behavior |
| 5. Archival Performance Data | Use of existing information, such as files or reports |

outcomes and measures.[42] Questionnaires are most often used in HRD evaluation because they can be completed and analyzed quickly. Figure 7-2 shows an example of a questionnaire that might be used to gather participant feedback (such questionnaires are sometimes called "smile sheets"). For instance, the question "I would recommend this program to others" is a question meant to capture trainee reactions.[43] Some guidelines for writing effective questionnaires are listed in Figure 7-3. Jeffrey Berk of KnowledgeAdvisors provides some useful information and guidance concerning paper-based, online, and e-mail versions of training evaluations.[44]

Any or all of these methods are appropriate for collecting evaluation data, depending on their relevance to the questions being asked. For example, if an HRD professional is interested in assessing trainee reactions to a seminar on pension benefits, interviews or questionnaires might be good choices. Alternatively, if management wanted to know whether the seminar affected interest in the company's pension plan, the number of inquiries employees make to the HR department about the pension plan could be tracked through direct observation or archival data. Some advantages and disadvantages of using various data collection methods are listed in Table 7-4.

Cheri Ostroff developed an interesting way to measure whether trainees use what they have learned back on the job.[45] One problem with supervisors' observations has been the difficulties supervisors often have in recalling specific behaviors that an employee has engaged in. Ostroff presented supervisors or other observers with a scripted situation and asked them to check off which of several behaviors the employee has engaged in or would be most likely to perform.

Ostroff compared this technique to more traditional behavior and performance measures in assessing the effectiveness of a training program for school principals (see Figure 7-4). Only the scripted situation method revealed the significant effects of the training program. Further research is needed to assess the effectiveness and generalizability of the scripted situation method.[46] However, Ostroff's findings represent the kind of research that will make data collection and evaluation more accurate and feasible in organizational settings.

**FIGURE 7-2**     **A PARTICIPANT REACTION QUESTIONNAIRE**

Title of the session:_____

The purposes of this rapid-feedback evaluation are to find out how you are doing, to find out how we are doing as facilitators of your learning experience, and to get your opinions about the content of the course and the training methods we are using together.

Please circle the number on the 1–5-point scale that best expresses your opinion for each question.

|  | No, waste of time | | It was useful | | Yes, very worthwhile |
|---|---|---|---|---|---|
| 1. Do you think that this session was worthwhile? | 1 | 2 | 3 | 4 | 5 |
|  | Not at all | | It was useful | | Very much |
| 2. How much did you personally need this session? | 1 | 2 | 3 | 4 | 5 |
|  | Not at all | | To some degree | | Completely |
| 3. To what extent were you able to participate actively in the learning experience? | 1 | 2 | 3 | 4 | 5 |
|  | Poorly | | Well | | Very well |
| 4. How well did the trainer(s) do the job? | 1 | 2 | 3 | 4 | 5 |

5. What did you like most about this session?

6. What did you like least, and how could we improve?

7. Do you have any comments or suggestions?

SOURCE: From N. L. Weatherby & M. E. Gorosh (1989). Rapid Response with Spreadsheets. *Training and Development Journal, 43*(9), p. 76. Reprinted by permission. Copyright © September 1989 from Training & Development Journal by Weatherby, N. L., & Gorosh, M. E. Reprinted with permission of American Society for Training & Development.

## CHOOSING DATA COLLECTION METHODS

Three vital issues to consider when deciding which data collection method to use are reliability, validity, and practicality. **Reliability** has to do with the consistency of results, and with the freedom from error and bias in a data collection method. A method that has little or no error or bias is highly reliable, whereas the results of a method that has significant error or bias is unreliable and cannot be trusted. Decisions based on unreliable information are likely to be poor ones.

For example, suppose employee leadership skills are judged by having supervisors watch employees interact with each other in a role-playing exercise. If one of the supervisors assigns consistently harsher scores than the others, that personal bias and error will be reflected in low leadership ability scores for certain employees who might otherwise be considered excellent leaders.

**FIGURE 7-3** **GUIDELINES FOR WRITING EFFECTIVE QUESTIONNAIRES**

1. **Write simply and clearly, and make the meaning obvious.**
   Good example:  How often does your boss give you feedback on your job performance?
   Bad example:   To what extent do administrative superiors provide information regarding the quality of performance of people on your level?

2. **Ask discrete questions.**
   Good example:  1. The organization's goals are clear.
                  2. My role within the organization is clear.
   Bad example:   The organization's goals and your role within the organization are clear to you.

3. **Provide discrete response options and explain them.**
   Good example:  During the past three months, how often did you receive feedback on your work?

   | not once | about every month | about once/ week | about every day or so | several times a day |
   |----------|-------------------|------------------|-----------------------|---------------------|
   | 1        | 2                 | 3                | 4                     | 5                   |

   Bad example:   During the past three months, how often did you receive feedback on your work?

   | rarely | | occasionally | | frequently |
   |--------|---|-------------|---|-----------|
   | 1      | 2 | 3           | 4 | 5         |

4. **Limit the number of response options.**
   Good example:  What percent of the time are you generally sure of what the outcomes of your work efforts will be?

   | 0–20% | 21–40% | 41–60% | 61–80% | 81–100% |
   |-------|--------|--------|--------|---------|
   | 1     | 2      | 3      | 4      | 5       |

   Bad example:   What percent of the time are you generally sure of what the outcomes of your work efforts will be?

   | 0–20 | 21–30 | 31–40 | 41–50 | 51–60 | 61–70 | 71–80 | 81–90 | 91–100 |
   |------|-------|-------|-------|-------|-------|-------|-------|--------|
   | 1    | 2     | 3     | 4     | 5     | 6     | 7     | 8     | 9      |

5. **Match the response mode to the question.**
   Good example:  To what extent are you generally satisfied with your job?

   | not at all | a little | some | quite a bit | very much |
   |------------|----------|------|-------------|-----------|
   | 1          | 2        | 3    | 4           | 5         |

   Bad example:   Are you generally satisfied with your job?
                  YES          NO

6. **Get all of the important information.**

SOURCE: From J. H. Maher, Jr., & C. E. Kur (1983). Constructing Good Questionnaires. *Training and Development Journal,* 37(6), 106. Reprinted by permission. Copyright © June 1983 from Training & Development Journal by Maher, Jr., J. H., & Kur, C. E. Reprinted with permission of American Society for Training & Development.

**TABLE 7-4**

## ADVANTAGES AND LIMITATIONS OF VARIOUS DATA COLLECTION METHODS

| Method | Advantages | Limitations |
|---|---|---|
| Interview | Flexible<br>Opportunity for clarification<br>Depth possible<br>Personal contact | High reactive effects<br>High cost<br>Face-to-face threat potential<br>Labor intensive<br>Trained observers needed |
| Questionnaire | Low cost<br>Honesty increased if anonymous<br>Anonymity possible<br>Respondent sets pace<br>Variety of options | Possible inaccurate data<br>On-job responding conditions not controlled<br>Respondents set varying paces<br>Return rate beyond control |
| Direct Observation | Nonthreatening<br>Excellent way to measure behavior change | Possibly disruptive<br>Reactive effect possible<br>May be unreliable<br>Trained observers needed |
| Written Test | Low purchase cost<br>Readily scored<br>Quickly processed<br>Easily administered<br>Wide sampling possible | May be threatening<br>Possible low relation to job performance<br>Reliance on norms may distort individual performance<br>Possible cultural bias |
| Simulation/Performance Test | Reliable<br>Objective<br>Close relation to job performance | Time consuming<br>Simulation often difficult<br>High development cost |
| Archival Performance Data | Reliable<br>Objective<br>Job-based<br>Easy to review<br>Minimal reactive effects | Lack of knowledge of criteria for keeping or discarding records<br>Information system discrepancies<br>Indirect<br>Need for conversion to usable form<br>Record prepared for other purposes<br>May be expensive to collect |

SOURCE: Reprinted from *Handbook of training evaluation and measurement methods*, J. J. Phillips, p. 92, Copyright 1983, with permission from Elsevier.

**FIGURE 7-4**

## THE SCRIPTED SITUATION DATA COLLECTION METHOD: ITEM FROM A SCHOOL PRINCIPAL PERFORMANCE SURVEY

The administrator receives a letter from a parent objecting to the content of the science section. The section topic is reproduction. The parent objects to his daughter having exposure to such materials and demands that something be done. The administrator would most likely (check one):

_____ Ask the teacher to provide handouts, materials, and curriculum content for review.

_____ Check the science curriculum for the board-approved approach to reproduction and compare board guidelines to course content.

_____ Ask the head of the science department for his/her own opinion about the teacher's lesson plan.

_____ Check to see if the parent has made similar complaints in the past.

SOURCE: From C. Ostroff (1991). Training effectiveness measures and scoring schemes: A comparison. *Personnel Psychology, 44,* 360. Reprinted by permission.

Another issue to consider in selecting a data collection method is validity. **Validity** is concerned with whether the data collection method actually measures what we want it to measure, that is, are we hitting the right target? For example, suppose a trainer decides to use a written test to measure whether trainees have learned the procedure for completing travel expense forms. The test is valid to the extent that the scores on the test indicate whether the employee actually knows how to complete the forms. If the focus of training was on knowing which information to report on the expense form, yet the items on the test focus more on performing calculations, the test scores may be measuring the wrong thing. If this is the case, use of such a test will likely lead to poor decisions.

Reliability and validity are complex issues, and assessing them often requires knowledge of statistics and measurement concepts. HRD professionals who are unfamiliar with these concepts should read more about the topic or consult other members of the organization, knowledgeable professors, or consultants who are familiar with these issues.[47]

In addition to being reliable and valid, data collection methods must also be *practical*, given the constraints of the organization. **Practicality** concerns how much time, money, and resources are available for the evaluation method. For example, conducting interviews with all supervisors to assess employee job behavior may take more time than the staff has available. In this case, interviewing a sample of supervisors or using a questionnaire may be practical alternatives. As mentioned earlier, realistic and creative trade-offs can ensure that the evaluation effort is carried out and yields useful information.

### TYPES OF DATA

At least three types of data are available for evaluating HRD effectiveness: individual performance, systemwide performance, and economic.[48] Individual performance data emphasize the individual trainee's knowledge and behaviors (Kirkpatrick's Levels 2 and 3). Examples of these kinds of data include an employee's test scores, number of units produced, timeliness of performance, quality of performance, attendance, and attitudes. Systemwide performance data concern the team, division, or business unit in which the HRD program was conducted, and could include data concerning the entire organization. Examples of systemwide data include productivity, rework, scrap, customer and client satisfaction, and timeliness. Economic data report the financial and economic performance of the organization or unit, that is, the bottom line, and include profits, product liability, avoidance of penalties (such as fines for noncompliance with laws and regulations), and market share. Economic data is what ROI and utility calculations are generally seeking to provide.

A complete evaluation effort is likely to include all three types of data. Different questions demand different kinds of information. For example, Robinson and Robinson list possible data choices to determine whether a sales training program has impacted an organization's operations, including ratio of new accounts to old accounts, call-to-close ratio, average sale size, items per order, and add-on sales.[49] These and other data could be tracked for individuals, organizational units, or an entire organization. Another useful source for systemwide measures is a recent book by Tesoro and Tootson.[50] Again, the key is to carefully examine the questions being asked or the decisions being made when selecting which data to use.

## THE USE OF SELF-REPORT DATA

**Self-report data,** or data provided directly by individuals involved in the training program, is the most commonly used type of data in HR evaluation.[51] Recall that trainee reactions (Kirkpatrick's Level 1) remain the most widely used evaluation measure. Self-reports can offer personality data, attitudes, and perceptions and can provide information to measure the effectiveness of HRD or other programs. For example, the trainer may measure learning by asking trainees to judge how much they knew before training and how much they feel they know after training. Information collected this way, whether through interviews or questionnaires, can be useful and meaningful. However, Podsakoff and Organ identify two serious problems that can occur when relying on self-report data:

1. **Mono-method bias.** If both reports in a before-and-after evaluation come from the same person at the same time (say, after training), conclusions may be questionable. The respondents may be more concerned about being consistent in their answers than about providing accurate responses.

2. **Socially desirable responses.** Respondents may report what they think the researcher (or boss) wants to hear rather than the truth. For example, employees may be fearful or embarrassed to admit that they learned nothing in a training program.[52]

In addition, there can be what is referred to as a **response shift bias,** in which respondents' perspectives of their skills before training change during the training program and affect their after-training assessment.[53] For example, trainees may discover during training that their pretraining judgment of skill was unrealistically high and then adjust their posttraining evaluations accordingly. As a result, the data may show no improvement of skill after training, even though such an improvement may have occurred.

Self-report data can be useful in HRD evaluation, but relying on self-report data alone can be problematic. Depending on the question being asked, direct observation by trained observers (like supervisors), tests, or simulations can often yield better, more conclusive information than self-reports.

## RESEARCH DESIGN

A **research design** is a plan for conducting an evaluation study. Research design is a complex topic. To inform yourself of all the issues surrounding research design, you could read whole books on the topic. Barring that, we hope that you would read and understand a summary of key points on this topic. However, we also recognize that not every student (or instructor) sees the value of studying this information. So, for the most comprehensive treatment of this topic, we urge you to consult the resources listed in the following endnote.[54] For those seeking thorough, though condensed coverage of research design issues, we provide an appendix to this chapter that goes into more detail than we do here. We have often found that students are more interested in this material when they are faced with a project on the job, and they are looking for reference material to help them make choices for a project they are designing ("What was it you said again was the minimal acceptable design for a training evaluation study?"), and the appendix provides you with some key information that can inform your decisions concerning the most appropriate research design to use for particular situations. At the minimum, however, there are some critical issues that every HRD student should understand. We present these below. While this is far from a complete treatment of the topic, we hope to convey the importance of research design issues to effective HRD evaluation.

Research design is critical to HRD evaluation. It specifies the expected results of the evaluation study, the methods of data collection, and how the data will be analyzed. Awareness of research design issues and possible design alternatives can help managers and HRD professionals do a better job of conducting evaluations and critiquing the results of evaluation studies.

When evaluating any HRD effort, the researcher or HRD professional would like to have a high level of confidence that any changes observed after the program or intervention were due to that intervention, and not to some other factor (such as changes in the economy, the organization, or the reward structure in place). This is the basic notion of validity, that is, are we confident in the accuracy of our conclusions?

Unfortunately, it still remains quite typical that, if outcomes are measured at all, they are only collected *after* the training program has been completed. The basic picture is as follows:

Training provided                Evaluation measures collected

The trainer would obviously like to see high values on each measure collected, for example, positive reactions, high scores on the learning measures, and positive indications of behavior change and results. But what might be some problems of collecting measures only *after* the training has been completed? For one thing, such a one-shot approach may not be measuring the most important things. Recall our earlier discussions of how evaluation should be tied directly to the objectives determined via the needs assessment process. An evaluation measure that is too broad or generic may not capture real changes that have occurred as a result of training. A second drawback of this after-only approach is that one can't be certain that the outcomes attained were due to the training. Simply put, this approach to evaluation doesn't give any indication of trainees' initial skill or knowledge level, that is, where they started. To have greater confidence that the outcomes observed were brought about by the training (and not some other extraneous factor), the following practices should be included in the research design:

1. **Pretest and posttest** — Including both a pretest and a posttest allows the trainer to see what has changed after the training. If the majority of trainees already knew the material covered in training before they started it, then high scores on the posttest measure of learning become much less impressive.

2. **Control group** — A control group is a group of employees similar to those who receive training, yet who don't receive training at the same time as those who are trained. However, this group receives the same evaluation measures as the group that is trained, and this allows for a comparison of their scores. The ideal scenario is where the training group and the control group have similar scores before training, and then the scores for the training group increase after training, while those of the control group remain constant. This provides fairly strong evidence that the training (and not some other factor) was responsible for the changes on the outcome measures.

Combining these two points creates what can be called the "pretest-posttest with control group" research design. We view this as the minimum acceptable research design for most training and HRD evaluation efforts. There may be times when trainers have to get by with less, but the degree of confidence in one's findings will always be lower if one or both of these factors is missing (though see the Appendix for research by Sackett and Mullin).[55]

Two other factors should be included in a strong research design. First, if a control group is used, the trainer should ensure that the training and control groups are as similar as possible. For example, it would be unacceptable if the group receiving training had greater existing knowledge, skills, or abilities than the control group, as this would bias the results that were obtained after training. If the trainer is using existing or intact groups, he or she should use archival data to show that the two groups do not differ in any significant way (e.g., test scores, years of experience). Further, if it is possible, it is advantageous if individuals can be randomly assigned to the training and control groups. Such **random assignment** further increases the confidence one can have that training brought about the observed changes (and, in this case, not some characteristic that differed between the two groups). It must be pointed out that in many real-life training settings, random assignment is impractical, and is thus not widely used. However, random assignment increases the likelihood of obtaining valid results from one's evaluation efforts.

A second factor to consider is the collection of data over time. Such an approach, called a **time series design,** allows the trainer to observe patterns in individual performance. For example, if performance is relatively steady over time, and then shows a clear spike after training, and then remains at this higher level over time, this would again suggest that the result was due to the training, and not some other factor.

A final point to make here has to do with sample size. Researchers and practitioners often get frustrated with one another over this issue, as the number of people providing data for a training evaluation is often lower than what would be recommended for purposes of statistical analysis. That is, there are practical limitations in many training situations that limit the number of people receiving training (or in the control group) to a relatively small number. One study of research on training evaluation found that the median sample size across these studies was forty-three people.[56] Yet, having low numbers of trainees is often disastrous for statistical analyses, because small sample sizes make it difficult to attain statistically significant results, *even when the training has in fact had an impact*. It is generally recommended that, as a bare minimum, the training and control groups each need at least thirty individuals to have even a moderate chance of obtaining statistically significant results. However, many researchers would prefer to see a number much higher than this, for example, at least 100 people in each condition (some researchers would go even higher). This is difficult to attain in many situations. One approach is to pool data within an organization (such as collecting data from the same training program offered over time). Also, recent efforts to combine data from different research studies via **meta-analysis** have also helped to determine the impact (or effect size) of various training interventions. For example, in a widely cited meta-analytic study, Burke and Day combined the results from many different studies to find the "average" effectiveness of numerous managerial training methods.[57] The main point, however, is that HRD professionals need to give careful thought to sample size issues *before* they undertake training and evaluation. When sample sizes are small, it is much harder to show that the training intervention had a positive impact on desired individual and organizational outcomes.

Another vital topic for training evaluation has to do with ethics. Choices concerning evaluation often force the trainer or researcher to make difficult ethical decisions. These are discussed next.

## ETHICAL ISSUES CONCERNING EVALUATION RESEARCH

Many of the decisions supervisors and HRD professionals make have ethical dimensions.[58] This is a far larger issue than we will address here.[59] Resolving the paradoxes inherent in ethical dilemmas is no easy task. Yet, it is vital that these issues be addressed. In terms of training evaluation, actions such as assigning participants to training and control groups, reporting results, and the actual conduct of the evaluation study all raise ethical questions. Schmitt and Klimoski identified four ethical issues relating to HRD evaluation: informed consent, withholding training, the use of deception, pressure to produce findings.[60] To this list, we add the issue of confidentiality.

## CONFIDENTIALITY

Some evaluation research projects involve asking participants questions about their own or others' job performance. The results of these inquiries may be embarrassing or lead to adverse treatment by others if they are made public. For example, if evaluation of a management development seminar involves asking participants their opinion of their supervisors, supervisors may become angry with participants who report that they don't think the supervisors are doing a good job. Similarly, employees who perform poorly or make mistakes on important outcome measures (like written tests or role-playing exercises) may be ridiculed by other employees.

Wherever possible, steps should be taken to ensure the confidentiality of information collected during an evaluation study. Using code numbers rather than names, collecting only necessary demographic information, reporting group rather than individual results, using encrypted computer files, and securing research materials are all ways to maintain confidentiality. As a result of such efforts, trainees may be more willing to participate in the evaluation project.

## INFORMED CONSENT

In many research settings, such as hospitals and academic institutions, evaluation studies are monitored by a review board to ensure that participants are aware that they are participating in a study and know its purpose, what they will be expected to do, and the potential risks and benefits of participating. In addition, participants are asked to sign a form stating that they have been informed of these facts and agree to participate in the study. This is called obtaining the participants' **informed consent.**

Review boards and informed consent are not common in industrial settings; often the norm in these organizations is that management has control over and responsibility for employees. We agree with Schmitt and Klimoski that ethical considerations and good management are compatible.[61] Wherever possible, informed consent should be obtained from employees who participate in an evaluation study. Involving them in this way motivates researchers to treat the employees fairly, and it may actually improve the effectiveness of the training intervention by providing complete information.[62]

## WITHHOLDING TRAINING

Research designs involving control groups require that some employees receive training while others do not. This apparent partiality can be problematic if the training is believed to improve some employees' performance, which could lead to organizational benefits like a raise or promotion, or if the training could increase some employees' well-being, as in health-related programs. If the training is expected to be effective, is it fair to train some employees and not others just for purposes of evaluation?

There are at least three possible resolutions to this dilemma.[63] First, an unbiased procedure, such as a lottery, can be used to assign employees to training groups. Second, employees who are assigned to a control group can be assured that if the training is found to be effective, they will have the option of receiving the training at a later time. Third, the research design can be modified so that both groups are trained, but at different times. One possible design is illustrated below.

| Group 1: | Measure | Training | Measure | Measure |
| Group 2: | Measure | Measure | Training | Measure |

In fact, when a large number of people are going to be trained in small groups over a period of time, this type of design is quite feasible. However, whatever approach is used, dealing with the issue of withholding training is often a matter of practicality, in addition to an ethical matter. It is possible, for example, that employees assigned to a control group may refuse to participate in the study or be less motivated to complete the outcome measures.

## USE OF DECEPTION

In some cases, an investigator may feel that the study will yield better results if employees don't realize they are in an evaluation study, or if they are given some false or misleading information during the study. This is most often the case when the training is conducted as part of a formal research experiment, and less likely with more typical organizational evaluation practices. Nonetheless, we believe this practice is generally unethical and should be used only as a last resort. Employees who are deceived may become angry with management, damaging a trust that is difficult to reestablish. Any benefits of the HRD program are likely to be undermined by the effects on employees who feel they have been betrayed.

Alternatives to deception should be considered. If deception is used, it should be as minimal as possible, and employees in the study should be informed of the deception and the reasons for it as soon as their participation in the study ends.[64]

## PRESSURE TO PRODUCE POSITIVE RESULTS

HRD professionals and their managers may feel pressure to make certain that the results of their evaluation demonstrate that the program was effective. This may be one reason why rigorous evaluation of HRD programs is not done more often. The HRD people are the ones who design and develop (or purchase), deliver, and evaluate the program. If the evaluation shows the program was not effective, the HRD department may lose funding and support and have its activities curtailed.

Although the possibility exists for fraud in the form of doctoring results, reporting partial results, or setting up biased studies, it is unclear how often this occurs in HRD evaluation. However, given that reports of evaluation fraud in other areas of organizational life are fairly common, one cannot help but have concerns about the state of affairs in HRD evaluation.

Professional standards and ethical conduct call for those conducting HRD evaluations to report complete results. That having been said, it is no doubt difficult for many people to face the potential consequences of bad results. This leads to our last major topic in this chapter, namely, how to demonstrate that a training intervention has had a positive impact on important organizational measures.

## ASSESSING THE IMPACT OF HRD PROGRAMS IN DOLLAR TERMS

Following both Kirkpatrick and Phillips, one of the more important issues to examine is the effect of an HRD program on the organization's effectiveness. This assessment can be done using a variety of performance indexes, such as productivity, timeliness, and cost savings. It is important to demonstrate effectiveness on the reaction, learning, and job behavior levels, but HR managers and HRD professionals may be at a disadvantage when their results are compared to those of other divisions that are able to express their results in monetary terms.

One of the goals of translating the effects of HRD programs into dollar terms is to make clear that the programs are *investments* and as such will lead to payoffs for the organization in the future. Although many managers and supervisors pay lip service to this idea, they often see HRD and other HR interventions primarily as *costs* — exemplified by the fact that HR programs are often the first programs cut when financial and economic pressures force the organization to reduce its expenses.

It has long been argued that HR programs are difficult to assess in financial terms, but the evaluation of training costs (including ROI) and utility analysis are two practical ways to determine the financial impact of various HRD programs.

### EVALUATION OF TRAINING COSTS

Evaluation of training costs compares the costs incurred in conducting an HRD program to the benefits received by the organization, and can involve two categories of activities: cost-benefit evaluation and cost-effectiveness evaluation.[65] **Cost-benefit analysis** involves comparing the monetary costs of training to the benefits received in nonmonetary terms, such as improvements in attitudes, safety, and health. **Cost-effectiveness analysis** focuses on the financial benefits accrued from training, such as increases in quality and profits, and reduction in waste and processing time. A framework offered by Cullen et al. distinguishes between structured and unstructured training, and it lists possible training costs (training development, materials, time, and production losses) and benefits (improvements in time to reach job competency, job performance, and work attitudes).[66]

Robinson and Robinson developed a model that divides training costs into five categories: direct costs, indirect costs, development costs, overhead costs, and compensation for participants (see Table 7-5).[67] These costs are then compared to benefits as measured by improvements in operational indicators, such as job performance, quality, and work attitudes.

The general strategy for evaluating training costs is to measure cost and benefit indicators in dollar terms (or translate them to dollar terms) and then compare

---

**TABLE 7-5**                                                    **TRAINING PROGRAM COSTS**

To calculate the cost of a training program, an HRD professional should consider five categories of expenses.

**Direct costs**

These are costs directly associated with the delivery of the learning activities. They include course materials (reproduced or purchased), instructional aids, equipment rental, travel, food and other refreshments, and the instructor's salary and benefits.

Such costs are so directly tied to the delivery of a particular program that if you canceled the program the day before you planned to conduct it, you would not incur them. (While program materials may have been reproduced or purchased, they would not be consumed, and so they would be available for a future program.)

**Indirect costs**

These costs are incurred in support of learning activities, but cannot be identified with any particular program. Even if the program were canceled at the last minute, such costs could not be recovered.

Examples would be costs for instructor preparation, clerical and administrative support, course materials already sent to participants, and time spent by the training staff in planning the program's implementation. Expenses for marketing the program (for example, direct-mail costs) would also be considered indirect costs. Marketing may have cost $2,000. If there is insufficient registration and if the program is canceled, the $2,000 cannot be recovered.

**Development costs**

All costs incurred during the development of the program go in this category. Typically, they include the development of videotapes and computer-based instructional programming, design of program materials, piloting of the program, and any necessary redesign. This category also includes the cost of the front-end assessment, or that portion of the assessment directly attributed to the program. In addition, the costs of evaluation and tracking are included.

If a program is to be conducted for a few years, the cost is often amortized over that period. For example, one-third of the development cost may be charged off in the first year of implementation, one-third in the second year, and one-third in the last year. Otherwise, there is a real "bulge" in the budget, because of development costs during the first year.

**Overhead costs**

These costs are not directly related to a training program, but are essential to the smooth operation of the training department.

If you have audiovisual equipment that has been purchased specifically for your department, there is a cost to maintain that equipment. Some portion of that annual cost should be charged to

*continued*

| TABLE 7-5 | CONTINUED |
|---|---|

the various training programs. If you have classroom space available to you, there is an overhead cost for supplying heat and lighting. The cost of supporting that space for days when the classroom is used for particular courses should be charged to those programs.

**Compensation for participants**

These costs comprise the salaries and benefits paid to participants for the time they are in a program. If the program is two days long, salaries and benefits for your participants for those two days are costs of the program.

   Typically, HRD professionals do not know what individual people earn, but can obtain that information by asking the compensation department to provide a figure for an average salary paid to the various levels of people who will be attending. The average salary is then multiplied by the number of people attending the program, to derive a compensation estimate.

SOURCE: From D. G. Robinson & J. Robinson (1989). Training for impact. *Training and Development Journal, 43*(8), 39. Reprinted with the permission of American Society for Training & Development.

them. For example, a program's **return on investment (ROI)** can be calculated by dividing total results by total benefits:

$$\text{Return on investment} = \frac{\text{Results}}{\text{Training costs}}$$

The greater the ratio of results to costs, the greater the benefit the organization receives by conducting the training program. For example, Bank of America recently conducted a training program designed for its in-house trainers. Positive reaction, learning, and behavior measures were obtained. Additionally, a 1.15 (or 115 percent) ROI was determined for this program. For this, the company received an Excellence in Practice citation from ASTD in 2003.[68]

   If the ROI ratio is less than 1, then the training program costs more than it returns to the organization. Such a program needs to be either modified or dropped (there may, of course, be times when some noneconomic or legally mandated reason exists to continue a certain training program; even here, however, if the ROI for the program is negative, some rethinking or reworking of the program is likely in order).

   Table 7-6 shows how Robinson and Robinson applied their model to calculate the costs for a training program they conducted at a wood-panel producing plant. Table 7-7 shows how they calculated the results and return on investment for the same plant.[69]

*ISSUES IN COMPUTING AND USING ROI ESTIMATES.* Using ROI estimates to express the contribution of an HRD program has received increased attention. For example, Jack Phillips published three articles that advocated using ROI ratios and offered advice on how HRD practitioners could do this.[70] (Recall that Phillips proposed a modification of Kirkpatrick's four-level evaluation model to include ROI as Level 5.) Patti and Jack Phillips have written a recent article addressing ROI

**TABLE 7-6**

## EXAMPLE OF TRAINING COST ANALYSIS

Direct costs: The travel and per-diem cost is zero, because training took place adjacent to the plant. There is a cost for classroom space and audiovisual equipment, because these were rented from a local hotel. Refreshments were purchased at the same hotel. Because different supervisors attended the morning and afternoon sessions, lunch was not provided.

Indirect costs: The clerical and administrative costs reflect the amount of clerical time spent on making arrangements for the workshop facilities, sending out notices to all participants, and preparing class rosters and other miscellaneous materials.

Development costs: These costs represent the purchase of the training program from a vendor. Included are instructional aids, an instructor manual, videotapes, and a licensing fee. The instructor-training costs pertain to the one-week workshop that the instructor attended to become prepared to facilitate the training. Front-end assessment costs were covered by the corporate training budget.

Overhead costs: These represent the services that the general organization provides to the training unit. Because figures were not available, we used 10 percent of the direct, indirect, and program development costs.

Compensation for participants: This figure represents the salaries and benefits paid to all participants while they attended the workshop.

**Direct Costs**

| | |
|---|---:|
| Outside Instructor | 0 |
| In-house instructor — 12 days × $125 | $ 1,500.00 |
| Fringe benefits @ 25% of salary | $ 375.00 |
| Travel and per-diem expenses | 0 |
| Materials-56 × $60/participant | $ 3,360.00 |
| Classroom space and audiovisual equipment — 12 days @ $50 | $ 600.00 |
| Food; refreshments $4/day × 3 days × 56 participants | $ 672.00 |
| **Total direct costs** | **$ 6,507.00** |

**Indirect Costs**

| | |
|---|---:|
| Training management | 0 |
| Clerical/administrative | $ 750.00 |
| Fringe benefits — 25% of clerical/ administrative salary | $ 187.00 |
| Postage, shipping, telephone | 0 |
| Pre- and postlearning materials $4 × 56 participants | $ 224.00 |
| **Total indirect costs** (rounded to nearest dollar) | **$ 1,161.00** |

**Development Costs**

| | |
|---|---:|
| Fee to purchase program | $ 3,600.00 |
| Instructor training | |
| Registration fee | $ 1,400.00 |
| Travel and lodging | $ 975.00 |
| Salary | $ 625.00 |
| Benefits (25% of salary) | $ 156.00 |
| **Total development costs** | **$ 6,756.00** |

**Overhead Costs**

| | |
|---|---:|
| General organization support | 10% of direct, indirect, and development costs |
| Top management's time | |
| **Total overhead costs** | **$ 1,443.00** |

**Compensation for Participants**

| | |
|---|---:|
| Participants' salary and benefits (time away from the job) | |
| **Total compensation** | **$16,696.00** |
| **Total training costs** | **$32,564.00** |
| **Cost per participant** | **$ 581.50** |

SOURCE: From D. G. Robinson & J. Robinson (1989). Training for impact. *Training and Development Journal, 43*(8), 40. Reprinted with the permission of American Society for Training & Development.

| TABLE 7-7 | | EXAMPLE OF CALCULATING TRAINING RETURN ON INVESTMENT | | | |

| Operational Results Area | How Measured | Results Before Training | Results After Training | Differences (+ or −) | Expressed in $ |
|---|---|---|---|---|---|
| Quality of panels | % rejected | 2% rejected 1,440 panels per day | 1.5% rejected 1,080 panels per day | .5% 360 panels | $720 per day $172,800 per year |
| Housekeeping | Visual inspection using 20-item checklist | 10 defects (average) | 2 defects (average) | 8 defects | Not measurable in $ |
| Preventable accidents | Number of accidents | 24 per year | 16 per year | 8 per year | |
| | Direct cost of each accident | $144,000 per year | $96,000 per year | $48,000 | $48,000 per year |
| | | | | Total savings: | $220,800.00 |

$$\text{ROI} = \frac{\text{Return}}{\text{Investment}} = \frac{\text{Operational Results}}{\text{Training Costs}}$$

$$= \frac{\$220,800}{\$32,564} = 6.8$$

SOURCE: From Training for impact; D. G. Robinson & J. Robinson; Copyright © 1989; *Training and Development Journal*, *43*, 41. This material is used by permission of John Wiley & Sons, Inc.

issues in the public sector.[71] Jack Phillips also published a very useful book on HRD evaluation.[72] For example, he offered the following process for collecting the information needed to calculate ROI:

1. Collect Level-4 evaluation data: Ask, Did on-the-job application produce measurable results?
2. Isolate the effects of training from other factors that may have contributed to the results.
3. Convert the results to monetary benefits.
4. Total the costs of training.
5. Compare the monetary benefits with the costs.[73]

Steps 1 and 2 focus on research design issues. With regard to step 3, Phillips advocates collecting both hard and soft data (e.g., units produced and accident cost, employee attitudes, and frequency of use of new skills) that demonstrate a program's effectiveness. This step would obviously be part of the evaluation study. Once this collection is done, Phillips provides suggestions concerning how to convert the data to monetary terms (e.g., using historic costs and estimates from various sources). In a similar vein, Parry provides a worksheet that HRD professionals can use to identify and summarize the costs and benefits associated with an HRD program.[74] More recently, Parry provided several helpful worksheets to assist in the calculation of both ROI and cost-benefit estimates.[75]

Phillips made several suggestions regarding how to increase the credibility of ROI estimates and the cost estimates they are built on.[76] These include using conservative estimates of costs, finding reliable sources for estimates, explaining the assumptions and techniques used to compute costs, and relying on hard data whenever possible. Beyond this, Parry suggests having managers and supervisors calculate training costs.[77] He sees their involvement as a way to remove the potential suspicion that an HRD professional may try to place the data in the most favorable light to his or her own area.

The second line of thinking regarding ROI estimates focuses on whether and when ROI estimates should be used. Recognizing the time and cost involved in creating ROI estimates, Phillips observed that some organizations set targets for how many HRD programs should be evaluated at this level. He cites evaluating 5 percent of an organization's HRD programs at the ROI level as an example of a target that could be used.[78] Willyerd sounds a cautionary note on the use of ROI estimates.[79] She points out that some writers (e.g., Kaplan and Norton) question the overreliance on accounting and financial measures in business in general, and instead call for using an approach to performance measurement that balances a number of perspectives (e.g., financial, customer, internal process, and innovation and learning).[80]

Willyerd suggests that HRD professionals would be wise to follow Kaplan and Norton's notion of a *balanced scorecard* when presenting the effectiveness of HRD programs, and that they collect and communicate data from each of the four perspectives.[81] Doing this, she argues, avoids the shortcomings of relying strictly on financial measures, while still communicating the impact of the HRD program on all of the organization's strategic dimensions. A recent book by Lynn Schmidt emphasizes a training scorecard for training evaluation that goes beyond financial measures alone.[82] Others have made similar arguments as well.[83]

We hope this surge of interest in ROI will encourage HRD practitioners to attempt to use ROI estimates as *one* of the ways they communicate the value of HRD programs. In January 2004, ASTD held an ROI Network Conference in Scottsdale, Arizona. At this conference, Merrill Anderson was honored as ROI practitioner of the year, and Accenture received the ROI impact study award.[84] However, we again stress that such estimates should be used carefully, and that it is important to build the credibility of such estimates in the eyes of management. After all, HRD evaluation is about supporting decisions. Different decisions call for different supporting data, and building credibility can ensure that decision makers will actually heed and use the data provided.

*UTILITY ANALYSIS.* The results of an evaluation study often express the effect of an HRD program in terms of a change in some aspect of the trainee's performance or behavior. For example, if untrained employees average 22.5 units produced (per day, or per hour) and trained employees average 26 units produced, the gain due to training is 3.5 units per employee. **Utility analysis** provides a way to translate these results into dollar terms. One popular approach to utility analysis is the Brogden-Cronbach-Gleser model.[85] This model computes the gain to the organization in dollar terms $\Delta U$, or "change in utility") using the following variables:

N  = Number of trainees
T  = Length of time the benefits are expected to last
$d_t$  = An effect size, which expresses the true difference of job performance between the trained and untrained groups (expressed in standard deviation units)
$SD_y$ = Dollar value of job performance of untrained employees (expressed in standard deviation units)
C  = Costs of conducting the training

Wayne Cascio combined these elements into a formula to compute the dollar value of improved performance due to training.[86] The left side of the equation estimates the benefits of training, while the right side presents the cost. The formula is:

$$\Delta U = (N)(T)(d_t)\,(SD_y) - C$$

Some terms in the equation can be directly measured, such as **N, C,** and $d_t$, but others, such as **T** and $SD_y$, typically must be estimated. More complicated versions of this formula have been developed to account for other factors that may affect the real monetary value of the benefits accrued, such as attrition and decay in the strength of training effects over time.[87]

Cascio suggests a method for incorporating the results of utility analysis into cost-benefit analysis for training and HRD programs.[88] Drawing upon techniques of capital budgeting, the three phases of Cascio's approach are as follows:

1. Compute the minimum annual benefits required to break even on the program (e.g., how much of a payback must the program generate in order to cover its costs?).

2. Use break-even analysis to determine the minimum effect size ($d_t$) that will yield the minimum required annual benefit (how much of an improvement in job performance must the trained employees show for the program to generate the payback needed to break even?).

3. Use the results from meta-analytic studies to determine the expected effect size and expected payoff from the program (what is the likely degree of improvement in job performance that the HRD program being proposed has shown in previously conducted research on this program or method?).

The goal of such cost-benefit analyses is to put HRD professionals on a more equal footing with other managers, so they can demonstrate the expected gains of their programs and compare these gains to either the gains from other programs or other potential investments (like the purchase of a new piece of equipment).

Although the computational formulas for this approach are somewhat complex, Cascio points out that they can be computerized, thereby requiring only that the HRD manager or professional determine and input the values that correspond to each of the key parameters (like cost, benefits, and effect size). We urge you to complete the utility calculation exercise at the end of the chapter.

While utility analysis can help to translate the benefits of training programs into dollar terms, many training professionals have concerns about the practicality of such efforts. Further, some researchers have questioned its value because of the nature of the estimates used to determine some of the factors in the formula.[89] Latham reports that economists have not accepted this form of analysis.[90] It is also unclear to what extent HRD professionals use utility analysis to communicate the effectiveness of HRD programs. Given that utility analysis is intended to help managers see HRD programs as an investment and to make more informed decisions about HRD programs, it is reasonable to ask whether their decisions are influenced by utility estimates.

Research on this question has produced mixed results. On one hand, Latham and Whyte found that managers are not influenced in the way HR practitioners would hope.[91] They found that including utility analysis information actually *reduced* managers' support for a valid employee selection program. Similarly, Hazer and Highhouse observed that "the degree to which managers accept the notion that the effectiveness of HR programs can be measured in terms of dollars remains an open question" (p. 110).[92] On the other hand, Morrow, Jarret, and Rupinski report that having a senior management team that (1) is interested in a demonstration that HRD programs are a worthwhile investment and (2) preapproves the utility model and procedures to be used will lead to acceptance of utility information as legitimate.[93]

We believe that utility analysis (in addition to ROI and cost estimates) presents an opportunity for HRD professionals to provide information to decision makers in dollar terms. However, we agree that simply providing managers with the dollar estimates generated by utility analysis will not by itself be sufficient to gain acceptance or use.[94] As with ROI estimates, gaining management acceptance appears to be a key consideration. Michael Sturman recently proposed a number of modifications to the equations that are used to calculate utility estimates. He concludes his article by stating that "for a complex decision making tool to be useful, the users of the decision aid must desire the information it provides and be trained in its use" (p. 297).[95] Commenting on the Whyte and Latham results mentioned earlier, Sturman continues, "We should not be surprised that an individual untrained with a use of a decision aid fails to adhere to the results of the aid" (p. 297).[96] Toward that end, we provide a list of recommendations offered by various authors that should increase the chances that management will accept and use utility information:

- Involve senior management in determining the utility model and procedures to be used.
- Train HR professionals and managers in the details of utility analysis.
- Offer an explanation of the components of the utility model.

- Involve management in arriving at estimates.
- Use credible and conservative estimates.
- Admit that the results of utility analysis are often based on fallible but reasonable estimates.
- Use utility analysis to compare alternatives, rather than to justify individual programs.[97]

Finally, it is important to remember that not all decision makers, and not all HRD programs, require justification in dollar terms. We agree with Latham's suggestion that HRD professionals find out from senior managers what they consider when determining the value of HRD programs and provide management with information in those terms.[98] For some organizations, this may include the dollar value, while in others demonstrating positive improvements in nonmonetary terms may be preferred. A lively debate concerning the inclusion of "values" (other than financial return) in HRD evaluation was presented in *Human Resource Development Quarterly*.[99] Interested readers are encouraged to look further into these issues, as they again remind us of the ethical issues involved in all evaluation efforts. Finally, we present you with an interesting situation where researchers moved *away from* utility analysis and ROI calculations, and still managed to provide meaningful organizational-level data on the impact of training (see the boxed insert nearby)

## A CLOSING COMMENT ON HRD EVALUATION

HRD professionals should recognize the importance of evaluating HRD programs and the variety of ways evaluation can be conducted. Given the many constraints placed on HRD efforts, Grove and Ostroff recommend the following:

1. Perform a needs analysis.
2. Develop an explicit evaluation strategy.
3. Insist on specific training objectives.
4. Obtain participant reactions.
5. Develop criterion instruments (to measure valued outcomes).
6. Plan and execute the evaluation study.[100]

Not every program needs to be evaluated to the same extent. New programs and those with high visibility and expense should be evaluated more thoroughly than proven programs and those that are offered less frequently. The key is to have a well-planned evaluation strategy that sets the stage for how and to what extent each program will be evaluated. While those with little evaluation experience may see this task as daunting and burdensome, it remains an essential aspect of human resource development. The challenges now faced by organizations, and the importance of HRD in meeting those challenges, demand serious and sustained evaluation efforts — and results.[101]

## Measuring Organizational Results without Measuring ROI

St. Luke's Medical Center is a large healthcare provider in northeastern Pennsylvania. It began a major team-building initiative in the early 1990s and was able to show early on that trainees liked the program, and that behavioral change was taking place. In attempting to demonstrate the value of this training to the organization, Robert Weigand and Richard Wagner considered using utility and ROI formulas similar to those presented in this chapter. They ended up using a simpler approach, which was based on determining what organizational outcomes had changed as a result of the changed behaviors produced by the training initiative. Some of the organizational consequences that they hypothesized (and found) to be impacted by training included:

- changes in turnover rates
- fewer employees needed to staff various shifts and departments
- increased patient return rates (due to satisfaction with the service provided)
- patient recommendations of the medical center to others

It is significant that, in most cases, the medical center was already able to provide the data needed to make such evaluations, that is, no HRD professional or researcher needed to collect new information. Finding tangible changes in the organization is especially critical for a team-building project, where such "soft" skills as listening, delegating, and decision making are emphasized. Using the organization's own measures to capture the value of such training was sufficient in this case to demonstrate the positive impact of training on the organization. While this takes nothing away from efforts to convert such measures into "dollar metrics" (as in ROI or utility analysis), this example suggests that, with some common sense and hard work, Level 4 evaluation is doable — and is being done.

SOURCES: Weigand, R. J. & Wagner, R. J. (1999). Results-oriented training evaluation. *The Quality Resource, 18*(4), July/August, 1–5; Wagner, R. J. & Weigand, R. (1998). Evaluating an outdoor-based training program — A search for results: St. Luke's Hospital. In D. L. Kirkpatrick (Ed.), *Evaluating training programs: The four levels,* (2nd ed., pp. 204–220). San Francisco: Berrett-Koehler.

### RETURN TO OPENING CASE

The challenge faced by Dave Palm at LensCrafters was to show a clear link between training and the organization's bottom-line financial results. This is what Jack Phillips has referred to as Level 5 evaluation, emphasizing how the monetary value of training exceeds the costs.

Your instructor has additional information on what was done at LensCrafters to meet this challenge to provide evidence for the effectiveness of company training.

SOURCE: Purcell, A. (2000). 20/20 ROI. *Training & Development, 54*(7), July, 28–33.

### SUMMARY

In this chapter, we introduced the last phase of the HRD process: evaluation. HRD evaluation is defined as the systematic collection of descriptive and judgmental information necessary to make effective HRD decisions. The purposes of HRD evaluation include determining whether the programs have achieved their objectives, building credibility and support for programs, and establishing the value of HRD programs.

We discussed a number of frameworks and models of the evaluation process to emphasize the many options available when evaluating HRD programs. Kirkpatrick's approach, which is the earliest and most popular, proposes four levels of evaluation: participant reaction, learning, behavior, and results. Many of the other frameworks (e.g., CIPP, Brinkerhoff, Phillips) build upon Kirkpatrick's approach, and expand the focus of evaluation beyond measuring postprogram effectiveness, or include elements not explicitly stated by Kirkpatrick, or seek to do both. In addition, two models (Kraiger et al. and Holton) are attempts to create evaluation models that are more strongly theory- and research-based.

Data collection is central to HRD evaluation. Among the types of information that may be collected are individual, systemwide, and economic data. Some of the data collection methods used in HRD evaluation include interviews, surveys, observation, archival data, tests and simulations.

Options for designing the evaluation study were also presented. The research design provides a plan for conducting the evaluation effort. It spells out the types of information to be collected, how it will be collected, and the data analysis techniques to be used. The design should balance the need for making valid conclusions with practical and ethical concerns. We presented several issues that should be addressed in choosing an appropriate design.

HRD professionals are often asked to justify the allocation of resources. This involves a financial assessment of the impact of HRD programs. This assessment can be done by evaluating training costs using cost-benefit or cost-effectiveness analysis or by translating a trained employee's productivity into dollar terms through utility analysis. More and better efforts are needed at demonstrating the impact of HRD programs on the effectiveness of the organization as a whole.

## KEY TERMS AND CONCEPTS

| | |
|---|---|
| control group | reliability |
| cost-benefit analysis | research design |
| cost-effectiveness analysis | response shift bias |
| HRD evaluation | return on investment (ROI) |
| informed consent | self-report data |
| internal validity (Appendix) | statistical power (Appendix) |
| meta-analysis | time series design |
| practicality | utility analysis |
| pretest-posttest | validity |
| random assignment | |

## QUESTIONS FOR DISCUSSION

1. Even though most HRD professionals agree that HRD evaluation is valuable, why isn't it practiced more frequently by organizations? Identify and

describe at least two reasons why evaluation might not be done. How could these objections to evaluation be overcome?

2. Describe the four levels of evaluation that make up Kirkpatrick's framework of evaluation. Identify one example of data at each level that might be collected to provide evidence for the effectiveness of a class or training program in which you have participated.

3. What do the CIPP and Brinkerhoff models of evaluation add to evaluation that is not included in Kirkpatrick's model? What benefit, if any, is there to viewing evaluation in this way?

4. What do the Kraiger et al. and Holton models of evaluation add to evaluation that is not included in Kirkpatrick's model? What benefit, if any, is there to viewing evaluation in this way?

5. Suppose you have been asked to design a program intended to train airline flight attendant trainees in emergency evacuation procedures. You are now designing the evaluation study to show that the flight attendants understand the procedures and use them on the job. Which data collection methods do you think would be the most useful in providing this evidence? How might the type of learning outcome affect your choice of measuring learning? Support your choices.

6. Identify and describe three potential problems with using self-report measures (e.g., participant questionnaires) in HRD evaluation. How can these problems be minimized?

7. Why is the issue of statistical power important to HRD evaluation(see Appendix)? Describe two ways a researcher can increase power while controlling the cost of evaluation.

8. Identify and describe at least three ethical considerations in conducting evaluation research. How do these factors affect the evaluation effort?

9. What is the advantage, if any, to expressing the benefits of conducting HRD programs in dollar terms? Briefly describe the return on investment (ROI) and utility analysis approaches. What are the limitations to using these approaches? How can they be overcome?

10. What is the idea of a balanced scorecard? How can this be applied to HRD and training?

11. Using the information in the appendix, compare and contrast experimental and quasiexperimental research designs. Is one type of design superior to the other? Support your answer.

## EXERCISE: CALCULATING THE COSTS AND BENEFITS OF TRAINING

Assume you work in the HRD function for a large manufacturing facility. Employees have been placed into work teams, and top management is now considering providing additional formal cross-training to team members, so that people will be able to do a variety of different tasks within the team. However, the lowest possible cost available for a high-quality training program is determined to be $2,000 per employee. In light of this cost, management has asked you to estimate the potential value (utility) of this training program. Initial training will be provided to thirty team members, and their performance will be compared to thirty other employees who have not been trained. To be conservative, you've decided to assume that the effects of training last for one year (though you obviously hope the impact lasts much longer).

Two critical items that you need to calculate a utility estimate are $d_t$ and $SD_y$. After training, you find that the trained employees can now produce an average of 26 units per day, while the untrained employees produce 22.5. To calculate $d_t$, you need to take the difference between these two numbers and divide this number by the standard deviation in units produced for the untrained group. In this case, the standard deviation in units produced turns out to be 5 units per day. The other critical item to determine is $SD_y$. In a manufacturing setting such as this, you can look at actual productivity levels for all employees in this job category and calculate the difference between an employee at the mean or average productivity level, and an employee one standard deviation above the mean. From company records, you determine that this number is $10,000.

You now have all the information you need to calculate a utility estimate for this situation. Using the formula from Cascio (see below), what is the projected benefit to the organization of training these thirty team members? What was the cost? What is the estimated change in utility of this training? How would you present this information to top management, as they consider whether to use this training program for others employees in the organization?

$$\Delta U = (N)(T)(d_t)(SD_y) - C$$

## INTEGRATIVE CASE: What Went Wrong at University Hospital?

Pat Rowe, Vice President of University Hospital, recently attended a conference session that discussed the problems of integrating computer technology into the work practices of health care professionals. The session lecturer argued that implementation often fails because staff do not receive proper training in the use of the new equipment and software. This seemed plausible to Pat. In the last year, the hospital's senior management team had decided to purchase thousands of dollars of equipment that was supposed to "redesign the delivery of patient care." However, word was getting around that staff were disgruntled with the new equipment and were not using it.

Upon returning to the hospital, Pat called the director of training and development, Wei Lee, to discuss the insights gained at the conference. Pat said to Wei, "I think I know why staff aren't using the computer equipment. They didn't receive adequate training."

Wei replied, "I seem to recall that the manufacturer did provide training, but I'm not entirely sure what was included. Do you want me to look into it?"

"Yes, that's a good idea. But I still think we need to train them. Why don't you get them in here to do some more training."

Wei immediately called the computer equipment manufacturer and learned that 10 months ago, as part of the implementation process, two design engineers had conducted numerous lectures with unit staff on how to work with the new equipment and software.

These sessions were poorly attended and were conducted using a lecture and overhead format. Wei decided that the poor attendance was probably responsible for the problems, and so she asked the manufacturer to re-run the training session. This time, staff would be offered free coffee and doughnuts to encourage attendance.

Staff were sent a memo from the training department encouraging them to attend one of the sessions. Unit managers, who were not invited to attend the training, were asked to mention the sessions in staff meetings and highlight the free coffee and doughnuts. Unfortunately, attendance was only marginally better.

The latest training sessions were again conducted by design engineers, but this time they used a new teaching device — a laptop computer hooked up to an overhead projector. This allowed them to "walk through" the various screens and options of the program with staff in a real-time simulation. At the end of the session, staff were given a manual describing the computer hardware and software. It was suggested to staff that they read the manual on their own time and consult it when they had problems. Walking out of the session, one staff member was heard saying, "Computers scare the heck out of me. I can't possibly learn this stuff. And to top it all off, I don't think anybody really cares if I do use this new system."

SOURCE: Brown, T. C., Li, S. X., Sargent, L. D., & Tasa, K., What went wrong at University Hospital? An exercise assessing training effectiveness. *Journal of Management Education, 27*(4), pp. 485–496, Copyright © 2003. Reprinted by Permission of Sage Publications, Inc.

Visit *http://werner.swlearning.com* for links to informative websites for this chapter.

## REFERENCES

1. Goldstein, I. L. (1980). Training in work organizations. *Annual Review of Psychology, 31,* 229–272, quotation from p. 237.

2. Phillips, J. J. (1983). *Handbook of training evaluation and measurement methods.* Houston, TX: Gulf.

3. Zenger, J. H., & Hargis, K. (1982). Assessment of training results: It's time to take the plunge! *Training and Development Journal, 36*(1), 11–16.

4. Goldstein, I. L., & Ford, J. K. (2002). *Training in organizations: Needs assessment, development, and evaluation.* Belmont, CA: Wadsworth.

5. Saari, L. M., Johnson, T. R., McLaughlin, S. D., & Zimmerle, D. M. (1988). A survey of management training and education practices in U.S. companies. *Personnel Psychology, 41,* 731–743.

6. *2003 State of the Industry Report* (2003). Alexandria, VA: ASTD.

7. Salas, E., & Kosarzycki, M. P. (2003). Why don't organizations pay attention to (and use) findings from the science of training? *Human Resource Development Quarterly, 14*(4), 487–492; Goldstein (1980), *supra* note 1; Latham, G. P. (1988). Human resource training and development. *Annual Review of Psychology, 39,* 545–582; Wexley, K. N. (1984). Personnel training. *Annual Review of Psychology, 35,* 519–551.

8. Salas & Kosarzycki (2003), *supra* note 7.

9. Saari et al. (1988), *supra* note 5; *2003 State of the Industry Report* (2003), *supra* note 6.

10. Goldstein (1980), *supra* note 1.

11. Brinkerhoff, R. O. (1987). *Achieving results from training.* San Francisco: Jossey-Bass; Bushnell, D. S. (1990). Input, process, output: A model for evaluating training. *Training and Development Journal, 44*(3), 41–43; Galvin, J. C. (1983). What trainers can learn from educators about evaluating management training. *Training and Development Journal, 37*(8), 52–57; Kirkpatrick, D. L. (1967). Evaluation. In R. L. Craig & L. R. Bittel (Eds.), *Training and development handbook* (87–112). New York: McGraw-Hill; Kirkpatrick, D. L. (1987). Evaluation. In R. L. Craig (Ed.), *Training and development handbook* (3rd ed., pp. 301–319). New York: McGraw-Hill; Kirkpatrick, D. L. (1994). *Evaluating training programs: The four levels.* San Francisco: Berrett-Koehler; Warr, P., Bird, M., & Rackham, N. (1970). *Evaluation of management training.* London: Gower Press.

12. Kirkpatrick (1967, 1987, 1994), *supra* note 11; Kirkpatrick, D. L. (2004). A T&D classic: How to start an objective evaluation of your training program. *T&D, 58*(5), May, 16–18.

13. Arthur, W., Bennett, W., Edens, P. S., & Bell, S. T. (2003). Effectiveness of training in organizations: A meta-analysis of design and evaluation features. *Journal of Applied Psychology, 88*(2), 234–245.

14. Sinclair, R. C., Smith, R., Colligan, M., Prince, M., Nguyen, T., & Stayner, L. (2003). Evaluation of a safety training program in three food service companies. *Journal of Safety Research, 34*(5), December, 547–558.

15. *2003 State of the Industry Report* (2003), *supra* note 6.

16. *Ibid.*

17. Bushnell (1990), *supra* note 11.

18. Holton, E. F. III (1996). The flawed four-level evaluation model. *Human Resource Development Quarterly, 7,* 5–21.

19. Kraiger, K., Ford, J. K., & Salas, E. (1993). Application of cognitive, skill-based, and affective theories of learning outcomes to new methods of training evaluation. *Journal of Applied Psychology, 78,* 311–328.

20. Alliger, G. M., & Janak, E. A. (1989). Kirkpatrick's levels of training criteria: Thirty years later. *Personnel Psychology, 42,* 331–342.

21. Kirkpatrick, D. L. (1996). Invited reaction: Reaction to Holton article. *Human Resource Development Quarterly, 7,* 23–325.

22. Kaufman, R., & Keller, J. M. (1994). Levels of evaluation: Beyond Kirkpatrick. *Human Resource Development Quarterly, 5,* 371–380.

23. Tan, J. A., Hall, R. J., & Boyce, C. (2003). The role of employee reactions in predicting training effectiveness. *Human Resource Development Quarterly, 14*(4), 397–411.

24. Warr, P., & Bunce, D. (1995). Trainee characteristics and the outcomes of open learning. *Personnel Psychology, 48,* 348–374.

25. Phillips, J. J. (1996). ROI: The search for the best practices. *Training & Development, 50*(2), 43–47.

26. Kaufman & Keller (1994), *supra* note 22.

27. Galvin (1983), *supra* note 11.

28. Warr et al. (1970), *supra* note 11.

29. Brinkerhoff (1987), *supra* note 11.

30. Kraiger et al. (1993), *supra* note 19.

31. Holton (1996), *supra* note 18.

32. Kaufman & Keller (1994), *supra* note 22; Warr & Bunce (1995), *supra* note 24; Phillips (1996), *supra* note 25.

33. Kaufman & Keller (1994), *supra* note 22.

34. Brinkerhoff (1987), *supra* note 11.

35. Alliger & Janak (1989), *supra* note 20; Alliger, G. M., Tannenbaum, S. I., Bennett, Jr., W., Traver, H., & Shotland, A. (1997). A meta-analysis of the relations among training criteria. *Personnel Psychology, 50*, 341–358.

36. Alliger et al. (1997), *supra* note 35.

37. Werner, J. M., O'Leary-Kelly, A. M., Baldwin, T. T., & Wexley, K. N. (1994). Augmenting behavior-modeling training: Testing the effects of pre- and post-training interventions. *Human Resource Development Quarterly, 5*(2), 169–183.

38. Holton (1996), *supra* note 18.

39. Stoel, D. (2004). The evaluation heavyweight match. *T&D, 58*(1), 46–48.

40. Campbell, D., & Graham, M. (1988). *Drugs and alcohol in the workplace: A guide for managers.* New York: Facts on File.

41. *Ibid*; Robinson, D. G., & Robinson, J. (1989). Training for impact. *Training and Development Journal, 43*(8), 34–42.

42. Kraiger, et al. (1993), *supra* note 19.

43. Werner et al. (1994), *supra* note 37.

44. Berk, J. (2004). Training Evaluations. *T&D, 58*(9), September, 39–44.

45. Ostroff, C. (1991). Training effectiveness measures and scoring schemes: A comparison. *Personnel Psychology, 44,* 353–374.

46. Curphy, G. J., Gibson, F. W., Macomber, G., Calhoun, C. J., Wilbanks, L. A., & Burger, M. J. (1998). Situational factors affecting peer reporting intentions at the US Air Force Academy: A scenario-based investigation. *Military Psychology, 10*(1), 27–43; Haccoun, R. R., & Saks, A. M. (1998). Training in the 21st century: Some lessons from the last one. *Canadian Psychology, 39*(1–2), 33–51.

47. Anastasi, A. (1982). *Psychological testing.* New York: Macmillan; Cook, T. D., & Campbell, D. T. (1979). *Quasi-experimentation: Design and analysis issues for field settings.* Chicago: Rand-McNally; Cook, T. D, Campbell, D. T., & Peracchio, L. (1990). Quasi-experimentation. In M. D. Dunnette & L. M. Hough (Eds.), *Handbook of industrial and organizational psychology* (2nd ed., Vol. 1, pp. 491–576). Palo Alto, CA: Consulting Psychologists Press; Sackett, P. R., & Larson, J. R. Jr. (1990). Research strategies and tactics in industrial and organizational psychology. In M. D. Dunnette & L. M. Hough (Eds.), *Handbook of industrial and organizational psychology* (2nd ed., Vol. 1, pp. 419–489). Palo Alto, CA: Consulting Psychologists Press; Schmitt, N. W., & Klimoski, R. J. (1991). *Research methods in human resources management.* Mason, OH: Thomson/South-Western.

48. Phillips (1983), *supra* note 2; Phillips, J. J. (1996). How much is the training worth? *Training & Development, 50*(4), 20–24; Robinson & Robinson (1989), *supra* note 41.

49. Robinson & Robinson (1989), *supra* note 41.

50. Tesoro, F., & Tootson, J. (2000). *Implementing global performance measurement systems: A cookbook approach.* San Francisco: Jossey-Bass/Pfeiffer.

51. Podsakoff, P. M., & Organ, D. W. (1986). Self-reports in organization research: Problems and prospects. *Journal of Management, 12,* 531–544.

52. *Ibid.*

53. Sprangers, M., & Hoogstraten, J. (1989). Pretesting effects in retrospective pretest-posttest designs. *Journal of Applied Psychology, 74,* 265–272.

54. Campbell, D. T., & Stanley, J. C. (1966). *Experimental and quasi-experimental designs for research.* Chicago: Rand McNally; Cook & Campbell, (1979), *supra* note 38; Sackett, P. R., & Larson, J. R. Jr. (1990). Research strategies and tactics in industrial and organizational psychology. In M. D. Dunnette & L. M. Hough (Eds.), *Handbook of industrial and organizational psychology* (2nd ed., Vol. 1, pp. 419–489). Palo Alto, CA: Consulting Psychologists Press; Schmitt & Klimoski, (1991), *supra* note 47.

55. Sackett, P. R., & Mullen, E. J. (1993). Beyond formal experimental design: Towards an expanded view of the training evaluation process. *Personnel Psychology, 46,* 613–627.

56. Arvey, R. D., Cole, D. A., Hazucha, J. F., & Hartanto, F. M. (1985). Statistical power of training evaluation designs. *Personnel Psychology, 38,* 493–507.

57. Burke, M. J., & Day, R. R. (1986). A cumulative study of the effectiveness of managerial training. *Journal of Applied Psychology, 71,* 232–245.

58. Hatcher, T. (2002). Ethics and HRD: A new approach to leading responsible organizations. Cambridge, MA: Perseus.

59. Russ-Eft, D., & Hatcher, T. (2003). The issue of international values and beliefs: The debate for a global HRD code of ethics. *Advances in Developing Human Resources, 5*(3), 296–307.

60. Schmitt & Klimoski (1991), *supra* note 47.

61. *Ibid.*

62. Hicks, W. D., & Klimoski, R. J. (1987). Entry into training programs and its effects on training outcomes: A field experiment. *Academy of Management Journal, 30,* 542–552.

63. Cook & Campbell (1979), *supra* note 47.

64. Fromkin, H. L., & Streufert, S. (1976). Laboratory experimentation. In M. D. Dunnette (Ed.), *Handbook of industrial and organizational psychology* (415–465). New York: Rand McNally.

65. Cascio, W. F. (2000). Costing human resources: The financial impact of behavior in organizations (4th ed.). Mason, OH: Thomson/South-Western.

66. Cullen, J. G., Swazin, S. A., Sisson, G. R., & Swanson, R. A. (1978). Cost effectiveness: A model for assessing the training investment. *Training and Development Journal, 32*(1), 24–29.

67. Robinson & Robinson (1989), *supra* note 41.

68. Dade, S. (2004). The business needs drive training evaluation at Bank of America. *ASTD Links,* February. Retrieved October 1, 2004 from http://www.astd.org/astd/Publications/ASTD_Links/February2004/InPractice_Feb04_Dade.htm

69. Robinson & Robinson (1989), *supra* note 41.

70. Phillips (1996), *supra* note 25; Phillips, J. J. (1996). Was it the training? *Training & Development, 50*(3), 28–32.

71. Phillips, P. P., & Phillips, J. J. (2004). ROI in the public sector: Myths and realities. *Public Personnel Management, 33*(2), 139–149.

72. Phillips, J. J. (1996). *Accountability in human resource management.* Houston: Gulf.

73. Phillips (1996, p. 20), *supra* note 48.

74. Parry, S. B. (1996). Measuring training's ROI. *Training & Development, 50*(5), 72–77.

75. Parry, S. B. (2000). *Training for results.* Alexandria, VA: ASTD.

76. Phillips (1996), *supra* note 48.

77. Parry (1996), *supra* note 74.

78. Phillips (1996), *supra* note 25.

79. Willyerd, K. A. (1997). Balancing your evaluation act. *Training, 51*(3), 52–58.

80. Kaplan, R. S., & Norton, D. P. (January-February, 1992). The balanced scorecard — measures that drive performance. *Harvard Business Review,* 71–79.

81. *Ibid.*

82. Schmidt, L. (2003). *In action: Implementing training scorecards.* Alexandria, VA: ASTD.

83. Goldwasser, D. (2001). Beyond ROI. *Training, 38*(1), January, 82–87.

84. ASTD presents ROI awards to Dr. Merrill Anderson and Accenture (2004). Retrieved October 1, 2004, from http://www.astd.org/NR/rdonlyres/77CE7CA2-24FA-4C1F-812C-4B59190F5994/0/2003ROIAwardspressrelease.pdf

85. Brogden, H. E. (1949). When testing pays off. *Personnel Psychology, 2,* 171–185; Cronbach, L. J. (1965). Comments on "A dollar criterion in fixed-treatment employee selection programs" in L. J. Cronbach & G. C. Gleser (Eds.), *Psychological tests and personnel decisions* (2nd ed.). Ubana, IL: University of Illinois Press; Schmidt, F. L., Hunter, J. E., & Pearlman, K. (1982). Assessing the impact of personnel programs on workforce productivity. *Personnel Psychology, 35,* 333–347.

86. Cascio (2000), *supra* note 65.

87. Cronshaw, S. F., & Alexander, R. A. (1985). One answer to the demand for accountability: Selection utility as an investment decision. *Organizational Behavior and Human Decision Processes, 35,* 102–118; Cascio, W. F. (1989). Using utility analysis to assess training outcomes. In I. L. Goldstein and Associates, *Training and development in organizations* (63–88). San Francisco: Jossey-Bass; Boudreau, J. W. (1983). Economic considerations in estimating the utility of human resource productivity improvement programs. *Personnel Psychology, 36,* 551–576.

88. Cascio (1989), *supra* note 87.

89. Dreher, G. F., & Sackett, P. R. (Eds.). (1983). *Perspectives on employee staffing and selection.* Homewood, IL: Richard D. Irwin.

90. Latham, G. P. (1988). Human resource training and development. *Annual Review of Psychology, 39,* 545–582.

91. Latham, G. P., & Whyte, G. (1994). The futility of utility analysis. *Personnel Psychology, 47,* 31–46; Whyte, G., & Latham, G. P. (1997). The futility of utility analysis revisited: When even an expert fails. *Personnel Psychology, 50,* 601–610.

92. Hazer, J. T., & Highhouse, S. (1997). Factors influencing managers' reactions to utility analysis: Effects of $SD_y$ method, information frame, and focal intervention. *Journal of Applied Psychology, 82,* 104–112.

93. Morrow, C. C., Jarrett, M. Q., & Rupinski, M. T. (1997). An investigation of the effect and economic utility of corporate-wide training. *Personnel Psychology, 50,* 91–119.

94. Hazer & Highhouse (1997), *supra* note 92; Latham (1988), *supra* note 90.

95. Sturman, M. C. (2000). Implications of utility analysis adjustments for estimates of human resource intervention value. *Journal of Management, 26,* 281–299.

96. *Ibid.*

97. Hazer & Highhouse (1997), *supra* note 92; Latham (1988), *supra* note 90; Latham & Whyte (1994), *supra* note 91; Morrow et al. (1997), *supra* note 90; Shultz, K. S. (1996). Utility analysis in public sector personnel management: Issues and keys to implementation. *Public Personnel Management, 25*(3), 369–377; Sturman (2000), *supra* note 95.

98. Latham (1988), *supra* note 90.

99. Parsons, J. G. (1997). Values as a vital supplement to the use of financial analysis in HRD. *Human Resource Development Quarterly, 8,* 5–13; Brinkerhoff, R. O. (1997). Invited reaction: Response to Parsons. *Human Resource Development Quarterly, 8,* 15–21.

100. Grove, D. A., & Ostroff, C. (1991). Program evaluation. In K. N. Wexley (Ed.), *Developing human resources.* Washington, DC: BNA Books.

101. Haccoun & Saks (1998), *supra* note 46.

7-1

# APPENDIX TO CHAPTER 7:
# MORE ON RESEARCH DESIGN

A research design provides a plan or blueprint for conducting an evaluation study. Research design is a complex topic, and much has been written about it.[1] Our goal in this section is to go beyond our brief coverage in the chapter, and introduce the reader to important issues in research design, and discuss some of the possibilities available when evaluating HRD programs.

Research design is a critical aspect of any evaluation effort. Awareness of research design issues and possible research design alternatives can help a manager or HRD professional conduct effective evaluations, and also critique the results of the evaluation studies done by others.

## RESEARCH DESIGN VALIDITY

The validity of a research design depends on the extent to which one can be confident that the conclusions drawn from it are true.[2] Validity of a design is judged on a continuum from high (high confidence that the design yields truthful conclusions) to low (doubtfulness about the design's conclusions).

Research design validity has at least four aspects: internal, external, construct, and statistical conclusion.[3] Typically, the most important of these aspects for HRD evaluation is internal and statistical conclusion validity, and we will emphasize these in this appendix. Briefly, external validity has to do with the ability to generalize the evaluation results to other individuals or other settings. Construct validity has to do with ensuring that your measuring instruments are capturing what you are claiming to measure, e.g., a scale tapping "openness to experience" is measuring this construct and not something else (such as positive affect).

**Internal validity** concerns a judgment as to whether conclusions about the relationship between the variables being studied could have been due to some other variable. In the case of HRD evaluation, if an increase in employee performance is observed after an HRD program, we want to assess whether the program was responsible for the change, rather than some other factor such as experience or work rules.

For example, when a sales training program is being evaluated to determine whether it improves sales, one hopes to conclude that any observed increases in sales are a result of the training program. However, there are other factors that could encourage sales, such as economic conditions, the sales territory, or an employee's years of experience in selling. If the evaluation study does not control for these factors (i.e., ensure they don't affect the results), we cannot be sure whether any increases in sales are due to the training program or not. So, if sales after the training program are 15 percent higher than before, but the HRD evaluation did not control or adjust for economic conditions or trainee experience, it will not be clear whether the training or something else caused the increase in sales. Therefore, the study's internal validity is low, and we cannot be confident that any conclusions based on this study are true.

Cook and Campbell identified a number of factors that can threaten or reduce internal validity. Appendix Table 7-1 lists these threats to internal validity of HRD evaluations.[4]

Any of these factors, if present or not controlled for by the research design, can undermine the results of the study. An HRD professional should always seek to select a research design that will ensure that valid conclusions can be drawn. Many conditions present within an organization can make it difficult to ensure a high degree of validity. Concerns over validity and rigor in research design can inhibit people from conducting training evaluation. However, as suggested by Goldstein, creatively matching the research effort to the organizational constraints can ensure that evaluation is done and meaningful conclusions are drawn.[5] We now discuss three categories of research designs, namely, nonexperimental, experimental, and quasi-experimental designs.

## NONEXPERIMENTAL DESIGNS

A *nonexperimental research design* leaves a great deal of doubt as to whether the HRD program has in fact caused a change in the trainees' skills, knowledge, or performance. Such designs include the case study, relational research, and the one-group pretest-posttest design.[6] Traditional thinking suggests that each of these designs is poorly suited for making conclusive statements about training effectiveness. There are simply too many plausible alternative explanations for any observed changes when using these methods to be able to confidently conclude that an HRD program has caused an observed change. However, this thinking assumes that internal validity is always the paramount concern of the evaluation researcher. As Sackett and Mullen suggest, this is not always the case. We first describe these designs and then address the issue of their appropriateness for use in HRD evaluation.[7]

*CASE STUDY.* The *case study research design* involves an intensive, descriptive study of a particular trainee, training group, or organization to determine what has occurred and reactions to it. If diagrammed, this design would look like this:

Training ⟶ Posttraining measures and descriptions

**APPENDIX TABLE 7-1**      **FACTORS THAT CAN AFFECT INTERNAL VALIDITY**

1. **History**    Unrelated events occurring during the training period that can influence training measurements.
2. **Maturation**    Ongoing processes within the individual, such as aging or gaining job experience, which are a function of the passage of time.
3. **Testing**    The effect of a pretest on posttest performance.
4. **Instrumentation**    The degree to which criterion instruments may measure different attributes of an individual at two different points in time.
5. **Statistical Regression**    Changes in criterion scores resulting from selecting extreme groups on a pretest.
6. **Differential Selection**    Using different procedures for selecting individuals for experimental and control groups.
7. **Experimental Mortality**    Differential loss of respondents from various groups.
8. **Interaction of Differential Selection and Maturation**    Assuming that experimental and control groups were different to begin with, the compounding of the disparity between the groups by maturational changes occurring during the experimental period.
9. **Interaction of Pretest with the Experimental Variable**    During the course of training, something reacting with the pretest in such a way that the pretest affects the trained group more than the untrained group.
10. **Interaction of Differential Selection with Training**    When more than one group is trained, because of differential selection, the groups are not equivalent on the criterion variable to begin with; therefore, they may react differently to the training.
11. **Reactive Effects of the Research Situation**    When the research design itself so changes the trainees' expectations and reactions that results cannot be generalized to future applications of the training.
12. **Multiple Treatment Interference**    Differential residual effects of previous training experiences.

SOURCE: From W. F. Cascio (1991). *Applied Psychology in Personnel Management* (4th ed, p. 395). Adapted by permission of Pearson Education, Inc. Upper Saddle River, NJ.

The sources of data frequently used in case studies usually include archival data and reports of participants and observers. Because no pretraining information is collected, and there is no untrained comparison group, many threats to internal validity exist. However, a carefully conducted case study can create a record of the training program.

*RELATIONAL RESEARCH. Relational research* involves measuring two or more variables in an attempt to describe or explain their relationship to one another.[8] For example, a manager may distribute a questionnaire to managers who attended an assessment center asking them to rate the value of each of the activities conducted during the program (such as a leaderless group discussion or in-basket exercise).

Typically, relational research includes computing correlation coefficients (a numerical index of a relationship between two variables) between the variables measured.

While the pattern of correlations can give an idea of how the variables are related, the conclusions drawn can only be suggestive because measurements are taken at only one point in time. This makes it difficult to assess the direction of the relationships measured. For example, suppose a study shows a strong relationship between attitude toward training and attitude toward one's supervisor. Did one's feeling about the supervisor affect feelings toward the training, or did one's feeling toward training affect feelings toward the supervisor? Correlational data cannot answer such questions.

*ONE-GROUP PRETEST-POSTTEST DESIGN.* In this design, the trainees are assessed on the variables being observed before training and again after training. That is

$$Pretest \longrightarrow Training \longrightarrow Posttest$$

This design can help to determine whether the trainees have changed as a result of the training program. For example, if a customer service program is intended to improve the trainees' attitudes toward customers, the tests would measure their attitudes toward customers before and after training. However, if a change is noticed, this design does not show whether the *training program* was the cause of the change. Many factors could threaten its internal validity, such as history, maturation, and instrumentation.

*RECONSIDERATION OF NONEXPERIMENTAL RESEARCH DESIGNS.* As can be seen from the descriptions of the nonexperimental designs, they are highly vulnerable to threats to internal validity. As such, these designs have been seen as poor ways to assess HRD program effectiveness, and most writers caution against using them except as a way to gather details about a program and as the basis for ideas to be investigated in future studies. Given this recommendation against these simple designs and the barriers that many HRD professionals see as preventing them from using more rigorous designs (e.g., no access to control groups or inability to randomly assign participants to groups), it is not terribly surprising that many HRD programs are not evaluated in any serious way.

However, Sackett and Mullen call for a reconsideration of the appropriateness of nonexperimental designs in HRD evaluation.[9] They argue that these designs are appropriate for answering *some* of the questions an HRD professional has about a program and its participants, and they identify some of the considerations and constraints to using these designs. Sackett and Mullen begin their argument by pointing out that HRD professionals conduct evaluations to answer various types of questions, and they argue that the research design to be used should depend on the question being asked. In particular, two types of questions may be of interest:

1. How much change has occurred?
2. Has a particular target level of knowledge, skill, or performance been achieved by trainees?

According to Sackett and Mullen, if the HRD professional must answer the first question (e.g., in order to establish the utility of an HRD program or compare the effectiveness of two HRD programs), then internal validity is the foremost concern, and a research method that can control for threats to internal validity is likely called for. Ordinarily, this would make a nonexperimental design a poor choice. But if the HRD professional wants to answer the second question (which assesses the effectiveness of both the program and the individuals who participated in it), then internal validity is not the foremost concern, and a nonexperimental design may be appropriate.

Being able to answer the question "Has a particular level of performance been achieved?" requires that a clear target level of performance exists and that the organization is interested in establishing the level of performance achieved by each participant. In this case, a one-group posttest-only design (i.e., the case study) or one-group pretest-posttest design can be used to answer this question. Although one could not conclude whether the performance level was reached *because* of the HRD program, one can confidently state the trainees' level of achievement.

Even in the case where the question "How much change has occurred?" is the focus of evaluation, Sackett and Mullen argue that it is possible to account for some potential threats to internal validity while using a nonexperimental design. For example, if the HRD professional can obtain knowledge about the events occurring in the organization while the program is being conducted, it may permit an assessment of the extent to which history effects threaten internal validity.

We agree with Sackett and Mullen's arguments in this regard. They provide an excellent example of how creative thinking can expand our view of HRD evaluation and increase the chances HRD practitioners will choose to evaluate their programs.

## EXPERIMENTAL DESIGNS

*Experimental designs* are constructed to show that any effects observed in the study have resulted from training and not from other factors. These designs include two significant factors:

1. A *control group* that does not receive training
2. *Random assignment* of participants to the training and control groups

Use of a control group allows the researcher to rule out the effects of factors outside of training (like maturation and history). Usually, the hopes are that the group receiving training improves and the control group does not.

However, if the training and control groups differ on some important factor, such as experience, prior training, gender, or educational level, then the comparison of the groups is compromised — these factors may be the cause of observed changes. The easiest way to select equivalent control groups is to randomly assign participants to the two groups. Random assignment permits the researcher to assume the groups are equivalent.[10]

Alternatively, a matching strategy could also create equivalent groups, by:

1. identifying the factors, such as experience or job category, that are likely to affect the groups on the variables being measured

2. measuring potential participants on those factors
3. assigning subjects to balance each group on those factors

For example, if women are found to be better listeners than men, and listening skills may have an effect on learning what is being trained, the proportion of men and women in both the experimental and the control groups should be the same.

Experimental designs include the pretest-posttest, with control design, the posttest-only, with control design, and the Solomon four-group design.

*PRETEST-POSTTEST WITH CONTROL DESIGN.* This design allows control for outside influences by including a group that is not trained as a comparison group.

Group 1: Pretest ⟶ Training ⟶ Posttest

Group 2: Pretest ⟶ Posttest

This design allows the researcher to make three comparisons:

1. Are the two groups in fact equivalent before training? This is assessed with the pretest.
2. Did training improve the trainees? This is assessed by comparing Group 1's pretest and posttest scores.
3. Did the untrained group remain unchanged during the course of the study? This is assessed by comparing Group 2's pretest and posttest scores.

If the answer to all three questions is yes, it is safe to conclude that training has had an effect.[11]

*POSTTEST-ONLY WITH CONTROL DESIGN.* Sometimes, there is not enough time to gather pretest measurements. Also, the use of some pretest procedures may affect the outcome of training. For example, if one is measuring attitudes toward sexual harassment before a workshop about sexual harassment, simply answering questions about the topic may motivate the trainees to seek out more information or be more sensitive to the issue. Therefore, it is possible that changes in attitudes may be the result of the pretraining measure rather than the training. Alternatively, if the same test (such as a test on pricing procedures) is used as both a pretest and posttest, participants may remember the items, casting doubt on the results of the posttest.

To resolve these situations and still have the benefit of an untrained comparison group, a *posttest-only with control design* could be used.

Group 1: Training ⟶ Posttest

Group 2: ⟶ Posttest

The effectiveness of this design relies on the assumption that the two groups are equivalent (using a method like random or matched assignment) before the study.

*SOLOMON FOUR-GROUP DESIGN.* Solomon was one of the first researchers to point out how a pretest can affect the results of an evaluation study.[12] His research design therefore uses one experimental group and three different groups to control for the effects of the pretest.

            Group 1: Pretest  ⟶  Training  ⟶  Posttest

            Group 2: Pretest  ⟶  Posttest

            Group 3:  ⟶  Training  ⟶  Posttest

            Group 4:  ⟶  Posttest

This design is a combination of the two research designs just described. It allows the researcher to make strong conclusions about the effectiveness of the HRD program. While it is the most elegant or attractive design from a research standpoint, its main disadvantage is that the number of participants it requires prevents many organizations from being able to use it.

It should be noted that multiple posttest measures can be taken if an experimenter is concerned about whether the effects of training are long lasting or if it may take a while for training to take effect. Multiple measures work best with routine data collection methods that do not affect employee performance, such as personnel (e.g., attendance) or operations data.

Although experimental designs are the most rigorous of the research designs and permit the greatest confidence in conclusions drawn from them, organizational constraints can make it difficult to use them. In many organizations, it is difficult to use random assignment to groups. If employees work in distant locations or if training some employees and not training others will cause friction among employees, using a pure experimental design is not possible.

## QUASI-EXPERIMENTAL DESIGNS

Some people feel that if rigorous adherence to an experimental design cannot be achieved, then evaluation is not worth doing. This is shortsighted. Campbell and Stanley and Cook and Campbell have offered *quasi-experimental designs* as a viable way to conduct evaluations.[13] In these designs, the researcher attempts to control as many threats to validity as possible, while matching evaluation research concerns to organizational constraints. Two quasi-experimental designs include the nonequivalent control group design and the time series design.

*NONEQUIVALENT CONTROL GROUP DESIGN.* In a nonequivalent control group design, one cannot assume that the two groups — the control group and the group about to receive training — are equivalent. For example, if employees in one location are the trainees and employees at another location make up the control group, any number of factors may lead to nonequivalence, such as years of experience, economic conditions, and equipment.

The threats to validity most likely to affect conclusions from a nonequivalent control group design are selection-maturation interaction, testing-training interaction, and regression effects.[14] The burden for the evaluation researcher is to attempt to discover the factors on which the groups differ and then attempt to control for them, either statistically or in the way the experiment is conducted.

*TIME SERIES DESIGN.* In the time series design, the researcher takes multiple measures on the variables of interest (e.g., skill operating a lathe) before and after training. This can be done using a training group alone, or with a training and control group.

Simple Time Series Design

$$\text{Group 1: } M_1\ M_2\ M_3\ M_4\ M_5 \longrightarrow \text{Training} \longrightarrow M_6\ M_7\ M_8\ M_9\ M_{10}$$

Multiple Time Series Design

$$\text{Group 1: } M_1\ M_2\ M_3\ M_4\ M_5 \longrightarrow \text{Training} \longrightarrow M_6\ M_7\ M_8\ M_9\ M_{10}$$

$$\text{Group 2: } M_1\ M_2\ M_3\ M_4\ M_5 \longrightarrow M_6\ M_7\ M_8\ M_9\ M_{10}$$

In the previous diagrams, the M indicates the criterion or outcome measure. Multiple measures allow the researcher to have a better idea of the employee's standing on the criterion both before and after training. The measurements can be graphed to help determine any change or trends before and after training. If a change is observed, the training program is likely to be the cause.

Time series designs are well suited for handling the validity threat of history, but they may be susceptible to an instrumentation threat if the measurement method can affect employee performance on the criterion measure. As with all quasi-experimental designs, the researchers must be vigilant for possible threats to validity and attempt to control for them.

## STATISTICAL POWER: ENSURING THAT A CHANGE WILL BE DETECTED IF ONE EXISTS

Statistical analysis is the primary way researchers summarize the information collected in a study and is often the basis for drawing conclusions about training effectiveness. This raises the issue of statistical conclusion validity. In general, *statistical conclusion validity* refers to the extent to which the research design and statistical analyses performed can lead to false conclusions.[15] To the extent that the design and analyses are appropriate, one can be confident in the results of the study (keeping in mind the issues of internal, external, and construct validity).

Of particular interest in HRD evaluations is the notion of **statistical power.** In a training evaluation study, statistical power is the probability of concluding there is a difference between the training and control groups (or the scores trainees achieve on a pretest and posttest) *when a difference actually exists.* The higher the power of a design or analysis, the greater the chances of finding a difference; the lower the power, the greater the chances that a true difference between the groups will go undetected.

Clearly, HRD professionals should be aware of statistical power and make sure that they use designs and analyses that have adequate power.[16] Yet, it is unlikely that HRD practitioners consider issues of statistical power when designing evaluation studies. A study investigating the statistical power of studies reported in leading management and applied psychology journals concluded that the power in published research is low.[17] Mone et al. also surveyed study authors and found that researchers did not perceive a strong need for statistical power in their studies. If the academic researchers publishing in leading journals (who are likely more skilled in research design and methodology issues than the typical HRD practitioner) are using low-power designs and do not perceive a strong need for power, it is probably safe to assume that power is not a significant consideration among HRD practitioners, either. This is a serious oversight. Why go through the time and effort of doing an evaluation if one cannot be confident that the results are true?

One of the best ways to increase statistical power is to increase the number of participants in a study. All things equal, the greater the number of participants in each group, the greater the statistical power will be. However, many organizations do not have this option, given the number of employees available or the cost of including additional participants or both. Arvey et al. reported that the median sample size in training evaluation is 43.[18] Studies with this number of participants have relatively low statistical power (which can be modified somewhat according to the statistical analysis procedure used). This means that in many organizations, reliance on low-power research designs may lead to the mistaken conclusion that training is ineffective.[19]

In discussing the trade-offs that exist between the four aspects of research design validity, statistical conclusion validity is typically viewed as being less important than internal validity. Yet, several authors have questioned the conventional wisdom. Sackett and Mullen put the issue this way:

> We would like to offer the proposition that statistical conclusion validity needs to take first priority in applied training evaluation research. The question, Is there a difference between trained and untrained groups? needs to be answered before addressing, Can the difference be attributed to the training intervention? What follows from this proposition is that it may be reasonable to trade off internal validity for statistical conclusion validity.[20]

Sackett and Mullen suggest that dividing a limited number of participants equally into a training group and a control group reduces statistical power; yet if no control group were used and the same limited number of participants were all placed into the training group (e.g., as in the nonexperimental one-group pretest-posttest design), statistical power would increase dramatically. This would increase the chances that a difference would be detected, even though it would be difficult to attribute any difference between the groups to the training. Depending on the question the organization wanted to answer, this trade-off may be the preferred course of action. As mentioned earlier, it may be possible to assess the impact of some of the threats to internal validity using existing knowledge about the participants and the organization.

Yang, Sackett, and Arvey offer a second suggestion for increasing the statistical power of a design: use unequal numbers of participants in the training and control groups.[21] In a paper that addresses the issue of the cost of training evaluation, Yang et al. point out that a trade-off exists between the power of an evaluation design and the cost of implementing the design. Although increasing the number of participants in both the control and training groups equally increases statistical power, it also increases the cost of doing the study, potentially to a prohibitive level. This is because participants in the training group must be trained as well as have their performance assessed. Yang et al. argue that increasing the total number of participants in the study by placing a greater number in the control group keeps the overall cost of the study down, while reaching power levels similar to those using a lower total number of participants divided equally among the two groups. Building on the work of Arvey, Maxwell, and Salas, Yang et al. developed formulas that can be used to identify the optimal ratio of control group size to training group size in an unequal-group-size design.[22]

Yang, Sackett, and Arvey also suggest a third way the sample size could be increased by making another cost-related trade-off: using less expensive, less valid measuring devices (called proxy measures) than one might otherwise use (called the target criterion measure).[23] This trade-off would permit assessing more participants for the same cost, thus increasing power. For example, suppose one was interested in assessing the job-security perceptions of trainees in an evaluation of a career development workshop. Although using a one-item job-security measure would be less valid and less reliable than a lengthier multi-item questionnaire, it would be quicker and less expensive to administer and process. This would allow the researcher to assess more study participants for the same cost, which would increase statistical power. Yang et al. state that as long as one can make the assumption that "any effects of training on the proxy are due to the effects of training on the target (i.e., training target proxy) . . . it is possible to make inferences about the effects of training on the target criterion from a study using the less expensive proxy criterion" (p. 652). They go on to demonstrate the cost savings that could be achieved and offer a series of step-by-step guidelines to help an HRD practitioner figure the cost savings that could be achieved by using a less valid proxy measure.

We find these ideas appealing because they provide some specific suggestions as to how HRD practitioners can take creative steps to conduct meaningful evaluation studies that address important methodological issues. In addition, they represent some concrete ways to move beyond the "experiment or nothing" mind-set that can inhibit practitioners from evaluating HRD programs.

## SELECTING A RESEARCH DESIGN

As we have indicated, there are a number of possible research designs to use when conducting an HRD evaluation study. Therefore, what factors should an HRD professional consider when selecting a design to use for an evaluation study?

Obviously, the validity of the conclusions drawn from the study is an important concern. Without valid conclusions, the evaluation effort is compromised. But other issues besides validity also need to be considered. Schmitt and Klimoski offer four additional criteria: conceptual issues, the costs associated with making a decision error, resources, and the value system and skills of the investigator.[24]

Conceptual issues concern the purpose of the evaluation study and previous research conducted on the training program being evaluated. The design used should permit the investigators to answer the questions they are charged with asking. Recall Sackett and Mullen's arguments regarding matching the design to the questions one must answer.[25] In addition, if previous research indicates that certain factors may affect training effectiveness (like experience or gender), the research design should address these factors.

Second, it is possible that the investigator will make an incorrect conclusion based on the study. The study may show that the training program did not improve job performance, when in fact it did. Or the study may show a high degree of transfer of training, while employees actually apply little of what they learned to their jobs. When selecting a research design, the investigator must consider the costs associated with making an incorrect decision based on the study. If the costs are very high (that is, the organization will spend a large amount of money using the program or will exclude employees from promotions if they do not successfully complete training), validity of the design becomes more important.

Third, certain designs, such as a pretest-posttest design or the Solomon four-group design, use more resources than others. The investigator may have limited time, money, facilities, and subjects for the evaluation effort. Evaluation should be as valid as possible within resource constraints. As we have discussed, it is possible to make cost-related trade-offs to improve various aspects of research design validity.[26]

Fourth, some organization members may be more committed and able to conduct some approaches to evaluation research (e.g., more or less rigorous) than other approaches. The expertise and attitudes of those involved in the evaluation effort should be considered.[27]

All in all, even though research design can be complicated, it obviously has a major impact on the success of most evaluation efforts. HRD professionals and others concerned with evaluation ignore research design issues at their own (and their organization's) peril.

## APPENDIX REFERENCES

1. Campbell, D. T., & Stanley, J. C. (1966). *Experimental and quasi-experimental designs for research.* Chicago: Rand McNally; Cook, T. D., & Campbell, D. T. (1979). *Quasi-experimentation: Design and analysis issues for field settings.* Chicago: Rand-McNally; Sackett, P. R., & Larson, J. R., Jr. (1990). Research strategies and tactics in industrial and organizational psychology. In M. D. Dunnette & L. M. Hough (Eds.), *Handbook of industrial and organizational psychology* (2nd ed., Vol. 1, pp. 419–489). Palo Alto, CA: Consulting Psychologists Press; Schmitt, N. W., & Klimoski, R. J. (1991). *Research methods in human resources management.* Mason, OH: Thomson/South-Western; Goldstein, I. L., & Ford, J. K. (2002). *Training in organizations: Needs assessment, development, and evaluation.* Belmont, CA: Wadsworth.

2. Cook, T. D., & Campbell, D. T. (1976). The design and conduct of quasi-experiments and true experiments in field settings. In M. D. Dunnette (Ed.), *Handbook of industrial and organizational psychology* (pp. 223–326). New York: Rand McNally.

3. *Ibid.*

4. *Ibid*; Cook & Campbell (1979), *supra* note 1.

5. Goldstein, I. L. (1980). Training in work organizations. *Annual Review of Psychology, 31,* 229–272.

6. Schmitt & Klimoski (1991), *supra* note 1.

7. Sackett, P. R., & Mullen, E. J. (1993). Beyond formal experimental design: Towards an expanded view of the training evaluation process. *Personnel Psychology, 46,* 613–627.

8. Schmitt & Klimoski (1991), *supra* note 1.

9. Sackett & Mullen (1993), *supra* note 7.

10. Cook & Campbell (1976), *supra* note 2.

11. Schmitt & Klimoski (1991), *supra* note 1.

12. Solomon, R. L. (1949). An extension of the control group design. *Psychological Bulletin, 46,* 137–150.

13. Campbell & Stanley (1966), *supra* note 1; Cook & Campbell (1976), *supra* note 2; Cook & Campbell (1979), *supra* note 1.

14. Cascio, W. F. (1991). *Applied psychology in personnel management* (4th ed.). Englewood Cliffs, NJ: Prentice-Hall.

15. Cook, T. D, Campbell, D. T., & Peracchio, L. (1990). Quasi-experimentation. In M. D. Dunnette & L. M. Hough (Eds.), *Handbook of industrial and organizational psychology* (2nd ed., Vol. 1, pp. 491–576). Palo Alto, CA: Consulting Psychologists Press.

16. Arvey, R. D., Cole, D. A., Hazucha, J. F., & Hartanto, F. M. (1985). Statistical power of training evaluation designs. *Personnel Psychology, 38,* 493–507.

17. Mone, M. A., Mueller, G. C., & Mauland, W. (1996). The perceptions and usage of statistical power in applied psychology and management research. *Personnel Psychology, 49,* 103–120.

18. Arvey et al. (1985), *supra* note 16.

19. Cascio (1991), *supra* note 14.

20. Sackett & Mullen (1993), *supra* note 7, p. 623.

21. Yang, H., Sackett, P. R., & Arvey, R. D. (1996). Statistical power and cost in training evaluation: Some new considerations. *Personnel Psychology, 49,* 651–668.

22. Arvey, R. D., Maxwell, S. E., & Salas, E. (1992). The relative power of training designs under different cost configurations. *Journal of Applied Psychology, 77,* 155–160; Yang et al. (1996), *supra* note 21.

23. Yang et al. (1996), *supra* note 21.

24. Schmitt & Klimoski (1991), *supra* note 1.

25. Sackett & Mullen (1993), *supra* note 7.

26. Haccoun, R. R., & Saks, A. M. (1998). Training in the 21st century: Some lessons from the last one. *Canadian Psychology, 39*(1–2), 33–51; Yang et al. (1996), *supra* note 21.

27. Schmitt & Klimoski (1991), *supra* note 1.

# PART 3

# HUMAN RESOURCE DEVELOPMENT APPLICATIONS

**8**

# Employee Socialization and Orientation

## Learning Objectives

*After reading this chapter, you should be able to:*

1. Discuss the content, outcomes, and process of organizational socialization.

2. State the challenges faced by new employees entering an organization and the things they need to be successful.

3. Describe the realistic job preview approach to recruiting, and explain how it can benefit organizations and new employees.

4. Define and explain the goals of employee orientation.

5. Identify the characteristics of an effective orientation program.

6. Learn the key elements necessary to design, implement, and evaluate an effective orientation program.

## OPENING CASE

New employee orientation is one of the most commonly used HRD approaches, but popularity is no guarantee that programs will be of high quality and effectiveness. As we will discuss in this chapter, the challenges to providing effective orientation programs are significant, and problems with these programs are common. Ideally, an orientation program should provide new employees with the information they need in a way that helps them adjust to the organization as soon as possible. In addition, the orientation period is an opportune time to allay concerns, reinforce the organization's values, and energize new employees about their new assignments. Yet, many organizations fail to take full advantage of this opportunity. Instead, they inundate recruits with information, including information they may not need or which may be contradictory. Further, many organizations often see orientation primarily as a way to process new employees (i.e., completing paperwork) rather than as a way to inspire them and make them feel good about the choice they have made to join the organization.

Consider the situation of International Sematech, a research consortium based in Austin, Texas. Sematech (short for **SE**miconductor **MA**nufacturing **TECH**nology) was formed by leading semiconductor manufacturers such as Hewlett-Packard, IBM, Intel, Lucent Technologies, Motorola, Philips, and Texas Instruments. Sematech currently has approximately 500 employees. What makes Sematech unique is that 70 percent of their employees are assignees on loan to Sematech from the member companies. After one to two years with Sematech, these assignees then return to their member company. In some years, turnover has exceeded 35 percent. The challenge that Sematech faced was in finding ways to get new employees (both direct hires and assignees) up to speed in as short a time as possible.

*Question: If you were in charge of orientation for Sematech, what approach would you recommend? What information is most critical to convey during orientation? What types of learning or training methods would you recommend? How long should the orientation last?*

## INTRODUCTION

Have you ever:

- *gone through a formal orientation program for a job you've held?*
- *been asked to assist in the orientation of a new employee (either as a supervisor or as a coworker)?*
- *given much thought to how new employees adjust or become socialized into a new organization?*
- *started a new job, only to discover that what you were told about the job and organization didn't match the way things really were?*

*If your answer to any of these questions was yes, what was the best (and worst) orientation experience you've ever had? Why?*

Using the building analogy introduced in Chapter 1, Part One of this book was meant to provide the foundation for effective HRD. Part Two provided the solid framework or structure for HRD. In Part Three, we will discuss numerous HRD applications. These can be compared to various rooms within the HRD structure. The first such "room" is the entryway or lobby. It is critical that new employees make a positive start with the organization. Organizational socialization processes and orientation programs are intended to do just that. This is the focus of Chapter 8.

Starting a new job can be stressful. Newcomers often find themselves in an unfamiliar work environment surrounded by people they do not know. To be successful in a new position, the new employee must establish relationships and learn new behaviors, facts, procedures, expectations, and values. New employees can also expect surprises along the way that require further adaptation, such as not anticipating the emotional impact of greater responsibility or underestimating the difficulty of adjusting to a new work schedule. In addition to learning new things, new employees may also need to "unlearn" things that helped them succeed in previous settings (such as in prior jobs or in school), but would be maladaptive in their new setting.[1]

The process of adjusting to a new organization is called *organizational socialization*. Socialization is a complex, lengthy process. It may take new employees weeks or months to understand what is expected from them on the job and how to behave in order to be accepted by other organization members. Successful socialization of new members is critical to both the individual and to the organization. At stake are:

- the new employee's satisfaction, performance, and commitment to the organization
- the work group's satisfaction and performance
- start-up costs invested in the new employee (such as recruiting, selection, training, and the time until the employee is up to full speed)
- the likelihood the employee will remain with the organization
- the costs of replacing the employee if he or she leaves

Despite the importance of socialization, some organizations do little to introduce and integrate new members, forcing them to learn on their own. Some employees may flourish under this sink-or-swim approach, but even they will likely experience anxiety and frustration during their early tenure. Fortunately, many organizations recognize the importance of successful socialization and act to facilitate the newcomers' transition into the organization.[2] This chapter provides a discussion of organizational socialization and the nature of this complex process. We will then identify two common approaches to facilitating employee socialization — the *realistic job preview (RJP)* and *employee orientation* — and explain how they can be used to benefit both the individual and the organization.

## SOCIALIZATION: THE PROCESS OF BECOMING AN INSIDER

**Organizational socialization** is defined as "the process by which an individual acquires the social knowledge and skills necessary to assume an organizational role."[3] The net result of this process is that someone who was considered by organization members to be an outsider is transformed into a productive and accepted insider. While this obviously applies to new hires, it can also apply to transferred and promoted employees as well. Unlike new hires, those who are transferred or promoted begin their socialization as insiders to the larger organization, with an understanding of its goals and values. Yet, like new hires, they are "outsiders" to the group they will be joining and face the challenge of gaining their new colleagues' acceptance and establishing themselves in a new role.

Before we discuss the socialization process itself, it is important that we explore three fundamental concepts: organizational roles, group norms, and expectations.

## SOME FUNDAMENTAL CONCEPTS OF SOCIALIZATION

*ORGANIZATIONAL ROLES.* A **role** is a set of behaviors expected of individuals who hold a given position in a group.[4] Roles define how a person fits into the organization and what he or she must do to perform effectively. For example, when we encounter a receptionist, we expect that person to perform certain functions of that role, such as greeting us, providing us with information, and directing us to those in the organization we wish to see. When newcomers enter a new group, they must learn what roles they are expected to fulfill in order to fit in and perform effectively.

Edgar Schein described three dimensions of organizational roles. These are:

1. *inclusionary* — a social dimension (e.g., outsider, probationary status, permanent status)
2. *functional* — a task dimension (e.g., sales, engineering, plant operations)
3. *hierarchical* — a rank dimension (e.g., line employee, supervisor, middle manager, officer)[5]

A new role requires learning to perform in ways that fulfill the social, functional, and hierarchical dimensions of that role. For example, a patrol officer who is promoted to shift sergeant will not be completely effective until he or she knows the tasks a sergeant must do, is able to do those tasks, and is accepted by others in the sergeant's role.

Van Maanen and Schein suggest that there are boundaries along these dimensions that employees cross during their careers.[6] The socialization process becomes much more intense and presents greater challenges just before and after the employee moves across a boundary. Crossing each boundary requires learning new attitudes and behaviors and carries with it the risk of failed socialization and negative outcomes, such as dissatisfaction and turnover.

Role communication and role orientation are two important issues for organizational socialization. Ideally, an individual's role would be communicated clearly and agreed upon by all concerned parties (including management, peers, and the individual). Unfortunately, roles are often not communicated clearly. Perception plays an important part in how roles are defined and communicated, and the individual, his or her coworkers, the immediate supervisor, and upper management are all likely to perceive a given role differently. Although many organizations consider a job description to be the official statement of an individual's role, job descriptions are often vague and open to interpretation.

The perceptual nature of organizational roles can lead to the following three situations:

1. **role overload** — when the employee perceives the role as being more than he or she can reasonably do

2. **role conflict** — when the employee receives mixed messages about what is expected of him or her by others, such as a boss and coworkers

3. **role ambiguity** — when the employee feels the role is unclear; this is often the result of assuming a newly created position

Research has shown that role overload, role conflict, and role ambiguity are all related to stress,[7] which in turn relates to job satisfaction, job performance, and other outcomes valued by the organization, including turnover and absenteeism.[8]

The individual's role orientation is also important to socialization. Individuals do not always conform completely to the role prescribed for them. **Role orientation** is the extent to which individuals are innovative in interpreting their organizational roles.[9] Role orientation exists on a continuum, with a custodial orientation (conforming closely to established ways of doing things) at one extreme, and an innovative orientation (taking considerable initiative in redefining the role) at the other.[10] For example, a market research analyst who has an innovative orientation may include educating managers in the ethics of marketing as a part of his or her role, even though other analysts in the organization do not perform this function. It is often beneficial for employees to creatively redefine their roles (i.e., have an innovative orientation) in ways that improve their own and the organization's effectiveness. However, this creativity and innovation will often challenge some of the organization's accepted beliefs and established ways of doing things.

Van Maanen and Schein suggest that the tactics an organization uses to socialize newcomers will influence an individual's role orientation.[11] Research supports this suggestion, which we will return to in our discussion of people processing tactics later in this chapter.[12]

*GROUP NORMS.* **Norms** are the rules of conduct (typically unwritten) that are established by group members to influence or control behavior within the group. Group norms are an important part of the socialization process because they indicate the behaviors that insiders agree are appropriate. Newcomers generally must learn to behave in ways that are consistent with group norms if they are to be accepted as an insider.

Groups do not develop or enforce norms for all possible behaviors and situations, but only for significant behaviors.[13] Schein suggests that organizations distinguish employee behaviors in terms of three levels of importance: *pivotal* (behaviors essential to organizational membership), *relevant* (behaviors that are desirable but not essential), and *peripheral* (unimportant behaviors).[14] Organizations are more likely to focus on pivotal and relevant behaviors during socialization and less likely to teach peripheral behaviors to the employee or pay attention to them. Similarly, Daniel Feldman observed that groups will enforce norms that facilitate group survival, express central values, make expected behaviors simpler or more predictable, or help members avoid interpersonal embarrassment.[15]

Learning a group's norms is not always easy. Norms are usually informal and unwritten — and also varied! They can differ from group to group within the same organization. Organizations can facilitate the socialization process by providing ways to help newcomers learn organization and group norms, such as in realistic job previews and orientation programs.

*EXPECTATIONS.* Expectations are also central to organizational socialization. An **expectation** is a belief about the likelihood that something will occur. Expectations can encompass behaviors, feelings, policies, and attitudes. Newcomers have expectations about how they will be treated, what they will be asked to do, and how they will feel in the new organization, among other things. Expectations are important for a variety of organizational issues, including motivation and decision making. Research suggests that newcomers' expectations can affect their satisfaction, performance, commitment, and tendency to remain with the organization.[16]

Unfortunately, recruiting practices often result in recruits having inflated expectations of their jobs and organizational life.[17] Unrealistically high expectations are not likely to be met, leading recruits to be dissatisfied and increasing the chances they will leave the organization. John Wanous argued that adjusting newcomer expectations to more reasonable (lower) levels reduces turnover.[18] In general, unmet expectations (whether realistic or not) can lead to dissatisfaction, which can eventually result in individuals quitting their jobs.[19] In a longitudinal study, Irving and Meyer reported effects for *any* discrepancy between what newcomers expect and what they encounter. This was not just for expectations that were unrealistically high.[20] A newcomer may have realistic expectations about an organization's social policies (like allowing time off for family issues), but discover that the policies are different than expected (e.g., requiring that time off be earned).

Newcomers develop and test expectations throughout the socialization process. The expectations that an individual will develop depend on a number of factors and a variety of sources, including the organization and its representatives, coworkers, friends, family, the media, as well the newcomer's own personality, attitudes, values, and prior experiences.

Organizations should be aware of the impact that expectations have on the newcomer's performance and satisfaction and take steps to ensure that the information they provide leads to realistic, attainable expectations. While organizations can help adjust newcomer expectations, surprise cannot be completely eliminated from the newcomer's experience, in part because newcomers may not be aware of how they feel about certain things until they experience them.[21] For example, telling an applicant from another geographic area about the climate in your area is not the same as having the applicant actually experience it (say, 20 degrees Fahrenheit with wind chill in the winter, or 100 degrees with high humidity in the summer).

## CONTENT OF SOCIALIZATION

Organizational socialization can be viewed as a learning process, in that newcomers must learn a wide variety of information and behaviors to be accepted as an organizational insider. Cynthia Fisher divides the content of socialization into five categories of learning:

1. *preliminary learning* — including the discovery that learning will be necessary, what to learn, and whom to learn from
2. *learning about the organization* — including the goals, values, and policies of the organization
3. *learning to function in the work group* — including the values, norms, roles, and friendships within the group
4. *learning how to perform the job* — including the necessary skills and knowledge for a particular job
5. *personal learning* — learning from experience with the job and organization, including self-identity, expectations, self-image, and motivation[22]

Newcomers who learn in each of these content areas should undergo attitude and behavioral changes. Similarly, Feldman proposed that socialization learning includes acquiring a set of appropriate role behaviors, developing work skills and abilities, and adjusting to the work group's norms and values.[23]

Georgia Chao and colleagues drew upon prior theory and research to propose six dimensions for organizational socialization: performance proficiency, politics, language, people, organizational goals and values, and history.[24] They developed a thirty-four-item questionnaire to measure these dimensions. Chao et al. tested the questionnaire and found support for their typology. They also conducted a longitudinal study and reported that each dimension was related to career effectiveness in a sample of engineers and managers. Jill Haueter and colleagues have developed an alternative questionnaire.[25]

Taken together, these categorization schemes make it clear that newcomers often face a difficult challenge. As we discussed in Chapter 3, learning different content areas often requires different mechanisms (recall Robert Gagné's views on this). Thus, it follows that organizations should use multiple approaches to facilitate the learning that must occur during successful socialization.

## OUTCOMES OF SOCIALIZATION

Socialization researchers have suggested a wide variety of affective, cognitive, and behavioral outcomes of the socialization process.[26] Our discussion of socialization to this point has mentioned a number of possible outcomes, both positive (e.g., organizational commitment, innovation) and negative (e.g., dissatisfaction, turnover, poor performance). Other possible outcomes of socialization include role overload, role conflict, and role ambiguity (discussed earlier). In general, successful socialization means that the newcomer develops (1) greater knowledge of the organization and work group; (2) attitudes that make performing, fitting into, and remaining with the organization and work group possible; and (3) behaviors that lead to personal and organizational effectiveness. Unsuccessful socialization is generally believed to result in unmet expectations, dissatisfaction, lack of commitment, and turnover.

We still do not have a strong understanding of how and when specific outcomes change during the socialization process.[27] Several studies have shown that early socialization experiences have a lasting impact on socialization outcomes,[28] and it appears that socialization continues over time.[29] In addition, information gained from supervisors and peers is highly valued by newcomers and has been found to have a significant effect in early socialization.[30] More research along these lines is needed, and future work should help to further clarify these processes.

So far, we have discussed what socialization is, some foundational concepts underlying socialization, and the content and proposed outcomes of socialization. Before discussing HRD practices that can be used to facilitate socialization, we consider a model of the socialization process, the "people processing" tactics that organizations use to socialize newcomers, and the role that newcomers play in socialization.

## VARIOUS PERSPECTIVES ON THE SOCIALIZATION PROCESS

### STAGE MODELS OF SOCIALIZATION

Many theorists who have written about organizational socialization have described the process using *stage models* that depict the steps or stages involved in the process.[31] Many stage models have been proposed.[32] Our discussion will focus on a representative three-stage model developed by Daniel Feldman, which is depicted in Figure 8-1.[33]

The first stage, **anticipatory socialization,** begins *before* the individual joins the organization. In this stage, the person forms an impression about what membership in an organization is like. Information about organizations is available from a variety of sources, such as rumors, anecdotes, advertisements, the media, employment recruiters, and increasingly through the Internet. For example, image advertising, such as Proctor & Gamble's "Touching Lives — Improving Life" or the U.S. Army's "An Army of One" campaigns, send messages about those organizations. Media also play a role in helping organizations establish reputations. Reports and ads about Microsoft, for example, communicate the message that this organization is an intellectually stimulating place to work where dedicated employees put in long hours. On the other hand, U.S. government antitrust cases against Microsoft have resulted in considerable negative publicity for the organization.

These impressions influence expectations that may in turn affect an individual's behavior. For example, people's expectations when looking for jobs may attract them to one organization, reject another organization from their consideration, and affect their decision to remain at an organization where they initially choose to work. As mentioned earlier, it is important that managers provide accurate information and help correct inaccurate expectations to avoid the potential negative consequences for performance, satisfaction, and tenure.

Also during the anticipatory socialization stage, individuals may be examining the extent to which their skills, abilities, needs, and values match those that they perceive the organization to require or prefer. These judgments can affect their behavior, both in terms of whether they will attempt to join the organization and how they may interact with organization members.

## FIGURE 8-1 — FELDMAN'S MODEL OF ORGANIZATIONAL SOCIALIZATION

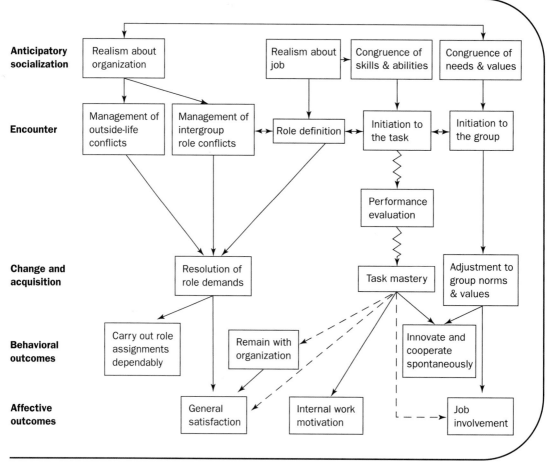

SOURCE: ACADEMY OF MANAGEMENT REVIEW by FELDMAN, D. C. Copyright 1981 by ACAD OF MGMT. Reproduced with permission of ACAD OF MGMT in the format Textbook via Copyright Clearance Center.

The **encounter** stage of the socialization process begins when a recruit makes a formal commitment to join the organization. A formal commitment may mean signing an employment contract or simply accepting an offer of employment or membership. At this point, an individual crosses the inclusionary boundary separating the organization from the outside environment and begins to discover what the organization is really like. During this stage, preemployment expectations may be confirmed or rejected. This can lead to some unpleasant surprises. An employee who joined an organization because of an impression that advancement into and through the management ranks will be rapid may find promotions come slowly and are fewer in number than expected. During this stage, new employees must manage conflicts between lifestyle and work, resolve any role conflicts within the work group, define and clarify their own roles, become familiar with the dynamics of the work group and job, and learn and perform the tasks required by the job.

The third and last stage in this process is called **change and acquisition.** This stage occurs when new employees accept the norms and values of the group, master the tasks they must perform, and resolve any role conflicts and overloads. Employees who successfully complete this stage will likely be satisfied, internally motivated and involved in the job, perform their jobs dependably, and remain with the organization.

These three stages have also been labeled "getting in," "breaking in," and "settling in." As shown in Figure 8-1, it is predicted that successful movement through all three stages will lead to positive affective and behavioral outcomes.

It is important to recognize that socialization does not occur in a vacuum. The process is affected by the dynamics within the group, as well as by on-the-job learning, career development, and life development.[34] Furthermore, it should be clear from the preceding discussion that socialization is a two-way street. Events during the socialization process change not only the newcomer but organizational insiders as well.

Two other caveats about stage models of socialization should be mentioned. First, stage models provide a framework describing what happens to a typical or average individual. A variety of issues, including the rate of socialization and whether individuals progress through the stages in a lock-step order, have not been adequately addressed.[35] Second, stage models are not the only way to view the socialization process. For example, Meryl Rice Louis developed a process model of events that might occur within the encounter stage.[36] In her view, surprises are typical, and socialization occurs as newcomers find ways to explain these events and use these explanations to predict what will happen in the future. Therefore, it is important to view such models more as suggestions rather than absolutes.

## PEOPLE PROCESSING TACTICS AND STRATEGIES

Even if the effort is not deliberate or part of a planned program, all organizations influence the adjustment of new members. Van Maanen calls these actions **people processing strategies,** and suggests seven pairs of tactics organizations may use when processing or socializing newcomers (see Table 8-1).[37]

The particular tactics an organization uses are often the result of tradition rather than a conscious choice.[38] Van Maanen argues that whatever people processing strategies an organization uses, they will have a strong impact on newcomers' attitudes, behaviors, and beliefs. Further, Van Maanen, Schein, and others have hypothesized that various combinations of people processing tactics lead newcomers to develop a particular role orientation.[39] Specifically, they suggested the following:

1. A process that is sequential, variable, serial, and involves divestiture practices will lead newcomers to develop a *custodial orientation* (they will define their roles as the organization traditionally has defined them). A strong example of this approach is the Marine Corps basic training program.

**TABLE 8-1**  PEOPLE PROCESSING STRATEGIES

1. **Formal Versus Informal**  Involves the newcomer's role and whether the setting in which the activity occurs is segregated from the ongoing work content. Formal processes are segregated and make the newcomer's role explicit. Informal processes take place within the work context, do not clearly delineate the newcomer's role, and are usually unstructured. In a formal strategy, all newcomers will likely have very similar experiences (whether they are processed together or individually), whereas in an informal strategy, each newcomer's experience will likely be unique.

2. **Individual Versus Collective**  The degree to which newcomers are socialized individually or as a group. In a collective (or group) strategy, newcomers tend to develop a collective sense of the organization and possibly a sense of camaraderie ('we're all in this together"). Here, newcomers can test out their own ideas with one another and form a consensus. Individual strategies will likely be more expensive.

3. **Sequential Versus Nonsequential**  Sequential strategies contain a series of stages (such as probationary appointment, associate, or partner) through which newcomers must progress before they gain a recognized role and status within the organization. A nonsequential process contains one stage in which the complete transition occurs (such as a promotion to supervisor after completing a two-week training program).

4. **Fixed Versus Variable**  The time frame for completing the transition period. In a fixed process, the newcomer knows in advance when the transition period will end (e.g., three years in an apprenticeship program to be considered a journeyman). In a variable process, newcomers are not aware of when the process will end, and in fact, the time it takes to complete the process may vary from individual to individual.

5. **Tournament Versus Contest**  In tournament processes, newcomers are sorted according to their potential, ambition, background, or other factors, and then assigned to separate "tracks" accordingly. For example, some systems separate new management recruits into either a fast track or a regular track. Contest processes, however, do not make such early distinctions among newcomers. Newcomers enter the process together, and they progress through various channels according to their own observed abilities and interests.

6. **Serial Versus Disjunctive**  Serial strategies involve having senior organization members work with newcomers to groom them to assume similar roles (as in a mentor program). In disjunctive strategies, newcomers are socialized by organization members who are not a part of their work group (as with trainers). Serial strategies are predicted to perpetuate established values and norms, while disjunctive strategies are more likely to increase innovation.

7. **Investiture Versus Divestiture**  The degree to which the socialization process is designed to preserve or strip away the newcomer's identity. Investiture strategies reinforce the uniqueness and viability of the newcomer's individual characteristics and are commonly used when socializing recruits for senior management positions. Divestiture strategies attempt to suppress certain characteristics of newcomers (such as their attitudes and self-confidence) and replace them with characteristics deemed of value to the organization, as is done during basic training in military organizations.

SOURCE: Reprinted from *Organizational Dynamics*, 7, Van Maanen, J., People Processing: Strategies of Organizational Socialization, 18–36, Copyright 1978, with permission from Elsevier.

2. A process that is collective, formal, random, fixed, and disjunctive will lead to a *content innovation* role orientation (newcomers will make changes and improvements in their roles, but still consider their mission from the organization's traditional perspective). An example of this is General Motors Corporation's Saturn division, which was created as a way for the company to redefine how automobiles would be designed and built within their organization.

3. A process that is individual, informal, random, disjunctive, and uses investiture practices will lead to a *role innovation* orientation (creatively redefining the mission and goals of the role, going beyond merely improving the knowledge base or practices within the role). Senior managers who are hired from outside an organization are likely to be socialized in this way, taking advantage of their unique set of qualities to introduce major changes in the organization.

Several studies have tested these hypotheses. Gareth Jones studied MBA recipients.[40] He classified socialization tactics as either institutionalized (collective, formal, sequential, fixed, serial, and investiture) or individualized (individual, informal, random variable, disjunctive, and divestiture). Jones changed two of Van Maanen and Schein's predictions: he predicted fixed tactics and investiture tactics would decrease innovation. His findings support the notion that institutionalized tactics lead to a custodial role orientation, and that individualized tactics lead to an innovation role orientation. Allen and Meyer, also using MBA recipients, replicated Jones's findings, and further found that the serial-disjunctive dimension was the best predictor of role orientation.[41] In a related study, Ashford and Saks found that institutionalized tactics reduced newcomers' uncertainty and anxiety and led to stronger attachments to the job and organization, but that individualized tactics were associated with stronger performance and reduced intentions to quit.[42] Their findings raise the possibility that there could be a trade-off between using individualized or institutionalized socialization tactics. While these studies offer initial support for the effect that socialization tactics can have on newcomer attitudes and behavior, further research using different samples and methods (beyond using self-report data) is needed before firm conclusions can be made.

## NEWCOMERS AS PROACTIVE INFORMATION SEEKERS

A third perspective on organizational socialization emerged in the 1990s. Early socialization theories tended to portray newcomers as reacting to socialization processes and events. However, it has been suggested that this view is incomplete.[43] Newcomers often actively seek out the information they need, to be able both to master their environment and to fill in the gaps left by supervisors, coworkers, and other sources. This perspective explicitly recognizes that socialization is a two-way street, and it is not necessarily something that organizations do "*to*" people.

A series of longitudinal studies demonstrate that newcomers actively seek out information.[44] It also appears that information seeking has an impact on socialization outcomes.[45] The dynamics of the information-seeking process are only beginning to be investigated. For example, two studies found that newcomers tended to use different information-seeking tactics and sources of information for different types of information.[46]

A growing body of research has emphasized workplace learning as an overarching goal of HRD.[47] This has also been linked to employee socialization and orientation efforts.[48] We welcome more work in this area, as it clearly aligns well with the learning emphasis in the HRD field that was described in Chapter 3. That is, employee socialization should focus on the learning processes of new employees. It is valuable to emphasize ways in which new employees can be facilitated as active rather than merely passive learners in the socialization process.

Research on newcomers' proactive role in socialization has significant implications for practice. For example, if newcomers tend to seek out some information by observing others and experimenting to see what works and what doesn't, organizations should encourage them to do so. This could be done by minimizing the risks newcomers face for experimenting, by training supervisors and peers to support newcomers' attempts to gather information, and by creating orientation programs that include information-seeking activities and reinforcement for newcomers who engage in them.

## WHAT DO NEWCOMERS NEED?

So far, we have described the socialization process in terms of the key concepts involved, content, outcomes, stages, and people processing strategies. Given this knowledge, we must now ask: What do newcomers need to be successfully socialized? A good way to approach this question is to compare what insiders have to what newcomers lack. Insiders typically have a clear idea of their role in the organization, the group and organization's norms and values, the KSAOs and experience that permit them to perform their work effectively, and they have adjusted to their roles, the work group, and the organization to the point that they have chosen to remain with the organization. In addition, insiders possess three essential elements:

1. *Accurate Expectations* — Insiders normally know what to expect of the situations in which they find themselves, so there are fewer surprises to confront them. Newcomers' expectations are more likely to differ from organizational reality.

2. *Knowledge Base* — When surprises do occur, insiders have the knowledge base (from history and experience in the setting) to more accurately make sense of the surprising event. Newcomers generally lack this knowledge.

3. *Other Insiders* — Insiders have coworkers with whom to compare their judgments and interpretations of organizational events. Newcomers have not yet developed the relationships with insiders they can trust and draw upon to help them interpret organizational events.[49]

Insiders are less frequently surprised by organizational events than newcomers, and they have the means available to make more accurate interpretations of such events. Newcomers are more likely to make inappropriate or dysfunctional interpretations, potentially leading to anxiety and behaviors and beliefs that differ from those of the insiders. For example, suppose the supervisor of a group of prison guards yells at several guards who arrived late for a shift, threatening them with disciplinary action. The supervisor may typically handle rule violations this way, but may rarely carry out these threats. Therefore, insiders would interpret this event as their boss "blowing off steam," and carry on with the shift. A newcomer to the group may view this episode differently, and may become apprehensive and worried about doing everything by the book.

Therefore, newcomers need clear information on expectations, roles, norms, and values, as well as assistance in developing the KSAOs and experience needed to perform the job effectively. Also, following Louis's view, newcomers need help interpreting events in the organization (especially surprises) and could benefit from insiders who are genuinely willing to share their knowledge and judgments.[50] In addition, newcomers will also need help in forming accurate expectations about the organization and finding ways to cope with their new roles, both at work and in their personal lives.

As we have seen, theory and research on organizational socialization provides managers and HRD professionals with a rich base upon which to develop programs and practices to assist newcomers in making the transition to become effective, accepted insiders. The challenge is to make practical application from this research literature. We now turn our attention to two practical approaches used by organizations to apply these theories to increase newcomer effectiveness and satisfaction.

## THE REALISTIC JOB PREVIEW

A **realistic job preview (RJP)** involves providing recruits with complete information about the job and the organization. While an RJP may seem like common sense, it actually stands in contrast to the traditional approach to recruiting, sometimes referred to as the "flypaper approach,"[51] in which the organization tries to attract applicants by selectively presenting only positive aspects of the job and downplaying any negative aspects. In an RJP, the recruit is given both positive and negative information — in essence, the whole truth. Thus if a job involves long hours and extensive travel, this information would not be withheld or glossed over, but rather discussed openly.

According to John Wanous, the goal of an RJP is to increase newcomers' satisfaction and commitment and the likelihood that they will remain with the organization.[52] A model of the RJP process (see Figure 8-2) suggests four interrelated mechanisms: vaccination, self-selection, coping, and personal commitment.[53]

1. *Vaccination Against Unrealistically High Expectations* — Providing accurate information to outsiders is similar to vaccinating people against a disease. Recruits are given information that permits them to adjust their expectations to the reality of the job. For example, a realistic portrayal of typical overtime or weekend work may assist applicants in understanding all that will be required of them in a given job.

FIGURE 8-2

## REALISTIC JOB PREVIEW EFFECTS

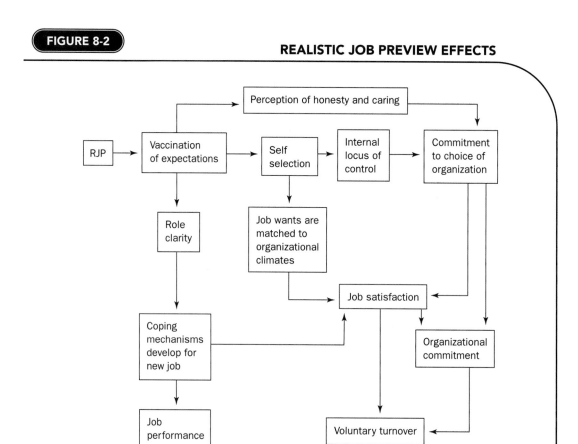

SOURCE: From Wanous, J. P. (1978). Realistic job previews: Can a procedure to reduce turnover also influence the relationship between abilities and performance? *Personnel Psychology, 31,* 251. Reprinted by permission.

2. *Self-Selection* — Realistic expectations enable recruits to decide whether the job and the organization match their individual needs. If they are incompatible, the recruit will probably not accept the position, thus saving the organization from hiring someone who would likely be dissatisfied and quit. The model suggests that self-selecting individuals are more likely to be satisfied employees. **Self-selection** obviously assumes that the organization has enough other applicants that it can afford to let applicants select themselves out of the hiring process.

3. *Coping Effect* — Realistic expectations help newcomers develop a clear idea of their roles, which in turn enables them to develop coping strategies for performing their jobs effectively.

4. *Personal Commitment* — A recruit who makes a decision to join an organization based on a realistic perspective will likely develop a stronger personal commitment to that choice. This encourages job satisfaction and a long-term commitment to remain with the organization.

Although the RJP occurs during the recruitment process, it can also be considered an HRD intervention in that it shares many of the same goals and techniques as other HRD approaches. As we described earlier, the socialization process really begins *before* an employee formally joins the organization, and the RJP addresses its initial step (i.e., anticipatory socialization) by attempting to adjust unrealistic impressions and reinforce accurate expectations.

## HOW REALISTIC JOB PREVIEWS ARE USED

The first step in developing an RJP is to assess the need for one. Interviews, questionnaires, and organizational records can be used to assess the satisfaction, commitment, and turnover of new employees in an organization.[54] In addition, questions should be asked about whether recruits' expectations were realistic and the extent to which the organization met their expectations. Employees who voluntarily leave the organization should be interviewed to determine their reasons for leaving (this is typically done in an exit interview). Often, employees leave for reasons that are unrelated to their job satisfaction (including following a spouse/partner to a new location, a change of heart about a career choice, returning to school, or receiving a better job offer elsewhere); in these cases, an RJP would likely do little to reduce the turnover.

Furthermore, it is important to consider the performance level of individuals who voluntarily leave the organization.[55] Some turnover may be desirable, for example, if the organization's poorest performers are the ones who are leaving. However, if this is not the case, and the organization would like to improve the situation (as when it is difficult to find new recruits), an alternative selection or training approach would likely be more effective than an RJP.

Advocates have suggested a number of conditions in which an RJP can be both useful and effective, including:

- when job candidates can be selective about job offers, especially during times of low unemployment
- when the selection ratio is low (the organization has many more job applicants than positions available)
- when the recruits are unlikely to have enough information available to them to develop realistic expectations (such as with entry level, complex, or "unique" jobs)
- when replacement costs are high[56]

A variety of media for delivering an RJP have been suggested, including printed materials (like booklets), audiovisual presentations (videos), discussions with a representative of the organization (usually a recruiter or job incumbent), oral presentations, and interviews.[57] Given that an RJP can be seen as a philosophy of recruiting rather than simply as a specific program, other media are also possible, including job advertisements, recruiting literature, direct observation of the work environment (such as a tour), work simulations, and actual work experience for the recruit (such as a co-op or internship).[58]

Unfortunately, most of the research conducted to date has focused primarily on booklets and videotapes, with little research comparing the relative effectiveness of various media. An exception is a study by Colarelli, which found that a two-way discussion between the recruit and a job incumbent proved more effective than an RJP booklet in reducing turnover.[59] Although it can be argued that using media that provide greater realism and immediacy (like videos or DVDs) and opportunities for two-way communication may be more effective than static approaches (like booklets), the expense of using such media may outweigh the benefits. Further research that examines both the effectiveness and utility of various media is needed. For an interesting example of an organization providing realistic information to prospective applicants on its website, see the "Living in Corning" example shown in the following endnote.[60]

In addition to selecting what media one will use to present the RJP, its content must be chosen. The following issues should be considered in determining RJP content:

- *Descriptive or Judgmental Content* — Descriptive content focuses on factual information, while judgmental content communicates incumbents' feelings.

- *Extensive or Intensive Content* — Extensive content contains all pertinent information, while intensive content implies selective information that is presented more briefly and forcefully.

- *Degree of Content Negativity* — Should the content of the RJP be highly negative, moderately negative, or somewhere in between?

- *Message Source* — if an audiovisual medium is used, should actors, job incumbents, or other organization members, such as supervisors or trainers, present the message?[61]

Wanous recommended using content that is judgmental, intensive, moderately negative, and presented by job incumbents. In addition, he also suggests that (1) recruits be explicitly encouraged to self-select themselves out of the selection process, (2) the RJP message have high credibility and match the medium used, and (3) the information presented match the organizational climate.[62] These recommendations seem reasonable, but the research remains insufficient to draw firm conclusions. Those preparing RJPs are advised to review the available literature and to examine the issues and arguments in light of their needs, budget, and available resources.

Timing is critical to the RJP. According to theory, RJPs should be given as early as possible (before a job offer is made) in order to activate important mechanisms like vaccination and self-selection. However, this can be an expensive proposition, depending on the number of recruits and the media used. In addition, senior management may be less likely to approve using negative information if the RJP is given early (such as in a recruiting video) rather than late in the process (after an offer is made).[63]

Research does not offer clear guidance on the timing of RJPs because in many of the studies the RJP was presented later in the process (e.g., after an offer or after the recruit accepted an offer). Although these studies have shown that RJPs are effective in lowering expectations and turnover, it may be that the timing used in these studies has led to conservative estimates of effectiveness.[64] Early delivery of the RJP seems to be the best approach, using multiple forms of media — such as job ads, recruiting brochures, and videos, DVDs, or online multimedia presentations — to communicate realistic information throughout the organizational entry process. Then, more expensive approaches can be used later, if necessary, when there are fewer individuals to process.

## ARE REALISTIC JOB PREVIEWS EFFECTIVE?

A variety of choices are available to help organizations evaluate the effectiveness of their RJP, including the criteria listed in Table 8-2. We recommend that organizations evaluate their RJPs and communicate the results of their evaluations through the scientific and practitioner literature. This will serve to expand the knowledge base upon which HRD professionals can make more informed decisions about designing and implementing RJPs.

**TABLE 8-2**

**EVALUATION CRITERIA FOR THE REALISTIC JOB PREVIEW**

| Stage of Entry | Evaluation Criteria |
| --- | --- |
| Preentry | 1. Ability of the organization to recruit newcomers |
| Entry | 2. Initial expectations of newcomers |
|  | 3. Choice of organization by the individual, (specific job wants being matched with climates) |
| Postentry | 4. Initial job attitudes |
|  | Satisfaction with the job |
|  | Commitment to the organization |
|  | Descriptive statements about the job (to be compared with expectations held as an outsider) |
|  | Thoughts about quitting |
|  | 5. Job performance |
|  | 6. Job survival and voluntary turnover rates |

SOURCE: Wanous, J. P. (1992). *Organizational entry: Recruitment, selection, orientation, and socialization of newcomers* (2nd ed., p. 72). Reading, MA: Addison-Wesley. Adapted by permission.

A relatively large number of studies examining the effectiveness of RJPs have been conducted, including a number of meta-analyses that review and combine the findings of multiple studies.[65] In general, research has shown that RJPs reduce inflated expectations and have a beneficial effect on turnover, satisfaction, and commitment. The average reduction of turnover has been between 5 and 10 percent.[66] Although much research has been done, many of the studies have had design flaws.[67] Thus, while it appears that RJPs are effective, better-designed studies that examine both underlying theory and practical issues will be of great benefit.

It should be noted that providing recruits with realistic information can only be expected to go so far in improving newcomers' attitudes and behaviors. An organization should examine what it can do to *improve* the conditions in which employees work and correct the problems that it can. For example, new employees may often be disappointed by the lack of responsibility and challenge in early assignments. Simply telling newcomers that this is the case may help lower their expectations, but Irving and Meyer found that providing newcomers with positive work experiences has a greater impact than altering expectations.[68] Similarly, reducing the need for unscheduled overtime may be more effective than simply telling people about the "overtime issue."

To summarize, while the magnitude of effectiveness demonstrated thus far is not as high as advocates had hoped for, RJPs offer a practical, relatively inexpensive, and ethical way to facilitate socialization for new employees. In today's economic environment, even moderate reductions in turnover can have a significant impact on organizational productivity. We encourage HRD practitioners to consider integrating RJPs within their organization's socialization processes.

## EMPLOYEE ORIENTATION PROGRAMS

**Employee orientation** programs are designed to introduce new employees to the job, supervisor, coworkers, and the organization. Orientation programs typically begin after the newcomer has agreed to join the organization, frequently on the individual's first day at work. According to John McGilllicuddy, "One of the first and most lasting impressions new employees have of their employers is how they are greeted and treated on their first day of work."[69] However, unlike realistic job previews, which affect primarily the anticipatory stage of socialization, employee orientation programs focus on the *encounter* stage of socialization, which is the period during which the newcomer finds out what the job and life in the organization are really like.

Commonly cited objectives of orientation programs include the following:

■ reduce the newcomer's stress and anxiety
■ reduce start-up costs
■ reduce turnover
■ reduce the time it takes for the newcomer to reach proficiency (training and break-in time)
■ assist the newcomer in learning the organization's values, culture, and expectations

- assist the newcomer in acquiring appropriate role behaviors
- help the newcomer adjust to the work group and its norms
- encourage the development of positive attitudes[70]

Orientation programs are common in organizations of all sizes. Surveys of HRD professionals reveal that between 70 and 96 percent of responding organizations conduct some form of orientation program.[71] Orientation programs exist for a wide variety of jobs and occupations. A recent issue of *Training* discussed orientation efforts at organizations such as Verizon, Sprint, Eddie Bauer, Wells Fargo, Hewlett-Packard, and Fairmont Hotels.[72] Other programs have been reported for employees at the Ritz-Carleton Hotel Company,[73] the Student Loan Marketing Association,[74] National Semiconductor,[75] Sematech,[76] county government workers in Mecklenburg County, North Carolina,[77] and temporary employees at a direct-marketing call center.[78] A recent ASTD survey suggested that 7 percent of all training and development expenditures were spent on orientation.[79]

## ASSESSMENT AND THE DETERMINATION OF ORIENTATION PROGRAM CONTENT

Ideally, orientation programs should follow the same assessment-design-implementation-evaluation (A DImE) framework that we have highlighted in Chapters 4 through 7. This means that organization representatives will do a careful assessment of exactly what content should be provided in orientation, as well as the best means for providing that content. This should then be followed up with a systematic evaluation effort, to determine how successful the orientation program was.

In general, orientation programs typically cover information about the company as a whole, which may be provided by the HRD staff, as well as job-specific information, which would more likely be provided by the newcomer's immediate supervisor. *Company information* might include an overview of the company, key policies and procedures, the mission statement, company goals and strategy, as well as information concerning compensation, benefits, safety and accident prevention, employee or union relations, and the physical facilities. *Job-specific information* could include the function of the department or work group, job duties and responsibilities, policies, rules, and procedures, a tour of the department, and introduction to department employees.[80]

Given the nature of organizational socialization, it is important that organizations clearly communicate job expectations to new employees. Such things as job responsibilities, tasks, reporting lines, accountability, and performance standards should be explained. All too often, a job description is viewed as the primary means for communicating this information, but as mentioned earlier, important job characteristics may be missing from this description. For example, work rules, working conditions, and relationships with coworkers, clients, and customers all play roles in establishing expectations, and all of these should be discussed.

The new employee should be given an overview of the organization's mission, goals, structure, culture, and products. These issues are critical. The organizational mission statement serves to reinforce basic values and the organization's place in its industry and in society. An employee who understands the importance of the mission is more likely to behave in accordance with it. Some organizations use a credo to communicate the core mission and reinforce this in company policies and goals. Many organizations try to simplify these statements and refer to them in a variety of official documents (such as the employee manual and business reports).

Compensation and benefits policies should also be explained during orientation. Some organizations devote a portion of the orientation period to completing compensation and benefit forms to make sure employees know what they are entitled to and are enrolled in the appropriate programs.

Orienting newcomers to the department in which they will be working provides them with a better understanding of how different jobs fit together within the whole of that unit, as well as how the unit or department fits into the larger organization. Workflow, coordination, and the like should be discussed. Finally, the physical layout of the workplace should also be explained, including the locations of supplies, facilities (like the cafeteria and rest rooms), emergency exits, and any unusual features.

A wide range of training methods and media are used in orientation programs, including lectures, videos/DVDs, printed materials, and discussions. For example, at Apple Computer, computer software is used as a primary means to deliver orientation content. This provides a greater degree of learner control of the orientation process than is true of most formal orientation programs, and this program was designed to maintain a high level of participant interest and enthusiasm.[81] Corporate intranets (internal computer networks that are modeled after the Internet) also offer a unique and powerful opportunity to provide newcomers with a wide range of information about the organization and its people whenever they want it (see the exercise at the end of the chapter).[82] Verizon Wireless makes use of online, classroom, and team settings to conduct its orientation program.[83] For a description of a cross-cultural orientation program for foreign college faculty in Oman that emphasizes lectures and discussion, see Al-Lamki.[84]

The length of orientation programs varies, from a few hours to several days to periodic sessions scheduled over several months. Table 8-3 provides a checklist of topics that are recommended for inclusion in most orientation programs. Table 8-4 shows a timetable of events for an extensive orientation program developed by Corning Corporation.[85]

## ORIENTATION ROLES

One of the most important elements of an effective orientation experience is frequent interaction between the newcomers and their supervisors, coworkers, and other organization members. Arnon Reichers suggests that these interactions are the primary vehicle through which socialization occurs, because it is these insiders who can provide newcomers with much of the information that they need to make sense of the organization.[86] She argues that the rate of socialization during the encounter stage is dependent on the frequency of these interactions: the more interaction, the faster the newcomer becomes socialized. In one study, new employees rated interactions with peers, supervisors and senior coworkers to be the most

| TABLE 8-3 | A CHECKLIST OF COMMON TOPICS TO INCLUDE IN AN ORIENTATION PROGRAM |
|---|---|

- schedule for the employee's first week on the job
- company history, philosophy, and an overview of what the company does
- organizational chart or charts
- overview of the industry or industries in which the organization operates
- review of the benefits package (e.g., health insurance, vacation/sick/personal leave policies, tuition reimbursement, retirement)
- summary of performance appraisal or performance management system, that is, how, when, and by whom employees will be evaluated, as well as general performance expectations
- review of compensation procedures: pay periods, direct deposit, and how and where to complete time sheets, time cards, and so on
- review of a current position or job description, including specific job requirements
- information about scheduling an employee physical exam (if required), and what to expect during such an exam
- career development information, for example, potential promotion opportunities, career paths, career resources and information available
- basic ergonomics and safety training
- overview of the employee handbook, policies and procedures, financial/credit union information
- information about obtaining an organizational identification card/badge, keys, setting up an e-mail account, computer password, telephone, parking permit, office supplies, and so on
- a tour of the facility and a map or listing of relevant businesses in the surrounding community (restaurants, shopping, dry cleaning, places to walk, etc.)
- technical or job-specific information (or how to schedule training for such information with the appropriate supervisor or coworker)
- dress code (e.g., casual dress Fridays)
- extracurricular activities (e.g., sports teams, special events)

SOURCES: Adapted from Hacker, C. A. (2004). New employee orientation: Make it pay dividends for years to come. *Information Systems Management, 21*(4), Winter, 89–92; Robbins, R. L. (2002). Orientation: Necessity or nightmare? *Supervision, 63*(10), October, 8–9; Hicks, S. (2000). Successful orientation programs. *Training & Development*, April, 59–60; Lindo, D. K. (1999) New employee orientation is your job! *Supervision, 60*(8), 6–9; Belaiche, M. (1999). A well planned orientation makes a difference. *Canadian Manager*, Spring, 23–24; Tyler, K. (1998). Take employee orientation off the back burner. *HR Magazine*, May, 54.

helpful (out of ten sources) in their socialization.[87] Furthermore, these interactions were correlated with newcomer attitudes (job satisfaction, organizational commitment, and intention to stay). By contrast, formal orientation programs (listed separately in the study) were considered only moderately helpful and correlated only with organizational commitment. The research that was cited earlier on

**TABLE 8-4**

## A TIMETABLE OF EVENTS FOR CORNING'S ORIENTATION PROGRAM

### Material Distribution

As soon as possible after a hiring decision is made, orientation material is distributed:

- The new person's supervisor gets a pamphlet titled *A Guide for Supervisors*.
- The new person gets an orientation plan.

### The Pre-Arrival Period

During this period the supervisor maintains contact with the new person, helps with housing problems, designs the job and makes a preliminary MBO (management by objectives) list after discussing this with the new person, gets the office ready, notifies the organization that this has been done, and sets the interview schedule.

### The First Day

On this important day, new employees have breakfast with their supervisors, go through processing in the personnel department, attend a **Corning and You** seminar, have lunch with the seminar leader, read the workbook for new employees, are given a tour of the building, and are introduced to coworkers.

### The First Week

During this week, the new employee (1) has one-to-one interviews with the supervisor, coworkers, and specialists; (2) learns the "how-tos, wheres, and whys" connected with the job; (3) answers questions in the workbook; (4) gets settled in the community; and (5) participates with the supervisor in firming up the MBO plan.

### The Second Week

The new person begins regular assignments.

### The Third and Fourth Weeks

The new person attends a community seminar and an employee benefits seminar (a spouse or guest may be invited).

### The Second Through the Fifth Month

During this period, assignments are intensified and new people have biweekly progress reviews with their supervisors, attend six 2-hour seminars at intervals (on quality and productivity, technology, performance management and salaried compensation plans, financial and strategic management, employee relations and EEO, and social change), answer workbook questions about each seminar, and review answers with their supervisors.

### The Sixth Month

The new employee completes the workbook questions, reviews the MBO list with the supervisor, participates in a performance review with the supervisor, receives a certification of completion for Phase I orientation, and makes plans for Phase II orientation.

### The Seventh Through the Fifteenth Month

This period features Phase II orientation: division orientation, function orientation, education programs, MBO reviews, performance reviews, and salary reviews.

SOURCE: PERSONNEL ADMINISTRATOR by E. J. McGarrell, Jr. Copyright 2005 by SOC FOR HUMAN RESOURCE MGMT. Reproduced with permission of SOC FOR HUMAN RESOURCE MGMT in the format Textbook via Copyright Clearance Center. Reprinted with permission of *Personnel Administrator* published by the Society for Human Resource Management, Alexandria, VA.

newcomers as proactive information seekers reinforces the idea that new employees value information from supervisors and coworkers.[88] Thus, these findings suggest that the newcomers' orientation experience should include frequent contact with their supervisors, coworkers, and the HRD staff.

*THE SUPERVISOR.* The supervisor plays a pivotal role in the orientation process, serving as both an information source and a guide for the new employee. The supervisor can help the newcomer overcome feelings of anxiety by providing factual information and clear and realistic performance expectations and by emphasizing the employee's likelihood of succeeding in the organization. For example, an orientation program was designed to reduce anxiety by communicating four key points ("Your opportunity to succeed here is very good"; "Disregard 'hall talk'"; "Take the initiative in communication"; and "Get to know your supervisor"). This program was found to significantly reduce turnover, training time, absenteeism, waste and rejects, and cost.[89]

In addition, the supervisor can assist new employees by encouraging their acceptance by coworkers. In some organizations, the supervisor judiciously assigns the new employee a "buddy," who is responsible for helping the new employee adjust to the job environment. Mentorship programs, which pair junior members of the organization with experienced senior members, can also be used for this purpose (see Chapter 12). Also supervisors (and coworkers) can assist newcomers in developing their roles in the organization. Major et al. reported that doing so reduces the negative effects of unmet expectations.[90]

Other important supervisor orientation functions include:

1. providing (or arranging for) training in job specifics
2. buffering the newcomer from demands outside the work group for a period of time to facilitate job learning
3. providing challenging initial assignments
4. conducting timely, constructive performance evaluations
5. diagnosing problems at work that create conflicts
6. using the newcomer's arrival as an opportunity to reallocate tasks or redesign work to improve effectiveness and employee satisfaction with the work system[91]

It is essential that supervisors receive training to help them fulfill their orientation responsibilities effectively. At Corning, for instance, supervisors receive a written guide and a copy of the new employee workbook and attend a three-hour workshop in which they learn about the orientation system, the logic behind it, their role, and how to perform their role effectively.[92] Similarly, it is recommended that supervisors be given a standardized first-day curriculum, informing them of the issues that should be discussed with new employees on their first day at work.[93] Others go beyond this to make recommendations for the first week and beyond.[94] For example, George Cadwell says, "Orientation is a two-week process and maybe a six-month process, depending on the organization and the job."[95] In addition to training the supervisors concerning orientation, it is also desirable to plan the interactions between supervisors and newcomers that should occur throughout the socialization process.[96]

*COWORKERS.* Organizational newcomers view interactions with coworkers as particularly helpful in their socialization to the organization, by providing support, information, and training.[97] In addition, coworkers are in a particularly good position to help newcomers learn the norms of the work group and organization. Coworkers can also relieve newcomers' anxiety by discouraging **hazing** activities, in which new employees are targets of practical jokes or are harassed because they lack certain information. One example of hazing involves sending the new employee on an errand to get something everyone but the new employee knows doesn't exist. Although some people feel incidents of hazing are part of the socialization ritual and can lead to bonding ("welcome to the club, we've all been through it"), more often the result is increased anxiety and antagonism, which can prolong the socialization period. Using coworkers as a support system for new employees may reduce the amount of hazing that occurs.

As we mentioned, one way that organizations can facilitate interaction between newcomers and their coworkers is to establish a buddy system in which newcomers are paired with experienced coworkers.[98] Coworkers designated as buddies should be given materials and training that can help them fulfill their roles.[99]

*THE HRD STAFF.* The primary role of the HRD staff in new employee orientation is to design and oversee the orientation program. Specifically, this may include producing or obtaining materials (such as workbooks and seminar leader guides), conducting training sessions, designing and conducting the evaluation study, and in some cases conducting parts of the orientation program itself (focusing on such things as available services, employee rights, benefits, and workplace rules).

HRD staff members can also play an important role in encouraging all levels of management to become involved in the orientation program and support it. Establishing a steering committee and finding ways for key managers to stay involved in the process (e.g., meeting with newcomers, conducting orientation sessions) are two ways this can be accomplished. Furthermore, HRD staff members should take steps (such as interviewing and surveying newcomers and supervisors) to ensure that the orientation program is being carried out as planned and that the program is current and effective.

*THE NEWCOMER.* The newcomer should be encouraged to play the lead role in the orientation process by being an active learner. Research on adult learning (recall our discussion in Chapter 3) suggests that adults should be comfortable in this role, in that they typically seek out information that is relevant to their situation and to the goals they are trying to achieve. In research on the effectiveness of orientation programs at Corning and Texas Instruments, newcomers were put in the position of guiding the learning process. At Corning, the entire orientation system was based on the principle of guided self-learning, with HRD staff members, supervisors and managers, coworkers, and resource materials playing supporting roles.[100] At Texas Instruments, newcomers were encouraged to take the initiative in communication and in getting to know their supervisor.[101] Both studies demonstrated the effectiveness of this approach. These findings mesh with research showing how newcomers actively seek out information during socialization.

Newcomers should be explicitly encouraged to seek out both information and relationships they feel will help them in adjusting to the organization. Similarly, organizations should attempt to establish a climate in which this kind of behavior by newcomers is welcomed and reinforced.[102] For example, France and Jarvis describe an orientation program that uses a variety of techniques and exercises to place newcomers in an active role throughout the program, encouraging participants to build collaborative skills and reinforcing the importance of proactivity and diversity in the organization.[103]

## PROBLEMS WITH ORIENTATION PROGRAMS

Many problems or criticism of orientation programs have been identified:

- too much emphasis on paperwork
- information overload (giving newcomers too much information too quickly)
- information irrelevance (general or superficial information that is not directly relevant to the newcomer's job assignment)
- scare tactics (heavy emphasis on failure rates or the negative aspects of the job)
- too much selling of the organization
- emphasis on formal, one-way communication (using lectures and videos without giving newcomers a chance to discuss issues of interest or ask questions)
- one-shot mentality (e.g., limiting the orientation program to only the first day at work)
- no diagnosis or evaluation of the program
- lack of follow-up[104]

**Information overload** is a particularly common problem, as many orientation programs cram a large amount of information into a short period. This is done for convenience and practicality purposes. However, a person can absorb only so much information in a given time period before learning efficiency drops and stress increases (remember the maxim: "The mind can only absorb what the seat can endure!"). Program designers and deliverers should be sensitive to this issue and try to prevent information overload by:

1. including only essential information during the initial phase of orientation

2. providing written materials that trainees can take with them and review later (or look up online), especially for complex benefits plans and important topics such as the company mission and work rules

3. conducting the program in phases to space out presentation of the material (e.g., Southwest Airlines holds its orientation program once a week, rather than for one week straight)[105]

4. following up with the newcomers to make sure they understand major issues and to answer any additional questions they may have

Needs assessment activities (discussed in Chapter 4) are one way that program designers can determine what information newcomers want and need. It can then be determined when in the process it would be beneficial to provide it. For example, National Semiconductor used benchmarking to identify best practices in other leading companies (e.g., Walt Disney, Corning) to determine the content and structure of its orientation programs.[106] The University of Minnesota's Facilities Management Department conducted focus groups with randomly selected new employees to identify what information they wanted to know.[107] Needs assessment information like this can make sure that newcomers get what they want when they need it, reducing the chances overload will occur.

## DESIGNING AND IMPLEMENTING AN EMPLOYEE ORIENTATION PROGRAM

The orientation problems we have cited can be avoided by paying attention to the basic principles that should guide any HRD intervention: needs assessment, design, implementation, and evaluation. Many issues must be considered when designing an orientation program.[108] Corning provides a good model for developing an orientation program.[109] Corning followed ten steps in designing its program:

1. Set objectives. Corning's objectives included:
   a. Reduce turnover in the first three years of employment by 17 percent.
   b. Reduce time to learn the job by 17 percent.
   c. Provide newcomers with a uniform understanding of the company.
   d. Build a positive attitude toward the company and communities.

2. Form a steering committee.

3. Research orientation as a concept.

4. Interview recently hired employees, supervisors, and corporate officers.

5. Survey the orientation practices of top companies (the program at Texas Instruments proved particularly helpful).

6. Survey existing company orientation programs and materials.

7. Select content and delivery method.

8. Pilot and revise materials.

9. Produce and package print and audiovisual materials.

10. Train supervisors and install the system.

The timetable of orientation events shown in Table 8-4 is a result of the program Corning devised. Note that this orientation program begins even before the new employee's first day at work. Before then, the recruit receives material about the community, the job, and the work environment. The program is then continued for fifteen months, through seminars, meetings, goal setting, and performance reviews. An evaluation study revealed that this program met or exceeded all of its objectives, including reducing voluntary turnover by 69 percent.

## EVALUATION OF ORIENTATION PROGRAM EFFECTIVENESS

There is relatively little published research on the effectiveness of orientation programs overall, nor has the relative effectiveness of various approaches been adequately assessed. A recent note in *Training* magazine reported anecdotal evidence of reduced turnover at several organizations after new orientation programs were implemented.[110] A study by Arthur Andersen found that a majority of companies used either a limited system — or no formal system — to evaluate the effectiveness of their orientation programs. Yet, as Andersen partner Gary Moran states, "If you can't measure program impact, you can't control its effectiveness."[111] Unfortunately, much of the orientation literature contains suggestions for how programs can or should be conducted without the necessary data to support these suggestions.

Despite this lack of research, some guidelines can be helpful to those planning employee orientation. Aspects of effective orientation programs are listed in Table 8-5.[112] For an example of a well-done evaluation of an organization's orientation program, see the boxed insert nearby, "News Flash: An Orientation Program is Evaluated, and a Research Article About It Gets Published."[113] For a longitudinal study of organizational entry, see Kammeyer-Mueller and Wanberg.[114]

Given that orientation programs are generally aimed only at new employees, they can frequently be invisible to longer-term employees. It has been suggested that organizations use their company newsletters to feature new or interesting content that is being presented in orientation. For example, Steelcase runs a front-page feature entitled, "Getting to know you: Employees get acquainted with Steelcase." This column serves as a refresher for new hires, but also serves as a training tool for "the most grizzled company veterans."[115] The Hudson Highland Group uses its online orientation program to provide information not just to new hires, but also to existing employees about changes and developments in their organization.[116]

In closing, it should be clear that newcomers face a significant challenge when joining an organization, and it benefits both the individual and the organization to facilitate the socialization process. While we have focused our discussion on realistic job previews and employee orientation, socialization continues throughout an employee's career. HRD practitioners should not ignore other training and career development activities that facilitate this ongoing socialization process. New employees need support throughout their early tenure with the organization in the form of meaningful and timely performance reviews and challenging assignments, and all employees can benefit from coaching and training, counseling to cope with stress and personal problems, and assistance in developing their careers. We explore these topics in later chapters of the text.

**TABLE 8-5**  **DESIGN ELEMENTS COMMON TO EFFECTIVE ORIENTATION PROGRAMS**

1. Well-run orientation programs are run on a "need to know" principle. Employees are given the information they need as they need it, and are subjected to neither cram courses nor superficial treatments of topics. The most relevant and immediate kinds of information are given first.

2. Effective orientation programs take place over a period of days and weeks. While the intensity of the orientation program is greatest on the first day, all the objectives of the orientation program cannot be met in that time frame. Good orientation programs begin even before new recruits arrive, and continue well after the first day.

3. The content of orientation programs should present a healthy balance of technical information about the job with the social aspects.

4. Orientation programs are generally more effective if they allow a lot of two-way interaction between managers and new employees. Successful socialization depends very heavily on the establishment of helpful, trusting superior-subordinate relationships.

5. The first day has a major impact on new employees: they remember those first impressions for years. Therefore, the running of that initial orientation program should be carefully planned and implemented by individuals with good social skills. Filling out paperwork should be kept to the bare minimum that day.

6. Well-run orientation programs assign the responsibility for new recruits' adjustment to their immediate supervisors. While human resource professionals and other staff can serve as important resources to new recruits, one steady source of guidance and support is critical. Moreover, the immediate supervisor is in the best position to see potential problems the recruit is facing and to help him or her solve those issues.

7. Orientation programs can facilitate new recruits' adjustment by helping them get settled in the community and in new housing. When the logistics of living are up in the air, it is difficult for new hires to fully concentrate on their work assignments. For this reason, many organizations provide assistance to new recruits in house hunting and include spouses or partners in several orientation activities.

8. New employees should be gradually introduced to the people with whom they will work rather than given a superficial introduction to all of them on the first day. Get the new employee involved in relevant team meetings as soon as possible.

9. New employees should be allowed sufficient time to get their feet on the ground before demands on them are increased.

10. Well-run orientation programs are relaxing. Their focus is on celebration. They decrease anxiety, not increase it. They seek to create positive attitudes toward the company by helpful and supportive behavior on the part of colleagues, not through high-toned speeches.

11. Finally, organizations should systematically diagnose the needs of new recruits and evaluate the effectiveness of their orientation programs. New topics and issues can be added to orientation programs when needed, and peripheral parts of the orientation program can be pruned.

SOURCE: Adapted from Feldman, D. C. (1988). *Managing careers in organizations* (p. 90). Glenview, IL: Scott, Foresman; Hacker, C. A. (2004). New employee orientation: Make it pay dividends for years to come. *Information Systems Management, 21*(4), Winter, 89–92. Reprinted with permission.

## News Flash: An Orientation Program is Evaluated, and a Research Article About it Gets Published[1]

As we have noted, academic research on orientation programs has not been extensive. A recent exception to this general state of affairs is a study by Howard Klein and Natasha Weaver. They studied the orientation program used for staff at The Ohio State University (faculty and students were not included in this program). As we noted in Chapter 7, it is preferable when subjects can be randomly assigned to "training" and "control" groups in a research project. This is often not feasible in "real" training efforts such as the orientation program used at this university. What Klein and Weaver did was to compare outcomes for fifty-five new hires who went through a voluntary orientation program to the outcomes reported by sixty-one new hires who did not attend orientation (in the Appendix to Chapter 7, this was referred to as a "quasiexperimental" research design). The researchers sought to rule out as many competing explanations for why the two groups might differ in terms of the outcome variables they measured, that is, job classification, race, gender, or education level.

The degree of socialization was measured using six scales developed by Georgia Chao and colleagues (these were mentioned earlier in the chapter).[2] Importantly, these measures were taken for both groups both before and after the "training" group went through orientation (this is a pretest-posttest, with control research design). The researchers predicted that orientation would impact the posttest measures for three of the six scales, namely the goals/values, history, and the language used in the organization. Statistically significant differences were found between those who attended orientation and those who did not on two of the three hypothesized measures: goals/values and history. Additionally, those going through orientation also reported higher scores on the "people" scale. These results also fully explained the difference between the two groups in terms of their affective commitment to the university. Those who had gone through the orientation felt more of an emotional commitment to the university, and this could be attributed to the changes that occurred in their socialization scores over time.

While there were some limitations of this study (which the authors duly note), it remains a noteworthy example of efforts to link the research on socialization with a practical orientation program. We hope the coming years will produce further efforts to blend research and practice, especially to improve orientation programs and how they are evaluated.

[1]Klein, H. J., & Weaver, N. A. (2000). The effectiveness of an organizational-level orientation training program in the socialization of new hires. *Personnel Psychology, 53*, 47–66.

[2]Chao, O'Leary-Kelly, Wolf, Klein, & Gardner (1994), *supra* note 24.

### RETURN TO OPENING CASE

For many years, Sematech used a traditional form of orientation training, in that trainees received an "information dump." According to Phil Pierce, director of total quality at Sematech, "We used the fire hose approach: We'd turn on a fire hose of information and say, 'Here! Take a drink.'" Because of widespread dissatisfaction with this approach, major changes were made. Your instructor has additional information available concerning what was done in this case.

D. R. France, & R. L. Jarvis (1996). Quick starts for new employees. *Training & Development, 50*(10), 47–50.

## SUMMARY

New employees face a considerable challenge when joining an organization. They must learn the skills and behaviors necessary to perform their jobs effectively, while at the same time learning the norms and expectations of the organization and work group. Research on organizational socialization describes how outsiders to the organization are transformed into accepted and productive insiders. The success of socialization has a significant effect on outcomes that are important to both the new employee and the organization, including job satisfaction, job performance, and turnover.

Models of the socialization process often describe it in stages, for example: (1) anticipatory socialization, in which individuals form impressions and expectations about an organization before joining it; (2) encounter, the period after the individual joins the organization and discovers what life in the organization is really like; and (3) change and acquisition, which, if successfully completed, results in changes that permit the newcomer to perform effectively, be satisfied, and gain the acceptance of organization members.

Organizations use a variety of socialization tactics to integrate newcomers into the organization, and evidence suggests that the tactics used will influence the attitudes and behaviors of new employees. Yet, newcomers do not just passively react to organizational attempts to socialize them. More recent research has demonstrated that newcomers are proactive information seekers, using different strategies and different information sources to learn about various aspects of the organization and the roles they are expected to play.

Two ways to assist employees in making the transition to productive and accepted insiders are realistic job previews and employee orientation programs. RJPs involve providing recruits with a balanced view of job expectations and life within an organization, including both positive and negative attributes. This method facilitates socialization by adjusting any unrealistic expectations employees might have, thus offering them the opportunity to join the organization (or decline to join) with a clear idea of what to expect. Orientation programs are used to introduce new employees to the organization, their work group, and their job. Orientation programs facilitate socialization by providing employees with information, skills, and relationships that help them adjust their expectations, understand group norms, and learn their new jobs.

## KEY TERMS AND CONCEPTS

| | |
|---|---|
| anticipatory socialization | people processing strategies |
| change and acquisition | realistic job preview (RJP) |
| employee orientation | role |
| encounter | role ambiguity |
| expectation | role conflict |
| hazing | role orientation |
| information overload | role overload |
| norms | self-selection |
| organizational socialization | |

## QUESTIONS FOR DISCUSSION

1. What are the differences between organizational roles and group norms? How are they similar?

2. Why are role ambiguity, role conflict, and role overload detrimental to the success of individuals and the organization?

3. Using Feldman's three-stage model of organizational socialization, how would you describe the way you were socialized into an organization where you have worked? How well does the model fit your experience?

4. If newcomers actively seek out information, what impact should this have on the socialization process and socialization outcomes? Make at least one recommendation for how an organization can use this fact to increase the effectiveness of an orientation program.

5. What three things do organizational insiders have to help them interpret organizational events that newcomers lack? How can organizations help newcomers gain these things?

6. Why might some managers resist using a realistic job preview (RJP)? What evidence could you offer to convince such managers to use one?

7. What are the benefits of using multiple forms of media (such as recruiting ads, booklets, multimedia, and discussions with potential coworkers) in an RJP program?

8. Which two aspects of an orientation program do you think are the most important in socializing new employees? Support your choices.

9. Identify and describe three potential problems common to orientation programs. How can each of these problems be overcome?

10. What is the supervisor's role in employee orientation? What could be done to convince or encourage a skeptical supervisor to fulfill this role in orientation?

11. Define hazing and describe how it can be prevented. In your opinion, should hazing ever play a role in socialization? Defend your answer.

## EXERCISE: DESIGNING A TECHNOLOGY-ENHANCED ORIENTATION PROGRAM

Imagine yourself as the only HRD professional working at the corporate offices of a 500-person global staffing firm. Your headquarters are in the United States, but you have employees working in many different locations (and even in different countries). Bringing people together in one location for new employee orientation isn't practical, so you are considering setting up an online orientation program. What specific orientation *content* would you include in such a program? What training *media* would you want to use (see Chapters 5 and 6 to review)? What specific *computer/technology* issues must be addressed to make this program work? Your instructor has additional information on this scenario.

*Visit http://werner.swlearning.com/ for links to informative websites for this chapter.*

## REFERENCES

1. Louis, M. R. (1980). Surprise and sensemaking: What newcomers experience in entering unfamiliar organizational settings. *Administrative Science Quarterly, 25,* 226–251.

2. Sims, D. M. (2002). *Creative new employee orientation programs.* New York: McGraw-Hill; H. J. (2002). Beyond the binder: Orientation highlights. *Training, 39*(8), August, 36–37.

3. Van Maanen, J., & Schein, E. H. (1979). Toward a theory of organizational socialization. In B. Staw (Ed.), *Research in organizational behavior* (pp. 209–264). Greenwich, CT: JAI Press, p. 211.

4. Vecchio, R. P. (1991). *Organizational behavior* (2nd ed.). Hinsdale, IL: The Dryden Press.

5. Schein, E. H. (1971a). The individual, the organization, and the career: A conceptual scheme. *Journal of Applied Behavioral Science, 7,* 401–426.

6. Van Maanen & Schein (1979), *supra* note 3.

7. Jackson, S. E., & Schuler, R. S. (1985). A meta-analysis and conceptual critique of research on role ambiguity and role conflict in work settings. *Organizational Behavior and Human Decision Processes, 36,* 16–78.

8. Sullivan, S. E., & Bhagat, R. S. (1992). Organizational stress, job satisfaction, and job performance: Where do we go from here? *Journal of Management, 18,* 353–374.

9. Van Maanen & Schein (1979), *supra* note 3.

10. Jones, G. R. (1986). Socialization tactics, self-efficacy, and newcomers' adjustments to organizations. *Academy of Management Journal, 29,* 262–279.

11. Van Maanen & Schein (1979), *supra* note 3.

12. Jones (1986), *supra* note 10; Allen, N. J., & Meyer, J. P. (1990). Organizational socialization tactics: A longitudinal analysis of links to newcomers' commitment and role orientation. *Academy of Management Journal, 33,* 847–858.

13. Shaw, M. (1981). *Group dynamics* (3rd ed.). New York: McGraw-Hill.

14. Schein, E. H. (1971b). Occupational socialization in the professions: The case of the role innovator. *Journal of Psychiatric Research, 8,* 521–530.

15. Feldman, D. C. (1984). The development and enforcement of norms. *Academy of Management Review, 9,* 47–53.

16. Porter, L. W., & Steers, R. M. (1973). Organizational, work, and personal factors in employee turnover and absenteeism. *Psychological Bulletin, 80,* 151-176; Wanous, J. P. (1980). *Organizational entry.* Reading, MA: Addison-Wesley; Wanous, J. P., Poland, T. D., Premack, S. L., & Davis, K. S. (1992). The effects of met expectations on newcomer attitudes and behaviors: A review and meta-analysis. *Journal of Applied Psychology, 77,* 288–297.

17. Wanous, J. P. (1976). Organizational entry: From naive expectations to realistic beliefs. *Journal of Applied Psychology, 61,* 22–29; Wanous (1980), *supra* note 16.

18. Wanous (1976), *supra* note 17.

19. Porter & Steers (1973), *supra* note 16, p. 152.

20. Irving, P. G., & Meyer, J. P. (1994). Reexamination of the met-expectations hypothesis: A longitudinal analysis. *Journal of Applied Psychology, 79,* 937–949.

21. Louis (1980), *supra* note 1.

22. Fisher, C. D. (1986). Organizational socialization: An integrative review. In K. Rowland and G. Ferris (Eds.), *Research in personnel and human resources management* (Vol. 4, pp. 101–145). Greenwich, CT: JAI Press.

23. Feldman, D. C. (1981). The multiple socialization of organization members. *Academy of Management Review, 6,* 309–318.

24. Chao, G. T., O'Leary-Kelly, A. M., Wolf, S., Klein, H. J., & Gardner, P. D. (1994). Organizational socialization: Its content and consequences. *Journal of Applied Psychology, 79,* 730–743.

25. Haueter, J. A., Macan, T. H., & Winter, J. (2003). Measurement of newcomer socialization: Construct validation of a multidimensional scale. *Journal of Vocational Behavior, 63*(1), 20–39.

26. Fisher (1986), *supra* note 22.

27. Kammeyer-Mueller, J. D., & Wanberg, C. R. (2003). Unwrapping the organizational entry process: Disentangling multiple antecedents and their pathways to adjustment. *Journal of Applied Psychology, 88*(5), 779–794; Feldman, D. C. (1989). Socialization, resocialization, and training: Reframing the research agenda. In I. L. Goldstein and Associates (Eds.), *Training and development in organizations* (pp. 376–416). San Francisco: Jossey-Bass; Fisher (1986), *supra* note 22.

28. Ashford, B. E., & Saks, A. M. (1996). Socialization tactics: Longitudinal effects on newcomer adjustment. *Academy of Management Journal, 39,* 149–178; Bauer, T. N, & Green, S. G. (1994). Effect of newcomer involvement in work-related activities: A longitudinal study of socialization. *Journal of Applied Psychology, 79,* 211–223; Morrison, E. W. (1993). Longitudinal study of the effects of information seeking on newcomer socialization. *Journal of Applied Psychology, 78,* 173–183.

29. Chao et al. (1994), *supra* note 24.

30. Major, D. A., Kozlowski, S. W. J., Chao, G. T., & Gardner, P. D. (1995). A longitudinal investigation of newcomer expectations, early socialization outcomes, and the moderating effects of role development factors. *Journal of Applied Psychology, 80,* 418–431; Ostroff, C., & Kozlowski, S. W. J. (1992). Organizational socialization as a learning process: The role of information acquisition. *Personnel Psychology, 45,* 849–874.

31. Feldman, D. C. (1976). A contingency theory of socialization. *Administrative Science Quarterly, 21,* 433–452; Feldman, D. C. (1976). A practical program for employee socialization. *Organizational Dynamics, 5*(2), 64–80; Feldman (1981), *supra* note 23; Schein, E. H. (1978). *Career dynamics: Matching individual and organizational needs.* Reading, MA: Addison-Wesley; Van Maanen, J. (1978). People processing: Strategies of organizational socialization. *Organizational Dynamics, 7*(1), 18–36.

32. Buchanan, B. (1974). Building organizational commitment: The socialization of managers in work organizations. *Administrative Science Quarterly, 19,* 533–546; Feldman (1976), *supra* note 31; Feldman (1981), *supra* note 23; Porter, L. W., Lawler, E. E. III, & Hackman, J. R. (1975). *Behavior in organizations.* New York: McGraw-Hill; Schein (1978), *supra* note 31; Wanous (1980), *supra* note 16.

33. Feldman (1981), *supra* note 23.

34. Feldman (1989), *supra* note 27; Schein (1978), *supra* note 31; Wanous, J. P. (1992). *Organizational entry: Recruitment, selection, orientation, and socialization of newcomers* (2nd ed.). Reading, MA: Addison-Wesley; Wanous, J. P., Reichers, A. E., & Malik, S. D. (1984). Organizational socialization and group development: Toward an integrative perspective. *Academy of Management Review, 9,* 670–683.

35. Wanous (1992), *supra* note 34.

36. Louis (1980), *supra* note 1.

37. Van Maanen (1978), *supra* note 31; Van Maanen & Schein (1979), *supra* note 3.

38. Van Maanen (1978), *supra* note 31.

39. Van Maanen & Schein (1979), *supra* note 3.

40. Jones (1986), *supra* note 10.

41. Allen & Meyer (1990), *supra* note 12.

42. Ashford & Saks (1996), *supra* note 28.

43. Morrison (1993), *supra* note 28; Ostroff & Kozlowski (1992), *supra* note 30.

44. Ashford, S. J., & Black, J. S. (1996). Proactivity during organizational entry: The role of desire for control. *Journal of Applied Psychology, 81,* 199–214; Morrison (1993), *supra* note 28; Ostroff & Kozlowski (1992), *supra* note 30.

45. Morrison (1993), *supra* note 28; Ostroff & Kozlowski (1992), *supra* note 30.

46. *Ibid.*

47. Garavan, T. N., Morley, M., Gunnigle, P., & McGuire, D. (2002). Human resource development and workplace learning: Emerging theoretical perspectives and organizational practices. *Journal of European Industrial Training, 26*(2–4), 60–71; Elsey, B., & Leung, S.-K. (2004). The role of the international manager in facilitating organizational change through workplace learning with Chinese employees. *Journal of General Management, 29*(3), 53–75.

48. Reio, T. G., Jr., & Wiswell, A. (2000). Field investigation of the relationship among adult curiosity, workplace learning, and job performance. *Human Resource Development Quarterly, 11*(1), 5–30; Ardts, J., Jansen, P., & van der Velde, M. (2001). The breaking in of new employees: Effectiveness of socialization tactics and personnel instruments. *Journal of Management Development, 20*(2), 159–167; Thomas, H. C., & Anderson, N. (2003). How to design induction programmes. *People Management, 9*(9), May 1, 42–43.

49. Louis (1980), *supra* note 1.

50. *Ibid.*

51. Schneider, B., & Schmitt, N. W. (1986). *Staffing organizations* (2nd ed.). Glenview, IL: Scott, Foresman.

52. Wanous (1980), *supra* note 16.

53. Wanous, J. P. (1978). Realistic job previews: Can a procedure to reduce turnover also influence the relationship between abilities and performance? *Personnel Psychology, 31,* 249–258; Wanous (1992), *supra* note 34.

54. Wanous (1992), *supra* note 34.

55. *Ibid.*

56. *Ibid*; Breaugh, J. A. (1983). Realistic job previews: A critical appraisal and future research directions. *Academy of Management Review, 8,* 612–619; Breaugh, J. A. (1992). *Recruitment: Science and practice.* Boston: PWS Kent.

57. Wanous (1992), *supra* note 34.

58. Breaugh (1992), *supra* note 56.

59. Colarelli, S. M. (1984). Methods of communication and mediating processes in realistic job previews. *Journal of Applied Psychology, 69,* 633–642.

60. Corning (2004). Retrieved October 6, 2004, from http://www.corning.com/careers/living_in_corning/welcome.asp

61. Wanous, J. P. (1989). Installing a realistic job preview: Ten tough choices. *Personnel Psychology, 42,* 117–134.

62. Wanous (1992), *supra* note 34.

63. Wanous (1989), *supra* note 61.

64. Breaugh (1992), *supra* note 56.

65. McEvoy, G. M., & Cascio, W. F. (1985). Strategies for reducing employee turnover: A meta-analysis. *Journal of Applied Psychology, 70,* 342–353; Premack, S. L., & Wanous, J. P. (1985). A meta-analysis of realistic job preview experiments. *Journal of Applied Psychology, 70,* 706–719; Reilly, R. R., Brown, B., Blood, M. R., & Malatesta, C. Z. (1981). The effect of realistic previews: A study and discussion of the literature. *Personnel Psychology, 34,* 823–834; Wanous, J. P. (1977). Organizational entry: Newcomers moving from outside to inside. *Psychological Bulletin, 84,* 601-618; Wanous (1980), *supra* note 16; Wanous (1992), *supra* note 34; Wanous, J. P., & Colella, A. (1989). Organizational entry research: Current status and future directions. In K. Rowland & G. Ferris (Eds.), *Research in personnel and human resources management* (Vol. 7, pp. 59–120). Greenwich, CT: JAI Press.

66. Premack & Wanous (1985), *supra* note 65; Wanous (1992), *supra* note 34.

67. Rynes, S. L. (1991). Recruitment, job choice, and post-hire consequences: A call for new research directions. In M. D. Dunnette & L. M. Hough (Eds.), *Handbook of industrial and organizational psychology* (2nd ed., Vol. 2, pp. 400–444). Palo Alto, CA: Consulting Psychologists Press.

68. Irving & Meyer (1994), *supra* note 20.

69. McGillicuddy, J. (1999). Making a good first impression. *Public Management,* January, 15–18.

70. Feldman, D. C. (1980). A socialization process that helps new recruits succeed. *Personnel, 57*(2), 11–23; Gomersall, E. R., & Myers, M. S. (1966). Breakthrough in on-the-job training. *Harvard Business Review, 44*(4), 62–72; Ivancevich, J. M., & Glueck, W. (1986). *Personnel/human resource management* (4th ed.). Plano, TX: Business Publications, Inc.

71. Grossman, M. E., & Magnus, M. (1989). The $5.3 billion tab for training. *Personnel Journal, 68*(7), 54–56; Tyler, K. (1998). Take new employee orientation off the back burner. *HR Magazine,* May, 49–57; *2003 State of the Industry Report* (2003). Alexandria, VA: ASTD.

72. e.g., Schettler, J. (2002). Wells Fargo: The first six months. *Training, 39*(8), 40.

73. Hays, S. (1999). Exceptional customer service takes the 'Ritz' touch. *Workforce, 78*(1), 99–102.

74. George, M. A., & Miller, K. D. (1996). Assimilating new employees. *Training & Development, 50*(6), 49–50.

75. Starcke, A. M. (1996). Building a better orientation program. *HR Magazine,* November, 107–114.

76. France, D. R., & Jarvis, R. L. (1996). Quick start for new employees. *Training & Development, 50*(10), 47–50.

77. McGillicuddy (1999), *supra* note 69.

78. West, K. L. (1996). Effective training for a revolving door. *Training & Development, 50*(9), 51–52.

79. *2003 State of the Industry Report* (2003). Alexandria, VA: ASTD.

80. St. John, W. D. (1980). The complete employee orientation program. *Personnel Journal, 59*(5), 373-378.

81. Brechlin, J., & Rossett, A. (1991). Orienting new employees. *Training, 28*(4), 45–51.

82. Tyler (1998), *supra* note 71; Ellis, K. (2004). Authoring tools. *Training, 41*(8), 20–25.

83. Schettler, J. (2002). Verizon Wireless: Joining the journey. *Training, 39*(8), 38–39.

84. Al-Lamki, S. M. (2002). Orientation: The essential ingredient in cross-cultural management. *International Journal of Management, 19*(4), 568–575.

85. McGarrell, E. J., Jr. (1984). An orientation system that builds productivity. *Personnel Administrator, 29*(10), 75–85.

86. Reichers, A. E. (1987). An interactionist perspective on newcomer socialization rates. *Academy of Management Review, 12*, 278–287.

87. Louis, M. R., Posner, B. Z., & Powell, G. N. (1983). The availability and helpfulness of socialization practices. *Personnel Psychology, 36*, 857–866.

88. Morrison (1993), *supra* note 28; Ostroff & Kozlowski (1992), *supra* note 30.

89. Gomersall & Myers (1966), *supra* note 70.

90. Major et al. (1995), *supra* note 30.

91. Feldman (1980), *supra* note 70.

92. McGarrell (1984), *supra* note 85.

93. Reinhardt, C. (1988). Training supervisors in first-day orientation techniques. *Personnel, 65*(6), 24–28.

94. Lindo, D. K. (1999) New employee orientation is your job! *Supervision, 60*(8), 6–9.

95. Tyler (1998), *supra* note 71, p. 52.

96. George & Miller (1996), *supra* note 74.

97. Louis et al. (1983), *supra* note 87.

98. Zarowin, S. (2004). Golden business ideas. *Journal of Accountancy, 198*(3), September, 108.

99. Federico, R. F. (1991). Six ways to solve the orientation blues. *HR Magazine, 36*(6), 69–70; Ostroff & Kozlowski (1992), *supra* note 30.

100. McGarrell (1984), *supra* note 85.

101. Gomersall & Myers (1966), *supra* note 70.

102. Ostroff & Kozlowski (1992), *supra* note 30.

103. France & Jarvis (1996), *supra* note 76.

104. Feldman, D. C. (1988). *Managing careers in organizations*. Glenview, IL: Scott, Foresman.

105. Tyler, (1998), *supra* note 71, p. 57.

106. Starcke (1996), *supra* note 75.

107. *Ibid.*

108. Sims (2002), *supra* note 2; Cohen, C. (2003). Make a good impression. *CA Magazine, 136*(5), June/July, 41–42; Saylor, T. (2003). Training: The single most significant event in the life of a franchise relationship. *Franchising World, 35*(4), May/June, 13–14; New employee orientation programs make cents (2004). *Commercial Law Bulletin, 19*(3), May/June, 6.

109. McGarrell (1984), *supra* note 85.

110. H. J. (2002). Orientation ROI. *Training, 39*(8), August, 38.

111. McShulskis, E. (1997). Monitor career development and orientation programs. *HR Magazine, 42*(11), 25.

112. Feldman (1988), *supra* note 104; Hacker, C. A. (2004). New employee orientation: Make it pay dividends for years to come. *Information Systems Management, 21*(4), Winter, 89–92.

113. Klein, H. J., & Weaver, N. A. (2000). The effectiveness of an organizational-level orientation training program in the socialization of new hires. *Personnel Psychology, 53,* 47–66.

114. Kammeyer-Mueller & Wanberg (2003), *supra* note 27.

115. Make sure all employees — even the veterans — learn from new-employee orientation. (2000). *Ragan's Strategic Employee Publications,* March, 5.

116. Ellis (2004), *supra* note 82.

**9**

# SKILLS AND TECHNICAL TRAINING

## Learning Objectives

*After reading this chapter, you should be able to:*

1. Identify and describe basic workplace competencies.

2. Explain the need for remedial basic skills training programs.

3. Explain the role of apprenticeship programs in today's work environment.

4. Describe a typical technical skills training program.

5. Describe a typical interpersonal skills training program.

6. Understand the professional development and education practices common in many organizations.

## OPENING CASE

In the 1980s, American consumers criticized the auto industry in the United States because it was not competing with the quality, cost, and customer satisfaction achieved by many Japanese auto manufacturers. Japanese manufacturers, led by Toyota, Nissan, and Honda, captured a large share of the U.S. small-car market. The message was clear — if U.S. auto manufacturers did not change the manner in which they produced and sold their products, they would continue to lose market share.

General Motors (GM), the largest U.S. auto manufacturer, sought to challenge the Japanese where they were the strongest — in the small-car market. GM managers felt that if they were going to compete successfully with the Japanese, they could not just make adjustments, but would have to do things entirely differently: create a new division from the ground up using a different management philosophy. Accordingly, in 1983, GM launched the Saturn Corporation, and in 1990, they produced their first vehicles from their plant in Spring Hill, Tennessee. A partnership was formed between General Motors and the United Auto Workers (UAW). This meant that production workers at Spring Hill were members of the UAW, but operated under a different contract than other UAW workers at GM. Saturn's philosophy embraced five core principles, that is, commitments to (1) customer satisfaction,

(2) excellence, (3) teamwork, (4) trust and respect for the individual, and (5) continuous improvement. Saturn management felt that the best means of communicating these principles would be comprehensive training programs at all levels and functions within Saturn.

Within the retail and wholesale operations, Saturn management wanted to emphasize the commitment to "customer enthusiasm and teamwork." In order to take a fresh approach, Saturn management looked outside the organization for a training partner, a vendor with commitment to these principles. They selected Maritz Communications Company. Saturn and Maritz committed approximately 130 training professionals (e.g., designers, writers, and automotive experts) to the task of designing their retail and wholesale operations training program. The Saturn/Maritz team was given the following challenge: "to take an ideal — a belief in a better way to sell cars — and change basic attitudes enough to make it a reality."

*Questions: If you were part of the Saturn training team, what issues would you emphasize in preparing and designing training for salespeople at Saturn dealerships? Would you recommend anything different for managers in both the manufacturing and retail arms of Saturn? How about for production workers at the Spring Hill plant?*

## INTRODUCTION

In this chapter, we will deal with the following types of questions:

- *Is there a literacy problem in the U.S. workplace, and if so, how severe is it?*
- *What types of training are available to individuals through the federal government?*

- *What kinds of apprenticeships are available today?*
- *What issues should trainers attend to when providing computer training?*
- *What makes for an effective training program concerning safety, quality, or team building?*
- *What role can labor unions play in skills and technical training?*
- *What forms of continuing education and professional development are available to employees after they have received their basic training?*

Organizations have become increasingly dependent on skilled technical and professional employees, and this trend is expected to continue. For example, the Bureau of Labor Statistics has projected the thirty fastest growing occupations between 2002 and 2012. Fourteen of those thirty jobs are in the medical/health fields; ten are technical/computer/safety positions, and six are service positions.[1] The increasing number of "technical" positions has resulted from such developments as technological advances, changing organizational goals, and organizational restructuring. These changes include the need for more cognitive skills (e.g., problem-solving and decision-making skills), as well as greater interpersonal skills (e.g., teamwork). Whether the changes result from plant modernization, computerization, or other innovations, they have helped create a shift away from jobs requiring low skill levels to jobs demanding higher skill levels.

In this chapter, we will discuss basic workplace competencies and then review some of the types of training programs used to improve these competencies. There are many ways that skills training programs can be categorized. For this chapter, we organize our discussion around three categories: basic skills/literacy education, technical training, and interpersonal skills training. **Basic skills/literacy education** refers to training that focuses on upgrading the reading, writing, and computation skills needed to function in most any job. **Technical training** refers to training that involves the process of upgrading a wide range of technical skills (such as computer skills) needed by particular individuals in an organization. **Interpersonal skills training** refers to training that focuses on an individual's relationships with others, including communication and teamwork. As you might imagine, training in all of these areas can be of critical importance to organizations. Table 9-1 lists the categories of skills training programs and the subcategories included within them. We will discuss programs used in each of these categories and subcategories.

## BASIC WORKPLACE COMPETENCIES

As mentioned in Chapter 1, a major problem facing employers today is the *skills gap* — the difference between the skill requirements of available jobs and the skills possessed by job applicants.[2] The skills gap is the result of at least three factors: (1) the skill level achieved by many high school and college graduates; (2) the growing number of racial minorities and non-English-speaking immigrants in the labor market (many of whom are concentrated in the worst-performing schools and school systems in the country); and (3) the increased sophistication of jobs due to increased reliance on information technology.[3] The skill levels of high school — and

| **TABLE 9-1** | CATEGORIES AND SUBCATEGORIES OF SKILLS AND TECHNICAL TRAINING |

| Training Category | Subcategories |
| --- | --- |
| Basic skills/Literacy | Remedial/basic education |
| Technical | Apprenticeship training |
| | Computer training |
| | Technical skills/knowledge training |
| | New methods/procedures |
| | Safety training |
| | Quality training |
| Interpersonal | Communications/interpersonal training |
| | Customer relations/services training |
| | Sales training |
| | Team building/training |

even some college — students, particularly at a time when organizations require increasingly skilled workers, has generated much criticism of public education systems in the United States.[4] A 2002 survey found that 73 percent of employers said that recent high school graduates lacked grammar and spelling skills, 63 percent of employers felt graduates lacked basic math skills, and 47 percent of employers said these students couldn't speak English properly; similar percentages were obtained when professors rated college freshman.[5] Many employers are finding that graduates with basic skill deficiencies must be given remedial training before they are job-ready. For example, this decline prompted the Los Angeles School District to issue a written warranty with each of its high school diplomas since 1994, stating that if an employer finds a graduate to be deficient in any basic skill, the school will provide remedial training at no cost to the employer.[6] This type of commitment reflects the urgency of the problem and demonstrates how some school administrators are trying to confront the issue.

The number of racial minorities in the labor market is predicted to be over one-third of the labor force by 2012.[7] This change in the demographics of the labor force is expected to be gradual. By 2012, Hispanics are predicted to increase to 14.7 percent of the labor force; African-Americans will make up about 12.2 percent; and Asians will be 5.5 percent, with 2 percent other (non-White/multiple racial categories).[8] Further, a sizable portion of these new workers will be immigrants who lack proficiency in English, and who also may lack basic skills. Thus, two kinds of training may be necessary to get them job-ready: basic skills and basic English-as-a-second-language training (ESL).[9] These deficiencies represent a major challenge to potential employers who must rely on these workers.

The increased sophistication of jobs, particularly as a result of the information technology explosion, has affected almost every industry. The trend toward increasingly powerful computer hardware and user-friendly computer software systems has led to a proliferation of high-technology applications, including robotics, decision-support systems, electronic mail systems, and communications networks. Continuous technical training will likely be necessary for those occupations that rely on information technology and are directly affected by the constant changes in hardware and software.

## BASIC SKILLS/LITERACY PROGRAMS

As discussed earlier, the basic competency skills include reading, writing, and computational skills. While the assessment of these skills is not always standardized, deficiencies in these skills are widely reported. In 1992, the U.S. Department of Education estimated that roughly 20 percent of adults living in the United States could be classified as functionally illiterate, that is, lacking sufficient literacy skills to meet daily needs in their workplaces and families.[10] Literacy experts have challenged this estimate as unduly harsh, and a follow-up survey will be released in 2005.[11] Nevertheless, it is clear that literacy issues pose major challenges for employers. If employees cannot read or compute at sufficient skill levels, it is extremely difficult to install new equipment that requires operators to read instructions and make decisions.[12]

Worldwide, the greatest number of illiterate adults can be found in developing nations, especially in rural areas. However, many industrialized nations also face challenges. For example, a 1995 report by the Organization for Economic Cooperation and Development estimated that 21 percent of U.S. adults had reading proficiency levels that were *below* primary school; this figure was worse than the estimates for most other countries surveyed.[13]

When creating a program to address basic skill deficiencies, employers should operationally define each basic skill. Kirsch and Jungeblut provide an example of how to operationally define literacy skills.[14] In their study of literacy among young adults (ages 21 through 25), literacy skills were defined according to three broad categories (p. 64):

1. *Prose literacy* — Skills and strategies needed to understand and use information from texts that are frequently found in the home and the community.

2. *Document literacy* — Skills and strategies required to locate and use information contained in nontextual materials that include tables, graphs, charts, indexes, forms, and schedules.

3. *Quantitative literacy* — Knowledge and skills needed to apply the arithmetical operations of addition, subtraction, multiplication, and division (either singly or sequentially) in combination with printed materials, as in balancing a checkbook or completing an order form.

The measurement of these skills was accomplished by devising a large number of simulated tasks that were then administered to a nationwide sample. A sizable number of young adults had low literacy scores, with an even greater number of young minority adults ranking below average. A recent book presents similar evidence.[15]

## ADDRESSING ILLITERACY IN THE WORKPLACE

Many organizations have recognized literacy issues among their workers. It is estimated that 61 percent of organizations conduct basic skills programs.[16] Companies like Motorola, Ford, Xerox, Polaroid, and Kodak have already instituted comprehensive basic skills programs.[17] The following are examples of some programs.

1. The California State Department of Education assisted nineteen area companies by developing a literacy program, involving 600 hours of development time, aimed at improving employee skills for reading work materials, entering required data, making numerical calculations, and using correct technical vocabulary in their speech.[18]

2. Chrysler Corporation (now DaimlerChrysler) invested $5 million in teaching basic skills to 3,000 to 4,000 workers in order to advance them to an eighth-grade level in reading, writing, and math.[19]

3. Federal government agencies have also recognized the literacy problem. For example, the Basic Skills Education Program (BSEP) was developed by the U.S. Army to deal with illiteracy issues among the troops.[20]

## DESIGNING AN IN-HOUSE BASIC SKILLS/LITERACY PROGRAM

The design of basic skills/literacy programs varies widely from organization to organization. There are at least two common characteristics: (1) an aptitude test and (2) small-group and one-on-one instruction. An *aptitude test* is important for assessing the current ability level of each trainee. For example, a basic skills program developed by the Palo Verde Nuclear Generating Station begins with an assessment of each trainee's learning ability before he or she is assigned to an intensive six-month study skills program.[21] These data are essential for developing an individualized lesson plan that allows the trainer to pinpoint learning objectives and to select the best training methods, techniques, and materials for each trainee.

*Small-group instruction* and *one-on-one tutoring* are important for supplying feedback to the trainee, as well as for conducting remedial work in any areas of deficiency. Zaslow suggests using supervisors as writing coaches by training them to give feedback to employees on such things as writing techniques.[22] To supplement small-group instruction, some organizations are using self-paced, computer-interactive programs that provide opportunities for employees to practice basic concepts. Many organizations now offer these programs in CD-ROM format or through their intranet. Self-pacing allows a trainee to practice at his or her own rate, without the pressures of a classroom, and to repeat or skip steps or sequences in the program as necessary. Perhaps this is obvious, but this approach is best used for trainees who are highly motivated to learn.

The methods used for in-house basic skills training programs also vary. Training manuals, tutorial disks, and videotapes/DVDs are the least costly methods to use because they do not require a classroom or an instructor, although these methods also have significant disadvantages.[23] However, when a trainer and classroom are used, the cost increases. The most costly programs are those that are customized, because they require considerable time and expertise to design.

As with most HRD interventions, support from management is an important ingredient of a successful basic skills training program. Yet, that support is not always easy to obtain. For example, an ASTD survey reported that the majority of HRD professionals believed "there is a problem and that many people in the organization are affected," while the majority of top management believed "there is a problem but that few people were affected."[24] This suggests that HRD professionals will likely need to inform and educate top management about the extent of the basic skills problem in their own organization if they expect to receive the necessary funding and support for their basic skills programs.

## FEDERAL SUPPORT FOR BASIC SKILLS TRAINING

The federal government has long recognized its role in supporting private training initiatives that are targeted toward the unemployed, displaced, and economically disadvantaged. From 1983 to 2000, the **Job Training and Partnership Act (JTPA)** was the largest federal skills training program. The JTPA replaced the Comprehensive Employment and Training Act (CETA). The goal of Title IIA of the JTPA was to provide training opportunities to the unemployed, displaced, and economically disadvantaged in order to help them obtain permanent jobs. Beginning July 1, 2000, the JTPA was replaced by the Workforce Investment Act (described more fully later in this section).

Under the JTPA, approximately $4 billion was available every year from the federal government. This money was funneled through 600 individual private industry councils (PIC) to private training institutes and employers in order to fund skills training.[25] Local government officials appoint the PICs, which are composed of representatives from business, education, community-based agencies, and others. The role of a PIC is to oversee the distribution of the funds and to ensure that state JTPA standards and guidelines are followed.

Most employer-based training programs involve basic skills and job-specific training. While most of the training is conducted on-site in a classroom, JTPA sponsored on-the-job training programs, as long as the employer agreed to hire the trainees once they complete their training. The success of JTPA programs was dependent, in part, on how well these programs were coordinated with the work of other social service agencies. For example, potential trainees could be identified and referred to a training agency by a community-based social agency that served the economically disadvantaged target population. This was the case when the Atlanta Marquis Hotel trained fifty-nine people; thirty-nine were referred by Goodwill Industries, a community-based nonprofit agency, and twenty were referred by the local PIC.[26]

In addition, the JTPA was tied to the **Worker Adjustment and Retraining Notification (WARN) Act.** The WARN Act requires employers with 100 or more employees to give sixty-days advance notice of a plant closure to both employees and unions. When plant closings or mass layoffs are imminent, JTPA funds were to be made available to set up "rapid response teams" that will work with unions and companies to administer retraining and worker-displacement programs.[27]

Despite successful JTPA programs, such as that of the Atlanta Marquis, two problems were identified. First, several private institutions and employers received funds fraudulently, that is, some employers used JTPA funds to hire workers whom they would recruit even under normal conditions.[28] Second, JTPA funds provided training for only a fraction of the eligible displaced and unemployed workers. This was due in part to the JTPA budget being decreased from $1.4 billion in 1983 to $0.9 billion in 1997. The funding of JPTA-type programs was also affected by the Personal Responsibility and Work Opportunity Reconciliation Act of 1996. A main goal of this act was to move people from welfare to work through a process known as workfare. The act mandates that welfare recipients work a minimum of twenty hours per week (the minimum was increased to thirty hours in 2002).

The JPTA was one of 150 federal education and training programs that together cost the taxpayers $25 billion a year. According to Judy and D'Amico, these programs were "notoriously ineffective . . . or at least extremely expensive, when their meager results are considered" (p. 133).[29] For example, a federal program attempted to retrain 4,500 laid-off garment workers in El Paso, Texas. While the program spent $25 million in almost two years, only 375 trainees were placed in jobs.[30] An empirical study of sixteen JTPA sites studied the impact of JTPA training on posttraining earnings. Eligible individuals were randomly assigned to either a training or a control condition, and JTPA training was found to have a positive, but modest (and statistically nonsignificant) impact on earnings ten months after training.[31] Beyond these concerns, the U.S. General Accounting Office (GAO) found that the narrow focus of the patchwork of federal education and training programs frustrates and confuses employers, program administrators, and those seeking assistance.[32] The GAO recommended that these programs be overhauled and consolidated to streamline services and make program administrators more accountable.

In response to this, the **Workforce Investment Act (WIA)** was passed in 1998. The goal of this act was to consolidate more than seventy federal education and training programs into block grants that are designed to give states more flexibility in meeting their constituents' education and training needs. The three major funding streams are for youth, adults, and displaced workers (that is, workers who have lost their jobs through layoffs, downsizing, etc.). The Act is designed to give greater control to local boards and the private sector, and to increase the accountability of all training providers for the outcomes of their efforts. While there is optimism about the potential for more positive use of federal training dollars, it is too early to determine what impact this new law is having on federally funded training efforts.[33] Clearly, though, federal funding for basic training will continue; it is imperative that these funds be used as effectively as possible to reach the populations targeted for assistance. It is hoped that the performance standards and performance management system built into the WIA will encourage greater accountability and successful outcomes for federally funded job training programs.

## TECHNICAL TRAINING

Technical training, as discussed earlier, is a generic term that can encompass a wide range of programs. For convenience, we will limit our discussion to five categories of technical training programs: apprenticeship training, computer training, technical skills/knowledge training, safety training, and quality training.

## APPRENTICESHIP TRAINING PROGRAMS

**Apprenticeship training** began during the Middle Ages as a way of passing on the knowledge of individuals working in skilled trades and crafts. The primary purpose of these early programs was preservation of the industrial and crafts guilds. Today, the focus of apprenticeship programs is to provide trainees with the skills needed to meet continually changing job requirements. With the challenges of the global economy and the scarcity of skilled employees, it is imperative that apprenticeship programs be more responsive to these needs.

Apprenticeship programs represent a unique partnership between employers, labor unions, schools, and government agencies. In 2003, there were over 850 different apprenticeship programs enrolling 488,297 registered apprentices.[34] Of this total, over half of all apprenticeships were in construction trades. A typical apprenticeship program requires a minimum of 2,000 hours of on-the-job training (OJT) experience.[35] In addition to the OJT experience, all programs require a minimum of 144 hours of classroom training. Classroom training may be given at a local vocational/technical school or community college. For example, the Community College of Rhode Island conducts the classroom portion of the Plastics Process Technician Apprenticeship Program for area employers. The four-year program is broken into 1,050 hours of classroom training and 8,000 hours of OJT training.[36] At the end of the program, the students receive not only certification as journeymen, but also an associate's degree in plastics process technology.

The U.S. apprenticeship system is regulated by the Office of Apprenticeship Training, Employer and Labor Services (OATELS) of the U.S. Department of Labor (DOL). OATELS was formerly called the Bureau of Apprenticeship and Training (BAT). There is an OATELS office in every state.[37] In addition, many states have apprenticeship councils that oversee apprenticeships in their state. A well-planned, properly administered apprenticeship program should lead to many positive outcomes for employers and employees. Table 9-2 lists some of these positive outcomes.

There are, however, some problems with the present apprenticeship system. For example, the National Center on Education and the Economy identified four major concerns: (1) learning is based on time requirements rather than competency, (2) programs are isolated from other education and training institutions, (3) programs are concentrated in traditional blue-collar occupations, and (4) the system has not adjusted to requirements for the period after the initial apprenticeship.[38] In addition, most apprenticeship programs begin after someone has completed high school, that is, they can be considered "adult" apprenticeships.

Some of these problems were addressed by an initiative called Apprenticeship 2000, started by the U.S. Department of Labor. Based on the successes of countries like Germany, one purpose of the program was to expand the apprenticeship concept and link it to secondary schools. For example, in 1991, the Wisconsin legislature passed an act that emphasized youth apprenticeships and technical preparation programs. Also around this time, Oregon redesigned its vocational high school curriculum to allow eleventh-grade students to enter an apprentice-type training program with businesses that guaranteed the students jobs after they graduated.[39] Such efforts are referred to as **school-to-work programs.** The success of the programs in Wisconsin and Oregon prompted other states, such as Rhode Island, New York,

| TABLE 9-2 | POSITIVE OUTCOMES OF A SUCCESSFUL APPRENTICE PROGRAM |

A well-planned and administered apprenticeship program will:

1. Attract adequate numbers of highly qualified applicants.
2. Reduce absenteeism.
3. Reduce turnover.
4. Increase productivity.
5. Reduce cost of training.
6. Facilitate compliance with federal and state Equal Employment Opportunity requirements.
7. Ensure availability of related technical instruction.
8. Enhance problem-solving ability of craftworkers.
9. Ensure versatility of craftworkers.
10. Address industry's need to remain competitive by investing in the development and continuous upgrade of the skills of its workforce.

SOURCE: Benefits for Program Sponsors. U.S. Department of Labor, Employment & Training Administration. Retrieved October 11, 2004, from http://www.doleta.gov/atels_bat/empbenef.cfm

North Carolina, and South Carolina, to seek similar reforms. These programs are distinct from more traditional adult apprenticeship programs, in that they target high school students, particularly those who are not likely to enroll in four-year colleges.

In response to the success that many states had with school-to-work initiatives, the U.S. Congress enacted the *School-to-Work Opportunities Act* in 1993. The act created a fund through which the federal government made grants available to states to cover the costs of implementing school-to-work programs. For example, Wisconsin received $27 million to support implementation of a variety of school-to-work programs, including youth apprenticeship, over a five-year period.[40] The Wisconsin youth apprenticeship program now offers apprenticeships in twenty-two occupational areas, including engineering, manufacturing, health services, automotive technician, and banking. First-year enrollment in the program was 700 (representing only 1 percent of high school students).[41] In 2004, roughly 2,200 students were involved in youth apprenticeships, with an even higher number of students in co-op education programs.[42] Funding cuts are blamed for the relatively low numbers of students involved.[43]

The success of a school-to-work program depends on the coordinated effort of all participants.[44] Schools should administer vocational assessment tests so that they can properly advise students on which program is best for them. In addition, schools should also ensure that their curriculum sufficiently prepares students in the fundamentals needed to learn advanced skills in the apprenticeship program. Other organizations involved in program administration, such as state government and labor unions, should provide technical support and advice to employers and help coordinate activities to ensure that programs runs smoothly. Finally, employers should ensure that the work assignments provide meaningful learning experiences for each student to build the competencies needed to complete the apprenticeship program.

Benefits to employers from school-to-work programs include access to a trained labor pool, a better public image, and potential eligibility for wage subsidies and tax credits.[45] These benefits, however, should be weighed against the potential costs. The direct costs include wages and benefits paid to students. The indirect costs include the time spent on the programs by HRD professionals and other employees who are responsible for coordinating the program, orienting and training the staff, and training and supervising the students. However, given the continuing shortage of skilled workers, school-to-work programs would seem to be a vital element in national efforts to reduce the skills gap noted earlier.

## COMPUTER TRAINING PROGRAMS

Computer skills training has become extremely popular. A 2003 survey by *Training* magazine found that 96 percent of companies conducted training on computer systems and applications.[46] Some computer training is more introductory in nature. *Introductory* programs introduce trainees to computer hardware and software. Such programs focus primarily on mastering basic software application, such as how to navigate the operating system. They do this through the use of manuals and *tutorials* (software programs themselves) that provide hands-on, interactive learning. These courses are designed to help trainees overcome their fear of computers and better understand how computers work.

*Applications training* covers specific software applications available within an organization.[47] Unlike introductory courses, which can be offered to an entire organization, applications training is typically provided on an as-needed basis. With the availability of online capabilities via an intranet, employees can access online computer training at any time of the day (or any day of the week — 24/7).

Given the range of options for conducting computer skills training, which approaches do employees prefer? One survey revealed that both experienced and less experienced trainees preferred to learn to use software by experimenting or through trial and error.[48] The more traditional training methods, including lectures and seminars, ranked near the bottom of the list of trainee preferences.

Researchers are exploring a number of learning issues involved in computer skills training. For example:

■ *Self-efficacy* — Self-efficacy is an individual's belief that he or she can successfully perform a given behavior (recall our discussion of self-efficacy in Chapter 3). Research has shown that a behavior modeling approach to software training resulted in higher self-efficacy scores and higher scores on an objective measure of computer software mastery than a tutorial approach.[49]

■ *Cognitive playfulness* — Cognitive playfulness includes the spontaneity, imagination, and exploratory approach that a person brings to task performance and learning.[50] Martocchio and Webster found that trainees higher in cognitive playfulness were more likely to exhibit higher learning, positive mood, and satisfaction with feedback.[51] However, they also found that positive feedback was more beneficial for employees who were lower in cognitive playfulness.

■ *Training format* — There is evidence that the use of behavior modeling for software training is more effective in producing computer skills learning and application than either of the more commonly used self-paced and lecture approaches.[52]

The results of empirical studies like the ones cited earlier can provide useful guidelines for designing and implementing computer skills training programs. This kind of ongoing research on learning-related issues underscores the need for HRD professionals to keep abreast of developments that could help them improve the design and implementation of computer skills training (and all HRD programs).

## TECHNICAL SKILLS/KNOWLEDGE TRAINING

When organizations introduce new technology (e.g., by modernizing plants or computerizing operations), they typically need to update the skills of the workers who must use it. Organizations often do this through job-specific technical skills/knowledge training programs. One recent survey found that technical skills/knowledge training is conducted by 90 percent of organizations, and training in new equipment operation by 85 percent.[53] Such training is often specific to a job, process, or piece of equipment, but can also be more general. For example, a training program used to teach clerical workers how to operate a new telephone system would be classified as job-specific. A training program used to train employees on new policies and procedures pertaining to waste disposal and given to all workers would be classified as general.

There are different levels of technical skills/knowledge training. At the lowest level, the goal is to prepare entry-level employees to perform basic functional responsibilities. These programs are similar to basic skills programs and combine classroom instruction with on-the-job training (OJT). As an example, Stanley-Bostitch Inc., a manufacturer of staples and fasteners, conducts a twenty-eight-week, entry-level operator training program of six modules, encompassing basic math, basic measurement skills, blueprint reading, shop practices, basic tooling, and basic machines. The last three modules involve intensive OJT. Successful trainees are expected to operate new, advanced equipment. In a similar situation, IBM assigns entry-level clerical workers to a two-week, sixty-eight-hour training program divided into fourteen modules that include automated procedures, time management, problem solving, and stress management.[54]

Beyond apprenticeship training, unions may also help provide training, such as with joint labor-management training programs designed to update union members' skills. For example, the Laborers' International Union and the Associated General Contractors (AGC) formed the Laborers-AGC Education and Training Fund.

One example of training provided by the Laborers-AGC group was an eighty-hour certificate course in hazardous-waste removal. Goodman reports that almost 9,000 of 500,000 union members had completed the training qualifying them to work on hazardous-waste removal projects.[55]

## SAFETY TRAINING

It is estimated that 77 percent of organizations conduct some form of **safety training**.[56] The need for such training increased dramatically after the passage of the 1970 **Occupational Safety and Health Act (OSHA).** For example, over $40 billion dollars is spent annually in the United States on organizational safety and health programs.[57] The Act established the **Occupational Safety and Health Administration** (also known as **OSHA**). OSHA (the administration) has four primary areas of responsibility, namely to (1) establish safety standards; (2) conduct safety inspections; (3) grant safety variances for organizations that are unable to comply with standards; and (4) cite organizations where standards are being violated. If an organization is cited for safety violations, safety training may be required to prevent future accidents. OSHA-mandated safety training focuses on safety equipment devices, handling of toxic chemicals, safe work habits, and actions to be taken in case of an accident. For more excessive violations, OSHA has the power to levy fines, shut down an operation, or even prosecute the management (or the owner).

In 2003, OSHA issued 83,539 citations for safety violations, plus an additional 59,861 for serious violations.[58] In data from 2000, OSHA attributed over half of all violations to "less-than-adequate training" as a contributing factor.[59] As one example, in 2003, a drilling rig company was fined over $68,000 for, among other things, failing to train crane operators on the types of cranes they would operate.[60] Further, the impact of inadequate training in an organization can be stated in quantifiable terms. Three of the most common metrics to portray the safety status of a site are:

- *Lost Work Day Index (LWDI)* — Number of workdays missed due to personal injury per 100 employees, divided by total number of employees × 100

- *OSHA Recordable Rate* — Number of OSHA Recordables/200,000 hours (the hours that 100 employees work with forty-hour weeks, and fifty weeks a year)

- *Lost Time Rate* — Number of Lost Time Accidents/200,000 hours

According to OSHA, the national LWDI average for private-sector organizations is 2.6 workdays missed per 100 employees.[61] The National Safety Council has established a $30,000 daily rate as an average to quantify a missed workday in dollars (based on a Fortune 500 energy company). Using these figures, and calculating the dollar impact of ten lost workdays, the total annualized costs associated with this can be determined to be:

10 lost workdays × 2.6 LWDI × $30,000 per lost workday = $780,000

In this hypothetical example, if a solution could be implemented (such as improved safety training) that could reduce lost workdays by even 10 percent, this would result in an annual savings of $78,000.[62] Certainly, greater savings than this are desirable and to be sought after.

OSHA regulations were expanded to include hazard-communications standards in 1988. These standards superceded right-to-know laws at the state level, and require organizations to (1) establish written hazard-communications policy, (2) replace old state posters with OSHA's posters, (3) establish procedures for obtaining **material safety data sheets (MSDS)** from manufacturers, (4) create notebooks containing MSDS and make them accessible to employees, (5) label hazardous materials and state the effects of such materials, (6) provide orientation for new employees and ongoing training for other employees, and (7) prepare a safety manual.[63]

Even with these regulations in place, injuries and illnesses are still common. For example, in 1989 there were approximately 6.5 million industrial accidents and illnesses on the job.[64] In 2002, the nonfatal occupational injury and illness rate for all industries was 5.3 per 100 employees, with approximately 4.7 million injuries and illnesses reported.[65] Agricultural, landscaping, meatpacking, and fishing industries had the highest accident rates. Over 5,500 worker deaths were reported in 2002 as well. This suggests that organizations still need to work diligently to reinforce safety standards and desired employee work behaviors. Some practical guidelines for safety training are provided in Table 9-3. Other desirable characteristics of an effective safety management program include:

1. top management support and reinforcement of safety standards[66]

2. employee involvement in suggesting safer work procedures and the selection of equipment[67]

3. regular and recurring safety training programs that reinforce safety standards and behaviors[68]

4. effective monitoring systems to ensure standards and behaviors are being practiced and to correct any unsafe conditions[69]

Because of OSHA regulations, industries that have historically had the highest incidence of work-related accidents now provide workers with ongoing safety training. The focus of this training is on prevention and emergency procedures. In addition, because of the right-to-know provisions described earlier, all organizations must orient and train employees on such things as the identification of toxic chemicals and how to use the MSDS system that explains how to neutralize possible negative side effects of chemical exposure.

In addition to OSHA-mandated training, some companies routinely conduct safety training and retraining in order to keep liability insurance premiums to a minimum. Such training can help a company to become "certified" as a safe company. Also, being designated as a safe company can help boost employee morale and make employees feel more secure.

Safety training is particularly important for production workers. They need training in the following areas: (1) recognizing, avoiding, and preventing unsafe conditions in their job and work areas; (2) procedures and rules relating to the use, transport, and storage of dangerous machinery, tools, and substances; (3) rules for

| TABLE 9-3 | TEN STEPS TOWARD AN EFFECTIVE SAFETY PROGRAM |
| --- | --- |

1. Determine the training objective. All training programs should seek to modify some employee behavior. Determine exactly what you want your employees to be able to do at the end of training.
2. Develop a list of competencies. What must each employee be able to do at a given level of training?
3. Create a trainee profile. Determine who will be undergoing training. Consider their age, gender, education, learning skills, and so on. Knowing your audience helps determine the language you use, making the training easier to follow.
4. Have the training manager determine an outline of the subject matter to be covered based on the competencies and trainee profiles.
5. Expand the outline for completeness and proper sequencing at least once.
6. Develop training based on the outline.
7. Test the training on experts.
8. Test the training on actual trainees to determine usability, understandability, and effectiveness.
9. Correct the training content based on feedback and reviews.
10. Evaluate your testing to make sure all questions are good. A question missed by many students may indicate the question is poorly written, or that the point was not covered well enough in the training.

SOURCE: Ten steps toward an effective safety program (1999). *CEE News, 51*(5), 10.

the use of protective clothing, systems, and devices for hazardous machinery, tools, and chemicals; and (4) methods of controlling hazards of any type, including the use of a fire extinguisher and other emergency equipment.

Safety training programs should be conducted both in the classroom and on the job site. Classroom training can focus on safety regulations, accident-reporting procedures, and other general information. Classroom training typically includes the most common approaches to safety training, that is, live instructors and video presentations, but can also include computer-based interactive training.[70] Computer-based training (CBT) programs can be classified as (1) computer-assisted instruction (CAI), in which the program provides drill and practice; (2) computer-managed instruction (CMI), in which the program evaluates the student's test performance, guides him or her to appropriate instructional resources, and tracks progress; and (3) computer-enriched instruction (CEI), in which the computer serves as a simulator or programming device.[71] Research has shown that safety trainees using CBT demonstrate equal or better achievement when compared to those who receive traditional instruction, and do so in less time, regardless of age, type of CBT used, or type of computer used. However, OSHA clearly states that while interactive CBT can be a valuable tool in a training program, its use alone does not meet the intent of most OSHA training requirements. They believe employees must be given the opportunity to ask questions, which requires access to a qualified trainer.[72]

On-site training can focus on actual safety standards and behaviors. **On-site safety observations (OSO)** are a way for organizations to take a proactive approach to improve their safety training efforts. An OSO is a formal, structured approach for conducting a safety needs assessment. Typically, the safety instructor will visit the worksite to gather critical data about workplace conditions, safe work procedures, and to conduct behavioral observations. This information is then used as the basis for developing training programs, better enabling the instructor to craft and tailor materials that are more relevant to trainees in a particular class.[73] Many organizations use behavior modeling as a training technique to reinforce desirable behaviors. As with any form of training, trainee transfer is a critical issue in safety training. Organizations should coordinate and reinforce safety training with other HRM procedures, such as performance evaluation and rewards systems, to motivate employees to put their safety training to use.

The effectiveness of safety training can be assessed by determining whether the safety standards and behaviors are being practiced. OSHA emphasizes evaluating training effectiveness in the short run by using a posttraining test of safety standards and procedures and monitoring behaviors. Long-run effectiveness can be determined by whether incidences of accidents, illness, and death decline.[74] In an effort to help organizations meet the demands of proper safety training, OSHA has developed a **Voluntary Protection Program.** This program encourages organizations to work in conjunction with OSHA to establish workplace safety programs. In return, OSHA provides free (and confidential) consulting services and assists with employee safety training. Participants are then exempted from OSHA inspections concerning the issues raised through the voluntary program.[75] As one example, the pulp and paper industry has recently become much more involved with the Voluntary Protection Program, with companies such as International Paper, Champion, and Weyerhaeuser working to earn VPP certification for particular worksites. Safety executives from these companies report improved safety performance, as well as greater overall performance, at their VPP worksites.[76] Further information on this topic can be found at OSHA's VPP website.[77]

Since the early 1990s, OSHA has focused less on random inspections and emphasized instead a smaller number of more targeted inspections. As a result, heavier penalties have been levied against fewer, but more serious offenders. For example, in 1989, OSHA conducted 52,255 inspections. In 1996, they conducted 25,850.[78] More recently, that number has begun to rise again. U.S. OSHA inspections from 2000 to 2003 were:

| Year | # U.S. OSHA Inspections |
|------|-------------------------|
| 2000 | 36,555 |
| 2001 | 35,974 |
| 2002 | 37,614 |
| 2003 | 39,798[79] |

It is important to note that while management and training professionals are traditionally responsible for training their workers in safety, other effective sources can be used. For example, safety training programs initiated by unions have gained strength and numbers over the past fifteen years. In addition, successful peer training programs are in place in a number of organizations. Peer trainers have played a major role in safety training, as evidence builds about how effective and credible fellow workers can be in this function.[80]

Ultimately, employee safety hinges on both improving the safety of the working conditions in which employees operate and increasing the amount of safe work behaviors engaged in by employees. Sadly, many workplace accidents are caused by employees acting in an unsafe manner (e.g., removing guards from machines, not wearing required protective gear, or not using equipment in the proper way). OSHA safety rules and regulations, protective gear, and other safety devices can all work to reduce the number of unsafe working conditions faced by employees. However, well-done safety training can be one of the most important elements to ensure that employees have both the skills and the motivation to perform their jobs as safely as possible.

## QUALITY TRAINING

Since the 1980s, organizations have placed special emphasis on increasing organizational productivity and quality. The guiding principles from W. Edwards Deming have served as the foundation for many quality improvement initiatives, first in Japan, and later in the United States and elsewhere. One outgrowth of Deming's fourteen principles is the concept of total quality management (TQM), defined as a set of principles and practices aimed at continually improving organizational effectiveness and efficiency.[81] It is a process designed to empower *all* employees to seek continuous improvements in quality. For employees, a change to TQM requires them to learn and embrace two fundamental skills: (1) the ability to work effectively with others in a team, and (2) the collection, analysis, and evaluation of quantitative data in decision making.[82] TQM has become a primary vehicle for introducing quality improvement in all kinds of organizations, including nonprofits and those in private industry and government. Depending on the industry, between 60 percent and 90 percent of U.S. companies have adopted some form of TQM.[83] One of the keys to successful TQM programs is **quality training.** The 2003 Industry Report by *Training* estimated that 65 percent of organizations provide training in quality and process improvement.[84]

It is important to follow an orderly process in the early stages of any TQM initiative.[85] A critical first step in developing a quality training program is for top management to agree on what quality means to the organization and on a set of metrics for measuring it. Table 9-4 identifies eight primary areas of concern prevalent in organizations that implement TQM.[86] The TQM philosophy argues that this first step should be conducted with input from people throughout the organization, especially frontline workers, and from the customers and clients the organization serves.

Quality can be defined from many perspectives, including product quality, service quality, and customer quality.[87] *Product quality* is defined as the degree to which products achieve or exceed production standards. Indicators of product quality can include things like the number of defects, recalls, and scrap, as well as the adherence to design specifications. *Service quality* is how well the organization responds to the

| TABLE 9-4 | MAJOR AREAS OF CONCERN FOR QUALITY IMPROVEMENT EFFORTS |

- the role of management leadership and quality policy
- training
- process management
- employee relations
- product/service design
- supplier quality management
- the role of the quality department
- quality data and reporting

SOURCE: Mandal, P., Howell, A., & Sohal, A. S. (1998). A systemic approach to quality improvements: The interactions between the technical, human and quality systems. *Total Quality Management, 9,* 79–99.

customers' needs after the product or service is delivered. It can be viewed as an attitude based on the customer's perceptions of performance.[88] This can be measured by noting things such as service response time, service backlog, and customer satisfaction ratings. *Customer quality* can be defined as the extent to which the organization has met or surpassed overall customer expectations. Such things as customer surveys and tracking customer complaints can measure this. Customer quality should not be ignored. Even when the product or service is technically perfect, it may fail in the marketplace if it does not meet customer expectations.[89]

It can be advantageous to implement quality training in two phases: quality awareness training and in-depth quality process and skills training. In the first phase, *awareness*, managers are introduced to the concept of quality improvement and how it will change their role. Awareness sessions should be led by a top manager who must demonstrate his or her long-term commitment to change, and make sure that other managers understand their "new" role in this approach, and the kind of support that will be expected from each manager. For example, some organizations, like Rockwell International, ensure that middle management has a vested interest in TQM by linking the program to their reward structure.[90] In turn, these managers are expected to conduct quality awareness sessions in their own units. Some organizations create a new organizational unit that is given direct responsibility for implementing the TQM program, including training programs. In addition, some organizations appoint task groups or "change committees" to oversee the process of organizational change (organizational change processes will be discussed in more detail in Chapter 14).

The next phase of TQM generally involves more *in-depth training* in process skills and quality skills. *Process skills* refer to ways to improve work coordination, solve problems, and resolve conflicts. *Quality skills* refer to the techniques and tools that can be used for tracking quality improvements. There are at least seven quality tools that can be used: process flow analysis, cause-and-effect diagrams, run charts, statistical process control, scattergrams, histograms, and Pareto charts.

These tools can be used for cause-and-effect analysis, problem solving, monitoring results, and recommending courses of action.

Of the quality tools just mentioned, **statistical process control (SPC)** has been most widely applied in various organizational settings (though more heavily in manufacturing than in service organizations). The principle underlying SPC is that most processes demonstrate variations in output and that it is important to determine whether the causes of such variation are normal or abnormal.[91] SPC focuses on training employees to be able to discern abnormal variations, so that adjustments can be made to the process to improve quality. Employees must learn to monitor output using control charts so that they can see variations.

In terms of the outcomes or effectiveness of TQM, there are a number of published evaluation studies of TQM, but only a few isolate the effects of the quality training program. One study, conducted by Motorola, evaluated the company's program using a multiple-group research design.[92] Trainees were assigned to three research groups: (1) those using the entire quality training curriculum (both process skills and quality skills) followed with reinforcement from senior managers; (2) those emphasizing either process or quality skills and followed up by senior managers; and (3) those using one or both methods, with no follow-up. Outcomes for the three groups were as follows: (1) the first yielded a $33 return for every dollar spent on training; (2) the second broke even; and (3) the third had a negative return.[93] These results would indicate that quality training should be comprehensive (covering both process and quality skills), and must be followed up by management.

Other factors often cited as necessary for successful TQM implementation are visionary leadership, upper management commitment and support for the transition to TQM, widespread employee involvement, integrated reward and compensation plans for quality improvements, and a performance evaluation process that is aligned with the nature of a TQM organization.[94] Of the unsuccessful attempts at TQM, case studies show that trained employees often fail to transfer their new skills to the workplace for the following reasons: (1) general employee resistance to change; (2) management failure to articulate clear objectives; and (3) few rewards for on-the-job use of new skills.[95] TQM will be discussed further in Chapter 14.

*QUALITY TRAINING AND THE ISO 9000 FAMILY OF STANDARDS.* A major boost for the quality movement was the establishment of uniform quality standards by the International Organization for Standardization (ISO). ISO is the international nongovernmental agency that has been established to improve the international exchange of goods and services and to develop international cooperation in intellectual, scientific, technological, and economic activity.[96] The U.S. affiliate of the ISO is the American National Standards Institute (ANSI).[97] Before ISO, organizations attempting to trade internationally faced different sets of standards for product quality. The primary purpose of ISO was to establish and monitor a set of quality standards that would serve as a common reference point for international trade.[98] The ISO standards have been revised a number of times.

One set of standards, referred to as **ISO 9000,** is directed at the quality of the processes used in creating a product or service.[99] These standards were most recently revised in 2000. In addition to the ISO 9000 family of quality process standards, there are other standards, for example, QS 9000, specifically targeted at the automotive industry, and TL 9000, aimed at reducing the cost of poor quality production within the global telecommunications industry.[100] A different set of standards, ISO 14000, was established concerning environmental management.[101] Because standards concerning the ISO 9000 family are more prevalent and encompassing, our discussion will focus on them.

Companies that comply with ISO 9000 standards are eligible to be officially registered and can use that designation in their trading activities and advertisements. To become ISO-registered (or certified), companies must be able to create and document a systematic program for delivering a product or service. There are three phases to implementing ISO 9000: document writing, implementation of a quality system, and system assessment for effectiveness. The second stage — implementation — takes up about half the time needed for registration, and this is where training takes place.[102] Initially, as U.S. companies became registered, they had a significant advantage over their domestic competition when doing business overseas, particularly in Europe. Today, ISO registration still offers organizations a marketing tool, worldwide recognition, and the ability to demonstrate the company's commitment to quality over competitors who are lacking the ISO designation. However, with many thousands of U.S. companies having earned this distinction, it is no longer a luxury; ISO has become almost a necessity for doing business in the international marketplace.

Based on numerous studies covering the ISO registration process, company-wide employee involvement through training is the quickest, most cost-effective way to achieve and maintain certification.[103] One of the ISO 9000 requirements has to do with an organization's quality training practices. Specifically, this requirement (1) focuses on how the organization identifies the training needs of employees who have a direct impact on quality, and (2) requires documentation of the training provided. ISO standards require that the organization conduct a job analysis to update job descriptions, including the qualifications needed to perform the work. For example, suppose that an analysis revealed that one of the knowledge requirements (KSAOs) for a particular job was knowledge of statistical process control techniques. The organization must ensure that job incumbents receive the appropriate training and that the training effort is documented.

The ISO monitors compliance by having ISO-certified auditors visit each ISO 9000-registered organization every six to twelve months to review whether the standards are being maintained, including reviewing the organization's training records. Basically, the auditors are checking to make sure that employees are performing a specific task according to the work instructions given. If they are, the employee is deemed to be adequately trained. This holds true for illiterate and handicapped employees as well. If the employee is able to explain the steps of the work instructions, and can demonstrate the necessary skills, the training is deemed adequate.[104] Noncompliance could potentially result in the loss of registration.

HRD professionals in organizations that are ISO 9000 registered (or want to be) must be aware of the ISO 9000 standards and help ensure that their organization is in compliance with them. In many organizations, the HRD professional is responsible for the training element. However, in some organizations, responsibility for ISO 9000 compliance may be given to a "quality assurance" unit, in which case

HRD professionals could serve as partners in training-related compliance activities. In any case, it is imperative that HRD professionals take a proactive role in ensuring that training activities meet ISO standards. For greater detail about ISO 9000 and other international standards, we urge you to seek out further information.[105]

## INTERPERSONAL SKILLS TRAINING

As discussed earlier, a number of basic workplace competencies involve working effectively with other people. These skills, sometimes referred to as "soft" skills, include communication, customer relations, selling, and teamwork. All can be improved through training. It is estimated that interpersonal/communication skills training is offered by 89 percent of organizations.[106] Interpersonal skills training programs cover a wide range of topics, with the most common ones being team building (67 percent), listening skills (63 percent), and delegation skills (61 percent).

Three trends have increased the need for interpersonal skills training. The first trend is a movement by organizations toward team-based approaches to accomplishing work, which usually involve team training with a strong interpersonal component. Second, high school and college graduates often lack the communication skills that organizations require, and third, many organizations are becoming more multicultural. With changing labor market demographics and the growth of multinational organizations, more and more organizations are developing cultural diversity programs. These courses are intended to change some of the incorrect assumptions, values, and beliefs people have about other cultures, with the desired outcome being the development of more effective cross-cultural interpersonal skills. These programs will be discussed in more detail in Chapter 15.

Interpersonal skills training programs offered by organizations vary in content. For example, at Motorola University in Schaumburg, Illinois, employees receive training in such topics as interpersonal communications, parenting, and weight management. Tech Central, an Edina, Minnesota-based temporary services firm, provides training in customer service, conflict resolution, interpersonal relations, and teamwork. At SAS Institute, a software developer in Carey, North Carolina, employees are trained on business ethics, time management, and leadership skills.[107] Finally, Duke Energy, in Charlotte, North Carolina, includes two interpersonal training courses (Personal Development and Relationship Development) in its professional development core curriculum.[108] These courses emphasize providing trainees with a better understanding of themselves and the handling of workplace relationships. In this section, we discuss three types of training that can be considered interpersonal skills training: sales training, customer service training, and teamwork training.

### SALES TRAINING

Traditional sales techniques (e.g., the "hard sell") are increasingly being abandoned for more consultative approaches that build trust, solve customers' problems, provide product and service options, and admit limitations.[109] This newer approach is intended to build customer loyalty and improve long-term customer relations.

The key to adopting new sales approaches is sales training. It is estimated that 55 percent of all organizations offer some type of sales training.[110] Training varies widely, from traditional sales techniques to the new consultative approaches. Some organizations, following the lead of Saturn Corporation, are overhauling entire retail and wholesale operations through comprehensive sales training programs. For example, at Motorola University, training goes hand in hand with all sales activity. Motorola involves sales managers as part of the "knowledge community" that is used to support their salespeople. These managers are coached on how to question, monitor, and review the efforts of salespeople to ensure that their training is being utilized. Salespeople must post account plans that are reviewed and revised by sales managers or sales trainers. The idea behind their sales training integration plan is to involve trainers at every step of the process, to measure results as soon after training as possible, and ultimately eliminate the differentiation between training and coaching on the job.[111]

Most organizations, however, are not willing to make such drastic changes. Some supplement sales training with other types of training (e.g., customer service training) that are intended to equip employees with the interpersonal skills needed to be effective. Many organizations also combine sales training with customer relations/service training. A sales training program should be tailored to an organization's needs. In particular, sales training objectives should be operationally defined based on the organization's goals (particularly their marketing goals) and should include input from sales representatives.[112] The following are six general objectives of high-performance sales training programs. An organization could use these as the basis to tailor company specific objectives:

- increased sales productivity
- lower turnover
- enhanced communication within and between all organizational levels
- better morale
- increased self-management of sales teams
- better customer relations

The specific objectives that an organization defines must be clear and must be understood by all employees.[113]

## CUSTOMER RELATIONS/SERVICE TRAINING

The increased emphasis on quality improvement has led organizations to emphasize customer relations and customer service. It is estimated that 81 percent of organizations conduct some form of **customer service training.**[114] In almost any job, customer service skills are important to achieving success, and people skills form the foundation for good customer service. Such skills include interpersonal relations, problem solving, leadership, and teamwork (discussed in the next section). People skills can foster a positive attitude, effective communication, courteous and respectful interaction and the ability to remain calm and in control in difficult situations.[115]

Any employee who interacts with a customer, even if indirectly, represents the organization, and each customer's perception of the quality of that interaction may influence how the organization's products and service are perceived. For example, a survey of over 1,300 retail customers concluded that (1) good service keeps customers coming back, while poor service drives them away; (2) organizations should continuously monitor customers' perceptions of their service; and (3) job skills of customer-service employees most likely need to be enhanced through training.[116]

The notion that *good service keeps customers coming back* is the crux of many customer service programs. For example, Guaranteed Eateries in Seattle instituted a customer guarantee program, referred to as "Your Enjoyment Guaranteed," which involved giving free drinks and even entirely free meals if certain service guidelines were not met. The frontline employees were empowered to grant these guarantees. While the program is estimated to cost about $10,000 per month, sales have risen 25 percent and profits have doubled.[117]

*Continuously monitoring customers' perceptions of service* is also critical. Organizations must be able to get feedback from their customers to determine if their needs were met. For example, Norand Corporation got "closer to the customer" by instituting a customer feedback system through monthly in-depth telephone surveys that were tabulated and circulated to each sales and service manager.[118] The results of such surveys can be used as part of the needs assessment process.

While customer service training varies considerably across both industries and companies, it has some common components. Stum and Church suggest that it should include four elements:[119]

1. *Introduce customer service training organization-wide.* Organization-wide customer service training can be a key component of a business turnaround. For example, a turnaround at Scandinavian Airlines Systems was attributed to the fact that, among other things, "they put 27,000 employees through a company-wide (customer service) training program."[120] Most leading service companies place such training on a similar high level of importance by including it in standard employee orientation programs.[121]

2. *Frontline employees need to be trained in customer relations skills, including interpersonal skills and operational practices.* This training is necessary for two reasons. First, customer contact employees (e.g., sales associates, customer service representatives, recruiters, secretaries, account executives) must have the skills and abilities to successfully relate to customers. Important interpersonal skills include the ability to listen and speak effectively. Second, the training should reinforce the notion that the long-term health of the organization depends, in part, on frontline employees exceeding customer expectations.[122] This is an important point. Customer-contact employees must be able to understand each customer's needs so that they can "shape" expectations. To do this, organizations must empower frontline employees to guarantee customer satisfaction, even if this means incurring additional costs.

3. *Service managers need training in how to coach employees and enforce new customer service standards.* Desatnick suggests that developing a customer-oriented workforce requires the hiring of service managers to train, develop,

and motivate employees.[123] Organizations should provide training to service managers to ensure they understand their roles and the need to monitor and reinforce customer service standards. The term *service manager* is used in a wider context here to include any supervisor whose employees interact with customers and other outsiders, from the sales manager to the office manager supervising secretaries who greet and interact with customers and clients.

4. *Provide incentives for supporting and sustaining the new customer service philosophy, including (but not limited to) recognition systems, compensation, and upgrading.* Customer service training should include employee incentives (or disincentives) that serve to reinforce desired behaviors. A wide range of individual and group incentives can be used for this purpose. Historically, organizations have relied on individual incentives, such as commissions, to motivate employees. However, in recent years, more and more organizations are making increasing use of group incentives, such as employee involvement and gains-sharing programs.

Some organizations have highly developed and formalized customer training curricula. For example, Tiffany & Co., a respected jewelry seller, has very high standards concerning what constitutes exceptional customer service. New salespeople must complete six to eight weeks of training before they ever meet with their first customer. All new sales representatives must go through knowledge, skills (customer service is a part of skills training at Tiffany), and product training. They then visit and tour corporate headquarters and the customer service/distribution center for a week of "graduate" coursework. The skills training here consists of telephone skills, presentation skills, and consultative selling. The customer service training process is essential and allows Tiffany "to uphold the unique tradition and culture" for which it is so widely known.[124] As another example, Fidelity Institutional Retirement Services Company (FIRSCo) created the Service Delivery University (SDU). The SDU is organized into five separate "colleges": Customer Service, Operations Management, Risk Management, Sales and Marketing, and Leadership and Management Development. Associates are required to complete the curriculum in all five colleges. The most critical college is the Customer Service College. Its purpose is "to create a company-wide dialogue about service excellence and how it is best delivered" so that after employees have completed training, they will "share a common language of service delivery," which is essential in a heavily regulated industry such as they are in.[125]

## TEAM BUILDING/TRAINING

Another recent development (partly growing out of the quality improvement movement) is the increasing emphasis on the use of teams as the basic organizational unit. Today, a large number of organizations have employees working in teams.[126] Team-based structures require that workers be adaptable and able to form and reform relationships with coworkers quickly and smoothly. Furthermore, *team training* is popular.[127] The *2003 Industry Report* estimated that 82 percent of organizations provide team building training.[128]

A team is defined as a group of "individuals who see themselves and who are seen by others as a social entity, who are embedded in one or more larger social systems (e.g., community, organizations), and who perform tasks that affect others (such as customers or coworkers)."[129] Five common types of work teams are quality circle, cross-functional, semiautonomous, self-managed, and self-designed teams.[130] As you might expect, self-managed and self-designed teams are the least commonly used.

There are at least two sets of team-related skills — task skills and process skills. *Task skills* are skills necessary for accomplishing the work assigned to the group. In a typical organization, employees will likely have the appropriate task-related skills and knowledge, but they must be able to apply those skills in a group setting. In addition, they may need to be cross-trained in skills other members have in order to perform group tasks together. For example, a team of mechanics and technicians that is charged with servicing an airplane will each bring unique and complementary talents to the task. Each member has a specific role to perform, and some roles must be performed in conjunction with other team members. However, to function as a team, members must understand each other's roles and see how they fit together into the overall task. *Process skills* are those skills that primarily have to do with working together as a team and maintaining the team relationships that are essential for teamwork. Interpersonal skills are among the most important process skills, and this includes skills in communication, negotiation, and conflict resolution.

A common form of team training is called **team building.** Team building can be viewed as an effort to unify varied individual energies, direct these energies toward valued goals and outputs, and link these efforts to organizational results.[131] It typically refers to a collection of techniques that are designed to build the trust, cohesiveness, and mutual sense of responsibility that make for an effective team. Most team-building interventions are led by a facilitator (sometimes called a change agent) whose role is to help the team improve its ability to work together effectively, communicate better, improve problem-solving capabilities, and make better decisions.[132]

Teams should not be formed just for the sake of having them. Teams should have a specific purpose, and be formed to accomplish a goal that needs the attention of a diverse group of people within an organization. Organizations should consider forming teams under conditions such as the following:

- A specific goal (or set of goals) needs a multifaceted group of people with complementary talents.
- A specific project is best addressed by cross-functional and multidepartmental coworkers who offer different perspectives.
- Broad-based perspectives are needed to develop and carry out the vision of growing a department or organization.[133]

Team-based approaches are fairly widespread, and teams have been shown to be an effective organizational intervention.[134] In Table 9-5, four approaches or models for building teams are presented. Under appropriate conditions, each approach can be an effective organizational intervention.[135] There is a growing literature on team effectiveness.[136] For example, Table 9-6 presents five variables that are predicted to

**TABLE 9-5**

## FOUR MODELS OF TEAM BUILDING

| Model | Emphasis | Team-member objective |
|---|---|---|
| Goal Setting | Setting objectives and developing individual and team goals | Involved in action planning to identify ways to achieve the goals that have been set |
| Interpersonal Relations | An increase in teamwork skills (mutual supportiveness, communication, sharing ideas) | Develop trust in each other and confidence in the team |
| Problem Solving | Identification of major problems in the team | Become involved in action planning for the solution of problems, as well as implementing and evaluating the solutions |
| Role Clarification | Increased communication among team members regarding their respective roles within the team | Achieve better understanding of their and others' respective roles and duties within the team |

SOURCE: Salas, E., Rozell, D., Mullen, B., & Driskell, J. E. (1999). The effect of team building on performance: An integration. *Small Group Research, 30,* 309–329.

**TABLE 9-6**

## VARIABLES PREDICTED TO INCREASE TEAM EFFECTIVENESS

| Variable | Definition |
|---|---|
| | *The extent to which:* |
| Team Structure | ■ team members understand and are committed to team goals |
| | ■ team roles are clearly defined |
| | ■ group norms are in place |
| Team Spirit | ■ a team has confidence in its ability to be effective |
| | ■ team members invest energy on behalf of the team |
| Social Support | ■ team members have positive interactions and provide support for one another |
| Workload Sharing | ■ work is equally divided among team members |
| Communication within the Group | ■ team members give and receive information |
| | ■ team members manage conflict in a healthy manner |

SOURCE: Werner, J. M., & Lester, S. W. (2001). Applying a team effectiveness framework to the performance of student case teams. *Human Resource Development Quarterly, 12*(4), 385–402.

increase team effectiveness.[137] However, more research is needed concerning the efficacy of **team training** that would help guide practitioners in designing training systems.[138] HRD professionals should rely on the HRD process (i.e., assess, design, implement, evaluate) in designing and delivering team-training programs, be vigilant about new research, and make judicious use of scientific and practical knowledge that is available. Teams will be discussed further (as a means to promote organization development) in Chapter 14.

## ROLE OF LABOR UNIONS IN SKILLS AND TECHNICAL TRAINING PROGRAMS

Historically, labor unions have been concerned with promoting the interests of union members, which includes keeping their skills and competencies current. As the demand for higher skilled workers has increased, unions have often taken an active role in providing training for their members, including both developing and sponsoring a wide variety of training programs.[139] Some unions have joined together to establish regional or statewide training centers. Many of these centers receive additional funding from public and private sources. Unions have also sought collaboration with schools and employers to meet the training needs of their members. These efforts are generally referred to as joint training programs.

### JOINT TRAINING PROGRAMS

A joint training program is an extension of the management-labor union relationship in which the goal is to provide meaningful training and personal developmental opportunities for union members. Unlike employer-sponsored HRD programs, which are under an employer's control and are available to a range of employees, joint training programs are administered by both the employer and the union and are usually available only to union members. Joint training programs vary in content. A study of 152 programs revealed that the four most common content areas were (1) safety and health (22 percent), (2) job skills training (17 percent), (3) communication skills (16 percent), and (4) assistance for displaced workers (11 percent).[140]

Most joint training programs comprise individual courses or programs that are fairly simple to administer, but some are very large, complex programs. One example is the Alliance for Employee Growth and Development, Inc., which was created in 1986 by AT&T, the Communications Workers of America (CWA), and the International Brotherhood of Electrical Workers (IBEW). The Alliance is administered by two coexecutive directors (one from AT&T and one from CWA) who report to a six-member Board of Trustees (three from each side).[141] The staff is dispersed among three regional headquarters in New Jersey, Texas, and Georgia. According to Treinen and Ross:

> The backbone of the Alliance organization is the local committees . . . made up of about six persons, three each from the company and unions. It is their job to raise the awareness of the Alliance in the eyes of their work force; to survey the work force to identify

training needs; to identify potential vendors of services within the local community; to work for Alliance staff to negotiate contracts with vendors; to monitor training activities for quality and relevant outcomes; and to perform posttraining analysis to ensure that programming is ongoing and fits the needs of the workers themselves.[142]

In the wake of the layoffs that resulted from the divestiture of AT&T in 1984, the first challenge to the Alliance was to address the needs of almost 100,000 displaced workers. To deal with this, the Alliance established displacement projects, relocation assistance, job placements, and a host of retraining opportunities. In addition to an array of ongoing training and education programs, the Alliance developed a comprehensive career and skills assessment process to provide displaced employees with meaningful information to develop individual development plans. Treinen and Ross viewed the Alliance's efforts as experimental and an opportunity to try and evaluate ways cooperation can benefit all parties concerned.[143]

The following are other examples of joint partnership programs:

1. In response to concerns about literacy among its members, the Laborers International Union collaborated with the Associated General Contractors to develop a Learn-At-Home video literacy program. The program was completed by 3,000 laborers in a two-year period.[144]

2. In response to the growing need for entry-level employment in the service industry, union and casino officials partnered together to offer a two-week training program to provide the skills needed to garner these jobs. The Southern Nevada Joint Management Culinary and Bartenders Training Fund, whose board included both casino and union officials, supported the effort. The center successfully trained more than 2,400 workers.[145]

3. A training trust was set up in Ohio, where the Communications Workers of America Local 4340 partnered with various employers to help pay for the training and certification of journeyman telecommunications technicians. Both the local union and the employers each pay into the program 12 cents an hour of each member's wages. With this partnership, a person successfully completing the training program is "basically guaranteed" to get hired, as the demand for technicians is high.[146]

These kinds of programs are examples of what can happen when labor unions, employers, state governments, and other institutions collaborate and focus their energies on improving workplace competencies. Joint training programs benefit the participating union members, and they can foster better relationships between union leaders and management. A recent study found that apprentices in joint programs were considerably more likely to complete the program than those in non-joint programs, that is, a difference in completions rates of 58.4 versus 30.2 percent.[147]

Joint training programs have implications for HRD professionals. First, if union leaders and management have a strong adversarial relationship, HRD professionals may find resistance from either side when proposing programs that are intended to benefit union members. Either side may suggest that these programs should be part of contract negotiations. However, in general, joint programs are best accomplished if they are outside of normal collective bargaining structures. Second, by having union leaders as active partners, HRD professionals should be able to better identify the needs of union members and, as a result, improve the design, implementation, and scheduling of training. Also, program announcements could be disseminated through the union's normal communication channels (e.g., union newsletter). Third, collaborating with unions on a single joint program provides an opportunity for HRD programs to promote other programs to union leaders as well.

## PROFESSIONAL DEVELOPMENT AND EDUCATION

A profession is an occupation that is based on an abstract body of knowledge.[148] Sharma describes the essence of a profession this way: a profession is an occupation in which workers "apply in their work a body of knowledge and techniques acquired through training and experience, have a service orientation and distinctive ethics, and have a great deal of autonomy and prestige."[149] Examples of professions include medicine, law, accounting, teaching, and engineering. Professional associations exist in most professions. A **professional association** is a private group that exists to advance and protect the interests of the profession and to offer services to its members (e.g., certification, publications, educational opportunities).

The domain of knowledge that an individual must master in order to be "officially" considered a professional in a given field is typically defined by the professional association (and, in some cases, state governments). In many professions, a credential such as **licensure** or **certification** is required for the individual to practice in that field. Generally speaking, state governments administer licensing, whereas professional associations administer certification. In both cases, the criteria an individual must typically meet include attainment of a degree, a given level of practical experience, and a passing score on an examination. For example, to earn the *Professional in Human Resources (PHR)* designation, an individual must pass a standardized test (administered by the Human Resource Certification Institute), and have a minimum of two years of exempt-level experience in human resources.

Because effectiveness as a professional is based on applying a body of knowledge, it is critical that professionals keep current with the latest ideas and techniques in their field. Professional associations and licensing agencies typically require license or certificate holders to engage in continuing education to maintain this credential. For example, the American Institute of Certified Public Accountants has adopted a national standard that requires practicing CPAs to attend a minimum of forty hours mandatory continuing professional education courses per year.[150] Continuing education opportunities are offered by at least three sources — college and universities, professional associations, and the organizations that employ professionals. We will briefly describe each.

### CONTINUING EDUCATION AT COLLEGES AND UNIVERSITIES

Many colleges and universities offer courses to meet the **continuing education** needs of professionals. Some benefits that can come out of this arrangement are

(1) organizations are able to use the expertise available at colleges, (2) organizations can sometimes assist the schools in designing courses that are job-specific, (3) organizations can choose instructors, and (4) college credit may be granted, making it possible for employees to obtain a college degree. Whether these benefits are realized depends on the demand for the courses and the flexibility of the academic institution to meet the needs of professionals and organizations.

There are many examples of joint programs between colleges and professional organizations. For instance, the Center for Financial Studies at Fairfield University in Fairfield, Connecticut, developed a cooperative venture with the National Council of Savings Institutions, which offers workshops to area banks and other financial organizations. Companies like NCR, Pacific Bell, and Control Data have developed college-credit courses approved by the American Council on Education Program on Non-collegiate Sponsored Instruction (ACE/PONSI), which uses administrators and faculty from local colleges to evaluate programs.[151] American College offers specialized training for insurance professionals, including those from John Hancock Financial Services.[152]

Some states have experimented with partnership programs. The state of New York began an experiment in 1983 with the Public Employees Federation, a government employees' union, in which public administration courses were designed and offered at area colleges and universities. The uniqueness of this program was that it was tied to the union contract, and thus had greater protection from budget cuts.[153] Similarly, the Governmental Services Center at Kentucky State University provides mandatory training and career-management workshops to a full spectrum of public-sector employees.[154]

## CONTINUING EDUCATION BY PROFESSIONAL ASSOCIATIONS

The main way professional associations provide continuing education opportunities is by sponsoring conferences, meetings, and workshops for their members. The program for these gatherings typically includes speeches by leading experts, discussion of current issues, and presentation of research findings. One of the primary benefits of these events is the opportunity to meet and share experiences with other professionals.

Another way professional associations try to keep their members current is by publishing journals, magazines, and newsletters that communicate ideas and practices in the field. Increasingly, professional associations are using the World Wide Web to disseminate this information. For example, the websites for the American Society for Training and Development and the Society for Human Resource Management are useful resources for HRD professionals.[155]

Some professional associations also offer precertification workshops to help members achieve certification. Precertification programs can be offered at the association's training center or at local colleges. For instance, the insurance industry sponsors two precertification programs leading to the chartered life underwriter (CLU) and chartered financial consultant (ChFC) designations at the American College.[156]

## COMPANY-SPONSORED CONTINUING EDUCATION

Organizations also play an important part in offering continuing education opportunities for the professionals they employ. Some organizations have developed college-like curricula within their own training centers. At the same time that many organizations are moving toward decentralizing the delivery of training programs, there appears to be a continuing trend toward developing on-site **corporate universities**. It is estimated that over 2,000 organizations have developed centralized training curricula, called "university," "college," or "institute of learning."[157] These on-site programs generally include a core curriculum that can be completed in stages so that it can be managed along with employees' jobs. The Service Delivery University at FIRSCo, discussed earlier, would fit this description. Staffing of these on-site programs varies. Some organizations rely exclusively on employees. Organizations like Motorola hire faculty for their on-site programs, both from among their senior professionals (many of them at retirement age) and from outside experts. This arrangement makes the program organization-specific, and enables it to incorporate training in the latest technology. For an interesting example of company-sponsored continuing education, see the boxed inset nearby, "NCR Offers Education for All in Dundee, Scotland." As in all other areas of HRD, it is vitally important that the effectiveness of corporate universities be measured to demonstrate a positive organizational impact.[158]

## HRD DEPARTMENT'S ROLE IN CONTINUING EDUCATION

The HRD department has three distinct roles to play with respect to continuing education — as an enabler, a resource provider, and a monitor. As an *enabler*, the HRD department must establish policies and procedures that foster an effective and equitable distribution of continuing education throughout the organization. As a *resource provider*, the HRD department should consider program-support options, including tuition reimbursement, educational leave, paid professional association fees, and compensation of travel expenses to off-site professional development sites. A tuition-reimbursement program is an important part of a professional-development program because it increases the chances employees will continue their education. Tuition reimbursement programs are offered by an estimated 95 percent of large organizations.[159] Most programs reimburse educational expenses, including tuition and fees, provided the course is job related and the employee receives a specified grade (e.g., B or better). Many feel that such programs will make employees more valuable to the organizations because, through it, they will become more creative, innovative, or entrepreneurial.[160]

While not as common, education leaves or sabbaticals offer employees an opportunity to continue their education or conduct research while they continue to receive pay for up to 12 months. Such programs are generally made available after a certain length of employment within the organization. Some organizations also offer these leaves to senior managers so that they can pursue other interests (e.g., teaching, volunteering time in a nonprofit organization, or writing). There are usually conditions that must be met by the employee to qualify for such leave, such as

## NCR offers Education for All in Dundee, Scotland

A significant development over the past twenty-five years has been the emergence of the Automated Teller Machine, or ATM, for obtaining cash and performing other basic banking transactions. U.S.-based NCR has been a leading manufacturer of ATMs, and one of their major manufacturing plants is in Dundee, Scotland. The Dundee plant has won numerous awards for its ATM design and manufacturing.

In the early 1990s, a program entitled, "Education for All" was started at the Dundee facility. The goal was to enhance the plant's capacity to grow through continuous innovation, customer focus, and cost competitiveness. The emphasis at Dundee has been more broadly on employee education, rather than focusing strictly on employee skills. Learning centers were set up in the plant, and links were established with local colleges and universities. Employee self-development as well as career development was encouraged. NCR paid for any educational courses that were broadly related to the company's business, and gave employees time off work to take such courses.

In 1991, 9 percent of all employees participated in at least one course through Education for All. By 1998, that figure had risen to 20 percent. Courses have included both undergraduate and graduate work in electronics, engineering, and other topics.

NCR Dundee enjoyed strong sales and a high degree of job security for many years.

However, in 1998, a decision was announced to lay off 200 of the plant's 1,500 employees, as a portion of their production process was going to be outsourced to other plants.

Judy Pate and her colleagues conducted research in 1999 at the Dundee plant. They surveyed employees who had participated in at least one Education for All course since 1995, and compared these surveys with others taken from a matched sample of employees who had not taken such courses (a control group). As predicted, employees who had used the Education for All program responded that they had used the knowledge and skills learned in their classes to enhance their work performance, that is, that learning transfer had occurred. Another interesting finding was that job satisfaction and organizational commitment were high for both groups. The researchers suggest that the Education for All program had produced a positive effect on employee attitudes — even after a layoff announcement, and even for employees who had not used the program.

Overall, this case study suggests that, at least for NCR Dundee, a commitment to employee education had both a direct and an indirect payoff. Employees obviously benefited from this continuing education program, but it would appear that NCR did as well.

Pate, J., Martin, G., Beaumont, P., McGoldrick, J. (2000). Company-based lifelong learning: What's the payoff for employers? *Journal of European Industrial Training*, 24(2/3/4), 149–158.

not having other means of support (e.g., another job) while on leave. In addition, return to the former job or organization is mandatory, as well as the production of a detailed report, conducting of seminars, or some other evidence to show that the leave was used productively.

Employers may also pay fees and expenses to allow employees to attend professional meetings and seminars. These sessions provide an opportunity to share ideas and discuss common issues. Such meetings are invaluable to employees who want to remain current in their fields and who want to write and present professional papers. Because of limited resources for such activities, an equitable process of approving these kinds of expenditures must be established. To be equitable, the policy should specify how employees can qualify for programs, provide justification for expenditures, and be approved by management. This policy should be made known throughout the organization.

Finally, the HRD department serves as a *monitor* by ensuring that the professional development process is working as planned. As we have stated many times already, evaluation is a critical part of any HRD effort. For instance, General Foods has a professional development process that requires supervisors to develop skills-assessment and development plans with each subordinate. These are used to organize training and development efforts in critical skill areas. They also allow HRD staff to monitor changes in the skills base of the individual unit or entire department.[161]

## RETURN TO OPENING CASE

Saturn Corporation made a commitment to extensive training for new employees. Topics included technical skills, problem solving, interpersonal skills, teamwork, and continuous improvement techniques. Also, production workers received extensive ongoing training after the initial training efforts were completed. For employees in the retail side of Saturn, a special program was established, entitled Saturn Training and Partnership (STEP). Your instructor has additional information on what was included in STEP to train employees at the Saturn dealerships.

## SUMMARY

The need for skilled and technical workers continues to rise. Employers often express concern that many young adults are graduating from schools lacking the skills needed to perform current jobs. We reviewed three categories of skills and technical training — basic skills, technical, and interpersonal. The level of illiteracy within the workforce has created a demand for basic skills programs. The content of these programs focuses on improving basic competencies, including reading, writing, and computational skills.

Technical training programs include apprenticeships and programs in computers, technical skills/knowledge, safety, and quality. Apprenticeship training, the most formalized employer-based program, involves both on-the-job (OJT) and classroom training. Computer training typically involves either introductory or applications training. Technical skills/knowledge programs are generally job-specific and are offered organization-wide. Quality and team-training programs are typically part of a larger quality improvement agenda and may include training needed for the organization to become ISO 9000 registered (or some other quality designation).

Interpersonal training programs include communication, sales, customer relations, and team building and team training. Many of these programs focus on increasing productivity and improving the quality of products, customer service, and customer relations.

We also reviewed professional development and education programs. In many professions, professional workers are required to participate in continuing education in order to gain or renew a license or certification. Continuing education opportunities are offered by a variety of providers, including colleges and universities, professional associations, and the organizations that employ professional workers.

## KEY TERMS AND CONCEPTS

apprenticeship training
basic skills/literacy education
certification
continuing education
corporate universities
customer service training
interpersonal skills training
ISO 9000
Job Training and Partnership
   Act (JTPA)
licensure
material safety data sheets
   (MSDS)
Occupational Safety and Health
   Act (OSHA)

Occupational Safety and Health
   Administration (OSHA)
on-site safety observations (OSO)
professional association
quality training
safety training
school-to-work programs
statistical process control (SPC)
team building
team training
technical training
Voluntary Protection Program
Worker Adjustment and Retraining
   Notification (WARN) Act
Workforce Investment Act (WIA)

## QUESTIONS FOR DISCUSSION

1. Explain why skills training programs are important for the long-term vitality of organizations.

2. Describe the nature and extent of the literacy problem facing organizations today. How might this problem affect an organization's attempt to introduce new technology (e.g., a computer-aided manufacturing system)? What are the possible solutions?

3. If you were responsible for designing a basic skills/literacy training program, what approach would you take? How would you determine the effectiveness of this program?

4. Colleges and universities are primarily service enterprises. What key components would you include in customer service training for college employees, such as security or records office staff, who interact with students?

5. Identify two ways that advances in information technology have affected organizations today. What are the implications of these advances for HRD professionals in ensuring that workers will be able to make the most of them?

6. If your organization were contemplating using a team-based approach to increase productivity and reduce cost, what training issues would the organization be likely to face? How could the organization address these issues?

7. Explain why continuing education for professionals is important to both organizational and individual success. What kinds of program options would you provide for professionals — such as accountants and dietitians — who need professional certification?

8. Explain and report back on the continuing education offerings (and requirements) in your area of study.

## EXERCISE: EVALUATING A CLASS PROJECT TEAM [162]

Select a student group that you are a part of this semester (if there is a group project in this class, use that as your target group). Visit the text website (*http://werner. swlearning.com*), and fill out the Student Team Audit Instrument in terms of how much you think each of the statements on this instrument is true of your group. If requested by your instructor, compile the results from your group for each scale. Once this has been completed, spend some time discussing your findings. What strengths or weaknesses do these findings reveal about your team? What could you do differently in the future to address any concerns or weaknesses of your team?

Visit *http://werner.swlearning.com* for links to informative websites for this chapter.

## REFERENCES

1. Fastest growing occupations, 2002–2012. Bureau of Labor Statistics. Retrieved October 9, 2004, from http://www.bls.gov/emp/emptab3.htm

2. Dole, E. (1990). "Ready, set, work," says labor secretary. *Training and Development Journal, 44*(5), 17–22.

3. Steck, R. N. (1992). The skills gap and how to deal with it. *D & B Reports, 40*(1), 47–48.

4. Hoff, D. J. (2002). Conferees urge Washington to tend to bettering high school. *Education Week, 21*(30), April 10, 9; Study says H.S. grads not ready for college. (2002). *Community College Week, 15*(3), September 16, 3.

5. Johnson, J., & Duffett, A. (2002). Reality check 2002. *Education Week, 21*(25), March 6, S1–S8.

6. *Ibid.*

7. Toossi, M. (2004). Labor force projections to 2012: The graying of the U.S. workforce. *Monthly Labor Review,* February, 37–57. Retrieved October 9, 2004, from http://www.bls.gov/opub/mlr/2004/02/art3full.pdf

8. *Ibid,* Table 6, p. 53.

9. Kogut, B. H. (2004). Why adult literacy matters. *Phi Kappa Phi Forum, 84*(2), Spring, 26–28.

10. Tyler, K. (1996). Tips for structuring workplace literacy programs. *HR Magazine, 41*(10), 112–116.

11. Manzo, A. V. (2003). Literacy crisis or Cambrian period: Theory, practice, and public policy implications. *Journal of Adolescent & Adult Literacy, 46*(8), 654–661; Kogut (2004), *supra* note 9.

12. Stone, N. (1991). Does business have any business in education? *Harvard Business Review, 69*(2), 46–62.

13. Fiske, E. B. (1997). Adults: The forgotten illiterates. *Christian Science Monitor, 89*(129), May 30, 18.

14. Kirsch, I. S., & Jungeblut, A. (1986). *Literacy: Profiles of America's young adults.* National Assessment of Educational Progress. Princeton, NJ: Educational Testing Service.

15. McCabe, J. (2003). *The wasted years: American youth, race, and the literacy gap.* Lanham, MD: Scarecrow Education.

16. 2003 Industry Report. (2003). *Training, 40*(9), 21–38.

17. Berger, M. A. (1983). In defense of the case method: A reply to Argyris. *Academy of Management Review, 8,* 329–333.

18. Kuri, F. (1996). Basics skills training boosts productivity. *HR Magazine, 41*(9), 73–79.

19. Filipczak, B. (1992). What employers teach. *Training, 29*(10), 43–55.

20. Wilson, L. S. (1990). An on-line prescription for basic skills. *Training and Development Journal, 44*(4), 36–41.

21. Carlisle, K. E. (1985). Learning how to learn. *Training and Development Journal, 39*(3), 75–80

22. Zaslow, R. (1991). Managers as writing coaches. *Training and Development Journal, 45*(7), 61–64.

23. Callaghan, D. R. (1985). Realistic computer training. *Training and Development, 39*(7), 27–29.

24. Rothwell, W. J., & Brandenburg, D. C. (1990). *Workplace literacy primer* (p. 56). Amherst, MA: Human Resource Development Press.

25. Laabs, J. J. (1996). Leading organizational change. *Personnel Journal, 75*(7), 54–63.

26. *Ibid.*

27. Holley, W. H., Jr., Jennings, K. M., & Wolters, R. S. (2005). *The labor relations process* (8th ed.). Mason, OH: Thomson/South-Western, p. 113.

28. *Business Week/Reinventing America* (1992).

29. Judy, R. W., & D'Amico, C. (1997). *Workforce 2020: Work and workers in the 21st century.* Indianapolis: Hudson Institute.

30. Templin, N. (2000, February 11). Anatomy of a jobs training program that went awry. *Wall Street Journal*, pp. B1, B4.

31. Barnow, B. S. (2000). Exploring the relationship between performance management and program impact: A case study of the Job Training Partnership Act. *Journal of Policy Analysis and Management, 19,* 118–141.

32. Pantazis, C. (1996). The state of lifelong learning. *Training & Development, 50*(8), 36–40.

33. Workforce Investment Act of 1998 (http://usworkforce.org/wialaw.txt); Irwin, D. (2000). New era ahead for work-force development. *Inside Tucson Business*, *10*(4), April 17, 1–2.

34. The National Registered Apprenticeship System. Programs and Apprentices: Fiscal Year 2003. Retrieved October 11, 2004, from http://www.doleta.gov/atels_bat/pdf/statsheet03.pdf; Crosby, O. (2002). Apprenticeships. *Occupational Outlook Quarterly*, *46*(2), Summer, 2–21.

35. Crosby (2002), *supra* note 34.

36. Woodberry, P. (1997, July 15). Personal communication.

37. See the Crosby (2002) article above (note 34) for contact information in each state.

38. Carnevale, A. P., & Johnston, J. W. (1989). *Training America: Strategies for the nation.* Alexandria, VA: ASTD.

39. Graves, B. (1993, February 14). Oregon school plan aims for big change. *The Oregonian*, p. A21.

40. Stamps, D. (1996). Will school-to-work? *Training, 33*(6), 72–81.

41. *Ibid*, quote from p. 74.

42. Christee, J. (2000, December 28). State of Wisconsin Youth Apprenticeship Director, Personal communication.

43. Davis, A. (2002, June 2). As support dwindles, schools re-examine apprenticeship programs. *Milwaukee Journal Sentinel*. Retrieved October 11, 2004, from http://www.jsonline.com/news/state/jun02/53650.asp

44. Jackson, G. B., & Wirt, J. G. (1996). Putting students to work. *Training & Development, 50*(11), 58–60.

45. *Ibid*.

46. 2003 Industry Report (2003), *supra* note 16.

47. Hall-Sheey, J. (1985). Course design for PC training. *Training and Development Journal, 39*(3), 66–67.

48. Harp, C. (1996). Winging it. *Computerworld, 30*(43), 107–109; Harp, C., Satzinger, J. and Taylor, S. (1997). Many paths to learning software. *Training & Development, 51*(5), 81–84.

49. Gist, M. E., Schwoerer, C., & Rosen, B. (1989). Effects of alternative training methods on self-efficacy and performance in computer software training. *Journal of Applied Psychology, 74*, 884–891; Fagan, M. H., Neill, S., & Wooldridge, B. R. (2003). An empirical investigation into the relationship between computer self-efficacy, anxiety, experience, support and usage. *Journal of Computer Information Systems 44*(2), 95–104.

50. Martocchio, J. J., & Webster, J. (1992). Effects of feedback and cognitive playfulness on performance in microcomputer software training. *Personnel Psychology, 45*, 553–578; Woszczynski, A. B., Roth, P. L., & Segars, A. H. (2002). Exploring the theoretical foundations of playfulness in computer interactions. *Computers in Human Behavior, 18*(4), 369–388.

51. *Ibid*.

52. Simon, S. J., & Werner, J. M. (1996). Computer training through behavior modeling, self-paced, and instructional approaches: A field experiment. *Journal of Applied Psychology, 81*, 648–659; Bolt, M. A., Killough, L. N., & Koh, H. C. (2001). Testing the interaction effects of task complexity in computer training using the social cognitive model. *Decision Sciences, 32*(1), 1–20; Davis, F. D., & Yi, M. Y. (2004). Improving computer skills training: Behavior modeling, symbolic mental rehearsal, and the role of knowledge structures. *Journal of Applied Psychology, 89*, 509–523.

53. 2003 Industry Report (2003), *supra* note 16.

54. Henneback, C. (1992). Instant secretaries: Just add training. *Training & Development, 46*(11), 63–65.

55. Goodman, F. F. (1992). A union trains for the future. *Training & Development, 46*(10), 23–29.

56. 2003 Industry Report (2003), *supra* note 16.

57. Hilyer, B., Leviton, L., Overman, L., & Mukherjee, S. (2000). A union-initiated safety training program leads to improved workplace safety. *Labor Studies Journal, 24*(4), 53–66.

58. Nash, J. L. (2004). Agency says inspections, citations rose in 2003. *Occupational Hazards, 66*(1), January, 12.

59. Franta, B. A. (2000). Bottom line figures quantify safety training initiatives. *Houston Business Journal, 31*(11), 31.

60. Drilling rig company cited for violating safety standards following a fatal accident in Quitman, La. (2003, June 20). OSHA Regional News Release, Region 6. Retrieved October 11, 2004, from http://www.osha.gov/pls/oshaweb/owadisp.show_document?p_table=NEWS_RELEASES&p_id=10258

61. OSHA's list of low-hazard industries will remain the same for additional year. (2004, February 17). *U.S. Newswire*, p. 1.

62. Franta (2000), *supra* note 59.

63. Rothwell, W. J. (1989). Complying with OSHA. *Training and Development Journal, 43*(5), 52–54.

64. Hackey, M. K. (1991). Injuries and illness in the workplace, 1989. *Monthly Labor Review, 114*(5), 34–36.

65. OSHA Facts (2004). Retrieved October 11, 2004, from http://www.osha.gov/as/opa/oshafacts.html

66. Thompson, B. L. (1991). OSHA bounces back. *Training, 28*(1), 45–53.

67. Jenkins, J. A. (1990). Self-directed work force promotes safety. *HR Magazine, 35*(2), 54–56.

68. Rothwell, W. J. (1989). Complying with OSHA. *Training and Development Journal, 43*(5), 52–54.

69. Kimmerling, G. F. (1985). Warning: Workers at risk, train effectively. *Training and Development Journal, 39*(4), 50–55.

70. Ten steps toward an effective safety program (1999). *CEE News, 51*(5), 10.

71. Janicak, C. A. (1999). Computer-based training: Developing programs with the knowledge-based safety training system. *Professional Safety*, June, 34–36.

72. *Ibid.*

73. Flick, J. P., Radomsky, M. C., & Ramani, R. V. (1999). On-site safety observation: The Penn State Approach to site-specific health and safety training. *Professional Safety*, October, 34–38.

74. Kimmerling (1985), *supra* note 69; Sinclair, R. C., Smith, R., Colligan, M., Prince, M., Nguyen, T., & Stayner, L. (2003). Evaluation of a safety training program in three food service companies. *Journal of Safety Research, 34*(5), 547–558.

75. Hoover, S. K. (1999, September 17). OSHA program reflects new focus. *CityBusiness: The Business Journal of the Twin Cities, 17*(16), 16.

76. Atkinson, W. (1999). OSHA's Voluntary Protection Program motivates mill safety improvements. *Pulp and Paper, 73,* 97–103.

77. Voluntary Protection Programs (2004). Retrieved October 11, 2004, from http://www.osha.gov/dcsp/vpp/index.html

78. *Ibid.*

79. OSHA Facts (2004), *supra* note 65; Nash (2004), *supra* note 58.

80. Hilyer et al. (2000), *supra* note 57.

81. Routhieaux, R. L., & Gutek, B. A. (1998). TQM/CQI effectiveness at team and department levels. *Journal of Quality Management, 3,* 39–62.

82. Hartmann, L. C., & Patrickson, M. (1998). Individual decision making: Implications for decision training in TQM. *International Journal of Quality & Reliability Management, 15,* 619–633.

83. Bennett, J. B., Wayne, E. K., & Forst, J. K. (1999). Change, transfer climate, and customer orientation. *Group & Organization Management, 24,* 188–216.

84. 2003 Industry Report (2003), *supra* note 16.

85. Hartmann & Patrickson (1998), *supra* note 82.

86. Mandal, P., Howell, A., & Sohal, A. S. (1998). A systemic approach to quality improvements: The interactions between the technical, human and quality systems. *Total Quality Management, 9,* 79–99.

87. Miller, T. O. (1992). A customer's definition of quality. *Journal of Business Strategy, 13*(1), 47.

88. Nowak, L. I., & Washburn, J. H. (1998). Antecedents to client satisfaction in business services. *Journal of Services Marketing, 12,* 441–452.

89. *Ibid.*

90. Vasilash, G. S. (1992). Driving beyond satisfaction at Rockwell Automotive. *Production, 104*(4), 40–43.

91. Mainstone, L. E., & Levi, A. S. (1989). Fundamentals of statistical process control. *Organization Behavior Management, 9*(1), 5–21.

92. Wiggenhorn, W. (1990 July–August). Motorola U: When training becomes an education. *Harvard Business Review,* 71–83.

93. *Ibid.*

94. Routhieaux & Gutek (1998), *supra* note 81; Kassicieh, S. K., & Yourstone, S. A. (1998). Training, performance evaluation, rewards, and TQM implementation success. *Journal of Quality Management, 3,* 25–38.

95. Bennett et al. (1999), *supra* note 83.

96. Kelley, S. (1998, December 11). All types of businesses can benefit from ISO use. *Dallas Business Journal, 22*(16), p. B4.

97. ANSI. Retrieved October 11, 2004, from http://www.ansi.org/default.aspx

98. Reimann, C. W., & Hertz, H. S. (1996). The Baldrige Award and ISO 9000 registration compared. *Journal for Quality & Participation, 19*(1), 12–19.

99. Elmuti, D. (1996). World class standards for global competition: An overview of ISO 9000. *Industrial Management, 38*(5), 5–9.

100. Another industry gets specific. (1999). *Export Today*, *15*(4), 72.

101. ISO 9000 and ISO 14000 in brief. Retrieved October 11, 2004, from http://www.iso.org/iso/en/iso9000-14000/index.html

102. Larson, M. (1999). Set up ongoing training. *Quality*, *38*(13), 56–57.

103. Geisler, C. D., & Justus, R. (1998). Training: A strategic tool for ISO and QS-9000 implementation. *IIE Solutions*, *30*(4), 24–27.

104. Larson (1999), *supra* note 102.

105. Internet Resources Review. Retrieved October 11, 2004, from http://www.ansi.org/internet_resources/overview/overview.aspx?menuid = 12#information; American Society for Quality. Retrieved October 11, 2004, from http://www.asq.org/portal/page?_pageid = 33,32429, 33_32554&_dad = portal&_schema = PORTAL

106. 2003 Industry Report (2003), *supra* note 16.

107. Oleson, M. (1999). What makes employees stay. *Training & Development*, *53*(10), 48–52.

108. Carnevale, A. P., Gainer, L. J., Villet, J., & Holland, S. L. (1990). *Training partnerships: Linking employers and providers.* Alexandria, VA: ASTD.

109. Mikula, J. (2004). Sales Training. Alexandria, VA: ASTD Press; Callahan, M. R. (1992). Tending the sales relationship. *Training & Development, 43*(12), 31–55.

110. 2003 Industry Report (2003), *supra* note 16.

111. Keenan, Jr., W. (2000). Sales training ROI? *Industry Week*, *249*(11), June 12, 23.

112. Peterson, R. T. (1990). What makes sales training programs successful? *Training & Development*, *44*(8), 59–64.

113. Mescon, M. H., & Mescon, T. S. (1999). Training is lacking in many sales departments. *Orlando Business Journal*, *15*(49), April 30, 28–29.

114. 2003 Industry Report (2003), *supra* note 16.

115. Evenson, R. (1999). Soft skills, hard sell. *Techniques: Making Education & Career Connections*, *74*(3), 29–31.

116. Becker, W. S., & Wellins, R. S. (1990). Customer-service perceptions and reality. *Training and Development Journal*, *44*(3), 49–51.

117. Firnstahl, T. W. (1989). My employees are my guarantee. *Harvard Business Review, 67*(4), 28–31.

118. Miller (1992), *supra* note 87.

119. Stum, D. L., & Church, R. P. (1990). Hitting the long ball for the customer. *Training and Development Journal, 44*(3), 45–48.

120. Albrecht, C. (1985). Achieving excellence in service. *Training and Development Journal, 39*(12), 64–67, quote from p. 64.

121. Desatnick, R. L. (1987). Building the customer-oriented work force. *Training and Development Journal, 41*(3), 72–74.

122. Cone, J. (1989). The empowered employee. *Training and Development Journal, 43*(6), 96–98.

123. Desatnick (1987), *supra* note 121.

124. Lorge, S. (1998). A priceless brand. *Sales & Marketing Management, 150*(10), 102–110.

125. McColgan, E. A. (1997). How Fidelity invests in service professionals. *Harvard Business Review,* January-February, 137–143, quote from p. 138.

126. Industry Report. (1996). Who's learning what? *Training, 33*(10), 55–66.

127. Prager, H. (1999). Cooking up effective training. *Training & Development, 53*(12), 14–15.

128. 2003 Industry Report (2003), *supra* note 16.

129. Guzzo, R. A., & Dickson, M. W. (1996). Teams in organizations: Recent research on performance and effectiveness. *Annual Review Psychology, 47,* 307–338, quote from pp. 308–309.

130. Banker, R. D., Field, J. M., Schroeder, R. G., & Sinha, K. K. (1996). Impact of work teams on manufacturing performance: A longitudinal study. *Academy of Management Journal, 39,* 867–890.

131. De Vany, C. (1999). Championship team-building: Ready, coach? *Journal of Property Management, 64*(2), 92–93.

132. Schwarz, R. M. (2002). *The skilled facilitator: Practical wisdom for developing effective groups.* San Francisco: Jossey-Bass.

133. *Ibid.*

134. Banker et al. (1996) *supra* note 130; Cohen, S. G., & Ledford, Jr., G. E. (1994). The effectiveness of self-managing teams: A quasi-experiment. *Human Relations, 47,* 13–43; Schilder, J. (1992). Work teams boost productivity. *Personnel Journal, 71*(2), 67–71; Musselwhite, E., & Moran, L. (1990). On the road to self-direction. *Journal of Quality & Participation,* 58–63.

135. Salas, E., Rozell, D., Mullen, B., & Driskell, J. E. (1999). The effect of team building on performance: An integration. *Small Group Research, 30,* 309–329.

136. Batt, R. (2004). Who benefits from teams? Comparing workers, supervisors, and managers. *Industrial Relations, 43*(1), 183–212; Trent, R. J. (2004). Becoming an effective teaming organization. *Business Horizons, 47*(2), 33–40.

137. Werner, J. M., & Lester, S. W. (2001). Applying a team effectiveness framework to the performance of student case teams. *Human Resource Development Quarterly, 12*(4), 385–402.

138. Cannon-Bowers, J. A. Tannenbaum, S. I., Salas, E., & Volpe, C. E. (1995). Defining Competencies and establishing team training requirements. In R. A. Guzzo, E. Salas, & Associates (Eds.), *Team effectiveness and decision making in organizations* (pp. 333–380). San Francisco: Jossey-Bass; Tannenbaum, S. I., & Yukl, G. (1992). Training and development in work organizations. *Annual Review of Psychology, 43,* 399–441.

139. A work order for big labor (2004, September 13). *Business Week,* Issue 3899, p. 128.

140. Hoyman, M., & Ferman, L. A. (1991). Scope and extent of joint training programs. In L. A. Ferman, M. Hoyman, J. Cuthcher-Gershenfeld, & E. J. Savoie, (Eds.), *Joint partnership programs.* Ithaca, NY: ILR Press.

141. Treinen, D., & Ross, K., (1991). The Alliance for Employee Growth and Development, Inc. In L. A. Ferman, M. Hoyman, J. Cuthcher-Gershenfeld, & E. J. Savoie, (Eds.), *Joint Partnership Programs.* Ithaca, NY: ILR Press.

142. *Ibid.*

143. *Ibid.*

144. Goodman (1992), *supra* note 55.

145. Jones, A. (1999). Unions take on the role of training for new jobs. *National Catholic Reporter, 35*(38), September 3, 5.

146. Ettorre, J. (1999). Unions labor to draw more. *Crain's Cleveland Business, 20*(35), August 30, M10-11.

147. Bilginsoy, C. (2003). The hazards of training: Attrition and retention in construction industry apprenticeship programs. *Industrial and Labor Relations Review, 57*(1), 54-67.

148. Abbot, J. (1988). The multicultural workforce: New challenges for trainers. *Training and Development Journal, 42*(8), 12-13.

149. Sharma, A. (1997). Professional as agent: Knowledge asymmetry in agency exchange. *Academy of Management Review, 22*, 758-798, quote from p. 763.

150. Walley, E. N. (1996). Is it time to take another look at CPE? *CPA Journal, 66*(2), 26-31.

151. Forsyth, S., & Galloway, S. (1988). Linking college credit with in-house training. *Personnel Administrator, 33*(11), 78-79.

152. Crosson, C. (1990). Hancock enlists American College for courses. *National Underwriter, 94*(12), 7, 36.

153. Faerman, S. R., Quinn, R. E., & Thompson, M. P. (1987). Bridging management practice and theory: New York's public service training program. *Public Administration Review, 47*(4) 310-319.

154. Childress, G. W., & Bugbee, J. A. (1986). Kentucky's across-the-board effort at making HRD work. *Public Personnel Management, 15*(4), 369-376.

155. ASTD. Retrieved on October 11, 2004, from http://www.astd.org/astd; Society for Human Resource Management. Retrieved on October 11, 2004, from http://www.shrm.org/

156. Crosson (1990), *supra* note 152.

157. Allen M. (2002). *The corporate university handbook: Designing, managing & growing a successful program.* New York: AMA; Barron, T. (1996). A new wave in training funding. *Training & Development, 50*(8), 28-33.

158. Johnson, G. (2003). 9 tactics to take your corporate university from good to GREAT. *Training, 40*(7), 38-41.

159. Gutteridge, T. G., Leibowitz, Z. B., &. Shore, J. E. (1993). *Organizational career development: Benchmarks for building a world-class workforce.* San Francisco: Jossey-Bass.

160. Russell, I. (2004). A refreshing absence. *Supply Management, 9*(10), May 13, 19; Toomey, E. L., & Connor, J. M. (1988). Employee sabbaticals: Who benefits and why. *Personnel, 65*(4), 81-84.

161. Courtney, R. S. (1986). A human resources program that helps management and employees prepare for the future. *Personnel, 63*(5), 32-40.

162. Werner & Lester (2001), supra note 137. Applying a team effectiveness framework to the performance of student case teams. *Human Resource Development Quarterly, 12*(4), 386-402.

**10**

# COACHING AND PERFORMANCE MANAGEMENT

## Learning Objectives

*After reading this chapter, you should be able to:*

1. Define coaching and performance management, and explain the need for such activities in organizations.

2. Explain how to analyze employee performance to set the stage for a coaching discussion.

3. Describe the steps involved in coaching to improve poor performance.

4. Explain how coaching can be used to maintain effective performance and encourage superior performance.

5. Identify the skills necessary for effective coaching.

6. Identify the critical elements in a performance management system.

7. Describe the evidence supporting the effectiveness of coaching and performance management.

■

## OPENING CASE

Consider the following scenario: you are working for a large pharmaceutical firm, and you have been asked to serve as a coach to the following two individuals. Both have been successful in their careers to this point, yet with both individuals, issues have been raised concerning their interpersonal skills. There is concern on the part of top management in the organization that both need to change their style of communicating to be effective in their current positions, as well as to advance further in the organization. After you read over the two scenarios, consider the questions at the end of the case.

**Scenario 1:** Jane is one of your senior researchers. She has a brilliant scientific mind, and is considered one of the top researchers in her field. She has received numerous promotions in your organization. Recently, however, her entire staff quit all at once. They described her as "impossible to work with," "insensitive to others," "abrasive," and "mean." In looking into the situation, you find that Jane's primary focus has been on getting the job done. She admits to you that she cares very little about the personal needs of her subordinates and that she gets very impatient with anyone who

cannot keep up with her fast-paced style of management.

**Scenario 2:** John is an accomplished middle-level manager in your organization. He is very good within his functional area, but has been told that he will not be promoted further unless he learns how to manage people more effectively. When you speak with John's administrative assistant, he complains about John's constant sarcasm and insincerity. In speaking with John yourself, it seems as if he is not really listening to you as you seek to discuss this issue with him. His facial expressions and body language come across as quite negative.

*Questions: If you were seeking to coach each of these individuals, where would you begin? What types of actions and activities would you engage in, and why? Are there any communication tools or exercises that you would recommend for either of these individuals? Finally, does it matter whether you are coaching these individuals as their immediate supervisor, or as an "outsider" (e.g., either as an HRD professional in this organization, or as an outside consultant)?*

## INTRODUCTION

To what extent do you agree or disagree with the following statements?

- *Most employees already know what they should do and how to do it.*

- *Performance management is simply a matter of expecting tasks to be done correctly and on time.*

- *If a problem occurs, the appropriate action is to give the employee a stern lecture or to threaten punishment. The problem will then go away — after all, the employee already knows what should be done and how to do it.*

- *If the problem does not go away, the employee must be stupid, lazy, or have a "bad attitude." Therefore, punishment is called for.*

- *If punishment fails, the only reasonable course of action is to terminate or transfer the employee.*

## THE NEED FOR COACHING

Managers and supervisors sometimes take a narrow, reactive, and negative view of their role in managing employee performance. As Michael Scott has written, "Many managers I've provided counsel to over the years are stuck in what I refer to as the 'punitive paradigm' of handling poor performers" (p. 12).[1] Such an approach to managing performance can actually create or compound performance problems, rather than solve them. This view can include beliefs such as those listed earlier. However, managers and supervisors who attempt to manage employees this way are frequently frustrated because their interventions are often ineffective or create additional opportunities for conflict. In such situations, performance management becomes aversive to both supervisors and employees. Therefore, many managers and supervisors choose to ignore poor performance and poor performers altogether. Instead, they may choose to assign the work to effective employees or even to do it themselves. This approach can lead to further problems, such as feelings of inequity and low morale among the employees assigned the extra work, while the initial problem remains unresolved.

Furthermore, this negative approach may lead to frustration when changes in the organization's goals demand higher levels of employee performance. Managers who believe that all they need to do to improve employee performance is to relay the orders issued from above and give employees a pep talk are stymied when these actions fail to achieve the goal. These actions may seem sensible to the manager who thinks employees already know what they are doing and how to do it. Unfortunately, if improvement does not occur, yelling, threats, or punishment may be the next, seemingly logical, course of action.

The reality is that sometimes employees know what to do and how to do it, but sometimes they do not. It could be that the recruiting and selection process is flawed; or that orientation and training have been done poorly (if at all). In addition, changes in the task, organization, or environment may prompt the need for new knowledge or skills. Even the supervisor's own behavior may undermine employee motivation. For example, if superior performance is neither noticed nor rewarded, a climate may exist in which effective performance is actually discouraged. Conflicting, confusing, or incomplete requests will also cause employees to wonder what the manager really expects.

Further, taking a negative approach to managing performance may mean that the only time the supervisor discusses performance with employees is when there is a problem or a request (demand) for improvement. Effective performance is ignored because it is expected. Employees may resent this treatment, and the employees' supervisor misses opportunities to encourage effective performance and prevent problems.

## COACHING: A POSITIVE APPROACH TO MANAGING PERFORMANCE

Effective managers and supervisors realize that they must take an *active* and *positive* role in employee performance to ensure that goals are met. These managers and supervisors realize that they are paid not so much for what they do, but for what their subordinates do. Therefore, they define their role in managing employee performance as one of empowering employees. Their role is to ensure that employees know specifically what to do, can actually do it, and do not face unnecessary obstacles or disincentives to effective performance. When changes in the environment, goals, or tasks occur, employees are informed and given the opportunity for training so they can adapt to the changes.

Effective managers and supervisors also make sure employees know how they are performing on a regular basis and that effective performance is rewarded when it occurs. They do not intervene only to correct problems or increase production. Therefore, performance discussions are less likely to be seen primarily as opportunities for conflict.

In short, managing employee performance effectively requires that managers and supervisors become *coaches* rather than controllers. We believe *coaching* is one of the most important functions a manager or supervisor can perform. A manager can be a superb planner, organizer, and decision maker, but without the effective management of employee performance that coaching provides, objectives will be difficult to achieve. Coaching can create a partnership between a supervisor and an employee that is dedicated to helping employees get the job done. The current popularity of various **participative management** approaches (e.g., employee empowerment and self-directed teams) requires supervisors, managers, and even executives to function primarily as coaches for those who report to them.[2] In this chapter, we discuss what is involved in coaching and describe how it can be used to improve poor performance and ensure continued effective performance. We also describe the skills and training necessary to be an effective coach. First, however, we need to distinguish between coaching and performance management.

## COACHING AND PERFORMANCE MANAGEMENT

A majority of organizations today have some sort of formal **performance appraisal** system. Such systems typically make use of a standardized rating form that is used to evaluate various aspects of employee performance.[3] Numerical values or ratings are generally assigned to each performance dimension. Most formal appraisals are done annually, though there is evidence that employees would prefer to be evaluated more frequently than this.[4] In fact, both supervisors and employees frequently express considerable dissatisfaction with the whole performance appraisal process.[5] Garold Markle has described performance appraisal as the poorest performing, most ineffective, and least efficient human resource practice.[6] Trainer and consultant Dick Grote has noted humorously that "There is probably no management process that has been the subject of more Dilbert lampoons than performance appraisal" (p. 14).[7] A recent large-scale survey by the Mercer consulting firm found that 42 percent of employees said their managers gave them regular feedback on their performance, 29 percent thought they were rewarded when they did a good job, and 25 percent said their managers coached them to improve their performance.[8]

In response to such dissatisfaction, an increasing number of organizations have begun to emphasize performance management.[9] **Performance management** goes beyond annual appraisal ratings and interviews, and incorporates employee goal setting, feedback, coaching, rewards, and individual development.[10] As such, performance management focuses on an ongoing process of performance improvement, rather than primarily emphasizing an annual performance review. A survey of employee preferences found a slight preference for receiving informal feedback on the job over formal feedback through an appraisal interview (53 percent to 47 percent). The authors of this study interpreted this as suggesting that most employees want both types of information, that is, they still want the information provided by a formal appraisal process, but they want this to be supplemented by an ongoing process of evaluation and feedback.[11] Furthermore, a benchmarking study conducted by Development Dimensions International placed performance management as the second highest priority for global business (right behind leadership development).[12]

There is a growing body of literature emphasizing the compensation and reward aspects of performance management.[13] These are critical issues for organizations to address. Reward issues fall outside the bounds of coverage for a textbook on human resource development, and thus we will stress the coaching, feedback, and goal-setting aspects of performance management in our discussion to follow. Nevertheless, we wholeheartedly agree with the point made in the broader literature that performance management and coaching must be connected to the goals and strategies of the organization as a whole.[14] As Jerry Gilley and colleagues point out, what is required is an organization-wide approach to performance improvement, with coaching and employee development as critical aspects of this effort.[15] Among other things, this also means that an organization's recognition and reward system must function in a way that managers and supervisors are in fact rewarded for effective coaching. The system should also be as user-friendly and automated as possible.[16] We will return to these points in our concluding comments. Next, however, let us look at the coaching process itself.

## DEFINITION OF COACHING

There is no single agreed-upon definition of coaching. Some authors define it narrowly as a performance-improvement technique. For example, Fournies defines coaching as a face-to-face discussion between a manager and a subordinate to get the subordinate to stop performing an undesirable behavior and begin performing desirable behaviors.[17] Similarly, Kinlaw defines coaching as a "mutual conversation between a manager and an employee that follows a predictable process and leads to superior performance, commitment to sustained improvement, and positive relationships" (p. 31).[18] In Kinlaw's view, effective coaching becomes a matter of learning how to conduct the coaching discussion.

Other authors see coaching in broader terms and draw upon similarities between organizational managers and athletic coaches. For example, Kirkpatrick and Zemke argue that sports coaches and managers have similar responsibilities (e.g., gathering data, providing feedback, recruiting, motivating, ensuring results, working with individuals and the team), and work under similar conditions (e.g., limited resources, time constraints).[19] Therefore, many of the characteristics of an effective athletic coach should also be present in the effective manager-coach.[20] These characteristics include optimism, a strong sense of moral values, honesty, humility, warmth, self-confidence, and trustworthiness. Some books expounding this view have been written by successful athletic coaches, such as Don Shula, the former head coach of the National Football League's Miami Dolphins.[21]

Evered and Selman take the model of "manager as athletic coach" one step further.[22] They argue that it is the "context of committed partnership" in which athletic coaching occurs that is the key to defining management coaching. The communication and relationship between coach and performer that spring from this partnership are the essence of coaching. They contend that to coach effectively, there must be a shift from seeing management as controlling employees to management as empowering or enabling employees. Similarly, Peters and Austin describe the manager-coach as one who brings individuals together and "encourages them to step up to responsibility and continued achievement, treating them as full-scale partners and contributors" (p. 325).[23]

To complicate matters further, some authors use the term *coaching* to describe both a broad approach to performance management and a specific technique to facilitate it. Peters and Austin define coaching broadly (as described earlier) as an overall approach to performance management, while at the same time naming five distinct though related roles that together make up coaching.[24] One of these five roles is given the name *coaching;* the other roles are called educating, sponsoring, counseling, and confronting. The coaching role is likened to leadership, whereas the other roles involve teaching (educating), mentoring (sponsoring), dealing with personal problems (counseling), or getting employees to face up to performance problems (confronting). Gilley and Boughton make a similar distinction, labeling the overall performance management process "performance coaching," and defining the roles a performance coach must play as training, mentoring, confronting, and career coaching.[25] Kinlaw sees coaching as both problem solving and performance improvement, and argues that it is made up of four functions: counseling, mentoring, tutoring, and confronting.[26]

Finally, some authors view coaching as something that is done primarily as a means for executive development or to help "problem" executives and professionals get back on track. Waldrop and Butler define coaching as "helping to change the behaviors that threaten to derail a valued manager" (p. 111).[27] Olesen describes coaching as helping senior executives recognize that they have a performance problem and assisting them in dealing with it.[28] Hellervik, Hazucha, and Schneider describe an extensive coaching program aimed at helping "managers and professionals with more serious skill deficiencies achieve significant changes in work behavior" (p. 878).[29]

So what is coaching? It would be easy to narrow the use of the term to refer to a specific performance-management technique. The disadvantage of this would be to risk creating the assumption that a manager can be controlling and manipulative and still effectively use coaching to improve performance. This is not likely to be the case. Fournies, as well as Evered and Selman, argues that effective coaching requires an optimistic, humanistic belief in the desire of employees to be committed to the task and the organization without coercion.[30] Coaching encompasses more than mere technique; it is a day-to-day approach to managing performance. Acting as a coach makes the manager or supervisor a partner with employees and a facilitator of their performance. Manager-coaches thus see themselves as serving employees and as getting paid for what the employees achieve, whereas traditional managers tend to assume monitor or controller roles, in which they "use" and control employees as they would any other resource.[31] At its heart, coaching requires managers to take an interest in and interact with subordinates to encourage effective performance.

We define **coaching** as a process used to encourage employees to accept responsibility for their own performance, to enable them to achieve and sustain superior performance, and to treat them as partners in working toward organizational goals and effectiveness. This is done by performing two distinct activities: (1) *coaching analysis,* which involves analyzing performance and the conditions under which it occurs, and (2) *coaching discussions,* or face-to-face communication between employee and supervisor both to solve problems and to enable the employee to maintain and improve effective performance.[32]

## ROLE OF THE SUPERVISOR AND MANAGER IN COACHING

It should now be clear that an employee's direct supervisor or manager bears the primary responsibility for coaching. While other managers in the organization can serve as mentors, teach a new skill, or help overcome a specific problem, coaching most often occurs within the context of an ongoing relationship between employee and supervisor. It is the supervisor's responsibility to ensure that his or her unit meets its goals, and that means ensuring that employees perform their tasks effectively. The supervisor delegates assignments, establishes standards, and monitors performance, and is therefore uniquely equipped with sufficient information, opportunity, and authority to carry out coaching effectively. Someone outside the work unit who does not perform these tasks lacks sufficient information, opportunity, and authority to coach effectively. Kinlaw has suggested that, in high performing teams, team members will also act as coaches.[33] However, while team members may have the information and opportunity to function as coaches, in many cases they lack the clear authority to do so. One of the challenges of using self-managed teams is to define the role for the manager or supervisor to whom the team reports, as well as the roles for team members. Often, one of the primary roles of managers and supervisors in team-based organizations is that of coach.[34]

## THE HRD PROFESSIONAL'S ROLE IN COACHING

HRD professionals can help managers and supervisors become effective coaches by providing training in the coaching process and ensuring that the coaches have the interpersonal skills needed to be effective. In addition, other HRD interventions, such as training, may solve problems uncovered by a coaching analysis. HRD professionals can also help management create a climate that encourages coaching through the use of organizational development (OD) techniques (see Chapter 14).

As we will see, resolving performance problems may require the use of HRM or other management activities beyond human resource development. For example, a performance problem may be caused by an inadequate reward system, and thus should be resolved by revising the compensation and reward system. Similarly, if a manager discovers the same skill deficiency in all employees, the recruiting or selection system may need to be changed, rather than relying on training to ensure that new employees can perform the job. If the information or production system contributes to or causes the problems, such as poorly maintained or outdated equipment or erroneous reports, correcting these systems should ultimately lead to improved performance. This is the premise behind Total Quality Management, which we discussed in Chapter 9.

We believe it is important that HRD professionals understand the coaching process and the skills necessary to conduct it well. While they may not have to conduct coaching themselves, they can help managers and supervisors prepare for this challenging and rewarding responsibility.

Finally, we would remind you of the basic point that coaching is an HRD intervention. It is easy to equate human resource development and training, and in fact, many of the examples and chapters in this book deal with training programs as HRD interventions. Remember, though, from Chapters 1 and 2 that HRD includes activities in addition to training that provide employees with the necessary skills and motivation to meet current and future job demands. Supervisors may need training to be effective coaches, and employees may need training to deal with performance issues uncovered by a coaching analysis. However, our point here is to emphasize that coaching, by itself, is an HRD intervention. HRD professionals must ensure that the coaching and performance management systems in their organizations are functioning effectively and contributing to organizational effectiveness.[35]

## COACHING TO IMPROVE POOR PERFORMANCE

Some amount of poor performance seems to be a fact of life in most (if not all) organizations. While most employees perform as expected, there will always be some who fail to meet expectations. According to Viega, "If there is one universal truth about managers, it is that all of them have problem subordinates" (p. 145).[36]

There are many reasons for poor performance. It is a manager's job to confront and deal with poor performance and to create conditions that minimize the chances that it will occur again. Coaching is one way to do this. In this section, we will address three issues: (1) the definition of poor performance, (2) how coaching analysis can be conducted to determine the cause of performance problems or issues, and (3) how the coaching discussion can be used to improve performance.

## DEFINING POOR PERFORMANCE

Defining what sorts of behavior constitute poor or unacceptable performance is not a simple matter. A given behavior, such as the time one arrives at work or the number of apartments a sales agent rents in a given month, is itself neither good nor bad. A behavior must be evaluated with respect to some standard or expected level of performance before it may be labeled good or poor. If the behavior meets or exceeds the standard, then it is typically considered good. If the behavior fails to meet the standard, it may be considered poor.

Yet, how far must a behavior deviate from what is expected before it is considered poor performance? The answer depends both on who is making the evaluation and on how that person perceives the situation. Supervisors may differ as to how large a deviation from the standard can be tolerated. Furthermore, the same supervisor may tolerate different deviations at different times for different employees. For example, it may be more acceptable for a salesperson to fail to reach a sales goal during traditionally slow seasons than during other times of the year. Similarly, a supervisor may ignore deviations from performance standards from an employee who is having personal problems, while at the same time holding other employees rigidly accountable for their behavior.

Furthermore, employees and supervisors may interpret performance differently either because they apply different standards to the same behavior or because they selectively attend to different aspects of the same behavior. For example, suppose a chef uses more expensive ingredients to prepare dishes than the restaurant manager authorizes. The chef may define this as effective behavior because it satisfies customers and may induce them to return. The manager, meanwhile, may interpret this as poor performance because it reduces the profit margin on the meals the chef prepares; the manager may consider the chef's behavior an instance of not following the rules.

In short, what is poor performance is not as clear-cut as it first appears; it depends on the standards established for performance and how those standards are applied. The following definition of **poor performance** takes these issues into account: "Specific, agreed-upon deviations from expected behavior" (p. 205).[37] This definition makes two important points. First, the extent of the deviation from a performance standard to be considered poor must be specifically defined. If absolutely no deviation will be tolerated, then this must be stated. If some deviation will be tolerated (e.g., two absences per quarter), then this amount must be made clear. Second, both the evaluator and the performer should agree to the amount of deviation that constitutes poor performance. This is not to say every performance standard must be negotiated; rather, the performer must be made aware of what the standard is and understand that it will be used to evaluate performance. The employee must agree that the standard is legitimate.

This definition of poor performance does not restrict the type of standard that may be used. For example, a supervisor can use an *absolute* standard, which would be applied to all subordinates, or a *relative* standard, which considers an employee's progress or performance in light of the performance of other employees. Requiring all employees to achieve an error rate of no more than 1 percent is an absolute standard; requiring an employee to be in the top 50 percent of his or her training class to be eligible for a permanent position is a relative standard. The choice of the standard should be guided by the organization's (and unit's) goals and methods used to achieve those goals (e.g., policies, practices, and the task itself). However, the use of relative standards has been criticized for not providing enough specificity concerning what an employee is doing well (or poorly). Further, employees often resist feedback that is based solely upon comparisons to other employees.[38] In contrast, absolute standards can provide more specific feedback to employees concerning their performance, and is generally more acceptable as well.[39]

Finally, although our discussion has tended to focus primarily on task-related behaviors, poor performance can also include other deviant workplace behaviors, depending on the organizational norm one uses as a referent. **Deviant workplace behavior** can be defined as "voluntary behavior that violates significant organizational norms, and in doing so threatens the well-being of an organization, its members, or both" (p. 556).[40] Robinson and Bennett created a typology of deviant workplace behaviors that categorizes deviant behaviors according to their severity (minor versus serious) and the nature of the behavior (organizational or interpersonal). The typology proposes four types of deviant workplace behavior:

1. production deviance (e.g., leaving early, intentionally working slowly)
2. property deviance (e.g., sabotaging equipment, lying about hours worked)
3. political deviance (e.g., showing favoritism, blaming or gossiping about coworkers)
4. personal aggression (e.g., sexual harassment, verbal abuse, endangering or stealing from coworkers)

Recent research suggests that expressions of deviant workplace behavior are related to perceptions of injustice in the workplace, as well as to the ethical climate prevailing in organizations.[41]

## RESPONDING TO POOR PERFORMANCE

Once a supervisor has determined that poor performance has occurred, he or she must diagnose the cause of the deviation and select an appropriate response.[42] One way to do this is to conduct a coaching (or performance) analysis. Before we describe coaching analysis, two issues need to be discussed that affect how it is conducted:

■ Poor performance may have *multiple* causes.

■ The process of *causal attribution* may affect what the supervisor considers an appropriate response.

Poor performance often does not result from a single cause, and the same type of performance problem may be caused by different factors at different times. As discussed in Chapter 2, employee behavior has many causes. These causes may exist within the individual (such as motivation or attitudes), or the organization (such as coworkers or reward systems), or the outside environment (such as social or family events). Solving a performance problem depends on identifying and dealing with the proper cause (or causes) of the problem. For example, if a radiology technician is abrupt with patients because of anxiety over the prospect of being laid off or because of a family crisis, sending the technician to courtesy training will probably not eliminate the problem. Coaching analysis can help the supervisor identify the correct cause or causes of poor performance, and thus help determine the appropriate response.

**Causal attribution theory** describes the process by which people assign causes to their own and others' behavior. Attribution theory suggests that supervisors may use both rational information and biases in determining the cause of employee performance.[43] Weiner suggests that there are four categories of causes of performance, two within the employee (effort and ability) and two in the situation (task difficulty and luck).[44] A response to poor performance will depend on whether a supervisor concludes that the cause of employee performance is within the employee, or is in the situation.

One of the biases that may occur when attempting to find the cause for the employee's behavior is the **fundamental attribution error.** This error is the tendency to overattribute a behavior to a cause within a person (e.g., effort or ability) rather than to the situation (e.g., task difficulty or luck). A supervisor who commits this error is likely to overlook real environmental causes of poor performance and thus blame the employee for poor performance that was not under the employee's control. For example, suppose a manager notices a serious error in a contract drawn up by a subordinate. It could be that a tight time deadline or inadequate information provided by another employee led to the error. A manager who commits the fundamental attribution error will tend to overlook these possibilities and instead try to find a cause within the subordinate, such as laziness or carelessness. This oversight may lead the manager to choose punishment as a response, rather than more correctly focusing on making a change in the environment so the error is unlikely to occur in the future.

In addition, an employee's response to a performance problem may affect the way a supervisor evaluates and responds to it. Employees are likely to attribute their failures to factors beyond their control (e.g., task difficulty, obstacles in the environment), rather than to a lack of ability or effort on their part,[45] thereby seeking to maintain their self-esteem.[46] Furthermore, employees may select feedback-seeking strategies that minimize the amount of negative feedback they receive.[47] When discussing performance problems with supervisors, employees may volunteer information that they hope will deflect the responsibility for poor performance from themselves to the environment, hoping that the supervisor will view the poor performance less negatively.[48] There is some evidence that these attempts at deflecting blame are successful. For example, Gioia and Sims found that supervisors who heard employee explanations for their poor performance saw the employee as less responsible for the performance than before the discussion.[49] In addition, research suggests that supervisors who viewed employees in this way evaluated the employee less negatively and provided less negative performance feedback.[50]

A complete discussion of the attribution process is beyond the scope of this chapter. The main point to be made is that the judgments that supervisors make when diagnosing the causes of poor performance can be affected by biases. This means that the coaching analysis can be adversely affected by such biases. Supervisors should be trained to guard against bias, and to make sure that they correctly identify the cause for poor performance.

## CONDUCTING THE COACHING ANALYSIS

**Coaching analysis** is the process of analyzing the factors that contribute to unsatisfactory performance and deciding on the appropriate response to improve performance. Building on Mager and Pipe's model of performance analysis,[51] Fournies describes a nine-step process designed to identify both the causes of poor performance and possible solutions.[52] In each step, the supervisor answers a question about the performance incident and determines how to proceed. The steps are listed in Table 10-1.

The coaching analysis process is based on the assumption that poor performance can have multiple causes, some of which are within the employee's control and some of which are not. The process leads the supervisor to examine common causes for performance problems. If the answer to a question in the analysis reveals the cause, the supervisor should take the appropriate action and then monitor performance to determine whether it improves. If it does not, the supervisor should continue the analysis until the employee's performance improves. Some of the actions recommended in the coaching analysis process involve HRM and HRD actions such as providing **feedback,** removing obstacles to performance, or providing training. A description of the steps in the process follows:

| **TABLE 10-1** | **STEPS FOR SUPERVISORS TO USE TO CONDUCT A COACHING ANALYSIS CONCERNING EMPLOYEE PERFORMANCE** |
|---|---|

1. Identify the unsatisfactory employee performance.
2. Is it worth your time and effort to address?
3. Do subordinates know that their performance is not satisfactory?
4. Do subordinates know what is supposed to be done?
5. Are there obstacles beyond the employee's control?
6. Does the subordinate know how to do what must be done?
7. Does a negative consequence follow effective performance?
8. Does a positive consequence follow nonperformance?
9. Could the subordinate do it if he or she wanted to?

SOURCE: Fournies, F. F. (1978). *Coaching for improved work performance.* New York: Van Nostrand Reinhold.

*STEP 1: IDENTIFY THE UNSATISFACTORY EMPLOYEE PERFORMANCE.* Coaching cannot begin until the supervisor defines in specific behavioral terms what the employee is doing wrong or failing to do. While this may seem obvious, managers and subordinates are notoriously poor at identifying the specific behavior or performance result that makes up the poor performance.[53] Descriptions such as "She just won't listen" or "He's surly when dealing with customers" do little to provide insight to solve the real problem. A clear, specific description of the problem permits examination of exactly what is occurring and may yield ideas about what is causing it. Furthermore, a supervisor who knows specifically what is happening can better determine whether any action he or she takes improves the situation or worsens it. Without this information, it is impossible to accurately monitor change.

Describing the unsatisfactory performance requires careful observation and recording of a specific behavior or behavioral pattern. For example, if the supervisor is concerned with an employee's tardiness, details of late arrival should be observed and recorded, such as date and time of arrival in each instance. With this information, the supervisor can judge the extent of the problem, determine whether and by how much the employee has violated company policy, and gain insight as to the cause of the problem. When appropriate, multiple sources of data should be used. Information from peers, subordinates, customers, and others (as in *360-degree performance appraisal systems*) may help shed light on exactly what is going on and the effect it is having on performance and outcomes.[54] Information from such sources may need to be gathered at various stages of the coaching analysis, so that the manager can more accurately answer the question at hand.

*STEP 2: IS IT WORTH YOUR TIME AND EFFORT TO ADDRESS?* After the problem has been clearly defined, the supervisor can estimate its severity. At this point, the supervisor must determine whether the performance problem is worth fixing. The problem may not be as bad as was initially thought. For example, after charting an employee's tardiness, the supervisor may realize that the employee is only occasionally late, but this is not a consistent or serious problem. Furthermore, some employee behaviors may be annoying to the supervisor or may not be in keeping with the supervisor's preferences, but do not detract from individual or workgroup performance. For example, a supervisor may prefer that employees not wear perfume or cologne, or may disagree with an employee's political views as related to the company's business (e.g., clean-air policies in a manufacturing plant). The supervisor should identify specifically why he or she considers a problem important.[55] If the so-called problem does not hinder individual, unit, or organizational effectiveness, then the supervisor should ignore it. Spending time and effort on matters that do not affect results, violate important rules or policies, or interfere with coworkers may do nothing more tangible than please the supervisor. If the supervisor indulges in preferences, however, he or she may alienate the employee or waste time that could be better spent managing the things that make a real difference.

*STEP 3: DO SUBORDINATES KNOW THAT THEIR PERFORMANCE IS NOT SATISFACTORY?* One reason employees may perform poorly is that they do not realize that what they are doing constitutes a problem. For example, a shipping clerk may not realize that 10 percent of the orders he ships lack a packing list, especially if he is not provided with performance feedback or evaluation standards. In addition, without feedback, the employee may assume everything is going well and see no reason to change. Therefore, the employee should be asked if he or she realizes that what he or she is doing is wrong. Simply pointing out faulty behavior and requesting correct performance may be enough to solve the problem.

*STEP 4: DO SUBORDINATES KNOW WHAT IS SUPPOSED TO BE DONE?* Not knowing what to do and when to do it may be another reason employees fail to perform correctly. For example, an employee who has never prepared a quarterly quality report or has never seen what a finished quality report looks like is not likely to produce a satisfactory report. In this step of coaching analysis, supervisors should ask employees if they know what they are supposed to be doing. If the employee does not know, the supervisor should explain what is required, or see that the employee receives the necessary training. This may be enough to eliminate the problem performance.

*STEP 5: ARE THERE OBSTACLES BEYOND THE EMPLOYEE'S CONTROL?* Sometimes poor performance is due to factors beyond an employee's control. For example, a loan officer may make a bad loan based on incorrect information provided by the bank itself or because a credit-reporting agency provided the bank with erroneous information. Many times, the supervisor is in a position to remove the obstacles that are causing poor performance. For example, if a supplier is delivering parts late, or the just-in-time delivery system isn't working properly, the supervisor should take steps to correct this. Such actions may result in satisfactory performance.

*STEP 6: DOES THE SUBORDINATE KNOW HOW TO DO WHAT MUST BE DONE?* Many supervisors assume an employee who attends a training or orientation session will have learned the content of the session. As we discussed in Chapter 3, learning is a complex process. Not all training results in learning. It is also possible that if a task is performed infrequently, the employee's skills may become rusty. For example, the first presentation an employee performs after a break of several months is always the toughest. Therefore, employees who have received training may not know, or may have forgotten, how to execute performance correctly. If this is the case, the supervisor should ensure that the employee receives training (and/or opportunities to practice) and that the employee has learned what is needed to perform the task.

*STEP 7: DOES A NEGATIVE CONSEQUENCE FOLLOW EFFECTIVE PERFORMANCE?* It is possible that an employee knows what to do and how to do it, but has learned not to do the behavior because it is always followed by an unpleasant consequence. Recalling our discussion of motivation in Chapter 2, the law of effect states that behavior followed by an aversive consequence will be less likely to occur. Therefore, if effective performance is followed by an aversive consequence, the employee will learn not to perform effectively.

For example, suppose a computer programmer who writes clear documentation is frequently asked by her supervisor to write documentation for other programmers. If the programmer prefers doing other tasks (e.g., writing programs), being asked to write more than her share of documentation would be an aversive consequence to doing this task well. This is especially true if other programmers in the unit get to write less documentation as a result. Therefore, the programmer may change her behavior to avoid this consequence by writing documentation of poorer quality in hopes of being assigned less of it.

Supervisors should attempt to determine whether an unpleasant consequence follows effective behavior. If it does, the supervisor has two alternatives. First, if possible, the aversive consequence should be removed. Returning to our example, if the programmer understands that she will no longer be given other employees' documentation to write if she does her own well, she will likely go back to writing clear documentation. Second, if the aversive consequence cannot be removed (e.g., if it is a part of the task itself), then the supervisor should provide a pleasurable consequence that outweighs the aversive consequence. For example, cleaning restrooms can be an unpleasant but necessary part of the job for custodians. If the supervisor provides custodians who do this part of the job well with a reward, such as being able to leave work early or being given first choice of vacation periods, the custodians will have good reason to perform this part of the job well.

*STEP 8: DOES A POSITIVE CONSEQUENCE FOLLOW NONPERFORMANCE?* Sometimes employees engage in poor performance because a positive consequence follows it. In effect, they are rewarded for poor performance. Sometimes supervisors unwittingly reward poor performance. For example, suppose an employee who doesn't like to work weekends becomes disruptive during weekend shifts. If the supervisor remedies the problem by not assigning the employee to weekend shifts, the supervisor has shown the employee that the way to get what he wants is to be disruptive.

Supervisors should examine poor performance to see what consequence is reinforcing it. The supervisor should then seek to remove the positive consequence for poor performance, and arrange for a positive consequence to follow effective performance instead. This course of action should remove the reason the employee was performing poorly and give the employee a reason to engage in effective performance.

*STEP 9: COULD THE SUBORDINATE DO IT IF HE OR SHE WANTED TO?* Sometimes employees perform poorly because they lack the skills, knowledge, or ability to perform effectively. Some employees will not be effective even after extensive training. If this is the case, then the employee should be transferred to perform work that this employee is capable of doing well, or be terminated from the organization. This is not necessarily all bad for the employee. Some employees are relieved when given a way out of a situation they cannot handle. For example, if a salesperson is uncomfortable using the tactics necessary to close a sale or does not understand the technical nature of the products to be sold, that individual may be better suited to other kinds of work. A better match serves both the organization and the individual.

*ANOTHER QUESTION: CAN THE TASK OR JOB BE MODIFIED?* In addition to the issues just raised, Mager and Pipe suggest that the supervisor should determine whether the task or job could be modified or simplified to increase the chances it will be performed correctly.[56] For example, some tasks, such as maintenance checks, require multiple steps. While it may be reasonable to require that maintenance workers remember all of these steps, an easier way would be to provide them with a job aid, such as a checklist that would be completed each time the worker services a piece of equipment.

*WHAT IF THE PROBLEM PERSISTS?* If the employee is capable of performing effectively and if the coaching analysis has failed to improve performance, then a *coaching discussion* is called for. During this discussion, the employee and supervisor talk over the problem and its causes, and, it is hoped, agree on a course of action to improve performance. The mechanics of this discussion are discussed next.

## THE COACHING DISCUSSION

As stated earlier, the **coaching discussion** is designed to help the employee perform effectively. Such a discussion can be part of the organization's formal performance appraisal system, but can also be used to respond to employee performance issues as they occur. At least two approaches can be used to guide this discussion: a three-stage process recommended by Kinlaw, and a five-step process from Fournies.[57] Because both approaches have merit, we will discuss each.

*THE KINLAW PROCESS.* Kinlaw suggests a three-stage approach to the coaching discussion, as follows:

- confronting or presenting
- using reactions to develop information
- resolving or resolution[58]

The goals of the *confronting* or *presenting stage* are to limit any negative emotion the employee might feel toward the problem situation, to specify the performance to be improved, and to establish that the goal is to help the employee change and improve. Kinlaw argues this can be done by specifically describing the performance that needs to be changed, limiting the discussion to a specific problem behavior, and avoiding assignment of blame by focusing on the future.

After the employee has confronted the problem performance, the supervisor must help the employee examine the causes for poor performance. This is done during the second stage of the discussion, *using reactions to develop information.* Kinlaw notes that employees may resist dealing with the problem after being confronted with it, and argues that supervisors can reduce this resistance by focusing on the employee's concerns rather than their own. The supervisor may then develop information by attending to the employee's explanations, acknowledging important points, probing for information, and summarizing what has been discussed. At the end of this second stage of the coaching discussion, the employee and supervisor should be in a position to agree on the nature of the problem and its causes.

The third and final stage of Kinlaw's coaching discussion is called *resolving* or *resolution*. In this stage, the employee takes ownership of the problem and agrees upon the steps needed to solve it. Both parties at this point express commitment to improving performance and to establishing a positive relationship. This is done by examining alternative courses of action, reviewing key points of the session, and affirming that performance can be successfully improved.

THE FOURNIES PROCESS. Fournies suggests a five-step discussion process that assumes the supervisor has conducted a thorough coaching analysis (as described earlier), and has determined that the employee could perform the task if he or she wanted to.[59] *The goal of the discussion is to get the employee to agree that a problem exists and to commit to a course of action to resolve it.*

**Step 1: Get the employee's agreement that a problem exists.** Unless the employee believes there is a performance problem, he or she will have no reason to change. Phillips has stated that getting an employee to agree that there is a need for improvement is the "Achilles' heel of coaching," and that without this, there is little chance of permanent change.[60] Getting agreement involves describing the problem behavior and its consequences for the supervisor, coworkers, and the employee. Fournies recommends that the supervisor ask the employee questions designed to extract a statement of the problem behavior and its consequences (e.g., "And who has to take your calls when you come back late from lunch?" "What happens if these calls aren't taken?"). This approach ensures that the employee understands the situation.

   This first step ends when the employee explicitly agrees that a problem exists. This step may consume as much as 50 percent of the time taken for the coaching discussion, but Fournies is adamant that the discussion should not go forward without explicit agreement from the employee that a problem does indeed exist. At this point, Fournies asserts most employees will commit themselves to changing the behavior. But in dealing with those who will not, the supervisor must decide whether to (1) drop the problem as one not worth pursuing or (2) take disciplinary action. A supervisor who has already done the coaching analysis should have determined that the problem is important. If not, the supervisor is paying the price for not doing the necessary homework and will be faced with having to back out of a messy situation. In our view, employees who do not agree at this point that a problem exists should be handled according to the organization's disciplinary policies (e.g., with warnings, letters to file, suspension with or without pay). It is hoped that the disciplined employee will realize the consequences of his or her actions and agree to help resolve the performance problem. If not, the supervisor can feel that a good-faith effort to resolve the problem has been made and can view the prospect of removing the employee — by transfer or termination — as the necessary action it is.

**Step 2: Mutually discuss alternative solutions to the problem.** During this part of the discussion, the supervisor asks the employee for alternatives to solving the problem. If necessary, the supervisor should prompt the employee for ideas. Fournies believes that employees will more likely be committed to alternatives that they have suggested. The supervisor's role during this part of the discussion is to help the employee come up with and clarify alternatives.

**Step 3: Mutually agree on actions to be taken to solve the problem.** After sufficient alternatives have been discussed, the supervisor and employee can agree on which alternatives to pursue to solve the problem. At this point, both the employee and the supervisor should clearly understand what will be done and when it will happen. They should also agree on a specific time to follow up on the discussion to determine whether the agreed-upon actions have been taken. Fournies also suggests that the supervisor thank the employee for making an effort to solve the problem and express confidence that it will be solved.

**Step 4: *Follow up to measure results.*** It is imperative that the supervisor follows up at the arranged time to determine whether the agreed-upon actions have been taken and the problem is resolved. Without follow-up, the supervisor will not know what has happened, and the employee may conclude that the supervisor really doesn't care about the problem. As obvious as this step may seem, we find that it is often easy for busy supervisors to overlook it.

**Step 5: *Recognize achievements when they occur.*** Many performance problems will not disappear overnight. Even if a problem is not completely eliminated, the employee should be recognized for any effort and improvement made. The idea is to motivate the worker to further improvement. When necessary, further discussions should be held to determine additional steps needed to resolve the problem. Follow-up, recognition of improvement, and updated improvement planning should continue until the employee is performing effectively.

If the employee is unwilling to improve performance and fails to take action as agreed, the supervisor must decide whether to live with the problem, transfer the employee, or pursue employee termination. Not all performance problems can be successfully resolved through coaching.

*AN ANALYSIS AND SYNTHESIS OF THE TWO APPROACHES.* Kinlaw and Fournies have much in common in their approaches to the coaching discussion. Both emphasize the need to get employees to verbally accept responsibility for improving performance and to involve them in developing the courses of action needed to solve the problem. They differ most in terms of the assumptions made about employee willingness to address performance problems. Kinlaw highlights the emotional aspect of discussing performance problems with employees and offers more guidance to supervisors in how to deal with employees' emotions and resistance. Fournies places more emphasis on the rational, in that he maintains that an employee faced with evidence of a performance problem and its consequences will generally be willing to deal with it. He states that employee unwillingness must either be based on the supervisor doing an insufficient job of analyzing the performance (e.g., not dealing with a specific behavior, dealing with an unimportant behavior, the employee's disbelief that the supervisor or organization will actually do anything about poor performance), or that the subordinate is engaging in self-destructive behavior.[61]

We believe that both approaches offer constructive ways to discuss performance problems and that a supervisor can benefit from adopting either approach, or some combination of the two. One point that neither approach makes clear is the importance of *setting specific goals* for performance improvement. While this is implicit in each approach (e.g., agreeing on what will be done and when), we believe that the supervisor and subordinate must agree upon a clearly stated performance goal before generating alternative solutions to the problem. As mentioned in Chapter 2,

PART 3: HUMAN RESOURCE DEVELOPMENT APPLICATIONS

| TABLE 10-2 | STEPS FOR SUPERVISORS TO USE TO CONDUCT A COACHING DISCUSSION AND FOLLOW-UP |
|---|---|

1. Identify the employee performance issue to be discussed. Be specific, factual, respectful, and supportive in presenting this issue to the employee.
2. Seek the employee's reaction and response to the supervisor's presentation of the performance issue.
3. Seek out the employee's agreement that a performance problem exists.
4. Mutually discuss alternative solutions to the issue.
5. Mutually agree on goals to set, actions that will be taken, and the follow-up plan that will be used to resolve this issue.
6. Follow up on this issue at the agreed-upon time and in the agreed-upon way.
7. Recognize and reward employee improvements and achievements as they occur.

research has shown convincingly that specific performance goals lead to performance improvement. Establishing a performance goal can also provide a focus for the later steps of the discussion, where discussion of alternatives, an action plan, and follow-up are covered. Our synthesis of the steps to an effective coaching discussion is presented in Table 10-2.

*WHAT IF THE COACHING DISCUSSION FAILS?* There is no guarantee that the coaching process will resolve all performance problems. Some employees are unable or unwilling to improve performance even after being given an opportunity to do so. If the employee is unable to improve, the supervisor should either transfer the employee to work he or she can perform effectively or terminate the employee. If the employee is unwilling to improve performance, the supervisor should discipline the employee according to the organization's policies (and if that fails, pursue termination). One potential advantage of the coaching process is that it provides the employee with a fair opportunity to recognize performance that is poor and take steps to improve it. If termination is the only choice left to the supervisor after coaching fails, then the supervisor should have adequate documentation to justify the termination and withstand challenges by the employee of unfair treatment.

## MAINTAINING EFFECTIVE PERFORMANCE AND ENCOURAGING SUPERIOR PERFORMANCE

Supervisors and managers should be interested not only in eliminating poor performance but also in ensuring that good performers remain effective or become even better. This means they should reward effective performance and provide employees who want to become superior performers with the necessary support and opportunity. Motivational approaches, including **goal setting,** job redesign, employee participation programs, and the like, are ways of increasing employees' sense of ownership of their performance, thereby encouraging them to remain successful.

Coaching can also be an effective way to encourage and enhance effective performance. Evered and Selman suggest that managers must create an environment that acknowledges employee contributions to the organization and empowers them to move forward.[62] Managerial supportiveness, availability, and willingness to work with employees will create an environment where employees will demand coaching from their managers because they will be energized to improve. This is important because if the employee does not have the desire to improve, the coaching discussion will likely be perceived negatively, and the employee will resist the manager's efforts.

The manager-coach can provide employees with a unique perspective on employee performance.[63] Because it is difficult to observe oneself while performing a task, it is often difficult for employees to know exactly how they are doing during performance. The manager-coach can observe the employee, describe specifically what the employee is doing and how he or she is doing it, and then make suggestions for improvement. For example, a sales manager can accompany an employee on several sales calls to develop a complete description of the employee's approach to selling. The employee and sales manager can then review the description and discuss ways the employee can overcome problems, build on strengths, and try new approaches. This approach to coaching effective employees is similar to Peters and Austin's idea of "skill stretching"[64] and is an essential element of achieving expert-level performance.[65] Xerox Corporation has included coaching as an integral part of its sales training efforts. Its focus is on providing managers the tools they need to coach, and on creating a partnership between the salespeople and their managers to improve sales performance.[66]

Evered and Selman (and others, such as H. Peters) stress that communication and partnership are vital to effective coaching.[67] An employee who does not invite coaching may resent the manager's efforts and feel threatened or insulted. Instead of seeing the manager's actions as helpful, the employee will feel the manager is trying to monitor and control him or her.

Another way to encourage continued effective performance through coaching is to communicate and reinforce the organization's values. Peters and Austin call this aspect of coaching **value shaping**.[68] Value shaping begins with the recruitment and orientation of new employees and is continued through training and in the manner that the manager relates to employees every day. According to Peters and Austin, a manager must reinforce organizational values through recognition, storytelling, and work relationships, and never compromise in adherence to those values. They argue that values can serve as guides for behavior that help employees know what is expected and how to behave even in novel situations. Obviously, value shaping can only occur if the organization has a strong corporate culture and a clear set of values to begin with.

## SKILLS NECESSARY FOR EFFECTIVE COACHING

The skills needed to be an effective coach can be grouped into two categories: communication and interpersonal skills. **Communication skills** are essential for effective coaching. Unless a manager has the ability both to listen to employees and to get them to understand what effective performance is and how to achieve it, coaching will not succeed.

Fournies takes a more behavioral tack than others, and argues that the only way a manager knows whether an employee understands what has been said is if the employee restates it.[69] The process of getting employees to state what the problem performance is, why it is a problem, and what they are going to do to remedy the problem, and then having the manager express his or her agreement with what the employee has said, is called thought transmission.

In addition to active listening, managers need to be *specific and descriptive* in communicating with employees.[70] This can increase the chance that the employee will understand what is expected and will offer less resistance to coaching. If a coach is descriptive rather than evaluative, the employee will realize that the coach is trying to help him or her, rather than place blame.

An approach called microtraining can be used to train managers and supervisors in the communication skills necessary for effective coaching.[71] This approach, which has proven effective in developing face-to-face communication skills, isolates the specific verbal and nonverbal skills that make up effective communication, and then trains participants in each skill.[72] The skills developed in the microtraining approach that are relevant to coaching include basic attending skills (e.g., maintaining eye contact), feedback, paraphrasing, reflection of feeling, open and closed questions, and focusing. A list of these skills and the components that are taught in the program is provided in Table 10-3.

In addition to communication skills, interpersonal skills are also important to effective coaching. These **interpersonal skills** include:

1. indicating respect
2. immediacy (i.e., focusing on the present; dealing with problems as they occur)[73]
3. objectivity (i.e., emphasizing factual information over subjective opinion)
4. planning
5. affirming (i.e., commenting on the employee's successes and positive prospects for improvement)
6. consistency of behavior
7. building trust
8. demonstrating integrity[74]

Concerning point 7, the building of trust, a literature review found that managers were more likely to be viewed as trustworthy by their subordinates when managers demonstrated concern for their employees, behaved consistently, demonstrated behavioral integrity, shared control with employees, and provided accurate and open communication.[75] Notice the overlap here with the points listed previously (especially points 3, 5, 6, and 8). This suggests that many of the same skills required for effective coaching also serve to increase the interpersonal trust between managers and employees. Finally, it is vitally important to emphasize that managers must *demonstrate commitment to and respect for the employee*.[76] An employee who believes that his or her manager is genuinely interested in and cares about him or her is more likely to seek out coaching and make an honest effort to improve.

| TABLE 10-3 | THE SIX SKILLS OF MICROTRAINING IN FACE-TO-FACE COMMUNICATION |

1. **Basic attending skills** to help involve the employee in the discussion. These include:

   a. a slight, but comfortable, forward lean of the upper body and trunk

   b. maintaining eye contact

   c. speaking in a warm but natural voice

   d. using sufficient encouragers (e.g., head nods, saying yes, and uh-huh)

   e. staying on the topic

2. **Feedback**

   a. providing clear and concrete data

   b. using a nonjudgmental attitude

   c. using timely, present-tense statements (e.g., "Max, I just made some suggestions for how you can present your ideas more clearly. But you don't seem interested. How can I help you improve your presentations?" as opposed to, "Your last four presentations were disasters. I won't tolerate another one.")

   d. providing feedback that deals with correctable items over which the employee has some control

3. **Paraphrasing** a concise restatement, in your own words, of what the employee has just said. Paraphrasing helps clarify the issue, lets the employee know you understand what has been said, and encourages him or her to continue. Paraphrases should be nonjudgmental and matter-of-fact.

4. **Reflection of feeling** reinforces the employee for expressing feelings and encourages open communication. Identifying and recognizing an employee's feelings can help the supervisor establish a closer rapport. Reflections of feeling have a structure:

   a. employee's name or pronoun

   b. stem (e.g., "It sounds as if you feel . . .")

   c. label for the emotion

   d. final stem to check whether you understood employee correctly (e.g., "Am I right?")

   An example: "Maria, you seem very nervous about working in front of others. Would you like to talk about that?"

5. **Open and closed questions** to support your purpose.

   a. Open questions (e.g., those beginning with How, Would, Could, or Why) encourage employees to talk and share their ideas (e.g., "Why do you think that is?").

   b. Closed questions (e.g., those beginning with Did, Is, Are, or How many) invite a response of a few words, which can be used to clarify, identify specific points, and speed the discussion (e.g., "Did you close the sale?").

6. **Focusing** helps identify potential areas of organizational difficulty (person, problem, context, other, and self) and ways to deal with each.

SOURCE: Kikoski, J. F., & Litterer, J. A. (1983). Effective communication in the performance appraisal interview. *Public Personnel Management Journal, 12,* 33–42. Adapted by permission.

PART 3: HUMAN RESOURCE DEVELOPMENT APPLICATIONS

HRD staff members can design and conduct programs to help managers and supervisors develop and practice these skills. Training programs that use role playing and behavior modeling have been effectively used to build the skills needed for effective coaching. For example, Weyerhaeuser Company's coaching training program uses a combination of modeling films, role-playing activities, and workbook exercises to teach coaching skills.[77] Silverman describes a two-day performance-appraisal training program called ADEPT (Appraising and Developing Employee Performance Training) that includes a module on diagnosing and coaching employee performance.[78] The module teaches participants how to identify performance problems, diagnose causes, and reach agreement on steps to be taken to solve the problems using two video scenes and a role-play exercise. It also teaches participants to give positive reinforcement to effective employees.[79] Firms such as Allstate Insurance, Goodyear Tire and Rubber, and Ohio Edison have used ADEPT.[80]

## THE EFFECTIVENESS OF COACHING

A recent study of the use of coaching and behavioral management techniques in a manufacturing organization found that the feedback and coaching led to increased employee satisfaction and commitment, and reduced turnover intentions.[81] Overall, though, there is not a large empirical literature that directly addresses the effectiveness of coaching as a way to improve poor performance and encourage and enhance effective performance. Could it be that managers and professionals see the effectiveness of coaching as self-evident? ("Of course it works. Why test it?"). However, research on the performance appraisal interview (which has much in common with coaching) clearly demonstrates the effectiveness of many aspects of the coaching discussion.

The **performance appraisal interview** is a meeting between a supervisor and subordinate in which the supervisor reviews the evaluation of an employee's performance and seeks to help the employee maintain and improve performance. While some aspects of the performance appraisal discussion are not relevant to coaching (e.g., timing of the discussion, discussion of salary or promotions), many of the techniques used in coaching are also used in the performance-improvement portion of the appraisal interview or performance review session. In this section, we provide a sampling of the findings from empirical research on the performance appraisal interview that are relevant to the effectiveness of coaching.

### EMPLOYEE PARTICIPATION IN DISCUSSION

Studies have addressed the extent to which providing employees an opportunity to contribute during the discussion affects discussion outcomes. Research shows that the more an employee participates, the greater is the employee's satisfaction with the discussion and the manager, and the more likely it is that performance goals will be met.[82] Positive outcomes (e.g., feeling the supervisor is more helpful and constructive) have also been demonstrated when supervisors explicitly welcome employee participation during the discussion.[83] Employees are more likely to participate when they perceive that the threat from the supervisor is low.[84] Finally, subordinates see the performance discussion as fairer when they are given a chance for two-way communication, especially when they are given the opportunity to challenge or rebut their evaluation.[85]

## BEING SUPPORTIVE

Supportiveness is one of the recurring themes in the coaching literature. The extent to which the supervisor is helpful and supportive has been shown to affect employee acceptance of the performance evaluation and satisfaction with the manager.[86] Managerial supportiveness has also been shown to be associated with higher levels of employee motivation.[87] Furthermore, when employees perceive that the supervisor has constructive reasons for providing performance feedback, they are less likely to show anxiety and are more likely to see the feedback as valuable.[88]

## USING CONSTRUCTIVE CRITICISM

Advocates of coaching urge managers to adopt a descriptive, nonjudgmental approach and offer feedback that is specific and factual. Criticism during the performance appraisal interview has been shown to lead to high levels of anxiety.[89] Furthermore, a series of studies investigating the effects of destructive criticism (i.e., feedback that is delivered inconsiderately, that is vague, or that attributes poor performance to internal causes) has demonstrated that destructive criticism:

- increases employee anger and tension
- leads employees to intend to handle further disagreements with resistance and avoidance
- leads employees to set lower goals and report lower self-efficacy
- is cited by employees as an important cause of conflict[90]

Employees will accept some criticism, but it must be specific and behaviorally focused.[91]

## SETTING PERFORMANCE GOALS DURING DISCUSSION

Setting goals during the performance discussion leads to positive outcomes, such as satisfaction with the discussion,[92] perceived fairness and accuracy of feedback,[93] and perceived utility of feedback.[94] As was cited earlier, setting specific goals has been clearly shown to lead to positive behavioral change.[95]

## TRAINING AND THE SUPERVISOR'S CREDIBILITY

Training supervisors to discuss performance with employees has been shown to be important to the performance discussion.[96] Further, when employees perceive the supervisor as credible (e.g., knowledgeable about the employee's job and performance), they are more likely to accept the supervisor's evaluation,[97] perceive the feedback as accurate, perceive the supervisor as more helpful, and report that they intend to use the feedback.[98]

## ORGANIZATIONAL SUPPORT

There needs to be strong organization-wide support for coaching and performance management. In particular, senior management must be active in their support, as compared to passively tolerating such efforts.[99] Further, the coaching and performance management system must be linked to the organization's strategy, mission, and values. According to Grote, "the performance management system is the primary driver for ensuring that [an organization's] mission, vision, and strategy are achieved" (p. 19).[100] This includes clear linkages to the organization's compensation and rewards system.[101]

## CLOSING COMMENTS ON COACHING AND PERFORMANCE MANAGEMENT

Taken together, research on performance appraisal supports the effectiveness of many of the components used in coaching, as we have described it in this chapter.[102] Thus, it appears that coaching can indeed be an effective way to manage employee performance. Having the employee participate in the discussion, setting goals for improvement, offering specific, behavioral feedback, being supportive and helpful, training supervisors, and ensuring the supervisor is knowledgeable about the employee's job and performance are all related to positive outcomes. Table 10-4 lists some recommendations for organizations and HRD professionals seeking to ensure the effectiveness of coaching as part of a well-run performance management system.

| TABLE 10-4 | RECOMMENDATIONS TO PROMOTE EFFECTIVE COACHING |

For coaching to be most effective, top managers and HRD professionals must ensure that:

1. An effective performance management system is operating within the organization (see Table 10-5). Among other things, this means that the organization's recognition and rewards system properly rewards managers and supervisors for effective coaching.
2. All managers and supervisors are properly trained in coaching skills and techniques.
3. A thorough coaching analysis has been done before employee performance issues are discussed with employees.
4. Supervisors prepare in advance for the coaching discussion.
5. Supervisor comments are constructive, helpful, and supportive.
6. Supervisors provide specific and behavioral feedback on employee performance.
7. Employees are involved in the coaching discussion.
8. Specific goals are set during the discussion.
9. An action plan is jointly established between the employee and the supervisor.
10. Coaching discussions are followed up, to ensure that the employee is following the action plan, and to recognize performance improvements when they occur.

| TABLE 10-5 | RECOMMENDATIONS FOR EFFECTIVE PERFORMANCE MANAGEMENT SYSTEMS |
|---|---|

For performance management systems to be most effective, it is recommended that:

1. The system must reflect the organization's culture and values.
2. Senior management must be committed to, and actively participate in, the performance management system.
3. The system should focus on the most important (or "vital few") performance measures.
4. Employee job descriptions should be linked to the performance management system.
5. Managers need to differentiate between employee performance levels, yet do so in a fair and objective manner.
6. Managers need thorough training in all aspects of the performance management process (evaluating, goal setting, giving feedback, coaching, linking to rewards; see Table 10-4).
7. The performance management system needs to be linked to the organizational compensation and rewards system.
8. There should be clear expectations and action planning concerning employee development (coming out of the performance management process).
9. The administrative burden should be minimized (e.g., via "e-HR").
10. The effectiveness of the performance management system should be regularly tracked, with adjustments to the system made as necessary.

SOURCES: Lawler, E. E., III, & McDermott, M. (2003). Current performance management practices: Examining the varying impacts. *WorldatWork Journal, 12*(2), 49–60; O'Neill, C., & Holsinger, L. (2003). Effective performance management systems: 10 key design principles. *WorldatWork Journal, 12*(2), 61–67; Weatherly, L. A. (2004). Performance management: Getting it right from the start. *2004 SHRM Research Quarterly*, March, retrieved October 28, 2004, from http://www. shrm.org/research/quarterly/0401perfmanagement.asp

Table 10-5 lists recommendations for the performance management system as a whole. However, while we at present have some confidence concerning the effectiveness of coaching and performance management, further research devoted specifically to these topics will help to establish these conclusions more firmly.[103] For an interesting case study on the effectiveness of coaching in a challenging organizational environment, see the boxed insert nearby, "Coaching for Change in a Difficult Environment."

We close this chapter with a quote from James Waldroop and Timothy Butler. They end their article, "The Executive as Coach," with the following comments:

> Successful executives often tell us that when they were in business school, they considered the quantitative "hard" subjects, such as finance and operations management, to be the most important topics they studied; they had little respect for the "soft" subjects, such as organizational behavior and human resources management. Fifteen or 20 years later, however, those same executives recognize that it is their people management skills — working with and developing people — that have been the key to both their personal success and to that of their business. Being an effective coach is one essential part of that key to success."[104]

## Coaching for Change in a Difficult Environment

Peter Clute describes a major change effort that took place at an oil refinery in the mid-western United States. This refinery was part of an international oil company. There were approximately 500 employees at this site, with roughly 300 represented by a labor union. This particular plant was described as a "difficult place to work," "uncooperative with other units," "mediocre in terms of operating standards," and having a workforce that was "stubborn and resistant to change." Given all this, it was viewed as a "marginal asset" within the corporation's overall business portfolio. This meant that its future was precarious.

A major change effort was undertaken from 1996–1998, based upon Peter Senge's principles concerning learning organizations (see Chapter 1). This change effort, entitled the Pacesetter Project, was particularly challenging, as two earlier change efforts had been attempted (and resisted) in 1990 and 1993, and members of this refinery had a "high degree of cynicism about anything that looked like a culture-change process" (organizational change will be discussed further in Chapter 14).

Mr. Clute had worked previously as an organization development consultant for this oil company and was hired as a learning leader for the project at this refinery. Two consultants from a consulting firm were also assigned to work on this project. A number of changes were made over an eighteen-month period to improve overall performance at the refinery. Part of this included involving the local union leadership in the design and implementation of the overall change effort (in the past, the relationship between management and the union had been adversarial).

Another aspect of the change effort wa[s] personal coaching provided to the facility['s] business unit manager by Mr. Clute. A partic[ular] emphasis was the manner in which thi[s] manager conducted "town hall" meetings i[n] the facility. For example, at a dinner for sixt[y] influential individuals at the plant to kick of[f] the Pacesetter Project, the manager wa[s] videotaped in his presentation, for purpose[s] of providing him with feedback as to how h[e] was communicating. According to Clute, "this set a visible example of 'If the boss i[s] willing to learn how to be better, we can lear[n] how to be better.'"

A number of other aspects were part of thi[s] change effort. However, Clute concludes tha[t] one of the main lessons in this case was tha[t] "coaching worked." The unit manager was re[-]ceptive and willing to learn and in fac[t] changed his behavior as a result of this inten[-]sive coaching effort. The local union leade[r] commented on improvements in communica[-]tion from management, as well as an in[-]creased level of trust between managemen[t] and the union. In terms of refinery perfor[-]mance, there was a marked improvement i[n] safety, operational performance, and prof[-]itability in 1997 and 1998. Anecdotal evidenc[e] attested to a dramatic change in the mind-se[t] and attitudes of most refinery employees.

While not every coaching project an[d] change effort ends so successfully, this articl[e] highlights the power of coaching to brin[g] about positive behavioral change, and con[-]tribute to a turnaround at a troubled oi[l] refinery.

Clute, P. W. (1999). Change at an oil refinery: Toward the creation of a learning organization. *Human Resource Planning, 22*(2), 24–38.

### RETURN TO OPENING CASE

Both of these scenarios are based on actual situations faced by executive com-munications consultant Merna Skinner. Skinner argues that all managers need to understand their own dominant style of communicating, and that a guided self-discovery process is needed to assist managers in doing this. Your instructor has additional information concerning what was done in each of these situations.

Skinner, M. (2000). Training managers to be better communicators. *Employment Relations Today, 27*(1), 73–81.

## SUMMARY

One of a manager's primary responsibilities is to ensure that employees perform their tasks effectively. Many managers choose to notice only poor performance and attempt to remedy it using threats and punishment. Performance management is an ongoing process that emphasizes employee goal setting, coaching, rewards, and individual development. It is more than just a new name for the performance appraisal process.[105] Organizations are increasingly using online systems to manage both the evaluative and the developmental aspects of performance management.[106] It has also been argued that performance management practices provide the needed link between employee and organizational performance.[107]

In this chapter, we emphasized the coaching, goal setting, and feedback aspects of performance management. Coaching can be viewed as a positive problem-solving approach to performance management that requires managers to enter into a partnership with employees. Managers who are effective coaches are more knowledgeable about employee performance and can help employees adjust to changes in goals, tasks, and expectations.

Coaching is defined as the process a manager or supervisor uses to encourage employees to accept responsibility for performance, enable them to achieve (and sustain) superior performance, and treat them as partners in working toward organizational goals. It involves both analyzing performance and conducting discussions with employees to solve performance problems and determine ways to enhance performance.

A coaching or performance analysis involves clearly defining a performance problem, examining the factors that affect poor performance, and determining the action required to ensure effective performance. Some of the factors that are examined in a coaching analysis include the importance of the behavior in question, whether employees know their performance is unsatisfactory and know what should be done about it, the presence of environmental obstacles to effective performance, the consequences of both effective and ineffective performance, and the employee's ability to perform the required tasks.

The chapter presents two main views of the coaching discussion. In Kinlaw's three-stage approach, the supervisor confronts the employee and presents the performance problem, uses the employee's reactions to develop information about possible causes and solutions, and agrees with the employee about what will be done to solve the problem. The Fournies approach involves getting the employee to agree that a problem exists, discussing alternative solutions, agreeing on actions to be taken, following up to measure results, and recognizing achievements. A synthesis of these two approaches was also presented. Coaching to maintain effective performance and encourage superior performance should focus, in part, on increasing the employee's sense of ownership of performance.

Coaching draws upon a supervisor's skills in analyzing employee performance and in using effective communication and interpersonal skills, including objectivity, immediacy, indicating respect, affirming, building trust, and demonstrating integrity. Training programs that use role playing and behavioral modeling can help supervisors and managers acquire these skills. The most effective coaching is likely to take place within a well-functioning performance management system. Recommendations for such systems were also presented.

## KEY TERMS AND CONCEPTS

causal attribution theory
coaching
coaching analysis
coaching discussion
communication skills
deviant workplace behavior
feedback
fundamental attribution error

goal setting
interpersonal skills
participative management
performance appraisal
performance appraisal interview
performance management
poor performance
value shaping

## QUESTIONS FOR DISCUSSION

1. What is meant by the term *performance management,* and how is this different from the performance appraisal practices that are common in many organizations?

2. Why is it important to coach employees with performance problems, as well as employees who are performing well?

3. Imagine that you are an HRD professional who has just finished conducting a training program for a group of supervisors at an air-conditioner manufacturing plant. When you ask if there are any questions, one of the supervisors says, "You seem so good at this coaching business. Why can't you coach my people for me?" How would you respond to that supervisor? Support your reasoning.

4. Describe the things that are necessary in order to define poor performance. What do you feel is difficult about defining performance as poor? Make one practical recommendation that you believe could make this task easier for managers. Support your choice.

5. Think about the last time you had a problem with your own performance, either on the job or in one of your classes. Using the nine-step performance analysis model from Fournies, try to identify the cause or causes of this problem, and state what you think could be done to correct it.

6. Many managers and supervisors find coaching difficult to do or are reluctant to do it. What do you believe are at least two important reasons for this? How do you think the obstacles you identify can be overcome?

7. During the coaching discussion, explain why it is necessary for the supervisor to get the employee to verbally agree that a performance problem exists.

8. Suppose you are a restaurant manager who is conducting a coaching discussion with one of your servers about the server's repeated failure to complete store-closing operations before leaving for the night. You have conducted a coaching analysis and have determined that the server is able to complete these responsibilities, that all obstacles to doing so have been removed, and that this is an important part of a server's job in your restaurant. Describe how you would get the server to agree that a problem exists, and what you would do if the server refuses to acknowledge that a problem exists. Describe the options available to you in dealing with this situation. Which option would you select? Support your choice.

9. In addition to coaching, what other aspects do you think are necessary for an organization to have an effective performance management system? Why?

## EXERCISE: DESIGN YOUR OWN PERFORMANCE MANAGEMENT SYSTEM

Assume that you are part of a task force charged with making changes to your organization's performance management system. Your organization currently requires that supervisors conduct annual performance appraisals for all of their employees. A rating form is completed and signed by both the supervisor and employee after the appraisal interview has been completed. Unfortunately, there has been very little guidance given to supervisors concerning how to conduct these interviews, or concerning what should be done after they have been completed. There seems to be very little consistency across supervisors as to the extent to which they include goal setting, coaching, and employee development issues in their appraisal interviews. Although the stated objectives for appraisals are that they should be linked to the organization's rewards system, there is no formal means for doing this, either.

*Your task*: Consider the following topics: annual appraisal ratings, appraisal interviews, feedback, goal setting, coaching, linkages to employee development, and linkages to organizational rewards. Using as many of these elements as you wish, design what you think would be an effective performance management system. If pressed to pick three topics or areas that you think are *most* important to do well, which topics would you emphasize? Why?

Visit http://werner.swlearning.com for links to informative websites for this chapter.

## REFERENCES

1. Scott, M. (2000). Seven pitfalls for managers when handling poor performers and how to overcome them. *Manage*, February, 12–13.

2. Geber, B. (1992). From manager into coach. *Training, 29*(2), 25–31; Kiechel, W., III (1991, November 4). The boss as coach. *Fortune*, pp. 201, 204; Latham, G. P. (1995). Whither

industrial and organizational psychology in a changing world of work? *American Psychologist, 50,* 928–939; Waldroop, J., & Butler, T. (2000). The executive as coach. *Harvard Business Review,* November-December, 111–117.

3. Bohlander, G., & Snell, S. (2004). *Managing human resources* (13th ed.). Cincinnati: Thomson/South-Western.

4. Gosselin, A., Werner, J. M., & Hallé, N. (1997). Ratee preferences concerning performance management and appraisal. *Human Resource Development Quarterly, 8,* 315–333.

5. Rice, B. (1985, September, 30–36). Performance review: The job nobody likes. *Psychology Today;* Longenecker, C. O., & Goff, S. J. (1990). Why performance appraisals still fail. *Journal of Compensation and Benefits, 6*(3), November/December, 36–41.

6. Markle, G. L. (2000). *Catalytic coaching: The end of the performance review.* Westport, CT: Quorum Books.

7. Grote, D. (2000). The secrets of performance appraisal. *Across the Board, 37*(5), May, 14–20.

8. Bates, S. (2003). Performance appraisals: Some improvement needed. *HR Magazine, 48*(4), April, 12.

9. Schneier, C. E., Shaw, D. D., & Beatty, R. W. (1991). Performance measurement and management: A tool for strategy execution. *Human Resource Management, 30,* 279–301; Rogers, R. W., Miller, L. P., & Worklan, J. (1993). *Performance management: What's hot, what's not.* Pittsburgh, PA: Developmental Dimensions International.

10. Cardy, R. L. (2004). *Performance management: Concepts, skills, and exercises.* Armonk, NY: M. E. Sharpe; Lawler, E. E., III, & McDermott, M. (2003). Current performance management practices: Examining the varying impacts. *WorldatWork Journal, 12*(2), 49–60; The benefits of performance management (1998). *Worklife Report, 11*(2), 10–12.

11. Gosselin, Werner, & Hallé (1997), *supra* note 4.

12. Wellins, R., & Rioux, S. (2000). The growing pains of globalizing HR. *Training & Development, 54*(5), 79–85.

13. Lawler, E. E., III (2003). Reward practices and performance management system effectiveness. *Organizational Dynamics, 32*(4), 396–404; Kerr, S. (1999). Organizational rewards: Practical, cost-neutral alternatives that you may know, but don't practice. *Organizational Dynamics, 28*(1), 61–70; Taylor, P. J., & Pierce, J. L. (1999). Effects of introducing a performance management system on employees' subsequent attitudes and effort. *Public Personnel Management, 28*(3), 423–452; Stivers, B. P., & Joyce, T. (2000). Building a balanced performance management system. *Advanced Management Journal, 65*(2), 22–29; Heneman, R. L., & Thomas, A. L. (1997). The Limited, Inc.: Using strategic performance management to drive brand leadership. *Compensation & Benefits Review, 27*(6), 33–40.

14. O'Neill, C., & Holsinger, L. (2003). Effective performance management systems: 10 key design principles. *WorldatWork Journal, 12*(2), 61–67; Gagne, K. (2002). Using performance management to support an organization's strategic business plan. *Employment Relations Today, 28*(4), 53–59; Schneier, Shaw, & Beatty (1991), *supra* note 8; Heneman & Thomas (1997), *supra* note 12.

15. Gilley, J. W., Boughton, N. W., & Maycunich, A. (1999). *The performance challenge: Developing management systems to make employees your organization's greatest asset.* Reading, MA: Perseus Books.

16. Gagne (2002), *supra* note 14; U.S. workers give performance management programs a failing grade. (2004). *PA Times, 27*(5), May, 13.

17. Fournies, F. F. (1978). *Coaching for improved work performance.* New York: Van Nostrand Reinhold.

18. Kinlaw, D. (1989). *Coaching for commitment: Managerial strategies for obtaining superior performance* (p. 31). San Diego, CA: University Associates, Inc.

19. Kirkpatrick, D. L. (1982). *How to improve performance through appraisal and coaching.* New York: AMACOM; Zemke, R. (1996). The corporate coach. *Training, 33*(12), 24–28.

20. Riley, P. (1994). *The winner within: A life plan for team players.* New York: Berkley Publishing Group.

21. Shula, D., & Blanchard, K. (1995). *Everyone's a coach: You can inspire any one to be a winner.* New York: HarperBusiness.

22. Evered, R. D., & Selman, J. C. (1990). Coaching and the art of management. *Organizational Dynamics, 18*(2), 16–32.

23. Peters, T., & Austin, N. (1985). *A passion for excellence: The leadership difference.* New York: Random House.

24. *Ibid.*

25. Gilley, J. W., & Boughton, N. W. (1996). *Stop managing and start coaching! How performance coaching can enhance commitment and improve productivity.* Chicago: Irwin Professional Publishing.

26. Kinlaw (1989), *supra* note 16.

27. Waldroop & Butler (1996), *supra* note 2.

28. Olesen, M. (1996). Coaching today's executives. *Training & Development, 50* (3), 22–27.

29. Hellervik, L. W., Hazucha, J. F., & Schneider, R. J. (1992). Behavior change: Models, methods, and a review of evidence. In M. D. Dunnette & L. M. Hough (Eds.), *Handbook of industrial and organizational psychology* (2nd ed., Vol. 3, pp. 823–895). Palo Alto, CA: Consulting Psychologists Press.

30. Fournies (1978), *supra* note 15; Evered & Selman (1990), *supra* note 20.

31. Fournies (1978), *supra* note 15.

32. Fournies (1978), *supra* note 15; Kinlaw (1989), *supra* note 16.

33. Kinlaw, D. C. (2000). Encourage superior performance from people and teams through coaching. *Women in Business, 52*(1), January/February, 38–41.

34. Geber (1992), *supra* note 2; Wellins, R. S., Byham, W. C., & Wilson, J. M. (1991). *Empowered teams: Creating self-directed work groups that improve quality, productivity, and participation.* San Francisco: Jossey-Bass.

35. Weatherly, L. A. (2004). Performance management: Getting it right from the start. *2004 SHRM Research Quarterly*, March, retrieved October 28, 2004, from http://www.shrm.org/research/quarterly/0401perfmanagement.asp; Gilley, Boughton, & Maycunich (1999), *supra* note 14.

36. Viega, J. F. (1988). Face your problem subordinates now! *Academy of Management Executive, 2,* 145–152.

37. Mitchell, T. R., & O'Reilly, C. A. (1983). Managing poor performance and productivity in organizations. *Research in Personnel and Human Resources Management, 1,* 201–234.

38. Bates, S. (2003). Forced ranking. *HR Magazine, 48*(6), June, 36, 38.

39. Noe, R. A., Hollenbeck, J. R., Gerhart, B., & Wright, P. M. (2000). *Human resource management: Gaining a competitive advantage* (3rd ed.). Boston: Irwin McGraw-Hill.

40. Robinson, S. L., & Bennett, R. J. (1995). A typology of deviant workplace behaviors: A multidimensional scaling study. *Academy of Management Journal, 38*, 555–572.

41. Ambrose, M. L., Seabright, M. A., & Schminke, M. (2002). Sabotage in the workplace: The role of organizational injustice. *Organizational Behavior & Human Decision Processes, 89*(1), 947–965; Peterson, D. K. (2002). Deviant workplace behavior and the organization's ethical climate. *Journal of Business & Psychology, 17*(1), 47–61.

42. Mitchell & O'Reilly (1983), *supra* note 35.

43. *Ibid.*

44. Weiner, B., Frieze, I., Kukla, A., Reed, L., Nest, S., & Rosenbaum, R. (1972). Perceiving the causes of success and failure. In E. Jones, D. Kanouse, H. Kelley, R. Nisbett, S. Balins, & B. Weiner (Eds.), *Attribution: Perceiving the causes of behavior.* Norristown, NJ: General Learning Press.

45. Mitchell, T. R., Green, S. G., & Wood, R. E. (1981). An attributional model of leadership and the poor performing subordinate: Development and validation. In L. L. Cummings & B. M. Staw (Eds.), *Research in organizational behavior* (Vol. 3, pp. 197–234). Greenwich, CT: JAI.

46. Larson, J. R., Jr. (1977). Evidence for a self-serving bias in the attribution of causality. *Journal of Personality, 45,* 430–441.

47. Larson, J. R., Jr. (1989). The dynamic interplay between employees' feedback-seeking strategies and supervisors' delivery of performance feedback. *Academy of Management Review, 14,* 408–422.

48. Gioia, D. A., & Sims, H. P. (1986). Cognition-behavior connections: Attribution and verbal behavior in leader-subordinate interactions. *Organizational Behavior and Human Decision Processes, 37,* 197–229.

49. *Ibid.*

50. Knowlton, W. A., Jr., & Mitchell, T. R. (1980). Effects of causal attributions on supervisor's evaluations of subordinate performance. *Journal of Applied Psychology, 65,* 459–466; Ilgen, D. R., & Knowlton, W. A., Jr. (1980). Performance attributional effects on feedback from supervisors. *Organizational Behavior and Human Decision Processes, 25,* 441–456.

51. Mager, R. F., & Pipe, P. (1970). *Analyzing performance problems.* Belmont, CA: Fearon Publishers.

52. Fournies (1978), *supra* note 15.

53. Mager & Pipe (1970), *supra* note 47; Viega (1988), *supra* note 34.

54. Sue-Chan, C., & Latham, G. P. (2004). The relative effectiveness of external, peer, and self-coaches. *Applied Psychology — An International Review, 53*(2), 260–278.

55. Mager & Pipe (1970), *supra* note 47.

56. *Ibid.*

57. Fournies (1978), *supra* note 15; Kinlaw (1989), *supra* note 16.

58. Kinlaw (1989), *supra* note 16.

59. Fournies (1978), *supra* note 15.

60. Phillips, K. R. (1998). The Achilles' heel of coaching. *Training & Development, 52*(3), March, 41–44.

61. Fournies (1978), *supra* note 15.

62. Evered & Selman (1990), *supra* note 20.

63. *Ibid.*

64. Peters & Austin (1985), *supra* note 21.

65. Ericsson, K. A., & Charness, N. (1994). Expert performance: Its structure and acquisition. *American Psychologist, 49,* 725–747.

66. Fox, D. (1983). Coaching: The way to protect your sales training investment. *Training & Development Journal, 37*(11), 37–39.

67. Evered & Selman (1990), *supra* note 20; Peters, H. (1996). Peer coaching for executives. *Training & Development, 50*(3), 39–41.

68. Peters & Austin (1985), *supra* note 21.

69. Fournies (1978), *supra* note 15.

70. Kinlaw (1989), *supra* note 16; Fournies (1978), *supra* note 15.

71. Kikoski, J. F., & Litterer, J. A. (1983). Effective communication in the performance appraisal interview. *Public Personnel Management Journal, 12,* 33–42.

72. Ivey, A., & Authier, J. (1978). *Microcounseling.* Springfield, IL: Charles C. Thomas; Ivey, A., & Litterer, J. (1979). *Face to face.* Amherst, MA: Amherst Consulting Group.

73. Pampino, R. N., MacDonald, J. E., Mullin, J. E., & Wilder, D. A. (2003). Weekly feedback vs. daily feedback: An application in retail. *Journal of Organizational Behavior Management, 23*(2–3), 21–43.

74. Kinlaw (1989), *supra* note 16; Peters & Austin (1985), *supra* note 59; Zemke (1996), *supra* note 17.

75. Whitener, E. M., Brodt, S. E., Korsgaard, M. A., & Werner, J. M. (1998). Managers as initiators of trust: An exchange relationship framework for understanding managerial trustworthy behavior. *Academy of Management Review, 23,* 513–530.

76. Evered & Selman (1990), *supra* note 20; Waldroop & Butler (1996), *supra* note 2.

77. Wexley, K. N., & Latham, G. P. (1991). *Developing and training human resources in organizations* (2nd ed.). New York: HarperCollins.

78. Silverman, S. B. (1990). Individual development through performance appraisal. In K. N. Wexley & J. R. Hinrichs (Eds.), *Developing human resources* (120–151). Washington, DC: Bureau of National Affairs.

79. *Ibid.*

80. Wexley & Latham (1991), *supra* note 71.

81. Luthan, F., & Peterson, S. J. (2003). 360-degree feedback with systematic coaching: Empirical analysis suggests a winning combination. *Human Resource Management, 42*(3), 243–256.

82. Latham, G. P., & Yukl, G. A. (1975). A review of research on the application of goal setting in organizations. *Academy of Management Journal, 18,* 824–845; Nemeroff, W. F., & Wexley, K. N. (1979). An exploration of the relationships between the performance feedback interview characteristics and interview outcomes as perceived by managers and subordinates. *Journal of Occupational Psychology, 52,* 25–34; Wexley, K. N., Singh, J. P., & Yukl, G. A. (1973). Subordinate personality as a moderator of the effects of participation in three types of appraisal interviews. *Journal of Applied Psychology, 58,* 54–59.

83. Burke, R. J., & Wilcox, D. S. (1969). Characteristics of effective employee performance review and development interviews. *Personnel Psychology, 22,* 291–305; Burke, R. J., Weitzel, W., & Weir, T. (1978). Characteristics of effective employee performance review and development interviews: Replication and extension. *Personnel Psychology, 31,* 903–919; Greller, M. M. (1975). Subordinate participation and reaction in the appraisal interview. *Journal of Applied Psychology, 60,* 544–549.

84. Basset, G. A., & Meyer, H. H. (1968). Performance appraisal based on self-review. *Personnel Psychology, 21,* 421–430; French, J. R. P., Kay, E., & Meyer, H. (1966). Participation and the appraisal system. *Human Relations, 19,* 3–20.

85. Greenberg, J. (1986). Determinants of perceived fairness of performance evaluations. *Journal of Applied Psychology, 71,* 340–342.

86. Burke & Wilcox (1969), *supra* note 76; Burke et al. (1978), *supra* note 76; Kay, E., Meyer, H. H., & French, J. P. R., Jr. (1965). Effects of threat in a performance appraisal interview. *Journal of Applied Psychology, 49,* 311–317; Nemeroff & Wexley (1979), *supra* note 75.

87. Dorfman, P. W., Stephan, W. G., & Loveland, J. (1986). Performance appraisal behaviors: Supervisor perceptions and subordinate reactions. *Personnel Psychology, 39,* 579–597.

88. Fedor, D. B., Eder, R. W., & Buckley, M. R. (1989). The contributory effects of supervisor intentions on subordinate feedback responses. *Organizational Behavior and Human Decision Processes, 44,* 396–414.

89. Kay, Meyer, & French (1965), *supra* note 79.

90. Baron, R. A. (1988). Negative effects of destructive criticism: Impact on conflict, self-efficacy, and task performance. *Journal of Applied Psychology, 73,* 199–207.

91. Latham, G. P., & Wexley, K. N. (1994). *Increasing productivity through performance appraisal* (2nd ed.). Reading, MA: Addison-Wesley; Cascio, W. F. (1982). *Applied psychology in personnel management.* Reston, VA: Reston Publishing.

92. Burke & Wilcox (1969), *supra* note 76; Burke et al. (1978), *supra* note 76; Greller (1975), *supra* note 76; Greller, M. M. (1978). The nature of subordinate participation in the appraisal interview. *Academy of Management Journal, 21,* 646–658.

93. Burke et al. (1978), *supra* note 76; Landy, F. J., Barnes, J. L., & Murphy, K. R. (1978). Correlates of perceived fairness and accuracy of performance evaluation. *Journal of Applied Psychology, 63,* 751–754.

94. Greller (1978), *supra* note 85.

95. Locke, E. A., & Latham, G. P. (1990). *A theory of goal setting and task performance.* Englewood Cliffs, NJ: Prentice Hall.

96. DeCotiis, T., & Petit, A. (1978). The performance appraisal process: A model and some testable propositions. *Academy of Management Review, 3,* 635–646; Landy, F. J., & Farr, J. L. (1980). Performance ratings. *Psychological Bulletin, 87,* 72–107.

97. Stone, D. L., Gueutal, H. G., & McIntosh, B. (1984). The effects of feedback sequence and expertise of the rater on perceived feedback accuracy. *Personnel Psychology, 37,* 487–506.

98. Bannister, B. D. (1986). Performance outcome feedback and attributional feedback: Interactive effects on recipient responses. *Journal of Applied Psychology, 71,* 203–210.

99. Markle (2000), *supra* note 6; Latham, G. P., & Wexley, K. N. (1981). *Increasing productivity through performance appraisal.* Reading, MA: Addison-Wesley.

100. Grote (2000), *supra* note 7.

101. Stivers & Joyce (2000), *supra* note 12; Heneman & Thomas (1997), *supra* note 12.

102. Latham & Wexley (1994), *supra* note 84.

103. Taylor & Pierce (1999), *supra* note 12; Kueng, P. (2000). Process performance measurement system: a tool to support process-based organizations. *Total Quality Management, 11*(1), 67–85; Curtright, J. W., Stolp-Smith, S. C., & Edell, E. S. (1999). Strategic performance management development of a performance measurement system at the Mayo Clinic. *Journal of Healthcare Management, 45*(1), January/February, 58–68.

104. Waldroop & Butler (1996), *supra* note 2.

105. Cederblom, D., & Pemerl, D. E. (2002). From performance appraisal to performance management: One agency's experience. *Public Personnel Management, 31*(2), 131–140.

106. Neary, D. B. (2002). Creating a company-wide, on-line, performance management system: A case study at TRW Inc. *Human Resource Management, 41*(4), 491–498; Lawler & McDermott (2003), *supra* note 10; Benson, A. D., Bothra, J., & Sharma, P. (2004). A performance support tool for Cisco training program managers. *TechTrends, 48*(2), March/April, 54–58, 78.

107. Jasica-Mercola, J., McIntyre, B. J., & Womack, J. W. (2003). Maximizing business results through performance management. Towers Perrin. Retrieved October 29, 2004, from http://www.towersperrin.com/hrservices/webcache/towers/United_States/publications/Capability_Brochures/HRDS_PerfMgmt/perfmgmnt0303.pdf

PART 3: HUMAN RESOURCE DEVELOPMENT APPLICATIONS

# 11

# EMPLOYEE COUNSELING AND WELLNESS SERVICES

## Learning Objectives

*After reading this chapter, you should be able to:*

1. Explain the need for employee counseling in organizations and why counseling is an HRD activity.

2. Describe the typical activities included in employee counseling programs.

3. Describe the focus and effectiveness of three types of employee counseling programs: employee assistance programs, stress management interventions, and employee wellness/ health promotion programs.

4. Describe the role of supervisors in the various types of employee counseling programs.

5. Explain the legal and ethical issues raised by employee counseling, assistance, and health and wellness programs.

## OPENING CASE

Lovelace Health Systems is a managed care organization that serves approximately 158,000 people in New Mexico (roughly 10 percent of the statewide population). It employs 3,300 people in one hospital, several specialty clinics, and many primary care clinics located in various communities in the state. Seventy percent of its employees are also health plan members, that is, they receive their health coverage through Lovelace.

The state of New Mexico has a death rate from cirrhosis of the liver that is nearly twice the national average, and in 1998, had the highest rate of drug-induced deaths per capita in the nation. This led leaders at Lovelace to look for ways to reduce and prevent substance abuse among their employees. The health system already had two voluntary programs in place, an employee assistance program and an employee wellness program. In 1997, they also began mandatory drug testing of all applicants who were offered employment.

In 1998, Lovelace sought to enhance what it was already doing with a new program called Project WISE. WISE stood for Workplace Initiative in Substance Education. The particular emphasis of Project WISE was an effort to reduce what was termed "risky" drinking. Employees completed a health risk appraisal, which included questions concerning alcohol use (as well as heart disease, stress, depression, diabetes, nutrition, and cancer risk). Employees whose answers to the alcohol use questions placed them in either the moderate- or high-risk categories were targeted for the new intervention (see Table 11-1 for details).

*Questions: If you were an HRD professional involved in setting up Project WISE, what issues would you emphasize as you designed and implemented this new program? What ideas do you have for ways to increase awareness of the dangers of risky drinking? How about concerning ways to change employee drinking behaviors? How might you evaluate the success of Project WISE? Are there any potential concerns in regards to collecting employee data that will be used to evaluate whether changes have occurred as a result of the new intervention?*

## INTRODUCTION

Have you ever witnessed any of the following from someone in a work setting?

- *showing up for work under the influence of alcohol or drugs*
- *struggling to maintain satisfactory job performance because of severe anxiety or depression*
- *refusing medical or other assistance for a treatable condition (e.g., obsessive-compulsive disorder, bipolarity, depression)*
- *burnout or fatigue as a response to ongoing work pressures and stress*
- *involvement (or noninvolvement) in organizational efforts to promote good health (e.g., fitness, nutrition, weight control, or control of high blood pressure)*

Personal problems are a part of life. Stress, alcohol and drug abuse, cardiovascular disease, obesity, mental illness, and emotional problems abound in modern society. Whether these problems are chronic, as in the case of alcoholism, or situational, as in the case of financial problems, they can affect behavior at work as well as one's personal life. Such problems contribute to accidents, absenteeism and turnover, poor decisions, decreases in productivity, and increased costs. Estimates of losses incurred due to the problems experienced by troubled workers are staggering.[1] One estimate placed the lost productivity costs at over $100 billion dollars annually — and that was for substance abuse alone.[2]

Rising healthcare costs are one reason organizations are so interested in helping employees with their personal problems. Healthcare costs in the United States have risen sharply over the past four decades, from $26.9 billion in 1960, to $247 billion in 1980, to $1.15 trillion in 1998, to a projected 1.92 trillion in 2005.[3] In addition to reducing healthcare costs, employers' efforts to improve employees' well-being are also purported to reduce workers' compensation costs, tardiness, absenteeism, turnover, lost time from work because of illness and injury, and accidents, while enhancing morale, loyalty, creativity, productivity, decision-making effectiveness, labor relations, recruiting, and company image.[4] Given the potential gains, it is not surprising that organizations are looking for ways to enhance the well-being of their employees.[5]

Another factor promoting organizational interest in employees' well-being is a shortage of skilled workers. Given the reduced birthrate following the baby boom, labor is less plentiful than it was when the baby boom generation was entering the workforce. Shortcomings in the educational system have only exacerbated the problem. As a result, many organizations have adopted the HR strategy that it is better to retain and help workers with problems than to discard them and be faced with recruiting new ones. This extra attention to retaining employees has persisted, even when many companies simultaneously face the need to downsize some portion of their business.[6]

How are organizations addressing the issue of employee well-being? In addition to traditional HR activities like training and motivational programs, organizations are also making a major investment in providing **employee counseling services** as a way to promote employees' well-being. In the literature describing employee counseling services, the term **counseling** has been used to refer to a variety of activities, from informal discussions with a supervisor to intensive one-on-one discussions with a trained professional.[7] Dale Masi's four-part definition of mental health counseling provides a good general description of some of the different types of activities that are typically involved in this activity at the workplace:

> (1) a relationship established between a trained counselor and the employee; (2) thoughtful and candid discussion of personal problems experienced by the employee; (3) an appropriate referral that secures the necessary assistance; and (4) the provision of short-term counseling, when a referral is not necessary. (p. 117)[8]

Employee counseling services have existed since the turn of the century. For example, in 1917, Macy's Department Store established an employee assistance program to help workers deal with personal problems, and by 1920, over 100 of the largest companies in the United States employed a welfare secretary, and a part of this individual's responsibilities included employee counseling.[9] Recently, growth in wellness-related activities has been explosive. Estimates in the early 1990s suggested that there were over 20,000 employee assistance programs, which dealt with substance abuse and mental health problems, and over 50,000 health promotion programs, which typically focus on physical health and well-being.[10] While recent trends indicate considerable consolidation in the number of programs currently offered, a 1998 survey suggested that over 48 million individuals in the United States were enrolled in employee assistance programs.[11] It is obvious from these numbers that many organizations strongly support employee counseling as an effective way to ensure employees' well-being.

## EMPLOYEE COUNSELING AS AN HRD ACTIVITY

Even with all the information we present in this chapter, this can be an intensely personal chapter to read, because many of us have experienced negative consequences resulting from the personal problems discussed in this chapter — either our own problems, or those of someone close to us. We hope this chapter provides useful guidance to you, whether as an employee, a supervisor, or an HRD professional. However, we would stress here the fact that employee counseling *is* an HRD activity. That is, employee counseling serves the same goal as any other HRD activity: to ensure that each employee is a positive contributor to the organization's effectiveness, and that he or she will continue to contribute in the future. Employee assistance and health promotion programs often use the same techniques as other HRD interventions. These techniques include workshops, role playing, behavior modeling, discussions, lectures, coaching, and audiovisual presentations. In addition, the process of delivering counseling services is the same as that of other HRD interventions, and includes needs assessment, planning/design, implementation, and evaluation. Designing, delivering, and evaluating employee counseling programs offer ample opportunity for HRD professionals to use their expertise (i.e., the "core" systems framework presented in Chapters 4 through 7).

## THE LINK BETWEEN EMPLOYEE COUNSELING AND COACHING

In the last chapter, we discussed employee coaching as a means by which supervisors in particular could identify and address work-related problems that employees are experiencing. Much of the focus of coaching analysis and discussion is on the employee's work performance, and how this can be improved. Clearly, however, many work performance problems are related to employees' personal lives, for example, an employee's habitual tardiness may be linked to that employee's use of drugs or alcohol outside of work. The focus of employee counseling is on addressing these personal problems, particularly as they impact employee work performance. In reality, coaching and counseling are often intertwined, as supervisors may find themselves confronted with employee personal problems as they seek to address a performance issue with an employee. However, for most employee personal problems, especially those that are more serious (e.g., depression, substance abuse), supervisors are generally encouraged to provide early identification and referral to a trained professional or counseling service, and not try to solve or resolve the employee's problem themselves.[12] Most managers and supervisors are not properly trained to deal with serious employee personal problems, and as we will discuss later, there are also legal issues to consider pertaining to employee counseling. A trained professional is most likely to be aware of the legal issues involved, and to ensure that any actions taken with an employee comply with all relevant laws and regulations.[13]

## AN OVERVIEW OF EMPLOYEE COUNSELING PROGRAMS

Organizations use a wide variety of activities and programs to help ensure the emotional and physical health of their employees. These activities range from health-risk appraisals to on-site counseling and stress reduction workshops, as well as other ways to promote employee health. They may take the form of a one-session discussion, a series of sessions, or an ongoing organizational activity. In this section, we discuss the components of a typical program, the providers of such services, and characteristics of an effective counseling program.

### COMPONENTS OF THE TYPICAL PROGRAM

While employee counseling programs vary in terms of problems addressed and specific techniques used, six activities are typical of such programs: (1) problem identification, (2) education, (3) counseling, (4) referral, (5) treatment, and (6) follow-up.

*PROBLEM IDENTIFICATION.* Problem identification usually involves the use of a screening device (e.g., a questionnaire or diagnostic test) and/or the training of employees and supervisors in the identification of problems. For example, employees may volunteer to have their cholesterol level assessed as part of a wellness program, or supervisors may be trained to identify the behavioral patterns that indicate possible substance abuse. Table 11-1 provides an example of a screening device concerning alcohol use.

*EDUCATION.* Education typically includes providing information about the nature, prevalence, likely causes and consequences of the problem, and ways the problem can be prevented. For example, a program focusing on hypertension (high blood pressure) might use pamphlets, videos, or a lecture to raise employees' awareness of the problem and how it can be treated or prevented.

*COUNSELING.* At a minimum, counseling involves a person with whom employees can discuss difficulties and/or seek further help. The type of counseling can vary from a frank discussion with a supervisor about work-related performance problems to meeting with a mental health professional skilled in diagnosing and treating problems such as depression or substance abuse.

*REFERRAL.* Referral involves directing the employee to the appropriate resources for assistance. For example, an employee who shows signs of cocaine addiction may be referred to a drug treatment facility that specializes in treating that addiction.

## TABLE 11-1    HEALTH RISK APPRAISAL CONCERNING ALCOHOL USE

### Questions

1. On average, how often do you drink beer, wine, liquor, or other beverages containing alcohol?
2. On days when you drink, how many drinks do you usually have? (One drink equals a 12-ounce beer, a 4-ounce glass of wine, or a shot of liquor.)
3. During the past thirty days, on how many days did you have five or more drinks on the same occasion?
4. In the next six months, do you want to reduce the amount of alcohol that you drink?

### Feedback

1. Low-risk drinking is using alcohol in a way that does not harm your health. Research suggests that, on any one day, more than four drinks for men and more than three for women can cause problems. Having more than twelve drinks a week can cause problems over time. Also, drinking alcohol every day may cause problems. Unless you limit your intake to one drink each day, you are advised to drink no more than four to five days a week.
2. Risk assessment categories:

    a. Low risk — drink less than seven days a week and no more than one to two drinks per occasion

    b. Moderate risk — drink up to three to four drinks per occasion or drink every day

    c. High risk — usually or occasionally drink five or more drinks per occasion

SOURCE: From Lapham, S. C., Chang, I., & Gregory, C. (2000). Substance abuse intervention for health care workers: A preliminary report. *Journal of Behavioral Health Services & Research, 27*(2), 131–143.

*TREATMENT/INTERVENTION.* Treatment includes the actual intervention to solve the problem. For example, a nutrition program may include cooking classes or the offering of healthy foods in the cafeteria and nutritious snacks in vending machines.

*FOLLOW-UP.* As with any other HRD activity, some form of monitoring is needed to ensure that the employee is carrying out the treatment and to obtain information on employee progress. For example, if the employee agrees to seek alcohol abuse treatment as part of an agreement to improve his or her performance, it is necessary to determine whether the employee actually attends and completes treatment.

Clearly, not all employee counseling programs make use of all six types of activities. Which activities an organization uses depends on the type of problem addressed, the appropriate response to the problem, and the resources the organization chooses to commit to the program. Take the example of a program to address employee physical fitness. One organization may choose to renovate part of its facility or build a new structure to house a fitness center, complete with a trained staff, locker room, showers, athletic courts, and exercise equipment. Another organization may offer employees free or reduced-fee membership in a local health club. An even less expensive option would be to make fitness information available and encourage employees to exercise on their own time.

## WHO PROVIDES THE SERVICE?

An organization may offer a counseling program in-house or contract it out. In-house (or on-site) programs involve using current employees or hiring specialists, such as psychologists, social workers, or other trained individuals, to operate the program. For example, the post office in northern England established a mental health improvement program staffed internally by full-time specialists in counseling whose responsibilities covered confidential counseling to employees and advising management on mental health-related issues.[14] Contracting the service out to a third party involves hiring a local specialist or organization to provide the service. For example, an organization may decide to use a freestanding employee assistance program to help employees deal with substance abuse issues, or work with local psychologists in private practice to help employees deal with emotional problems.

Each approach has a number of advantages and disadvantages.[15] Advantages attributed to in-house programs include (1) internal control of the program, (2) familiarity with the organization (e.g., its policies, procedures, and workforce characteristics), (3) better coordination of treatment and follow-up, (4) a sense of ownership of the program, and (5) greater awareness and credibility with supervisors. However, disadvantages of in-house programs can include (1) real or perceived problems with confidentiality, (2) lack of resources needed, (3) reluctance of some employees to use the service (e.g., a vice president of finance may be reluctant to go to a lower-level employee to admit a drinking or marital problem), and (4) possible limitations in staff skills and expertise.

An advantage of contracting the service out is that the organization can rely on the services of trained professionals whose business it is to treat the problem in question. In addition, confidentiality may be easier to maintain, cost may be lower, and there may be better identification and use of community resources. Disadvantages include the lack of on-site counseling, possible communication problems, and lack of knowledge of the organization and its employees. We will say more about the advantages and disadvantages of both approaches as we discuss employee assistance programs later.

## CHARACTERISTICS OF EFFECTIVE EMPLOYEE COUNSELING PROGRAMS

Communicating the program's services to managers, supervisors, and employees, and following up with them, is critical in getting organizational members to use it. For example, one survey found that employee willingness to use an employee assistance program was related to their familiarity with and trust in the program, and the personal attention provided by it.[16] Similarly, a study of four wellness programs found that programs using systematic outreach and follow-up counseling were more effective than those that did not.[17]

It is also important that managers and supervisors receive training in identifying problems and in how to counsel or refer employees to seek treatment when needed.[18] In many counseling programs, especially those dealing with addiction and mental health, the supervisor's role in helping the employee seek treatment and supporting the treatment effort is critical to success (we will discuss the supervisor's role in counseling in greater detail later in the chapter).[19] Other necessary ingredients for an effective counseling program include:

1. top management commitment and support
2. a clearly written set of policies and procedures outlining the program's purpose and its function within the organization
3. cooperation with local union(s), if they are present in the organization
4. a range of care (e.g., referral to community resources, follow-up)
5. a clear and well-enforced policy concerning employee confidentiality
6. maintenance of records for program evaluation
7. health insurance benefit coverage for services
8. family education[20]

## EMPLOYEE ASSISTANCE PROGRAMS

**Employee assistance programs (EAPs)** are defined as "job-based programs operating within a work organization for the purposes of identifying troubled employees, motivating them to resolve their troubles, and providing access to counseling or treatment for those employees who need these services."[21] EAPs have their origins in the occupational alcoholism programs begun in the 1940s. In the 1970s, they expanded to cover other issues, particularly drug and other substance abuse issues.[22] Since then, EAPs have expanded their coverage to also help employees with mental health issues, such as anxiety, depression, eating disorders, and compulsive gambling, as well as other personal, marital, or financial problems that may be affecting their work.[23] Possible outcomes that may be affected by EAPs include productivity, absenteeism, turnover, unemployment costs, treatment for substance abuse, accidents, training and replacement costs, and insurance benefits.[24] As mentioned earlier, the number of EAPs in the United States has grown dramatically since the 1970s. In 2004, the Employee Assistance Professionals Association had approximately 5,000 members.[25] Most large organizations provide an EAP,[26] with an estimated 82 percent of employees in the largest firms having access to EAP services.[27] Overall, approximately 33 percent of all private, nonagricultural worksites with fifty or more full-time employees offer EAP services to their employees.[28] In this section, we will (1) discuss the extent of the problem organizations face with respect to substance abuse and mental health, (2) describe the approach taken by EAPs, and (3) discuss the effectiveness of EAPs in dealing with these problems.

### SUBSTANCE ABUSE

Reports of the prevalence of alcohol and drug abuse and the problems they create are commonplace. Federal, state, and local governments spend billions of dollars dealing with the problems brought on by substance abuse, from crime to sickness.

It is clear that substance abuse has a powerful impact on modern society and on business and industry.

It is estimated that 19.4 million Americans abuse alcohol or drugs. Fully 77 percent of these individuals (14.9 million) are employed either full- or part-time, and this constitutes more than 10 percent of both the full- and part-time workforces.[29] It is estimated that 47 percent of industrial injuries and 40 percent of industrial fatalities can be linked to alcohol consumption and alcoholism.[30] Reported rates of on-the-job alcohol use vary by industry and culture, and even within a given industry.[31] Consider these examples:

1. A study of the relationship of drinking to workplace problems at a Fortune 500 manufacturing facility found that 24 percent of hourly workers reported drinking at work at least once during the previous year, with roughly 5.5 percent having four or more drinks before work. Workers who drank on the job or just before work were more likely than those who didn't to be criticized by a supervisor, argue with a supervisor, or have an argument or fight. Finally, those who were hungover at work were more likely to report having felt sick, having an argument or fight, having been criticized by a supervisor, having trouble doing the job, or having fallen asleep on the job.[32]

2. A survey of over 9,000 retail, manufacturing, and hospital organization employees found that 6.5 percent of respondents admitted to having come to work while under the influence of drugs or alcohol in the previous year. Just over 1 percent reported they came to work under the influence weekly or daily.[33]

3. A separate survey found that 8 percent of respondents reported being under the influence of marijuana, and 5 percent reported being inebriated at work at least once during the last year.[34]

Exactly how much substance abuse costs business in terms of lost productivity is difficult to determine. Some estimates place the amount at over $100 billion overall for alcohol and drug abuse,[35] though a recent estimate placed the figure for alcohol abuse alone at $134 billion per year.[36] It has been estimated that companies lose over $7,000 per year for every employee who abuses alcohol or drugs.[37] Studies have shown that marijuana and cocaine users are at greater risk for accidents, injuries, disciplinary problems, and involuntary turnover, although the level of risk is less than previously thought.[38] To combat this, the **Drug-Free Workplace Act of 1988** has promoted drug-free awareness programs among federal contractors and grant receivers, and this includes informing employees about the availability of drug counseling, rehabilitation, and employee assistance programs.[39]

## MENTAL HEALTH

The National Institute of Mental Health has estimated that 18.8 million adults in the United States experience a depressive illness in any given year, and that this constitutes 9.5 percent of the U.S. population.[40] Two research studies estimate that approximately 23 percent of the U.S. population has some type of diagnosable mental disorder in a given year, though only half of these individuals report impairment of their daily functioning due to the disorder.[41] It is also estimated that 5.4 percent of American adults have a serious mental illness that substantially interferes with one or more major life activities, including eating, managing money, and functioning in social, family, work, and educational settings.[42] Up to 25 percent of medical claims filed can be tied to mental and emotional illnesses,[43] and in 1998, over 25 percent of all hospital admissions in the United States were psychiatric admissions.[44] Among the emotional and mental health issues commonly seen by counselors in industry are the following:

- individual adjustment problems (neurosis to psychosis)
- external factors such as battering, incest, rape, or crime
- sexual problems, including impotence
- divorce and marital problems
- depression and suicide attempts
- difficulties with family or children
- sexual harassment in the workplace
- legal and financial problems[45]

An additional mental health issue that has gained attention recently is pathological or problem gambling. According to the National Council on Problem Gambling, 2 million U.S. adults can be classified as pathological gamblers (displaying a serious lack of control and disregard for the negative consequences of their continued gambling). An additional 4 to 6 million people are thought to be problem gamblers (i.e., gambling has disrupted an important life function for them).[46] Gambling is increasingly being included within the coverage of EAPs.[47] For example, the EAP at the University of Texas at Austin includes a Gambler's Anonymous Self-Assessment Questionnaire.[48]

Mental health problems may be brought into the workplace from employees' personal lives, and work itself can lead to a decline in mental health. Two studies of factory workers in the United Kingdom showed that employees in simplified jobs who felt their skills were underused and who spent a great deal of time daydreaming had poorer mental health than other employees in the study.[49]

Organizations are affected by employee mental health problems in the form of absenteeism, poor work habits, low job satisfaction, interpersonal conflicts, and indecisiveness.[50] For example, it is estimated that businesses lose $3 to $5 billion per year as a result of absenteeism due to spouse abuse.[51]

The issue of mental illness at work has been highlighted recently by three federal regulatory actions. First, in May 1997, the U.S. Equal Employment Opportunity Commission (EEOC) issued guidelines that were intended to help employers comply with the **Americans with Disabilities Act (ADA) of 1990** in the area of psychiatric disabilities (the ADA will be discussed in more detail later in the chapter). The guidelines explain issues employers may face when dealing with employees or applicants who have a mental impairment, and make general suggestions for how to deal with them. Second, the **Mental Health Parity Act of 1996** took effect on

January 1, 1998. This law states that private employers with more than 50 employees who offer mental health coverage (and roughly 80 percent of medium and large establishments do)[52] must offer annual and maximum lifetime dollar limits equal to those for "regular" medical benefits.[53] The Act does not cover treatment for substance abuse or chemical dependency, and does not mandate that private employers include mental health benefits in their health insurance plans. However, if mental health coverage is provided, it is impermissible to have lower payment caps for mental illnesses (such as bipolar disorder) than for other diseases (such as diabetes or heart disease).[54] Since 2001, this law has been extended on a year-by-year basis.[55] There have been efforts in the U.S. Congress since 2002 to pass a new bill, the Mental Health Equitable Treatment Act. This would require mental health coverage equal to other forms of coverage (this is often referred to as full parity). Third, shortly before leaving office in January 2001, President Clinton signed an executive order that required equal coverage or parity for mental health benefits offered to federal employees, their dependents, and to federal retirees. This executive order is expected to cover 9 million individuals.[56] Taken together, these actions require employers to pay attention to mental health issues and highlight the need for organizations to carefully manage and address them.

## THE EAP APPROACH TO RESOLVING EMPLOYEE PERSONAL PROBLEMS

EAPs are based on the notion that work is very important to people and that work performance should be used to identify employee personal problems and motivate employees to seek help.[57] Originally developed to deal with alcohol abuse, the EAP approach assumes — as does the Alcoholics Anonymous (AA) movement — that substance abusers will deny their problem until they are faced with a crisis. From the EAP point of view, that crisis is created by confronting the employee with evidence of substandard work performance, meanwhile making counseling available and attempting to motivate the employee to seek help.[58] Although this may seem surprising, Dale Masi argues that the workplace is, in fact, an ideal place for employees to receive treatment for mental health problems. Her argument is that many of the obstacles to seeking help, such as transportation and time off, are removed in the workplace.[59] A conceptual framework for the EAP approach is shown in Table 11-2 and Masi's framework for delivering mental health services is shown in Table 11-3.

An important aspect of the modern treatment of substance abuse and other personal problems in the workplace is that the employee problem is operationally defined in terms of *job performance,* rather than clinically defined in terms of addiction or psychiatric disorder. For example, the pattern of behaviors that indicate a substance-abuse problem typically include absenteeism, erratic performance, poor quality work, poor judgment, and complaints by clients or customers. Table 11-4 suggests behaviors that supervisors should monitor to help them identify changes in employee appearance or behavior that may indicate impairment due to substance abuse.

In most EAPs, supervisors are trained to use the **constructive confrontation** approach in dealing with troubled employees. This is, in fact, one of the seven

**TABLE 11-2**

## CONCEPTUAL FRAMEWORK FOR EMPLOYEE ASSISTANCE PROGRAMS

1. EAPs are based on the premise that work is very important to people; the work itself is not the cause of the employee's problem. Consequently, the workplace can be a means to get people help.

2. The supervisor plays a key role in getting help for the employee. Often, however, the supervisor denies the problem and even enables the troubled employee to continue the problem behavior. The supervisor is critical in the confrontational process with the troubled employee. Therefore, education is necessary to eliminate the supervisor's tendency to enable the employee by denying the problem.

3. Information about the employee's job performance is extremely important in diagnosis and treatment. It can be used to measure and track whether treatment is successful.

4. Workplace peers and union stewards are very important; however, they too can deny the problem and enable the employee to continue the behavior. Teaching them to confront and consequently break the denial barrier is an important element.

5. Job leverage is the key ingredient in helping an employee. The counselor must be able to use this in conjunction with the supervisor.

6. EAPs concentrate on job performance issues. They are not intended to be medical programs.

7. Cost-effectiveness is an important consideration and must be addressed with upper management.

8. The EAP professional's knowledge about addiction is paramount. Every EAP should be staffed by licensed professionals who are familiar with addictions and other employee personal problems.

SOURCE: *AMA handbook for developing employee assistance and counseling programs* by Masi, Dale A. © 1992 by AM MGMT ASSN/AMACOM (B). Reproduced with permission of AM MGMT ASSN/AMACOM (B) in the format Textbook via Copyright Clearance Center.

workplace practices that make up the "Core Technology" recommended by the Employee Assistance Professionals Association.[60] The constructive confrontation process is described as follows:

> This strategy calls for supervisors to monitor their employees' job performance, confront them with evidence of their unsatisfactory performance, coach them on improving it, urge them to use the EAP's counseling service if they have personal problems, and emphasize the consequences of continued poor performance. Constructive confrontation proceeds in progressive stages; at each stage, employees must choose whether to seek help from the EAP, manage their problems themselves, or suffer the consequences of their actions.[61]

According to this approach, the supervisor need not, and perhaps should not, say that the employee has a drug or alcohol problem. Rather, the supervisor should treat the problem like any other performance problem and leave it for the employee to seek help from the appropriate source. With this approach, recommending that the employee contact an EAP or other agency "if you need to" should be the extent of the supervisor's intervention. You should see that this approach is consistent with our discussion of employee coaching in the previous chapter.

| TABLE 11-3 | MASI'S FRAMEWORK FOR DELIVERING EAP AND MENTAL HEALTH SERVICES IN INDUSTRY |
|---|---|

1. Counseling in the workplace is short term. Long-term therapy is appropriate in the community.

2. There are logistical as well as legal problems when families are included. Although EAP programs often offer services to families, they are based on self-referral and supervisory-referral.

3. The manager or supervisor is the key person in the client's work life. The work associates are similar to family members. The counselor should learn their configuration and how these individuals interact with and impact the employee.

4. The counselor assumes the role of a "broker" or go-between for the employee between the supervisor and the therapist in the community.

5. The counselor should have skills in management consultation, that is, meeting with supervisors to determine whether they have a problem employee, advising them on a course of action, and supporting them through the referral and after-care process.

6. Crisis counseling (to deal with emergency episodes such as suicide attempts) should be available in the workplace.

7. The counselor must have special skills in confrontation to break the denial of the employee appropriately, especially the addicted person.

8. Confidentiality is an even greater issue in the workplace than it is in a community mental health clinic or social agency because of the uniqueness of the work setting. Competition for jobs, as well as an environment that does not necessarily understand employees' personal problems, mandate a clearly defined and enforced confidentiality policy.

9. Record-keeping procedures need to be carefully developed and delineated, so that employees are assured of their privacy. This is not as necessary to explain to clients in a hospital or social agency; it is accepted in such situations. Employees worry about who will read their records (especially HR professionals). The Privacy Act, Alcohol and Drug Regulations, and other relevant laws are guideposts that all EAPs should follow to protect their employees.

10. The counselor must also design and implement educational programs in the workplace.

11. The unique work system (including HR and company physicians) can be used to help the employee. The counselor needs to understand how these systems work.

12. Counselors need to be able to work with labor unions in the workplace, as appropriate.

SOURCE: From Masi, D. A. (1984). *Designing employee assistance programs* (pp. 119–120). New York: AMACOM.

**TABLE 11-4**

## BEHAVIOR PATTERNS THAT COULD INDICATE A POTENTIAL SUBSTANCE ABUSE PROBLEM

**Absenteeism**

- Taking many absences without authorization.
- Using vacation days to cover frequent absences.

**On-the-Job Absences**

- Often away from one's work area.
- Frequent tardiness after lunch or breaks.

**High Accident Rates**

- Accidents off the job that affect work performance.
- Accidents on the job due to carelessness, inattentiveness, etc.

**Job Performance Issues**

- Complaints from coworkers or clients.
- Missing deadlines.
- Frequent shifts between high and low performance.
- Difficulty understanding instructions or new information.

**Poor Relationships with Coworkers**

- Extreme reactions to real or implied criticism.
- Large mood swings.
- Avoiding coworkers and friends.
- Increasing irritability or argumentativeness.

SOURCE: Adapted from Campbell, D., & Graham, M. (1988). *Drugs and Alcohol in the Workplace: A Guide for Managers.* NY: Facts on File, pp. 100–101.

However, referral by a supervisor is not the only method by which employees may contact an EAP. Employees with personal problems may contact the EAP directly and receive counseling without the supervisor's knowledge. Some have argued that this is the preferred referral strategy, because the employee receives help before job performance is affected.[62] It is also possible for one employee to encourage a peer with a problem to seek help from an EAP. In fact, some success with Member Assistance Programs (MAPs) has been reported, where union representatives are actively involved in the administration of the assistance program.[63] It is argued that union representatives can intervene in a potential work performance problem before it becomes severe enough that the employer must deal with it.

The components of the typical EAP can vary in terms of organizational policy, referral method, use of in-house and external resources, types of problems treated, and staffing.[64] In general, though, the typical EAP consists of the following:

- a policy and procedures statement that makes clear the responsibilities of both the organization and the employee concerning health and personal problems impacting the job

- employee education campaigns, which may include letters, poster campaigns, or extensive training programs

- a supervisory training program that teaches problem recognition and performance documentation

- clinical services that may be provided by a professional in-house staff, or by off-site or community agencies

- follow-up monitoring to ensure real problem resolution has occurred[65]

A national survey revealed that the internal (or on-site) EAPs on average offer more services than external (off-site) EAPs, that is, 5.22 versus 3.74 services provided.[66] It has been estimated that, of the work sites that have EAPs, 17 percent have an internal EAP, 81 percent have an external EAP, and about 3 percent have both.[67] Table 11-5 shows estimates for the type of service provided by internal and external EAPs. In 1997, the reported average cost per eligible employee was $26.59 for internal EAPs and $21.47 for external EAPs.[68] The higher cost for internal EAPs could be because they offer more services than external EAPs. However, a recent survey of fifty-four Fortune 500 companies found that supervisors were much more likely to make referrals to internal EAPs, and that internal EAPs were better able to identify employees with substance abuse problems.[69] Finally, a research study on an internal EAP at a multinational company found three variables that predicted positive reactions to the EAP among EAP users as well as nonusers: perceived confidentiality, perceived support by other employees, and a belief that EAP use would not negatively affect one's career.[70]

Examples of EAPs have appeared frequently in the literature. Some of these include EAPs for employees of General Electric, players and staff of professional sports organizations, members of the Association of Flight Attendants, and schoolteachers and school employees.[71] In 2004, the largest provider of EAP services in the United States was Magellan Behavioral Care Management, which

| TABLE 11-5 | NATIONAL ESTIMATES OF EAP SERVICE PROVISION BY TYPE OF EAP | |
|---|---|---|

| Services Usually Provided by the EAP | Internal | External |
|---|---|---|
| Consultation with supervisors* | 88% | 58% |
| Participation in constructive confrontations with employees* | 63% | 30% |
| Short-term counseling* | 76% | 91% |
| Assessment and referral | 92% | 90% |
| Contact providers to determine progress of EAP clients in treatment | 77% | 75% |
| Contact of supervisors to determine success of clients after treatment* | 65% | 40% |
| Involvement in health promotion activities* | 65% | 37% |
| Average number of services provided* | 5.22 | 3.74 |

Note: *Difference significant at the 0.01 level.

SOURCE: Adapted with permission from French, M. T., Zarkin, G. A., Bray, J. W., & Hartwell, T. D. (1997). Costs of employee assistance programs: Findings from a national survey. *American Journal of Health Promotion, 11*, 220.

linked with EAP providers to supply over 20 percent of the EAP services offered nationwide.[72]

Another way that organizations can assist employees and their families with mental health issues is to provide mental health benefits in the employee benefit package.[73] As mentioned earlier, 80 percent of medium-sized and large establishments offer mental health insurance benefits. In addition, it should be noted that many organizations are turning to preemployment drug screening as a way to avoid hiring substance abusers while deterring substance abuse in the workplace,[74] with some success.[75] However, such programs are beyond the focus of this text. We encourage the interested reader to consult other sources.[76]

## EFFECTIVENESS OF EAPs

While the effectiveness of EAPs is generally accepted, there is some controversy about this.[77] Evaluation studies have used a wide range of outcomes to measure success, including percentage of employees entering treatment, percentage returning to work following treatment, changes in the nature of the problem following treatment, improvements in work performance, cost savings, attitudes and knowledge about alcohol problems, and inclination to refer problem employees for medical assistance.[78] A review of the literature on the effectiveness of such programs reported that most studies claim a 50 to 85 percent success rate.[79] Reported estimates of cost savings have ranged from $2 to $20 per dollar invested in the program.[80] Reports of EAP effectiveness include results such as:

- A research study randomly assigned 227 workers to one of three treatment groups: mandatory attendance at Alcoholics Anonymous (AA) meetings, compulsory inpatient treatment, or a choice of treatment options provided along with "nondirective" advice from EAP professionals.[81] The researchers tracked the employees for two years. With regard to job performance, they found that all three groups improved, with no difference among treatment groups. With regard to drinking and drug abuse, the inpatient group was most improved, followed by the choice group and the AA group, respectively. Furthermore, 63 percent of the AA group required additional inpatient treatment, compared to 38 percent of the choice group and 23 percent of the inpatient group. Given these results and the low cost differential in inpatient costs between the three groups (only 10 percent), the researchers recommend that giving employees the choice of treatment or sending them to AA initially is riskier than inpatient treatment, and should be followed by monitoring for indications of relapse.

- Absenteeism was reduced by 52 percent in EAP users and workers' compensation and healthcare costs were cut by 74 percent and 55 percent, respectively.[82]

- Sick leave usage among users was reduced by 74 to 80 percent.[83]

- Some 75 percent of problem drinkers improved work performance as a result of constructive confrontation and counseling.[84]

However, critics charge that this evidence is tainted because many EAP evaluation studies suffer from serious methodological and design flaws, such as lack of comparison groups and random assignment to treatments.[85] Luthans and Waldersee argued that much of the evidence is anecdotal and based on testimonials.[86] Flaws such as these make it difficult to determine whether results are in fact due to the EAP.

Furthermore, success rates reported in EAP literature exceed those reported for governmental and social service agencies that treat problem drinkers.[87] Studies that have examined the effectiveness of other alcoholism treatment programs report far lower rates of success than EAPs. For example, Madsen reported that AA programs help only one out of eighteen alcoholics,[88] and Polich and colleagues found that four years after treatment, only 28 percent of alcoholics who completed a formal treatment program had abstained from drinking in the past six months.[89] A recent large-scale study of three treatment options (i.e., a twelve-step facilitation therapy, cognitive-behavioral coping skills therapy, and motivational enhancement therapy) found that all three groups improved similarly on measures of drinking after twelve months: 35 percent of subjects in the treatment groups reported complete abstinence from drinking during the follow-up period, while 65 percent reported slipping or relapsing.[90] The discrepancies between these studies may be due to the lack of common definitions of success (e.g., most studies rely on self-reported measures of drinking behavior and abstinence rather than on physiological measures), insufficiently long follow-up periods in some cases, and the mislabeling of those entering treatment in the EAP studies. The masking of symptoms for long periods by employees hoping to avoid dismissal may also skew results.[91]

Two other criticisms of the EAP approach deserve note. Weiss states that the job behaviors commonly used to identify alcoholic employees have not been clearly supported by the literature.[92] He also claims that by using job performance to identify employees with substance-abuse problems, "it is possible a poor-performing person could be labeled an alcoholic, treated for alcoholism, and be pronounced rehabilitated with no necessary reference at any point in the process to consumption of alcohol (but merely to working harder)."[93] However, while the research on constructive confrontation is not plentiful, the evidence so far offers support for its efficacy in dealing with both substance abuse and other problems.[94]

EAP advocates have addressed some of these concerns. For example, Blum and Roman argue that EAPs are not alone among those HR interventions that need more rigorous evaluation research.[95] Further, they claim that "all of the published studies indicate that EAPs are cost-effective. There is no published evidence that EAPs are harmful to corporate economies or to individual employees" (p. 12). They conclude by saying that "despite the lack of definitive studies of the outcomes of EAPs, there is an impressive accumulation of evidence across a variety of worksites about EAP effectiveness" (pp. 12–13). Studies compiled by the Employee Assistance Professionals Association suggest that the net savings for companies exceeds the costs paid for EAPs.[96]

What are we to conclude, then, about the effectiveness of EAPs? Given the number of EAPs currently in operation, it is obvious that organizational decision makers perceive some level of effectiveness for EAPs in dealing with troubled employees. However, flaws in much of the EAP evaluation literature make it difficult to unequivocally claim that they are effective. While the rigorous evaluation studies called for by critics would help resolve the issue, the obstacles to conducting such studies (e.g., limited access to EAPs by researchers, confidentiality of records, reluctance to use random assignment to study groups) are formidable.[97] Further, there may be reduced motivation for alcohol-intervention researchers to publish their findings in peer-reviewed journals that apply the rigorous standards necessary for building a firm base of scientific knowledge.[98] Given these constraints, we agree with Harris and Heft that research on various aspects of EAPs, such as constructive confrontation, is possible and would offer useful evidence.[99] Some of the research that we have cited is moving in this direction.[100] More research like this is definitely needed.

Industry's commitment to EAPs and other programs (e.g., preemployment drug screening) makes it clear that the motivation and resources to deal with substance abuse and troubled employees are available; we owe it to all concerned to use them in the most effective way possible. HRD professionals who are considering adopting an EAP for their organization should determine whether it is likely to be a cost-effective solution for their organization, and if so, determine the types of programs needed.[101] They can make these decisions by (1) calculating the per-person cost of treating problems to obtain the desired outcomes and (2) comparing those costs to the cost of replacing the person rather than offering treatment.[102]

Detailed advice for establishing an EAP, including substance-abuse policies, procedures, and training, can be found in Thompson and Masi and in a series of documents published by the Employee Assistance Professionals Association (EAPA).[103] The EAPA also administers a certification examination for EAP professionals, the Certified Employee Assistance Professional, or CEAP. Further information can be found at the EAPA website: http://www.eap-association.com.

While the need for EAP services remains high, recent trends in health care and the law are bringing many changes to this area. For example, many **managed care** organizations (such as Magellan Health Services) have purchased or started their own EAP services. This has led many EAP services to fall under the broader heading of "behavioral health care management."[104] The upside of this is a greater integration of EAP services with other initiatives, such as stress management, employee wellness and health promotion (to be discussed later). A potential downside, however, is that, as we have noted, EAPs have emphasized "constructive confrontation," meaning that employees must first deal with the impact of their problem on their work performance, and then pursue treatment for their problem. Healthcare organizations typically have not dealt directly with work performance issues, especially for employees who are not voluntarily seeking treatment, that is, those referred to an EAP because of a work performance issue. The concern here is that the distinctive EAP approach may get lost when EAPs are placed under the umbrella of behavioral health care.[105]

Legally, under the Americans with Disabilities Act, an employee whose manager *perceives them to be disabled* is covered under the law. This has led the EAPA to take the position that EAPs should serve primarily as an assessment and referral service, and that other trained professionals should do the counseling. It remains unresolved whether a supervisor's referral of an employee to an EAP constitutes a "perceived disability" that would be covered under the ADA.[106] Recently, a lawsuit was filed under the ADA against the assistance program in use at UPS; however, supervisory referral was not an issue in that case.[107] Legal issues will certainly have a strong impact on the issues raised in this section of the chapter.

## STRESS MANAGEMENT INTERVENTIONS

For many years, stress and its effects has been among the most popular topics in both the popular and research literature. For example, commenting on the hectic pace of modern work, the *Wall Street Journal* recently ran a series of articles under the heading, "Can Workplace Stress Get *Worse*?"[108] Additionally, a review of the stress literature identified over 300 scholarly articles published on that topic, with hundreds more articles in the popular press and in trade journals.[109] Stress is estimated to cost the U.S. economy over $300 billion a year.[110]

While the methodological limitations of much stress research (e.g., reliance on self-reports of stress and its effects, rather than objective measurements) have made it difficult to pronounce firm cause-effect statements about the relationship of work stress to other factors (such as mental and physical health, job performance, and job satisfaction), the research to date strongly suggests such a relationship.[111] For example, a review of stress factors in organizations noted that:

Stress is a common aspect of the work experience. It is expressed most frequently as job dissatisfaction, but it finds expression also in more intense and aroused affective states — anger, frustration, hostility, and irritation. More passive, but perhaps no less negative, are such responses as boredom and tedium, burnout, fatigue, helplessness, hopelessness, lack of vigor, and depressed mood. Consistent with these feelings are relationships between job stress and lowered self-confidence and self-esteem. Complaints about health can be considered among psychological responses to stress or they can be treated as indicative of some illness; whichever interpretation we make, responses to job stress include somatic complaints and health symptoms. Finally, some of these responses suggest explicit consequent behavior. Alienation from the organization and lack of commitment to it, for example, are consistent with reported intent to leave (intended turnover) (p. 608).[112]

Kahn and Byosiere offer five categories of behavioral responses to stress: degradation/disruption of the work role itself (e.g., accidents and errors), aggressive behavior at work (e.g., stealing), flight from the job (e.g., absenteeism), degradation/disruption of other life roles (e.g., spouse abuse), and self-damaging behaviors (e.g., smoking or alcohol or drug use).[113] Again, despite methodological concerns, they conclude that in general "work-generated stressors have behavioral effects, that those effects are manifest both on the job and away from it, and that they impose substantial costs on work organizations" (p. 610).

**Stress management programs or interventions (SMIs)** are defined as "any activity, program, or opportunity initiated by an organization, which focuses on reducing the presence of work-related stressors or on assisting individuals to minimize the negative outcomes of exposure to these stressors."[114] SMIs are a popular form of employee counseling program, with roughly 40 percent of organizations estimated to have such interventions.[115] Companies such as John Hancock Insurance and General Electric have been cited for their exemplary stress management programs.[116] The techniques used to treat stress vary widely, including education, time management, physical exercise, assertiveness training, biofeedback, meditation, and communications training.[117] While stress management interventions are popular, two important issues have yet to be completely addressed: the definition of stress and the effectiveness of SMIs.

## DEFINING STRESS

Stress has been difficult to define. Matteson and Ivancevich found hundreds of definitions of stress in the literature.[118] This lack of an agreed-upon definition limits our ability to compare results across studies, because what is called stress in one study may differ from what is called stress in another. Despite this, there is some agreement that **stress** includes three main components:

- some environmental force affecting the individual, which is called a **stressor**
- the individual's psychological or physical response to the stressor
- in some cases, an interaction between the stressor and the individual's response[119]

**TABLE 11-6**

**ORGANIZATIONAL STRESSORS**

1. Factors intrinsic to the job
     role conflict or ambiguity
     workload
     insufficient control

2. Organizational structure and control
     red tape
     politics
     rigid policies

3. Reward systems
     faulty and infrequent feedback
     inequitable rewards

4. Human resource systems
     inadequate career opportunities
     lack of training

5. Leadership
     poor relationships
     lack of respect

SOURCE: From J. M. Ivancevich (1990). Worksite stress management interventions. *American Psychologist, 45,* 254. Copyright 1990 by J. M. Ivancevich. Reprinted by permission.

Stressors can include a wide variety of stimuli both within and outside the organization. Organizational stressors can be such factors as poorly defined rules, lack of control, inconsistent policies, work overload, and inadequate rewards.[120] A list of possible organizational stressors is shown in Table 11-6.

Research has also examined a wide range of variables that may moderate the effect of stress on organizationally valued outcomes. Possible moderators include the individual's sense of competence, self-esteem, Type A behavior, perceived control, locus of control, job characteristics, social support, and organizational level.[121]

The way a person cognitively evaluates stress can play an important role in how stress is experienced. A force that feels like overwhelming stress to one person may be experienced as stimulating by another individual. For example, some employees may prefer loosely defined job roles because they then have the freedom to determine the activities that can be legitimately performed in their job. Other employees may experience a poorly defined role as stressful because they are confused about what they should and should not be doing. Some SMIs take advantage of this by providing employees with new ways of evaluating the stressors in their lives. For example, employees can be taught to view assignments that require them to use new skills as opportunities for growth rather than opportunities for failure.

The way individuals cope with stress can also have an effect on whether the stressor has a negative effect on performance. Learning relaxation exercises that help employees dissipate anxiety experienced when they are under stress can reduce the physical effects of the stressor (e.g., headaches, rapid breathing) and help the employee view the stressor in a more realistic way, rather than inflating its significance.

## A MODEL OF STRESS MANAGEMENT INTERVENTIONS

SMIs can be categorized as either educational or skill-acquisition oriented.[122] **Educational interventions** are designed to inform the employee about the sources of stress, what stress feels like, how stressors can be avoided, and how the individual can better cope with stress. **Skill-acquisition interventions,** such as time management or assertiveness training, are designed to provide employees with new ways to cope with stressors affecting their lives and performance and help keep the effects of stress in check.

Ivancevich and colleagues developed a model of SMIs that depicts the targets of the intervention, the type of intervention, and likely outcomes.[123] Their model, shown in Figure 11-1, categorizes SMIs as focusing on the individual (e.g., goal setting), the organization (e.g., job redesign), or the individual-organizational interface

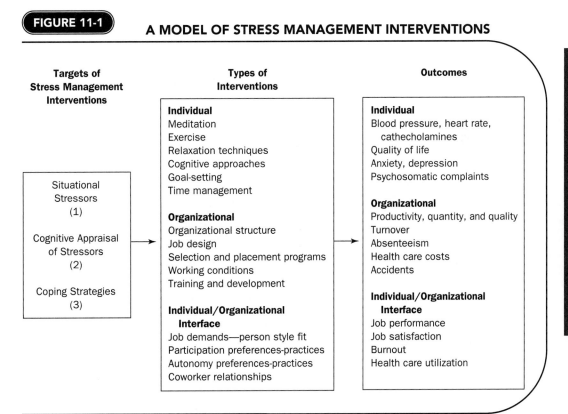

**FIGURE 11-1**     **A MODEL OF STRESS MANAGEMENT INTERVENTIONS**

| Targets of Stress Management Interventions | Types of Interventions | Outcomes |
|---|---|---|
| Situational Stressors (1)  Cognitive Appraisal of Stressors (2)  Coping Strategies (3) | **Individual**<br>Meditation<br>Exercise<br>Relaxation techniques<br>Cognitive approaches<br>Goal-setting<br>Time management<br><br>**Organizational**<br>Organizational structure<br>Job design<br>Selection and placement programs<br>Working conditions<br>Training and development<br><br>**Individual/Organizational Interface**<br>Job demands—person style fit<br>Participation preferences-practices<br>Autonomy preferences-practices<br>Coworker relationships | **Individual**<br>Blood pressure, heart rate, cathecholamines<br>Quality of life<br>Anxiety, depression<br>Psychosomatic complaints<br><br>**Organizational**<br>Productivity, quantity, and quality<br>Turnover<br>Absenteeism<br>Health care costs<br>Accidents<br><br>**Individual/Organizational Interface**<br>Job performance<br>Job satisfaction<br>Burnout<br>Health care utilization |

SOURCE: From Ivancevich, J. M. (1990). Worksite stress management interventions. *American Psychologist, 45*, figure 2, 254. Copyright 1990 by American Psychological Association. Reprinted by permission.

(e.g., coworker relationships). Currently, most workplace SMIs focus on helping the individual cope with stress through activities such as meditation (or mental imaging), exercise, and time management.[124] However, researchers are increasingly recommending that SMIs should focus on the characteristics of the work environment that cause stress.[125] We agree. SMIs that focus on work environment factors may yield significant benefits to both the individual and the organization, and may also be a way for organizations to assume their responsibility in creating and managing stress.

## THE EFFECTIVENESS OF STRESS MANAGEMENT INTERVENTIONS

The picture for SMIs is similar to that for EAPs: not enough rigorously conducted studies exist to allow firm conclusions.[126] A number of reviews of SMI research have been conducted.[127] While many anecdotal reports suggest that SMIs are effective in helping employees manage stress and saving organizations money, much SMI research has been lacking in scientific rigor. In contrast to this, however, a comprehensive review of sixty-four studies published in peer-reviewed journals between 1974 and 1994 found that many of the studies were well conducted; at least half were true experiments, and another quarter were judged to be properly conducted but without using randomized assignment to groups.[128]

The well-conducted studies that do exist provide evidence to support the effectiveness of commonly used SMI tactics.[129] For example, Murphy concluded that the effectiveness of SMIs varied according to the outcome measured.[130] He found that muscle relaxation was most effective in producing physiological outcomes, and cognitive-behavioral-skills interventions were most effective in affecting psychological outcomes. In addition, Murphy noted that combinations of techniques (e.g., of cognitive-behavioral skill and muscle relaxation) were the most commonly studied SMIs and the most effective over all of the outcomes measured. A study of ten stress reduction programs in the Netherlands indicated that they reduced absenteeism, and that the organizational benefits of these programs exceeded their costs.[131] A study of injured workers found that stress management techniques facilitated the reintegration of injured workers into the work environment.[132] Results such as these suggest that SMIs are in fact effective. Further studies that use sound methodology and examine SMIs within a well-developed theory or model will provide the information needed to make informed choices about which SMIs are most effective for dealing with work stress. Briner suggests that the following issues should guide stress management efforts:

- Look for specific issues with employees — instead of talking generally about "stress," determine what specifically is going on with employees.
- Assessment — what evidence is there of a problem, and how widespread is it?
- Specific and focused solutions — what will work in a particular organization? Where should the intervention be targeted?
- Strategic intervention — how does this intervention relate to other HR and organizational practices? Do other things in the organization need to change first?

■ Evaluation and feedback — what will be evaluated, and how will this guide future actions?[133]

## EMPLOYEE WELLNESS AND HEALTH PROMOTION PROGRAMS

**Employee wellness programs (EWPs)** or **health promotion programs (HPPs)** are made up of activities that promote employee behavior and organizational practices that ensure employee health and fitness.[134] Unlike disease prevention and health protection programs, HPPs and wellness programs are based on the premise that **wellness** is more than the mere absence of disease. These programs attempt to encourage individuals to adopt lifestyles that maximize overall well-being.[135] While stress management may be a component of an HPP, HPPs also deal with nonstress issues, such as obesity and smoking cessation.[136] Interest in health promotion and fitness is very strong. It is estimated that there are over 50,000 programs that promote physical fitness among employees,[137] and the number is growing.[138] According to a survey by Hewitt Associates, the percentage of worksites that have implemented at least some form of health promotion activity grew to 91 percent in 1997, with wellness programs offered by 89 percent.[139] According to one national survey, some of the most common health promotion activities are exercise/fitness, smoking cessation, stress management, blood pressure education, and back problem prevention.[140]

O'Donnell describes three levels at which fitness and wellness programs can be implemented.[141] *Level I* programs primarily cover educational activities and may not attempt to directly change employee behavior. Techniques used in Level I programs include newsletters, posters, classes, and health screening. *Level II* programs are those that attempt to bring about direct behavioral change. The activities in such programs may include supervised exercise classes, memberships in fitness centers, and classes on how to properly perform physical work tasks, such as lifting. *Level III* programs try to create an organizational environment that helps employees maintain healthy lifestyles. Two widely publicized examples of Level III programs are Johnson and Johnson's Live for Life program[142] and Control Data's Staywell program,[143] which the company also sells to other organizations. For an example of an exemplary wellness program, see the boxed insert nearby. A recent survey of health promotion experts emphasized the need to link health promotion efforts with an organization's goals and strategy.[144]

Heirich and colleagues described ten dimensions of worksite wellness programs. These dimensions are:

1. establishing a constructive policy for wellness
2. conducting wellness screening — health risk appraisals
3. establishing working relationships with community resources
4. referral of employees to treatment and health-improvement interventions
5. providing health-improvement interventions using a menu approach
6. outreach and follow-up counseling, done on a regular and ongoing basis
7. wellness events done for the entire organization

## An Exemplary Wellness Program at Central States Health & Life

Central States Health & Life Company of Omaha, a medium-sized life and health insurance firm founded during the Depression, may seem an unlikely place for the beginning of a revolution. But for over thirty years, the company has been in the vanguard of the employee wellness movement in the United States. It has demonstrated that helping employees stay well can yield benefits for employer and employee alike.

This revolution did not happen overnight. The wellness program at Central States began out of a concern for the company's claims and loss ratio. CEO William M. Kizer became interested in the reasons why many policyholders were hospitalized or died prematurely. The answer was that, in many cases, hospitalization and early death were due to policyholders' lifestyles. Factors within an individual's control, such as smoking and obesity, appeared to be the main culprits. Kizer thought that if these factors were addressed, many self-induced illnesses could be prevented — a view that has since been supported by scientific evidence.

While he couldn't do much to alter the health of policyholders, Kizer realized that he could help his own employees avoid such problems. Beginning with small steps, such as providing executives with an opportunity to exercise during the lunch period, Central States has created a wellness program that has become a model for other organizations to follow. Kizer hit upon a way that even small- and medium-sized businesses can create relatively inexpensive and effective wellness programs for their employees.

He calls his model the SANE approach. SANE stands for the four components of their wellness program: *S*moking, *A*lcohol, *N*utrition, and *E*xercise.

Central States began its smoking cessation program by establishing a company smoking policy, which created smoking and nonsmoking areas and smoking-cessation classes. These activities set the stage for a smoking ban, which was introduced later. The alcohol portion of the program also started inexpensively with a written policy on the use of alcohol at company-sponsored events. This was followed by a program to help employees who had alcohol- or substance-abuse problems get help. Central States uses an outside provider that is skilled in treating such problems and maintains confidentiality for those who seek help. The firm followed that action by instituting a drug and alcohol testing program to catch problems early, and then introduced an alcohol- and drug-abuse education program.

The nutrition portion of Central States' SANE approach focuses on food at the worksite, offering employees healthy snack alternatives in vending machines and making refrigerators and microwave ovens available to encourage employees to bring healthy foods for lunch. And, while Central States provides a relatively expensive, fully equipped fitness center for employees, Kizer points out there are less expensive ways to encourage exercise, for example, subsidizing memberships in a YMCA or health club, or sponsoring competitions, such as Central States' "Walk 100 Miles in 100 Days for $100" incentive campaign. Central States has found that such competitions effectively increase employee participation. The walking campaign resulted in a participation rate of more than one-third of its employees.

Central States also ensured that its program enjoyed both management support and employee ownership through its More Life Committee, which was made up of a cross-section of Central States employees and managers.

Has the company's wellness program paid off? It resulted in controlled health insurance premium costs at a time when other organizations struggled with rising premiums.

From Schott, F. W., & Wendel, S. (1992). Wellness with a track record. *Personnel Journal, 71*(4), 98–104.

8. consultation on worksite policies and systems, and organizational-level changes

9. ongoing evaluation of the process used to carry out the wellness program, as well as any reductions in employees' health risks

10. periodic evaluation based on work performance and benefit use[145]

In addition, they suggest two other important issues: turning fitness centers into wellness centers, and involving employees' family members in the activities of the wellness program.

Table 11-7 lists activities that might take place in employee wellness or health promotion programs. The sequence of events common to many such programs can be described as follows:

> The program begins with employee health screening, results of the health screen are fed back to the employee in some type of counseling session, employees are advised to participate in one or more health promotion activities consistent with their current health status, and follow-up counseling and health assessment reinforces and maintains employee involvement.[146]

| TABLE 11-7 | ACTIVITIES THAT MAY BE INCLUDED IN AN EMPLOYEE WELLNESS OR HEALTH PROMOTION PROGRAM |

| Screening Programs | Educational Programs | Behavioral Change Programs |
|---|---|---|
| Annual medical exam | Alcohol and drug use | Exercise and fitness |
| Blood analysis | Breast self-exam | Aerobics |
| Cervical cancer | Cancer prevention | Calisthenics |
| Colon and rectal cancer | Coronary disease risk factors | Recreational sports |
| Diabetes | Cardiopulmonary | Competitive sports |
| Fitness assessment | resuscitation | Weight training |
| Health fairs | Weight control | Exercise instruction |
| Health-risk appraisal | Exercise and fitness | EAPs |
| Height and weight | First aid | Healthy back |
| High blood pressure | Cancer detection | Self-defense |
| Preemployment medical | Low back pain | Smoking cessation |
| exams | Nutrition | Stress management |
| Pulmonary function tests | Seat-belt use | Weight loss |
| Screening for job-specific | Smoking cessation | Cooking classes |
| health | Stress | |

SOURCE: From Davis, M. F., Rosenberg, K., Iverson, D. C., Vernon, T. M., & Bauer, J. (1984). Worksite health promotion in Colorado. *Public Health Reports, 99*, 2.

Four common components of HPPs are exercise and fitness, smoking cessation, nutrition and weight control, and control of hypertension (high blood pressure). We will examine each of these components and their effectiveness next.

## EXERCISE AND FITNESS INTERVENTIONS

Corporate exercise and fitness programs are among the most popular employee well-being interventions, especially among large employers, 83 percent of whom offer an exercise-for-fitness program.[147] These programs can supply a range of services for employees, from jogging trails and on-site fitness centers to exercise breaks and company-sponsored sports leagues. Companies such as Xerox, Kimberly-Clark, Goodyear Tire and Rubber, Blue Cross of Indiana, and Tenneco have sponsored such programs.[148]

One of the driving forces behind the strong interest in exercise and fitness programs is evidence that the risk of developing coronary heart disease, cancer, and other leading causes of death can be reduced by adopting a healthy lifestyle.[149] Unfortunately, it has been estimated that fewer than 10 percent of adults in North America engage in regular activity at a level that could achieve or maintain cardio respiratory fitness.[150] This is despite the fact that even a modest increase in aerobic fitness beyond the level of a sedentary middle-aged adult is related to a significant reduction in the risk of dying prematurely.[151] Organizations supporting fitness and health programs expect to generate benefits such as a greater ability to attract and retain employees, more positive employee attitudes, and increased productivity through reduced absenteeism, turnover, and a heightened physical capacity to perform work.[152] Organizations also use fitness programs as a way to cut rising health-care costs.[153]

The physical and psychological benefits of well-designed workplace exercise and fitness programs have been demonstrated. For example, Shepard reviewed fifty-two studies of work site exercise and fitness programs reported in peer-reviewed journals.[154] He summarized the impact of these programs on a variety of health, fitness, and life satisfaction and well-being outcomes as follows:

> It seems clear from the research that a well-designed worksite program can enhance the health-related fitness of program participants. Body mass can be decreased by 1% to 2% (probably more if dietary counseling is included), body fat can be diminished by 10% to 15% relative to initial values, and aerobic power, muscle strength, and flexibility can each be augmented by as much as 20%. Nevertheless, such gains are shown only in employees who become regular program participants, typically only a small proportion of eligible persons . . . Cardiac and other health risks are diminished by participation in worksite exercise programs . . . Many uncontrolled studies have claimed that exercise programs increase life satisfaction and general well-being. (p. 450)

Similar to other programs cited in this chapter, many studies evaluating workplace fitness and exercise programs are limited by methodological concerns.[155] Even so, it appears that these fitness and exercise programs are effective in improving employee health, attitudes, and job behavior and reducing turnover and absenteeism.[156]

The major obstacle to the effectiveness of fitness and exercise programs may be persuading the employees who would most benefit from them to participate. Participation rates in fitness and exercise programs tend to be low, around 30 percent or less,[157] with rates for blue-collar workers tending to be much lower than those for white-collar workers, that is, about 3 to 5 percent.[158] This problem is exacerbated by the fact that many participants in such programs tend to be those who are already physically active.[159]

Organizations that use fitness programs should identify the needs of all employees and provide incentives to ensure that those at greatest risk also participate.[160] Systematic outreach and follow-up counseling have also been found to increase the effectiveness and cost-effectiveness of fitness programs.[161] Other aspects of an effective fitness and exercise program include establishing goals and objectives, obtaining management commitment, hiring quality staff, developing an evaluation strategy, and recruiting participants.[162] Finally, it does not appear that a large investment in equipment and facilities is needed. One review of worksite fitness programs found that combining outreach, individual counseling, and a supportive organizational environment with a moderately well-equipped facility was an effective (and cost-effective) approach.[163]

## SMOKING CESSATION

Smoking is one of the most publicized health risks in society and the workplace. It has been amply demonstrated for some time that smoking is linked to greater incidence of coronary heart disease, stroke, cancer, and emphysema.[164] Even so, it is estimated that 22.5 percent of U.S. adults still smoke, which is down from 42.4 percent in 1965, but is still high.[165] Evidence continues to mount concerning the increased health risks that befall smokers, as well as nonsmokers exposed to cigarette smoke (i.e., second-hand smoke). The additional annual cost of employing smokers and allowing smoking in the workplace has been estimated to be $2,853 per smoker.[166]

Organizations have increased their sponsorship of smoking cessation programs as a way to help employees, reduce costs, and provide a safer workplace. In many cases, state and local laws banning smoking in public areas have also prodded organizations to help employees quit smoking. Fifty-nine percent of worksites with fifty or more employees, and 85 percent of medium-sized and large worksites have a formal policy that prohibits or severely restricts smoking in the workplace.[167] A survey of private worksites found that 35 percent of respondents had a smoking cessation program.[168] Organizations can either sponsor smoking cessation programs in-house, as part of an EAP, stress management, or wellness program, or can refer interested employees to an outside organization, such as the American Cancer Society or a local hospital.

Two related measures of the success of smoking cessation programs are the quit rate and the percentage of smokers who participate in the program. An impressive quit rate is less significant to the organization if only a small proportion of smoking employees enter the program. Quit rates reported in the literature are typically in the area of 25 to 60 percent,[169] although more recent studies have reported quit rates between 12 and 25 percent.[170] Participation rates are not reported as frequently as quit rates, but are typically lower than quit rates.[171] If incentive programs such as competitions are used, participation rates can be much higher.[172] For example, an 88 percent participation rate was reported in a program that pitted employees of four banks against each other in a smoking cessation competition.[173] Finally, smoking cessation programs can be cost-effective. One study estimated that worksite smoking cessation programs can yield a cost-benefit ratio of 8.75, that is, over $8 gained for every $1 spent on the program.[174]

## NUTRITION AND WEIGHT CONTROL INTERVENTIONS

Approximately 64 percent of U.S. adults can be considered either overweight or obese. Overweight is defined as being 25 to 29.9 percent or more over one's "ideal" body weight (based on height and gender).[175] Obesity is defined by a body mass index (BMI) of 30 or more. According to recent census data, 34 percent of U.S. adults are overweight, and an additional 30 percent are obese.[176] Over the past twenty years, the trends toward increasing obesity in the U.S. population are dramatic and troubling. Obesity has been causally associated with musculoskeletal problems, hypertension, high levels of blood sugar and cholesterol, and some forms of cancer.[177] Because of the health and cost consequences of obesity and because of employee concerns about appearance, workplace weight control and nutrition interventions are becoming more common.[178] It is estimated that 37 percent of worksites with 50 or more employees and 85 percent of worksites with over 750 employees have a nutrition education and/or weight management program.[179]

The content of such programs varies widely and can include educational activities such as newsletters, leaflets, cooking demonstrations, weigh-ins, and advice on developing weight-loss programs. Organizations may also stock cafeterias and vending machines with healthy, low-fat foods and post nutritional information concerning food sold in their cafeteria.[180]

Worksite weight control programs can be effective in helping participants achieve short-term weight loss (that is, one to two pounds per week), but their effectiveness with regard to long-term weight loss and their health and productivity benefits have not been established.[181] Similarly, worksite nutrition and cholesterol programs can lead to short-term benefits for participants (e.g., attitude and dietary change, decreased cholesterol level), with more intensive programs that used individual counseling and follow-up leading to better results.[182]

In each of these types of programming, more and better conducted studies can help establish causal links to improved health and behavior. For example, results of two well-conducted, large-scale health promotion programs have recently been reported.[183] Both interventions led to reduced fat intake and increased fruit and vegetable consumption. As is the case with other health improvement programs, employee participation is an important aspect of program effectiveness. It does seem to be the case that competition serves to improve both participation and the success rate of such programs.[184]

Finally, we end this section with a cautionary note. Negative attitudes toward overweight individuals are widespread in our society. A review by Mark Roehling demonstrated substantial evidence of bias and employment discrimination against overweight people.[185] There are obvious psychological and economic implications here for overweight individuals, but also potential legal implications for employers. The point we would stress is that organizational efforts to assist individuals in losing weight can be good and beneficial to both the employee and the organization. However, organizations and their representatives need to make sure that their nutritional and weight control interventions are kept free of negative stereotypes and negative job outcomes for participants, unless the participant's weight is truly related to their ability to perform a given job (see Roehling for guidance here).[186]

## CONTROL OF HYPERTENSION

Approximately 29 percent of U.S. adults suffer from **hypertension**, with an additional 31 percent classified as prehypertensive (i.e., at risk for hypertension).[187] Health problems linked to hypertension include a significantly greater incidence of heart disease and stroke.[188] It has been estimated that organizations lose 52 million workdays per year because of heart and vascular disease.[189] Despite the potentially devastating effects of hypertension, it can often be controlled through exercise, weight reduction, medication, stress reduction, and a low-salt diet.[190] The high incidence of hypertension and the relative ease with which it can be detected and controlled have made hypertension screening and control programs popular in the workplace. Thirty-two percent of worksites with fifty or more employees and 78 percent of large worksites offer blood pressure screenings, while 29 percent of worksites with fifty or more employees and 68 percent of large worksites, respectively, offer information regarding blood pressure control. Of those offering screening, 72 percent refer employees with high blood pressure to a physician, and almost 40 percent monitor and/or follow up on these employees.[191]

Organizations need not have a full-blown fitness or health promotion program to help employees reduce hypertension. A typical screening and control program may include:

- provision of educational materials
- blood pressure screenings to identify hypertensive employees
- referral of such employees for treatment
- installation of blood pressure screening equipment for employees to use to monitor their own blood pressure
- low-salt foods available in both cafeteria and vending machines
- periodic monitoring of employee progress[192]

The effectiveness of workplace hypertension programs in reducing blood pressure and increasing participant knowledge appears to be well established.[193] Success rates of hypertension control programs in the workplace, as measured by percentages of employees who manage to control blood pressure over a period of time, range from 50 to 75 percent, which is often superior to programs offered in other settings.[194] Such programs also appear to be cost-effective. Foote and Erfurt reported a benefit of $1.89 to $2.72 in reduced healthcare claims per dollar spent on running a hypertension control program.[195]

### OVERALL EFFECTIVENESS OF HEALTH AND WELLNESS PROGRAMS

It is recommended that organizations have multiple components to their health and wellness programs, that is, covering as many of the topics identified earlier as possible. A recent compilation of the results of over forty studies of the impact of such programs demonstrated reductions in sick leave, health plan costs, and workers' compensation costs of over 25 percent. Further, an average cost-benefit ratio of 5.93 was obtained, suggesting that the benefits of such programs far outweigh the costs.[196] This is fairly impressive evidence of overall effectiveness. It would seem that the challenge now is to get more organizations to implement such inclusive wellness programs, and then to see more individuals take part in them.

## ISSUES IN EMPLOYEE COUNSELING

Each of the employee counseling approaches discussed previously is affected by a common set of issues, including effectiveness, ethical and legal issues, responsibility, and unintended negative consequences. We will discuss each of these general issues next.

### EFFECTIVENESS OF EMPLOYEE COUNSELING INTERVENTIONS

A common theme among the interventions cited previously is a general lack of scientifically sound studies demonstrating effectiveness. While a considerable amount of the evidence to support these interventions is based on anecdotes and testimonials, the trend is toward more rigorous studies. However, until a greater number of such studies are conducted and reported, the evidence cited earlier should be seen as more suggestive than conclusive. Table 11-8 summarizes the findings of a series of reviews of peer-reviewed studies that examined various health promotion activities.

Several factors make it difficult for rigorous research to be conducted on these topics. First, the personal nature of many problems addressed by counseling, such as substance abuse and mental illness, may make organizations reluctant to allow researchers access to the data needed. Second, defining success and effectiveness for many of these problems is a difficult task. In the case of alcohol abuse, for example, many programs define alcoholism indirectly, in terms of changes in job behavior, rather than directly, in terms of the volume or pattern of alcohol consumption. Is an alcohol abuse program effective if treated employees return to normal working patterns, even if the employees still drink? Similarly, what period of time is suitable to establish that a problem has been resolved? Does a reduction of stress for six months signify success? The prevention of relapse is a significant factor, whether in the case of weight control, hypertension, or fitness interventions. We would suggest that effectiveness be defined using multiple criteria, including cost-effectiveness, short- and long-term behavior and attitude changes, participation rates, and direct impact on the cause of the problem.[197] It would also be beneficial to conduct more longitudinal studies that use multiple worksites and interventions and to examine organizational-level interventions and outcomes.[198]

Third, the reasons an organization has begun an intervention in the first place may affect whether research is done and how effectiveness is defined. Some organizations launch employee counseling programs because they believe it is the right thing to do or because the program is consistent with the organization's philosophy. Other organizations implement such programs to enhance the organization's image, both internally and externally. Effectiveness data in these cases may not affect whether the organization continues to offer the program; the fact that the program is being offered is the key concern.

One way to encourage organizations to evaluate their programs is to provide a model that identifies the data needed for sound evaluation. Gebhardt and Crump describe a strategy for evaluating wellness programs that we believe could be used as a guideline for evaluating EAPs and SMIs as well.[199] Their strategy includes these steps:

1. Determine the demographics of the organization (age, sex, etc.).
2. Determine expected participation rates.
3. Estimate program start-up and maintenance costs needed to meet objectives.
4. Implement a testing and tracking system to quantify program outcomes.
5. Measure pre- and postprogram changes for relevant outcomes.
6. Analyze program variables separately by relevant demographic groups and by measuring participation versus nonparticipation in the program.
7. Perform cost-benefit analyses of present and future benefits, expressed in current-dollar value.

Following this framework is not easy, as it is often hard to identify all the costs and benefits of a program and to express them in economic terms.[200] However, conducting an evaluation based on this strategy can provide the data needed to make informed decisions about the program. We refer interested readers to a recent study by Musich and colleagues, where the economic returns of a health promotion program were demonstrated.[201]

## LEGAL ISSUES IN EMPLOYEE COUNSELING PROGRAMS

Federal and state legislation has had a significant impact on employee counseling programs, especially in the area of alcohol and drug abuse. Federal laws such as the Federal Rehabilitation Act of 1973, the Drug-Free Workplace Act of 1988, and Executive Order 12564 (called the Drug-Free Federal Workplace Act) have generally served to encourage the adoption of EAPs.[202] For example, the Drug-Free Workplace Act requires federal contract and grant recipients of more than $100,000 to have a written policy regarding drug use in the workplace and to notify employees of the availability of related counseling, rehabilitation, and employee assistance programs. State laws, such as Rhode Island's, and federal agency rules, such as those of the Department of Transportation, require drug testing programs to be accompanied by EAPs or some other form of rehabilitation counseling.[203]

Some proponents of employee counseling programs cite a legal advantage to such programs, pointing out that they help the organization comply with existing laws such as the *Rehabilitation Act of 1973* and the *Americans with Disabilities Act of*

## TABLE 11-8 — SUMMARY OF INTERVENTIONS, METHODOLOGY, EFFECTS, AND RATING OF THE PEER-REVIEWED LITERATURE THAT EXAMINED THE EFFECT OF WORKSITE HEALTH PROMOTION ACTIVITIES ON HEALTH-RELATED OUTCOMES

| Area | Interventions Evaluated | Study Methods/Designs |
|---|---|---|
| Exercise | Self-regulated program, fitness class (usually 30–45 minutes, 2–3 times/week), programs include compliance strategies | 10% used experimental designs, 27% used quasi-experimental with matched controls, pre-/postmeasures, primarily short-term measures (end of program to 12 months), primarily self-report, some biomedical measures |
| Health risk appraisal (HRA) | HRA followed by educational program or materials | 44% used experimental designs, primarily pre-/postmeasures, measured short-term effects (end of program to one year), used both self-report and biomedical measures |
| Nutrition/ cholesterol | Nutrition: group education, group education and individual counseling, cafeteria-based. Cholesterol: individual counseling, group education, media, combination of all three | 42% used experimental designs, primarily pre-/postmeasures, measured short-term effects (end of program to one year) and long-term (up to six years for cholesterol) effects. Nutrition: primarily self-report, direct observation, biomedical measures for cholesterol. Cholesterol: biomedical measures |
| Weight control | Programs centered on behavior modification, education topics, and incentive system | 18% used experimental designs, primarily pre-/postmeasures, short-term effects (end of program to one year), self-report and biomedical measures |
| Hypertension | Two main program formats: (1) screening, treatment, long-term monitoring and (2) group education and training | 35% used experimental designs, pre-/post design with longitudinal tracking, measured both short-term (end of program) and long-term effects, biomedical measures |
| Alcohol | Two main program formats: (1) assessment, referral, follow up and (2) general education | 7% used experimental designs, primarily measured short-term effects usually pre-/postintervention or referral, self-report measures |
| HIV/AIDS | Group education | 9% used experimental design, primarily pre-/postmeasures, measured short-term effects (end of program to six weeks), self-report measures |
| Stress management | Broad categories: progressive relaxation, meditation, cognitive-behavioral skills, combination of techniques, others; 73% were prevention programs | 53% used experimental designs, pre-/postmeasures (end of program to one year), psychological measure or self-report |

*continued*

**TABLE 11-8**                                                                              **CONTINUED**

| Methodological Problems | Documented Effects | Overall Rating |
|---|---|---|
| Hawthorne effect?, self-selection bias, attrition, small sample sizes | Decrease in body mass, skinfolds, % body fat, blood pressure, total cholesterol, smoking level, and absenteeism; increased muscle strength and endurance, and life satisfaction and well-being | Suggestive |
| Self-selection bias, self-report measures, attrition | Decrease total cholesterol, blood pressure, smoking levels, weight, and health age; increase physical activity and seat-belt use | Weak |
| Self-selection bias and attrition for both, lack of valid measures for nutrition | Nutrition: attitude and dietary change, decrease cholesterol level. Cholesterol: decrease cholesterol level and weight, dietary change | Suggestive/indicative for both |
| Self-selection bias, attrition | Weight loss, decrease attrition | Indicative |
| Self-selection, attrition | Decreased blood pressure (systolic and diastolic), increase in knowledge | Conclusive |
| Reliance on self-report, self-selection bias, attrition, sampling problems | Decrease in alcohol/drug consumption, increase in job performance, attitude change | Suggestive |
| Self-selection bias, lack of valid and reliable measures, self-report measures | Increase in knowledge, and behavioral intent; attitude change | Weak |
| Self-selection bias, small sample sizes | Decrease blood pressure and anxiety, increase job satisfaction | Indicative |

PART 3: HUMAN RESOURCE DEVELOPMENT APPLICATIONS

SOURCE: Adapted with permission from M. G. Wilson (1996). A comprehensive review of the effects of worksite health promotion on health-related outcomes: An update. *American Journal of Health Promotion, 11,* 108.

*1990 (ADA)*. These laws prohibit employers from discriminating against individuals with disabilities and require that employers make "reasonable accommodations" to help such employees perform their job functions. Both of these laws cover employees with alcohol and drug problems (e.g., the ADA includes in its definition of disability such individuals who have successfully completed or are currently using a supervised drug rehabilitation program and who are no longer using illegal drugs).

The Rehabilitation Act, which applies to federal contractors and government-supported organizations, specifies that employees with disabilities may be discharged only for job-performance reasons. An alcoholic employee may not be fired because of his or her alcoholism, but only for the negative effects the alcoholism has had on work performance. In addition, it is unlawful to simply permit the employee's performance to deteriorate to a level that would justify termination. According to the law, the employer must make reasonable accommodations that help the employee resolve the problem and improve performance. In the case of substance abuse, "**reasonable accommodation**" has been interpreted to mean the employee must be offered the opportunity for treatment and permitted the time necessary for the treatment to take effect before firing for poor performance is justified.[204] Some authors see EAPs as a way to prevent lawsuits relating to wrongful discharge or reasonable accommodation.[205]

The ADA, which took effect in July 1992, broadly defines reasonable accommodation to include modification of facilities, materials, procedures, and jobs, and states that employers must take such action provided these modifications do not create an "undue hardship" on the organization (e.g., significant difficulty or expense). The impact of the ADA has been greater than that of the Rehabilitation Act because it applies to all employers of fifteen or more employees. The ADA created considerable concern among employers who feared the cost of complying with the act and felt that its definitions of disability, reasonable accommodation, and undue hardship were too vague to provide clear guidance on compliance. While the ADA does not explicitly mention counseling services, it is likely some employers will see EAPs, SMIs, and/or wellness or HPPs as ways to help them comply with the law. As mentioned earlier, the EEOC's 1997 *Enforcement Guidance on the Americans with Disabilities Act and Psychiatric Disabilities* offers information concerning mental health issues.

The potential legal advantage of using counseling programs to comply with existing laws may be offset to the extent that the counseling program exposes employers to lawsuits charging erroneous assessment for failure to refer either to appropriate treatment or to any treatment.[206] Further, in the case of fitness and wellness programs, litigation may also be encountered if an employee becomes injured while participating in company-sponsored events or while working out in its fitness facility.

Clearly, there are both legal pros and cons to engaging in employee well-being programs. The rapid growth of these programs may indicate that such problems are either not prevalent or are not considered significant by many organizations. Nevertheless, legal issues should be examined when an organization is planning and implementing any counseling programs.

## WHOSE RESPONSIBILITY IS EMPLOYEE COUNSELING?

Employees, the organization, supervisors, and unions all have a role to play in employee well-being. As stated earlier, organizations stand to gain significant benefits from efforts to improve employee mental and physical health. It should be noted that labor unions have played a role in employee well-being also. Several unions, such as the Association of Flight Attendants, have sponsored EAPs to assist members with alcohol- and drug-abuse problems.[207] Proponents of union involvement in employee counseling contend that union-sponsored programs can help reduce members' negative perceptions of counseling.[208] In addition, union-based programs can take advantage of peer pressure and referrals to encourage troubled employees to seek assistance.[209] Furthermore, employees may be more likely to seek help from a union than an employer, perceiving the union's interest in offering help as a genuine concern, while the employer's interest may be seen as self-serving.[210]

Observers have noted that management has typically involved unions in counseling programs such as EAPs almost as an afterthought.[211] We believe opportunities exist for joint counseling programs that can motivate increased employee use (and therefore the effectiveness) of these programs. The Member Assistance Programs mentioned in our discussion of EAPs are an example of such joint efforts.[212] However, critics note that union cooperation will not necessarily facilitate the effectiveness of EAPs,[213] and adoption of an EAP has at times been hindered by union involvement.[214]

Obviously, the individual bears primary responsibility for his or her own well-being. Given the impact of lifestyle choices on health and longevity, individuals are ultimately responsible for the course of their lives. Still, many of the factors leading to stress and poor coping result from an interaction between the organization and the individual.[215] Individuals should be trained to recognize these sources so that they can determine when help is needed.

Finally, supervisors and managers play a key role in the effectiveness of any employee counseling effort. Because supervisors are in regular contact with employees, are responsible for their development and evaluation, and are ultimately held responsible for their performance, they occupy a unique position. The supervisor's primary responsibility is to ensure the effective functioning of the work unit. Supervisory counseling should focus on awareness of employee performance problems that might be the result of personal problems, supporting troubled employees by helping them obtain the care they need to improve performance, motivating the employee to improve, and monitoring performance to ensure that improvement does occur.

Confronting problem employees and dealing with them sensitively and effectively is a challenging task. Care must be taken to train supervisors and managers to fulfill the counseling role. A supervisor who is too harsh or zealous in undertaking counseling can be as counterproductive as one who avoids the role completely.[216] Training programs should help supervisors acquire both the skills and attitudes needed to fulfill this important role. Suggestions for the content of a supervisory counseling training program that addresses these issues are shown in Table 11-9.

| TABLE 11-9 | POSSIBLE CONTENT OF A SUPERVISORY COUNSELING TRAINING PROGRAM |
| --- | --- |

1. Identification of the supervisor's initial reactions to the prospect of counseling (e.g., using comfort reaction questionnaire)
2. Lecture and discussion of various counseling topics, which may include:
   a. emotional needs of individuals
   b. potential signs of employee problems
   c. signs of overinvolvement in counseling (e.g., loss of objectivity, focusing beyond job performance, guidelines for giving advice)
   d. structure of a counseling session, including decisions to be made therein
   e. counseling terminology to facilitate discussion of feelings, reactions, and behaviors
   f. nonverbal communication
3. Training in counseling skills, perhaps using case studies and behavior modeling
4. Role play of counseling sessions
5. Discussion of the relationship between counseling and coaching/performance management
6. Evaluation of counseling options and resources available

SOURCE: From Ramsey, K. B. (1985). Counseling employees. In W. R. Tracey (Ed.), *Handbook of human resource management and development* (pp. 829, 832). New York: AMACOM.

### ETHICAL ISSUES IN EMPLOYEE COUNSELING

Two ethical issues relating to employee counseling services merit discussion: confidentiality and the nature of participation (i.e., whether mandatory or voluntary).[217] Each is discussed here.

**Confidentiality** is a key concern in all types of employee counseling interventions. We emphatically agree with the position taken by Matteson and Ivancevich:

> Simply put, all records of program utilization should be held in the strictest confidence, should be maintained separate and apart from an employee's personnel file, and should be released only with the express permission of the employee. (p. 293)[218]

While data generated by participation in, for example, a nutrition program may be less sensitive than that gained from a drug treatment program, it is nevertheless important to guarantee the confidentiality of all employee counseling records. Program policy statements should include an explicit description of the confidentiality policy and the steps involved in implementing it.

A second ethical consideration concerns whether participation in a counseling program should be voluntary or mandatory. While organizations stand to gain greater benefits if all members of a target group participate in a program (e.g., all smokers, or all obese employees), we believe participation should be voluntary. Employees should have the right to determine their lifestyle, and should not be forced to engage in behavior change other than that relating to performance of their jobs. Even an employee with a substance abuse problem should be free to choose whether and how to deal with that problem. The organization can offer assistance in treating the problem, but it should not attempt to force acceptance of treatment. If the employee's substandard performance does not improve after he or she has had ample opportunity to improve, then the organization should pursue its regular procedures concerning discipline and discharge.

## UNINTENDED NEGATIVE OUTCOMES OF EMPLOYEE COUNSELING PROGRAMS

It is possible that participating in a counseling or fitness program can have unintended negative consequences. This is particularly true of health promotion programs. Some potential unintended negative consequences could include (1) workers' compensation cost increases; (2) employees participating in fitness programs may experience scheduling problems, increased fatigue and accidents, and lower performance; or (3) smoking bans may lead to conflicts between smokers and nonsmokers.[219] There is little research on this topic to guide organizations in making decisions. Decision makers concerned about such consequences may find some help by investigating the experiences of other organizations.

## CLOSING COMMENTS

Both organizations and employees have much to gain from workplace counseling interventions. While the numbers of active programs indicate that employers already are acting upon this opportunity, we need to know more about what works, how well it works, and under what conditions it works. Economic conditions and changing business strategies often lead to cost-cutting initiatives, and counseling programs (like all others) will be closely examined. As we have emphasized throughout this book, HRD professionals have the skills and expertise (in needs assessment, program design and implementation, and evaluation) to provide this information and to help see that their organizations' resources are used wisely.

EAPs, wellness programs, and other health promotion programs continue to develop and change. We have noted the efforts to consolidate more of these programs, rather than running them as independent entities. We expect to see more integration and consolidation in the coming years. One interesting proposal is that employers get more involved in "behavioral risk management," that is, in more proactively looking for ways to spot potential for workplace conflict and violence. As Dale Tidwell states,

> If an EAP is willing to audit the organization for violence potential and conflict problems, work with managers, intervene with interpersonal conflicts and meet with troubled employees one-on-one instead of over an 800 line, it can have a tremendous preventive impact on violence and other behavioral risks.[220]

At some point in our lives, most of us will be impacted by the issues raised in this chapter. This may be through personal experience, or through the experiences of someone close to us, such as a close friend or family member. The workplace is certainly not the only place to look for remedies to employee personal problems. However, healthy work environments cannot be expected to occur without healthy employees. In our view, managers and HRD professionals should be concerned with promoting the broadest forms of employee health and well-being. This chapter has provided many practical ways of accomplishing this task.

## RETURN TO OPENING CASE

Lovelace Health Systems began Project WISE in June 1998. Both the intervention and the evaluation efforts were carefully planned out. Your instructor has further details about what was done in this intervention, and what outcomes have been observed to date.

Lapham, S. C., Chang, I., & Gregory, C. (2000). Substance abuse intervention for health care workers: A preliminary report. *Journal of Behavioral Health Services & Research, 27*(2), 131–143.

## SUMMARY

Employee well-being affects the ability, availability, and readiness of employees to perform their jobs. The effects of problems with alcohol and drug abuse, mental health, smoking, gambling, and stress are widespread and cost organizations billions of dollars in lost productivity. Both the organization and its employees stand to gain from employers' attempts to provide information and programs that help employees deal with these problems.

Employee counseling programs, which can include employee assistance programs, stress management programs, and wellness and health promotion programs, include activities such as problem identification and diagnosis, education, counseling or advising, referral to appropriate treatment, actual treatment, and follow-up. Employee counseling can be viewed as an HRD activity because it seeks to ensure that employees are now and will continue to be effective contributors to organizational goals.

While each of these programs is believed to be effective in helping at least some participants, the data available have frequently come from studies that lack scientific rigor. Although the data indicate that these programs can yield benefits to both individuals and organizations, more rigorous research is needed to determine the true effectiveness of these interventions. Solving the problem of how to increase employee participation from those who would most benefit from using these programs is an important issue.

Supervisors play a key role in an effective counseling program and must be aware of what programs are available to their employees and what employees need to do to participate. In addition, for many programs, such as alcohol-abuse counseling, the supervisor often serves as the person who first recognizes that an employee may be in trouble and refers the employee for treatment. In addition, the supervisor is also in a position to participate in the follow-up effort to determine whether the employee is carrying out the treatment and whether the problem is under control or has been solved. Training supervisors to perform this form of counseling role is an important part of ensuring overall program effectiveness.

Employee counseling programs face legal and ethical issues. Laws and regulations have both fueled the growth of counseling programs and raised questions about the role counseling programs may play in providing disabled employees (and those perceived to be disabled) with "reasonable accommodations" to perform their job duties. Ensuring the confidentiality of an employee's participation in counseling and the nature of participation (e.g., whether voluntary or mandatory) are two ethical issues that must be dealt with, as is the possible presence of negative consequences from participation.

## KEY TERMS AND CONCEPTS

Americans with Disabilities Act
   of 1990 (ADA)
confidentiality
constructive confrontation
counseling
Drug-Free Workplace Act
   of 1988
educational interventions
employee assistance program
   (EAP)
employee counseling services

employee wellness program (EWP)
health promotion program (HPP)
hypertension
managed care
Mental Health Parity Act of 1996
reasonable accommodation
skill-acquisition interventions
stress
stress management intervention (SMI)
stressor
wellness

## QUESTIONS FOR DISCUSSION

1. Explain why employee counseling services can be considered HRD programs. Describe two elements counseling programs have in common with other HRD programs.

2. What are the similarities and differences between employee coaching (Chapter 10) and employee counseling (discussed in this chapter)?

3. Suppose you were asked by your employer to develop a proposal for an employee assistance program (EAP). Which approach would you recommend: an in-house program run by employees of your organization, or a service provided by an outside contractor? Support your choice. Suppose financial constraints limited the company to offering only two areas of service (e.g., mental health, substance abuse, gambling, financial problems). Which services do you think are most important? Support your choices. Describe how you would make sure that you select the services that would provide the company and employees with the most benefits.

4. There is some disagreement about the effectiveness of EAPs and the constructive confrontation approach in treating alcohol abuse. Present the

positions supporting both sides of the argument. Given what you have learned about this issue, where do you think the truth lies? Support your choice.

5. Stress management interventions commonly focus on helping employees find ways to deal with the stressors in their lives. Yet, some experts believe organizations should modify jobs or other organizational attributes (e.g., management style) to remove or reduce the impact of such stressors themselves, rather than teaching coping skills alone. What is your opinion on this matter? Support your position.

6. Some people believe that programs like wellness programs infringe on an individual's right to choose his or her own lifestyle, maintaining that an individual has the right to smoke cigarettes, eat junk food, and avoid exercise if he or she wants to. What argument can you make to support the use of workplace wellness and health promotion programs? What argument would support the critics of workplace wellness programs? If you were a director of a workplace wellness program at a large banking firm, for example, how would you balance the needs of the company with the rights of individuals? Support your position.

7. Employee counseling programs of all types are popular in the United States, despite the relative lack of scientific evidence that conclusively supports the efficacy of these programs. If managers are such bottom-line decision makers, why do they continue to offer these programs when an ironclad case for their effectiveness has not yet been made? Describe two reasons why it is difficult to conduct conclusive scientific studies as to the effectiveness of employee counseling services.

### EXERCISE: HOW ARE YOU DEALING WITH WORK STRESS?

An organization called Job Stress Help Counselors has a survey available online that asks you to describe a specific job-related stress that you are experiencing. This survey can be found at http://www.jobstresshelp.com/survey.htm.

Consider a stressful experience that you have had in a past or present job. Then, take this confidential online survey. Was this survey and the follow-up information helpful to you in thinking about this situation? What has worked best for you in dealing with stress in your life? Your instructor will give you further instructions concerning other requirements to complete this assignment.

> Visit http://werner.swlearning.com for links to informative websites for this chapter.

### REFERENCES

1. Everly, G. S., Feldman, R. H. L., & Associates (1985). *Occupational health promotion: Health behavior in the workplace.* New York: Wiley; Harwood, H. J., Napolitano, D. M., Kristiansen, P. L., & Collins, J. J. (1985). *Economic costs to society of alcohol and drug abuse and mental*

*illness: 1980.* (Publication No. RTI/2734/00-01FR). Research Triangle Park, NC: Research Triangle Institute; Maiden, R. P. (1988). Employee assistance program evaluation in a federal government agency. In M. J. Holosko & M. D. Feit (Eds.), *Evaluation of employee assistance plans* (pp. 191–203). New York: Haworth Press; Symonds, W. C., Ellis, J. E., Siler, S. F., Zellner, W., & Garland, S. B. (1991, March 25). Is business bungling its battle with booze? *Business Week,* pp. 76–78.

2. Collins, K. (2000). EAPs: Better onsite or offsite? *Behavioral Health Management, 20*(2), 42–46.

3. U.S. Census Bureau (1999). *Statistical abstract of the United States: 1999* (119th ed.). Washington, DC: U.S. Government Printing Office; Centers for Medicare & Medicaid Services (2004). Retrieved November 1, 2004, from http://www.cms.hhs.gov/statistics/nhe/projections-2003/t1.asp

4. Wojcik, J. (2004). Wellness in favor as employers aim to lower costs. *Business Insurance, 38*(13), March 29, 4–5; Donaldson, S. I. (1995). Worksite health promotion: A theory-driven, empirically based perspective. In L. R. Murphy, J. J. Hurrell, Jr., S. L. Sauter, & G. P. Keita (Eds.), *Job stress interventions* (pp. 73–90). Washington, DC: American Psychological Association; Terborg, J. (1986). Health promotion at the worksite: A research challenge for personnel and human resources management. In K. H. Rowland & G. R. Ferris (Eds.), *Research in personnel and human resources management, 4,* 225–267.

5. Berry, L. L., Mirabito, A. M., & Berwick, D. M. (2004). A health care agenda for business. *Sloan Management Review, 45*(4), Summer, 56–64.

6. Masi, D. A., & Reyes, P. J. (1999). *Productivity lost: Alcohol and drugs in the workplace.* Horsham, PA: LRP Publications; Caudron, S. (1996). Low unemployment is causing a staffing drought. *Personnel Journal, 75*(11), 58–67; Walker, J. W. (1988). Managing human resource in flat, lean and flexible organizations: Trends for the 1990s. *Human Resource Planning, 11*(2), 124–132; Walker, J. W. (1989). Human resource roles for the 90s. *Human Resource Planning, 12*(1), 55–60.

7. Cairo, P. C. (1983). Counseling in industry: A selected review of the literature. *Personnel Psychology, 36,* 1–18.

8. Masi, D. A. (1984). *Designing employee assistance programs.* New York: AMACOM.

9. Popple, P. R. (1981). Social work practice in business and industry. *Social Service Review, 6,* 257–269.

10. Glasgow, R. E., & Terborg, J. R. (1988). Occupational health promotion programs to rescue cardiovascular risk. *Journal of Consulting and Clinical Psychology, 56,* 365–373.

11. Prince, M. (1998). EAPs becoming part of larger programs. *Business Insurance, 32*(24), 14–15; Oss, M. E., & Clary, J. (1998). The evolving world of employee assistance. *Behavioral Health Management, 18*(4), 20–24.

12. Collins (2000), *supra* note 2.

13. Yandrick, R. M. (1998). The EAP struggle: Counselors or referrers? *HR Magazine, 43*(9), 90–95.

14. Sadu, G., Cooper, C., & Allison, T. (1989). A post office initiative to stamp out stress. *Personnel Management, 21*(8), 40–45.

15. Phillips, D. A., & Older, H. J. (1981). Models of service delivery. *EAP Digest, 1*(May-June), 12–15.

16. Harris, M. M., & Fennell, M. L. (1988). Perceptions of an employee assistance program and employees' willingness to participate. *Journal of Applied Behavioral Science, 24,* 423–438.

17. Erfurt, J. C., Foote, A., & Heirich, M. A. (1992). The cost-effectiveness of worksite wellness programs for hypertension control, weight loss, smoking cessation, and exercise. *Personnel Psychology, 45,* 5–27.

18. Masi, D. A. (1992). Employee assistance programs. In D. A. Masi (Ed.), *The AMA handbook for developing employee assistance and counseling programs* (pp. 1–35). New York: AMACOM; Swanson, N. G., & Murphy, L. R. (1991). Mental health counseling in industry. In C. L. Cooper & I. T. Robertson (Eds.), *International review of industrial and organizational psychology* (Vol. 6, pp. 265–282). Chichester: Wiley.

19. Trice, H. M., & Beyer, J. M. (1984). Work-related outcomes of the constructive confrontation strategy in a job-based alcoholism program. *Journal of Studies on Alcohol, 45,* 393–404.

20. Swanson & Murphy (1991), *supra* note 18; Wolfe, R. A., & Parker, D. F. (1994). Employee health management: Challenges and opportunities. *Academy of Management Executive, 8*(2), 22–31; Wilson, M. G., Holman, P. B., & Hammock, A. (1996). A comprehensive review of the effects of worksite health promotion on health-related outcomes. *American Journal of Health Promotion, 10,* 429–435.

21. Sonnenstuhl, W. J., & Trice, H. M. (1986). *Strategies for employee assistance programs: The crucial balance* (p. 1). Ithaca, NY: ILR Press.

22. Becker, L. R., Hall, M., Fisher, D. A., & Miller, T. R. (2000). Methods for evaluating a mature substance abuse prevention/early intervention program. *Journal of Behavioral Health Services & Research, 27*(2), 166–177.

23. Mann, S. E., & Kelly, M. J. (1999). EAP: A beneficial benefit for agents and clients. *LAN: Life Association News, 94*(10), 118–120; Masi (1992), *supra* note 18; Sonnenstuhl, W. J. (1988). Contrasting employee assistance, health promotion, and quality of work life programs and their effects on alcohol abuse and dependence. *The Journal of Applied Behavioral Science, 24,* 347–363.

24. Cascio, W. F. (2000). *Costing human resources: The financial impact of behavior in organizations* (4th ed.). Mason, OH: Thomson/South-Western.

25. http://www.eap-association.com

26. Mental and Physical Health Programs Proliferate (1995, May). *HRFocus, 72,* 12; Blum, T. C., & Roman, P. M. (1995). *Cost-effectiveness and preventive implications of employee assistance programs.* (DHHS Publication No. SMA 95-3053). Washington, DC: U.S. Government Printing Office.

27. Oss & Clary (1998), *supra* note 11.

28. *Ibid.*

29. National Survey on Drug Use and Health (2003). U.S. Department of Labor. Retrieved November 1, 2004, from http://www.dol.gov/asp/programs/drugs/said/WhatsNew.asp?ID=1667

30. Alcohol and Drug Abuse in America Today (2004). U.S. Department of Labor. Retrieved November 1, 2004, from http://www.dol.gov/asp/programs/drugs/workingpartners/stats/wi.asp

31. Hollinger, R. C. (1988). Working under the influence (WUI): Correlates of employees' use of alcohol and other drugs. *Journal of Applied Behavioral Science. 24,* 430–454.

32. Ames, G. M., Grube, J. M., & Moore, R. S. (1997). The relationship of drinking and hangovers to workplace problems: An empirical study. *Journal of Studies on Alcohol, 58,* 37–47.

33. Hollinger (1988), *supra* note 31.

34. Mensch, B. S., & Kandel, D. B. (1988). Do job conditions influence the use of drugs? *Journal of Health and Social Behavior, 29,* 169–184.

35. Collins (2000), *supra* note 2.

36. Brink, S. (2004). The price of booze. *U.S. News & World Report, 136*(4), February 2, 48–50.

37. Cited in Lapham, S. C., Chang, I., & Gregory, C. (2000). Substance abuse intervention for health care workers: A preliminary report. *Journal of Behavioral Health Services & Research, 27*(2), 131–143.

38. Normand, J., Salyards, S., & Mahoney, J. (1990). An evaluation of pre-employment drug testing. *Journal of Applied Psychology, 75,* 629–639; Zwerling, C., Ryan, J., & Orav, E. J. (1990). The efficacy of preemployment drug screening for marijuana and cocaine in predicting employment outcome. *Journal of the American Medical Association, 264*(20), 2639–2643.

39. Drug Free Workplace Advisor (2004). Retrieved November 1, 2004, from http://www.dol.gov/elaws/asp/drugfree/screen4.htm

40. Depression (2000). National Institute of Mental Health. Retrieved November 1, 2004, from http://www.nimh.nih.gov/publicat/depression.cfm#ptdep1

41. Rouse, B. A. (1995). *Substance abuse and mental health statistics sourcebook.* (DHHS Publication No. SMA 953064). Washington, DC: U.S. Government Printing Office; Regier et al. (1993). The de facto mental and addictive disorders service system. Epidemiologic catchment area prospective one year prevalence rates of disorders and services. *Archives of General Psychiatry, 50*(2): 85–94.

42. Kessler, R. C. et al. (1998). A methodology for estimating the 12-month prevalence of serious mental illness. In R. W. Manderscheid & M. J. Henderson, *Mental Health, United States, 1999,* 99–109. Rockville, MD: Center for Mental Health Services; http://www.nami.org/fact.htm

43. Lee, F. C., & Schwartz, G. (1984). Paying for mental health care in the private sector. *Business and Health, 1*(19), 12–16.

44. Center for Mental Health Services (1998). *Survey of Mental Health Organizations and General Mental Health Services.* Rockville, MD: Center for Mental Health Services.

45. Masi (1984), *supra* note 8, p. 118.

46. Annual Report (2003). National Council on Problem Gambling. Retrieved November 1, 2004, from http://www.ncpgambling.org/media/pdf/ncpg_03_ap.pdf

47. Mann & Kelly (1999), *supra* note 23.

48. EAP Tools and Resources (2004). Retrieved November 1, 2004, from http://www.utexas.edu/hr/eap/resources.html

49. Clegg, C., Wall, T., & Kemp, N. J. (1987). Women on the assembly line: A comparison of main and interactive explanations of job satisfaction, absence, and mental health. *Journal of Occupational Psychology, 60,* 273–287; Clegg, C., & Wall, T. (1990). The relationship between simplified jobs and mental health: A replication study. *Journal of Occupational Psychology, 63,* 289–296.

50. President's Commission on Mental Health (1978). *Report to the president* (Vol. 1). Washington, DC: U.S. Government Printing Office.

51. Engleken, C. (1987). Fighting the costs of spouse abuse. *Personnel Journal, 66*(3), 31–34.

52. U.S. Bureau of the Census (1999), *supra* note 3.

53. Bachman, R. E. (1997). Time for another look. *HR Magazine, 42*(3), 93–96.

54. Goldstein, D. B. (1999, July). Mental health parity and beyond. *Medical Reporter.* Retrieved November 1, 2004, from http://medicalreporter.health.org/tmr0799/parity.html

55. Rosenbaum, M. D., & Scheidt, K. S. (2004). Extension of the Mental Health Parity Act. *Employee Benefit Plan Review, 58*(9), March, 27.

56. Goode, E. (2001, January 1). Equal footing: A special report; 9 million gaining upgraded benefit for mental care. *New York Times*, p. A1.

57. Masi & Reyes (1999), *supra* note 6; Masi (1992), *supra* note 18.

58. Sonnenstuhl (1988), *supra* note 23.

59. Masi (1992), *supra* note 18.

60. Yandrick (1998), *supra* note 13.

61. Sonnenstuhl, W. J., Staudenmeier, W. J., Jr., & Trice, H. M. (1988). Ideology and referral categories in employee assistance program research. *The Journal of Applied Behavioral Science, 24,* 383–396, p. 385.

62. Santa-Barbara, J. (1984). Employee assistance programs: An alternative resource for mental health service delivery. *Canada's Mental Health, 32,* 35–38.

63. Becker et al. (2000), *supra* note 22; Taurone, D. (1999). Labor partnership maps out behavioral health ROI. *Employee Benefit News, 13*(12), 76–77.

64. Walsh, D. C., & Hingson, R. W. (1985). Where to refer employees for treatment of drinking problems. *Journal of Occupational Medicine, 27,* 745–752.

65. Luthans, F., & Waldersee, R. (1989). What do we really know about EAPs? *Human Resource Management, 28,* 385–401.

66. French, M. T., Zarkin, G. A., Bray, J. W., & Hartwell, T. D. (1997). Costs of employee assistance programs: Findings from a national survey. *American Journal of Health Promotion, 11,* 219–222.

67. Substance Abuse and Mental Health Services Administration (1993). *National household survey on drug abuse: Main findings 1991.* Rockville, MD: Substance Abuse and Mental Health Services Administration.

68. French et al. (1997), *supra* note 66.

69. Collins (2000), *supra* note 2.

70. Harlow, K. C. (1998). Employee attitudes toward an internal employee assistance program. *Journal of Employment Counseling, 35*(3), September, 141–150.

71. Stuart, P. (1993). How McDonnell Douglas cost-justified its EAP. *Personnel Journal, 72*(2), 48; Walsh, D. C., Hingson, R. W., Merrigan, D. M., Levenson, S. M., Cupples, L. A., Herren, T., Coffman, G. A., Becker, C. A., Barker, T. A., Hamilton, S. K., McGuire, T. G., & Kelly, C. A. (1991). A randomized trial of treatment options for alcohol-abusing workers. *New England Journal of Medicine, 325,* 775–782; Dickman, F., & Hayes, B. (1988). Professional sports and employee assistance programs. In F. Dickman, B. R. Challenger, W. G. Emener, & W. S. Hutchinson, Jr. (Eds.), *Employee assistance programs: A basic text* (pp. 425–430). Springfield, IL: Charles C Thomas; Feuer, B. (1987). Innovations in employee assistance programs: A case study at the association of flight attendants. In A. W. Reilly & S. J. Zaccaro (Eds.), *Occupational stress and organizational effectiveness* (pp. 217–227). New York: Praeger; Emener, W. S. (1988). School teachers and school personnel. In F. Dickman, B. R. Challenger, W. G. Emener, & W. S. Hutchinson, Jr. (Eds.), *Employee assistance programs: A basic text* (pp. 443–453). Springfield, IL: Charles C Thomas.

72. Magellan Health Services (2004). Retrieved November 1, 2004, from http://www.magellanhealth.com/about/fastfacts.asp?leftmenu=3&sub=none; Prince (1998), *supra* note 11.

73. Rosen, R. H., & Lee, F. C. (1987). Occupational mental health: A continuum of care. In A. W. Reilly & S. J. Zaccaro (Eds.), *Occupational stress and organizational effectiveness* (pp. 245–267). New York: Praeger.

74. Axel, H. (1990). *Corporate experiences with drug testing programs.* New York: The Conference Board.

75. For a review, see Harris, M. M., & Heft, L. L. (1992). Alcohol and drug use in the workplace: Issues, controversies, and directions for future research. *Journal of Management, 18,* 239–266.

76. Gatewood, R. D., & Feild, H. S. (2001). *Human Resource Selection* (5th ed.). Fort Worth, TX: Harcourt College Publishers; Axel (1990), *supra* note 74; Harris & Heft (1992), *supra* note 75.

77. Blum, T., & Bennett, N. (1990). Employee assistance programs: Utilization and referral data, performance management, and prevention concepts. In P. M. Roman (Ed.), *Alcohol problem intervention in the workplace* (pp. 144–162). New York: Quorum Books; Blum & Roman (1995), *supra* note 26; Roman, P. M., & Blum, T. C. (1996). Alcohol: A review of the impact of worksite interventions on health and behavioral outcomes. *American Journal of Health Promotion, 11,* 136–149; Roman, P. M., & Blum, T. C. (2002). The workplace and alcohol problem prevention. *Alcohol Research & Health, 26*(1), 49–57.

78. Swanson & Murphy (1991), *supra* note 20; Roman & Blum (1996), *supra* note 77.

79. Tersine, R. J., & Hazeldine, J. (1982). Alcoholism: A productivity hangover. *Business Horizons, 25*(11), 68–72.

80. Cascio (2000), *supra* note 24; Mann & Kelly (1999), *supra* note 23.

81. Walsh et al. (1991), *supra* note 71.

82. Skidmore, R. A., Balsam, D. D., & Jones, O. (1974). Social work practice in industry. *Social Work, 19,* 280–286.

83. Wrich, J. T. (1984). *The employee assistance program.* Center City, MN: Hazelden Educational Foundation.

84. Trice & Beyer (1984), *supra* note 19.

85. Kurtz, N. R., Googins, B., & Howard, W. C. (1984). Measuring the success of occupational alcoholism programs. *Journal of Studies on Alcohol, 45,* 33–45; Luthans & Waldersee (1989), *supra* note 65.

86. Luthans & Waldersee (1989), *supra* note 65.

87. Tersine & Hazeldine (1982), *supra* note 79; Wagner, W. G. (1982). Assisting employees with personal problems. *Personnel Administrator, 61*(11), 59–64.

88. Madsen, W. (1976). Alcoholics Anonymous as a crisis cult. *Journal of Studies on Alcohol, 37,* 482.

89. Polich, J. M., Armor, D. J., & Braker, H. B. (1981). *The course of alcoholism: Four years after treatment.* New York: Wiley.

90. Project MATCH Research Group (1997). Matching alcoholism treatments to client heterogeneity: Project MATCH posttreatment drinking outcomes. *Journal of Studies on Alcohol, 58,* 7–29.

91. Luthans & Waldersee (1989), *supra* note 65.

92. Weiss, R. M. (1987). Writing under the influence: Science versus fiction in the analysis of corporate alcoholism programs. *Personnel Psychology, 40,* 341–355.

93. Weiss (1982), reported in Weiss (1987), *supra* note 92, p. 348.

94. Sonnenstuhl, W. J. (1992). The job-treatment balance in employee assistance programs. *Alcohol Health & Research World, 16*(2), 129–133; Trice & Beyer (1984), *supra* note 19.

95. Blum & Roman (1995), *supra* note 26.

96. Cited in Moran, T. (1999). Assistance programs help workers during crisis. *Crain's Detroit Business, 15*(21), May 24, E-2.

97. Swanson & Murphy (1991), *supra* note 18.

98. Blum & Roman (1995), *supra* note 26.

99. Harris & Heft (1992), *supra* note 75.

100. See, for example, Becker et al. (2000), *supra* note 22; Harlow (1998), *supra* note 70; Lapham et al. (2000), *supra* note 37.

101. Luthans & Waldersee (1989), *supra* note 65.

102. *Ibid.*

103. Thompson, R., Jr. (1990). *Substance abuse and employee rehabilitation.* Washington, DC: BNA Books; Masi & Reyes (1999), *supra* note 6; Masi (1984), *supra* note 8; Masi (1992), *supra* note 18.

104. Prince (1998), *supra* note 11.

105. Prince (1998), *supra* note 11; Yandrick (1998), *supra* note 13; Collins, E. J. (1994). EAPs vs. MCOs: Resolving the conflict. *Behavioral Health Management, 14*(4), 12–20.

106. Bahls, J. E. (1999). Handle with care. *HR Magazine, 44*(3), March, 60–66; Yandrick (1998), *supra* note 13.

107. de Miranda, J. (2004). ADA lawsuit challenges UPS employee assistance program. *Alcoholism & Drug Abuse Weekly, 16*(32), 5.

108. Hymowitz, C., & Silverman, R. E. (2001). In this economy — you bet. Add financial uncertainty to general job overload; Costello, D. (2001). Incidents of "desk rage" disrupt America's offices; Lublin, J. S. (2001). Mergers often trigger lower morale; Maher, K. (2001). At Verizon call centers, stress is seldom on hold. All appearing in the *Wall Street Journal, 237*(11), January 16, B1, B4, B12; Extreme job stress: Survivors' tales (2001); Dunham, K. J. (2001). Seeking the new, slimmed-down workday: 9 to 5. Both appeared in the *Wall Street Journal, 237*(12), January 17, B1, B4.

109. Ganster, D. C., & Schaubroeck, J. (1991). Work stress and employee health. *Journal of Management, 17,* 235–271.

110. Schwartz, J. (2004, September 5). Always on the job, employees pay with health. *New York Times,* p. 1.1.

111. Ganster & Schaubroeck (1991), *supra* note 109; Kahn, R. L., & Byosiere, P. (1992). Stress in organizations. In M. D. Dunnette & L. M. Hough (Eds.), *Handbook of industrial and organizational psychology* (2nd ed., Vol. 3, pp. 571–650). Palo Alto, CA: Consulting Psychologists Press; Sullivan, S. E., & Bhagat, R. S. (1992). Organizational stress, job satisfaction, and job performance: Where do we go from here? *Journal of Management, 18,* 353–374.

112. Kahn & Byosiere (1992), *supra* note 111.

113. *Ibid.*

114. Ivancevich, J. M., Matteson, M. T., Freedman, S. M., & Phillips, J. S. (1990). Worksite stress management interventions. *American Psychologist, 45,* 252–261, p. 252.

115. Krohe, J., Jr. (1999). Workplace stress. *Across the Board, 36*(2), February, 36–42.

116. Crane, J. (1999). Firms take lead on stress management for workers. *Boston Business Journal, 19*(41), November 19, 34–35.

117. Everly, G. S. (1984). The development of occupational stress management programs. In G. S. Everly & R.H.L. Feldman (Eds.), *Occupational health promotion* (49–73). New York: Wiley; Ivancevich et al. (1990), *supra* note 114; Murphy, L. R. (1996). Stress management in work settings: A critical review of health effects. *American Journal of Health Promotion, 11,* 112–135.

118. Matteson, M. T., & Ivancevich, J. M. (1987). *Controlling work stress.* San Francisco: Jossey-Bass.

119. Ivancevich et al. (1990), *supra* note 114.

120. Matteson & Ivancevich (1987), *supra* note 118.

121. Kahn & Byosiere (1996), *supra* note 111; Sullivan & Bhagat (1992), *supra* note 111.

122. Matteson & Ivancevich (1987), *supra* note 118.

123. Ivancevich et al. (1990), *supra* note 114.

124. Ivancevich et al. (1990), *supra* note 114; Murphy (1996), *supra* note 117.

125. Ganster & Schaubroeck (1991), *supra* note 111; Murphy, L. R. (1986). A review of occupational stress management research: Methodological considerations. *Journal of Occupational Behavior Management, 8,* 215–228; Murphy, L. R., Hurrell, J. J., Jr., Sauter, S. L., & Keita, G. P. (Eds.). (1995). *Job stress interventions.* Washington DC: American Psychological Association.

126. Briner, R. (1999). Against the grain. *People Management, 5*(19), September 30, 32–38.

127. DeFrank, R. S., & Cooper, C. L. (1987). Worksite stress management interventions: Their effectiveness and conceptualization. *Journal of Managerial Psychology, 2,* 4–10; Ivancevich, J. M., & Matteson, M. T. (1986). Organizational level stress management interventions: Review and recommendations. *Journal of Occupational Behavior Management, 8,* 229–248; Ivancevich et al. (1990), *supra* note 114; Matteson & Ivancevich (1987), *supra* note 118; Murphy, L. R. (1984). Occupational stress management: A review and appraisal. *Journal of Occupational Psychology 57,* 1–17; Murphy (1986), *supra* note 125; Murphy (1996), *supra* note 117; Newman, J. D., & Beehr, T. (1979). Personal and organizational strategies for handling job stress: A review of research and opinion. *Personnel Psychology, 32,* 1–43.

128. Murphy (1996), *supra* note 117.

129. Murphy (1996), *supra* note 117; Ivancevich et al. (1990), *supra* note 114; Jex, S. M. (1998) *Stress and job performance.* Thousand Oaks, CA: Sage.

130. Murphy (1996), *supra* note 117.

131. Kompier, M.A.J., Guerts, S.A.E., Gründemann, R.W.M., Vink, P., & Smulders, P.G.W. (1998). Cases in stress prevention: The success of a participative and stepwise approach. *Stress Medicine, 14*(3), July 1, 155–168.

132. Jones, D. L., Tanigawa, T., & Weiss, S. M. (2003). Stress management and workplace disability in the U.S., Europe, and Japan. *Journal of Occupational Health, 45*(1), 1–7.

133. Briner (1999), *supra* note 126; Briner, R. B., & Reynolds, S. (1999). The costs, benefits, and limitations of organizational level stress interventions. *Journal of Organizational Behavior, 20*(5), 647–664.

134. Gebhardt, D. L., & Crump, C. E. (1990). Employee fitness and wellness programs in the workplace. *American Psychologist, 45,* 262–272; Terborg (1986), *supra* note 4.

135. Terborg (1986), *supra* note 4; Wolfe & Parker (1994), *supra* note 20.

136. Fielding, J. E., & Piserchia, P. V. (1989). Frequency of worksite health promotion activities. *American Journal of Public Health, 79,* 16–20; Wilson, M. G. (1996). A comprehensive review of the effects of worksite health promotion on health-related outcomes: An update. *American Journal of Health Promotion, 11,* 107–108.

137. Driver, R. W., & Ratliff, R. A. (1982). Employers' perceptions of benefits accrued from physical fitness programs. *Personnel Administrator, 27*(8), 21–26; Driver, R. W., & Ratliff, R. A. (1982). Employers' perceptions of benefits accrued from physical fitness programs. *Personnel Administrator, 27*(8), 21–26.

138. Public Health Service (1995). *Healthy people 2000: Midcourse review and 1995 revisions.* Washington, DC: U.S. Department of Health and Human Services.

139. Carbasho, T. (1999). Employee health programs become standard. *Pittsburgh Business Times, 18*(30), February 12, 25–26.

140. Public Health Service (1992), *1992 national survey of worksite health promotion activities: Summary report,* pp. 3–21, Washington, DC: Public Health Service.

141. O'Donnell, M. P. (1986). *Design of workplace health promotion programs.* Royal Oak, MI: American Journal of Health Promotion.

142. Wilber, C. S. (1983). The Johnson & Johnson program. *Preventive Medicine, 12,* 672–681.

143. Fielding, J. E. (1984). Health promotion and disease prevention at the worksite. *Annual Review of Public Health, 5,* 237–265.

144. Chapman, L. S. (2004). Expert opinions on "best practices" in worksite health promotion (WHP). *American Journal of Health Promotion, 18*(6), July/August, 1–6.

145. Heirich, M. A., Erfurt, J. C., & Foote, A. (1992). The core technology of work-site wellness. *Journal of Occupational Medicine, 34,* 627–637.

146. Terborg (1986), *supra* note 4, p. 231.

147. Public Health Service (1992). *1992 National survey of worksite health promotion activities: Summary report.* Washington, DC: U.S. Department of Health and Human Services.

148. Shepard, R. J. (1996). Worksite fitness and exercise programs: A review of methodology and health impact. *American Journal of Health Promotion, 10,* 436–452.

149. Harris, P. R. (1981). *Health United States 1980: With prevention profile.* Washington, DC: U.S. Government Printing Office; Mattzarro, J. D. (1984). Behavioral health: A 1990 challenge for the health science professions. In J. D. Mattzarro, S. M. Weiss, J. A. Herd, N. E. Miller, & S. M. Weiss (Eds.), *Behavioral health: A handbook of health enhancement and disease prevention* (3–40). New York: Wiley; Miller, N. E. (1983). Behavioral medicine: Symbiosis between laboratory and clinic. *Annual Review of Psychology, 34,* 1–31.

150. Caspersen, C. J., & Merrit, R. K. (1995). Physical activity trends among 26 states: 1986–1990. *Medicine and Science in Sports and Exercise, 27,* 213–220.

151. Blair, S. N., Kohl, H. W., Paffenbarger, R. S., Clark, D. G., Cooper, K. H., & Gibbons, L. W. (1989). Physical fitness and all-cause mortality: A prospective case study of healthy men and women. *Journal of the American Medical Association, 262,* 2395–2401.

152. Howard, J., & Mikalachki, A. (1979). Fitness and employee productivity. *Canadian Journal of Applied Sport Sciences, 4,* 191–198; Public Health Service (1992), *supra* note 147.

153. Wolfe & Parker (1994), *supra* note 20.

154. Shepard (1996), *supra* note 148.

155. Falkenberg, I. (1987). Employee fitness programs: Their impact on the employee and the organization. *Academy of Management Review, 12,* 511–522; Shepard (1996), *supra* note 148.

156. Gebhardt & Crump (1990), *supra* note 134.

157. Fielding (1984), *supra* note 143; Shepard, R. J. (1983). Employee health and fitness: The state of the art. *Preventive Medicine, 12,* 644–653.

158. Gebhardt & Crump (1990), *supra* note 134.

159. Fielding, J. E. (1982). Effectiveness of employee health improvement programs. *Journal of Occupational Medicine, 24,* 907–916.

160. Conrad, P. (1987). Who comes to work-site wellness programs? *Journal of Occupational Medicine, 29,* 317–320.

161. Erfurt, Foote, & Heirich (1992), *supra* note 17.

162. Gebhardt & Crump (1990), *supra* note 134.

163. Heirich, M. A., Foote, A., Erfurt, J. C., & Konopka, B. (1993). Work-site physical fitness programs: Comparing the impact of different program designs on cardiovascular risks. *Journal of Occupational Medicine, 35,* 510–517.

164. Fielding (1984), *supra* note 143.

165. Smoking Prevalence Among U.S. Adults. Retrieved November 1, 2004, from http://www.cdc.gov/tobacco/research_data/adults_prev/prevali.htm

166. Cascio (2000), *supra* note 24.

167. National Center for Health Statistics. (1995). *Healthy people 2000 review, 1994.* (DHHS Publication No. PHS 95-1256-1). Washington, DC: U.S. Government Printing Office.

168. Fielding & Piserchia (1989), *supra* note 136.

169. Matteson & Ivancevich (1987), *supra* note 118.

170. Mankani, S. K., Garabrant, D. H., & Homa, D. M. (1996). Effectiveness of nicotine patches in a workplace smoking cessation program. *Journal of Occupational and Environmental Medicine, 38,* 184–189; Sorensen, G., & Stoddard, A. (1998). The effects of a health promotion-health protection intervention on behavior change: The Wellworks study. *American Journal of Public Health, 88*(11), 1685–1690; Sorensen, G. Beder, B. Prible, C. R., & Pinney, J. (1995). Reducing Smoking at the workplace: Implementing a smoking ban and hypnotherapy. *Journal of Occupational Medicine, 37,* 453–460; Sorensen, G., Lando, H., & Pechacek, T. F. (1993). Promoting smoking cessation at the workplace: Results of a randomized controlled intervention study. *Journal of Occupational Medicine, 35,* 121–136.

171. Matteson, M. T., & Ivancevich, J. M. (1988). Health promotion at work. In C. L. Cooper & I. Robertson (Eds.), *International review of industrial and organizational psychology* (pp. 279–306). London: Wiley.

172. Matson, D. M., Lee, J. W., & Hopp, J. W. (1993). The impact of incentives and competitions on participation and quit rates in worksite smoking cessation programs. *American Journal of Health Promotion, 7,* 270–280.

173. Klesges, R. C., & Glasgow, R. E. (1986). Smoking modification in the worksite. In M. F. Cataldo & T. J. Coates (Eds.), *Health and industry.* New York: Wiley.

174. Warner, K. E., Smith, R. J., Smith, D. G., & Fries, B. E. (1996). Health and economic implications of a work-site smoking-cessation program: A simulation analysis. *Journal of Occupational and Environmental Medicine, 38,* 981–992.

175. Centers for Disease Control (2004). Defining overweight and obesity. Retrieved November 2, 2004, from http://www.cdc.gov/nccdphp/dnpa/obesity/defining.htm

176. National Center for Health Statistics (2004). Age-adjusted prevalence of overweight and obesity among U.S. adults, age 20 years and over. Retrieved November 2, 2004, from http://www.cdc.gov/nchs/products/pubs/pubd/hestats/obese/obsefig1.GIF

177. Lee, I., Manson, J. E., Hennekens, C. H., & Paffenbarger, R. S. (1993). Body weight and mortality: A 27-year follow-up of middle-aged men. *Journal of the American Medical Association, 270,* 2823–2828; Lew, E. A., & Garfinkel, L. (1979). Variations in mortality by weight among 750,000 men and women. *Journal of Chronic Diseases, 32,* 563–576.

178. Terborg (1986), *supra* note 4.

179. Public Health Service (1992), *supra* note 147.

180. *Ibid.*

181. Hennrikus, D. J., & Jeffry, R. W. (1996). Worksite intervention for weight control: A review of the literature. *American Journal of Health Promotion, 10,* 471–489.

182. Glanz, K., Sorensen, G., & Farmer, A. (1996). The health impact of worksite nutrition and cholesterol intervention programs. *American Journal of Health Promotion, 10,* 453–470.

183. Sorensen & Stoddard (1998), *supra* note 179; Glanz, K., Patterson, R. E., Kristal, A. R., Feng, Z., Linnan, L., Heimendinger, J., & Hebert, J. R. (1998). Impact of work site health promotion on stages of dietary change: The Working Well study. *Health Education & Behavior, 25*(4), 448–463.

184. Feuer, D. (1985). Wellness programs: How do they shape up? *Training, 22*(4), 25–34; Brownell, K. D., Cohen, R. Y., Stunkard, A. J., Felix, M. R., & Cooley, N. B. (1984). Weight loss competitions at the worksite: Impact on weight, morale, and cost-effectiveness. *American Journal of Public Health, 74,* 1283–1285.

185. Roehling, M. V. (1999). Weight-based discrimination in employment: Psychological and legal aspects. *Personnel Psychology, 52,* 969–1016.

186. Ibid.

187. Greenlund, K. J., Croft, J. B., & Mensah, G. A. (2004). Prevalence of heart disease and stroke risk factors in persons with prehypertension in the United States, 1999–2000. *Archives of Internal Medicine, 164*(19), October 25, 2113–2118; Wang, Y., & Wang, Q. J. (2004). The prevalence of prehypertension and hypertension among U.S. adults according to the New Joint National Committee Guidelines: New challenges of the old problem. *Archives of Internal Medicine, 164*(19), October 25, 2126–2134.

188. Fielding (1984), *supra* note 143.

189. Cohen, W. S. (1985). Health promotion in the workplace. *American Psychologist, 40,* 213–216.

190. Fielding (1984), *supra* note 143.

191. Public Health Service (1992), *supra* note 147.

192. Terborg (1986), *supra* note 4.

193. Wilson, Holman, & Hammock (1996), *supra* note 20.

194. Matteson & Ivancevich (1988), *supra* note 171.

195. Foote, A., & Erfurt, J. C. (1991). The benefit to cost ratio of work-site blood pressure control programs. *Journal of the American Medical Association, 265*(10), 1283–1286.

196. Chapman, L. (2003). Meta-evaluation of worksite health promotion economic return studies. *American Journal of Health Promotion, 17*(3), January/February, 1–10.

197. Matteson & Ivancevich (1988), *supra* note 171; Luthans & Waldersee (1989), *supra* note 65.

198. Wilson, Holman, & Hammock (1996), *supra* note 20; Sorensen & Stoddard (1998), *supra* note 170; Glanz et al. (1998), *supra* note 182.

199. Gebhardt & Crump (1990), *supra* note 134.

200. Cascio (2000), *supra* note 24.

201. Musich, S. A., Adams, L., & Edington, D. W. (2000). Effectiveness of health promotion programs in moderating medical costs in the USA. *Health Promotion International, 15*(1), 5–15.

202. Masi (1992), *supra* note 18.

203. Axel (1990), *supra* note 74.

204. Luthans & Waldersee (1989), *supra* note 65.

205. Good, R. K. (1986). Employee assistance. *Personnel Journal, 65*(2), 96–101.

206. Loomis, L. (1986). Employee assistance programs: Their impact on arbitration and litigation of termination cases. *Employee Relating Law Journal, 12,* 275–288.

207. Feuer (1987), *supra* note 71.

208. Akabus, S. (1977). Labor: Social policy and human services. *Encyclopedia of Social Work,* 727–744; Feuer (1987), *supra* note 82; Perlis, G. (1980). Labor and employee assistance programs. In R. H. Egdahl & D. C. Walsh (Eds.), *Mental wellness programs for employees.* New York: Springer-Verlag.

209. Trice, H. M., Hunt, R., & Beyer, J. M. (1977). Alcoholism programs in unionized work settings: Problems and prospects in union-management cooperation. *Journal of Drug Issues, 7,* 103–115.

210. Steele, P. D. (1988). Substance abuse in the work place, with special attention to employee assistance programs: An overview. *Journal of Applied Behavioral Science, 24,* 315–325.

211. Trice, Hunt, & Beyer (1977), *supra* note 209.

212. Becker et al. (2000), *supra* note 22; Taurone, D. (1999), *supra* note 63.

213. Weiss (1987), *supra* note 92.

214. Fennell, M. (1984). Synergy, influence, and information in the adoption of administrative innovations. *Academy of Management Journal, 27,* 113–129.

215. Ivancevich et al. (1990), *supra* note 114.

216. Ramsey, K. B. (1985). Counseling employees. In W. R. Tracey (Ed.), *Human resource management and development handbook* (pp. 821–836). New York: AMACOM.

217. Matteson & Ivancevich (1988), *supra* note 171.

218. *Ibid.*

219. Terborg (1986), *supra* note 4.

220. Cited in Yandrick (1998), *supra* note 13.

# 12

# CAREER MANAGEMENT AND DEVELOPMENT

## Learning Objectives

*After reading this chapter, you should be able to:*

1. Define the term *career*, and explain the roles involved in career management and development.

2. Explain the effect that the "new employment relationship" is having on career management.

3. Describe how models of life and career development enhance our understanding of careers.

4. Explain what is involved in career management and describe several models of career management.

5. Describe five career management practices.

6. Describe four issues that affect career management.

7. Understand what is involved in designing a career management program.

■

## OPENING CASE

In the province of Quebec, Canada, the proportion of government or public sector jobs that are held by senior and middle managers has decreased. This has led to decreased advancement opportunities and an issue of "career plateauing" for many government workers. A concern is that workers who see little to no opportunity to advance will experience frustration, which could lead to decreased organizational commitment, decreased work performance, and increased exit from their organizations.

Assume that you are asked to advise senior managers in the Quebec public sector. Answer the following questions: *What information would you like to obtain from managers and professionals concerning their careers? What types of career management activities might be useful for such managers and professionals? Why did you pick the activities that you did?*

## INTRODUCTION

Have you ever wondered about any of the following questions?
- *What exactly are people talking about when they refer to a "new" employment relationship?*
- *If things are changing so rapidly within organizations and in the external environment, does it even make sense to talk about career development issues?*
- *Are there typical issues that employees face at particular ages or stages of their careers?*
- *What roles should employees, managers, and HRD professionals play in managing employees' careers?*
- *What types of career development activities are actually used by organizations?*

The study of careers and how they develop is one of the most active areas of inquiry in the social sciences. Psychologists, educators, sociologists, economists, and management scholars are all trying to understand how a person selects, works within, and makes decisions to change the focus of his or her working life. There are also many governmental, legal, and public policy issues that impact career development.[1] It is not surprising that careers should be the focus of such intensive study and governmental intervention. Most of us will spend a good portion of our lives working. The choices we make about what our work will involve determine to a large degree the success, happiness, and financial well-being of ourselves and our children.

Understanding and finding ways to influence the careers of employees in an organization is also an integral part of HRD. Career development provides a future orientation to HRD activities. It is a fact of life that people and organizations change. Organizational objectives and the blend of knowledge, skill, abilities, and other characteristics (KSAOs) it will take to reach those objectives change in response to challenges from the environment. This is especially true in the turbulent environment that has characterized the past two decades, an environment that has been typified by rapid change, increased competition, globalization, an employment relationship that is less loyalty based, and flatter, less hierarchical organizational structures. By the same token, as employees grow and change, the types of work they may want to do may change as well. If organizations can assist employees in making decisions about future work, they can better prepare employees for new responsibilities within the organization and, when appropriate, enhance the employability of the employees over the long haul. Similarly, if organizations understand how employees make decisions about future work, they can do a better job of planning to meet their human resource needs.

Career development is such a broad field that it is beyond the scope of this book to survey it in its entirety. Instead, we will focus on career development concepts and practices that managers and HR professionals can use to fulfill their role as developers of human resources.

## THE "NEW EMPLOYMENT RELATIONSHIP"

In Chapter 1, we outlined five issues that create challenges for HRD professionals: increasing workforce diversity, competing in a global economy, eliminating the skills gap, the need for lifelong learning, and facilitating organizational learning. As we will discuss, these issues affect career development as well. Before we get into the specifics of career development, it is useful to highlight an additional issue that has special impact on career development in organizations: the changes taking place in the nature of the employment relationship.

Traditionally, many employees believed that if they joined an organization, became competent, worked hard, and stayed out of trouble, they would have a job for as long as they would want it. Some have called this an "entitlement" mentality toward jobs, benefits, and the like, that is, that employers "owed" such things to their employees. Organizations often encouraged this view. Many adopted a paternalistic approach toward their employees, offering job security and stability in exchange for worker loyalty. Employers often used the term *family* as the metaphor for their relationship with employees. For example, until the mid-1980s, employees referred to the Metropolitan Life Insurance Company as Mother Met (a nickname management was proud of) because they believed that whatever happened, the company would take care of them.

In the context of this social contract, career development was seen primarily as the organization's concern. The goal was to ensure that the ranks of management would be filled with individuals who were prepared for these tasks and fit the organization's culture. The career development practices that were used primarily created an internal labor market to fulfill the organization's needs. Career progress was defined primarily in terms of promotion and pay increases within one organization.

Individuals often viewed career management within the confines of this approach. They would engage in career planning to the extent that they had vertical aspirations and were selected for or volunteered to participate in the organization's development activities. Moving up through the ranks of management was often the main career goal.

This kind of long-term relationship between employees and employers requires a stable, predictable environment and a hierarchically structured organization. As we all know, stability and predictability have given way to rapid change and uncertainty.[2] Peter Vaill has used the metaphor *permanent white water* to characterize this unstable environment.[3] Organizations have generally responded to this turbulence with downsizing, shrinking hierarchies, reorganization, cost cutting, outsourcing, mergers and acquisitions, technological innovation, and more performance-oriented HRM programs. Interventions like these may address short-term financial concerns for employers, but they also have eroded the traditional employment relationship. For example, a survey of workers in the Silicon Valley region in California, as well as Vancouver and Toronto in Canada, found that efforts to *minimize* layoffs was viewed as most likely to promote high levels of skill and effort among employees.[4]

As a result of organizational actions such as downsizing and outsourcing, the employment relationship has changed to one in which paternalism has more generally given way to an exchange relationship for the mutual benefit of both parties, from a promise of long-term security to a situation where employees have the primary responsibility for their own future, and from entitlement to the goal of obtaining opportunities to remain employable.[5] As an example of this new relationship, the following list was found on a bulletin board of a company going through widespread layoffs:

- We can't promise you how long we'll be in business.
- We can't promise you that we won't be acquired.
- We can't promise that there'll be room for promotion.
- We can't promise that your job will exist when you reach retirement age.
- We can't promise that the money will be available for your pension.
- We can't expect your undying loyalty, and we aren't even sure we want it.[6]

It should be noted that the traditional employment relationship did not exist everywhere and for everyone. Many industries and occupations, including the entertainment industry, agriculture, construction and related trades, and professional services (such as law, accounting, and architecture), have always had significant numbers of organizations and workers existing in short-term and medium-term relationships and career progressions that do not neatly fit the stereotypical corporate model.[7] However, for most people, the traditional paradigm and what came with it was seen as the prototype of a career, and working for an organization with this kind of relationship or working in a mainstream occupation was seen as having a "real job" or a "career."

For those who have entered the workforce believing in and expecting this more traditional form of employment relationship, the realization that things have changed can be unnerving and unsettling. Facing the realization that *they*, not the organization, are responsible for their own continued employability has created uncertainty for many people. In a recent review of articles published on this topic, there was widespread agreement that employees were increasingly expected to (1) assume responsibility for developing and maintaining their own skills, (2) add demonstrable value to the organization, and (3) understand the nature of their employer's business. At the same time, there was strong agreement that, under the new employment relationship, employers should provide (1) opportunities for skill development, training, and education and (2) employee involvement in decision making, assistance with career management (e.g., coaching and mentoring), and performance-based compensation.[8] Overall, the concept of a "boundaryless" career, that is, a career not bound to one organization or profession, has become quite popular.[9]

## IMPACT OF THE NEW EMPLOYMENT RELATIONSHIP ON ORGANIZATIONAL CAREER MANAGEMENT AND DEVELOPMENT

Given such changes in the typical employment relationship, does the concept of organizational career management and development still make sense? The answer is yes, for numerous reasons. First, there will continue to be a significant number of organizations (both large and small) that have long-term relationships with their employees, and it is in both the organizations' and the employees' best interest to plan and enact a mutually beneficial future. Career management and development can be a key part of this effort.

Second, the work many organizations must do to achieve their goals changes over time. Even organizations that use contingent workers, outsourcing, and partnership arrangements to get the work done need to maintain a core of employees with whom they have long-term relationships. It is in the organizations' interest to ensure that the employees who make up the core (especially managers) are prepared and willing to change to meet new demands. Third, within this "new" employment environment, the availability of career-enhancing assignments and career management activities can be used both as a recruitment tool to attract employees and contingent workers to work for the organizations, and as a motivational tool to gain their full effort, commitment, and creativity.

In our view, what should change, and what is changing, is that organizational career development should be designed to fit the responsibilities and needs of *both* individuals and organizations, providing the opportunities both need to prosper in a dynamic environment. Authors such as Carrie Leana and Daniel Feldman describe strategic, proactive ways that both individuals and organizations can react to this dynamic environment.[10] Mark Roehling and colleagues provide examples of how companies such as Allstate and Hallmark have clearly spelled out *mutual expectations* regarding the employer-employee relationship, that is, what they expect of their employees, as well as what employees can expect of them.[11] We will describe in more detail how career management and development can be done to meet both organizational and individual needs as we continue our discussion throughout the chapter.

## DEFINING CAREER CONCEPTS

### WHAT IS A CAREER?

What comes to mind when you think of the word *career*? The word *career* means many things to many people. It also has different meanings among researchers. Greenhaus[12] and Schein[13] described several themes underlying different definitions of the term, including:

1. *The property of an occupation or organization.* When used in this way, career describes the occupation itself (e.g., sales or accounting) or an employee's tenure within an organization (e.g., my college career).[14]

2. *Advancement.* In this sense, career denotes one's progression and increasing success within an occupation or organization.[15]

3. *Status of a profession.* Some use the term career to separate the "professions," such as law or engineering, from other occupations, such as plumbing, carpentry, or general office work. In this view, the lawyer is said to have a career, while the carpenter does not.[16]

4. *Involvement in one's work.* Sometimes career is used in a negative sense to describe being extremely involved in the task or job one is doing, as in "Don't make a career out of it."[17]

5. *Stability of a person's work pattern.* A sequence of related jobs is said to describe a career, while a sequence of unrelated jobs does not.[18]

Each of these definitions is limiting in that it defines career narrowly. Several authors have offered definitions that are more expansive.[19] We agree with Greenhaus and colleagues that a **career** is best described broadly as "the pattern of work-related experiences that span the course of a person's life."[20]

This definition includes both *objective* events, such as jobs, and *subjective* views of work, such as the person's attitudes, values, and expectations.[21] Therefore, both a person's work-related activities and his or her reactions to those activities are part of his or her career. Further, this definition is consistent with the notion that careers develop over time, and that all persons have careers, regardless of profession, level of advancement, or stability of work pattern.

By not being tied to advancement-oriented or career-as-organizational-property points of view, this definition also recognizes the multiplicity of work-related paths and experiences that people engage in and respond to throughout their lives. This definition of a career also underscores the influence and importance of the individual, organization, and the environment on the individual's work life. While the job and occupational choices an individual makes during a career are determined in large part by forces within the individual, the organization and other external forces (e.g., society, family, the educational system) also play important roles. The individual is driven toward particular job choices by his or her skills, knowledge, abilities, attitudes, values, personality, and life situation. Organizations provide jobs and information about jobs, as well as opportunities and constraints within which one may pursue other jobs in the future (especially if one chooses to remain employed within the same organization). Both the individual and organization have needs and priorities, and it is important to remember that *both* are critical to the development of one's career.

Finally, this definition of career takes the focus away from the stereotypical idea of a career as a stable, long-term, predictable, organization-driven sequence of vertical moves. It is broad enough to encompass many of the recent ideas that have been offered in the career development literature (and discussed later in the chapter), and it can liberate individuals, practitioners, and theorists to see the realities and possibilities that currently exist.

## RELATIONSHIP OF CAREER TO NONWORK ACTIVITIES

While the definition of career that we have chosen focuses on work-related events and the individual's reactions to those events, some career theorists also emphasize the importance of nonwork events to one's career. For example, Donald Super argues that to truly understand and manage careers, one must consider all of an individual's skills, abilities, and interests.[22] Placing the notion of career within the larger context of one's life, Super argues that organizations should offer employees opportunities to use all their talents — and thus attain real life satisfaction. He further suggests that if organizations do not attempt to understand the whole person, they may be less able to compete in the future as the mix of skills needed to reach organizational objectives changes. Parker echoes this point of view.[23] She suggests that career development activities should explicitly recognize the impact and value that relationships outside of work have on employees, such as having employees include their outside relationships during self-assessment and career exploration.

Even if one does not take as expansive a view of career management as Super and Parker do, it is difficult to ignore the impact of nonwork influences on an individual's career. People come to organizations for specific reasons, and those reasons often change as they age. Family and society have a strong influence on a person's interests and aspirations, and significantly influence the role that work and career play in the person's life. Ignoring these influences limits an organization's ability to understand and manage their employees' careers.

## CAREER DEVELOPMENT

Over the past thirty years, much attention has been given to addressing the question of how careers and adult lives develop over time. Research clearly supports the notion that careers develop in a predictable, common sequence of stages.[24] Researchers have found that at various ages, people generally face common issues and pressures that they attempt to resolve in their lives. The stages affect, and are affected by, the career activities and choices the individual has made.

The overall process of **career development** can be defined as "an ongoing process by which individuals progress through a series of stages, each of which is characterized by a relatively unique set of issues, themes, and tasks."[25] We will present several models of career development in the next section of this chapter. However, it is useful to distinguish between two sets of activities that can be subsumed within career development: career planning and career management.

## CAREER PLANNING AND CAREER MANAGEMENT

As stated earlier, both the individual and the organization have interests in an individual's career, and both parties may take actions to influence that career. These sets of related activities are referred to as *career planning* and *career management*. These activities can be viewed as existing along a continuum.[26]

**Career planning** is defined as "a deliberate process of 1) becoming aware of self, opportunities, constraints, choices, and consequences, 2) identifying career-related goals, and 3) programming work, education, and related developmental experiences to provide the direction, timing, and sequence of steps to attain a specific career goal."[27] Viewed in this way, career planning is an activity performed by the individual to understand and attempt to control his or her own work life. The individual need not perform these activities alone. Assistance from counselors, supervisors, and others within and outside the organization can be helpful, but the focus of career planning is on the individual. For example, completing a career awareness workbook that helps the employee understand his or her skills, abilities, and preferences would be considered a career planning activity. If career planning is done successfully, the individual will know what he or she wants and have a set of action steps that, if followed, should lead to the achievement of these goals.

On the other end of the continuum is **career management,** defined as "an ongoing process of preparing, implementing, and monitoring career plans undertaken by the individual alone or in concert with the organization's career systems."[28] Career management may include activities that help the individual develop and carry out career plans, but the focus is on taking actions that increase the chances that the organization's anticipated HR needs will be met. At its most extreme, career management is largely an activity carried out by the organization. An example of such an activity is *succession planning*, which is typically carried out by senior management to determine which employees can and should be prepared to replace people in positions of greater responsibility.

Figure 12-1 describes where various career development activities fit along the career development spectrum.[29] These activities vary according to (1) the amount of influence by the individual, (2) the amount of information provided to the individual, (3) the amount of influence by the organization, and (4) the amount of information provided to the organization. Career management and career planning activities can be complementary and can reinforce each other. For example, it is difficult to monitor the career plans of an individual who has not made specific plans. A balance between the two (management and planning) makes for effective career development.[30]

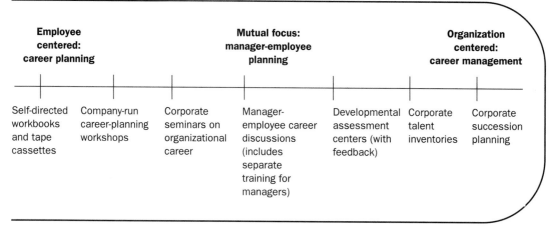

SOURCE: D. T. Hall (1986). An overview of current career development theory, research, and practice. In D. T. Hall and associates (eds.), Career development in organizations (4), San Francisco: Jossey-Bass. Copyright 1986 by Jossey-Bass, Inc. This material is used by permission of John Wiley & Sons, Inc.

The organization can support actions at any point on the spectrum, assisting the employee with career planning, as well as conducting career management activities.

Jeffrey Greenhaus and colleagues use the term *career management* to refer to all phases of career development activities, from gaining self-awareness, to developing career goals and plans, to enacting those plans.[31] Because planning is a significant activity within management, we adopt this more inclusive use of the term *career management* and use this model to form the framework of our discussion of how individuals and organizations can influence career development. Before discussing how one can influence the course of one's career, however, it is important to examine the career development process.

## STAGES OF LIFE AND CAREER DEVELOPMENT

One way to characterize a person's life or career is by identifying common experiences, challenges, or tasks most people seem to go through as their life or career progresses. For example, psychologists such as Freud and others have long argued that aspects of human nature such as personality, intelligence, and morality all develop in a predictable, common sequence closely tied to a person's age.[32] Research by Levinson[33] and Erikson[34] suggests that adult life follows a series of common stages. Work done by Schein,[35] Super,[36] and others suggests that careers also develop in stages.

Visualizing career development as unfolding in stages helps us to understand why some experiences occur, for example, difficulties in adjusting to one's first position, or experiencing midcareer problems, and why they are so common. From a practical perspective, a stage view helps both the individual and the organization to predict likely crises and challenges and therefore plan ways to resolve or minimize them. For example, if challenge in an initial job is an issue for most young, new employees, then these individuals can be assisted in understanding the nature of the problem, and organizations can ensure that initial assignments have sufficient challenge to overcome this problem.

It is also true that stage views of development have their limitations. First, they describe what happens to the typical individual. Of course, all individuals are unique and will not have the same experiences. For example, many people experience a period of self-questioning and reevaluation at midcareer, but not all people do. Levinson and colleagues found that 80 percent of the men they interviewed had experienced such a crisis, but 20 percent had not.[37] So when using a stage approach, one gets only an average view, not one that applies to all people.

In addition, many stage views use age or life experiences, or both, to define when a stage is likely to begin and end. Some criticize using age as a criterion, arguing that major life events such as marriage and one's first job occur at different ages for different individuals. However, Levinson argues that the age ranges he uses, while flexible, are based on empirical research evidence.[38] He states that it is hard to ignore the data, though more research needs to be done to confirm the validity of age anchors.

We believe that the usefulness of stage views outweighs the limitations. While age ranges may have to be interpreted liberally, and any given individual may not fit the stage model, there is enough evidence to support the usefulness of stage models as a way to understand and respond to career development.

## STAGE VIEWS OF ADULT DEVELOPMENT

A person's career is one part of life, influenced by (and influencing) major life events. Therefore, it is useful to briefly examine two stage models of adult development before we discuss a model of career development. Theorists Erik Erikson[39] and Daniel Levinson[40] have offered stage models of adult development that provide a meaningful basis for understanding career development.

*ERIKSON'S MODEL OF ADULT DEVELOPMENT.* Erikson proposed that people progress through eight stages during the course of their life.[41] These stages focus on both psychological and social issues, as depicted in Table 12-1. In each stage, the person is faced with a challenge that he or she must resolve in order to develop.

For example, the fifth stage, which occurs during adolescence, is defined by a conflict between *identity* and role confusion. If individuals successfully resolve this issue, they will enter adulthood with a clear sense of who they are in relation to others in the world. If they do not successfully resolve this issue, they will enter adulthood with confusion over who they are and what their role in the world is to be. It is the positive and negative experiences in each stage that determine its outcome.

The last three stages of Erikson's model focus on the issues facing adult development. As a young adult, one is faced with the challenge of developing meaningful relationships with others, or *intimacy.* If the individual successfully resolves this stage, he or she will be able to make a commitment to other individuals and groups; otherwise, the individual is likely to experience feelings of isolation.

In middle adulthood, the challenge is to develop the capacity to focus on the generations that will follow, which Erikson calls **generativity.** This can take the

| TABLE 12-1 | ERIKSON'S STAGES OF HUMAN DEVELOPMENT |

| Stage of Development (Issue) | Age Range (Years) |
| --- | --- |
| 1. basic trust versus mistrust | infancy |
| 2. autonomy versus shame and doubt | 1–3 |
| 3. initiative versus guilt | 4–5 |
| 4. industry versus inferiority | 6–11 |
| 5. identity versus role confusion | puberty and adolescence |
| 6. intimacy versus isolation | young adulthood |
| 7. generativity versus stagnation | middle adulthood |
| 8. ego integrity versus despair | maturity |

form of becoming more involved in the lives of one's children, social issues affecting future generations, or in serving as a mentor for younger colleagues. Erikson argues that failure to resolve this stage will lead to feelings of stagnation, in that one has made no contribution to the world that will last after he or she is gone.

Finally, in maturity, the individual faces issues of **ego integrity,** which involves developing an understanding and acceptance of the choices one has made in life. Successful development of ego integrity permits one to be at peace with one's life as one faces death. Failure at this stage can lead to despair over the meaninglessness of one's existence.

Erikson's view of adult development identifies issues (ego integrity, generativity, and intimacy) that can affect the career choices that employees make. Organizations can serve as places where individuals can resolve some of these challenges. For example, participating in mentoring programs serves the needs of young adults to develop meaningful relationships, as well as the needs of middle-aged adults to find a way to "give something back" to members of future generations.

Knowledge of these challenges also helps the organization understand some of the changes employees go through. Employees nearing retirement are facing many sources of stress (e.g., the loss of work and part of their social support system). **Preretirement counseling** and motivational programs geared toward older workers can yield benefits for both the individual and the organization. Finally, Erikson's model also provides evidence that there is a predictable order to the issues individuals face as they develop.

*LEVINSON'S "ERAS" APPROACH TO ADULT DEVELOPMENT.* Levinson and his colleagues developed a view of how adults develop based on the notion that adult lives progress through *seasons,* not unlike the seasons of the year.[42] He discovered these stages by collecting intensive biographical information from individuals in different walks of life over a period of years.

Levinson, like Erikson, argues that there is an underlying order to adult life called the *life cycle*. He uses the metaphor of seasons to indicate that major phases of a person's life (called *eras*) are like seasons of the year in the following ways:

1. They are qualitatively different.
2. Change occurs within each season.
3. There is a transitional period between each season that is part of both seasons.
4. No season is superior or inferior to another season.
5. Each season contributes something unique to life.
6. There are four seasons or eras in a person's life.[43]

The four eras proposed by Levinson are preadulthood, early adulthood, middle adulthood, and late adulthood. Each era contains a series of stable and transitional periods. The stable periods last about six years, and the within-era transitional periods last about four or five years. The transitional periods between eras, called *cross-era transitions*, last about five years and signal the end of one era and the beginning of a new one. Figure 12-2 depicts Levinson's eras model.

The general pattern of progress through life is not from an inferior mode of being to a superior one. Rather, the transitional periods raise issues that cannot be dealt with by the life structure that exists at the current stage of a person's life. During these transitions, the individual questions and reexamines that structure and searches for new, different ways of dealing with these issues. New life structures supplant the old until the next transition period.

Levinson also discovered that the stages of a person's life are closely related to age. For example, preadulthood, which ranges from infancy to age twenty-two, is a period in which individuals work to develop a sense of self. Levinson's research showed some variation in the age ranges among individuals, but also amazing constancy. Because careers occur primarily during Levinson's eras of young adulthood and middle adulthood, it is useful to examine each of these eras in more detail.

***Early Adulthood (Ages 17–45)*** Early adulthood includes four periods: the early adult transition (ages 17–22), entry life structure for early adulthood (ages 22–28), age 30 transition (ages 28–33), and the culminating life structure for early adulthood (ages 33–40). In general, early adulthood is a period of great energy and great stress. During this era, the person is at a biological peak and is striving to attain the goals and desires of youth. Finding a place in society, obtaining meaningful work, realizing a lifestyle, establishing meaningful relationships (including marriage for many individuals), and raising a family are all a part of this period. Many people experience occupational advancement during this period as well. However, the stresses present are also great. Family and society place demands on the individual at the same time he or she is dealing with individual ambitions and passions.

Of particular note in early adulthood is the age 30 transition. For those in Levinson's studies, this was a time of questioning and reappraisal about the path they had initially chosen and whether it was adequate for helping the individual realize major life goals. Levinson refers to major life goals as The Dream. If the age

**FIGURE 12-2** LEVINSON'S "ERAS" MODEL OF ADULT DEVELOPMENT

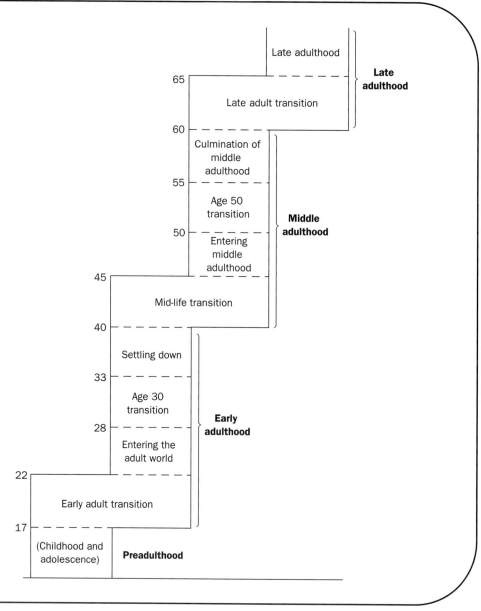

SOURCE: From D. J. Levinson, C. N. Darrow, E. B. Klein, M. H. Levinson, & B. McKee (1978). *Seasons of a man's life*. New York: Knopf (57). Copyright 1978 by Daniel J. Levinson. Reprinted by permission of Alfred A. Knopf.

30 transition is successfully resolved, the individual experiences a period of stability in which The Dream is vigorously pursued and work is done toward becoming "one's own person."

*Middle Adulthood (Ages 40–65)* The midlife transition (ages 40–45) leads from early adulthood to the beginning of middle adulthood. Research by Levinson and others shows that a person's life changes significantly between early and middle adulthood.[44] During this period, there is a major questioning of the life structure (goals, ambitions, etc.) and of The Dream that was so vigorously pursued at the end of early adulthood. Questions often asked during this transition include, "What have I done with my life? What is it I want to accomplish before I die? What do I want to leave behind for my family and others?" It is not surprising that this transition is so universal and so powerful. At this time in life, the individual is experiencing declines in physical functioning as his or her children are growing up or becoming adults. The individual's parents may be in significant physical decline or may die, and the individual may also witness the deaths of friends and peers.

The midlife transition can lead to an even stronger sense of self, allowing one to become more accepting of oneself and others, and more compassionate. Unsuccessful resolution of this transition, however, can lead to bitterness and stagnation (notice the similarity to Erikson's idea of generativity). The midlife transition is followed by a period of stability (ages 45–50), the age 50 transition (ages 50–55), and another stable period (ages 55–60) that leads to the end of middle adulthood. One's late forties and fifties can be a period of great satisfaction or great frustration as the individual becomes a senior member of the groups and organizations with which he or she has been involved.

*Late Adulthood (Age 60–Death)* Late adulthood begins with the late adulthood transition (ages 60–65). During this period, the individual faces additional major life events, typically including retirement, further physical decline, and the loss of family and loved ones. The major challenge in this era (similar to Erikson) is to come to terms with one's life and accept things as they have been, rather than dwell on what might have been. Less research has been done on this era than on the earlier ones.

CONTRIBUTIONS OF LEVINSON'S MODEL TO CAREER DEVELOPMENT Levinson's ideas are significant. His model is based on empirical evidence and expands upon earlier ideas (e.g., Erikson's) about adult life development. While Levinson acknowledges that the model must undergo additional testing and refinement, research supports the sequence of events that the model suggests and the age boundaries he has set. In addition, there is evidence that the model, which was developed initially with white men, also applies to black men, women, and those in other cultures.[45] In particular, research done with women from a variety of occupations (including homemakers) has provided evidence that the era model accurately describes the seasons in a woman's life,[46] although the content of the life structures differs in some cases from those of men.[47]

There are similarities between the Levinson and Erikson models. For example, they both rely on age ranges as markers for development, and they identify similar issues that all adults must deal with as they develop (e.g., identity and intimacy).

Levinson's model differs, however, in that it makes finer distinctions and describes adult development as progressing through alternating periods of stability and transition.

More important for our purposes, the notion that early adulthood, middle adulthood, and late adulthood represent a predictable sequence of life events provides a useful way to examine career development. A career is a part of a person's total life and will be affected by these life issues. HRD professionals can use these ideas to help identify the particular issues employees in their organizations may face and plan career development programs accordingly. In addition, Levinson's model also suggests that there are periods of stability in a person's life that can be both productive and satisfying. This notion challenges the traditional assumption regarding *career plateaus* (periods lacking significant increases in responsibility) as consistently problematic.[48]

## MODELS OF CAREER DEVELOPMENT

Just as it is possible to depict adult development as progressing through a series of stages, it is also possible to depict career development in this way. We will discuss two approaches to modeling career development: one traditional and the other more contemporary.

### TRADITIONAL MODELS OF CAREER DEVELOPMENT

Numerous models of career development have been offered to explain the sequence of stages that adults progress through during their work lives.[49] These models emphasize the notion of an orderly series of career stages linked to age ranges, place the career into the context of a person's life, and contain overlapping concepts.[50] Given the similarities among these models, Greenhaus and colleagues combined these approaches into a five-stage model, which is shown in Table 12-2.[51] Each stage is described here.

*STAGE 1: PREPARATION FOR WORK (AGE 0–25).* The major tasks during this period involve forming and defining an idea of the occupation one would like to engage in, and making necessary preparations for entry into that occupation. These activities include assessing possible occupations, selecting an occupation, and obtaining the necessary education. A great deal of research has been done to identify the factors that influence occupational choice.[52] The choices one makes during this stage represent initial decisions rather than final ones, and establish the first direction of the individual's career.[53]

*STAGE 2: ORGANIZATIONAL ENTRY (AGE 18–25).* At this stage, the individual selects a job and an organization in which to begin employment in the chosen career field. The amount and quality of information obtained can affect whether the initial job choice will be a fulfilling introduction to one's career or a disappointing false start. Among the obstacles the individual faces in this stage are initial job challenge (is it sufficient?), initial job satisfaction (typically lower than at later career stages,

| TABLE 12-2 | A FIVE-STAGE MODEL OF CAREER DEVELOPMENT FROM GREENHAUS AND COLLEAGUES |
|---|---|

**1. Occupational Choice: Preparation for Work**

| Typical Age Range: | Initially 0–25; then variable |
|---|---|
| Major Tasks: | Develop occupational self-image, assess alternative occupations, develop initial occupational choice, pursue necessary education. |

**2. Organizational Entry**

| Typical Age Range: | Initially 18–25; then variable |
|---|---|
| Major Tasks: | Obtain job offer(s) from desired organization(s), select appropriate job based on accurate information. |

**3. Early Career: Establishment and Achievement**

| Typical Age Range: | 25–40 |
|---|---|
| Major Tasks: | Learn job, learn organizational rules and norms, fit into chosen occupation and organization, increase competence, pursue The Dream. |

**4. Midcareer**

| Typical Age Range: | 40–55 |
|---|---|
| Major Tasks: | Reappraise early career and early adulthood, reaffirm or modify The Dream, make choices appropriate to middle adult years, remain productive in work. |

**5. Late Career**

| Typical Age Range: | 55–retirement |
|---|---|
| Major Tasks: | Remain productive in work, maintain self-esteem, prepare for effective retirement. |

SOURCE: From *Career Management* 3rd edition by Greenhaus. © 2000. Reprinted with permission of South-Western, a division of Thomson Learning: www.thomsonrights.com. Fax 800-730-2215.

due to the disparity between initial expectations and organizational realities), and organizational socialization (becoming an insider).

The last three career stages in the model are organized around Levinson's life eras (e.g., early adulthood, middle adulthood, and late adulthood). Greenhaus believes each of these eras presents significant issues that affect a career.

*STAGE 3: THE EARLY CAREER (AGE 25–40).* During this stage, the individual is dealing with finding a place in the world and pursuing his or her life dream; this also involves becoming established in a career and in an organization. The specific challenges that must be met to do this include becoming technically proficient and becoming assimilated into an organization's culture (i.e., learning its norms, values, and expectations). Successful resolution of these challenges can result in job satisfaction, advancement in terms of position and responsibility, and increased financial and social rewards. In short, the early career stage is about becoming established and "making it."

*STAGE 4: THE MIDCAREER (AGE 40–55).* Following Levinson, the midcareer stage begins at the same time as the midlife transition. Therefore, one of the tasks the individual faces at midcareer is a reexamination of the life structure and choices that were adopted during the early career. The individual may reaffirm or modify The Dream, make choices appropriate to middle adulthood, and remain productive at work. These challenges are congruent with the popular notion of a midcareer crisis. The crisis may be severe for some and not even seen as a crisis by others. Two events that often occur during midcareer are *plateauing* (a lack of significant increases in responsibility and/or job advancement) and *obsolescence* (finding one's skills are not sufficient to perform tasks required by technological change). As stated earlier, the individual who successfully resolves these challenges will remain productive, while one who does not will experience frustration and stagnation.

*STAGE 5: THE LATE CAREER (AGE 55–RETIREMENT).* The individual faces two challenges during the late career. First, he or she must strive to remain productive and maintain a sense of self-esteem. This can sometimes be hampered by the negative beliefs that society has regarding the performance and capabilities of older workers. Second, this individual faces the challenge of disengaging from work and retiring. Retirement brings many emotional, financial, and social changes and should be planned for well in advance of the actual retirement date. Given current trends in the Social Security system, the abolition of the mandatory retirement age for most jobs, and questions about the management of pension funds, many people will be facing a career without an adequately planned retirement. Rather than facing retirement, the individual may have to face occupational change at an age at which his or her parents were dealing with a shift from work to nonwork. Pressures toward early retirement by organizations trying to reduce labor costs may at the same time force some workers into retirement sooner than planned, creating an additional set of problems.

This model is useful for identifying the normal, or typical, sequence of events and experiences that occur within one's working life. Some individuals, such as those who begin new occupations late in life, will deviate from the age ranges suggested in the model. Even though the ages will vary, many of the challenges are likely to stay the same, but the individual will perceive and respond to them in light of the other issues he or she is facing at that particular stage of life.

*CONTEMPORARY VIEWS OF CAREER DEVELOPMENT.* Certainly, the trends in globalization, demographics, technology (both information and otherwise), the changing employment relationship, team-based work, and new organizational structures are having a significant impact on the way careers are viewed. In light of this changing landscape, some theorists have questioned the relevance of traditional notions of career stages.[54] These contemporary views of career development share the notion that individuals (and organizations) must be flexible and adaptable to succeed in a highly changeable and uncertain environment. Two sets of ideas illustrate this line of thinking.

For example, Hall and Mirvis advanced the idea of the **protean career.**[55] The protean career concept (named for the Greek god Proteus, who could change his shape at will) argues that individuals drive their own careers, not organizations, and that individuals reinvent their careers over time as needed. As individuals go through life, they are on a search for meaning and self-fulfillment, and their careers are made up of their choices and experiences (work, educational, and otherwise). Each person's career will be unique. Instead of progressing through a series of discrete and predictable changes, the protean career "encompasses any kind of flexible, idiosyncratic career course, with peaks and valleys, left turns, moves from one line of work to another, and so forth."[56]

That is not to say individuals do not have common elements in their careers. The protean view embraces the idea that lifelong learning and personal development are at the center of career development. As a result, a person's career will likely be made up of a "succession of 'ministages' (or short-cycle learning stages) of exploration-trial-mastery-exit, as they move in and out of various product areas, technologies, functions, organizations, and other work environments."[57] In this view, it is not a person's chronological age that is important, but the so-called career age, or number of years the individual has spent in a particular cycle. Therefore, the issues in the exploration part of the cycle, for example, will likely be the same each time the individual enters it.

The implication of the protean career is that career management must be *proactive*. While the protean career can be liberating and exhilarating, it also carries a dark side. This includes fear, uncertainty, a rapid pace of change, and a removal of the typical supports that individuals have used to identify themselves and make sense of the world (e.g., defining oneself by job title or in relation to one's employer).

A second example of a contemporary view of career development is the notion of differing career patterns, called the *multiple career concept model*.[58] This model suggests that there are four different patterns of career experiences, called **career concepts.** These four concepts differ in terms of the "direction and frequency of movement within and across different kinds of work over time. . . . Distinctly different sets of motives underlie each of the four concepts."[59] The four career concepts are:

- *Linear* — A progression of movement up an organizational hierarchy to positions of greater responsibility and authority; motivated by desire for power and achievement; variable time line; in the United States, this has been the traditional view of a "career."

- *Expert* — A devotion to an occupation; focus on building knowledge and skill within a specialty; little upward movement in a traditional hierarchy, more from apprentice to master; motivated by desire for competence and stability; rooted in the medieval guild structure.

- *Spiral* — A lifelong progression of periodic (seven to ten years) moves across related occupations, disciplines, or specialties; sufficient time to achieve a high level of competence in a given area before moving on; motives include creativity and personal growth.

- *Transitory* — A progression of frequent (three to five years) moves across different or unrelated jobs or fields; untraditional; motives include variety and independence.[60]

Brousseau and colleagues argue that these four concepts can be combined to form a wide variety of hybrid concepts.[61] They state that the traditional model of career management has favored individuals with a linear or expert career concept, but that the shifts going on in the world now tend to favor those with a transitory or spiral career concept. The challenge to organizations and individuals, then, is to conduct career management in what they call a pluralistic fashion that matches the organization's strategy and career culture with individuals' career concepts. (We will discuss this idea further in the section on career management.)

## RECONCILING THE TRADITIONAL AND CONTEMPORARY CAREER MODELS

At this point, it may be fair to ask which of the models best depicts our present reality. A glib, but not entirely wrong, response is that it depends on whom you are talking about and where that person works. Some organizations and some industries still fit the traditional model fairly well. For example, even in the face of technological change, competition, and political pressures, the U.S. Postal Service has remained relatively stable in terms of the employment security its employees enjoy. In other organizations and industries, the traditional model does not fit well. For example, in the information technology industry, the rapid pace of change has led to a proliferation of new organizational structures, nontraditional employment arrangements, unprecedented growth, and instability. Also, in some industries, there have always been alternatives to the traditional model. For example, in professional service firms (e.g., accounting, law) and the arts and entertainment (e.g., the film industry), career patterns have rarely fit the traditional hierarchical progression for many, if not most, employees (see Malos & Campion[62] and Jones & DeFillippi[63] for examples of career issues in professional service firms and the film industry, respectively).

We agree with those who argue that individuals, organizations, and theorists do not simply trade one set of ideas about careers for another; as mentioned earlier, there has been and always will be a multiplicity of views about careers.[64] In that sense, we welcome the contemporary ideas such as the protean career and various career concepts. We believe that such ideas open people's minds to look past stereotypes to the variety of possibilities available, and encourage individuals and organizations to come up with ways to manage and plan careers that will satisfy their needs and objectives. Clearly, one size does not fit all. Further, individuals should take responsibility for their lives and employability. Yet, organizations also bear a responsibility for career management, both for their own interests, and for the well-being of those who work within their organization.

That having been said, we believe it would be foolish to ignore age-based stage models of life and career. While we are all unique, we also share many common experiences. There seem to be events and transitions that many people experience at similar life and career stages, and the decisions and actions made at each stage should be studied. In addition, as mentioned, stage theories are not to be interpreted as narrow categorizations that must fit all individuals. Greenhaus and colleagues point out that "classification problems are inherent in all age-related theories of career development. But they may not be problems after all. Our aim is not merely to classify an individual into a particular stage but to understand how careers unfold and how people relate at different stages of their careers and lives" (p. 122).[65] We agree.

## LIFE STAGE AND CAREER MODELS AS THE CONCEPTUAL BASE FOR CAREER DEVELOPMENT

Taken together, models of life stages and careers provide a rich foundation for the practice of career management and development. By understanding the issues raised in these models, individuals can be better equipped to think about, anticipate, and manage the transitions they will experience during their lives. Similarly, this knowledge can help organizations develop strategies and tactics to manage the career transitions their employees will experience and create career management systems that will both meet the organizations' HR needs and satisfy the needs of employees.

## THE PROCESS OF CAREER MANAGEMENT

So far, we have discussed issues that provide a context within which career management occurs. We turn our attention now to the specific activities individuals and organizations can use to actively manage employee careers. As discussed earlier, career management involves both planning for career activities and putting those plans into action. First, we will present a model of career management that offers a prescriptive approach individuals can use to manage their careers. Then, we will present several models that focus on how organizations may structure their career management systems.

### AN INDIVIDUALLY ORIENTED CAREER MANAGEMENT MODEL

As discussed earlier, individuals face a number of decisions in managing their careers. Greenhaus and colleagues present a valuable model of how individuals should manage this process.[66] This is presented in Figure 12-3.

This model represents an ideal career management process — the way people should conduct career management, not a description of what the typical person actually does.[67] The model states that effective career management begins as the individual responds to the need to make a career decision. That response includes eight activities: career exploration, awareness of self and environment, goal setting, strategy development, strategy implementation, progress toward the goal, feedback from work and nonwork sources, and career appraisal. These activities are described in greater detail in Table 12-3. To perform them, the individual uses information, opportunities, and support from family, as well as from educational, work, and societal institutions. The model suggests that career management occurs in a series of steps, though the order of progression through these steps may vary. The process may be summed up this way:

> The career management cycle is a problem-solving, decision-making process. Information is gathered so individuals can become more aware of themselves, and the world around them. Goals are established, plans or strategies are developed and implemented, and feedback is obtained to provide more information for ongoing career management.[68]

**FIGURE 12-3**     **A MODEL OF CAREER MANAGEMENT**

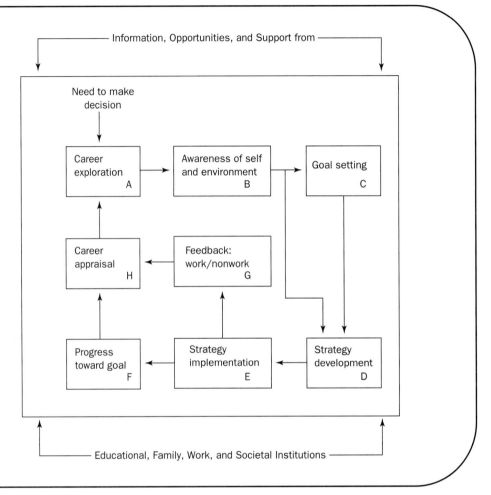

SOURCE: From *Career Management* 3rd edition by Greenhaus. © 2000. Reprinted with permission of South-Western, a division of Thomson Learning: www.thomsonrights.com. Fax 800-730-2215.

It is important to note that the career management process is cyclical and ongoing. The need to make career decisions can result from changes within the individual (e.g., questioning done at midcareer) and changes in the environment (e.g., organizational decisions such as firing and downsizing, or a merger or acquisition). As discussed earlier, individual advancement and satisfaction may not be reliable indicators of success. Effective application of the career management model, including knowledge of both self and the environment, realism of goals, career strategies, and continual feedback, are more meaningful indicators of career success.[69]

Following such a model can assist both employees and organizations in understanding what should be done to effectively manage careers. Obviously, employees benefit when they establish and work toward career goals. But it is also beneficial for organizations to encourage their employees to manage careers in this way. An

**TABLE 12-3**

# CAREER MANAGEMENT ACTIVITIES

1. **Career exploration.** Career exploration involves gathering information about one's self and the environment. For example, a young woman engaged in career exploration would collect information about her skills, values, and preferences as well as information about the possible jobs and organizations available to her in the environment.

2. **Awareness of self and environment.** Successful career exploration will lead the individual to a deeper self-awareness and an understanding of both opportunities and constraints present in the environment. This awareness of self and environment can lead the individual to set or revise career goals, or if such goals are already set, it would lead to strategy development.

3. **Goal setting.** A career goal is an outcome the individual decides to try to obtain. Such goals may be specific (e.g., I want to become a partner in my accounting firm by age 35) or general (e.g., I want to be a successful and respected chef). To the extent career goals are based on an awareness of the self and environment, they are likely to be realistic.

4. **Strategy development.** A career strategy is an action plan for accomplishing the career goal. An effective strategy should include the actions that should be carried out and a timetable for performing them. Many of the HRD practices and programs presented in this book can serve as part of an individual's career strategy. For example, a police officer whose career goal is to become a police sergeant may develop a strategy that includes attending college and other training courses and successfully completing the sergeant's examination. The strategy will be more effective if it is based on realistic self-awareness and environmental awareness. Greenhaus lists seven career strategies: competency in the current job, increased involvement in work, developing skills, developing opportunities, cultivating mentor relationships, image building, and engaging in organizational politics.

5. **Strategy implementation.** Strategy implementation involves carrying out the strategy the individual has developed. Following a realistic strategy as opposed to acting without a clearly defined plan increases the likelihood of attaining the career goal. It is easier to get where you want to go if you have a plan to follow. However, some people may develop elaborate plans, but then fail to implement them. Strategy implementation can lead to progress toward the goal and feedback from work and nonwork sources.

6. **Progress toward the goal.** This is the extent to which the individual is nearing the career goal.

7. **Feedback from work and nonwork sources.** Valuable information about the progress toward the career goal can be obtained from both work sources — such as co-workers, supervisors, and specialists, and nonwork sources — such as friends, family, and teachers.

8. **Career appraisal.** Feedback and information on progress toward the career goal permit the individual to appraise his or her career. This appraisal leads to reengagement in career exploration, and the career management process continues with another cycle of activities.

SOURCE: From *Career Management* 3rd edition by Greenhaus. © 2000. Reprinted with permission of South-Western, a division of Thomson Learning: www.thomsonrights.com. Fax 800-730-2215.

organization's needs change over time, given the loss of key employees through turnover and retirement, and in response to competitive and other environmental challenges. Assisting employees in conducting this process can help the organization ensure that the human resources available will be adequate to perform important tasks and accomplish organizational objectives.

## ORGANIZATIONALLY ORIENTED CAREER MANAGEMENT MODELS

As you have seen, the model from Greenhaus and colleagues is more individually focused. Other authors present models that are more organizationally focused.[70] These models share the idea that the organization's structure and needs should guide the organization's career management system. We will briefly describe three of these models.

*THE PLURALISTIC APPROACH.* As described earlier, Brousseau and colleagues believe that there are at least four career concepts that represent patterns employees' careers can take.[71] They argue that organizations can have career cultures that mirror these career concepts (i.e., linear, expert, spiral, and transitory). An organization's career culture is defined by the organization's structure, what forms of performance it values, and the rewards it offers employees. At the same time, the organization's career culture should support its strategic direction (e.g., an organization seeking diversification should adopt a spiral career concept culture).[72]

Brousseau and colleagues present a pluralistic approach as a way to align the organization and the individual. They state: "We suggest that both organizations and the workforce as a whole might benefit from a pluralistic approach that combines varied amounts and types of organizational structure with an array of quite different career experience opportunities. Organizations would retain sufficient structure to maintain certain core competencies and organizational leadership, while utilizing less structured arrangements to meet the demands of external change and flux" (pp. 55–56).

Operationally, Brousseau and colleagues offer three types of career management methods: (1) *counseling*, (2) individual career development program *contracts*, and (3) a *cafeteria* approach that includes a variety of "career-track options, training opportunities, performance evaluation schemes, and reward systems" (p. 62), from which employees may choose to fit their own career goals. Designing and managing a pluralistic career culture involves an ongoing process of assessing the gaps between the organization's strategy and employees' career concepts and motives, identifying the optimal organizational structure, and then identifying and implementing the proper career management practices.

*A SYSTEMS VIEW OF CAREER MANAGEMENT.* Nicholson proposes that there are three main elements of a career development system: (1) the *people system,* which includes the activities involved in selecting, nurturing, and motivating human resources; (2) the *job market system,* which includes the structure for developmental opportunities; and (3) the *management and information system,* which facilitates the exchange of people, ideas, and information.[73] Given the environmental forces most organizations now face, Nicholson believes that linking these three systems is vital to career management. He suggests "career management must link the *people system* and the *job market system* via the *management and information system*" (emphasis in original, p. 48).

This linkage could be made within organizations by ensuring that information is available and usable, and could include between-company cooperation in the form of creating and maintaining databases of people and jobs. Doing so would provide individuals and organizations with a way to gain and use knowledge to accomplish their goals. Nicholson suggests that individual outcomes of such a system would include better job-person fit, competency, and leadership. Organizational outcomes would include better teamwork, flexibility, and dynamism.

TEAM-BASED CAREER DEVELOPMENT. As many organizations are shifting toward more team-oriented structures, it is possible that team experiences can be used for career management. Cianni and Wnuck note that in team-based organizations, career development responsibility can be shared among the individual, the team, and the organization.[74] A team model for career development can enhance an individual member's growth and ensure that teams develop as well. Cianni and Wnuck suggest that the basic attributes of a team career model include the following:

- Team members serve as role models.
- Teams reward behaviors that enhance team performance and growth, and personal growth and development.
- Teams determine training opportunities both for the team and for individuals.
- The team moves collectively to higher organizational levels.
- People move laterally within the team.
- The organization evaluates the team; the team evaluates the individual.

The model offers different developmental activities for different team career stages. Stage 1, designed to integrate the individuals into the team, would include team competency and project management training, team building, and skill and personal style assessment. Stage 2, designed to continue team development, would include team problem solving and performance monitoring training, task rotation, and coaching. Finally, Stage 3, intended to make the team more independent and accountable, would include training in learning organization tools, leadership potential assessment, leadership rotation, and the possibility of having members lead a Stage 1 team.

Benefits of the team model should include higher productivity, commitment, organizational flexibility, and retention of high performers. However, not all teams would benefit from this approach. Cianni and Wnuck argue that this would most benefit cross-functional teams intended to help the organization expand into new markets or create new projects or services, as well as internal consulting teams charged with implementing change or serving internal customers.

These organizationally oriented career models emphasize the role of organizational structure and organizational goals as a driving force in career management, making career management a more strategic endeavor. They differ in terms of their applicability to particular organizations. While the pluralistic approach is intended to be used in a wide range of organizations, the career systems and team models will likely fit best in a particular range of organizations. Because these are new ideas, research and practical experience are needed to determine their effectiveness and the best way of using them. We find them intriguing and think they are expanding career development in new and exciting directions.

## ROLES IN CAREER MANAGEMENT

### THE INDIVIDUAL'S ROLE

Despite the melodrama of article and book titles proclaiming *You are Absolutely, Positively on Your Own*[75] and *We are All Self-Employed*,[76] it has always been true that each person bears the primary responsibility for his or her own career. The definition of *career* presented in this chapter makes it apparent that a career is an individual phenomenon. While many workers in the past felt they had the luxury of turning over responsibility for their career progress to their employers, the changes in the social contract between employers and their workers has necessitated that everyone should recognize and accept personal responsibility. The thrust behind many of the current wave of you-are-on-your-own articles is to get workers to see the changes that have taken place and to change their attitudes toward career management, from passive and complacent to proactive.

The career management model from Greenhaus and colleagues, which we discussed earlier, provides a useful framework for career planning and management. It is a rational model, in that it assumes that the best way to approach career management is through careful information gathering, planning and goal setting, decision making, action and follow-through, and follow-up.

What competencies are needed for effective career management? Hall emphasizes careers as a lifelong learning process, and argues that people must learn how to learn and gain self-knowledge, and must become more adaptable.[77] Other authors have suggested that individuals should make decisions and take assignments that provide them with an opportunity to learn and continuously develop new and existing skills.[78]

Jones and DeFillippi distilled six competencies that were possessed by people who successfully navigated the boundaryless careers and network-type of organizations found in the film industry, which they argue typify the new career landscape.[79] These competencies are:

- *Knowing What* — understanding the industry's opportunities, threats, and requirements
- *Knowing Why* — understanding the meaning, motives, and interests for pursuing a career
- *Knowing Where* — understanding the locations and boundaries for entering, training, and advancing within a career system
- *Knowing Whom* — forming relationships based on attraction and social capital that will gain access to opportunities and resources
- *Knowing When* — understanding the timing and choice of activities within one's career
- *Knowing How* — understanding and acquiring the skill and talents needed for effective performance in assignments and responsibilities

Each of these competencies creates challenges, such as dealing with uncertainty, managing career demands, creating a career path, mastering relationships, developing career timing, and enhancing collaboration. In fact, Jones and De-Fillippi and others argue that forming and working within relationships is one of the most essential tasks or competencies needed to successfully managing one's career.[80] The six competencies are interrelated. Jones and DeFillippi suggest that knowing what, where, and when form a map of the industry, while knowing why, how, and whom provide the self-knowledge and skill to navigate the career system.

We support this emphasis on learning. Many career development activities are based on acquiring and using these competencies. Even if you are in an organization or industry characterized by a traditional career system, developing these competencies will better enable you to attain your career goals.

## THE MANAGER'S RESPONSIBILITY

The career management process just described presents a number of opportunities for managers and supervisors to become involved. For example, during career appraisal, a supervisor can serve as a source of information about an employee's capabilities and limitations through the performance evaluation process. The supervisor can also provide accurate information about career paths and opportunities within the organization, support the employee's career plans (e.g., nominate the employee for training, adjust the employee's schedule to permit attendance in a training program), and serve as a key source of feedback to the employee on career progress.

Supervisory involvement has been cited as a key component of successful career development programs.[81] Based on an analysis of critical incidents gathered from employees, there are four roles that managers and supervisors should be trained to perform in order to fulfill their responsibility as career developers.[82] These roles include:

1. *Coach* — one who listens, clarifies, probes, and defines employee career concerns
2. *Appraiser* — one who gives feedback, clarifies performance standards and job responsibilities
3. *Adviser* — one who generates options, helps set goals, makes recommendations, and gives advice
4. *Referral Agent* — one who consults with the employee on action plans and links the employee to available organizational people and resources

## THE HRD AND CAREER DEVELOPMENT PROFESSIONAL'S RESPONSIBILITY

In many ways, an HRD professional's role is the same in career management as it is in any other HRD activity: to ensure that the organization has programs and activities that will help the organization and its employees to achieve their goals. This role involves all of the foundational activities in needs assessment, design, implementation, and evaluation.

In addition, in light of the changes in the career landscape, Hall offers the following suggestions for career development and HRD professionals to help individuals become "masters of their own careers":

1. Start with the recognition that each individual "owns" his or her career.

2. Create information and support for the individual's own efforts at development.

3. Recognize that career development is a relational process in which the career practitioner plays a broker role.

4. Become an expert on career information and assessment technologies.

5. Become a professional communicator about your services and the new career contract.

6. Promote work planning that benefits the organization as a whole, over career planning that is unrelated to organizational goals and future directions.

7. Promote learning through relationships at work.

8. Be an organizational interventionist, that is, someone willing and able to intervene where there are roadblocks to successful career management.

9. Promote mobility and the idea of the lifelong learner identity.

10. Develop the mind-set of using natural (existing) resources for development.[83]

Finally, HRD professionals must examine the employment practices used by their organization, and determine the extent to which these practice promote or work against the kinds of career management behavior they want employees to engage in.[84]

In the next section of this chapter, we will present some common career development practices and activities used by organizations. These practices can serve multiple purposes in the career management process.

## CAREER DEVELOPMENT PRACTICES AND ACTIVITIES

Organizations have a wide range of possible career development tools and activities from which to choose. Some of these, such as self-awareness workshops, are intended primarily for career planning and development, while others, such as recruitment, are a part of normal HR management activities. A study of career development activities at large organizations grouped career development activities into six categories: employee self-assessment tools, organizational-potential assessment processes, internal labor-market information exchanges, individual counseling or career discussions, job matching systems, and development programs.[85] Table 12-4 lists the categories, the career development practices included within each category, and the percentage of organizations employing each practice or planning to do so. For comparison purposes, data from three different countries are provided in this table. A recent survey of medium- to large-size organizations in India found that the most frequently used methods were succession planning, career counseling by supervisors, career counseling by HR professionals, and assessment centers.[86]

For clarity of presentation, we will use this framework for describing these activities and will discuss various types of career development practices separately. However, it is important to keep in mind that many organizations use these tools and activities as a part of an integrated or overall career development program. For example, organizations such as Amoco, Eastman Kodak, Boeing, Corning, and AT&T

**TABLE 12-4**

## ORGANIZATIONAL CAREER DEVELOPMENT TOOLS AND THEIR USAGE

| Career Development Practice | Percent Employing Practice | | |
|---|---|---|---|
| | United States sample (Gutteridge et al., 1993) | Canadian sample (Lemire et al., 1999) | United Kingdom sample (Baruch & Peiperl, 2000) |
| A. Employee self-assessment tools | | | |
| 1. Preretirement workshops | 46 | | 80 |
| 2. Career planning workshops | 34 | | 46 |
| 3. Career workbooks (stand-alone) | 18 | 27 | |
| 4. Computer software | 13 | | |
| B. Individual counseling or career discussions | | | |
| 1. Supervisor or line manager | 83 | | 93 |
| 2. Human Resource staff | 83 | | 86 |
| 3. Specialized counselor | | | |
| a. internal | 24 | 45 | |
| b. external | 17 | | |
| 4. Senior career advisors | 22 | | |
| C. Internal labor-market information exchanges | | | |
| 1. Career ladders or dual career ladders | 34 | 20 | 51 |
| 2. Career resource center | 22 | | |
| 3. Career information handbooks | 20 | 33 | 58 |
| 4. Other career information formats | 22 | | |
| D. Job matching systems | | | |
| 1. Job posting | 84 | 79 | 96 |
| 2. Replacement or succession planning | 65 | | 85 |
| 3. Internal placement systems | 56 | | |
| 4. Informal canvassing | 52 | | |
| 5. Skills inventories or skills audit | 37 | | |
| 6. Staffing committees | 24 | | |
| E. Organizational potential assessment processes | | | |
| 1. Interview process | 68 | | |
| 2. Job assignments | 65 | | |
| 3. Promotability forecasts | 46 | | |
| 4. Psychological testing | 34 | | |
| 5. Assessment centers | 14 | | 47 |
| F. Development programs | | | |
| 1. Tuition reimbursement | 95 | | |
| 2. In-house training and development programs | 92 | 72 | |
| 3. External seminars and workshops | 91 | | |
| 4. Employee orientation programs | 86 | 57 | |
| 5. Job rotation | 54 | 12 | |
| 6. Supervisor training in career discussions | 44 | | |
| 7. Job enrichment or job redesign | 41 | 85 | |
| 8. Mentoring systems | 21 | | 71 |
| 9. Dual-career couple programs | 8 | | |

SOURCES: Adapted from Gutteridge, T. G., Leibowitz, Z. B., & Shore, J. E. (1993). *Organizational career development: Benchmarks for building a world-class workforce* (p. 22). San Francisco: Jossey-Bass; Lemire, L., Saba, T., & Gagnon, Y.-C. (1999). Managing career plateauing in the Quebec public sector. *Public Personnel Management, 28*(3), 375–391; Baruch, Y., & Peiperl, M. (2000). Career management practices: An empirical survey and implications. *Human Resource Management, 39*(4), 347–366.

PART 3: HUMAN RESOURCE DEVELOPMENT APPLICATIONS

all have integrated career management and development programs that use a variety of these activities.[87]

## SELF-ASSESSMENT TOOLS AND ACTIVITIES

**Self-assessment activities,** such as self-study workbooks or career planning workshops, focus on providing employees with a systematic way to identify capabilities and career preferences. Self-assessment is best used as a first step in the process (i.e., at the stage of self-exploration) rather than as the only activity in a career management program.[88] Self-assessment activities can be done by an individual alone, in groups, or in some combination of the two. Effective self-assessment should (1) set the stage for the self-assessment experience and (2) help an individual explore his or her values, interests, skills, feelings, personal resources, goals for timing, and decision-making styles.[89] This information can help answer questions such as "Who am I?" "What do I want out of my life and my career?" and "How can I best achieve my career goals?"

Self-assessment workbooks provide information and a series of exercises to help an individual discover his or her values, abilities, and preferences. These workbooks can be purchased from a third party or designed specifically for an organization. For example, Richard Bolles' best-selling book *What Color is Your Parachute?* includes many self-discovery exercises, along with information about various occupations and job search skills.[90] Similarly, John Holland's *The Self-Directed Search* helps an individual reader identify his or her interests and suggests possible occupations that match these interests.[91]

The advantages of self-assessment exercises developed by third-party sources are that they are readily available and have been designed by career development experts. However, they are not designed to fit within an organization's specific HRD and career development strategy. The HRD staff may need to make modifications, or develop supplementary material to fill these gaps.

Workbooks designed to complement an organization's overall HRD strategy may do better at making employees aware of resources and opportunities within the organization. Such workbooks can include a statement of the organization's career development policy and associated procedures; information on the organization's structure, career paths, and job specifications; information about related training, education, and development programs; and instructions on how employees can obtain further information, such as names, addresses, and phone numbers of resource persons within the organization.[92]

The activities included within a workbook can also be delivered via computers and the Internet.[93] For example, the U.S. Army uses a microcomputer-based self-assessment system for officers called Officer Career Information and Planning System (OCIPS), and the American College Testing Program publishes a computer-based system called DISCOVER. Each of these programs provides career information and self-discovery exercises similar to those found in workbooks. One of the advantages of using self-assessment workbooks and computer programs is that they can be completed at the employee's convenience. However, it can also be beneficial to provide self-assessment information in an interactive group session where employees can share and discuss their insights. Career planning and preretirement workshops are well suited for this purpose.

Like other self-assessment approaches, career planning workshops provide a structured experience in which participants develop, share, and discuss personal information about their strengths, weaknesses, goals, and values.[94] Workshops can be made up of one or more sessions that focus on what career planning and management is all about, self-discovery, reality testing of insights gained during self-discovery through discussions with the facilitator and other participants, identification of possible career directions and opportunities, and career goal setting.[95]

The advantages of workshops include the ability to reach many people at once, opportunities to gain support from peers and to develop networks, and exposure to other people's ideas and reactions. In addition, feedback from the facilitator and other group members may help the individual recognize any self-deception or self-ignorance that might go undetected if a self-assessment workbook were used alone. Potential disadvantages include scheduling problems, difficulty in designing an experience that suits all the participants' needs (especially if they come from different organizational levels), and the possibility that some people may be intimidated by the group setting.[96]

If performed effectively, self-assessment activities can provide an individual with a sound basis on which to develop realistic career goals and strategies. As suggested above by Greenhaus and colleagues, self-assessment and evaluation of the environment are important first steps in establishing effective career goals and strategies. Career counseling and information about the internal labor market can also provide useful information for this task. These career management activities will be discussed next.

## INDIVIDUAL COUNSELING OR CAREER DISCUSSIONS

Individual career counseling involves one-on-one discussions between the employee and an organizational representative. One survey revealed that organizations primarily used HR professionals, supervisors, or line managers as career counselors.[97] Such counseling sessions can range from brief, informal talks, to the annual performance evaluation discussion, to a series of discussions with a manager or counseling professional.[98]

Individualized counseling can answer a wide range of questions and can either stand alone or supplement other career development activities. The career counseling process can be viewed in three stages:

1. *Opening and Probing* — This stage establishes rapport and determines the employee's goals for the counseling session(s).

2. *Understanding and Focusing* — This includes providing assistance in self-assessment and establishing career goals and strategies.

3. *Programming* — This stage provides support for implementing the career strategy.[99]

During this process, the counselor can suggest actions to the employee and provide support and feedback about the ideas and results of actions taken by the employee.

Counseling can be used for continuing employees as well as employees who are approaching retirement, are about to be laid off, or are terminated. **Outplacement counseling** focuses on assisting terminated employees in making the transition to a new organization.[100] The use of outplacement counseling has become widespread since the 1980s, especially in the wake of the downsizing, mergers, and acquisitions that organizations experienced during this period. These sessions can focus on job search skills, stress management, and career planning. Of all the forms of individualized counseling, outplacement counseling is the most likely to be performed by a counselor who is not an organization member. Many consulting firms offer outplacement services for hire.

*Preretirement counseling* and workshops involve activities that help employees prepare for the transition from work to nonwork. Retirement is often filled with great uncertainty on both the personal and the financial level. Preretirement counseling programs typically involve discussions about financial planning, social adjustment, family issues, and preparing for leisure activities.

An important issue in individualized counseling centers on the individual selected to be the counselor. In some ways, managers and supervisors are well suited to serve as counselors. They are knowledgeable about the organization and should be familiar with the employee's performance and his or her capabilities. In addition, they are in an ideal position to offer support and to follow up on actions taken by the employee. However, there are disadvantages to using supervisors and managers as career counselors. First, unless they receive training in career development issues and counseling skills such as listening, questioning, and clarification, they may lack the skills to perform effective counseling. Second, even with training, some supervisors and managers lack the abilities and/or desire to perform the task well. They may view it as an added burden and may not be rewarded by the organization for performing it. Finally, employees may be reluctant to discuss their career plans with current bosses or to take advice from a nonprofessional.[101]

If managers and supervisors are to be used as counselors, the following steps should be taken:

1. Their role in the career development process must be clarified.
2. They must be trained to perform this role.
3. They must have the opportunity to discuss their own career development concerns.
4. The role of counselor or developer should be incorporated into the organizational reward system (e.g., included in managers' performance evaluations).[102]

One element of this approach has been used at Metropolitan Life, where the performance evaluation process for managers and supervisors includes an evaluation of how well they are doing in developing their employees.

## INTERNAL LABOR MARKET INFORMATION EXCHANGES AND JOB MATCHING SYSTEMS

Employees engaged in career planning need accurate environmental information in addition to an accurate self-assessment. To this end, the organization should provide employees with information about job opportunities within the organization. Two commonly used methods for doing this are job posting systems and the establishment of career paths. (We will discuss succession planning in the next section.)

**Job posting,** is one of the most common career development activities. It involves making open positions in the organization known to current employees before advertising them to outsiders. In a typical job posting program, the organization publishes the job description, job requirements, pay range, and an application procedure for vacancies, and it provides a form for employees to submit. The vacancies can be posted in a common area, such as on a bulletin board reserved for that purpose. Increasingly, such postings are done online, using the organization's website or intranet. Interested employees can then apply and be considered for the vacant positions. Job posting systems are widely used in both government and private organizations.

Job posting is a source of career information as well as a recruiting and selection tool. Employees can learn which skills and abilities are needed for various positions and can use that information as a springboard for career development discussions and to establish career goals and strategies. If they are administered openly and fairly, job postings can help employees realize that they have a future in the organization, and this can improve morale. However, job posting systems can also create problems if employees suspect that only low-level or undesirable positions are being posted, or if the job requirements listed are rigged to ensure that an "inside" candidate is the only one qualified for a position.

A **career path** is a sequence of jobs, usually involving related tasks and experiences, that employees move through over time.[103] For example, a career path in a city police department may include the positions of patrol officer, desk sergeant, lieutenant, captain, and chief of police. Career paths communicate to employees the possibilities for job movement. Together with job descriptions and job specifications, these paths can aid the employee in developing a career strategy.

Career paths can be developed using either a traditional or a job/behavioral approach.[104] In the traditional approach, the career path represents what has typically happened in the organization and usually represents a consensus among managers about logical job movements within a particular department. For example, if computer operators typically become technical advisors before becoming supervisors, the career path will reflect this. In the job/behavioral approach, the path is created by analyzing the similarities and differences among jobs in the organization. For example, if the positions of market research analyst and human resource research analyst require similar skills, these jobs may be listed on the same career path, even though they exist in different departments. The job/behavioral approach can include jobs from throughout the organization and, as a result, open up more possibilities for movement than the traditional approach.[105]

Some organizations use a *dual career path* or dual-track system in which the path to greater responsibility includes both management and nonmanagement tracks. The presence of nonmanagement paths, with relatively equivalent esteem and pay, can serve the needs of employees who lack the skills or the desire to become managers. For example, the Exploration Division of British Petroleum established dual career paths for areas such as engineering and product development. Teams of managers and employees established the system, and trained colleagues in how to use the new system.[106] Such an approach opens up more possibilities than the traditional pyramid structure provides.

While career paths can help provide information to employees about career progression possibilities, they may rely too heavily on what the organization has typically done rather than on what it is likely to need in the future.[107] Given the changes in the career landscape that we noted earlier in the chapter, vertical progressions may be unavailable, or they may be shorter than have traditionally been available, unappealing to employees with spiral or transitional career concepts, or not in keeping with the organization's strategy and career culture. Therefore, career paths should be developed within the context of each organization's strategic and human resource planning activities. In addition, care should be taken to identify possible alternative paths, such as lateral career movement.[108] This is included in the career grid approach, in which career grids, based on job content, specify possible vertical and horizontal sequences of positions employees may hold.[109] The grids can communicate not only the potential paths but also the competencies required for each position in the paths and developmental ideas for moving through these positions.[110] From an organizational viewpoint, this approach is beneficial in that it provides skilled and valued employees (e.g., the organization's top engineers or accountants) with a career option that promises progression, while allowing them to remain in their specialty area. It also provides a learning and developmental incentive for employees who are not interested in becoming managers.

Beyond using career paths and job posting, internal information can also be supplemented by publishing booklets and flyers that inform employees of career enhancement possibilities. Knowledge of available resources such as upcoming training programs and tuition assistance programs can help employees develop and implement their career strategy.

Another source of internal labor market information is a *skills inventory*.[111] A skills inventory is a database that contains information about employee skills, education, performance evaluation, and career preferences. It is often part of an organization's human resource information system (HRIS). HRD professionals can use this information during the needs assessment phase to identify the capabilities of the workforce and pinpoint any skill shortages that should be addressed. Skills inventory information is usually collected from voluntary reports from employees. Potential shortcomings of voluntary self-reports include the possibility of incomplete, inaccurate, or outdated information, though the recent growth in network- and personal computer-based HRIS has made these issues easier to deal with than they once were.[112]

## ORGANIZATION POTENTIAL ASSESSMENT PROCESSES

Organizations have a vested interest in ensuring that they have individuals available who are ready to fill key positions when these positions become vacant. To this end, many organizations evaluate the *potential*, or *promotability*, of managerial, professional, and technical employees. Those judged as high-potential employees can then be "groomed" for these positions. Three ways that **potential assessment** can be done are through potential ratings, assessment centers, and by succession planning.

**Potential ratings** are similar to employee performance evaluations. An employee's manager or supervisor typically performs them. They measure multiple dimensions, and include a summary or overall rating of the employee's potential for advancement. The main difference between potential ratings and performance ratings is that potential ratings focus on the future rather than the past or present. This method requires the rater to judge whether an employee is likely to be successful in jobs requiring skills he or she may not currently use. Also, the results of potential evaluations are unlikely to be made known to the employee. Ratings of potential are subject to the same problems as performance evaluations (i.e., rating errors and biases). Raters should be trained in the proper way to conduct such an evaluation.

**Assessment centers,** which can be used as part of the employee selection process, can also be used to assess potential for advancement.[113] In an assessment center, small groups of employees perform a variety of exercises while being evaluated by a group of trained assessors. The exercises can include simulations, role plays, group discussions, tests, and interviews. The exercises should measure relevant skills and aptitudes for a given position. The assessors are typically managers who are one or two organizational levels above those being evaluated (assessees). Assessors should be specifically trained for this task. The assessors write a detailed report on each assessee and usually make an overall judgment about the assessee's promotability. When used for developmental purposes, the intensive assessment feedback is provided to the employee to increase self-awareness. The feedback from a developmental assessment center can be used by the employee to develop career goals and a plan for future development. While career development assessment centers can be expensive to use, they provide a rich source of data. Care should be taken in designing assessment center procedures to include assessment of skills that can be developed in a reasonable amount of time and to include exercises that permit multiple opportunities to observe participants in each dimension.[114] Examples of this approach include developmental assessment centers at AT&T[115] and Kimberly Brothers Manufacturing Company.[116]

**Succession planning** is a third way of conducting potential evaluations.[117] This process is most often done for upper-level management positions. It requires senior managers to identify employees who should be developed to replace them. Information generated during succession planning may not be communicated to the employee. If potential evaluations are made known to the employee and his or her superiors, this information can be used to create a self-fulfilling prophecy. That is, if managers believe the employee has a high potential for advancement, they may be more likely to evaluate the person favorably and promote him or her more quickly than actual performance warrants.[118] If succession plans are not communicated to the employee, the organization runs the risk of a mismatch between the employee's career plans and its plans for the employee. Making this information available to the employee can ensure that the employee develops realistic career plans[119] and reduces the chances that the person will refuse the position.

In the case of management development, the notion of *succession management* can be seen as a way for succession planning to better serve organizations in a rapidly changing environment.[120] One of the main properties of succession management is viewing the goal of the process as one of creating a cadre of individuals who have the competencies needed to work as part of a senior management team. Future competencies, in the form of a "leadership template," are used as the criteria toward which groups of individuals should be developed. The role of senior management is not to identify specific individuals to replace them, but to identify developmental opportunities, create challenging assignments that are central to the business and create a team/network orientation, and mentor and serve as role models for those who are being developed.

## DEVELOPMENTAL PROGRAMS

The final group of career management activities we will examine are developmental programs. These include job rotation, in-house HRD programs, external workshops and seminars, tuition assistance and reimbursement plans, and mentoring programs. These programs provide employees with opportunities to learn new ideas and skills, thus preparing them for future positions as well as introducing new challenges.

**Job rotation** involves assigning an employee to a series of jobs in different functional areas of the organization. These assignments are typically lateral rather than vertical moves, and can involve serving on task forces or moving from line to staff positions. Job rotation is a good way to introduce variety into an employee's career. In addition, it provides the employee with a chance to learn and use new skills and to better understand different organizational functions. It can also serve to help the employee build networks within the organization, and be better prepared for future promotion opportunities, when they become available.

There is some research to support the effectiveness of job rotation as a career development tool.[121] One study found that job rotation was related to outcomes such as salary, promotion, and satisfaction, and was perceived to be related to improved knowledge, skills, and other career benefits.[122] This study also reported that rotation tended to occur for employees early in their career and for employees who were performing well. Professional nonmanagerial employees were more interested in rotation than others. With regard to implementing job rotation, care should be taken to ensure that the job assignments used in job rotation offer developmental opportunities, rather than just the chance to do something different.[123]

**Mentoring** refers to a relationship between a junior and senior member of the organization that contributes to the career development of both members. Mentoring relationships can be important from both a life development and a career development perspective. From a life development perspective, recall from Levinson's era approach to adult development that young adults seek to establish meaningful relationships, while middle-aged adults often want to make an impact on the generation to follow them. From a career development perspective, the younger employee wishes to become established in the organization, while the middle-aged employee wants to remain productive at work. From either perspective, the mentoring relationship serves the needs of both members.

The mentoring relationship serves both career and psychosocial (e.g., social support) functions.[124] The mentor provides the protégé with career support — by opening doors, "teaching the ropes" of the organization, creating potential opportunities to demonstrate competence, enhancing visibility, and ensuring that the protégé has challenging work. The protégé provides the mentor with a meaningful, mutually reinforcing relationship that demonstrates the value and commitment of both parties to the organization. The mentor has a chance to serve as a role model and share what he or she knows with someone who can benefit from such knowledge. In return, the mentor receives respect, support, and in many cases, friendship.

In many organizations, mentoring relationships are formed as a result of the parties' mutual attraction. Some organizations, such as Apple Computer,[125] Federal Express,[126] and the Federal Reserve Bank of Chicago,[127] have created formal mentoring programs in which mentors and protégés are paired by the organization and provided with support for the relationship. An example of a formal mentoring program is shown in Table 12-5.

Research has shown that mentoring can yield numerous organizational benefits, including facilitating the socialization of new members into the organization, reducing turnover, minimizing midcareer adjustments, enhancing transfer of beneficial knowledge and values, and facilitating the adjustment to retirement.[128]

Mentoring relationships are complex. While they serve a variety of needs for both mentor and protégé, they are also subject to potential limitations and problems. Limitations of formal mentoring programs include the small number of mentor pairs that they can accommodate, and such unintended negative consequences

---

**TABLE 12-5**　　　　**EXAMPLE OF A FORMAL MENTORING PROGRAM**

**Sample Implementation**

1. Define a population for whom relationships should be established. Invite potential mentors and protégés to help define the criteria for matching pairs and the process for doing so.

2. Collect data on potential participants that are needed to maximize an effective matching process (such as career goals, performance records, developmental needs).

3. Assign juniors and seniors to each other or foster a voluntary selection process. Provide guidelines on goals of the program, role expectations, and staff support services, and encourage participation in relevant educational offerings.

4. Set up monitoring procedures for providing feedback to the organization concerning how the program affects employee development over time.

| Advantages | Disadvantages |
|---|---|
| ■ Ensures that juniors and seniors find each other. | ■ Individuals may feel coerced and confused about responsibilities. |
| ■ Increases the likelihood that matches will be good ones. | ■ Those who are not matched feel deprived and pessimistic about their futures. |
| ■ Provides ongoing support to the pairs. | ■ Assumes that volunteers can learn the requisite skills; some may be ill suited. |
| ■ Makes mentoring relationships legitimate and more accessible. | ■ Destructive dynamics may evolve within formal pairs or with immediate supervisors. |

SOURCE: From Kram, K. E. (1986). Mentoring in the workplace. In D. T. Hall & Associates (Eds.), *Career development in organizations* (p. 183). San Francisco: Jossey-Bass.

as dissatisfaction with the relationship and negative feelings of those not involved in the program.[129] It is not clear whether informal mentoring is superior to formal mentoring in terms of the depth and scope of the mentor-protégé relationship. While one research study found that the protégés in informal relationships received more career-related support and had better career outcomes,[130] a separate study found no difference.[131] Recent research by Eby and colleagues sought to understand negative experiences that protégés have with their mentors.[132]

It is also not clear the extent to which problems exist in cross-gender mentoring relationships. Earlier writers suggested that such problems exist.[133] Research supporting this contention has reported findings suggesting that:

1. Concern exists between the parties about intimacy and sexual attraction.[134]

2. There is an inclination for men and women to rely on sex-role stereotypes.[135]

3. Dissatisfaction with the role-modeling aspect of the relationship may be felt.[136]

4. The relationship is subject to public scrutiny (e.g., jealous spouses, office gossip).[137]

5. Peer resentment may occur.[138]

More recent studies have found no gender differences in the amount of career mentoring that protégés receive.[139] It may be that in male-dominated occupations, gender role has more to do with differences in the amount of mentoring received than biological sex.[140] Recent research also has found that women are just as likely as men to become mentors, report intentions to mentor, and to see the costs and benefits of entering a mentorship relationship similarly.[141]

Research on cross-racial mentoring suggests another source of potential problems. Thomas found that black protégés with white mentors reported less satisfaction with the mentoring relationship and less support than did members of same-race mentoring relationships.[142] Even within same-race and same-sex mentoring relationships, lack of support from the organization and incompatibility of the parties can undermine the relationship. For example, the way that participants in a cross-race developmental relationship prefer to deal with racial issues affects the dynamics of such relationships.[143] When both parties share the same strategy for addressing racial issues, the relationship has both career advancing and psychosocial elements (i.e., it becomes closer and more personally supportive). When the parties prefer different strategies for dealing with racial issues, the relationship is primarily oriented toward career advancement only, and lacks the psychosocial element.

Given the problems that can occur, some authors have questioned the value of mentoring. Clawson argued that mentoring is not essential and that employees can gain some of the same benefits by learning from their current supervisors, while seeking sponsorship at the appropriate time from someone else.[144] Kram suggests that it may not be necessary for employees to look for everything that mentoring can provide in a single relationship.[145] In addition, relationships with peers can also provide some of the same functions that mentors do (e.g., information, career strategies, emotional support, personal feedback), and may be more suitable for individuals without mentors or for those who do not want mentors.[146] Recent writing recommends the value of a mentoring network, where employees foster relationships with multiple mentors.[147]

Given the potential benefits for both the individual and the organization, we believe mentoring is a viable and appropriate career development strategy. If an organization chooses to develop a formal mentoring program, three conditions seem to increase the chances of success:

1. The program should be clearly linked to business strategy and existing HR policies and practices, so as to increase the chances that potential participants and senior management will accept and actively support the program.

2. Core components of the program (objectives, guidelines, training and education, communication strategy, monitoring and evaluation, and coordination) should be designed for effectiveness rather than expediency.

3. Voluntary participation and flexible guidelines are critical to success.[148]

In addition, formal mentoring programs should be used as one part of an organization's overall development strategy. Mentoring should be tied to strategic business needs and take advantage of natural learning opportunities in the organization, as well as HR systems that encourage mentoring.[149]

## ISSUES IN CAREER DEVELOPMENT

Several other issues should be considered when formulating or modifying an organization's career development program. These include generating career motivation, career plateauing, career development for nonexempt workers, and career development without advancement. We will discuss each of these issues briefly.

### DEVELOPING CAREER MOTIVATION

Developing career motivation is a significant career management goal.[150] According to Manuel London, **career motivation** affects how people choose their careers, how they view their careers, how hard they work in them, and how long they stay in them.[151] London sees career motivation as a set of characteristics grouped into three facets: career resilience, career insight, and career identity.[152] Each of these facets is defined in Table 12-6. A person can have a high, moderate, or low level of career motivation depending on his or her position in each of these categories. For example, a person with high career motivation will continue to pursue career goals in the face of obstacles and setbacks (career resilience), formulate and pursue realistic career goals (career insight), and be highly involved in work and aggressively pursue career goals (career identity).

While career motivation is partly determined by an individual's life experiences, career activities and practices can help develop a person's career motivation.[153] For example, self-awareness workbooks and personal journals can be used to build career insight. Because career motivation can affect both decision making and commitment to one's career, it would be beneficial for organizations to offer career development activities to enhance such motivation. Table 12-7 provides some suggestions for how this can be accomplished.

**TABLE 12-6**

## DEFINITIONS OF THE THREE FACETS OF CAREER MOTIVATION

1. **Career resilience.** The extent to which people resist career barriers or disruptions affecting their work. This consists of self-confidence, need for achievement, the willingness to take risks, and the ability to act independently and cooperatively as appropriate.

2. **Career insight.** The extent to which people are realistic about themselves and their careers and how these perceptions are related to career goals. This includes developing goals and gaining knowledge of the self and the environment.

3. **Career identity.** The extent to which people define themselves by their work. This includes involvement in job, organization, and profession and the direction of career goals (e.g., toward advancement in an organization).

SOURCE: From London, M., & Mone, E. M. (1987). *Career management and survival in the workplace* (p. 54). San Francisco: Jossey-Bass.

**TABLE 12-7**

## METHODS FOR INCREASING CAREER MOTIVATION

1. **To support career resilience**
   a. Build employees' self-confidence through feedback and positive reinforcement.
   b. Generate opportunities for achievement.
   c. Create an environment conducive to risk taking by rewarding innovation and reducing fear of failure.
   d. Show interpersonal concern and encourage group cohesiveness and collaborative working relationships.

2. **To enhance career insight**
   a. Encourage employees to set their own goals.
   b. Supply employees with information relevant to attaining their career goals.
   c. Provide regular performance feedback.

3. **To build career identity**
   a. Encourage work involvement through job challenge and professional growth.
   b. Provide career development opportunities, such as leadership positions and advancement potential.
   c. Reward solid performance through professional recognition and/or financial bonus.

SOURCE: From London, M. (1991). Career development. In K. N. Wexley & J. Hinrichs (Eds.), *Developing human resources* (pp. 5–159). Washington, DC: BNA Books.

Career motivation can be important in addressing the issues facing workers who have lost their jobs because of downsizing, layoffs, or some personal issue or setback.[154] Efforts to redeploy such workers can be more effective if career motivation issues are addressed, whether the methods are government and community programs to assist unemployed workers to obtain jobs, retraining for displaced employees, joint union-management retraining programs, or internal contingent workforces.[155] London offers a variety of suggestions concerning how managers and executives can address career motivation issues to successfully redeploy displaced workers, and for how organizations can support career motivation in older workers.[156]

## THE CAREER PLATEAU

The pyramidal structure of many organizations together with a shrinking number of management positions typically means that a time will come in an individual's career when he or she will no longer be able to "move up" in the organization. In addition, career progress is not likely to be a continuous upward journey, but rather one that includes periods of movement and periods of stability. These factors contribute to what has been termed a career plateau. A **career plateau** has been defined as "the point in a career where the likelihood of additional hierarchical promotion is very low" (p. 602).[157] Early writing on career plateaus suggested that this is a traumatic experience for many employees (especially those who desire career growth), accompanied by feelings of stress, frustration, failure, and guilt.[158] More recent writing suggests that a plateau can also be seen as a "time of change, transition, reevaluation, and reflection" (p. 229).[159]

The empirical research on the consequences of career plateaus has been mixed, with some verification of negative consequences of plateauing, coupled with other data suggesting that employees at such a plateau can be happy and productive.[160] At least two explanations for these mixed findings have been offered. First, Feldman and Weitz argued that the factors that lead to a plateau affect the consequences of the plateau. For example, if employees become plateaued because they lack the skills and ability to advance, they will likely exhibit poor performance and job attitudes. Alternatively, if the plateau occurs because of self-imposed constraints or a low need for growth, the employee will likely continue to perform well and have positive job attitudes. Feldman and Weitz suggest a model (presented in Table 12-8) that specifies six causes of career plateaus together with their impact on performance and attitudes and possible managerial interventions to address them. This model presents an encouraging approach to career plateaus. It has been used recently to discuss issues of career plateauing among auditors.[161]

Georgia Chao offered a second explanation for the mixed findings regarding the consequences of career plateaus. This explanation centers on the way the concept has been measured.[162] Studies have tended to define a career plateau operationally as a dichotomy (as in plateaued versus not plateaued) and have used job tenure (e.g., number of years since last promotion) to indicate whether the individual has plateaued. Chao observed that viewing plateaus as a dichotomy ignores the fact that individuals gradually become aware that their careers are plateaued, and that

**TABLE 12-8**

## CAUSES OF CAREER PLATEAUS AND SUGGESTED MANAGERIAL INTERVENTIONS

| Source of Career Plateaus | Impact on Performance and Attitudes | Managerial Interventions |
|---|---|---|
| **I. Individual Skills and Abilities**<br>Selection system deficiencies.<br>Lack of training.<br>Inaccurate perceptions of feedback. | Poor performance.<br>Poor job attitudes. | Redesign of selection system.<br>Improved training.<br>Improved performance appraisal and feedback systems. |
| **II. Individual Needs and Values**<br>Low growth need strength.<br>Career anchors of security and autonomy.<br>Self-imposed constraints. | Solid performance.<br>Good job attitudes. | Continue to reward, contingent on no downturn in performance.<br>Career information systems. |
| **III. Lack of Intrinsic Motivation**<br>Lack of skill variety.<br>Low task identity.<br>Low task significance. | Minimally acceptable job performance.<br>Declining job attitudes. | Combining tasks.<br>Forming natural work units.<br>Establishing client relationships.<br>Vertical loading.<br>Opening feedback channels. |
| **IV. Lack of Extrinsic Rewards**<br>Small raises, few promotions.<br>Inequities in reward systems.<br>Uncontingent rewards. | Poor performance.<br>Poor job attitudes. | Redesign of compensation system.<br>Redesign of promotion policies.<br>Encourage highly dissatisfied to leave. |
| **V. Stress and Burnout**<br>Interpersonal relationships on job.<br>Organizational climate.<br>Role conflict. | Poor performance.<br>Poor job attitudes. | Job rotation.<br>Preventive stress management. |
| **VI. Slow Organizational Growth**<br>External business conditions.<br>"Defender" corporate strategy.<br>Inaccurate personnel forecasts. | Continued good performance in short run.<br>Declining job attitudes. | Sabbaticals; off-site training.<br>Provide "stars" with increased resources.<br>Provide poorer performers with incentives to leave or retire. |

SOURCE: Reprinted with permission from Feldman, D. C., & Weitz, B. A. (1988). Career plateaus reconsidered. *Journal of Management*, 14, 71.

different levels of awareness may lead to different consequences.[163] Second, Chao argued that what is critical to defining career plateaus is the individual's *perception* of being plateaued, because the individual's perception of career progress will likely determine how he or she feels about it and reacts to it. Consequently, she hypothesized that a perceptual measure of career plateaus will better explain the consequences of being plateaued than the traditional job tenure approach. Chao developed a perceptual measure of plateauing and found that perception accounted for more variance in four outcomes (including satisfaction and career planning) than did job tenure.[164] Similar findings were obtained recently by Lee.[165] Chao also found that the negative effects of a plateau were worse during the early years of an employee's career. Other researchers have reported similar results.[166]

These findings suggest that career plateauing is more complex than previously thought. Based on this research, it is recommended that HRD professionals should (1) assess whether employees are plateaued by determining employees' perceptions of the extent to which their careers are stalled and attempt to identify the reasons for the plateau, and (2) tailor the action used to resolve an employee's problem according to the cause of the plateau.

Given the flattening of organizational hierarchies, some plateauing is inevitable, and it is important for organizations to find a way to maintain employees' motivation and effectiveness. Ettington found that managers can be *successfully plateaued* (i.e., exhibit effective job performance and satisfaction with the job and life). She argues that organizations should engage in HRM practices that facilitate successful versus unsuccessful plateauing. In the area of career development, Ettington suggests practices such as broadening opportunities to grow on the job, removing obstacles to lateral and downward career moves, and helping employees identify and prepare for new challenges.[167] Tremblay and Roger found that attitudes and behaviors were most positive for plateaued managers who felt that their jobs were richer, and that they had more opportunity to participate in decision making.[168]

## CAREER DEVELOPMENT FOR NONEXEMPT EMPLOYEES

Although much of the career development literature focuses on developing managers and professionals, the career development needs of blue-collar and nonexempt employees (e.g., clerical and support staff and technicians, who are paid hourly or weekly rates and are entitled to overtime) have been largely ignored. One reason for this disregard is an assumption by many researchers, managers, and HR professionals that these employees do not have long-term ambitions that need to be addressed.[169] However, given the large number of such employees and the critical role they play in organizational effectiveness, HRD professionals need to consider career development activities that allow organizations to better use the potential of these employees and serve their long-term needs.

Some HRD professionals are beginning to examine this issue. A survey of career development professionals about the development needs of nonexempt employees revealed the following:

1. Job satisfaction often comes from the work itself, which is problematic if the work is repetitive and unchallenging.

2. Changing current status (e.g., union to nonunion, blue collar to white collar) requires both a significant personal investment and a significant cultural adjustment. For example, white-collar positions may require higher education levels than blue-collar positions, and employees who cross the "collar line" may not receive the support they need from coworkers.

3. Nonexempt employees may become more frustrated during their careers than exempt employees because opportunities to make a vertical transition are more limited for them.[170]

Some organizations, such as Corning and Lockheed Marine, have implemented career development programs for nonexempt employees to better serve them and ensure that future employment needs of the organization will be met. Both programs recognize that nonexempt employees need to be encouraged to take the initiative in their career development and be supported by management for doing so. Lockheed Marine's program includes career/life planning workshops (open to all employees), a career development resource center, and support for lifelong learning activities (e.g., tuition reimbursement for relevant courses, in-house seminars).[171] Corning's program includes four components: career exploration and planning software, videos, information books describing career possibilities at Corning, and supervisory training in career counseling.[172] Both programs have been successful in terms of high levels of employee participation and greater levels of career development actions on the part of nonexempt employees. Both of these programs serve as good examples of how organizations can address both their own needs and the career development needs of this large pool of employees. It is our hope that these initiatives stimulate more research and practice in this area.

## ENRICHMENT: CAREER DEVELOPMENT WITHOUT ADVANCEMENT

Many organizations find themselves faced with the prospect of downsizing their workforces and reducing the numbers of management positions in response to competition and changing business conditions. However, even with fewer employees, organizations still have to engage in career development activities, because HR needs will change as business strategy and technology changes. These forces increase the likelihood that organizations will have to develop career development programs, without being able to offer upward movement or the promise of job security as benefits to employees.[173] Instead, career development efforts will have to focus on enriching employees in their current jobs or areas of expertise if they are to increase employee satisfaction, maintain the skill base the organization needs, and offer employees a sense of career security by providing them with the best chance of gaining meaningful employment if they are laid off.[174]

Career development options within an enrichment strategy include:

1. certification programs and mastery paths that specify selection criteria and identify performance expectations, and training requirements to move through various levels of expertise within a job

2. retraining programs

3. job transfers or rotation[175]

Enrichment programs raise the level of skills and professionalism of the workforce, and they can increase employees' sense of self-esteem and self-determination in guiding their own careers. Given the changes that are occurring in the organizational landscape, enrichment and other career development practices that encourage self-determination, continuous learning, and employability are especially important.

## DELIVERING EFFECTIVE CAREER DEVELOPMENT SYSTEMS

It should be clear by now that any HRD program has the best chance of succeeding if attention is paid to performing thorough needs assessment, design, implementation, and evaluation. The same is true for career development programs. Our earlier discussion highlights some of the relevant issues in the design and implementation of an effective system. Table 12-9 provides a systematic approach to creating and

**TABLE 12-9**

**A SYSTEMS APPROACH TO CREATING A CAREER DEVELOPMENT PROGRAM**

**Identify Needs**
1. Link career development to business strategy.
2. Align employee and organization needs.

**Build a Vision for Change**
3. Build systems and link them to other management and HR systems (e.g., quality initiatives, orientation, performance evaluation, compensation).
4. Use a variety of tools and approaches.

**Develop a Plan for Action**
5. Create a corporate infrastructure, but implement career development systems in individual business units or divisions.
6. Ensure line manager participation, starting with system development.

**Implement for Impact and Longevity**
7. Hold line managers accountable and give them the skills they will need to fulfill their responsibilities.
8. Follow up initial implementation with a series of activities that keep career development salient (e.g., information sharing, career action teams).

**Evaluate and Maintain Results**
9. Evaluate.
10. Continuously improve the career development effort.
11. Maintain high visibility and ongoing communication of career development.

SOURCES: Based on Leibowitz, Z. B., Farren, C., & Kaye, B. L. (1986). *Designing career development systems*. San Francisco: Jossey-Bass, and Gutteridge, T. G., Leibowitz, Z. B., & Shore, J. E. (1993). *Organizational career development: Benchmarks for building a world-class workforce*. San Francisco: Jossey-Bass.

delivering an effective career development system. Using this approach, it is critical to obtain senior management support and to conduct and evaluate pilot programs before implementing a full-blown program.

We have frequently noted that rapid changes in the environment (e.g., demographics, technology, competition) have led to changes in organizational operations, which then has an effect on employees (e.g., the advent of downsizing). Managing career development efforts well in the current turbulent environment makes it even more important that such activities be tied to an organization's strategic plan. As we noted in Chapter 4, this means that needs assessment data should include organization-level data on goals, strengths, weaknesses, resource availability, organizational climate, and on the current human resource plan. Career development, like all HRD activities, should fit into the overall HR strategy. Recruiting, selection, compensation, benefits, and HRD activities have an impact on career development, and all can be used to facilitate the process.

HRD practitioners should also consider benchmarking their career development practices by examining effective approaches used by other organizations. The practitioner literature (e.g., *T&D, Training, HR Magazine*) and some books regularly feature articles profiling effective practices.[176] Career development practices can also be benchmarked through discussions with other professionals and visits to leading organizations.

Another issue in developing and delivering career development activities is the attitude held by many people that career development is primarily an individual's responsibility, and therefore this is *not* a beneficial area for organizational activity. In our view, this takes the individual responsibility notion to an unhealthy extreme that could encourage employers to abdicate any involvement in the career development process. This attitude must be overcome if a career management system is to gain wide acceptance. One way to overcome this attitude and benefit both the organization and the individual is to make clear from the start what purpose the career development programs will serve. Are these programs intended to enhance employee growth and decision making? Address EEO and affirmative action pressures? Improve the organization's image? Ensure that the organization has the necessary talent to remain effective? Whatever the purposes, they should be clearly stated. Achievement of these goals should then be evaluated once the program is in operation. The use of a steering committee, together with input from a variety of employees as to the planning, design, and testing of these programs, can further build support, understanding, and commitment.

In addition, many organizations are finding that career management works best when activities are coordinated within an integrated career development system.[177] Examples of organizations that have effectively used this approach include 3M, Bechtel Group, Eastman Kodak Company, and Boeing.[178] According to Gutteridge, Leibowitz, and Shore, career systems like these have four elements in common: (1) involvement of senior management early to gain visible, up-front support; (2) establishment of guiding principles from the beginning; (3) development of the systems from the line upward, involving employees from all levels and areas of the organization; and (4) flexibility so that organizational units can tailor the system to fit their needs. A scale developed by Lee and Bruvold taps employee perceptions of organizational investments in employee development.[179] Items concerning both training and career management are included in this scale and may prove helpful as organizations seek to involve employees with designing and improving their career management systems.

On a more negative note, a recent large-scale survey of HR professionals in England provided some troubling findings:

- Less than 50 percent of these professionals said that their organization had a formal career management strategy.
- 26 percent said that their organization's career management strategy covered all employees.
- 34 percent thought that senior managers in their organization were "firmly committed" to career management.
- 56 percent felt that line managers do not take career management seriously.
- 5 percent reported that line managers in their organization are trained to support employee career development.[180]

Clearly, such findings suggest considerable room for improvement! Another topic that needs to be addressed more fully is the extent to which career development issues differ across diverse employee populations, for example, by gender, ethnicity, religion, age, and other considerations.[181] To tie things together, we close the chapter with recommendations concerning how to enhance organizational career development efforts:

1. Integrate individual developmental planning with organizational strategic planning.
2. Strengthen the linkages between career development and other HRM systems.
3. Move career development systems toward greater openness.
4. Enhance the role of managers in career development through both skill building and accountability.
5. Develop and expand peer learning and other team-based developmental approaches.
6. Stress on-the-job development; deemphasize traditional training programs that are isolated, one-shot events.
7. Emphasize enrichment and lateral movement.
8. Identify and develop transferable competencies.
9. Include values and lifestyle assessments in career development activities.
10. Implement a variety of career development approaches to accommodate different learning styles and the needs of a diverse workforce.
11. Tie career development directly to organizational quality initiatives.
12. Expand career development measurement and evaluation.
13. Continue to study best practices and organizational career development in a global context.[182]

## RETURN TO OPENING CASE

A survey of 192 managers and professionals in the Quebec public sector was conducted by Louise Lemire and colleagues.[1] They asked these individuals the extent to which they felt that their careers had plateaued, and they collected various other information as well. Your instructor has additional information concerning the results of this study.

[1] Lemire, L., Saba, T., & Gagnon, Y.-C. (1999). Managing career plateauing in the Quebec public sector. *Public Personnel Management, 28*(3), 375–391.

## SUMMARY

A career is the pattern of work-related experiences that span the course of a person's life. Each individual is ultimately responsible for his or her own career, which includes developing a clear understanding of self and the environment in order to establish career goals and plans. Organizations can assist the individual by providing information, opportunities, and assistance. By doing so, the organization can enhance its internal labor market and be more effective in recruiting and motivating employees (both contingent and long term). In turn, the individual gains an opportunity for enhanced employability. This is especially important given the changes that have occurred in the employment relationship over the past twenty-five years.

Erikson described our lives as progressing through a series of stages, with each stage presenting the individual with a challenge he or she must meet in order to develop further and achieve happiness and a clear sense of self. Levinson similarly described adult life as progressing through a series of stages, with each era representing a season in a person's life. In each season, the demands on the individual change, and the individual works to make changes in his or her life to meet those demands. Both models teach us that change is a normal and inevitable part of adult life and that the challenges faced in life will affect career plans and decisions. Several models of career development were presented, from a traditional age-related model, to others (e.g., protean careers and career concepts) incorporating current trends in the organizational landscape.

Greenhaus and colleagues describe the process of career management from the individual's perspective as one in which the individual (1) explores the environment, (2) develops a clear sense of environment and self-awareness, (3) sets career goals, (4) develops a strategy to reach the goal, (5) implements the strategy, (6) makes progress toward the goal, (7) obtains feedback on progress from work and nonwork sources, and (8) appraises his or her career.[183] Using this process can enable an individual to achieve career satisfaction and greater life happiness. Three organizationally focused models of career management, the pluralistic model, the systems model, and a team-based model, were presented as examples of how organizations may be able to link their career management process to the organization's structure and strategy.

The roles to be played by the individual, HRD practitioner, and manager in career development were also presented. In particular, we discussed the competencies, such as adaptability, learning how to learn, and relationship formation and maintenance, that individuals need to effectively manage their careers.

Organizations use a variety of tools and techniques to manage employee careers. These include self-assessment tools and activities, such as workbooks, workshops, and computer programs, individual career counseling, job posting exchanges, organizational potential assessment, and developmental programs such as job rotation and mentoring. These activities and practices help employees gather information to develop career awareness, formulate career plans, and offer opportunities to implement these plans.

Designing a career management program involves steps similar to those for developing any HRD intervention: conducting a needs analysis, identifying the goals and components of the program, establishing criteria to measure effectiveness, implementing the program, and evaluating its effectiveness. Because career management programs affect the human resource function in an organization, developers and deliverers of such programs must be aware of issues involved in HR planning, equal employment opportunity and affirmative action, and labor relations. In addition, organizations should consider the issues of career motivation, career plateaus, and career development for nonexempt workers when designing career development programs.

## KEY TERMS AND CONCEPTS

| | |
|---|---|
| assessment center | job posting |
| career | job rotation |
| career concepts | mentoring |
| career development | outplacement counseling |
| career management | potential assessment |
| career motivation | potential ratings |
| career path | preretirement counseling |
| career planning | protean career |
| career plateau | self-assessment activities |
| ego integrity | succession planning |
| generativity | |

## QUESTIONS FOR DISCUSSION

1. What can be gained by defining the term *career* broadly as the pattern of work-related experiences that span the course of one's life? That is, compare this definition with other commonly held notions of the term *career*.

2. How does Levinson's approach to adult development relate to Greenhaus and colleagues' five-stage model of career development? That is, compare and contrast the similarities and differences between these two models.

3. Using your knowledge of the stages of life and career development, explain how the career issues of a twenty-seven-year-old differ from those of a forty-five-year-old. What are the organizational implications of the issues you identified?

4. Protean careers and the career concepts model offer ideas that are intended to reconcile the idea of career development with the changes going on in the environment and in organizations. In your view, how do these ideas contribute to our understanding of career development? How well do they fit with your views of career development? Based on these ideas, identify and describe two actions you could take to increase the chances you will have the kinds of work experiences and lifestyle that you would like.

5. Describe ways in which career management can be viewed as a problem-solving and decision-making process.

6. Explain how both organizations and individuals can benefit from a well-designed career management system.

7. Discuss the value of self-assessment tools and activities to effective career development.

8. As a career development tool, mentoring has been linked to both potential benefits and problems for organizations and individuals. Given these potential benefits and problems, describe how you feel about the prospect of becoming involved in a mentoring relationship as part of your own career development. What would your concerns be, and what would you like to see an organization do to ensure that the mentoring experience is a positive one?

9. Recent research suggests that career plateaus are more complex than previously thought. Briefly explain why the individual's perception of being plateaued is important and how organizations may want to develop multiple ways for dealing with plateaued employees.

10. The flattening of many organizational structures is forcing many individuals and organizations to change their perceptions of what career advancement is all about. What are some alternatives to upward movement as a career option? How do you feel about the prospect of these alternatives as opposed to the traditional upward progress within your own career?

## EXERCISE: A CAREER PLANNING ESSAY[184]

Students in classes where this text is used have typically already prepared a formal resume. Some students will also have had experience outlining their career goals and/or job search strategies. For those without such experiences, the following exercise by Douglas Lyon and Eric Kirby should prove useful. An important concept behind such a project is that each person should seek to actively manage one's own career (the value of this notion is hopefully apparent to you after reading this chapter).

### Assignment
Each student should answer the following three general questions:

  a) Where do I want to be?

  b) Where am I now?

  c) How am I going to get there?

The primary end product of this assignment is an action plan concerning how you plan to close the gap between your current and desired situation. Consider the following issues and questions as you address each portion of the assignment:

a) **Where do I want to be?**

Some issues to consider here include:

- What are my short-term career objectives?
- What are my long-term career objectives?
- What sorts of lifestyle issues are important to me (e.g., location, hours worked)?
- What personal values are most important to me (e.g., alignment with personal ethics, time spent with family)?
- Are there life stage or career stage issues that are relevant to my current decision making?

b) **Where am I now?**

Two key issues should be addressed here:

- An assessment of my current personal values
- An assessment of my current knowledge, skills, abilities, and other qualifications compared to those required for a desired job

Self-reflection is most important here, though the opinions of people who know you, as well as the results of assessment surveys can also be very useful (most institutions of higher learning provide access to their students to various self-assessment devices through their careers services center, often free of charge).

c) **How am I going to get there?**

In this section, you should outline a plan of action to obtain your goals. This may be very specific if you are already very clear on your career goals, but may be more general, when your career objectives are less clear. In either case, the idea is to discuss ways of pursuing a career that is most consistent with your lifestyle goals and values.

> Visit http://werner.swlearning.com for links to informative websites for this chapter.

## REFERENCES

1. Werner, J. M. (2002). Public policy and the changing legal context of career development. In D. C. Feldman (Ed.), *Work careers: A developmental perspective* (pp. 245–273). San Francisco: Wiley/Jossey-Bass; Herr, E. L., & Shahnasarian, M. (2001). Selected milestones in the evolution of career development practices in the twentieth century. *Career Development Quarterly, 49*(3), 225–232.

2. Dany, F., Mallon, M., & Arthur, M. B. (2003). The odyssey of career and the opportunity for international comparison. *International Journal of Human Resource Management, 14*(5), 705–712.

3. Vaill, P. B. (1996). Learning as a way of being: Strategies for survival in a world of permanent white water. San Francisco: Jossey-Bass.

4. Charness, G., & Levine, D. I. (2000). When are layoffs acceptable? Evidence from a quasi-experiment. *Industrial and Labor Relations Review, 53*(3), 381–400.

5. Altman, B. W., & Post, J. E. (1996). Beyond the "social contract": An analysis of the executive view at twenty-five large companies. In D. T. Hall & Associates, *The career is dead — long live the career: A relational approach to careers* (pp. 46–71). San Francisco: Jossey-Bass.

6. Hall, D. T., & Mirvis, P. H. (1996). The new protean career: Psychological success and the path with a heart. In D. T. Hall & Associates, *The career is dead — long live the career: A relational approach to careers* (pp. 15–45). San Francisco: Jossey-Bass, p. 20.

7. Malos, S. B., & Campion, M. A. (1995). An options-based model of career mobility in professional service firms. *Academy of Management Review, 10,* 611–644; Jones, C., & DeFillippi, R. J. (1996). Back to the future in film: Combining industry and self-knowledge to meet career challenges in the 21st century. *The Academy of Management Executive, 10*(4), 89–103.

8. Roehling, M. V., Cavanaugh, M. A., Moynihan, L. M., & Boswell, W. R. (2000). The nature of the new employment relationship: A content analysis of the practitioner and academic literatures. *Human Resource Management, 39*(4), 305–320.

9. Pringle, J. K., & Mallon, M. (2003). Challenges for the boundaryless career odyssey. *International Journal of Human Resource Management, 14*(5), 839–853.

10. Leana, C. R., & Feldman, D. C. (2000). Managing careers. In E. E. Kossek & R. N. Block (Eds.), *Managing human resources in the 21st Century: From core concepts to strategic choice* (pp. 24.1–24.19). Mason, OH: Thomson/South-Western.

11. Roehling et al. (2000), *supra* note 8.

12. Greenhaus, J. H. (1987). *Career management.* Hinsdale, IL: The Dryden Press; Greenhaus, J. H., Callanan, G. A., & Godshalk, V. M. (2000). *Career management* (3rd ed.). Fort Worth, TX: Harcourt College Publishers.

13. Schein, E. H. (1987). Individuals and careers. In J. Lorsch (Ed.), *Handbook of organizational behavior* (pp. 155–171). Englewood Cliffs, NJ: Prentice Hall.

14. Dalton, G. W., Thompson, P. H., & Price, R. L. (1977). The four stages of professional careers: A new look at performance by professionals. *Organizational Dynamics, 6*(1), 19–42; Van Maanen, J., & Schein, E. H. (1977). Career Development. In J. R. Hackman & J. L. Suttle (Eds.), *Improving behavior at work: Behavioral science approaches to organizational change.* Santa Monica, CA: Goodyear.

15. Hall, D. T. (1976). *Careers in organizations.* Pacific Pallisades, CA: Goodyear; Van Maanen & Schein (1977), *supra* note 14.

16. Hall (1976), *supra* note 15.

17. Schein (1987), *supra* note 13.

18. Van Maanen & Schein (1977), *supra* note 14.

19. Greenhaus (1987), *supra* note 12; Feldman, D. C. (1989). Careers in organizations: Recent trends and future directions. *Journal of Management, 15,* 135–156.

20. Greenhaus et al. (2000), *supra* note 12, p. 9.

21. *Ibid.*

22. Super, D. E. (1986). Life career roles: Self-realization in work and leisure. In D. T. Hall & Associates (Eds.), *Career development in organizations* (pp. 50–94). San Francisco: Jossey-Bass.

23. Parker, V. A. (1996). Growth-enhancing relationships outside work (GROWs). In D. T. Hall & Associates, *The career is dead — long live the career: A relational approach to careers* (pp. 180–222). San Francisco: Jossey-Bass.

24. Hall, D. T. (1976). *Careers in organizations.* Pacific Pallisades, CA: Goodyear; Hall, D. T. (1986). An overview of current career development theory, research, and practice. In D. T. Hall & Associates (Eds.), *Career development in organizations* (pp. 1–20). San Francisco: Jossey-Bass; Levinson, D. J. (1986). A conception of adult development. *American Psychologist, 41,* 3–13; Levinson, D. J. (1996). *The seasons of a woman's life.* New York: Knopf; Levinson, D. J., Darrow, C. N., Klein, E. B., Levinson, M. H., & Mckee, B. (1978). *Seasons of a man's life.* New York: Knopf; Schein, E. H. (1978). *Career dynamics: Matching individual and organizational needs.* Reading, MA: Addison-Wesley; Schein (1987), *supra* note 10.

25. Greenhaus et al. (2000), *supra* note 12, p. 13.

26. Storey, W. D. (Ed.) (1976). *A guide for career development inquiry: State-of-the-art report on career development.* ASTD Research Series Paper No. 2. Madison, WI: American Society for Training and Development.

27. *Ibid,* cited in Hall (1986), *supra* note 24, p. 3.

28. *Ibid.*

29. Hall (1986), *supra* note 24.

30. Gutteridge, T. G. (1986). Organizational career development systems: The state of the practice. In D. T. Hall & Associates (Eds.), *Career development in organizations* (pp. 50–94). San Francisco: Jossey-Bass.

31. Greenhaus et al. (2000), *supra* note 12.

32. Freud, S. (1959). *Collected papers.* New York: Basic Books

33. Levinson (1986, 1996), *supra* note 24; Levinson et al. (1978), *supra* note 24.

34. Erikson, E. H. (1963). *Childhood arid society* (2nd ed.). New York: W. W. Norton.

35. Schein (1978), *supra* note 24; Schein (1987), *supra* note 13.

36. Super, D. E. (1980). A life-span, life-space approach to career development. *Journal of Vocational Behavior, 16,* 282–298.

37. Levinson et al. (1978), *supra* note 24.

38. Levinson (1986), *supra* note 24.

39. Erikson (1963), *supra* note 34.

40. Levinson (1986, 1996), *supra* note 24; Levinson et al. (1978), *supra* note 24.

41. Erikson (1963), *supra* note 34.

42. Levinson (1986, 1996), *supra* note 24; Levinson et al. (1978), *supra* note 24.

43. Levinson (1986), *supra* note 24.

44. *Ibid.*

45. *Ibid.*

46. Levinson (1996), *supra* note 24.

47. Caffarella, R., & Olson, S. (1993). Psychosocial development of women. *Adult Education Quarterly, 43*(3), 125–151; Levinson (1996), *supra* note 24.

48. Feldman, D. C., & Weitz, B. A. (1988). Career plateaus reconsidered. *Journal of Management, 14,* 69–80.

49. Hall, D. T., & Nougaim, K. (1968). An examination of Maslow's need hierarchy in an organizational setting. *Organizational Behavior and Human Performance, 3,* 11–35; Schein (1978), *supra* note 24; Super (1980), *supra* note 36; Super, D. E. (1992). Toward a comprehensive theory of career development. In D. H. Montross & C. J. Shinkman (Eds.), *Career development: Theory and practice* (pp. 35–64). Springfield, IL: Charles C Thomas.

50. Greenhaus et al. (2000), *supra* note 12.

51. *Ibid.*

52. Brown, D., Brooks, L., & Associates (Eds.) (1990). *Career choice and development* (2nd ed.). San Francisco: Jossey-Bass.

53. Greenhaus et al. (2000), *supra* note 12.

54. Hall (1986), *supra* note 24; Hall, D. T., & Mirvis, P. H. (1995). Careers as lifelong learning. In A. Howard (Ed.), *The changing nature of work* (pp. 323–361). San Francisco: Jossey-Bass; Hall & Mirvis (1996), *supra* note 4; Brousseau, K. R., Driver, M. J., Eneroth, K., & Larsson, R. (1996). Career pandemonium: Realigning organizations and individuals. *The Academy of Management Executive, 10*(4), 52–66.

55. Hall & Mirvis (1995), *supra* note 54; Hall & Mirvis (1996), *supra* note 6; Mirvis, P. H., & Hall, D. T. (1994). Psychological success and the boundaryless career. *Journal of Organizational Behavior, 15,* 365–380; Hall (1976), *supra* note 21; Hall (1986), *supra* note 24.

56. Hall & Mirvis (1996), *supra* note 6 p. 21.

57. *Ibid*, p. 33.

58. Driver, M. J. (1994). Workforce personality and the new information age workplace. In J. A. Auerbach & J. C. Welsh (Eds.), *Aging and competition: Rebuilding the U.S. workforce* (pp. 185–204). Washington, DC: National Council on the Aging and the National Planning Association; Brousseau et al. (1996), *supra* note 51.

59. Brousseau et al. (1996), *supra* note 54, p. 56.

60. *Ibid.*

61. *Ibid.*

62. Malos & Campion (1995), *supra* note 7.

63. Jones & DeFillippi (1996), *supra* note 7.

64. Nicholson, N. (1996). Career systems in crisis: Change and opportunity in the information age. *The Academy of Management Executive, 10,* 40–51.

65. Greenhaus et al. (2000), *supra* note 12.

66. *Ibid.*

67. *Ibid.*

68. *Ibid.*

69. *Ibid.*

70. Allred, B. B., Snow, C. C., & Miles, R. E. (1996). Characteristics of managerial careers in the 21st century. *The Academy of Management Executive, 10*(4), 17–27; Brousseau et al. (1996), *supra* note 54; Cianni, M., & Wnuck, D. (1997). Individual growth and team enhancement: Moving toward a new model of career development. *The Academy of Management Executive, 11*(1), 105–115; Nicholson (1996), *supra* note 64.

71. Brousseau et al. (1996), *supra* note 54.

72. *Ibid.*

73. Nicholson (1996), *supra* note 64.

74. Cianni & Wnuck (1997), *supra* note 70.

75. Morin, W. J. (1996, December 9). You are absolutely, positively on your own. *Fortune,* 222.

76. Hakim, C. (1994). *We are all self-employed.* San Francisco: Berrett-Koehler.

77. Hall, D. T. (1996). Protean careers of the 21st century. *The Academy of Management Executive, 10*(4), 8–16.

78. Fox, D. (1996). Career insurance for today's world. *Training & Development, 50*(3), 61–64.

79. Jones & DeFillippi (1996), *supra* note 7.

80. Hall, D. T. (1996). Implications: The new role of the career practitioner. In D. T. Hall & Associates, *The career is dead — long live the career: A relational approach to careers* (pp. 314–336). San Francisco: Jossey-Bass; Fletcher, J. K (1996). A relational approach to the protean worker. In D. T. Hall & Associates, *The career is dead — long live the career: A relational approach to careers* (pp. 105–131). San Francisco: Jossey-Bass.

81. Leibowitz, Z. B., Farren, C., & Kaye, B. L. (1986). *Designing career development systems.* San Francisco: Jossey-Bass; Leibowitz, Z. B., Feldman, B. H., & Mosley, S. H. (1992). Career development for nonexempt employees: Issues and possibilities. In D. H. Montross & C. J. Shinkman (Eds.), *Career development: Theory and practice* (pp. 324–335). Springfield, IL: Charles C Thomas; Russell, M. (1984). Career planning in a blue-collar company. *Training and Development Journal, 38*(1), 87–88.

82. Leibowitz, Z., & Schlossberg, N. (1981). Training managers for their role in a career development system. *Training and Development Journal, 35*(7), 72–79.

83. Hall (1996), *supra* note 80, pp. 318–325.

84. Arthur, M. B., Claman, P. H., & DeFillippi, R. J. (1995). Intelligent enterprise, intelligent careers. *The Academy of Management Executive, 9*(4), 7–22.

85. Gutteridge, T. G., Leibowitz, Z. B., &. Shore, J. E. (1993). *Organizational career development: Benchmarks for building a world-class workforce.* San Francisco: Jossey-Bass.

86. Budhwar, P. S., & Baruch, Y. (2003). Career management practices in India: An empirical study. *International Journal of Manpower, 24*(6), 699–719.

87. Gutteridge et al. (1993), *supra* note 85.

88. Gutteridge (1986), *supra* note 30; Leibowitz et al (1986), *supra* note 81.

89. Smith, C. B. (1988). Designing and facilitating a self-assessment experience. In M. London & E. M. Mone (Eds.), *Career growth and human resource strategies: The role of the human resource professional in employee development* (pp. 157–172). New York: Quorum Books.

90. Bolles, R. N. (2004). *What color is your parachute? 2004: A practical manual for job-hunters and career changers.* Berkeley, CA: Ten Speed Press.

91. Holland, J. L. (1977). *The self-directed search.* Palo Alto, CA: Consulting Psychologists Press.

92. Burack, N. L., & Mathys, N. J. (1980). *Career management in organizations: A practical human resource planning approach.* Lake Forest, IL: Brace-Park Press.

93. Savickas, M. L. (2003). Advancing the career counseling profession: Objectives and strategies for the next decade. *Career Development Quarterly, 52,* 87–96; DeFillippi, R. J., Arthur, M. B., & Parker, P. (2003). Internet odysseys: Linking web roles to career and community investments. *International Journal of Human Resource Management, 14*(5), 751–767; Harris-Bowlsby, J., & Sampson, J. P., Jr. (2001). Computer-based career planning systems: Dreams and realities. *Career Development Quarterly, 49,* 250–260.

94. Gutteridge (1986), *supra* note 30.

95. Leibowitz et al. (1986), *supra* note 81.

96. *Ibid.*

97. Gutteridge et al. (1993), *supra* note 85.

98. Gutteridge, T. G., & Otte, F. L. (1983). *Organizational career development: State of the practice.* Washington, DC: ASTD Press.

99. Burack & Mathys (1980), *supra* note 92.

100. Gutteridge (1986), *supra* note 30.

101. Leibowitz et al. (1986), *supra* note 81.

102. Gutteridge (1986), *supra* note 30.

103. Walker, J. W. (1976). Let's get serious about career paths. *Human Resource Management, 15*(3), 2–7.

104. Shippeck, M. A., & Taylor, C. (1985). Up the career path. *Training and Development Journal, 39*(8), 46–48.

105. *Ibid.*

106. Tucker, R., Moravec, M., & Ideus, K. (1992). Designing a dual career-track system. *Training & Development, 46*(6), 55–58.

107. Gutteridge (1986), *supra* note 30.

108. Kaye, B., & Farren, C. (1996). Up is not the only way. *Training & Development, 50*(2), 48–53.

109. Walker, J. W. (1992). Career paths in flexible organizations. In D. H. Montross & C. J. Shinkman (Eds.), *Career development: Theory and practice* (pp. 385–402). Springfield, IL: Charles C Thomas.

110. Tucker et al. (1992), *supra* note 106.

111. Kaumeyer, R. A. (1979). *Planning and using skills inventory systems.* New York: Van Nostrand Reinhold.

112. Pentland, B. T. (2000). Human resource information systems. In E. E. Kossek & R. N. Block (Eds.), *Managing human resources in the 21st Century: From core concepts to strategic choice* (pp. 7.1–7.27). Mason, OH: Thomson/South-Western.

113. Boehm, V. R. (1988). Designing developmental assessment centers. In M. London & E. M. Mone (Eds.), *Career growth and human resource strategies: The role of the human resource professional in employee development* (pp. 173–182). New York: Quorum Books.

114. Thornton, G. C. (1992). *Assessment centers in human resource management.* Reading, MA: Addison-Wesley.

115. Cairo, P., & Lyness, K. S. (1988). Stimulating high-potential career development through an assessment center process. In M. London & E. M. Mone (Eds.), *Career growth and human resource strategies: The role of the human resource professional in employee development* (pp. 183–194). New York: Quorum Books.

116. Thornton (1992), *supra* note 114.

117. Karaevli, A., & Hall, D. T. (2003). Growing leaders for turbulent times: Is succession planning up to the challenge? *Organizational Dynamics, 32*(1), 62–79.

118. Schein (1987), *supra* note 13.

119. Leibowitz et al. (1986), *supra* note 81.

120. Leibman, M., Bruer, R. A., & Maki, B. R. (1996). Succession management: The next generation of succession planning. *Human Resource Planning, 19*(3), 17–28.

121. Wailerdsak, N., & Suehiro, A. (2004). Promotion systems and career development in Thailand: A case study of Siam Cement. *International Journal of Human Resource Management, 15*(1), 196–218.

122. Campion, M. A., Cheraskin, L., & Stevens, M. J. (1994). Career-related antecedents and outcomes of job rotation. *Academy of Management Journal, 37,* 1518–1542.

123. White, R. P. (1992). Jobs as classrooms: Using assignments to leverage development. In D. H. Montross & C. J. Shinkman (Eds.), *Career development: Theory and practice* (pp. 190–206). Springfield, IL: Charles C Thomas.

124. Kram, K. E. (1986). Mentoring in the workplace. In D. T. Hall & Associates (Eds.), *Career development in organizations* (pp. 160–201). San Francisco: Jossey-Bass; Noe, R. A. (1988). Women and mentoring: A review and research agenda. *Academy of Management Review, 13,* 65–78; Scandura, T. A. (1992). Mentorship and career mobility: An empirical investigation. *Journal of Organizational Behavior, 13,* 169–174.

125. Coley, D. B. (1996). Mentoring two-by-two. *Training & Development, 50*(7), 46–48.

126. Lean, E. (1983). Cross-gender mentoring — downright upright and good for productivity. *Training and Development Journal, 37*(5), 60–65.

127. Thomas, D. A., & Carioggia, G. M. (2002). The Federal Reserve Bank of Chicago's mentoring program (A). Boston, MA: Harvard Business School Press.

128. Kram (1986), *supra* note 124.

129. Kram, K. E., & Bragar, M. C. (1992). Development through mentoring: A strategic approach. In D. H. Montross & C. J. Shinkman (Eds.), *Career development: Theory and practice* (pp. 221–254). Springfield, IL: Charles C Thomas.

130. Chao, G. T., Walz, P. M., & Gardner, P. D. (1992). Formal and informal mentorships: A comparison on mentoring functions and contrast with nonmentored counterparts. *Personnel Psychology, 45,* 620–636.

131. Tepper, B. J. (1995). Upward maintenance tactics in supervisory mentoring and nonmentoring relationships. *Academy of Management Journal, 38,* 1191–1205.

132. Eby, L., Butts, M., Lockwood, A., & Simon, S. A. (2004). Protégés' negative mentoring experiences: Construct development and nomological validation. *Personnel Psychology, 57,* 411–447.

133. Ragins, B. R. (1989). Barriers to mentoring: The female manager's dilemma. *Human Relations, 42,* 1–22.

134. Kram, K. E. (1985). *Mentoring at work.* Glenview, IL: Scott, Foresman; Bowen, D. W. (1985). Were men meant to mentor women? *Training and Development Journal, 39*(2), 31–34.

135. Kanter, R. M. (1977). *Men and women of the corporation.* New York: Basic Books.

136. *Ibid.*

137. Bowen (1985), *supra* note 134.

138. Kram (1985), *supra* note 134.

139. Dreher, G. F., & Ash, R. A. (1990). A comparative study of mentoring among men and women in managers, professional, and technical positions. *Journal of Applied Psychology, 75,* 539–546; Whitely, W., Dougherty, T. W., & Dreher, G. F. (1992). Correlates of career-oriented mentoring for early career managers and professionals. *Journal of Organizational Behavior, 13,* 141–154; Turban, D. B., & Dougherty, T. W. (1994). Role of protege personality in receipt of mentoring and career success. *Academy of Management Journal, 37,* 688–702.

140. Scandura, T. A., & Ragins, B. R. (1993). The effects of sex and gender role orientation on mentorship in male–dominated occupations. *Journal of Vocational Behavior, 43,* 251–265.

141. Ragins, B. R., & Scandura, T. A. (1994). Gender differences in expected outcomes of mentoring relationships. *Academy of Management Journal, 37,* 957–971; Ragins, B. R., & Cotton, J. L. (1993). Gender and willingness to mentor in organizations. *Journal of Management, 19,* 97–111.

142. Thomas, D. A. (1990). The impact of race on manager's experience of developmental relationships (mentoring and sponsorship): An intraorganizational study. *Journal of Organization Behavior, 11*(6), 479–491.

143. Thomas, D. A. (1993). Racial dynamics in cross-race developmental relationships. *Administrative Science Quarterly, 38,* 169–194.

144. Clawson, J. G. (1985). Is mentoring necessary? *Training and Development Journal, 39*(4), 36–39.

145. Kram (1986), *supra* note 124.

146. Kram, K. E., & Isabella, L. A. (1985). Mentoring alternatives: The role of peer relationships in career development. *Academy of Management Journal, 28,* 110–132.

147. de Janasz, S. C., Sullivan, S. E., & Whiting, V. (2003). Mentor networks and career success: Lessons for turbulent times. *The Academy of Management Executive, 17*(4), 78–91.

148. Kram & Bragar (1992), *supra* note 129.

149. *Ibid*; Kaye, B., & Jacobson, B. (1996). Reframing mentoring. *Training & Development, 50,* August, 44–47.

150. London, M. (1983). Toward a theory of career motivation. *Academy of Management Review, 8,* 620–630; London, M. (1985). *Developing managers: A guide to motivating people for successful managerial careers.* San Francisco: Jossey-Bass.

151. London (1985), *supra* note 150; London, M., & Mone, E. M. (1987). *Career management and survival in the workplace.* San Francisco: Jossey-Bass.

152. London (1985), *supra* note 150.

153. Borgen, W. A., Amundson, N. E., & Reuter, J. (2004). Using portfolios to enhance career resilience. *Journal of Employment Counseling, 41*(2), 50–59.

154. Rooney, M. C. (2004). Recovering from a career setback. *Healthcare Executive, 19*(2), 57–58.

155. London, M. (1996). Redeployment and continuous learning in the 21st century: Hard lessons and positive examples from the downsizing era. *The Academy of Management Executive, 10*(4), 67–79.

156. London, M. (Ed.). (1995). *Employees, careers, and job creation: Developing growth-oriented human resource strategies and programs.* San Francisco: Jossey-Bass, offers an excellent examination of how HRD programs such as career development can be used as an alternative to employee displacement and downsizing and to address societal issues and facilitate economic growth.

157. Ferrence, T. P., Stoner, J.A.F., & Warren, E. K. (1977). Managing the career plateau. *Academy of Management Review, 2,* 602–612, p. 602.

158. Latack, J. C. (1984). Career transitions within organizations: An exploratory study of work, non-work, and coping strategies. *Organizational Behavior and Human Performance, 34,* 296–322; Schein (1978), *supra* note 24.

159. Duffy, J. A. (2000). The application of chaos theory to the career-plateaued worker. *Journal of Employment Counseling, 37*(4), 229–236.

160. Feldman & Weitz (1988), *supra* note 48; Elsass, P. M., & Ralston, D. A. (1989). Individual responses to the stress of career plateauing. *Journal of Management, 15,* 35–47; Ettington, (1997). How human resource practices can help plateaued managers succeed. *Human Resource Management, 36,* 221–234.

161. Chau, C.-T. (1998). Career plateaus. *Internal Auditor, 55*(5), 48–52.

162. Chao, G. T. (1990). Exploration of the conceptualization and measurement of career plateau: A comparative analysis. *Journal of Management, 16,* 181–193.

163. *Ibid.*

164. *Ibid.*

165. Lee, P.C.B. (2003). Going beyond career plateau: Using professional plateau to account for work outcomes. *Journal of Management Development, 22*(5/6), 538–551.

166. Tremblay, M., Roger, A., & Toulouse, J. (1995). Career plateau and work attitudes: An empirical study of managers. *Human Relations, 48,* 221–237.

167. Ettington (1997), *supra* note 160.

168. Tremblay, M., & Roger, A. (2004). Career plateauing reactions: The moderating role of job scope, role ambiguity, and participation among Canadian managers. *International Journal of Human Resource Management, 15*(6), 996–1017.

169. Leibowitz et al. (1992), *supra* note 81.

170. *Ibid.*

171. Russell (1984), *supra* note 81.

172. Leibowitz et al. (1992), *supra* note 81.

173. Recent ideas about career development, such as the protean career and career concepts discussed earlier, also make clear that not all individuals would desire upward movement, even if it were available.

174. London, M. (1991). Career development. In K. N. Wexley & J. Hinrichs (Eds.), *Developing human resources* (pp. 152–184). Washington, DC: BNA Books.

175. *Ibid.*

176. Gutteridge et al. (1993), *supra* note 85.

177. Baruch, Y. (2003). Career systems in transition: A normative model for organizational career practices. *Personnel Review, 32*(1/2), 231–251.

178. *Ibid.*

179. Lee, C. H., & Bruvold, N. T. (2003). Creating value for employees: Investment in employee development. *International Journal of Human Resource Management, 14*(6), 981–1000.

180. Hirsh, W., & Rolph, J. (2003). Snakes and ladders. *People Management, 9*(9), May 1, 36–37.

181. Cook, E. P., Heppner, M. J., & O'Brien, K. M. (2002). Career development of women of color and white women: Assumptions, conceptualization, and interventions from an ecological perspective. *Career Development Quarterly, 50,* 291–305; Turban, D. B., Dougherty, T. W., & Lee, F. K. (2002). Gender, race, and perceived similarity effects in developmental relationships: The moderating role of relationship duration. *Journal of Vocational Behavior, 61*(2), 240–262; Baruch, Y. (2004). The desert generation: Lessons and implications for the new era of people management. *Personnel Review, 33*(2), 241–256; Bunker, K. A., Kram, K. E., & Ting, S. (2002). The young and the clueless. *Harvard Business Review, 80*(12), December, 81–87; Guichard, J. (2003). Career counseling for human development: An international perspective. *Career Development Quarterly, 51,* 306–321; Rainbird, H., & Munro, A. (2003). Workplace learning and the employment relationship in the public sector. *Human Resource Management Journal, 13*(2), 30–44.

182. Gutteridge et al. (1993), *supra* note 85, pp. 201–204.

183. Greenhaus et al. (2000), *supra* note 12.

184. Lyon, D., & Kirby, E.G. (2000). The career planning essay. *Journal of Management Education, 24*(2), 276–287.

# MANAGEMENT DEVELOPMENT

PART 3: APPLICATIONS OF HUMAN RESOURCE DEVELOPMENT

## Learning Objectives

*After reading this chapter, you should be able to:*

1. Define management development and describe the extent to which it is used in U.S. organizations.

2. Describe the approaches that have been taken to describe the managerial job.

3. Explain specific ways that management development can be linked to organizational goals and strategies.

4. Describe the options and trends in management education.

5. Explain how training and on-the-job experiences can be used to develop managers.

6. Describe the components of two approaches frequently used in management development programs: leadership training and behavior modeling training.

7. Use the HRD process model to design, implement, and evaluate management development programs.

**OPENING CASE**

Imagine yourself among the executives and managers of a large, urban hospital. Your hospital is a private, nonprofit hospital that serves a number of low-income neighborhoods. The long-standing mission of the hospital has been to provide quality service to the community, regardless of an individual's ability to pay. However, recent changes and turmoil in the healthcare industry have raised concerns about your hospital's ability to remain viable and financially solvent. As a top management team, you have decided to maintain your commitment to your existing clients. However, you also wish to attract more clients with the means (or insurance packages) to pay for your services. Add to this situation the fact that you are about to move into a new facility, which includes a new computer system designed to improve the overall efficiency of your hospital.

The question has come up about the advisability of offering a management training program. You might address the various changes and challenges in your external environment, for example, with so many other hospitals to choose from, how do you become the preferred healthcare alternative for this "new" population of clients? You are also thinking of ways to improve the internal environment, that is, how you can be more efficient by making the best use of the new technology that will be available in your new facility.

*Questions: If you were part of this top management team, do you think it is a good idea to offer management training at this time? If so, where would you start? What would be your focus? What particular challenges would you expect to face as you moved into this new facility?*

## INTRODUCTION

Do you think the following statements are true or false?

- *It is predicted that there will be fewer managers in the United States by the end of this decade than there are presently.*

- *Researchers have been able to describe the managerial job with a high degree of precision.*

- *The systems model of HRD (assess-design-implement-evaluate) is not very helpful when it comes to management development.*
- *Management education is a small and decreasing proportion of all the postsecondary educational opportunities that students in the United States are taking.*
- *Corporate universities are only popular among very large organizations.*
- *Behavior modeling training may work fine for entry-level training, but it has not been found to be very effective for management development efforts.*

For at least the past sixty-five years, managers have been viewed as a dynamic and important element of business organizations. Given the turbulence in today's environment, an organization must have a high-quality, flexible, and adaptive management team if it is to survive and succeed. This is true even for organizations that have chosen to restructure (e.g., with flatter hierarchies, and fewer permanent employees) and empower employees to be more a part of organizational decision making. It is managers who are ultimately responsible for making the decision to change their organizations' strategies and structures, and it is managers who must ensure that these new approaches are implemented, modified, and executed in a way that achieves the organizations' goals. While they may do this in a different way than they have in the past (e.g., less command and control, more leading and coaching), managers still play a critical role in organizations' adaptation and success. In essence, using fewer managers in an organization makes it *more* important that each manager is effective.

It should be noted that despite the popular press reports indicating that the number of managers is shrinking, the U.S. Bureau of Labor Statistics has estimated that the category of managerial occupations contained approximately 10.1 million people in 2002. Further, this category is expected to show a net gain of 1.2 million jobs between 2002 and 2012, or more than a 12 percent increase. As an occupational group, managers are expected to make up 6.8 percent of the total labor force in 2012, which is down slightly from its percentage of the total labor force in 2002 (7.0%).[1]

Management development is one major way for organizations to increase the chances that managers will be effective. While many have believed that the ability to manage (like the ability to lead) was primarily an inborn capability, the current prevailing view is that the KSAs (knowledge, skills, and abilities) required to be an effective manager can be learned or enhanced.[2]

**Management development** is a very popular HRD activity. Although management development has been defined in many ways, we feel the following definition captures the essence of management development as it can and should be practiced in organizations:

> An organization's conscious effort to provide its managers (and potential managers) with opportunities to learn, grow, and change, in hopes of producing over the long term a cadre of managers with the skills necessary to function effectively in that organization.[3]

First, this definition suggests that management development should be seen as specific to a particular organization. Although there appear to be roles and competencies that apply to managing in a variety of settings, each organization is unique, and its goal should be to develop individuals to be more effective managers within its own context.[4] Second, management development consists of providing employees with opportunities for learning, growth, and change. While there is no guarantee that particular individuals will take advantage of, or profit from, these opportunities, management development cannot occur unless opportunities are at least provided.[5] Third, management development must be a conscious effort on the part of the organization. Leaving development to chance greatly reduces the likelihood that the organization will achieve the kinds of changes it needs and desires. Fourth, management development (like all HRD activities) should be directly linked to the organization's strategy, that is, it must meet the organization's business needs if it is to be a sound investment. While many current management development programs do not conform to this definition, we think this serves as a benchmark to which such programs can and should aspire.

Management development has been described as having three main components: management education, management training, and on-the-job experiences.[6] **Management education** can be defined as "the acquisition of a broad range of conceptual knowledge and skills in formal classroom situations in degree-granting institutions."[7] As we will describe later, the "formal classroom situations" to which the definition refers include a wide range of activities, with the classroom setting increasingly being used to bring together and process the results of outside activities to draw conclusions about what has been learned. **Management training** focuses more on providing specific skills or knowledge that could be immediately applied within an organization and/or to a specific position or set of positions within an organization (e.g., middle managers).[8] **On-the-job experiences** are planned or unplanned opportunities for a manager to gain self-knowledge, enhance existing skills and abilities, or obtain new skills or information within the context of day-to-day activities (e.g., mentoring, coaching, assignment to a task force).

In this chapter, we will discuss a number of management development activities that are used within each of these three components.

## EXTENT OF MANAGEMENT DEVELOPMENT ACTIVITIES

As mentioned earlier, management development is one of the most commonly offered approaches to HRD. In a 2003 survey, 91 percent of organizations provided management development, 88 percent provided supervisory skills training, and 78 percent offered executive development. Strikingly, only 35 percent of all training dollars were spent on nonexempt employees, with the rest going to supervisors, managers, executives, and other exempt-level employees. The total cost of formal training aimed at management was estimated to be $19.1 billion.[9] The most frequently cited reasons for developing managers include broadening the individual and providing knowledge or skills.[10] Few organizations (5 percent in the survey just cited) cited intent to reward managers as a reason for providing them with developmental opportunities.

## ORGANIZATION OF THE CHAPTER

Management development comprises such a broad range of issues and approaches that it is not realistic to try to cover them all in a single chapter. Rather, we will focus our discussion on the following issues:

1. efforts to describe the managerial job, including *roles* managers must perform and the *competencies* necessary for performing them effectively

2. making management development strategic

3. options available for management education

4. options available for management training and using on-the-job experiences for management development

5. a description of two common approaches used to develop managers (leadership training and behavior modeling training for interpersonal skills)

6. the design of management development programs

## DESCRIBING THE MANAGER'S JOB: MANAGEMENT ROLES AND COMPETENCIES

Given that almost all organizations employ managers, the scrutiny under which managers operate, and the vast literature on management and its subfields, one would expect that we would have a clear idea of what managers do, the KSAs necessary to do those things effectively, and how to identify and develop those KSAs. Unfortunately, surprisingly little research has been conducted about what managers do, how they learn to do it, and how managers should be developed.[11] While it is true that popular conceptions of the manager's role and development are available, scientific research has yet to provide a clearly supported and accepted model that can be used to guide management development. Even among the best empirical studies in this area, such as the Management Progress Study conducted over a thirty-year period at AT&T, there are significant limitations (e.g., small sample sizes, analysis of only one organization) that make it difficult to confidently conclude what most or all managers do and how they develop.[12]

The changes that have occurred in organizations in the past two decades have only complicated this picture. Many of the research studies from the 1970s and before looked at management in hierarchically structured organizations that operated in relatively stable environments. As we have pointed out many times, organizations have had to respond to environmental challenges to stay competitive, and the structures and strategies they use have changed. The role of management has probably changed in many organizations as well. It is likely that the established views of the management job may be more relevant for some organizations than others.

This is not to say that what we learned in the past is useless. But we do need to know which aspects from the past are still relevant and descriptive of managing at the present time. This underscores the need for HRD professionals to identify what the management job is (and needs to be) in their *own organization* before they can design and deliver management development processes and programs that will meet the needs of their own business and contribute to its competitiveness and effectiveness. In this section of the chapter, we briefly describe several approaches to conceptualizing the management role to suggest a starting point in designing a reasonable management development program. As indicated in the definition of management development presented above, meaningful management development is likely to differ among organizations, considering the context and challenges facing each particular organization. Designers of such programs should begin their efforts by obtaining a clear understanding of the organization (including its external environment, goals, strategic plan, culture, strengths and weaknesses) and the characteristics of the target population (managers and managers-to-be). The research available on what managers do, how they do it, and how they develop the needed capabilities can provide a useful base from which to begin the needs assessment process. It is unrealistic, however, to expect such research, no matter how advanced, to provide the blueprint for any particular organization's management development strategy.

## APPROACHES TO UNDERSTANDING THE JOB OF MANAGING

Researchers who have examined the job of managing have done so from at least three perspectives: describing the characteristics of the job as it is typically performed, describing the roles managers serve, and developing process models that show how the various components of managing relate to each other.[13] The **characteristics approach** involves observing the tasks managers perform and grouping them into meaningful categories. McCall, Morrison, and Hannan reviewed the results of a group of observational studies and concluded that ten elements of managing were consistently present.[14] These elements indicate that the management job involves long hours of work (primarily within the organization), high activity levels, fragmented work (e.g., many interruptions), varied activities, primarily oral communication, many contacts, and information gathering. In addition, managers tend *not* to be reflective planners (given the variety of tasks and fragmented nature of the work) and do poorly in accurately estimating how they spend their time.

While these observations may be interesting, they do not provide much assistance in describing specifically what managers do, how they do it, and how they should be developed. A common conclusion from such studies is that important questions about the job remain unanswered (e.g., the relationship of the activities to each other) and that "knowing that the managerial job is varied and complex is not particularly helpful in the identification and/or development process."[15]

A second approach to describing the managerial job is to *identify the roles that managers are typically assigned.* This can be accomplished by using either an observational approach or an empirical approach. The observational approach is typified by Fayol's[16] five management functions (planning, organizing, commanding, coordinating, and controlling) and Mintzberg's[17] managerial roles: interpersonal (figurehead, leader, liaison), informational (monitor, disseminator, spokesperson), and decisional (entrepreneur, disturbance handler, resource allocator, and negotiator). While these categorizations are extremely popular, they too do not adequately describe what managers do. They also lack specificity.[18]

The empirical approach relies on a descriptive questionnaire (e.g., the Management Position Description Questionnaire) that is completed by managers themselves, and/or by others who work with them.[19] However, even this approach has failed to provide practical, meaningful descriptions of the job.[20] Taken together, the observational and empirical approaches to categorizing the managerial role have not proved useful as a definition of the managerial job or as a guide to developing managers.

One way researchers have tried to overcome the limitations of the previous approaches is to develop *process models* that take into account the relevant competencies and constraints involved in performing the management job. Two process models of particular note to the discussion of management development are the integrated competency model[21] and the four-dimensional model.[22] The **integrated competency model** is based on interviews of over 2,000 managers in twelve organizations. The model focuses on *managerial competencies,* that is, skills and/or personal characteristics that contribute to effective performance, rather than the roles managers perform.[23] The model identifies twenty-one competencies that are grouped into six categories: human resource management, leadership, goal and action management, directing subordinates, focus on others, and specialized knowledge.[24] Table 13-1 shows the specific competencies included in each cluster. The human resources, leadership, and goal and action clusters are seen as most central to managing.

A major contribution of this model from Boyatzis and colleagues is its attempt to describe the managerial job in terms of the competencies that contribute to performance and the relationships among these competencies. The integrated competency model is an example of a competency-based approach to management development. Competency-based approaches have become extremely popular, not only as the basis for management development programs,[25] but for other training and development programs and HR programs as well.[26]

A weakness of the integrated competency model is that the model is based on a narrow range of measuring devices, which are not likely to represent or reveal all of the traits, skills, and knowledge needed for managerial performance.[27] In addition, the method by which the competencies were identified has been sharply criticized. The instrument used, called the Behavioral Event Interview (BEI), asks managers to describe three job incidents they felt were effective and three job incidents they felt were ineffective.[28] Barrett and Depinet argue that this method is inappropriate for measuring competencies as Boyatzis describes them.[29] That is, Boyatzis described a competency as "an underlying characteristic of a person in that it may be a motive, trait, skill, aspect of one's self-image or social role, or a body of knowledge he or she uses" (p. 21), and said competencies may be unconscious and that an individual may be "unable to articulate or describe them" (p. 21).[30] Barrett and Depinet also contend that the validation process used to support the model was flawed.

The second process model of the managerial job that can contribute to designing management development efforts is the **four-dimensional model.**[31] Based on various information sources (e.g., managerial diaries, interviews, performance evaluation documents, observation), this model depicts the managerial role as having the following dimensions:

1. Six *functions* — forecasting and planning, training and development, persuasive communication, influence and control, expertise/functional area, and administration

2. Four *roles* — innovator, evaluator, motivator, director

| TABLE 13-1 | CLUSTERS AND COMPETENCIES ASSOCIATED WITH THE INTEGRATED COMPETENCY MODEL |

| Cluster | Competencies |
| --- | --- |
| Human Resource Management | Use of socialized power<br>Positive regard[a]<br>Managing group processes<br>Accurate self-assessment[a] |
| Leadership | Self-confidence<br>Use oral presentations<br>Conceptualization<br>Logical thought[a] |
| Goal and Action Management | Efficiency orientation<br>Proactivity<br>Concern with impact<br>Diagnostic use of concepts |
| Directing Subordinates | Use of unilateral power[a]<br>Spontaneity[a]<br>Developing others[a] |
| Focus on Others | Perceptual objectivity<br>Self-control<br>Stamina and adaptability<br>Concern with close relationships |
| Specialized Knowledge | Memory<br>Specialized job knowledge[a] |

Note: [a]Identified as "threshold competencies," that is, characteristics essential to performing a job, but not causally related to superior job performance.

SOURCE: From L. F. Schoenfeldt & J. A. Steger (1990). Identification and development of managerial talent. In G. R. Ferris & K. M. Rowland (Eds.), *Organizational entry* (p. 210). Greenwich, CT: JAI Press.

3. Five (relational) *targets* — peers, subordinates, superiors, external, and self
4. An unspecified number of managerial *styles* (attributes that describe the image and approach of the manager) — examples include objectivity, personal impact, leadership, energy level, and risk taking

The four-dimensional model states that managers interact with various targets (e.g., subordinates), carrying out an assortment of functions by performing specific roles (i.e., the roles that exist within each of the functions). The way they perform these functions and roles is consistent with their managerial style. For example, in performing the training and development function with a subordinate (the target), the manager may have to direct the subordinate, motivate him or her during training, and evaluate progress (all roles contained within the training and development function). The manager may do this by using a particular style (e.g., objectivity, which involves evaluating and responding to the subordinate in an unbiased manner).

The four-dimensional and integrated competency models include similar skills, roles, and activities and provide a solid basis for describing the managerial job and designing management development programs (see Schoenfeldt & Steger for a discussion of the relationships among the models).[32] These models provide a conceptual basis to view the role of managers within a specific organization and the competencies managers need to perform effectively. However, these models do not have a sizable body of empirical research to support their validity. Just as importantly, these models should not be viewed as substitutes for a thorough needs assessment.

## MANAGERS AS PERSONS: A HOLISTIC VIEW OF THE MANAGER'S JOB

The approaches we have presented to describing the manager's job all have one thing in common: they attempt to describe the manager's job by identifying its elements. This approach has its risks and limitations, according to authors such as Henry Mintzberg and Peter Vaill.[33] Mintzberg describes the problem as follows:

> If you turn to the formalized literature, you will find all kinds of lists — of tasks or roles or "competencies." But a list is not a model . . . and so the integrated work of managing still gets lost in the process of describing it. And without such a model we can neither understand the job properly nor deal with its many important needs — for design, selection, training, and support. . . . We have been so intent on breaking the job into pieces that we never came to grips with the whole thing.[34]

Vaill raises this concern in light of the turbulent environment in which managers must manage.[35] While he believes that naming the functions that managers must perform can "define the territory that leaders and managers are concerned with" (p. 114), the list-of-functions approach leaves out something essential: the performing of the managerial job. Vaill explains the problem this way:

> The list of functions approach forgets that action taking is a concrete process before it is anything else. Furthermore, it is a concrete process performed by a whole person in relation to a whole environment populated by other whole persons (that is, not other lists of functions). This whole process is embedded in time and is subject to the real time of its operation and to all the turbulence and change that surround it, that indeed suffuse it, because the turbulence and change are within action takers as much as they surround them. Simply to name the function to be performed as though it were the action ignores all of this richness of the actual action-taking process, and worst of all, ultimately masks the richness and leads to an empty model of what the action-taking *process* is (emphasis in original).[36]

Vaill uses the metaphor of "managing as a performing art" to show that the job of managing is more than the sum of its competencies, roles, and functions, just as, for example, a jazz band or dance troupe performance is more than the pieces or knowledge and skills that make it up. He criticized the competency movement, arguing that it is based on a set of assumptions that may not be true, in effect "presuming a world that does not exist, or that is at least quite improbable."[37]

**FIGURE 13-1**

## MINTZBERG'S "WELL ROUNDED" MODEL OF THE MANAGERIAL JOB

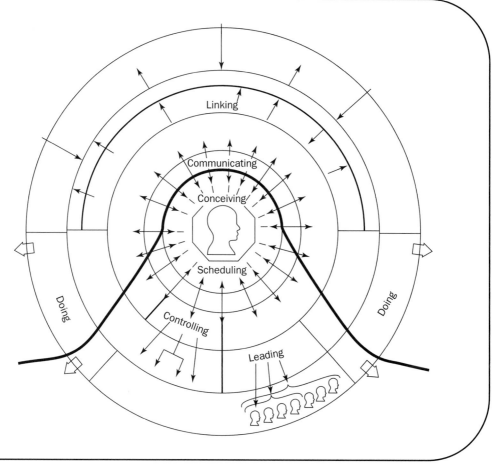

SOURCE: Reprinted from "Rounding out the manager's job" by H. Mintzberg, *MIT Sloan Management Review,* 36(1) 1994, pp. 23, by permission of publisher. Copyright 1994 by Massachusetts Institute of Technology. All rights reserved.

In response to these deficiencies, Mintzberg developed a model of the manager's job that attempts to bring together what has been learned about managing in a more holistic or integrated way.[38] His goal was to develop a model that reflects the richness and variety of styles individuals use in carrying out the managerial job. The model represents the manager's job as a framework of concentric circles, in what he calls a "well-rounded" job. Figure 13-1 shows a diagram of Mintzberg's well-rounded model. The words in the model refer to the seven interrelated roles Mintzberg sees as making up the managerial job: conceiving, scheduling, communicating, controlling, leading, linking, and doing.

At the center of the model is the *person in the job.* The person brings to the job a set of values, experiences, knowledge, competencies, and mental models through which he or she interprets environmental events. These components combine to form the individual's managerial style, which drives how the person carries out the job. The next circle contains the *frame of the job,* which is the "mental set the incumbent assumes to carry it out" (p.12). The frame includes the person's idea of the purpose of what he or she is trying to accomplish as well as the person's approach to getting the job done. Working within this frame involves the role Mintzberg calls conceiving. The heavy line curving around the frame of the job is meant to depict everything in the organization that is under the manager's control, that is, his or her span of control.

The next circle contains the *agenda of the work.* The agenda is made up of the issues that are of concern to the manager and the schedule (i.e., allocation of time) used to accomplish the work. Dealing with the agenda of the work involves the role of scheduling. The frame of the job and agenda of the work are surrounded by the *actual behaviors that managers perform,* both inside and outside of the unit they manage. Mintzberg sees three levels of action: managing through information (which involves the roles of communicating and controlling), managing through people (which involves the roles of linking and leading), and managing through direct action (which involves the role of doing tasks).

Mintzberg's central argument is that "while we may be able to separate the components of the job conceptually, I maintain that they cannot be separated behaviorally . . . it may be useful, even necessary, to delineate the parts for purposes of design, selection, training and support. But this job cannot be practiced as a set of independent parts" (p. 22). He points out that the manager's job will vary, depending on what is called for by the work and the particular approach or style a manager uses. The manager's style will affect his or her work through the roles he or she favors, the way in which the roles are performed, and the relationship that exists among the roles. Mintzberg states that interviews with managers he has met bear out his ideas of the variety and richness of the managerial job. Like the other approaches to describing the manager's job, Mintzberg's model should be seen as a work-in-progress, awaiting further development and validation through research.

What can HRD professionals take away from the ideas presented by Vaill and Mintzberg? We think the main contribution is that they remind us that the job of managing is a complex, multifaceted, and integrated endeavor. While competency models and lists of KSAs are useful in identifying what it takes to do the job and as focal points for management development programs, HRD professionals should not think that management development is only about developing roles and competencies. We need to remember that managers are people who perform work, not collections of competencies and KSAs. Some practical implications of this are that HRD professionals should:

1. recognize that one of the goals of management development is to develop the whole person, so that he or she can manage effectively within the context of the organization and external environment

2. design programs and processes that go beyond the one-shot event, and include ongoing activities that provide the opportunity to reinforce and refine what has been learned in the context of performing the work

3. build into programs and practices a recognition of the interrelationships between the "components" of managing, so that participants can see and feel

how what they are learning can be integrated into the whole of the management job

4. implement programs and processes in a way that recognizes and takes advantage of the values, knowledge, and experiences that participants bring to the management experience

5. consider what the person brings to the job of managing when dealing with learning and transfer of training issues

6. include recognition of these issues when conducting needs assessment and evaluation activities for management development programs

## IMPORTANCE OF NEEDS ASSESSMENT IN DETERMINING MANAGERIAL COMPETENCIES

As we stated in Chapter 4, needs assessment provides critical information in determining the conditions for training, where training is needed, what kind of training is needed, and who needs training. Given the fact that research on the managerial job has left many unanswered questions, the importance of conducting a thorough needs assessment before designing a management development program is amplified. Despite this, many organizations fail to conduct proper needs assessment. According to a survey of 1,000 organizations by Lise Saari and colleagues, only 27 percent of respondents reported conducting any needs assessment before designing management development programs.[39] A review of forty-four studies where needs assessment was discussed found that 36 percent analyzed organizational-level needs, with lower percentages for assessment of process, group, or individual-level needs.[40] The results of these two studies suggest that many organizations are leaving much to chance and are likely wasting critical resources.

Some organizations are doing a good job of needs assessment for management development and as a result have a clearer idea of the competencies and issues their development programs should address. For example, Aeroquip-Vickers had top managers identify the top twenty-five competencies that managers needed for future success. This was then used to form a managerial success profile that guided subsequent management development efforts in this organization.[41] As a second example, the Blanchard Valley Health Association, a healthcare system in Findlay, Ohio, used needs assessment to formulate its Leaders for Tomorrow program. This yearlong program includes classroom learning, small-group discussion, computer learning modules, and an "action learning" component, where managers work on job-related projects.[42] Third, the State of Idaho completed an intensive needs assessment before implementing its Certified Public Manager (CPM) program for state managers.[43]

Finally, after the court-ordered breakup of AT&T, New York Telephone found itself facing competition for the first time in its history.[44] Company officials needed to identify the required skills for managers to respond to this new competitive environment. Intensive work by a task force, as well as survey responses from over 3,000 managers, identified the twenty most important skills that managers needed. These were combined into six groups (personal, communications, organizing and planning, people and performance management, business, and independent thinking) and used to identify courses for the company's management skills curriculum.

We hope these examples illustrate the value of conducting a thorough investigation of the competencies needed to perform effectively before designing a management development program.

## THE GLOBALLY COMPETENT MANAGER

The advent of the global economy has led to recommendations that organizations create management development programs to produce globally competent managers.[45] Organizations such as Corning Glass, 3M, ITT, and General Electric have incorporated this perspective into their management development programs. We present three examples of how the competencies needed to be an effective global manager have been conceptualized.

Bartlett and Ghoshal argue that to succeed in a global environment, organizations need a network of managers who are specialists in global issues, and that organizations do not need to globalize all managers.[46] They suggest four categories of managers are needed:

1. *Business Managers* — This type of manager plays three roles, serving as "the *strategist* for the organization, the *architect* of its worldwide asset configuration, and the *coordinator* of transactions across national borders" (p. 125).

2. *Country Managers* — This type of manager, who works in the organization's national subsidiaries, also plays three roles, serving as "the *sensor* and interpreter of local opportunities and threats, the *builder* of local resources and capabilities, and the *contributor* to active participation in global strategy" (p. 128).

3. *Functional Managers* — These managers are functional specialists (e.g., in engineering, marketing, human resources) who "*scan* for specialized information worldwide, '*cross-pollinate*' leading-edge knowledge and best practice, and *champion* innovations that may offer transnational opportunities and applications" (p. 130).

4. *Corporate Managers* — These managers serve in corporate headquarters and orchestrate the organization's activities, playing the roles of *leader and talent scout* (i.e., by identifying potential business, country, and functional managers) and *developing* promising executives.

Bartlett and Ghoshal illustrate these roles by using case studies of managers at Procter & Gamble, Electrolux, and NEC.[47] They suggest that organizations need to develop management teams capable of performing these functions in concert to achieve the organization's goals. While this categorization provides some sense of how these roles interrelate, further research is needed to determine whether this approach can be a useful basis for developing global managers.

Adler and Bartholomew present a second point of view.[48] These authors identify seven transnational skills that they believe are necessary to managing effectively in a global environment: global perspective, local responsiveness, synergistic learning, transition and adaptation, cross-cultural interaction, collaboration, and foreign experience. They argue that transnationally competent managers need a broader set of skills than traditional managers. Adler and Bartholomew state that an organization's human resource management strategies must be modified in order to manage and develop such managers, and they conclude from a survey of fifty North American firms that these organizations' present HRM strategies are less global than their business strategies.[49] These authors provide recommendations for how HRM systems can be modified to become more global — for example, developmental activities should prepare managers to work "anywhere in the world with people from all parts of the world" (p. 59).

These two views of the globally competent manager differ in at least two ways. First, Bartlett and Ghoshal adopt a role-oriented view, while Adler and Bartholomew focus on the competencies managers need. Second, Adler and Bartholomew suggest that all managers become "globalized," while Bartlett and Ghoshal argue that global management requires a team of managers who perform different functions and roles (and who would require significantly different sets of competencies).[50]

Spreitzer, McCall, and Mahoney offer a third point of view on international competencies.[51] They argue that it is important to focus on *future* challenges that may require different competencies than those required today. Therefore, Spreitzer and colleagues emphasize competencies involved in *learning from experience* as a part of the set of competencies used to identify international executive potential and develop effective international managers. Spreitzer et al. identified fourteen dimensions that could predict international executive potential. The list includes:

- eight *end-state competency dimensions* — for example, sensitivity to cultural differences, business knowledge, courage to take a stand, bringing out the best in people, acting with integrity, insight, commitment to success, and risk taking

- six *learning-oriented dimensions* — for example, use of feedback, cultural adventurousness, seeking opportunities to learn, openness to criticism, feedback seeking, and flexibility

These authors developed an instrument, called *Prospector,* that rates managers on these dimensions to identify which managers had the greatest potential to be effective international executives. Using over 800 managers from various levels of six international firms in twenty-one countries, Spreitzer and colleagues provided evidence of the validity and reliability of the *Prospector* instrument as a way to predict international executive success.

The value of the approach taken by Spreitzer and colleagues is that it (1) gives HRD professionals ideas about what dimensions international management development programs should address, as well as possible ways to select which managers should participate in and most benefit from these activities, (2) reminds HRD professionals to consider future challenges managers may face that may take them beyond the competencies that have been needed in the past, and (3) provides an excellent model for how HRD professionals can take a scientific approach to identifying and generating supporting evidence for the sets of competencies they will use as the basis of management development.

Our purpose in raising these three points of view is not to suggest which is "correct" or would make the better foundation for describing the managerial job and the development of managers (although we believe the method used by Spreitzer and colleagues to be the most worthy of emulation).[52] These models (as well as other ideas about achieving global competency) require further research, testing, and modification.[53] These approaches illustrate how the global environment can impact the approach taken to developing an organization's managers. In addition, they underscore the need to consider an organization's business strategy and environment as foundations for management development efforts.

## WHAT COMPETENCIES WILL FUTURE MANAGERS NEED?

Just as Spreitzer and colleagues included consideration of learning-related dimensions to address competency areas that international managers will need in the future, other researchers are trying to estimate the competencies managers will need to navigate their careers in the twenty-first century.[54] For example, Allred, Snow, and Miles argue that new organizational structures will demand new sets of managerial competencies.[55] Based on a survey of managers, HR executives, and recruiters, Allred and colleagues concluded that five categories of KSAs will be important for managerial careers in this new century: (1) a knowledge-based technical specialty, (2) cross-functional and international experience, (3) collaborative leadership, (4) self-management skills, and (5) personal traits, including integrity, trustworthiness, and flexibility.

We mention this example to encourage HRD professionals to consider the question of what future competencies managers will need. It is important that management development activities prepare managers for the future. Estimates will have to be made, and should include trends and industry-specific issues that will likely affect the businesses that managers will have to manage. Most of all, it means that management development should be seen as a *long-term process*. Management development programs and the development process should not be seen as finished products, but as organic works in progress that are regularly evaluated and modified as trends, strategies, and conditions warrant. This approach is already being used in many organizations, including 3M, General Electric, TRW, and Motorola, to name just a few.[56]

Having explored the nature of the management job and the competencies that managing requires, we turn our attention to the issue of making management development strategic.

## MAKING MANAGEMENT DEVELOPMENT STRATEGIC

We have noted that management development should be tied to the organization's structure and strategy for accomplishing its business goals. Recall that this point was made back in Chapter 1, as we discussed the learning and performance wheel coming out of the ASTD study.[57] Before we describe the management development practices organizations use, it is useful to examine how these activities can be framed and delivered in a way that ensures that this strategic focus is maintained.

Seibert, Hall, and Kram suggest that three desired linkages should exist between the organization's strategy and its management development activities: (1) the link between the business environment and business strategy, (2) the link between business strategy and the organization's management development strategy, and (3) the link between the management development strategy and management development activities.[58] Based on an examination of management development practices at twenty-two leading organizations, Seibert et al. concluded that these organizations pay attention to the first and last links, but the middle linkage between the business strategy and the management development strategy was weak. They suggest that this linkage is weak because the HRD function has too often focused on itself rather than its customer, has been unable to respond rapidly enough to meet customer needs, and has a tendency to see a false dichotomy between developing individuals and conducting business.

Seibert and colleagues found that some organizations, such as 3M and Motorola, did make this link, by making sure that strategic business issues drove management development, ensuring that HRD professionals provided a timely response to business needs, and by integrating management development as a natural part of doing business. Based on their review, they proposed four guiding principles that can help HRD professionals make the necessary strategic links:

1. *Begin by moving out and up to business strategy* — This involves viewing the HRD professional's role primarily as implementing strategy, and secondarily as a developer of managers. Practical suggestions include becoming intimately familiar with the organization's strategic objectives and business issues, using these as a starting point for identifying management behaviors and competencies, and looking for developmental opportunities within the activities needed to accomplish strategic objectives.

2. *Put job experiences before classroom activities, not vice versa* — This involves using job experiences as the central developmental activity, with classroom activities playing the role of identifying, processing, and sharing the learning that is taking place on the job. This assumes that on-the-job experiences will be actively managed to ensure that learning will take place and strategic needs will be addressed.

3. *Be opportunistic* — Ensure that management development is flexible and open to respond to the business needs and issues the organization is facing and will likely face. This involves moving away from elaborate, rigid programs to programs that can change and are built to be responsive to the organization's changing needs.

4. *Provide support for experience-based learning* — This involves creating a culture that expects, supports, and rewards learning as a part of day-to-day challenges and that reinforces individuals for taking control of their own development as managers.

Burack, Hochwarter, and Mathys offer another approach to strategic management development.[59] Using a review of so-called "world-class" organizations, Burack et al. identified seven themes common to strategic management development: (1) a linkage between management development and the business plans and strategies; (2) seamless programs, which cut across hierarchical and functional boundaries; (3) a global orientation and a cross-cultural approach; (4) individual learning focused within organizational learning; (5) a recognition of the organization's culture and ensuring that the management development design fits within and creates or supports the desired culture; (6) a career development focus; and (7) an approach built on empirically determined core competencies.

3M is an example of an organization that has integrated its strategy of global competition into its management development program.[60] An overseas assignment is one element of the developmental process for individuals who are being groomed for senior management positions. These managers are assigned to positions as managing directors for 3M subsidiaries for a period of three to five years. During this time, the individual is responsible for conducting the ordinary business of the subsidiary. Individuals are assigned based on who would benefit most from the experience.

What is unique about 3M's approach to using global assignments is the way the assignments are managed. Specifically, this approach includes the following: (1) international assignments are requirements for promotion to senior positions, so resistance to these assignments disappears; (2) each expatriate has a senior management sponsor who provides orientation, annual review meetings, and on-going support; and (3) the assignments are changed as the business strategy and international situations change. For example, changing economic developments in Europe led 3M to change the position the expatriate is assigned to from managing director of a subsidiary to a product manager position on a European management action team to heading up a European business center. The managing director position approach was used in areas of the world for which it still made strategic sense (e.g., Latin America, Asia Pacific, Africa). This kind of flexible approach is a good example of keeping management development responsive to the changing needs of the organization, while making sure development and strategy achievement go hand in hand.[61]

The ideas offered by these authors highlight the strategic issues and offer common practices used in respected organizations.[62] They are not time-tested blueprints for success. Furthermore, the "best practices" and "leading organizations" approach to identifying principles and actions should be viewed with some caution. What is found is determined by whom the researchers have chosen to include in their sample and what they were able to discover. As was the case with the organizations profiled in the best-selling book *In Search of Excellence*,[63] not all organizations that meet the criteria for inclusion when the study is done continue to meet the criteria in later years.[64] The environment we live in is too turbulent for any set of principles to hold true in particular organizations for too long.

Finally, the suggestions offered in such studies should be viewed as suggestions and should not be copied unthinkingly.[65] The authors of the studies we cited express such caution in their writing, identify needs for future research to substantiate their suggestions, and remind readers that it is the practitioners' responsibility to ensure that what is done within their organizations should be based on needs assessment and a thorough knowledge of the organization and its environment.

## MANAGEMENT EDUCATION

As defined earlier, management education involves activities designed to help participants gain a broad range of conceptual knowledge and skills in formal classroom situations, most typically from degree-granting institutions. Management education continues to be an extremely popular activity. Enrollments in bachelor's and master's degree programs in the United States have grown rapidly since the 1980s.[66] It is estimated that approximately 281,000 bachelor's degrees, 121,000 master's degrees, and over 1,100 doctoral degrees were awarded in business during the academic year ending in 2002.[67] Business degrees remain by a wide margin the most popular bachelor's degrees awarded in the United States, the second most popular master's degree (behind education), and the eleventh most popular doctoral degree.[68] Excluding the more specialized doctoral programs, management education activities can be grouped into two categories:

1. bachelor's or master's programs in business administration (B.B.A. or M.B.A.) offered at colleges and universities
2. executive education, which can range from condensed M.B.A. programs to short courses delivered by colleges and universities, consulting firms, private institutes, and professional and industry associations

Each category is discussed next.

### BACHELOR'S OR MASTER'S DEGREE PROGRAMS IN BUSINESS ADMINISTRATION

Traditional management education offered at four-year colleges and universities, leading to a bachelor's or master's degree, generally focuses on management knowledge and general concepts. While there has been some debate as to whether to focus such management education programs on providing primarily conceptual knowledge (e.g., market research techniques, planning and decision models) or developing the skills (e.g., communication, interpersonal) that managers need to be successful, most business school programs seek to provide both. The curricula of many M.B.A. and B.B.A. programs follow the accreditation standards issued by the main accrediting body in management education, the Association for the Advancement of Collegiate Schools of Business (AACSB). The AACSB distinguishes between bachelor's and master's education in terms of scope. It sees bachelor's education as combining "general education with basic study of business," and master's education as providing a professional general managerial perspective.[69] The AACSB standards are mission based, in that they provide for flexibility in program content, structure, and delivery based on the institution's mission (e.g., the degree of emphasis on teaching and research).

According to the AACSB curriculum standards, the curricula of both bachelor's and master's programs should provide an understanding of the following issues and how they affect organizations: ethical, global, political, social, technological, legal and regulatory, environmental, and demographic diversity. Bachelor's programs should provide foundational knowledge in accounting, behavioral science, economics, mathematics, and statistics, along with a general education component that makes up at least half of the students' programs. Master's programs should be organized around a core of financial reporting, analysis and markets, domestic and global economic environments, creation of goods and services, and human behavior in organizations. Programs at both levels should provide training in written and oral communication, with master's programs ensuring that graduates have basic quantitative analysis and computer skills.[70]

Business schools were widely criticized as being ineffective during the late 1980s and early 1990s. The criticism prompted a comprehensive review of business school training by the AASCB, which addressed concerns that business schools were not satisfying the needs of organizations in terms of providing students with the education needed to become effective managers.[71] Concerns focused on the lack of cross-functional integration in coursework (e.g., finance, human resource management), perceptions of graduates' levels of "soft" skills (e.g., communication, interpersonal), lack of an international perspective, and a lack of breadth in the students' preparation (i.e., too much focus on business issues at the expense of providing a broad education). Business schools were urged to modify their curricula to address these shortcomings to make students and organizations more competitive.[72] These recommendations have far-reaching consequences both in terms of knowledge of subject matter needed by the faculty to develop the content of these programs and the educational techniques needed to deliver them.

Business schools have, by and large, responded to the challenge. For example, the Wharton School at the University of Pennsylvania became one of the first M.B.A. programs to completely overhaul its curriculum to meet what were perceived to be the realities of doing business in the next century. Rather than offering semester-long courses in separate disciplines, the Wharton program offers courses in four 6-week modules that integrate the disciplines to solve problems. The revised program also places a heavy emphasis on the development of "people skills," practical problem solving, and acquiring a global perspective. The curriculum, which was developed with the input of students, faculty, alumni, futurists, CEOs, and corporate recruiters, became both a model to be emulated and a stimulus for program innovations at other schools.[73]

Another example of innovation and change in business schools is the M.B.A. program redesign at the Weatherhead School of Business at Case Western Reserve University in Cleveland, Ohio.[74] Its program was designed to focus on learning outcomes, involve and serve the needs of all stakeholder groups (e.g., students, alumni, potential employers), stimulate students to think about issues in novel ways, expand students' capacity to think and act creatively, and place faculty in the role of managers of learning rather than teachers.[75] The program has six elements: (1) a managerial assessment and development course that provides students with a way to assess and develop the KSAs relevant to their management careers (using a competency-based approach); (2) development of an individual learning plan; (3) Executive Action Teams, which are groups of students who meet regularly with a local executive advisor to integrate learning across courses and from students experiences; (4) eleven core courses in management and business disciplines (e.g., accounting, finance, human resources, and labor policy); (5) multidisciplinary perspective courses organized around themes such as managing in a global economy, technology management, and the history of industrial development; and (6) advanced elective courses.[76] An evaluation study conducted over a two-year period showed evidence that the outcome-oriented, competency-based program "had a positive impact in helping students to improve their abilities between the time of entry and graduation."[77]

The Wharton and Weatherhead examples show the kinds of changes that have been going on in business schools in recent years. Student input into a wide range of issues, efforts to improve teaching and placement support, and cooperation with business have become commonplace at many business schools.[78] Innovations in teaching have also been implemented. Team-oriented and applied projects and assignments are now widely used. Many business schools use computer and telecommunication technology as a central part of courses, and courses (and even entire programs) taught completely online are becoming increasingly commonplace.[79] Both the *Journal of Management Education* and the *Academy of Management Learning and Education* include examples, ideas, and issues that management educators are developing and debating to keep business education responsive, relevant, and effective.[80]

It should be noted that degree programs at both the graduate and undergraduate levels should be seen as only one component of a manager's development. It is unreasonable to expect that education at these levels will result in a "whole manager" who has all the KSAs needed to manage effectively. At their best, business programs can provide a valuable foundation for a manager's development and a good way for practicing managers to reflect on their experiences and develop new skills and knowledge. Graduates of such programs should be seen as "works-in-progress," with the potential to become effective managers with further development and experience.[81]

## EXECUTIVE EDUCATION PROGRAMS

Because of the length of time it can take to complete an M.B.A. program and the crowded lives of many full-time managers, many institutions, both academic and otherwise, have developed a number of alternatives. These alternatives, which can range from condensed M.B.A. programs known as Executive M.B.A.s (E.M.B.A.s), to short courses on given topics and issues, to one-time sessions, can be referred to as **executive education** programs. Executive education has become big business for the universities and institutions that provide it. For example, it is estimated that INSEAD (in Fontainebleu, France), Harvard, and the Center for Creative Leadership earned annual revenues of $37 million, $30.1 million, and $23.5 million, respectively, from executive education programs.[82]

*EXECUTIVE M.B.A. PROGRAMS.* It is estimated that over 9,500 executives attend **executive M.B.A. (E.M.B.A.) programs** at 102 business schools in North America each year.[83] Most of these programs condense or accelerate the coursework, with courses meeting once per week (typically on weekends). These programs typically are designed to be completed in two years. Students tend to be older, full-time managers from a variety of organizations who have a significant amount of experience as managers.

Advantages of E.M.B.A. programs include the opportunity to interact with managers from other organizations, maximum input of new ideas, high quality of instruction, and the prestige afforded by having a university affiliation. Commonly perceived disadvantages include inadequate exposure to information specific to the organization's needs, the high price, and an insufficient numbers of instructors within a given program who are effective at teaching adults.[84] In addition, critics have charged that some programs are merely watered-down versions of M.B.A. programs, with poor quality of instruction and lax admission standards, and with the primary goal of generating income for the school.[85]

Are E.M.B.A. programs an effective approach to developing managers? There is little existing research to answer the question. Evaluations are generally based on anecdotal information. Typical results of the few evaluation studies of E.M.B.A. programs indicate that participants are generally satisfied with their experience, feeling that they have been broadened by their exposure to new ideas and people, and have gained increased levels of self-confidence.[86] Despite the lack of hard evidence, organizations continue to support such programs.

Most organizations use E.M.B.A. programs as one component of their executive development efforts in addition to other in-house and external activities (e.g., succession planning, short courses).[87] Organizations interested in using E.M.B.A. programs should carefully examine their development needs and investigate the programs they consider using. Discussions with administrators, faculty members, and alumni can yield useful information.

*OTHER APPROACHES TO EXECUTIVE EDUCATION.* Executive education need not be as comprehensive as an M.B.A. or E.M.B.A. program. Many providers offer courses in a wide range of management topics. These courses are generally focused on a particular topic, issue, or skill, and are freestanding (i.e., they do not exist within a degree-oriented curriculum). Before 1980, the dominant external provider of such programs was the American Management Association (AMA), which continues to offer hundreds of courses on a wide range of topics.[88] The current picture is different in that no single provider dominates the field. In addition to colleges and universities, organizations such as the Center for Creative Leadership, Wilson Learning, industry associations, and a host of consultants offer courses that can be used as part of a total management development program. The boxed insert nearby provides information on an innovative E.M.B.A. program at the Weatherhead School of Management at Case Western Reserve University.

The intent of many courses is to mix theory with a great deal of practical relevance in order to provide participants with information and tools that have immediate application to their current jobs. Advances in telecommunications, especially in satellite transmission, videoconferencing, and the Internet, are making long-distance learning a growing part of executive education that could lead to major changes in how executive education is provided. In 1996, it was estimated that 10 percent of all organizations and 22 percent of large organizations used commercial satellite distance learning networks to deliver training.[89] In 2003, it was estimated that 31 percent of all training was delivered outside of the traditional instructor-led classroom (this included distance education, instructor-less computer-based training, and other nonclassroom forms of training).[90] A special issue in the *Journal of Management Education* was devoted to the topic "Management education in the

## The Professional Fellows Program at the Weatherhead School of Management

At the Weatherhead School of Management at Case Western Reserve University in Cleveland, Ohio, an innovative approach to executive education has been developed. The program is aimed at midcareer professionals who have little formal management education, but who are entering or already in management positions. Enrollees in this program were designated as "Professional Fellows." It was decided that this would be a nondegree program rather than an M.B.A.-type program. There is a strong emphasis in the program on self-directed learning. Four distinctive elements make up the Professional Fellows Program, or PFP:

1. An initial course is taken that emphasizes individual assessment and development. Each participant must write up a personal learning plan that will guide his or her further studies and personal development over the next five to seven years.

2. Participants take a series of seminars on current challenges in leadership and management.

3. Each participant completes an individualized, intensive study of a particular topic (or topics) through a major research project and via course electives.

4. Participants take part in a "Society of Fellows," which is an active peer network that seeks to facilitate continuous, lifelong learning.

As of 1999, fifty-three people in four classes of Fellows had participated in the program. The aspect of the program that was cited as most helpful was the development of the individualized learning plan. In interviews, participants also cited the impact that the program had on their self-confidence. Some of the particular abilities that Fellows thought had been most enhanced by their involvement in the program were networking, planning, group management, initiative, and developing others.

The Weatherhead faculty who described this program view it as a successful work-in-progress. They close their article with three penetrating questions that are worth considering:

1. Can or should this process be expanded to other regions or professional schools?

2. Does the PFP have implications for other forms of management education, for example, E.M.B.A., M.B.A., or undergraduate management education?

3. Can universities view this as a legitimate program, and will faculty involvement in this program be treated as equal in value as involvement in degree-granting programs (M.B.A., undergraduate)?

You might recognize that this program is strongly influenced by the principles of adult learning that we presented in Chapter 3. Given our discussion there, what do you think about applying these principles in a bachelor's or master's program? In your opinion, would it work? Why or why not?

From Ballou, R., Bowers, D., Boyatzis, R. E., & Kolb, D. A. (1999). Fellowship in lifelong learning: An executive development program for advanced professionals. *Journal of Management Education, 23*, 338–355.

information age."[91] Colleges and universities are finding a growing market in beaming lectures and classes conducted by their "star" professors via satellite to remote locations (e.g., alumni clubs and company classrooms). Two examples of this trend include:

- a consortium of eight business schools brought together by Westcott Communications Inc., called the Executive Education Network, which has connections to over 100 classrooms in companies including Kodak, Walt Disney, and Texas Instruments
- the University of Michigan, which provides live video courses to companies in the United States, Europe, and Asia, in partnership with a consortium headed by British Telecom[92]

Advantages of using such courses offered by external providers include controlling the costs of in-house courses, the specialized expertise of the provider, the design and packaging of such courses, and a practitioner-oriented approach (particularly among courses not offered by universities).[93] In addition, satellite courses can be delivered at the convenience of the client and do not require participants to travel to attend the program.[94] One of the significant disadvantages of such courses is a lack of quality control. Operating in a highly competitive environment, many of these providers are under pressure to stay in business and may reduce their standards to ensure they generate sufficient business in the short term. While market forces will eventually (and ideally) weed out the poor quality programs, this may take time and many clients may purchase poor quality courses in the process.[95] Furthermore, as we discussed in Chapters 5 and 6, the content of the course needs to be matched to the medium used to deliver it. For example, given the current state of technology, satellite transmission may be better suited for knowledge transmission (because it typically uses a lecture format, with all of the associated advantages and disadvantages), while interpersonal skills courses would be better conducted in person.[96]

One potential disadvantage to short courses offered by colleges and universities is a real or perceived lack of relevance and practical orientation. One way some organizations are addressing these concerns is by working with colleges and universities to customize courses that will meet their specific needs. Colleges and universities are increasingly willing to customize courses to fit a particular client's needs. For example, Hoffman-LaRoche Inc., a New Jersey-based healthcare and pharmaceutical company, had the Massachusetts Institute of Technology (MIT) customize a course to provide managers with training in strategic management of technology, leadership, and quality.[97] Other similar partnerships exist between Ford Motor Company and the University of Michigan and IBM and Wharton. While this approach may resolve the issues of quality and relevance, it is expensive, with costs per program (e.g., a three- or four-day course) ranging from $50,000 to $80,000.[98] Hequet recommends that organizations interested in such an approach should "shop around" by discussing their needs with a variety of schools, explaining specifically what they want, and finding out what the school can offer (i.e., in terms of times, locations, instructors) and then negotiate to obtain a reasonable price.[99]

Customized or not, short courses offered by external providers are likely to remain a significant part of the management development scene in the future, especially in light of the convenience and variety of the options that are available. One of the best ways an organization can ensure that it purchases courses that will meet its needs is to conduct a thorough needs analysis and evaluate the programs both before and after they are used.

Vicere suggests the following guidelines be used in designing executive education initiatives:

- Effective executive education is a blend of experience, training, education, and other forms of development and does not rely solely on classroom-based techniques.

- Real-time interaction with real-life business issues is an integral element of effective executive education.

- Executive education should develop and revitalize both the participant and the organization.

- Executive education should instill a desire for continuous learning and knowledge creation on the part of both individuals and organizations.

- Effective executive education efforts should contribute to the development of both the individual talents of leaders and the collective knowledge base of the organization.

- Executive education should help establish a talent pool of leaders at all levels of the organization.[100]

Regardless of the type of management education provided (bachelor's, M.B.A., E.M.B.A., or other), the challenge facing all management educators today is to ensure the timeliness and "value-added" of what is presented.[101] Joseph Alutto has referred to this as "Just-in-time management education in the 21st century," and this is a useful description of what organizations are seeking from management education.[102] The dynamic social, political, economic, and technological changes occurring today require fundamental changes in the manner in which management education is conducted.[103] We expect further major changes in the shape and substance of management education in the next decade.

## MANAGEMENT TRAINING AND EXPERIENCES

Various surveys indicate that almost 90 percent of organizations provide training and on-the-job experiences as part of their efforts to develop managers.[104] The majority of organizations use a combination of externally provided and internally developed courses and programs to achieve this goal. In this section of the chapter, we focus briefly on company-specific management training approaches. A wide variety of possibilities exist.[105] To illustrate the options in use, we will discuss three approaches: company-designed courses, corporate universities, and on-the-job experiences.

## COMPANY-DESIGNED COURSES

Organizations frequently design their own courses and seminars as one way to develop their managers. Such courses have the advantage of being tailored to the specific issues, skills, and individual attributes of the organization and its managers. These efforts can range from a specific course focusing on one skill or issue (e.g., evaluating employee performance, budgeting) to a series of interconnected courses (e.g., a two-week-long series of workshops to expose key nonmanagers to all company divisions and products and acquaint them with the challenges the company faces). For example, General Electric (GE) developed a series of courses to prepare managers to compete successfully in a global environment. The program, offered at the company's Crotonville, New York, management development center, is made up of a core curriculum that includes courses offered in a five-stage developmental sequence — Corporate Entry Leadership Conferences, New Manager Development Courses, Advanced Functional Courses, Executive Programs, and Officers' Workshops. This program services employees ranging from new college hires to corporate officers.[106] The courses are tailored to the challenges faced by GE's managers, including the use of GE-specific issues to provide an opportunity for participants to solve problems.

The issues in designing and implementing such courses are the same as for any HRD program. It is particularly important to ensure that such courses fit within an overall framework for developing managers. The idea is to avoid redundancy and help participants see the relevance of the courses to their overall developmental plan. It also helps managers, who are responsible for developing their subordinates, to understand the relationships of the courses the organization offers to the overall development effort. For example, GE makes clear its expectation that 80 percent of development occurs through on-the-job experience, with only 20 percent taking place through formal development (e.g., such as the Crotonville courses).[107] This perspective emphasizes to managers that the bulk of their developmental efforts should be focused on providing subordinates with meaningful developmental experiences on the job.

Some organizations go beyond their own managers as participants in their management development courses. For example, GE invites managers and officials from key overseas customers (and potential customers), such as Aeroflot from Russia and a group of Chinese managers, to attend customized programs alongside GE managers at Crotonville. The purpose of these programs is to develop the skills and talents of the managers involved, form relationships that can lead to greater cooperation and increased business opportunities, and learn the way other organizations and countries conduct business.[108]

## CORPORATE UNIVERSITIES

A large number of organizations have concluded that a significant component of their management development strategy should include a company academy or college in which all managers at certain levels are required to complete a specific curriculum. It is estimated that over 2,000 organizations have their own corporate universities.[109] Organizations that have taken this approach include GE, IBM, McDonald's, Motorola, Intel, Dunkin' Donuts, Holiday Inn, and Xerox. The facilities used for these academies can be quite elaborate (e.g., hundred-acre, landscaped campuses with multiple buildings and residential facilities located away from other company facilities). They have a specific educational mission geared toward the organization's specific needs and preferred ways of doing things. For example, McDonald's, the worldwide fast-food chain, teaches managers its approach to ensuring quality, service, and cleanliness at Hamburger University in Oak Brook, Illinois. The courses at Hamburger University include operational procedures that reinforce the organization's philosophy. Hamburger University uses a wide range of training methods, including lecture and discussion, audiovisuals, and hands-on experiences with equipment.[110]

Xerox Corporation devotes a portion of its over 2,000-acre corporate living, learning, and fitness center in Leesburg, Virginia, to its corporate education center. The center is capable of handling 1,000 students at a time and offers curricula in sales training, service training, and management training. The management training curriculum focuses on teaching participants about the business, their jobs as managers, and about themselves. Faculty for the center is drawn from the company's employees, and course design is performed by a group of professionals (Educational Services) specifically trained in course design that has access to production facilities capable of creating courses using a wide range of technologies (e.g., video, computer-assisted instruction). Members of this group identify needs and develop courses in collaboration with clients, subject matter experts, and instructors.[111]

While not all company academies are as elaborate as those run by McDonald's or Xerox, they are an expensive component of management development. Some organizations permit members of outside organizations to use their facilities and attend their courses for a fee when space permits. Critics charge that the standardized curricula at corporate academies can lead to problems (e.g., unresponsiveness to the organization's needs, detachment from the realities of the operating divisions). Eurich suggests, however, that such curricula can be useful if they transmit knowledge and skills that all participants at a particular level should know and that some of the problems that accompany this approach can be mitigated by a "vigilant management and training staff to ensure that a curriculum admits new ideas and responds to change" (p. 167).[112] It should be noted that programs at many corporate universities have kept pace with the changes going on in the rest of HRD and management development, including changing delivery methods and an emphasis on serving the organization's strategic needs.[113] Recent articles describe the latest developments in corporate universities.[114]

## ON-THE-JOB EXPERIENCES

On-the-job experiences play an important role in the development of managers.[115] Many organizations use job assignments and experiences as an explicit part of their management development efforts. However, despite the importance of on-the-job experience to management development, too often organizations leave such development to chance, hoping managers discover the lessons to be learned on their own. In addition, not much is known about how these events influence development and how we can make the most of such experiences.[116] Some observers have noted that many on-the-job experiences tend to reinforce old attitudes and behaviors, rather than encourage managers to adopt new ones that can make them more effective.[117]

Clearly, research on the types of events that have developmental potential, the lessons they can teach, and how such lessons can be learned is needed if we are to harness the power of experience. An important step in that direction is a series of studies on the role of experience in executive development conducted at the Center for Creative Leadership (CCL).[118] Researchers from CCL studied 191 successful executives from six major organizations by asking them to describe the key events in their careers and explain what they learned from them. These inquiries yielded over 1,500 lessons executives learned. Content analysis of these statements resulted in thirty-two types of lessons that can be grouped into five themes: setting and implementing agendas, handling relationships, basic values, executive temperament, and personal awareness. The developmental events were summarized into five categories: setting the stage, leading by persuasion, leading on the line, when other people matter, and hardships. Table 13-2 lists the themes and the lessons that make up each theme, and Table 13-3 lists the categories of events and types of events that make up each category.

McCall, Lombardo, and Morrison observe that the lessons learned from on-the-job events are hard-won, involving emotion, reflection, and assistance from others to extract the meaning.[119] They conclude that it is management's responsibility (shared with the individual) to be vigilant for opportunities to develop subordinates (e.g., through task-force assignments and challenging assignments), and to provide the necessary support, resources, feedback, and time necessary for subordinates to learn from these events. While recognizing that firm conclusions are hard to come by, McCall and colleagues suggest that an effective management development system is one that is characterized by the following:

1. *Opportunism* — taking advantage of opportunities for growth and learning
2. *Individualism* — taking into account the unique attributes of the individuals being developed
3. *Long-term perspective* — taking the view that developing managers is a multiyear process (e.g., 10–20 years)
4. *Encouragement of self-motivation* — encouraging the individuals being developed to be self-motivated
5. *Online approach* — centered on learning on the job

The events approach described by the CCL research is intriguing and presents a variety of useful suggestions for using experiences deliberately to develop managers. We believe this research is an important step forward in this area. One way to make better use of on-the-job experiences for management development would be to have a method to assess the developmental components of jobs. A first step in that direction is the **Developmental Challenge Profile (DCP)**.[120] The DCP is a ninety-six-item questionnaire based on the research investigating job features that

**TABLE 13-2**                    POTENTIAL LESSONS OF EXPERIENCE

### Setting and Implementing Agendas

- Technical/professional skills
- All about the business one is in
- Strategic thinking
- Shouldering full responsibility
- Building and using structure and control systems
- Innovative problem-solving methods

### Handling Relationships

- Handling political situations
- Getting people to implement solutions
- What executives are like and how to work with them
- Strategies of negotiation
- Dealing with people over whom you have no authority
- Understanding other people's perspectives
- Dealing with conflict
- Directing and motivating subordinates
- Developing other people
- Confronting subordinate performance problems
- Managing former bosses and peers

### Basic Values

- You can't manage everything all alone
- Sensitivity to the human side of management
- Basic management values

### Executive Temperament

- Being tough when necessary
- Self-confidence
- Coping with situations beyond your control
- Persevering through adversity
- Coping with ambiguous situations
- Use (and abuse) of power

*continued*

**TABLE 13-2**                                                                          **CONTINUED**

**Personal Awareness**
- The balance between work and personal life
- Knowing what really excites you about work
- Personal limits and blind spots
- Taking charge of your career
- Recognizing and seizing opportunities

SOURCE: Reprinted with permission from *Key Event in Executives' Lives,* Technical Report No. 32 (Greensboro, NC: Center for Creative Leadership, 1987), p. 227.

**TABLE 13-3**                                                        **THE DEVELOPMENTAL EVENTS**

**Setting the Stage**
- Early work experience
- First supervisory job

**Leading by Persuasion**
- Project/task-force assignments
- Line to staff switches

**Leading on Line**
- Starting from scratch
- Turning a business around
- Managing a larger scope

**When Other People Matter**
- Bosses

**Hardships**
- Personal trauma
- Career setback
- Changing jobs
- Business mistakes
- Subordinate performance problems

SOURCE: Reprinted with the permission of The Free Press, a Division of Simon & Schuster Adult Publishing Group, from LESSONS OF EXPERIENCE: How Successful Executives Develop on the Job by Morgan W. McCall, Jr., Michael M. Lombardo, Ann M. Morison. Copyright 1988 by Lexington Books. All rights reserved.

PART 3: HUMAN RESOURCE DEVELOPMENT APPLICATIONS

could be developmental.[121] It contains fifteen scales organized around the following three categories of developmental features:

- *Job transition* — unfamiliar responsibilities, proving yourself
- *Task-related characteristics* — which includes nine scales in three areas:
  1. creating change — developing new directions, inherited problems, reduction decisions, problems with employees
  2. high level of responsibility — high stakes, managing business diversity, job overload, handling external pressure
  3. nonauthority relationships — influencing without authority
- *Obstacles* — adverse business conditions, lack of top management support, lack of personal support, difficult boss

The research done by McCauley and colleagues on the DCP found that it had high internal consistency and test-retest reliability, and validity evidence supported the relationship of the majority of the scales to "perceptions of the learning of fundamental managerial skills and ways of thinking" (p. 556). The DCP is still being refined, but McCauley and colleagues suggest that it has at least two practical uses for management development: (1) DCP feedback can provide managers with a better understanding of the learning opportunities that are available within their jobs, and (2) the DCP can be used to identify components that can be designed into jobs to improve the opportunities for development.

In addition to the "events" view, there are at least two other approaches to using on-the-job experiences systematically in management development: mentoring and action learning. *Mentoring* was discussed in Chapter 12, so we will not revisit that topic here. **Action learning** is a concept first attributed to British physicist Reg Revans that has become increasingly common in the United States.[122] Originally developed as a way to encourage line managers to provide input to modify operating systems,[123] action learning as it is currently practiced involves having participants select an organizational problem, write a case study describing the problem, and meet with a group of other managers who face similar problems to discuss ways the problem can be dealt with.[124] This idea is sort of a "living case" approach, where instead of analyzing situations that have been resolved in the past, participants deal with ongoing problems and issues. The most widely cited example of action learning (and likely the largest implementation) is the Work-Out program at GE.[125] It is estimated that over 220,000 people have participated in the action-learning Work-Outs.[126]

Among the potential advantages of an action-learning approach is the discovery of a structured way to examine and analyze on-the-job events. Action learning also provides the opportunity to motivate participants to seek additional development (e.g., negotiation skills) that will help them resolve the type of problem discussed. In addition, because participants focus on existing issues, their motivation to learn and seek further development may be stronger. And, in the process, action-learning participants are actually solving problems and implementing solutions, making management development an integral part of strategy implementation and yielding the organization tangible benefits beyond development. Most of the writing about action learning has been descriptive and anecdotal rather than empirical, but action learning is clearly a technique that is gaining wide use and enthusiastic reviews.[127] Lyle Yorks and colleagues conducted a well-done qualitative research study on action learning in a multinational corporation.[128] Alan Mumford has also provided helpful guidance on the uses and boundaries of action learning.[129]

A key to using on-the-job experiences for developmental purposes is to ensure that time and techniques are provided so that opportunities for learning are not overlooked. Several of the examples we have cited so far in the chapter highlight ways this can be addressed. In addition, Daudelin suggests that building time and methods for reflecting on work experiences into the management development process (and day-to-day work) can be a way to ensure that learning will occur.[130] She describes a number of methods for individual reflection (e.g., journal writing, business writing, assessment instruments, mediation, and spontaneous thinking during repetitive activities such as jogging) and reflection with another person or a small group (e.g., performance appraisal discussions, counseling sessions, project review meetings, mentoring, and informal discussions with friends or colleagues).

In summary, there are a variety of ways organizations can systematically use on-the-job experiences to develop managers. While there is much research to be done, on-the-job experience should be a significant component of an organization's management development strategy. We recommend that organizations examine the opportunities available to them in this area to determine how they can make the most of experiences in their managers' development.

## EXAMPLES OF APPROACHES USED TO DEVELOP MANAGERS

There are many options for conducting management training and development. Many training techniques are available (see Chapters 5 and 6) as well as many training topics, including leadership, motivation, interpersonal skills, decision making, cultural and global training, as well as technical knowledge. We will describe two commonly used management development programs: leadership training and the use of behavior modeling to develop interpersonal and other skills.

### LEADERSHIP TRAINING

Leadership has been one of the most heavily researched and popularly discussed topics in management. As any organizational behavior text will attest, there is a wide array of leadership theories seeking to describe and predict effective leadership attributes.[131] There is a widespread belief that leadership skills are essential to effective management, especially for organizations that are trying to implement changes. At any time, dozens of books and popular press articles are available to managers to help them learn how they can become more effective leaders. Some of the problems with advice in the popular press on leadership are that it is usually anecdotal, lacks a sound theoretical basis, and is often contradictory. Leadership training is one of the most commonly offered forms of training, with 85 percent of the organizations surveyed in 2003 offering such training.[132] We will discuss how many organizations are using a multifaceted approach to developing leaders that is based on the notion of transformational leadership, as well as a program focused on leaders developing other leaders.

*TRANSFORMATIONAL LEADERSHIP: THE MISSING PIECE OF THE LEADERSHIP PUZZLE?* For many people, a leader is someone who captures our attention, presents us with a vision of what could be, inspires us to pursue the vision, and shows us the way to get there.[133] These ideas are at the heart of what Bernard Bass refers to as **transformational leadership.**[134] The main elements of transformational leadership include charisma (offering a vision and raising the self-expectations of followers), intellectual stimulation (helping followers change their assumptions and focus on rational solutions), and individualized consideration (e.g., providing coaching and individual development). This view of leadership is in contrast to a transactional approach, where the emphasis in on the exchange relationship between leader and follower, that is, "You give me your time and effort, and I'll give you this salary, the chance for promotion, and so on."

Transformational leadership seems to fit most people's ideas of what "real leaders" do (especially when they are leading an organizational change effort; organizational change will be discussed in Chapter 14). There is some evidence to suggest that the elements of transformational leadership are related to organizational outcomes.[135] Transformational leadership training is being developed and tested.[136] For example, Barling and colleagues operationalized transformational leadership training into a one-day group-training session followed by four monthly individual booster sessions.[137] The emphasis was placed on helping participants become more intellectually stimulating (a key transformational leadership element). In the one-day session, participants examined their own views of leadership, received a presentation about transformational and other types of leadership, learned about goal setting, and used role plays to practice goal setting and other leadership behaviors within the context of the organization's mission statement. The booster sessions consisted of goal setting to improve participants' leadership behavior and generating and reviewing action plans. In a two-group pretest-posttest study of managers (total $N = 20$) in a bank branch setting, Barling and colleagues found that managers in the training group were perceived by their subordinates as higher on all three aspects of transformational leadership. In addition, subordinates of the trained managers showed increased organizational commitment, and there was some evidence to suggest that branches in which the trained managers worked had better financial outcomes.

While research on transformational leadership training is in its early stages, there has been a large amount of recent research on this topic. For example, consecutive issues of *Leadership Quarterly* were devoted entirely to charismatic and transformational leadership theories.[138] Some important criticisms have been made of theory and research in this area,[139] and responses and new directions have been proposed.[140] Such debate and dialogue is healthy. In general, this line of research offers a positive example of taking a theoretically based, scientific approach to leadership development. The exercise at the end of the chapter asks you to profile someone you think is an effective leader.

*LEADERSHIP DEVELOPMENT: THE STATE OF THE PRACTICE.* Leadership development in organizations, although not always theory based, has seen a number of high-profile changes that have been driven by organizations' need to compete in a turbulent, uncertain environment. While many examples have appeared in the popular and practitioner literature, we will describe two approaches to give the reader a sense of how practical concerns are driving the state of the practice.

One recent approach in leadership development can be referred to as *leaders developing leaders.* This trend is signified by the direct, frequent involvement of CEOs and senior managers in developing a cadre of leaders within their organizations. For example, at organizations such as Intel, PepsiCo, GE, AlliedSignal, Shell Oil, and the U.S. Navy SEALs, the chief officers see leadership development as one of their primary responsibilities.[141] Cohen and Tichy argue that transformational leadership is the type of leadership that investors are demanding of corporate executives.[142] After investigating best practices in leadership development approaches at a group of top organizations, Cohen and Tichy concluded that the key to these approaches is that leaders must develop leaders. This involves the following ideas on why and how to develop leaders (pp. 60–61):

- Winners are judged by their sustained success.
- Winning companies have leaders at every level.
- The best way to get more leaders is to have leaders develop leaders.
- To develop others, leaders must have a teachable point of view.
- Leaders create stories about the future of their organizations.

Two of these ideas deserve special note: a teachable point of view and storytelling. According to Cohen and Tichy, a teachable point of view focuses on four leadership areas: *ideas* about products, services, and the marketplace, and a real-world explanation of the leader's *values, edge* (making the tough, go-no go decisions), and *energy* (motivating and energizing others). The teachable point of view must then be articulated in the form of a business-oriented story based on the leader's experience. Cohen and Tichy argue that stories are an engaging, personal way to communicate a leader's vision for the future. The key elements of a leader's story appear to be making a case for change, presenting an idea of where the organization is headed, and showing how the organization will get there.

Cohen and Tichy offer examples of how a leadership development approach based on these ideas was implemented at Shell Oil Company at Shell's Learning Center.[143] The key role for HRD professionals in this approach is to "help leaders craft their teaching approaches. That requires HRD staff to play a different role by collaborating with the leaders and 'driving' the cultural mindset in which teaching and leadership are intertwined" (p. 73).

A second approach to leadership development is the Center for Creative Leadership's LeaderLab.[144] The goal of the program is to prepare and encourage leaders to act more effectively in the leadership situations they face.[145] The program is based on research done at CCL and elsewhere on the nature of leadership and leader development. It lasts six months, beginning with a weeklong session in which participants undergo a range of assessment and feedback exercises (including 360-degree feedback obtained in advance from their superiors, subordinates, and peers) and development of an action plan for leadership improvement. These sessions include working in teams with "change partners," action-oriented exercises, and nontraditional learning activities such as creating pieces of art. A second four-day session occurs three months later, in which the manager's progress and learning over the three months is reviewed, and the action plan is revised accordingly. The revised action plan is then implemented over the remaining three months.[146]

These are only two examples of the kinds of approaches organizations are taking to develop leaders. Given the importance many organizations and stakeholders place on leadership, it is critical that HRD professionals design and deliver leadership development approaches that advance their own organization's ability to compete and blend relevant theory and methodology with ongoing efforts at evaluation and modification.

## BEHAVIOR MODELING TRAINING

Behavior modeling training is a popular training technique that has been used primarily to train people to perform manual, interpersonal, and cognitive skills.[147] The technique is based on Bandura's social learning theory, which was applied to supervisory training by Goldstein and Sorcher.[148] The underlying rationale for this form of training is that people can learn by observing other people (models) perform a task provided they are shown clearly what the components of the behavior are, remember what the behavior is, actually perform the behavior, and are motivated to use what they have learned.[149]

**Behavior modeling** typically involves five steps: modeling, retention, rehearsal, feedback, and transfer of training. During the **modeling phase,** trainees are usually shown a video clip in which a model performs the behavior to be learned. The desired behavior is broken into a series of discrete **learning points,** or key behaviors that make up the overall behavior. For example, if supervisors were being trained to handle employee complaints, the video would show a supervisor handling complaints in the desired manner. The learning points for this behavior might include:

1. Listen openly.
2. Do not speak until the employee has had his or her say.
3. Avoid reacting emotionally (do not get defensive).
4. Ask for the employee's expectations about a solution to the problem.
5. Agree on specific steps to be taken and specific deadlines.[150]

In the **retention phase,** trainees perform activities to enhance the memory of what they have observed. These activities include reviewing the learning points, discussing the rationale underlying each point, and talking over the behaviors the model performed to illustrate those points. In the **rehearsal phase,** each trainee role plays the desired behavior with another trainee. For example, each trainee learning how to handle employee complaints would have an opportunity to role play resolving a complaint from another trainee representing the complaining employee.

During the **feedback phase,** each trainee receives feedback on his or her performance based on what was done well and what should be improved. Finally, in the **transfer of training phase,** trainees are encouraged to practice the newly learned behavior on the job. In some behavior modeling programs, trainees regroup later to discuss problems and successes in using their newly learned skills.

Two examples of behavior modeling training applied to the mastery of computer software programs were reported by Gist and colleagues, and Simon and Werner.[151] In the Gist et al. study, trainees observed a videotape in which the model illustrated the steps involved in performing each task to be learned. The video also reviewed key learning points and showed trainees the responses to expect from the program on the computer monitor. Following a demonstration of each step, the trainer stopped the videotape to allow trainees to perform it, with the responses from the program on the computer monitor providing feedback as to the correctness of the trainee's performance. In the Simon and Werner study, Navy personnel were trained to use a new computer system using three different approaches: a lecture approach (using Microsoft PowerPoint® slides), a self-paced approach (using individual workbooks), and a behavior modeling approach, where the instructor demonstrated ("modeled") the correct procedures on a computer display viewed by all trainees. Both learning and behavioral retention were significantly higher for trainees who received the behavior modeling approach than for those trained using the other two approaches.

Beyond these two studies, there is growing research evidence supporting the effectiveness of behavior modeling training. Research has generally supported the technique's effectiveness.[152] Burke and Day's meta-analysis of management training found that behavior modeling was among the most effective management training techniques for learning and behavioral change.[153] A separate meta-analysis found similar effects for learning and behavioral change, and also sizable effects from behavior modeling interventions on various results measures (from productivity changes to increased free-throw shooting accuracy for a women's basketball team).[154]

One of the reasons that behavior modeling seems to be effective is that it increases a trainee's feelings of self-efficacy, which is one's belief in his or her capacity to perform a particular task (see Chapter 2).[155] Individuals with high self-efficacy tend to perform better than individuals with low self-efficacy.[156]

Research has suggested how behavior modeling works and how it can be improved.[157] For example, a series of studies has demonstrated the importance of learning points in the process. *Learning points* keyed to important behaviors and demonstrated by the model result in greater recall and performance of those behaviors.[158] In addition, research suggests that learning points generated by trainees led to better performance than learning points generated by "experts."[159]

Baldwin examined two ways such training may be improved: by providing multiple scenarios during training and by exposing trainees to both positive and negative models.[160] Baldwin suggested that providing multiple scenarios may increase the chances trainees would generalize the skills they learn to apply them to other situations. He also theorized that providing negative models as well as positive models would help trainees not only learn new behaviors but unlearn prior, ineffective behaviors. Baldwin reported two significant findings: (1) that providing both positive and negative models led to greater generalization than using positive models only, but (2) that viewing only positive models led only to greater reproduction of the behavior learned than viewing both positive and negative models.[161] These results suggest that different approaches to using models in behavior modeling training may be needed, depending on the goals of the training (e.g., reproducing a behavior in a particular type of situation or being able to use the behavior in a variety of situations).

Behavior modeling is not without its critics. Parry and Reich argue that the technique can have several weaknesses, including the following:

1. Modeling uses simplistic behavior models.

2. Trainees may not get explanations of the theory underlying the need for the behaviors being taught. For example, suppose the training session focuses on handling abusive customers. If trainees are told they should let the customer vent his feelings, they should be told why.

3. The classes may be boring because they follow a similar format and have all trainees in a session perform the same role playing.

4. Examples of incorrect behavior are seldom used, even though they provide opportunities for learning.

5. If verbal behavior is being taught, then the use of film or video might interfere by adding extraneous stimuli. Written models may be better for these cases.

6. Many trainees engage in improvisational acting rather than true role playing.

7. While focusing on behaviors rather than underlying attitudes may be effective in the short run, it is important to change attitudes as well. Otherwise, employees will not stick with the newly learned behaviors over the long haul.[162]

Parry and Reich believe the technique can be effective if these limitations are overcome.[163] Rosenbaum replied to Parry and Reich's criticisms by suggesting, among other things, that the design and delivery of behavior modeling training requires rigorous technique, that models serve as points of reference rather than purporting to show the only way to handle a situation, and that modeling conforms to the tenets of adult learning.[164] This sort of debate is healthy, and combined with research on ways to improve modeling training, can lead to better ways of using behavior modeling to help managers (and others) improve their interpersonal (and other) skills.[165] Pescuric and Byham note that behavior modeling training is also amenable to an interactive, computer-based self-study format.[166] They suggest that classroom-based delivery, the traditional approach to behavior modeling training, is only one of four options that can be used. The other three include classroom training augmented by on-the-job practice under the guidance of a coach; self-study of the principles, model, and application components followed by practice in a classroom setting; and self-study followed by on-the-job practice. Those who wish to use the technique should consult Goldstein and Sorcher,[167] plus books written by Decker and Nathan, as well as Silberman, for specifics on how to develop a program.[168]

## DESIGNING EFFECTIVE MANAGEMENT DEVELOPMENT PROGRAMS

While this should not surprise you, management development programs need to be constructed the way any sound HRD program is: through needs assessment, design, implementation, and evaluation. The HRD process model (A DImE) emphasized so heavily in previous chapters needs to be applied to management education and development efforts as well. More specifically, the issues discussed in this chapter lead to several recommendations and reminders:

1. Management development must *be tied to the organization's strategic plan* to be responsive to the needs of the organization and those of the individuals being developed.

2. A *thorough needs assessment,* including investigating what managers in the organization do and the skills they need to perform effectively, is essential.

3. *Specific objectives*, both for the overall program and for each of its components, (e.g., on-the-job experiences, classroom training) should be established.

4. *Involvement in and commitment of senior management in all phases* of the process, from needs assessment to evaluation, is critical. Simply stated, it is management's responsibility to ensure that the organization has a high quality management team.

5. A *variety of developmental opportunities*, both formal and on the job, should be used. Further, as emphasized by action learning advocates, there must be a linkage between what is learned in the classroom and what people are actually doing in their jobs.

6. The program should be designed to ensure that the individuals to be developed are *motivated to participate* in such activities. The day-to-day demands placed on managers at all levels make it easy to put development issues on the back burner.

7. Action should be taken to *evaluate* the program regularly and *modify and update* it as needs change.

While this list contains nothing new or startling (especially coming in the thirteenth chapter of this text!), many management development programs do not conform to these basic expectations. We present you with the "ideal," realizing full well that reality often falls short of this. Ghoshal and colleagues have called for a new, more proactive role for managers in organizations and society.[169] In our view, effective management education and development efforts will be critical for managers to successfully take on this new role. Prescriptions such as those on our previous list take on added significance given the environmental turbulence currently facing organizations and their managers. As stated by Longenecker and Ariss, "The competitive climate of the twenty-first century dictates that organizations take a more proactive posture regarding management education and development in order to stay competitive" (p. 651).[170] Effective managers remain critical for organizational effectiveness, and management development is a primary means of ensuring that managers have the knowledge and competencies necessary to be effective, both now and in the future. Whether you manage other employees, or never wish to, we hope that you see the importance of this topic to your own lives and careers.

## RETURN TO OPENING CASE

This challenging situation was faced by a large community hospital in New York City. Two management consultants were hired who worked together with executives and human resource professionals at the hospital to design and implement a management training program. This program was first offered to executives, and then to seventeen middle-level hospital managers. A particular focus of the training was on linking the strategic needs of the organization with the individual training needs of participants. Your instructor has additional information on the program and the outcomes obtained by it.

## SUMMARY

Management development is one of the most widely offered and important forms of HRD. It should be deliberate, long-term oriented, specific to the organization, and tied to the organization's strategic plan.

While one would expect that existing research on the managerial job would provide a clear picture of what managers do, the competencies they need, and how they develop, there is much we still do not know. This chapter presented several ways this issue has been addressed and emphasized the importance of careful study by HRD researchers and practitioners to better answer questions about the managerial job when designing management development programs for their own organizations.

Options for management education include college and university degree programs and executive education. In addition, we also explored organizationally based training and experience methods, including courses and programs, corporate academies or universities, and on-the-job experiences.

To illustrate the content of some of the approaches used in management development, we described two common training programs: leadership training and behavior modeling training. Two approaches to leadership development were presented, transformational leadership, and leaders developing leaders. Behavior modeling training involves learning by observing a model perform the behavior in question. Trainees are usually shown a videotape of a model performing the behavior. They discuss the components of the behavior, practice the behavior by role playing, and receive constructive feedback on their performance. This form of training has been shown to be effective for both motor and interpersonal skills.

The chapter closed with a list of recommendations for designing effective management development programs.

## KEY TERMS AND CONCEPTS

action learning
behavior modeling
characteristics approach
Developmental Challenge
  Profile (DCP)
executive education
executive M.B.A. (E.M.B.A.)
  programs
feedback phase
four-dimensional model
integrated competency model

learning points
management development
management education
management training
modeling phase
on-the-job experiences
rehearsal phase
retention phase
transfer of training phase
transformational leadership

## QUESTIONS FOR DISCUSSION

1. Explain why management development is one of the most common HRD activities found in organizations today.

2. Given the current trends toward empowerment and employing fewer levels of management, how important do you believe management development will be in the next ten years? Support your answer.

3. Why is it important for an HRD practitioner to understand managerial roles and competencies? How are these assessed? How is this information used as a needs assessment in designing a management development program?

4. Efforts to accurately and completely describe the job of managing have met with considerable frustration. Why do you think the job of managing has proved so difficult to pin down? Which of the ideas and models offered so far do you believe to be the most useful in guiding management development? Support your choice.

5. Compare and contrast management education, management training, and on-the-job experiences. How can these be combined in a strategic management development program?

6. Briefly describe the key advantages and disadvantages of the three approaches to management education. Under what conditions would you recommend that an organization send its managers to an executive M.B.A. program?

7. Explain how management education prepares a manager for his or her role. What are the different forms of management education? Can they be substituted by training or on-the-job experiences? Why or why not?

8. Explain the role on-the-job experience plays in a manager's development. Identify two ways an organization can increase the chances that the on-the-job experiences its managers encounter will be developmental experiences.

PART 3: HUMAN RESOURCE DEVELOPMENT APPLICATIONS

9. Describe how managing in a global environment can differ from the traditional approach to managing. Describe one way that we can develop managers to be more successful in a global environment.

10. Briefly describe the components of the behavior modeling approach to training. Describe how you would use these components to design a behavior modeling session that trains supervisors to effectively obtain an employee's agreement for improved performance.

## EXERCISE: PROFILING AN EFFECTIVE LEADER[171]

Select an individual that you think is an effective leader. This can be someone real or fictitious, and can come from a movie, book, popular culture, or from history. You are urged to select someone whom you find personally compelling or interesting. In your opinion, what factors or attributes contributed to this person's effectiveness as a leader? How could people be trained to increase more of the attributes you identified in your target leader? Your instructor will give you guidance in terms of the length of the assignment you are to complete.

Visit *http://werner.swlearning.com* for links to informative websites for this chapter.

## REFERENCES

1. Bureau of Labor Statistics (2004). Retrieved November 12, 2004, from http://www.bls.gov/news.release/ecopro.t02.htm; see also, Judy, R. W., & D'Amico, C. (1997). *Workforce 2020: Work and workers in the 21st century.* Indianapolis: Hudson Institute.

2. Campbell, J. P., Dunnette, M. D., Lawler, E. E., & Weick, K. E., Jr. (1970). *Managerial behavior, performance, and effectiveness.* New York: McGraw-Hill.

3. McCall, M. W., Jr., Lombardo, M. M., & Morrison, A. M. (1988). *The lessons of experience: How successful executives develop on the job* (p. 147). Lexington, MA: Lexington Books.

4. Schoenfeldt, L. F., & Steger, J. A. (1990). Identification and development of management talent. In G. R. Ferris & K. M. Rowland (Eds.), *Organizational entry* (pp. 191–251). Greenwich, CT: JAI Press.

5. McCall et al. (1988), *supra* note 3.

6. Keys, B., & Wolfe, J. (1988). Management education and development: Current issues and emerging trends. *Journal of Management, 14,* 205–229; Wexley, K. N., & Baldwin, T. T. (1986). Management development. *Journal of Management, 12,* 277–294.

7. Keys & Wolfe (1988), *supra* note 6, p. 205.

8. *Ibid;* Wexley & Baldwin (1986), *supra* note 6.

9. Galvin, T. (2003). Industry Report 2003. *Training, 40*(9), 21–38.

10. Saari, L. M., Johnson, T. R., McLaughlin, S. D., & Zimmerle, D. M. (1988). A survey of management training and education practices in U.S. companies. *Personnel Psychology, 41,* 731–743.

11. Beatty, R. W., Schneier, C. E., & McEvoy, G. M. (1987). Executive development and management succession. *Personnel and Human Resources Management, 5,* 289–322; Schoenfeldt & Steger (1990), *supra* note 4.

12. Bray, D. W., Campbell, R. J., & Grant, D. L. (1974). *Formative years in business: A long-term AT&T study of managerial lives.* New York: Wiley; Howard, A., & Bray, D. W. (1988). *Managerial lives in transition: Advancing age and changing times.* New York: Guilford Press.

13. Schoenfeldt & Steger (1990), *supra* note 4.

14. McCall, M. W., Jr., Morrison, A. M., & Hannan, R. L. (1978). *Studies of managerial work: Results and methods.* (Tech Report No. 14). Greensboro, NC: Center for Creative Leadership.

15. Schoenfeldt & Steger (1990), *supra* note 4, p. 196.

16. Fayol, H. (1949). *General and industrial management* (C. Storrs, Trans.). London: Pitman.

17. Mintzberg, H. (1973). *The nature of managerial work.* New York: Harper & Row; Mintzberg, H. (1975). The manager's job: Folklore and fact. *Harvard Business Review, 53*(4), 49–61.

18. Carroll, S. J., & Gillen, D. J. (1987). Are the classical management functions useful in describing managerial work? *Academy of Management Review, 12,* 38–51.

19. Tornow, W. W., & Pinto, P. R. (1976). The development of a managerial job taxonomy: A system for describing, classifying, and evaluating executive positions. *Journal of Applied Psychology, GI,* 410–418.

20. Schoenfeldt & Steger (1990), *supra* note 4.

21. Boyatzis, R. E. (1982). *The competent manager: A model for effective performance.* New York: Wiley.

22. Manners, G., & Steger, J. A. (1976). Behavioral specifications of the R&D management role. *IEEE Transactions in Engineering Management, 23,* 139–141; Manners, G., & Steger, J. A. (1979). Implications of research in the R&D management role for the selection and training of R&D managers. *R & D Management, 9,* 85–92; Schoenfeldt, 1979 — no citing in references.

23. Albanese, R. (1988). Competency-based management education. *Journal of Management Development, 8*(2), 66–76.

24. Boyatzis (1982), *supra* note 21.

25. Smith, M. E. (1992). The search for executive skills. *Training & Development, 46*(11), 88–95.

26. McLagan, P. A. (1997). Competencies: The next generation. *Training & Development, 51*(5), 40–47.

27. Schoenfeldt & Steger (1990), *supra* note 4.

28. This is an example of the use of the critical incident technique, which we described in Chapter 4.

29. Barrett, G. V., & Depinet, R. L. (1991). A reconsideration of testing for competence rather than for intelligence. *American Psychologist, 46,* 1012–1024.

30. Boyatzis (1982), *supra* note 21.

31. Schoenfeldt & Steger (1990), *supra* note 4.

32. *Ibid.*

33. Mintzberg, H. (1994), Rounding out the manager's job. *Sloan Management Review, 36*(1), 11–26; Vaill, P. B. (1989). *Managing as a performing art: New ideas for a world of chaotic change.* San Francisco: Jossey-Bass.

34. Mintzberg (1994), *supra* note 33, p. 11.

35. Vaill (1989), *supra* note 33.

36. *Ibid*, pp. 114–115.

37. *Ibid*, p. 35.

38. Mintzberg (1994), *supra* note 33.

39. Saari et al. (1988), *supra* note 10.

40. Chiu, W., Thompson, D., Mak, W.-M., & Lo, K. L. (1999). Re-thinking training needs analysis: A proposed framework for literature review. *Personnel Review, 28*(1/2), 77–90.

41. LaHote, D., Simonetti, J. L., & Longenecker, C. O. (1999). Management training and development at Aeroquip-Vickers, Inc.: A process model, Part 1. *Industrial and Commercial Training, 31*(4), 132–135; LaHote, D., Simonetti, J. L., & Longenecker, C. O. (1999). Management training and development at Aeroquip-Vickers, Inc.: A process model, Part 2. *Industrial and Commercial Training, 31*(6), 213–218.

42. Salopek, J. J. (2004). Leading indicators: Leadership development in action. *T&D, 58*(3), March, 16–18.

43. Patton, W. D., & Pratt, C. (2002). Assessing the training needs of high-potential managers. *Public Personnel Management, 31*(4), 465–484.

44. Sutton, E. E., & McQuigg-Martinetz, B. (1990). The development partnership: Managing skills for the future. *Training and Development Journal, 44*(4), 63–70.

45. Adler, N. J., & Bartholomew, S. (1992). Managing globally competent people. *The Executive, 6*(3), 52–65; Bartlett, C. A., & Ghoshal, S. (1992). What is a global manager? *Harvard Business Review, 70*(5), 124–132; Bogorya, Y. (1985). Intercultural development for managers involved in international business. *Journal of Management Development, 4*(2), 17–25; Murray, F. T., & Murray, A. H. (1986). SMR forum: Global managers for global business. *Sloan Management Review, 27*(2), 75–80.

46. Bartlett and Ghoshal (1992), *supra* note 45.

47. *Ibid.*

48. Adler and Bartholomew (1992), *supra* note 45.

49. *Ibid.*

50. *Ibid;* Bartlett & Ghosal (1992), *supra* note 45.

51. Spreitzer, G. M., McCall, M. W., Jr., & Mahoney, J. D. (1997). Early identification of international executive potential. *Journal of Applied Psychology, 82*, 6–29.

52. *Ibid.*

53. Townsend, P., & Cairns, L. (2003). Developing the global manager using a capability framework. *Management Learning, 34*(3), 313–327.

54. Spreitzer et al. (1997), *supra* note 51.

55. Allred, B. B., Snow, C. C., & Miles, R. E. (1996). Characteristics of managerial careers in the 21st century. *The Academy of Management Executive, 10*(4), 17–27.

56. Downham, T. A., Noel, J. L., & Prendergast, A. E. (1992). Executive development. *Human Resource Management, 31,* 95–107; Seibert, K. W., Hall, D. T., & Kram, K. E. (1995). Strengthening the weak link in strategic executive development: Integrating individual development and global business strategy. *Human Resource Management, 34,* 549–567.

57. Davis, P., Naughton, J., & Rothwell, W. (2004). New roles and new competencies for the profession. *T&D, 58*(4), 26–36.

58. Seibert et al. (1995), *supra* note 56.

59. Burack, E. H., Hochwarter, W., & Mathys, N. J. (1997). The new management development paradigm. *Human Resource Planning, 20*(1), 14–21.

60. Seibert et al. (1995), *supra* note 56.

61. *Ibid.*

62. Seibert et al. (1995), *supra* note 56; Burack et al. (1997), *supra* note 59.

63. Peters, T. J., & Waterman, R. H. (1982). *In search of excellence: Lessons from America's best run companies.* New York: Warner Books.

64. Peters, T. (1996, Dec. 2). The search for excellence continues. *Forbes ASAP,* 239–240.

65. Seibert et al. (1995), *supra* note 56; Burack et al. (1997), *supra* note 59.

66. Porter, L. W., & McKibbin, L. E. (1988). *Management education and development: Drift of thrust into the 21st century?* New York: McGraw-Hill.

67. Digest of Education Statistics (2003). Tables 265, 268, and 271. Retrieved November 13, 2004, from http://nces.ed.gov/programs/digest/d03/list_tables3.asp#c3a_5

68. *Ibid.*

69. American Assembly of Collegiate Schools of Business (1996, July 23). Business accreditation standards. <wweb\stand5.html>

70. *Ibid.*

71. Porter & McKibbin (1988), *supra* note 66.

72. *Ibid.*

73. Byrne, J. A. (1991, May 13). Wharton rewrites the book on B-schools. *Business Week,* 43.

74. Boyatzis R. E., Cowen, S. S., & Kolb, D. A. (1995). Management of knowledge: Redesigning the Weatherhead MBA program. In R. E. Boyatzis, S. S. Cowen, D. A. Kolb, & Associates, *Innovation in professional education: Steps on a journey from teaching to learning* (pp. 32–49). San Francisco: Jossey-Bass.

75. *Ibid.*

76. *Ibid.*

77. Boyatzis R. E., Baker, A., Leonard, D., Rhee, K., & Thompson, L. (1995). Will it make a difference? Assessing a value-added, outcome-oriented, competency-based program. In R. E. Boyatzis, S. S. Cowen, D. A. Kolb, & Associates, *Innovation in professional education: Steps on a journey from teaching to learning* (pp. 167–202). San Francisco: Jossey-Bass, p. 179.

78. Byrne et al. (1996), *supra* note 65.

79. Phillips, V. (1998). Online universities teach knowledge beyond the books. *HR Magazine, 43*(8), July, 121–128.

80. For example, Chen, G., Donohue, L. M., & Klimoski, R. J. (2004). Training undergraduates to work in organizational teams. *Academy of Management Learning & Education, 3*(1), 27–40; Fairfield, K. D., & London, M. B. (2003). Tuning into the music of groups: A metaphor for team-based learning in management education. *Journal of Management Education, 27*(6), 654–672; Mello, J. A. (2003). Profiles in leadership: Enhancing learning through model and theory building. *Journal of Management Education, 27*(3), 344–361; O'Connell, D. J., McCarthy, J. F., & Hall, D. T. (2004). Print, video, or the CEO: The impact of media in teaching leadership with the case method. *Journal of Management Education, 28*(3), 294–318.

81. Linder, J. C., & Smith, H. J. (1992). The complex case of management education. *Harvard Business Review, 70*(5), 16–33.

82. Byrne, J. A. (1995, October 23). Virtual B-schools. *Business Week,* 64–68.

83. Byrne (1991), *supra* note 73.

84. Porter & McKibbin (1988), *supra* note 66.

85. Byrne (1991), *supra* note 73.

86. Andrews, K. R. (1966). *The effectiveness of university management development programs.* Boston: Harvard University; Hollenbeck, G. P. (1991). What did you learn in school? Studies of a university executive program. *Human Resource Planning, 14*(4), 247–260.

87. Fresina, A, J., & Associates. (1988). *Executive education in corporate America.* Palatine, IL: Anthony J. Fresina and Associates.

88. Eurich, N. P. (1990). *The learning industry: Education for adult workers.* Lawrenceville, NJ: Princeton University Press; Porter & McKibbin (1988), *supra* note 66.

89. Industry Report (1996). Who's learning what? *Training, 33*(10), 55–66.

90. Galvin (2003), *supra* note 9.

91. Mainstone, L. E., & Schroeder, D. M. (1999). Management education in the information age. *Journal of Management Education, 23,* 630–634.

92. Byrne (1995), *supra* note 82.

93. Porter & McKibbin (1988), *supra* note 66.

94. Byrne (1995), *supra* note 82.

95. Porter & McKibbin (1988), *supra* note 66.

96. Tham, C. M., & Werner, J. M. (2004). Designing and evaluating E-learning in higher education: A review and recommendations. *Journal of Leadership and Organizational Studies, 11*(2), 15–25.

97. Hequet, M. (1992). Executive education: The custom alternative. *Training, 29*(4), 38–41.

98. *Ibid.*

99. *Ibid.*

100. Vicere, A. A. (1996). Executive education: The leading edge. *Organizational Dynamics, 25*(2), August, 67–81.

101. Weir, D., & Smallman, C. (1998). Managers in the year 2000 and after: A strategy for development. *Management Development, 36*(1), 43–51.

102. Alutto, J. A. (1999). Just-in-time management education in the 21st century. *HR Magazine, 44*(11), 56–57.

103. Townsend & Cairns (2003), *supra* note 53; Bilimoria, D. (2000). Redoing management education's missions and methods. *Journal of Management Education, 24*, 161–166.

104. Lee, C. (1991). Who gets trained in what — 1991. *Training, 28*(10), 47–59; Saari et al. (1988), *supra* note 10.

105. Mabey, C. (2002). Mapping management development practice. *Journal of Management Studies, 39*(8), 1139–1160.

106. Tichy, N. M. (1989). GE's Crotonville: A staging ground for corporate revolution. *The Academy of Management Executive, 3*, 99–107.

107. *Ibid.*

108. Downham et al. (1992), *supra* note 56.

109. Allen, M. (2002). *The corporate university handbook: Designing, managing & growing a successful program.* New York: AMA; Corporate universities open their doors. (2000). *Manager Intelligence Report*, October, 6–8.

110. Eurich (1990), *supra* note 88; Odiorne, G. S., & Rummler, G. A. (1988). *Training and development: a guide for professionals.* Chicago: Commerce Clearing House.

111. Odiorne & Rummler (1988), *supra* note 110.

112. Eurich (1990), *supra* note 88, p. 167.

113. Meister, J. C. (1993). *Corporate quality universities: Lessons in building a world-class work force.* Burr Ridge, IL: Irwin Professional Publishing.

114. Gerbman, R. V. (2000). Corporate universities 101. *HR Magazine, 45*(2), February, 101–106; Meister, J. C. (1998). Ten steps to creating a corporate university. *Training & Development, 52*(11), November, 38–43; Corporate universities: The new pioneers of management education. (1998). *Harvard Management Update*, October, 5–7; Densford, L. E. (2000). Motorola University: The next 20 years. *Corporate University Review*, January/February, 15–23.

115. Digman, L. A. (1978). How well-managed organizations develop their executives. *Organizational Dynamics, 7*(2), 63–80; McCall et al. (1988), *supra* note 3; Zemke, R. (1985). The Honeywell studies: How managers learn to manage. *Training, 22*(8), 46–51.

116. McCauley, C. D., Ruderman, M. N., Ohlott, P. J., & Morrow, J. E. (1994). Assessing the developmental components of managerial jobs. *Journal of Applied Psychology, 79*, 544–560; Wexley & Baldwin (1986), *supra* note 6.

117. Keys & Wolfe (1988), *supra* note 6.

118. McCall et al. (1988), *supra* note 3.

119. *Ibid.*

120. McCauley et al. (1994), *supra* note 116.

121. *Ibid.*

122. Heller, F. (2003). Action learning worldwide: Experiences of leadership and organizational development. *Management Learning, 34*(3), 386–389; Keys & Wolfe (1988), *supra* note 6; Fulmer, R. M. (1997). The evolving paradigm of leadership development. *Organizational Dynamics, 25*(4), 59–72.

PART 3: HUMAN RESOURCE DEVELOPMENT APPLICATIONS

123. Morgan, G., & Ramirez, R. (1983). Action learning: A holographic metaphor for guiding social change. *Human Relations, 37,* 1–28; Revans, R. (1982). What is action learning? *Journal of Management Development, 1*(3), 64–75.

124. McGill, I., & Brockbank, A. (2004). *The action learning handbook: Powerful techniques for education, professional development, and training.* London: Routledge Falmer; Keys & Wolfe, 1988, *supra* note 6.

125. Cohen, E., & Tichy, N. (1997). How leaders develop leaders. *Training & Development, 51*(5), 58–73; Tichy, N., & Sherman, S. (1993). *Control your destiny or someone else will: How Jack Welch is making GE the world's most competitive corporation.* New York: Doubleday; Downham et al. (1992), *supra* note 56.

126. Fulmer (1997), *supra* note 122.

127. Hirst, G., Mann, L., Bain, P., Pirola-Merlo, A., & Richver, A. (2004). Learning to lead: The development and testing of a model of leadership learning. *Leadership Quarterly, 15*(3), 311–327; Mumford, A. (1987). Action learning (Special Issue). *Journal of Management Development, 6*(2), 1–70.

128. Yorks, L., O'Neil, J., Marsick, V. J., Nilson, G. E., & Kolodny, R. (1996). Boundary management in Action Reflection Learning TM research: Taking the role of a sophisticated barbarian. *Human Resource Development Quarterly, 7,* 313–329; see also a response to this article, Baldwin, T. T. (1996). Invited reaction: Comments on feature article. *Human Resource Development Quarterly, 7,* 331–334.

129. Mumford, A. (1993). *Management development: Strategies for action* (2nd ed.). London: IPM.

130. Daudelin, M. W. (1996). Learning from experience through reflection. *Organizational Dynamics, 24*(3), 36–48.

131. For example, Nelson, D. L., & Quick, J. C. (2006). *Organizational behavior* (5th ed.). Mason, OH: Thomson/South-Western.

132. Galvin (2003), *supra* note 9.

133. Levasseur, R. E. (2004). People skills: Change management tools — The modern leadership model. *Interfaces, 34*(2), 147–148.

134. Bass, B. M. (1985). *Leadership and performance beyond expectations.* New York: Basic Books; Bass, B. M. (1990). From transactional to transformational leadership: Learning to share the vision. *Organizational Dynamics, 18*(3), 19–36.

135. Barling, J., Weber, T., & Kelloway, E. K. (1996). Effects of transformational leadership training on attitudinal and financial outcomes: A field experiment. *Journal of Applied Psychology, 81,* 827–832.

136. Popper, M., Landau, O., & Gluskinos, U. M. (1992). The Israeli defense forces: an example of transformational leadership. *Leadership and Organizational Development Journal, 13*(1), 3–8; Barling et al. (1996), *supra* note 135.

137. Barling et al. (1996), *supra* note 135.

138. For example, Conger, J. A. (1999). Charismatic and transformational leadership in organizations: An insider's perspective on these developing streams of research. *Leadership Quarterly, 10*(2), 145–169; Hunt, J. G., & Conger, J. A. (1999). Overview — charismatic and transformational leadership: Taking stock of the present and future (Part II). *Leadership Quarterly, 10*(3), 331–334.

139. Shamir, B. (1999). An evaluation of conceptual weaknesses in transformational and charismatic leadership theories. *Leadership Quarterly, 10*(2), 285–305; Beyer, J. (1999). Taming and promoting charisma to change organizations. *Leadership Quarterly, 10*(2), 307–330.

140. Shamir, B. (1999). Taming charisma for better understanding and greater usefulness: A response to Beyer. *Leadership Quarterly, 10*(4), 555–562; Mumford, M. D., Zaccaro, S. J., Connelly, M. S., & Marks, M. A. (2000). Leadership skills: Conclusions and future directions. *Leadership Quarterly, 11*(1), 155–170.

141. Cohen & Tichy (1997), *supra* note 125; Sherman, S. (1995, November 27). How tomorrow's best leaders are learning their stuff. *Fortune,* 90–102.

142. Cohen & Tichy (1997), *supra* note 125.

143. *Ibid.*

144. Vicere (1996), *supra* note 100; Bongiorno, L. (1995, October 23). How'm I doing? *Business Week,* 72–73.

145. Vicere (1996), *supra* note 100.

146. *Ibid.*

147. May, G. L., & Kahnweiler, W. M. (2000). The effect of a mastery practice design on learning and transfer in behavior modeling training, *Personnel Psychology, 53*(2), 353–373.

148. Goldstein, A. P., & Sorcher, M. (1974). *Changing supervisor behavior.* Elmsford, NY: Pergamon Press.

149. Decker, P. J., & Nathan, B. R. (1985). *Behavior modeling training: Principles and applications.* New York: Praeger.

150. *Ibid,* p. 145.

151. Gist, M. E., Schwoerer, C., & Rosen, B. (1989). Effects of alternative training methods on self-efficacy and performance in computer software training. *Journal of Applied Psychology, 74,* 884–891; Simon, S. J., & Werner, J. M. (1996). Computer training through behavior modeling, self-paced, and instructional approaches: A field experiment. *Journal of Applied Psychology, 81,* 648–659.

152. Gist et al. (1989), *supra* note 151; Latham, G. P., & Saari, L. E. (1979). The application of social learning theory to training supervisors through behavior modeling. *Journal of Applied Psychology, 64,* 239–246; McGehee, W., & Tullar, W. L. (1978). A note on evaluating behavior modification and behavior modeling as industrial training techniques. *Personnel Psychology, 31,* 477–484; Meyer, H. H., & Raich, M. S. (1983). An objective evaluation of a behavior modeling training program. *Personnel Psychology, 36,* 755–761.

153. Burke, M. J., & Day, R. R. (1986). A cumulative study of the effectiveness of managerial training. *Journal of Applied Psychology, 71,* 232–245.

154. Werner, J. M., & Crampton, S. M. (1992). The impact of behavior modeling training on learning, behavior, and results criteria: A meta-analytic review. In M. Schnake (Ed.), *Proceedings* (pp. 279–284). Southern Management Association.

155. Bandura, A. (1986). *Social foundations of thought and action.* Englewood Cliffs, NJ: Prentice Hall.

156. Taylor, M. S., Locke, E. A., Lee, C., & Gist, M. E. (1984). Type A behavior and faculty research productivity: What are the mechanisms? *Organizational Behavior and Human Performance, 34,* 402–418.

157. Decker, P. J. (1983). The effects of rehearsal group size and video feedback in behavior modeling training. *Personnel Psychology, 36,* 763–773; Decker, P. J. (1984). Effects of different symbolic coding stimuli in behavior modeling training. *Personnel Psychology, 37,* 711–720; Latham & Saari (1979), *supra* note 152.

158. Latham & Saari (1979), *supra* note 152; Mann, R. B., & Decker, P. J. (1984). The effect of key behavior distinctiveness on generalization and recall in behavior-modeling training. *Academy of Management Journal, 27,* 900–909.

159. Hogan, P. M., Hakel, M. D., & Decker, P. J. (1986). Effects of trainee-generated versus trainer-provided rule codes on generalization in behavior-modeling training. *Journal of Applied Psychology, 71,* 469, 473.

160. Baldwin, T. T. (1992). Effects of alternative modeling strategies on outcomes of interpersonal skills training. *Journal of Applied Psychology, 77,* 147–154.

161. This study also illustrates the importance of evaluating training at different levels, as recommended in Chapter 7.

162. Parry, S. B., & Reich, L. R. (1984). An uneasy look at behavior modeling. *Training and Development Journal, 30*(3) 57–62.

163. *Ibid.*

164. Rosenbaum, B. L. (1984). Back to behavior modeling. *Training and Development Journal, 30*(11), 88–89; Parry & Reich (1984), *supra* note 162.

165. Werner, J. M., O'Leary-Kelly, A. M., Baldwin, T. T., & Wexley, K. N. (1994). Augmenting behavior-modeling training: Testing the effects of pre- and post-training interventions. *Human Resource Development Quarterly, 5*(2), 169–183.

166. Pescuric, A., & Byham, W. C. (1996). The new look of behavior modeling. *Training & Development, 50*(7), 24–30.

167. Goldstein, A. P., & Sorcher, M. (1974). *Changing supervisor behavior.* Elmsford, NY: Pergamon Press.

168. Decker & Nathan (1985), *supra* note 149; Silberman, M. L. (1999). *Active learning: A handbook of techniques, designs, case examples, and tips.* San Francisco: Jossey-Bass/Pfeiffer.

169. Ghoshal, S., Bartlett, C. A., & Moran, P. (1999). A new manifesto for management. *Sloan Management Review, 40*(3), Spring, 9–20.

170. Longenecker, C. O., & Ariss, S. S. (2002). Creating competitive advantage through effective management education. *Journal of Management Development, 21*(9), 640–654.

171. Adapted from Mello, J. A. (2003). Profiles in leadership: Enhancing learning through model and theory building. *Journal of Management Education, 27*(3), 344–361.

14

# ORGANIZATION DEVELOPMENT AND CHANGE

## Learning Objectives:

*After reading this chapter, you should be able to:*

1. Define organization development (OD).

2. Understand the basic theories and concepts of OD.

3. Describe the planned-change model.

4. Explain the roles of the change agent, manager, and people within the system in developing an intervention strategy.

5. Understand the basic steps involved in designing an implementation strategy.

6. Explain the different types of human process-based intervention strategies.

7. Explain the different types of technostructural intervention strategies.

8. Explain the different types of sociotechnical intervention strategies.

9. Explain the different types of organization

transformation intervention strategies.

10. Describe the role of HRD practitioners in OD interventions.

## OPENING CASE

Extrusion (a pseudonym) is a Norwegian organization that sought to flatten its organizational structure and increase the amount of employee participation in the organization. The new CEO of the company was very enthusiastic about this idea, and enlisted the help of a management professor to document the progress and changes that should occur as a result of this major change in the organizational structure.

*Questions: If you were a consultant working on this change project, what issues would you raise before the organization switched to a flatter, more participative organizational structure? What issues or problems might this organization face as it seeks to make such a change? What types of things can it do to try to minimize these problems?*

## INTRODUCTION

In this chapter, we will emphasize:

- HRD interventions that focus on the group or organizational level
- Theories about how individuals, groups, and organizations successfully deal with change
- A model of planned change that integrates individual, group, and organizational-level variables
- Several HRD efforts that promote transformation of the organization as a whole
- A view of organizations as high performance work systems, where all parts are integrated and working together toward common goals

Change has become a way of life for most organizations. Pressure from increasing competition, globalization, technological developments, and other forces has created an environment that rewards organizations that are capable of identifying trends and issues and responding quickly to them.[1] The element of HRD that can best enable organizations to embrace and manage change is organization development.

## ORGANIZATION DEVELOPMENT DEFINED

**Organization development** (OD) is a process used to enhance both the effectiveness of an organization and the well-being of its members through planned interventions.[2] Notice three key points here. First, OD enhances the effectiveness of the organization. Effectiveness, in this context, is defined as achieving organizational goals and objectives.[3] Second, OD enhances the well-being of organization members. Well-being refers to the perceived overall satisfaction each organization member feels toward his or her job and work environment. Generally speaking, "having challenging and meaningful work leads to high work satisfaction and, if rewarded by the organization, to higher satisfaction with rewards as well."[4] Thus, OD is intended to enhance both personal and work satisfaction.

Third, OD is used to enhance the effectiveness of organizations and individual well-being through planned interventions. Planned interventions refer "to sets of structured activities in which selected organizational units (target groups or individuals) engage with a task or sequence of tasks where the task goals are related directly or indirectly to organizational improvement."[5] Thus, planned interventions, or **intervention strategies,** are the primary means through which organizational improvement and changes take place.

## PLAN OF THE CHAPTER

The purpose of this chapter is to define organizational development theories and concepts. First, we will introduce and discuss a model of planned change. Then, we will discuss the various roles involved in planning and implementing change strategies. Next, we will discuss four types of change strategies and some of the specific techniques used in each. Finally, we will discuss the role of the HRD professional in introducing and managing change.

## ORGANIZATION DEVELOPMENT THEORIES AND CONCEPTS

OD theories have evolved primarily from four academic disciplines — psychology, sociology, anthropology, and management. OD theory can be divided into two categories — change process theory and implementation theory.

### CHANGE PROCESS THEORY

Change process theory seeks to explain the dynamics through which organizational improvement and changes take place.[6] Kurt Lewin depicted the change process as occurring in three stages — unfreezing, moving, and refreezing.[7] The unfreezing stage involves the process of getting people to accept that change is inevitable, and to stop doing certain things that resist change (e.g., clinging to an ineffective current policy, practice, or behavior). The moving stage involves getting people to accept the new, desired state (e.g., new policies and practices). The last stage, refreezing, involves

| TABLE 14-1 | SCHEIN'S THREE-STAGE MODEL OF THE CHANGE PROCESS |
|---|---|

**Stage 1**  *Unfreezing* — Creating motivation and readiness to change through:
   a. disconfirmation or lack of confirmation
   b. creation of guilt or anxiety
   c. provision of psychological safety

**Stage 2**  *Changing* through cognitive restructuring — Helping the individual to see, judge, feel, and react differently based on a new point of view obtained through:
   a. identifying with a new role model, mentor, and so on
   b. scanning the environment for new relevant information

**Stage 3**  *Refreezing* — Helping the individual to integrate the new point of view into:
   a. his or her total personality and self-concept
   b. significant relationships

SOURCE: From E. H. Schein (1987). *Process consultation* (vol. 2, p. 93). Reading, MA: Addison-Wesley.

making the new practices and behaviors a permanent part of the operation or role expectations. Lewin viewed change as deriving from two forces: (1) those internally driven (from a person's own needs) and (2) those imposed or induced by the environment. Environmental forces can be further distinguished between driving (pushing for change) and restraining forces (those seeking to maintain the status quo). For change to be environmentally imposed, driving forces must outnumber restraining forces.

Edgar Schein further delineated each stage of Lewin's model (see Table 14-1).[8] The emphasis of Schein's Change Model is on the dynamics of individual change and how a change agent assists with managing these changes. At Stage 1 (unfreezing), the change agent motivates the person to accept change by disconfirming his or her attitudes, behaviors, or performance. For example, for an employee to correct poor work habits, he or she must first accept that his or her performance is inappropriate. At Stage 2 (changing through cognitive restructuring), the emphasis is on getting the employee to see and do things differently and to actually believe that by changing work habits, his or her performance will improve. Finally, at Stage 3 (refreezing), the change agent helps the person to integrate these new behaviors (work habits) into his or her thought patterns. This stage focuses on helping the employee to reconfirm his or her self-concept and reinforce desired performance standards.

Trader-Leigh provides an interesting case study of resistance hindering change efforts at the U.S. State Department.[9] As a counterpoint, Dent and Goldberg challenge the notion that individuals universally resist change.[10] They argue that,

> People may resist loss of status, loss of pay, or loss of comfort, but these are not the same as resisting change. . . . Employees may resist the unknown, being dictated to, or management ideas that do not seem feasible from the employees' standpoint. However, in our research, we have found few or no instances of employees resisting change (p. 26).[11]

Dent and Goldberg argue that Lewin's notion of resistance to change has been misunderstood, and that the proper focus should be at the systems level. That is, work takes place within a system of roles, attitudes, norms, and other factors, and thus, resistance to change should be viewed as an issue or problem for the whole organizational system, rather than focusing on individual employees.[12] This argument is similar to that put forward by proponents of the High Performance Work System concept, which we will cover at the end of this chapter. Dealing with individual-level change is clearly vital, yet this also needs to be understood and handled within the context of changes and forces operating within the organization as a whole.

## IMPLEMENTATION THEORY

Implementation theory focuses on specific intervention strategies that are designed to induce changes. We will briefly discuss some of the underlying theories and concepts of four types of interventions: human process-based, technostructural, sociotechnical systems (STS) designs, and large systems. Later in the chapter, we will go into more detail about specific types of OD interventions within each of these categories.

*HUMAN PROCESS-BASED INTERVENTION THEORY.* Human process-based theories, also known as human processual theories, place a heavy emphasis on the process of change, and focus on changing behaviors by modifying individual attitudes, values, problem-solving approaches, and interpersonal styles. The theoretical underpinnings of this approach are drawn from the behavioral sciences, particularly the need, expectancy, reinforcement, and job-satisfaction theories (see Chapter 2). The application of these theories to change interventions was pioneered in the 1950s by Lewin, in collaboration with others such as Lippitt, White, Likert, and McGregor. Lewin was able to transfer his knowledge of the way planned interventions produce desired behavioral changes in a social setting to organizational settings.[13] Lewin hypothesized that interventions should be directed at the group level rather than at the individual level. He felt that changing an individual's behavior without first changing group norms would be fruitless, because that individual would be viewed as a deviate and pressured to return to his or her former behavior pattern. Lewin's work led to the development of several OD intervention techniques, including survey feedback and force field analysis, which will be discussed later in the chapter.

Chris Argyris, another early pioneer of human process-based intervention strategies, postulated that the basic requirements of an intervention activity are valid information, free choice, and internal commitment.[14] To facilitate change, the person involved in the change should have useful information with which to diagnose the situation and then act on that information. Free choice implies that the person involved in the change process has the autonomy, control, and motivation to implement the intervention activity. Internal commitment implies that the person or persons involved in the change process have "ownership" of the strategy and, by implication, "have processed valid information and made an informed free choice."[15] Argyris's early work led to the development of several team-building techniques, including process consultation, role clarification, and confrontation meetings. Team building will be discussed later in the chapter.

*TECHNOSTRUCTURAL INTERVENTION THEORY.* **Technostructural theory** focuses on improving work content, work method, work flow, performance factors, and relationships among workers.[16] One of the key concepts with this approach is job design. A job has several distinguishing characteristics, including individual tasks or duties, responsibilities, authority, relationships, and skill requirements. Hackman and Oldham hypothesized that certain job characteristics affect employee psychological states, which in turn affect work outcomes and satisfaction.[17] They believe that changing one or more of a job's characteristics — a strategy called job enrichment — can induce positive psychological changes resulting in improved performance and satisfaction. Hackman and Oldham's work has been primarily applied to job redesign (job enrichment programs), an intervention tool for increasing job satisfaction and productivity.

Another dimension of technostructural intervention strategies is the level of participation in the change process. Many practitioners readily accept that the design should be "participative" without first understanding the impact of participation on the individual or organization.[18] Statements like "people will participate if given the opportunity" or "people prefer participation to nonparticipation" are too simplistic.[19] One difficulty for practitioners is that participation is still a vaguely defined construct.

*SOCIOTECHNICAL SYSTEMS (STS) DESIGNS.* **Sociotechnical systems (STS) interventions** are "directed at the fit between the technological configuration and the social structure of work units . . . [which] results in the rearrangement of relationships among roles or tasks or a sequence of activities to produce self-maintaining, semiautonomous groups."[20] Most of the early research in the 1960s and 1970s focused on quality of work life interventions. The projects focused on such things as industrial democratization, participative management, job enrichment, and work rescheduling interventions. The underlying emphasis of these projects was on the impact of such interventions on worker satisfaction and productivity.

At the same time that STS designs were being developed, W. E. Deming was pioneering techniques of employee involvement geared toward improving quality. In the early 1950s, Deming introduced these new concepts to U.S. corporations, which were initially not very receptive to his approaches. Deming later spoke to a group of Japanese industrialists who found his message consistent with their general business philosophy. With the application of Deming's concepts to STS theory, STS interventions have begun to focus on "empowering" the worker to assume more lateral responsibility for the work. These innovations include quality circles, total quality management, and self-managed teams.

*ORGANIZATION TRANSFORMATION CHANGE.* The theory of **organization transformation** (OT) change was pioneered by Beckhard, who viewed organizations as complex, human systems, each possessing a unique character, culture, and value system, along with "information and work procedures that must be continually examined, analyzed, and improved if optimum productivity and motivation are to result."[21] His approach assumes that there are numerous challenges facing managers, including changes in mission, ways of doing business, ownership, and the impact of downsizing. To meet these challenges, organizational leaders must be able to develop a vision guided by beliefs and principles that can be translated into mission and goals. The mission and goals should form the basis for managing the organization, effectively using technology, and distributing rewards. To do this effectively, organizational leaders must understand such things as the nature of culture and what it takes to change it, the significant role of values in an organization's life, the general sociopolitical nature of the world, technology, and, finally, the concepts of managing change effectively and of balancing stability and change.[22]

## LIMITATIONS OF RESEARCH SUPPORTING OD THEORIES

As in many areas of HRD, there are limitations in the research that has been conducted to test the underlying theoretical constructs of OD and the effectiveness of OD interventions.[23] These limitations include:

1. the lack of true experimental designs in most OD research
2. the lack of resources available to many OD practitioners
3. the limitations of field research designs
4. potential bias by OD evaluators (who are often the designers of the intervention)
5. simply a "lack of motivation" by the OD evaluator to do the job correctly[24]

In particular, it is difficult to isolate causality in such research. Applying traditional experimental strategies, which attempt to isolate causation, to OD interventions forces researchers to focus on a single intervention episode and overlook the systematic nature of organizations.[25] In addition, most OD research results are measured by changes in attitudes and behaviors. This is a limitation because attitudinal and behavioral changes are considered intervening variables and may have very little to do with the improvements in group and organization performance that OD interventions are ultimately intended to achieve.[26]

One significant methodological development is the application of meta-analysis to OD research. Meta-analysis is a set of analytical techniques that statistically combines the results of studies that are investigating the same variable or intervention, making it easier to draw conclusions from prior research. In addition to examining the effects of change interventions on dependent variables, meta-analysis also makes it possible to examine the effects of moderator variables (e.g., the technology used in the organization, organization types, and the rigor of the research study).[27] Meta-analysis also makes it possible to statistically remove possible effects of things such as reviewer bias.[28] Meta-analytic studies of OD research have made it easier to determine what we can gain from prior research.

## MODEL OF PLANNED CHANGE

The lack of fundamental OD research has underscored the need for a universally accepted model of planned change.[29] Because of the lack of a generic model, change process and intervention theories are "recklessly combined and crossed levels of abstraction, levels of analysis, and narrowly defined discipline boundaries."[30] The purpose of this section is to present a model of planned change that attempts to provide a framework for integrating OD theory, research, and practice. The Porras and Silvers model of planned change provides a useful framework for introducing change within an organizational setting (see Figure 14-1).[31] Specifically, it addresses how planned interventions targeted at specific organization variables will result in positive organizational outcomes. There are four distinct parts to this model. First, it distinguishes two types of intervention strategies — OD and organization transformation (OT). Porras and Silvers feel that OT should be a separate entity because the underlying theories and concepts are not as well defined as OD.[32] In comparison, human process-based and technostructural theories have gained widespread acceptance among OD practitioners.

**FIGURE 14-1**      **MODEL OF PLANNED CHANGE**

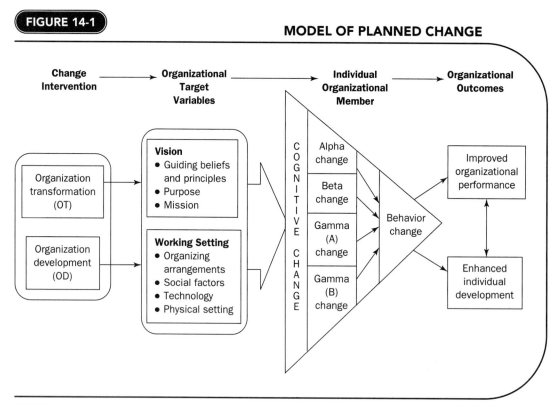

SOURCE: From J. I. Porras & R. C. Silvers. Organization development and transformation. Reprinted, with permission, from the *Annual Review of Psychology, Volume 43.* Copyright 1991 by Annual Reviews. www.annualreviews.org.

The second part of the model shows the relationship between change interventions and organizational target variables. The model shows two sets of target variables. The first is vision variables, which are the underlying organizational values, beliefs, and principles that guide management decisions and provide the foundation for the purpose and mission of the organization. The second type of target variables are identified as work setting variables, which are directly related to or influenced by OD interventions and vision variables. Work setting variables include policies, procedures, work rules, job descriptions, formal reporting lines, social factors, and communication patterns. In essence, these form the framework for organization structure.

The third part of the model focuses on the types of individual cognitive change. Porras and Silvers conceptualize cognitive change as the alteration of a person's perception of some existing organizational variable or paradigm.[33] An organizational paradigm can be defined as a generally accepted view or belief that is based on unexamined assumptions.[34] Cognitive change can occur at four levels:

1. **Alpha** changes are possible when individuals perceive a change in the levels of variables (e.g., a perceived improvement in skills) within a paradigm, without altering their configuration (e.g., job design).

2. **Beta** changes are possible when individuals perceive a change in the value of variables (e.g., a change in work standards) within an existing paradigm, without altering their configuration.

3. **Gamma (A)** changes are possible when individuals perceive a change in the configuration of an existing paradigm, without the addition of new variables (e.g., changing the central value of a "product-driven" paradigm from "cost-containment" to "total quality focus"; this results in the reconfiguration of all variables within this paradigm).

4. **Gamma (B)** changes are possible when individuals perceive a replacement of one paradigm with another that contains new variables (e.g., replacing a product-driven paradigm with a customer-responsive paradigm).[35]

As the definitions indicate, each level of cognitive change represents change as an occurrence on a broader scope, from individual to organizational. For example, suppose a shipping clerk attends a training program to improve her reading skill. An alpha change can be said to have occurred if at the end of training she perceives that her reading skill has improved. Further, suppose that the shipping manager attempts to improve productivity by reducing the standard for effective order processing time from forty-eight hours to twenty-four hours. A beta change can be said to have occurred if the shipping clerks accept this new standard as legitimate. This is so because the employees now define success as processing an order in less than twenty-four hours, as opposed to less than forty-eight hours.

Gamma A and B changes refer to changes occurring at the organization level. Gamma A changes are directed at the manner in which the operation's mission or philosophy is accomplished, but where the core mission remains intact. For example, if a product-driven organization introduced new cost-containment procedures, without changing its operation philosophy, a gamma A change would have occurred. Alternatively, gamma B changes are directed at the core mission or philosophy. For example, a gamma B change has occurred if the organization redefines itself from being product driven to being customer driven. Unlike a gamma A change, a gamma B change "alters existing behaviors, creates new behaviors, and gives individual employees a totally new of way of viewing their work."[36]

There are several benefits from distinguishing between levels of cognitive change. First, this can help the change agent to select the kind of intervention strategy that would be appropriate to achieve the desired change. Second, this approach provides a conceptual framework for evaluating OD interventions. Specifically, the level of change dictates the appropriate research designs and measurement techniques that should be used to assess it. Third, effectiveness can be reported as a change at one or more of the four cognitive levels, making communication of results clearer.

The fourth, and last, part of the model focuses on how individual behavioral changes can lead to two possible outcomes — improved organizational performance and enhanced individual development. Organizational performance, in this context, refers to improvements in efficiency, effectiveness, productivity, and profitability. Enhanced individual development refers to the alteration of behaviors or skills, or both, resulting in such things as improved work habits, increased commitment, and improved performance. These outcomes are consistent with the definition of OD presented earlier.

## DESIGNING AN INTERVENTION STRATEGY

The model of planned change that we just described provides a framework for integrating OD theory, research, and practice. In this section, we will discuss how OD practitioners go about designing an intervention strategy that targets specific organizational variables. We will first discuss specific roles in the design and implementation phases. Next, we will examine some steps in designing an intervention strategy. Last, we will look at the role of the HRD practitioner in this process.

### SPECIFIC ROLES

There are at least three distinct sets of roles that must be fulfilled when designing and implementing intervention change strategy — the change manager, the change agent, and the roles played by individuals within the system that is being changed.

*ROLE OF CHANGE MANAGER.* The **change manager** oversees the design of the intervention strategy. This person would have overall responsibility for assessing the need for change, determining the appropriate intervention activities, implementing the strategy, and evaluating the results. Some organizations elect to develop a parallel structure for introducing change — one person responsible for ongoing management functions and another person responsible for managing change. However, using a parallel structure may lead to a situation in which the change manager would not have sufficient power to create the conditions for change, particularly if others perceive the functional manager in the organization as not supporting the change process.

Rather than create a parallel structure, most organizations look to the functional manager to assume the additional duties of change manager. When using this approach, it is important that the manager who is selected to be the change manager be at the appropriate organizational level. For example, if a team-building intervention were going to be used in a single department, the change manager would be the department manager. Alternatively, if the target of the intervention were to change the mission of the organization, the appropriate change manager would be the CEO.

Managers must understand the nature of planned change as opposed to "forced" change. Forced change, which uses coercive tactics (e.g., threat of discipline), may produce immediate results, but these changes in behavior may not be permanent. Individuals may react immediately to forced change in order to avoid any negative consequences. However, when the threats of these consequences are removed, the person may revert to old habits or behaviors. Unfortunately, many managers will continue to use forced change until they learn to balance their short-term needs with the potential for the more permanent long-term benefits of planned change.

Fulfilling the role of the change manager is often difficult. The change manager must pay sufficient attention to the change initiative and see it through to its conclusion. According to one survey, executives attributed the failure of change initiatives to their own inattention to the change initiative.[37] In addition, managers and executives often lack knowledge of the change process and the impact the change has on individuals, and they often lack the skills to manage the human elements of change.[38] These findings suggest that organizations need to do more to prepare executives and other mangers to assume the change management role.

Some organizations have addressed this need. For example, Corning, Inc. developed a program (referred to as a tool kit), called Exercises for Managing Change, that provides information, activities, handouts, and other resources that help managers and executives to prepare for change, move through the change process, and live with change.[39] Programs like this help change managers to understand their role and encourage them to call on others to help them develop and implement a planned change strategy.

*ROLE OF CHANGE AGENT.* The **change agent** assists the change manager in designing and implementing change strategy. Among other things, the change agent has primary responsibility for facilitating all of the activities surrounding the design and implementation of the strategy. This person should have knowledge of OD theories, concepts, practices, and research results so that he or she can advise the change manager on implementation issues and the efficacy of different intervention strategies.[40]

The change agent can be an internal staff person (e.g., HRD practitioner) or an external consultant. Internal change agents generally are knowledgeable regarding the organization's mission, structural components, technology, internal politics, and social factors. This knowledge can be very important for establishing a trusting relationship with the change manager and members of the system that will undergo the change. However, system members may feel the internal change agent is too close to the existing situation and cannot be objective. In addition, the internal change agent may not possess the specialized knowledge needed for a particular intervention strategy. If this is the case, the organization may decide to hire an external consultant with specialized OD knowledge and skills.

External change agents are hired to fulfill a specific function or role for a specified period. The external change agent's role is determined by the change manager and is typically outlined in a contract. The contract should specify the exact nature of the work to be performed, the timetable for the work, length of service, method and amount of payment, and some way of evaluating the change agent's performance. Some organizations negotiate a performance clause, which gives the organization the right to evaluate the change agent's efforts at any time and provides that the contract can be terminated if the work is not up to the agreed-upon standards.

Warner Burke described eight roles that a change agent may play (see Table 14-2).[41] Each of these roles represents a different aspect of the relationship between the change agent and the change manager or client. For example, when a change agent assumes the advocate role (i.e., becomes highly directive), he or she is attempting

## TABLE 14-2 — CHANGE AGENT'S ROLES

| Role | Definition | When Appropriate |
|------|-----------|------------------|
| Advocate | Highly directive role in which the change agent tries to influence the client to use a certain approach. | When client is not sure of the approach to take and needs a lot of direction. |
| Technical Specialist | Provides specific technical knowledge on special problems. | When client seeks direction on a special problem. |
| Trainer or Educator | Provides information about OD or different intervention strategies. | When client needs training in some aspect of OD. |
| Collaborator in Problem Solving | Provides assistance in problem analysis, identifying solutions, and action steps. | When client needs assistance in decision making. |
| Alternative Identifier | Same as above, but does not collaborate. | When client needs assistance in developing a decision-making process. |
| Fact Finder | Serves as a research or data collector. | When client needs are very specific. |
| Process Specialist | Facilitates meetings and group processes. | When client's needs are for process consultation. |
| Reflector | Helps client to understand situation by reacting to information. | When client is not sure of the data and seeks clarification. |

SOURCE: From W. W. Burke (1987). *Organization development* (pp. 146–148). Reading, MA: Addison-Wesley.

to influence the change manager to select a certain strategy. At the other extreme, when the change agent assumes the role of a reflector (i.e., becomes nondirective), he or she is attempting to clarify information so that the change manager can make the decision. It is not unusual for a change agent to serve in several roles during the same intervention. For example, if during the initial stages of designing the intervention strategy, the change manager lacks understanding of some of the key concepts of planned change, the change agent may act as a trainer to ensure that these concepts are understood. Having gained sufficient knowledge, the change manager will likely look to the change agent to assume additional roles (e.g., fact finder or process specialist).

Since the 1990s, a number of consulting firms have promoted the concept of change management. These firms, including McKinsey & Co., Arthur D. Little, and Gemini Consulting, are promoting positive organizational change as well as their roles as external change agents. Some authors have gone so far as to suggest that "change management" will replace the term "organization development" as the heading for organizational-level interventions.[42] However, this notion has met with vigorous opposition.[43] Whatever the outcome of this debate, it is clear that external change agents (and consulting firms) are playing a leading role in many ongoing change efforts.

Many recent efforts have involved various types of team-based interventions. As a result, individuals who serve as change agents are increasingly being called upon to help change managers transform work groups into teams. To do so, they must have several sets of skills. First, the change agent must be able to perform a variety of team-building activities. Second, when working with the team leader (who may be the change manager), the change agent must be able to assist him or her in each of the elements of team development, including facilitating team meetings, managing conflicts, problem solving and decision making, and establishing team roles and expectations. Third, the change agent must have the diagnostic skills needed to understand the culture of the group or system that is targeted for change. Understanding the cultural aspects (e.g., values, norms, beliefs) of the group will enable the change agent to identify important "access leverage points" that can facilitate or impede the implementation of the change strategy.[44] For example, if an organization has a long-standing tradition of celebrating important milestones (e.g., the end of a production run, the completion of a training program, or the end of a seasonal sales period), a change agent should identify these customs and traditions and use them to support the change process. If important aspects of the culture are ignored, group members might resist the change. The relationship between culture and change is also important at the individual and organization levels.

*ROLES OF INDIVIDUALS WITHIN A SYSTEM UNDERGOING CHANGE.* The roles of individuals within the system that is the target of the intervention strategy are determined by the change manager. The system can be a small work group or the entire organization. Individuals or groups within the system may be asked by the change manager to take on a specific role in the change process. For example, some organizations create a change committee whose role is to work with both the change manager and the change agent in designing and implementing the intervention strategy. Committees or task forces are important to collect data, develop team skills, and define the emerging tasks and roles within the system.[45] Ideally, these individuals will be energized by their involvement, motivating them to put forth the extra effort needed for committee work.[46]

## STEPS FOR DESIGNING AN INTERVENTION STRATEGY

To design an intervention strategy, the change manager, with the help of the change agent and others in the system, must be able to diagnose the existing environment for change, develop and implement a plan of action, and evaluate the results of the intervention to determine if the desired (behavioral) changes have occurred. Each of these steps is discussed next.

*DIAGNOSE THE ENVIRONMENT.* Diagnosing the environment is an assessment process that focuses on determining the readiness of the target group to accept change. If the group is not ready, resistance will occur and change will likely fail. One way to determine readiness to accept change is by conducting force field analysis. Lewin developed **force field analysis** to analyze the driving and restraining forces of change. Figure 14-2 illustrates force field analysis graphically using the example of a company that plans to introduce new production standards. The change manager, change agent, and possibly a change committee or task force would diagnose the environment to determine possible forces both for and against change. These forces are shown as "force" lines. The length of the lines indicates the relative force — the longer the line, the greater the force. Theoretically, for change to take place, the accumulation of forces *for* change has to exceed the accumulation of forces *against* change. In the example in Figure 14-2, the restraining forces would

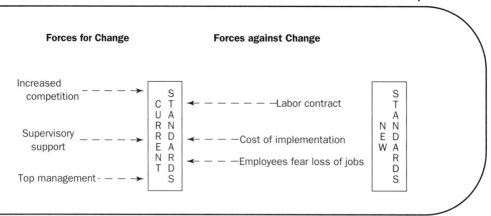

| FIGURE 14-2 | FORCE FIELD ANALYSIS (INTRODUCING NEW PRODUCTION STANDARDS) |

seem to prevent the introduction of new product standards unless the present situation were modified. Thus, the value of a force field analysis is that it allows the intervention strategists to pinpoint specific support and resistance to a proposed change program. In the example, the change manager must be able to reduce the resistance (e.g., restructure the labor contract) or increase the positive forces in favor of change. Force field analysis has recently been used to address change issues in professional accounting firms and hospitals.[47]

*DEVELOP AN ACTION PLAN.* Developing an action plan involves identifying specific target variables and determining the techniques that will be used to bring about change. Identifying specific target variables (e.g., resistance points, existing policies) allows the intervention strategists to better understand the relative complexity of the change program. Using the earlier example of changing production standards, the change manager may view the union, supervisors, and production workers as possible resisters to change. The union will have to agree to a change in production standards; supervisors must understand the need to change those standards and why their active support is critical to the outcome; and employees need to know that the change will not affect their job security. The next step is to determine the appropriate intervention techniques for instituting change. In the example, the following techniques may be considered:

1. Schedule a supervisory meeting and follow-up sessions to communicate the critical need for changing standards and impress key employees with the need to actively support the change.
2. Conduct meetings with union officials to determine their interpretation of the labor contract and whether they agree that management has the "right" to change production standards unilaterally. Depending on the results of the meetings, other sessions may be necessary.
3. Conduct an awareness/training session for production-level employees to set forth how the changes in production standards will affect them personally and how those changes will be implemented.

The **action plan** specifies the intervention strategy. Like any other plan, the action plan should specify the objective of each change activity, who will be involved, who is responsible, and when the activity will be completed. Implementation of the action plan involves carrying out each step in the intervention strategy. This may require at least as much energy and commitment of the change manager and change agent as all of the previous steps combined. Too often, people get bogged down with the planning process and see it as an end in itself, rather than as a means to an end. Thus, when the action plan is prepared, participants may be unwilling to see it through. The role of the change manager, with the assistance of the change agent, is to oversee the implementation of the plan and ensure that all steps are followed, that tasks are completed, and that deadlines are met. If there is any delay in carrying out an activity, the change manager should intervene and find out the cause of the delay. The change manager should continually confer with the members of the system to review results, get feedback, and make the appropriate adjustments.

*EVALUATION OF RESULTS OF THE INTERVENTION.* As indicated by our process model of HRD (first presented in Chapter 1), the results of an OD intervention must be evaluated to determine whether behavior has changed and whether problems have emerged (e.g., new standards may be in place, but the union wants the workers classifications or pay to be upgraded). It is important that members of the system be involved in these steps to determine whether the action plan was effective. Evaluation results should be provided to demonstrate the degree to which the intervention was effective. If there are other problems identified, the change manager may want to repeat the action planning process.

### ROLE OF HRD PRACTITIONERS IN THE DESIGN OF OD INTERVENTIONS

HRD practitioners have two primary roles in the design of OD interventions. First, they can serve as change agents. As discussed in Chapter 1, OD competencies are part of the overall competencies of an HRD professional (see Figures 1-2 and 1-5). In planned change situations, particularly those that involve HRD programs as intervention techniques, the HRD practitioner can help the change manager understand the full range of HRD programs and which ones work best under different conditions. In this role, the HRD practitioner can also facilitate some of the change activities (e.g., awareness sessions) that are part of the action plan.

The second role that an HRD practitioner can play in the design and implementation of OD interventions is to serve as the evaluator of intervention strategies. Even in situations where the HRD practitioner was not directly involved in the intervention strategy, he or she could be responsible for the evaluative component. Again, it is important that this person possesses the competencies to conduct the needed research and use the appropriate methodology to evaluate the effects of the change effort.

### THE ROLE OF LABOR UNIONS IN OD INTERVENTIONS

In unionized organizations, OD interventions and labor relations are inextricably linked. If union members generally mistrust management, it is not likely that they will be willing partners in a planned change program. Rather, they may attempt to obstruct the process. Some OD practitioners would argue that if an organization truly wants to bring about lasting change in a unionized work environment, management must first view union leaders as partners in change and emphasize that their commitment to long-term goals for change is as important as that of the top managers. Management and union leaders must share the reality that organizational changes must be made if the organization is to remain a viable entity and prosper. Furthermore, they must be willing to make fundamental changes in accountability and in the ways employees perform their jobs. This kind of arrangement is generally known as a *cooperative agreement.*

Cooperative agreements are usually accomplished within normal contract negotiations. Typically, unions make certain trade-offs as long as they appear to be in the best interest of the membership as a whole. During tough economic times, or when the organization faces financial or market problems, management and union leaders may be more willing to agree on a cooperative arrangement. In such circumstances, the union's priority is to ensure that jobs are saved and that there is little change to the wage structure, and management's priority is to see that business improves. But during stable times, or even boom times, the union may expect something in return for buying into the change.

Team-based approaches that emphasize empowerment (e.g., TQM, semi-autonomous or self-managing teams) have come under the scrutiny of unions and the National Labor Relations Board (NLRB). For example, the NLRB cited two companies for engaging in unfair labor practices by dominating or interfering with the formation of a labor organization.[48] The NLRB ruled that if an organization establishes employee committees that have authorization to set wages, hours, and conditions, this can be construed as a labor organization under the law, even if no labor union was present in the organization. The implications of this ruling for a given employer will depend largely on the existing relationship between employees and management (or union and management). If relationships are poor, this could essentially halt any efforts to involve employees (including union members) in most types of employee involvement processes and team-based approaches currently existing in organizations.

## TYPES OF INTERVENTIONS: HUMAN PROCESS-BASED

Most early OD interventions were **human process-based interventions.** These interventions are directed at improving interpersonal, intragroup, and intergroup relations. Two common human process-based intervention strategies that are still widely used are survey feedback and team building.[49]

### SURVEY FEEDBACK

**Survey feedback** is defined as "the systematic feedback of survey data to groups with the intent of stimulating discussion of problem areas, generating potential solutions, and stimulating motivation for change."[50] The data provide a snapshot of an existing situation, usually measuring some aspect of the group or organization. This data can then be used to compare an organization's current state with some desired state. Ideally, the result of survey feedback sessions is that changes will be attempted to bridge the gap between the current state and desired state.

There are many approaches to implementing survey feedback systems. For example, Alderfer and Holbrook's peer-intergroup model[51] has been used to supply feedback data to superiors and subordinates when relations are strained between them.[52] This approach involves two or more groups and focuses on organization-wide issues. The groups meet separately to discuss how the data reflect their concerns, and then they join the other groups to share their reactions. Significant concerns are then addressed through the development of action plans.

When using survey feedback as an intervention strategy, it is important for the change manager and change agent to be clear on (1) what organizational variables they are trying to measure, (2) how the survey will be designed and implemented to ensure the data will be reliable and valid, and (3) how best to present the survey results to the intended audience. There are many commercially produced (attitude or climate) surveys available that provide a range of normative items, along with comparative data.[53] Using commercially produced survey instruments can help the change manager address these issues. High-quality survey instruments (1) contain items that have been tested and refined to ensure clarity, (2) have undergone reliability studies to demonstrate their accuracy, and (3) permit the user to compare the results of his or her organization with the results of other organizations that have used the instrument.

## TEAM BUILDING

**Team building** is a process used to improve a work group's problem-solving ability and effectiveness.[54] Like individuals, groups experience problems. Groups can become dysfunctional when they experience problems that members cannot resolve or when they are unable to adapt to external changes (e.g., changes in technology). When a group becomes dysfunctional, relationships are strained, conflicts increase among the members, group output declines, and members are more likely to quit. A team-building intervention can be used to address some of these problems.

Even when groups are able to solve problems, management or members of the group (or both) may still feel that the group is not effective. Group effectiveness depends on at least three main elements:

1. the degree to which the group's productive output (its product or service) meets the standards of quantity, quality, and timeliness of the people who receive, review, and/or use the output

2. the degree to which the process of carrying out the work enhances the capability of members to work together interdependently in the future

3. the degree to which the group experience contributes to the growth and personal well-being of team members[55]

If one or more of these elements were missing, it would be possible to increase effectiveness through team building.

Before team building is attempted, several things should occur. First, there should be a preliminary diagnosis of the group's need for team building. Team building works best when there is a "strongly felt need to improve some basic condition or process that is interfering with the achievement of organizational goals."[56] Without a diagnosis of the group's need for team building, it is likely that some members of the group will resist any efforts to bring about change.

Second, a change agent should be selected who is able to use a wide range of OD skills and techniques to facilitate change. This is especially important given the things that the OD intervention is intended to change, for example, attitudes, norms, and habits. One valuable technique for team building is **process consultation** (PC), which is used by change agents to facilitate meetings and encounters with the work group. In this role, the change agent observes group activities and processes, and conducts a feedback session on those observations at the end of the meeting.

Third, the change manager and change agent should develop a general approach to the team-building sessions. Their roles should be specified clearly, in terms of who is going to facilitate different team-building activities. The approach should also specify the team-building cycle (e.g., action planning steps). Fourth, the change manager and change agent should establish a schedule outlining when these activities take place, including evaluation and follow-up sessions.

## EFFECTIVENESS OF HUMAN PROCESS-BASED INTERVENTIONS

There is some evidence that human process-based interventions can be effective in bringing about change. Two meta-analyses of the OD literature[57] showed, among other things, that:

1. team building was the most effective human process-based intervention for modifying satisfaction and other attitudes[58]
2. team building showed strong effects on productivity measures[59]

A recent meta-analysis found a small, but statistically significant positive effect of team-building interventions on subjective measures of performance; however, the effect on objective measures of performance was nonsignificant.[60] Thus, it still appears to be necessary to urge caution concerning the evidence for the effectiveness of team building on organizational performance.

## TYPES OF INTERVENTIONS: TECHNOSTRUCTURAL

The purpose of technostructural interventions is to (1) improve work content, work method, and relationships among workers[61] and (2) lower costs by replacing inefficient materials, methods, equipment, work-flow designs, and costly unnecessary labor with more efficient technology.[62] Given today's competitive climate, many organizations have turned to technostructural interventions to increase worker efficiency and satisfaction. The most common technostructural intervention strategies are job enlargement, job enrichment, and alternative work schedules.[63] We will discuss all three in this section.

### JOB ENLARGEMENT

**Job enlargement** interventions are "attempts to increase satisfaction and performance by consolidating work functions from a 'horizontal slice' of the work unit to provide greater variety and a sense of the whole task."[64] Job enlargement is generally carried out as a normal supervisory practice in most organizations. That is, a supervisor may observe boredom in a worker and diagnose that this person is not being challenged. The supervisor's normal coaching response, given no major obstacles (e.g., restrictions in a collective bargaining agreement), may be to reassign this person to a more challenging job. Thus, some job enlargement interventions are done informally.

There are, unfortunately, few published studies that isolate the effects of job enlargement from other interventions. One study, conducted by Campion and McClelland, examined whether using job enlargement on clerical jobs would have a desired effect on work outcomes (e.g., employee satisfaction).[65] They concluded that job enlargement had the greatest positive effect on employee satisfaction and customer service but had less effect on alleviating mental overload. Results from meta-analytic studies that compare job enlargement to other technostructural interventions will be presented at the end of this section.

## JOB ENRICHMENT

**Job enrichment** involves varying some aspect of the job in order to increase the potential to motivate workers. Probably the best developed approach to job enrichment is Hackman and Oldham's **job characteristics model.** The job characteristics model assumes that jobs have five core dimensions (i.e., skill variety, task identity, task significance, autonomy, and feedback). Hackman and Oldham argue that the core job dimensions affect work outcomes, such as job satisfaction and intrinsic motivation, by determining the extent to which employees experience:

1. *meaningfulness* of the work itself
2. *responsibility* for the work and its outcomes
3. *knowledge of actual results* of the work

Hackman and Oldham developed the *job diagnostic survey* (JDS), a self-report instrument, to measure workers' perception of each core job dimension. The scores on each core job dimension are combined into an overall *motivation potential score* (MPS) that is an indicator of the extent to which modifying one or more of the core job dimensions can enrich the job.

Job enrichment interventions based on this model have been the subject of considerable empirical testing and discussion. Overall, researchers have concluded that the model should be refined (e.g., clarifying the relationships among some variables, modifying calculation of the Motivational Potential Score).[66] Further, research suggests that the job characteristics included in the model are significantly related to job satisfaction[67] and to a lesser degree to job performance.[68] These relationships are stronger for individuals who have high growth need strength (that is, a desire to grow and learn within the job). Taken together, research supports the conclusion that the job characteristics approach to job enrichment can be an effective technostructural intervention.

## ALTERNATIVE WORK SCHEDULES

**Alternative work schedules** (AWS) allow employees to modify their work requirements to satisfy their personal needs. According to a study of 521 corporations, 93 percent of the responding organizations have some type of alternative work schedules.[69] The two most common AWS interventions are the *compressed workweek* and *flextime*.[70]

*COMPRESSED WORKWEEK.* The **compressed workweek** involves reducing the number of workdays in a week, usually from five to four. Typically, the compressed schedule provides an option to employees to work four 10-hour days, known as the 4/40 schedule. Research on the 4/40 plan seems to show a positive effect on employee attitudes, but its effects on work productivity are mixed.[71]

*FLEXTIME WORK SCHEDULE.* The **flextime schedule** allows employees some latitude in determining their starting and ending times in a given workday. Employees, particularly those with young children, may find it attractive to have the option of changing their working hours to conform to their family patterns. A substantial number of U.S. families have parents who both work. Further, according to one study, a single parent heads 19 percent of families, and 27 percent of these single parents are men.[72] Although some single parents may be on welfare, a significant majority of workers may have some time restrictions due to their parental responsibilities.

In most flexible work schedule arrangements, each employee must work some standard number of hours per day (e.g., eight hours) and all employees must be at work during a common core period of the day (usually during the middle of the day). On either side of the core time, usually four hours, each employee can decide when to begin and end the workday. A review of research suggests that flextime schedules are positively related to a number of factors, including organizational attachment, attendance, performance, stress, off-job satisfaction, and attitudes.[73] The effects of flextime were strongest on job attitudes (e.g., job satisfaction, satisfaction with work, and satisfaction with supervisor).

## EFFECTIVENESS OF TECHNOSTRUCTURAL INTERVENTIONS

Meta-analyses of technostructural interventions have shown:[74]

1. Alternative work schedules and job redesign had a moderate effect on measures of work output, such as quality and quantity of production.[75]

2. Work rescheduling interventions had a small but significant effect on measures of withdrawal behavior (e.g., absenteeism), whereas work redesign did not have a statistically significant effect on measures of withdrawal behavior.[76]

3. Overall, technostructural interventions had less effect than human process-based interventions.[77]

4. Alternative work schedules had a greater effect on attitude than did job design/enlargement or job enrichment.[78]

5. Job enlargement and job enrichment interventions brought about the same amount of overall change (42 percent change), with enrichment having a greater effect on productivity.[79]

It appears, then, that technostructural interventions can lead to changes, but that they are less effective overall than human process-based interventions. The general explanation for this difference is that human process-based interventions are intended to "affect changes in organizations through the employees rather than through modifications in the work or work environment (technostructural approaches)."[80] Of the three types of technostructural interventions, job design had the greatest effect on productivity, while alternative work schedules had the greatest effect on attitudes. All three types affected managerial/professional employees the most, an important point when considering using these techniques throughout an organization.

## TYPES OF INTERVENTIONS: SOCIOTECHNICAL SYSTEMS

Since the 1970s, organizations have used *sociotechnical systems* (STS) designs as a way to increase productivity and worker satisfaction. Whereas human process-based and technostructural interventions focus on interpersonal relationships and job design, STS interventions focus on the *combination* of organizational structural demands (e.g., work flow, task accomplishment, and performance) and social demands (e.g., relationships among workers).[81] This notion was first propounded by Eric Trist of the Tavistock Institute in Great Britain.[82] Today, STS interventions can be viewed as including quality circles, total quality management, and self-directed work teams. Each of these approaches is usually the focal point of a larger change strategy because the factors that determine effectiveness are linked to the nature and effectiveness of the entire organization.[83] STS interventions have been among the most widely implemented current OD interventions. Research suggests that STS interventions have had a greater effect on productivity than either human process-based or technostructural interventions.[84] We will discuss each one and describe the empirical evidence concerning their overall effectiveness.

### QUALITY CIRCLES

The **quality circle** (QC) approach gets employees involved in making meaningful work decisions including, but not limited to, solving job-related problems. While most QC programs are designed to meet unique organizational needs, there are some common features. First are the QC roles — the steering committee, the facilitator, and the circle leader. The steering committee, composed of key managers and employees, is responsible for implementing the QC process and making decisions about such things as resource allocation, production or operation changes, and employee assignments. The facilitator, selected by the steering committee, has responsibility for training the circle leaders and overseeing the operation of the circles. The facilitator must have OD competencies. Circle leaders, usually supervisors, are responsible for such things as calling meetings, encouraging active participation among members, and preparing reports for submission to the steering committee.

The second common characteristic of QCs is that participants receive training in group process, diagnosing problems, and problem-solving skills. Group leaders will generally be given additional training in group facilitation. A third common characteristic is that each circle meets on a regular basis to discuss issues like improvement of the work procedures and product quality, working conditions and facilities. Priority is usually given to problems in the work area of that QC, or under the direct control of the circle leader, or both. While participation is voluntary, employees are usually given time off to attend meetings. Finally, QCs make recommendations to management about how the issues they investigate can be addressed. They typically do not have the authority to implement the recommendations without management's approval.

The empirical evidence of the overall effectiveness of QCs is mixed. Steel and Lloyd studied the effects of participation in QC programs on several organizational variables.[85] They found the following:

1. There were significant effects on cognitive measures of a sense of competence and interpersonal trust, and on some measures related to properties of the task environment, such as goal congruence.

2. QC participants reported significantly greater attachment to the organization as the study progressed.

3. The QC process generally produced little overt enhancement in participants' work performance.

Park analyzed evaluative data from 154 QC programs in both private and public organizations and found that, overall, QC programs have shown an increase in organizational effectiveness and the empowerment of employees.[86] This conclusion was supported by Botch and Spangle, who found the QC to be a powerful employee development tool, primarily because participants perceived their involvement as a way of getting personal recognition.[87] Others disagree with these findings. They feel that while there are some decreases in operating costs, there is no evidence that productivity, quality, or attitudes have improved where QCs are used.[88]

Even with the mixed reviews of QCs, there seems to be a consensus among researchers that, for QC intervention strategies to be effective, they must include (1) comprehensive training for the facilitator, group leaders, and group members; (2) active support from top and middle management; (3) supervisors who possess good communications skills; and (4) inclusion of labor unions (where present).[89]

## TOTAL QUALITY MANAGEMENT

Faced with stiff competition, organizations have identified quality as a critical competitive factor. One way to improve quality is to design and implement a **total quality management** (TQM) program.

TQM is defined as a "set of concepts and tools for getting all employees focused on continuous improvement, in the eyes of the customer."[90] Based on the work of Deming, Juran, Crosby, and others, TQM seeks to make every employee responsible for continuous quality improvement. It usually involves a significant change in the way employees do their work.

Most TQM intervention strategies involve five basic components — total commitment from senior management, quality standards and measures, training for employees, communication, and reward, recognition, and celebration. Each of these components is discussed next. Senior management needs to guide the implementation of TQM. For example, Tenant Company found that managers are often isolated and need to be kept informed and involved.[91] A study of the TQM program at Digital Equipment Corporation revealed that the success of the program was dependent on how well management established clear quality goals and related them to business, communicated and reinforced them, and demonstrated behavior consistent with those values.[92]

Quality standards and measures serve as benchmarks for TQM. Organizations that establish quality goals must be able to quantify them according to defined standards. TQM emphasizes the role of each manager in terms of reducing cost, particularly nonconformance cost (which accounts for about 20 percent of revenues in most organizations) caused by deviations from performance standards.[93] According to McCormack, supervisors must be able to:

1. specify current performance standards
2. identify where outputs are at variance with standards
3. determine the causes of variances
4. identify and initiate actions to correct causes
5. specify desired performance
6. compare the desired standards to current standards and identify gaps
7. develop alternatives to close the gaps
8. institutionalize new standards[94]

Providing quality training to participants is critical to overall success. Therefore, organizations that seek to implement TQM must make a major investment in training. Training should begin with sensitizing managers at all levels to the philosophy and principles of TQM. All managers need training in both TQM awareness and how to implement TQM principles.[95] In addition, employees may need training in statistical process control (SPC) techniques.[96] Also, because problem-solving teams are almost always a part of a TQM intervention, team-building training should be included in quality training.[97]

Rewards, recognition, and celebration are used to keep employees energized and working toward the goals of total quality. Many organizations have linked TQM participation and success to three kinds of rewards: (1) individual monetary, (2) group monetary, and (3) nonmonetary rewards.[98] Individual monetary rewards, the more traditional form of compensation, are important for linking TQM to a manager's participation and success. However, because individual compensation systems "place a strong emphasis on individual performance, almost always creating a competitive situation among employees," some organizations have abandoned individual rewards.[99] Instead, many organizations are emphasizing gain-sharing programs.

There are several ways an organization can recognize individuals and groups for their contributions. These include awarding of plaques; naming of an employee (or group) of the week, month, or year; and celebrating with recognition luncheons and dinners. The organization can also be recognized for having a successful TQM program. The most prestigious award is the Malcolm Baldrige National Quality Award, which has been instrumental in promoting the concept of TQM. Organizations that want to be recognized must adhere to a nationally accepted set of criteria for evaluating their TQM program. In the public sector, NASA's Quality and Excellence Award is given annually to contractors, subcontractors, and suppliers who consistently improve the quality of their products and services.[100] Most organizations with TQM programs also recognize groups for their successes.

Communication begins with the CEO "going public" with a commitment to TQM and how it will change the direction of the company.[101] In addition, communication should be used to provide performance feedback and reviews. Another component should be a continuous flow of information on product and service quality improvements, so that employees can track their group progress. Many organizations display results on wall charts (or online) for this purpose.

Before considering TQM as an intervention strategy, the change manager should try to solve any preexisting problems that would derail the effort. If employees are dissatisfied with some other aspect of the organization, it will be very difficult for them to focus on quality issues. For example, the Wallace Company in Houston, Texas, a recipient of the Baldrige Award in 1990, took the advice of an external change agent and first addressed a problem that irritated employees before launching their TQM program.[102] Another preexisting condition that could delay implementing TQM is organizational **downsizing,** particularly at the management levels. Employees who fear losing their jobs may not be able to focus on TQM principles, unless they see them as a means of saving their jobs.

In addition to extensive applications in industry, many sectors of public service, including government, hospitals, and universities, have introduced TQM. The federal government has established the Federal Quality Institute, which offers quality seminars and in-house consulting to approximately thirty federal agencies.[103] State and local governments have also adopted TQM. For example, the city of Madison, Wisconsin, realized significant budgetary savings through TQM.[104] Hospitals across the United States have been adopting TQM as a means of improving patient care, performance, and market share.[105] In the face of declining budgets, universities and colleges are using TQM techniques to help focus on the needs of the market and ways to improve delivery systems. However, to be successful, colleges and universities need the cooperation of their faculty (and their labor unions) to change the tradition of lifelong tenure and peer review of their teaching.[106]

The practitioner literature suggests that there is a high rate of success with TQM, particularly from the organization's perspective. Many companies reported that TQM has led to significant improvements in product quality and service leading to increased market share, profits, and company image. For example, in 1987 Rockwell Tactical Systems was cited by the U.S. Army for having 1,744 quality problems in its Hellfire anti-armor missile production. But by applying TQM principles, they were able to save the existing program and, in 1990, won a new contract for 100 percent production of the missile.[107]

There is also evidence that suggests that TQM has not lived up to expectations. In a survey of organizations that had implemented TQM programs, 70 percent of the respondents indicated that TQM had not yielded benefits in proportion to their investment.[108] In line with this, Hodgetts, Luthans, and Lee state that people who expect improved quality must also expect costs to increase.[109]

Two of the reasons cited for why TQM has not lived up to expectations are the attitudes of top management and lack of visible support for the program.[110] However, even in situations where there is strong management support, lower level employees may be cynical and resist involvement in TQM because they perceive it as a "top-down" change program conceived by top management.[111]

There are many anecdotal examples in the practitioner literature of successful organizational outcomes of TQM interventions in both the private and public sectors. However, most of the literature measures global outcomes (e.g., improvement in error rates, assembly time, cost savings) and relies on case studies.[112] There is, unfortunately, little evidence from controlled studies showing effects on individual productivity and attitudes.[113]

Recently, Yusof and Aspinwall suggested that much of the research and theorizing on TQM has been done in the context of large organizations.[114] They propose a framework for the implementation of TQM in smaller organizations. Given the proliferation of entrepreneurial start-ups in the past decade, the application of TQM principles to smaller businesses is an area worthy of further attention and study by both researchers and practitioners.

## SELF-MANAGING TEAMS

As discussed in Chapter 9, **self-managed teams** (SMTs) are defined as formal groups in which the group members are interdependent and can have the authority to regulate the team's activities.[115] While most SMTs are designed to meet an organization's specific needs, they have some common characteristics, including the following:

1. There is an interdependent relationship between members of the team.
2. Members have discretion over such things as work assignment, work methods, work schedules, training, and dealing with external customers and suppliers.
3. Team members have a variety of skills that allow them to perform several tasks.
4. The team receives performance feedback.[116]

These characteristics represent a significant change over traditional supervisor-led work teams. In particular, many organizations reduce the numbers of supervisors and middle managers when they implement SMTs. In any case, the organization must establish a new role for the supervisors who remain. Some organizations transform the position of supervisor to "team advisor," "team facilitator," or "coach." In this arrangement, the individual's role is to help train team members and advise on such things as employee selection, budgeting, scheduling, performance evaluation, and discipline.[117]

Organizations typically use SMTs as part of a larger organizational transformation strategy directed at refocusing the organization, increasing employee involvement, increasing productivity, or reducing cost.[118] For example, Corning, Inc. launched a high performance work system program at its Blacksburg, Virginia, plant using the SMT approach, along with several other intervention activities (e.g., continuous improvement, work process designs).[119]

Education and training are critical components of implementing SMTs. Training should occur at several levels. First, awareness training should be used to introduce the process and explain the benefits to individuals. Second, skills training should be used to provide team members with the skills they will need to manage their team. These include budgeting and planning, problem solving, and communication. This can be difficult in organizations where the employee education level is low. Third, cross-training is provided by individual team members to other team members who are assigned shared tasks.

It is not clear how many large companies have implemented SMTs. Estimates range from 7 percent to 47 percent.[120] The effectiveness of the SMT approach is usually defined in terms of organizational-level performance indicators such as controlling cost and improvements in productivity and quality. Anecdotal evidence of the effectiveness of SMTs includes reports such as:

- At Northern Telecom's Morrisville, North Carolina, repair facility, revenue increased by 63 percent, sales by 26 percent, and earnings by 46 percent in the three years since implementing SMTs.[121]

- At General Electric's plant in Salisbury, North Carolina, part of the workforce of 24,000 was organized into SMTs, resulting in an increase of 250 percent in productivity.[122]

- At Johnsonville Foods in Sheboygan, Wisconsin, employee involvement in decision making increased greatly in 1982, and SMTs were established in 1986. Revenues went from $15 million in 1982 to $130 million in 1990. By 2004, revenues had exceeded $200 million, with a 500 percent increase reported in productivity in the past ten years.[123]

Beyond productivity increases, organizations have received other benefits of successful SMT applications. These include better quality products and services, higher employee morale, reduced or flatter management hierarchy, and more responsive organizational structures.[124]

Empirical evidence also appears to suggest that SMTs are effective. A meta-analysis conducted by Beekun found that autonomous work groups (SMTs) were more productive than semi-autonomous and nonautonomous groups.[125] Cohen and Ledford compared traditionally managed teams with self-managed teams over a two-year period and found that self-managed teams were more effective on a variety of indicators, including productivity, quality, safety, customer complaints, and absenteeism.[126]

There is other evidence that the results of SMTs are not always positive. Wall and colleagues conducted a long-term field experiment involving autonomous work groups in a manufacturing setting.[127] The intervention involved giving shop floor employees substantially more autonomy in carrying out their daily jobs. The results of the experiment showed positive results on intrinsic job satisfaction, but effects on motivation, organizational commitment, mental health, work performance, and turnover were not very positive.

One possible reason why self-managing teams sometimes fail to produce the expected productivity increases is the lack of effective work-team management or supervision.[128] This suggests that organizations that have implemented SMTs may not be committed to changing from a traditional hierarchical structure, or have not developed the proper support mechanisms (e.g., human resource systems, training). Therefore, it is important that other management systems reinforce team structure and team behavior.

## DIFFERENCES BETWEEN TQM AND SMT INTERVENTIONS

There are some significant differences between a TQM program and an SMT intervention. TQM is a participative process and "participation per se does not always equalize power and may even increase discrepancies."[129] In an SMT approach, each team is empowered with the authority to make decisions affecting the output of that team without the concurrence of a supervisor. Teams used within TQM are usually encouraged to participate in problem solving, but they do not have the authority to implement changes. TQM focuses primarily on quality, as compared with the SMT, in which quality is one of several goals.

The SMT approach requires significant changes in organizational structure, including accountability systems, policies, procedures, and job descriptions. Changing job descriptions may require collaboration with labor unions and possible changes in the collective bargaining agreement. Alternatively, use of TQM may also require minor structural changes that may need to be reflected in the labor contract.

Another difference between the two is the manner in which employees are trained. Using a TQM approach, the concept of lifelong training may be emphasized, but in reality, employees may only be trained in a limited number of TQM skills because teams tend to turn over.

## HRD PROGRAMS AS SOCIOTECHNICAL INTERVENTION TECHNIQUES

The role HRD professionals play in sociotechnical intervention techniques (STS) design changes is similar to their role with respect to human process-based and technostructural interventions. That is, there are three specific roles. First, HRD practitioners can be responsible for designing and implementing the training programs needed to make STS interventions work. Second, there is probably a strong need for HRD practitioners to help employees adjust to new roles within the STS design. With so much emphasis on productivity and quality improvement, there is considerable pressure on employees to change. HRD practitioners must be able to assist the change manager in correctly diagnosing the system's readiness to accept change and provide help in designing the appropriate change strategy that helps individual employees make the adjustments.

Third, because STS designs also emphasize participation, the HRD practitioner should also assist in determining the appropriate level of employee participation. There are two types of participation — representative and consultative. *Representative* programs allow employee participation on organizational committees such as advisory committees, employee councils, grievance committees, safety committees, and even boards of directors. Membership on these committees can be determined through appointment, self-selection, or election. If representatives are to be appointed, it is particularly important for the change manager to ensure that appointees understand and communicate the needs and concerns of the employees they represent. *Consultative* programs allow employees to participate directly in job-related issues that affect their daily work life. This is the approach used by most SMTs.

## TYPES OF INTERVENTIONS: ORGANIZATIONAL TRANSFORMATION

Generally speaking, organization transformation (OT) efforts focus on articulating a new vision for the organization, with the purpose of redefining the desired organizational culture, mission, and strategy. In this section we will discuss four types of OT interventions — cultural change, strategic change, learning organizations, and high performance work systems.

### CULTURAL INTERVENTIONS

**Organizational culture** is defined as a system of shared values, beliefs, and norms that are used to interpret elements in the environment and to guide all kinds of behavior.[130] Organizational culture is not something that is found in a mission statement or a corporate policy manual. Rather, organizational culture is communicated and reinforced through organizational mechanisms like the ones in Table 14-3.

Organizational cultural interventions involve more than simply restating values, beliefs, or norms, and communicating them to individuals. **Cultural changes** involve a complex process of replacing an existing paradigm or way of thinking with another. For example, if an organization wants to become multicultural (integrating aspects of other cultures into the fabric of the organization), it must be able to make some fundamental changes to existing organizational paradigms (e.g., valuing cultural differences). The organization will take on a new set of values (as espoused in the vision and mission) that will affect how individual workers relate to others, both in and outside their work setting. Gade and Perry recently described a largely unsuccessful effort to change the newsroom culture at a Midwestern newspaper.[131]

( **TABLE 14-3** )

**MECHANISMS THAT SUSTAIN ORGANIZATIONAL CULTURE**

1. what managers pay attention to
2. the ways managers react to critical incidents
3. role modeling, coaching, and organizational training programs
4. criteria for allocating rewards and status
5. criteria for recruitment, selection, promotion, and removal from the organization

SOURCE: From R. W. Woodman (1989). Organization change and development: New areas for inquiry and action. *Journal of Management*, 15(2), 217.

## STRATEGIC CHANGES

**Strategic change** is defined as any fundamental change in the organizational purpose or mission requiring systemwide changes. Systemwide changes can have three dimensions — size, depth, and pervasiveness.[132] The *size* of the change refers to the number of employees affected by the change. The *depth* of the change refers to the extent to which the change involves limited structural changes or goes to core values of the organization. The *pervasiveness* of the change refers to how many functions and hierarchical levels of the organization will be directly impacted by the change. As the organization moves along any or all of these dimensions, the change process becomes more complex.

Strategic interventions may be necessary when an organization is faced with external pressures to change and adapt. External pressures come from many sources, including the economic, social, legal, and political arenas.[133] Organizations unable to maintain a "dynamic fit" between themselves and the demands imposed by their environments will face decline and possible elimination.[134] Hodgkinson and Wright provide an interesting example of a top management team at a large organization that seemed unable to break out of their "strategic inertia" to face competitive changes.[135]

When organization transformation change involves reorganizing parts of the organization, the employees feel the effects. For example, between 1980 and 1986, General Electric acquired 338 businesses and sold off 232 — in addition to closing seventy-three plants — resulting in the loss of tens of thousands of jobs.[136] Beyond the elimination of jobs, *mergers* may require realignment of reporting lines, policies, procedures, allocation processes, and control systems. Depending on the size of the merging organizations, the effects can be very disruptive, particularly to the managers.

*Acquisitions* can also be disruptive. It is possible that operational components of the acquired organization will remain intact, though this is often not the case. Some acquisitions involve merging executive offices to establish command and control functions. In most acquisitions, the employees experience many job-related losses that may affect their ability to perform their jobs.[137] These are listed and explained in Table 14-4; the feelings they generate must be addressed as part of the overall change strategy.

## BECOMING A LEARNING ORGANIZATION

The earlier success with TQM and continuous improvement programs was the genesis of the learning organization approach. One of the key components of a successful TQM intervention is an emphasis on learning by everyone involved in the process. Managers and employees are asked to (1) learn a common language for improvement, (2) learn new tools and techniques, and (3) learn to take the initiative in improving work outcomes. TQM focuses on specific processes and tasks, which sometimes does not lead to the kinds of flexible and adaptive thinking that organizations need to compete in a turbulent environment. Further, the lessons learned are often not shared and applied outside of the specific area in which they

---

**TABLE 14-4**            **HOW EMPLOYEES FEEL ABOUT MERGERS**

| Feeling | Why? |
|---|---|
| 1. Loss of hierarchical status | Often the acquiring company becomes the "boss." |
| 2. Loss of knowledge of firm | Procedures and people change. |
| 3. Loss of trusted subordinates | People tend to be shifted around. |
| 4. Loss of network | New connections are formed. |
| 5. Loss of control | Acquiring company usually makes the decisions. |
| 6. Loss of future | No one knows what will happen. |
| 7. Loss of job definition | Most things are in flux for a while. |
| 8. Loss of physical location | Moving is typical in mergers. |
| 9. Loss of friends or peers | Often people leave, are fired, or transfer. |

SOURCE: Copyright © April 1990 from Training & Development Journal by Galosy, J. R. Reprinted with permission of American Society for Training & Development.

---

are learned. Some organizations have realized that they must be able to develop the capacity to transfer knowledge across the organization by collaborating and sharing expertise and information that is unbounded by status, space, and time. This emphasis on continuous learning, changing, and adapting led to the emergence of an OT intervention referred to as a *learning organization*.

*DEFINITION AND ORGANIZATION LEARNING LEVELS.* A **learning organization** is an organization in which "everyone is engaged in identifying and solving problems, enabling the organization to continuously experiment, improve, and increase its capability."[138] This approach involves a shift in an organizational paradigm — or gamma B change — because employees are expected to continuously learn as they produce. Learning can occur on at least three different levels:

1. *Single-loop* learning emphasizes the identification of problems and then taking corrective action[139]

2. *Double-loop* learning emphasizes understanding and changing the basic assumptions and core values that led to a particular problem[140]

3. *Deuterolearning* is directed at the learning process by improving how the organization performs single- and double-loop learning[141]

Chris Argyris makes the following point about learning:

> If learning is to persist, managers and employees must look inward. In particular, they must learn how the very way they go about defining and solving problems can be a source of problems in its own right. I have coined the terms single-loop and double-loop learning to capture a crucial distinction. To give a simple analogy: A thermostat that automatically turns on the heat whenever the temperature in a room drops below 68 degrees is a good example of single-loop learning. A thermostat that could ask, "Why

am I set at 68 degrees?" and then explore whether or not some other temperature might more economically achieve the goal of heating the room would be engaging in double-loop learning (p. 6).[142]

*Single-loop learning* is commonplace in continuous improvement programs, because employees are taught to identify problems and correct them. This type of learning is still important in the day-to-day performance of a learning organization. *Double-loop learning* represents a radical shift in the way employees learn, because it involves changing basic assumptions and core values about how they work. For example, a trainer may become frustrated when he finds out that several training programs were not well received by trainees. Upon reflection, the trainer might realize that these programs were designed five years ago and have become outdated. Further, the trainer might realize that the practice of HRD staff members relying on their own intuition and knowledge of the organization to determine training needs is not sufficient in these changing times. The trainer then surmises that if the training program is going to be effective in the future, the training design approach must be changed and updated. This realization should prompt the trainer to conduct a needs assessment and update the design. *Deuterolearning*, the highest level of learning, is essentially learning to learn. Returning to the example, deuterolearning will have taken place if the trainer encourages other staff members to view all of the organization's training programs as works-in-progress and adopt a mind-set of continually adapting programs to meet the organization's changing needs.

*ORGANIZATIONAL DIMENSIONS THAT SUPPORT A LEARNING ORGANIZATION.* Researchers and practitioners have an array of notions of what fosters learning in organizations. There are at least five different organizational dimensions of a learning organization: structure, information systems, HR and HRD practices, organization culture, and leadership.

1. *Structure.* One of the key dimensions of a learning organization is the reduction or removal of hierarchical barriers that divide managers and employees. In their place, learning organizations have implemented more collaborative structures like self-managed teams and cross-functional teams. Teams provide a natural setting for sharing and disseminating information. If teams develop a learning capacity, they become a microcosm for other teams in the organization. Teams can serve as an incubator for new ideas, because their limited size and focus permit them to mobilize their resources and experiment more efficiently than larger units. New knowledge gained through team learning can be propagated to other teams, although there is no guarantee this will occur.[143]

2. *Information acquisition, sharing, and retention.* While individuals and teams can learn, solve problems, and create new ideas, the organization will not have learned unless this new knowledge is acquired, stored, and made available to other organizational members, both now and in the future.[144] Indeed, there is a growing interest in the topic of "knowledge management."[145] To create a learning organization, management must institute structures and practices that encourage information sharing and retention. This includes innovative and state-of-the-art information systems. Knowledge can be

acquired from both internal and external sources. Internal sources would involve interactions between group members who can think insightfully about complex issues and are able to use their combined potential.[146] For example, General Electric's Corporate Executive Council meets quarterly to share information, ideas, and concerns and examine best practices both within and outside the industry "to stimulate broad-range thinking."[147] External sources would be unlimited, including organizational reports, industry reports, literature, and events. Knowledge sharing is continuous during all kinds of team interactions. Even if the team members are in different locations around the world, they can still share and communicate electronically.

3. *HRM practices.* There are a number of human resource management practices that are necessary to support a learning organization. For example, performance appraisal and reward systems that reinforce long-term performance and the development and sharing of new skills and knowledge are particularly important.[148] In addition, the HRD function in a learning organization may be radically changed to keep the emphasis on continuous learning. In a learning organization, every employee must take the responsibility for acquiring and transferring knowledge. Formal training programs, developed in advance and delivered according to a preset schedule, are insufficient to address shifting training needs and encourage timely information sharing. Rather, HRD professionals must become learning facilitators. Their role should be to assist, consult, and advise teams on how best to approach learning. They must be able to develop new mechanisms for cross-training peers — team members — and new systems for capturing and sharing information.[149] To do this, HRD professionals must be able to think systematically and understand how to foster learning within groups and across the organization.

4. *Organization culture.* As mentioned earlier, an organization's culture is made up of the shared beliefs, expectations, and behavioral patterns that define the organization's identity to its members. In a learning organization, the organizational culture contains elements that promote learning and knowledge sharing throughout the organization. For example, learning often requires some amount of risk. In a learning organization, risk taking in situations that represent opportunities to learn is not only encouraged, it is expected and rewarded. Mistakes are more likely to be viewed as opportunities to learn, rather than as failures. One of the challenges in becoming a learning organization is to move individuals and groups toward this new set of expectations and norms.[150]

5. *Leadership.* The role of the leader is critical to a learning organization. A leader in a learning organization is viewed as someone who can move the organization toward the kinds of culture, systems, and practices that are needed to support this philosophy. Peter Senge argues that this kind of leadership is needed not only at the top of a learning organization, but also at every level.[151] He advocates three essential types of leaders:

   a) *Executive leaders* are top should be managers who create a vision that embraces organizational learning principles, create a new culture, and provide support to local line leaders. These individuals are also the transformational leaders who teach, guide, and continually reinforce the organizational vision (see Chapter 13).

b) *Local line leaders*, or change managers, usually heads of divisions or major departments, provide the impetus for change by experimenting with new learning capabilities that may produce desired results. It is critical that they get actively involved in developing learning linkages throughout their unit to provide access to new information.

c) The *internal networkers* or *community builders*, or change agents, are "seed carriers" who assist local line leaders in experimenting and diffusing of new ideas. This is a role that HRD practitioners can fill.

*EFFECTIVENESS OF LEARNING ORGANIZATIONS.* There are many anecdotal examples describing organizations that have become learning organizations, including Motorola, Zytec, and Toyota.[152] However, empirical research demonstrating the effectiveness of learning organization interventions is sparse. One of the problems in the learning organization literature is that theorists and practitioners have projected a wide range of ideas and techniques onto this term. Consequently, it is difficult to design a learning organization intervention and difficult to combine research evidence from different studies. Despite these problems, there still seems to be considerable interest in the learning organization concept. Recent efforts to devise a reliable measure of this construct should encourage further research in this area.[153]

## HIGH PERFORMANCE WORK SYSTEMS

The high performance work system (HPWS) is another approach that has emerged from the experiences of companies involved in continuous improvement. There is no universal description of what constitutes a high performance workplace. Typically, HPWS are multifaceted, involving different combinations of the intervention strategies discussed earlier. According to Martha Gephart, some common characteristics of a HPWS intervention strategy include "self-managed teams, quality circles, flatter organizational structures, new flexible technologies, innovative compensation schemes, increased training, and continuous improvement."[154] However, these elements do not exist as separate initiatives. Rather, they are tied together as a *system* with a strategic focus and results-oriented work and management processes. According to Gephart, high performance work systems are organized around eight core principles:

1. They are aligned to an organization's competitive strategy.
2. Clear goals and outcomes are customer driven; individual, team, and organizational goals and outcomes are aligned.
3. Work is organized around processes that create products and services.
4. They include process-oriented tracking and management of results.
5. Organization is by work units that are linked to processes — which enhances ownership, problem solving, and learning.
6. Workplace structures and systems facilitate focus, accountability, cycle time, and responsiveness.

7. They are characterized by collaboration, trust, and mutual support.

8. Strategic change management is key.[155]

A framework for understanding high performance work systems can be seen in Figure 14-3.[156] As shown there, a high performance work system is argued to have alignment or fit in terms of overall strategy, organizational goals, and internal goals. That is, the organizational structure, management practices, HR systems, and other work practices all need to function together to produce high level outcomes for the organization, its employees, and its customers.

Xerox is one of the largest U.S. companies that has implemented the HPWS concept. It began its transformation in the early 1980s when faced with growing competition from the Japanese. The company began with the introduction of TQM (referred to as "leadership through quality") in 1984 and the introduction of self-managing teams in 1986. However, its strategy began to falter when the company realized that unless other organization systems changed as well, the transformation would not be successful. In particular, team members complained that they were still being evaluated and rewarded as individuals, but they were told to act as a team. This led to a complete refocusing of the organizational design to create a better fit between people, work, information, and technology. The company emphasized (1) customer-focused work, (2) clear organizational vision and goals, (3) continuous total process management, (4) accessible information, (5) enriched, motivating work, (6) empowered human resource practices, and (7) flexible and adaptable systems. The return on this significant investment of time and energy was that the company received more than twenty awards for its achievements and the company stock rose dramatically from \$29 a share in 1990 to \$160 a share in 1996.[157]

At Texas Instruments (TI), the introduction of self-managed teams led to some improvement in organizational efficiency and quality, but not as much as management had hoped for.[158] In 1991, a Higher Performing Organizational Development Unit was formed at TI. New initiatives included job enrichment, cross-functional teams, extensive cross-training, and strengthened individual incentives. The TI example emphasizes how the system of the HPWS should enhance the effectiveness of each of its components.

Although research exists about the separate component of an HPWS, there is little empirical research investigating these systems as a whole. Arup Varma and colleagues found that all thirty-nine organizations they surveyed reported net organizational gains from using HPWS practices. They conclude that high performance work systems "are primarily initiated by strong firms seeking to become stronger" (p. 33).[159] In terms of the specific practices that make up a high performance work system, Jeffrey Pfeffer has amassed considerable evidence for the effectiveness of practices such as self-managed teams, extensive employee training, and reduced barriers and status distinctions between management and employees.[160] Further, Edward Lawler and colleagues surveyed Fortune 1000 companies, and found that companies with high use of employee involvement and TQM practices had greater return on investment (14.6 percent versus 9.0 percent) than companies with low use of such practices.[161] More recently, Robert Vandenberg and colleagues studied the impact of various "high involvement" practices on the return on equity and employee turnover at forty-nine life insurance companies. One key finding of this

FIGURE 14-3          HIGH PERFORMANCE WORK SYSTEMS FRAMEWORK

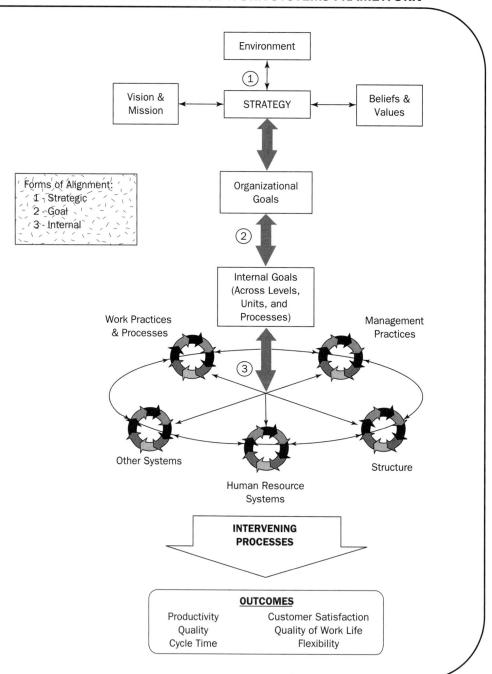

SOURCE: M. E. Van Buren & J. M. Werner (1996). High performance work systems. *Business & Economic Review*, *43*(1), October–December, 15–23. Reprinted by permission.

study was that the various high involvement practices (e.g., use of teams, incentives, training, and organizational goal clarity) were collectively related to organizational effectiveness, and this relationship was positive and statistically significant.[162] We expect further evidence to accumulate concerning the value to organizations of viewing themselves and their work practices as integrated high performance work systems.[163]

## EFFECTIVENESS OF ORGANIZATIONAL TRANSFORMATION CHANGE STRATEGIES

Many anecdotal reports describe successful OT strategies, but not enough is known about their overall effectiveness. The key to successful OT intervention is the articulation of an organizational vision that provides the guiding beliefs and principles (organization culture), explains the purpose of the organization (mission), and defines how the organization should fulfill its mission (strategy). A survey of executives from twenty countries found that (1) 98 percent perceived that a "strong sense of vision" would be the most important executive trait to be exhibited, (2) the most important executive skill would be "strategy formulation to achieve a vision," and (3) 90 percent perceive a lack of confidence in their own skills and ability to conceive a vision (p. 84).[164] The latter finding is somewhat disconcerting, given the number of organizations that have initiated OT interventions.

In their analysis of successful OT interventions, Trahant and Burke found that the strongest predictor of success "is strong committed leadership in the earliest stages of change — hands down."[165] Transformational leaders, as discussed in Chapter 13, emphasize emotional support and inspirational motivation as essential in creating a vision for the organization, hold middle management accountable for changes, and reshape management styles that meet the need of the workers.[166] Transformational leaders must also maintain a long-term view, and not just focus on short-term results, in order to bring about meaningful and lasting change. They must be willing to move from the traditional change mode that looks at isolated programs to one that sees all activities that can be continuously improved.[167] We urge the interested reader to consult a fascinating recent interview of Edgar Schein by Diane Coutu.[168] This article challenges leaders and other organizational members to do the hard work necessary to "genuinely reinvent themselves." Such "transformational learning" is portrayed as hard work, but necessary for effective change.[169]

## ROLE OF HRD PRACTITIONERS IN ORGANIZATIONAL TRANSFORMATION

To say that OT change will have an impact on employees is an understatement. With that in mind, there are several roles that can be assumed by HRD practitioners. First, they can serve on strategic change committees — not only to give advice on training and development, but also to help strategic planners look at various alternatives and their potential impact on people.[170] This role is key in all OT changes. Second, given the impact of mergers, acquisitions, and downsizing on workers, HRD practitioners must be involved in addressing these issues during the planning stages of such changes. Among other things, management must pay special attention to communicating with employees about the reasons for cutbacks and why they are being made. HRD practitioners can help facilitate awareness sessions. In this role, they can help employees deal with the realities of change. As discussed earlier, the role of the HRD professional needs to be more facilitative in OT interventions like high performance work systems.

Also, the traditional structure of the HRD function, with its separate goals, staff, and space, is generally inappropriate in organizations that implement the HPWS approach. Rather, the HRD function should be reorganized to ensure that training and development activities are integrated with other activities and functions so that learning opportunities are not missed.[171]

There are many different HRD programs and processes discussed in this book that can be used as part of an overall change strategy. OD and HRD are closely related. Because the intent of most planned interventions is to ultimately bring about changes in individual behavior, it is difficult to introduce change without using HRD programs and processes. While the relationship between OD and HRD is more apparent for human process-based and technostructural interventions, the need for HRD programs and processes is just as critical in organization transformation change interventions. Table 14-5 describes some examples of how HRD programs and processes contained in this text can be used as part of OD interventions.

## WHITHER ORGANIZATION DEVELOPMENT?

Organization development appears to be in a state of flux. As a field of study, it has long been known for its strong emphasis on employee well-being and humanistic values.[172] Yet, current efforts have sought to focus the field of OD more strongly on strategic business issues and on demonstrating its contributions to organizational

### TABLE 14-5 — HRD APPLICATIONS AS OD INTERVENTIONS

| Level | Emphasis | HRD Application |
|---|---|---|
| Human process-based | Human needs; job satisfaction | Career development; stress management; coaching |
| | Individual differences | Cross-cultural training |
| | Norms and values | Orientation; socialization |
| | Team effectiveness | Team training |
| Technostructural | Job competencies | Skills and technical training |
| Sociotechnical | Self-managed teams | Team training |
| | Total quality management | Quality training |
| Organization transformation | Reorganization (downsizing) | Employee assistance programs; management development |
| | Continuous learning | High performance work systems |

performance.[173] As one example, TRW was a pioneer in the implementation of organizational development techniques in the 1970s. However, by 1984, many line managers at TRW perceived HR and OD practitioners within their organization as having too little concern with business issues and organizational profitability.[174] TRW spent much of the 1980s and 1990s seeking to align HR (and OD) more closely with the strategic goals and direction of the organization. Quite frankly, we are skeptical that "change management" as a field of study will replace OD, as some have advocated.[175] Further, we agree with Burke, who argued that OD must not lose its focus on employee well-being.[176] However, the tension between employee focus and organizational performance will remain. In our view, the holistic approaches (such as high performance work systems) provide the best opportunities to maintain a distinctive focus on both individual and organizational issues. What happens to organization development as a field of study remains to be seen.[177] Clearly, technological developments will influence this field as it is influencing all others.[178] However, this much is clear: the need for successful organizational development interventions has never been greater. In our view, the forces driving organizations toward an increasing bottom-line emphasis are at present stronger than the restraining forces (or at least, those forces seeking to maintain a strong emphasis on employee well-being).[179] Organization development can play an active role in this situation.[180]

### RETURN TO OPENING CASE

This issue was studied over several years by Professor Bjorn Hennestad of the Norwegian School of Management. Initially, both the CEO and the employees of this organization were very enthusiastic about moving forward with the change to a more participative style of management. After announcing this change, an implementation date was set for five months later. Your instructor has additional information as to what was done in this particular situation.

Adapted from Hennestad, B. W. (2000). Implementing participative management: Transition issues from the field. *Journal of Applied Behavioral Science, 36*(3), September, 314–335.

### SUMMARY

Organization development (OD) is a process used to enhance the effectiveness of an organization and the well-being of its members through planned interventions. OD theory is divided into change process theory and implementation theory. Change process theory tries to explain the dynamics by which individuals, groups, and organizations change. Lewin viewed change as a three-stage process of unfreezing, transitional action (change), and refreezing. Implementation theory focuses on specific intervention strategies designed to induce changes. We discussed the underlying concepts of four different types of interventions: human process-based, technostructural, sociotechnical systems (STS), and organization transformations.

We introduced a model of planned change that consisted of four interrelated parts: (1) change interventions that alter (2) key targeted organizational variables that then affect (3) individual organizational members and their on-the-job behaviors, resulting in changes in (4) organizational outcomes. The focus of this model is on changing individual behaviors, which ultimately leads to improved organizational outcomes (e.g., performance), as well as individual development.

There are three roles that must be fulfilled when introducing organizational change — those of manager, change agent, and the individuals within the system being changed. The manager's role is to oversee the process. The influences generated within the system to promote change can vary, but the most important is that of members who participate directly in the process. The change agent's role is to consult, advise, and assist the manager in developing appropriate strategies for introducing change. In addition, some organizations hire external change agents (e.g., consultants).

We discussed some basic steps involved in designing a change strategy. To design an intervention strategy, the change manager, with the help of the change agent and others in the system, must be able to diagnose the existing environment for change, develop a plan of action, and evaluate the results of the action plan to determine if the desired changes have occurred. Force field analysis is a useful diagnostic tool for this process. HRD professionals have a definite role in this process. Among other things, an HRD professional can help the change manager understand the full range of HRD programs and processes and determine which works best under different conditions.

We described examples of the four types of planned interventions — human process-based, technostructural, sociotechnical, and organizational transformation. Human process-based interventions are directed at improving interpersonal, intragroup, and intergroup relations. Technostructural interventions focus on improving the work content, work method, and relationships among workers, and lowering cost by replacing inefficient materials, methods, equipment, work-flow designs, and costly unnecessary labor with more efficient technology. Sociotechnical interventions focus more on seeking innovative ways of increasing productivity and worker satisfaction through redesigning work-flow structures, work methods, and work content. Organization transformation interventions are used for large-scale strategic changes, cultural changes, learning organization efforts, and to promote high performance work systems. These approaches are very complex and need to be managed from the top of the organization.

## KEY TERMS AND CONCEPTS

action plan
alpha changes
alternative work
   schedules (AWS)
beta changes
change agent
change manager
compressed workweek

cultural change
downsizing
flextime schedule
force field analysis
gamma changes
human process-based
   interventions
intervention strategy

| | |
|---|---|
| job characteristics model | quality circle |
| job enlargement | self-managed teams |
| job enrichment | sociotechnical systems (STS) |
| learning organization | interventions |
| organizational culture | strategic change |
| organization development (OD) | survey feedback |
| organization transformation (OT) | team building |
| process consultation | technostructural theory |
| | total quality management (TQM) |

## QUESTIONS FOR DISCUSSION

1. Describe how an organization introduces change and how such changes can produce desired effects. Do you think that an organization can replicate another organization's procedure and get the same results? Why or why not?

2. Why is the role of the manager critical to the success of the intervention? Is it possible to have a successful intervention without the manager's direct involvement? If yes, under what conditions?

3. When are internal change agents more likely to be successful as compared to external change agents? If both are involved in the same intervention, what kinds of problems could arise? How are these problems resolved?

4. What change agent skills are necessary for helping a dysfunctional group become more effective? What if the problems are between managers? What happens if they refuse the help of the change agent?

5. Describe how the skills needed for designing and implementing human process-based interventions differ from those needed for technostructural interventions.

6. If you were a manager in a shoe manufacturing plant and you were asked to design and implement self-managed work teams, what kind of intervention strategy would you use? How would you involve first-line supervision in this process? What kinds of problems would you anticipate?

7. Is organization transformation change a necessity for maintaining an efficient organization? Why or why not? Even though there is limited empirical evidence to support organization transformation change intervention strategies, why do organizations still use this approach? Identify and describe a situation where you think that this approach would not be effective. Support your answer.

## EXERCISE: FORCE FIELD ANALYSIS AND YOU[181]

Your task: Select an issue that has been a concern or problem for students on your campus. For example, this could be an issue concerning classes, enrollment, health, safety, or dealing with faculty and staff at your institution. The main requirements are that this should be an issue that is important to you, and be one that has been raised before, but never adequately resolved.

Your tool: Refer back to Figure 14-2 and the discussion of force field analysis on p. 574. After reviewing this material, answer the following questions:

1. What is the current situation? Why is it a problem for students on your campus?

2. What is your ideal situation, that is, what would you like things to be like?

3. What are the forces *for* change, that is, what forces could lead to your ideal situation?

4. What are the forces *against* change, that is, the forces preventing change?

5. For the forces you listed in Steps 3 and 4, evaluate each one in terms of importance to this situation. Rate each force on a scale from 1–10, with a 10 rating for any force that is extremely strong, and a 1 rating for any force that is extremely weak.

6. For the situation you have selected, take the most important forces from Step 5, and construct a figure similar to Figure 14-2.

7. Looking at your figure, which side has the stronger forces? What does this suggest about the likelihood of change in this situation?

8. Suppose that the forces against change are stronger than the forces for change. To change this situation, you need to either increase the forces for change, or decrease the forces against change. What specific recommendations would you make that you or other students could do to increase the likelihood that a positive change will occur in this situation?

Visit http://werner.swlearning.com for links to informative websites for this chapter.

## REFERENCES

1. Hammer, M. (2004). Deep change: How operational innovation can transform your company. *Harvard Business Review, 82*(4), 84–93.

2. Alderfer, C. P. (1977). Organization development. *Annual Review of Psychology, 28,* 197–223; Beckhard, R. (1969). *Organization development: Strategies and models.* Reading, MA: Addison-Wesley; Beer, M., & Walton, E. (1990). Developing the competitive organization: Interventions and strategies. *American Psychologist, 45,* 154–161; French, W. L., & Bell, C. H., Jr. (1990). *Organization development.* Reading, MA: Addison-Wesley; Friedlander, F., & Brown, L. D. (1974). Organization development. *Annual Review of Psychology, 25,* 313–341.

3. Cummings, T. G., & Worley, C. G. (2005). *Organization development and change.* Mason, OH: Thomson/South-Western.

4. Locke, E. A., & Latham, G. P. (1990). *A theory of goal setting and task performance* (p. 16). Englewood Cliffs, NJ: Prentice Hall.

5. French & Bell (1990), *supra* note 2, p. 102.

6. Woodman, R. W. (1989). Organization change and development: New arenas for inquiry and action. *Journal of Management 15,* 205–228.

7. Lewin, K. (1958). Group decision and social change. In E. E. Maccoby, T. M. Newcomb, & E. L. Hartley (Eds.), *Readings in Social Psychology* (pp. 197–211). New York: Holt, Rinehart and Winston.

8. Schein, E. H. (1987). *Process consultation* (vol. 2). Reading, MA: Addison-Wesley.

9. Trader-Leigh, K. E. (2002). Case study: Identifying resistance in managing change. *Journal of Organizational Change Management, 15*(2), 138–155.

10. Dent, E. B., & Goldberg, S. G. (1999). Challenging 'resistance to change.' *Journal of Applied Behavioral Science, 35*(1), 25–41.

11. *Ibid.*

12. *Ibid.*

13. Bennis, W. G., Benne, K. D., & Chin, R. (1961). *The planning of change.* New York: Holt, Rinehart and Winston.

14. Argyris, C. (1970). *Intervention theory and method: A behavioral science view.* Reading, MA: Addison-Wesley.

15. *Ibid*, p. 20.

16. Friedlander & Brown (1974), *supra* note 2.

17. Hackman, J. R. & Oldham, G. R. (1975). Development of the Job Diagnostic Survey. *Journal of Applied Psychology, 60,* 159–170; Hackman, J. R., & Oldham, G. R. (1976). Motivation through the design of work: Test of a theory. *Organizational Behavior and Human Performance, 16,* 250–279; Hackman, J. R., & Oldham, G. R. (1980). *Work redesign.* Reading, MA: Addison-Wesley.

18. Cherns, A. (1987). Principles of sociotechnical design revisited. *Human Relations, 40,* 153–162.

19. Woodman (1989), *supra* note 6.

20. Nicholas, J. M. (1982). The comparative impact of organization development interventions on hard criteria measures. *Academy of Management Review, 7,* 531–542, p. 532.

21. Beckhard (1969), *supra* note 2, p. 3.

22. Beckhard, R., & Harris, R. (1987). *Organizational transitions: Managing complex change* (2nd ed., p. 8). Reading, MA: Addison-Wesley.

23. Alderfer (1977), *supra* note 2; Beer, M., & Walton, E. (1987). Organization change and development. *Annual Review of Psychology, 38,* 339–367; Bullock, R. J., & Svyantek, D. J. (1987). The impossibility of using random strategies to study the organization development process. *Journal of Applied Behavioral Science, 23,* 255–262; Porras, J. I., & Berg, P. O. (1977). The impact of organization development. *Academy of Management Review, 3,* 249–266.

24. Bullock & Svyantek (1987), *supra* note 23.

25. Beer & Walton (1987), *supra* note 23.

26. Nicholas (1982), *supra* note 20.

27. Neuman, G. A., Edwards, J. E., & Raju, N. S. (1989). Organization development interventions: A meta-analysis of their effects on satisfaction and other attitudes. *Personnel Psychology, 42,* 461–489.

28. Guzzo, R. A., Jette, R. D., & Katzell, R. A. (1985). The effects of psychologically based intervention programs on worker productivity: A meta-analysis. *Personnel Psychology, 38,* 275–291.

29. Bennis et al. (1961), *supra* note 13; Porras, J. I., & Hoffer, S. J. (1986). Common behavior changes in successful organization development efforts. *Journal of Applied Behavioral Science, 22,* 477–494.

30. Woodman (1989), *supra* note 6, p. 206.

31. Porras, J. I., & Silvers, R. C. (1991). Organization development and transformation. *Annual Review of Psychology, 42,* 51–78.

32. *Ibid.*

33. *Ibid.*

34. Golembiewski, R. T., Billingsley, K., & Yeager, S. (1976). Measuring change and persistence in human affairs: Types of change generated by OD designs. *Journal of Applied Behavioral Science, 12,* 133–157; Porras & Silver (1991), *supra* note 31; Thompson, R. C., & Hunt, J. G. (1996). Inside the black box of alpha, beta, and gamma change: Using a cognitive-processing model to assess attitude structure. *Academy of Management Review, 21,* 655–690.

35. Porras & Silver (1991), *supra* note 31, p. 57.

36. *Ibid,* p. 58.

37. Laabs, J. J. (1996). Leading organizational change. *Personnel Journal, 75*(7), 54–63.

38. Burke, W. W., Church, A. H., & Waclawski, J. (1993). What do OD practitioners know about managing change? *Leadership & Organization Development Journal, 14*(6), 3–11.

39. Demers, R., Forrer, S. E., Leibowith, Z., & Cahill, C. (1996). Commitment to change. *Training & Development, 50*(8), 22–26.

40. Doyle, M. (2002). From change novice to change expert — Issues of learning, development and support. *Personnel Review, 31*(4), 465–481.

41. Burke, W. W. (1987). *Organization development.* Reading, MA: Addison-Wesley.

42. Worren, N.A.M., Ruddle, K., & Moore, K. (1999). From organizational development to change management: The emergence of a new profession. *Journal of Applied Behavioral Science, 35*(3), 273–286.

43. Farias, G., & Johnson, H. (2000). Organizational development and change management: Setting the record straight. *Journal of Applied Behavioral Science, 36*(3), 376–379; though see the rejoinder by Worren, N. (2000). Response to Farias and Johnson's commentary. *Journal of Applied Behavioral Science, 36*(3), 380–381.

44. Pearce, C. L., & Osmand, C. P. (Winter 1996). Metaphors for change: The ALPs model of change management. *Organizational Dynamics, 24*(3), 23–35.

45. Beer & Walton (1987), *supra* note 23.

46. Kanter, R. M. (1983). *The change masters: Innovation for productivity in the American corporation.* New York: Simon & Schuster.

47. Aquila, A. J. (2004). Let the force be with you. *Accounting Today, 18*(10), June 7, 8–9; Baulcomb, J. S. (2003). Management of change through force field analysis. *Journal of Nursing Management, 11*(4), 275–280.

48. Hanson, R., Porterfield, R. I., & Ames, K. (1995). Employees empowerment at risk: Effects of recent NLRB ruling. *The Academy of Management Executive, 9*(2), 45–54.

49. Friedlander & Brown (1974), *supra* note 2; Guzzo et al. (1985), *supra* note 25; Neuman et al. (1989), *supra* note 27; Nicholas (1982), *supra* note 20; Nicholas, J. M., & Katz, M. (1985). Research methods and reporting practices in organization development: A review and some guidelines. *Academy of Management Review, 10,* 737–749.

50. Nicholas (1982), *supra* note 20.

51. Alderfer (1977), *supra* note 2.

52. Alderfer, C. P., & Holbrook, J. (1973). A new design for survey feedback. *Education Urban Society, 5,* 437– 464.

53. Lawler, E. E., III. (1986). *High-involvement management.* San Francisco: Jossey-Bass.

54. Nicholas (1982), *supra* note 20.

55. Hackman, J. R., & Walton, R. E. (1986). Leading groups in organizations. In P. S. Goodman & Associates (Eds.), *Designing effective work groups* (pp. 72–119). San Francisco: Jossey-Bass, pp. 78–79.

56. Dyer, W. G. (1987). *Team building* (p. 36). Reading, MA: Addison-Wesley.

57. Guzzo et al. (1985), *supra* note 28; Neuman et al. (1989), *supra* note 27.

58. Neuman et al. (1989), *supra* note 27.

59. Guzzo et al. (1985), *supra* note 28.

60. Salas, E., Rozell, D., Mullen, B., & Driskell, J. E. (1999). The effect of team building on performance. *Small Group Research, 30*(3), 309–329.

61. Friedlander & Brown (1974), *supra* note 2.

62. Gerstein, M. S. (1987). *The technology connection.* Reading, MA: Addison-Wesley.

63. Guzzo et al. (1985), *supra* note 28; Neuman et al. (1989), *supra* note 27; Nicholas (1982), *supra* note 20; Nicholas & Katz (1985), *supra* note 49.

64. Nicholas (1982), *supra* note 20.

65. Campion, M. A., & McClelland, C. L. (1991). Interdisciplinary examination of the costs and benefits of enlarged jobs: A job design quasi-experiment. *Journal of Applied Psychology, 76,* 186–198.

66. Fried, Y., & Ferris, G. R. (1987). The validity of the job characteristics model: A review and meta-analysis. *Personnel Psychology, 40,* 287–318.

67. Loher, B. T., Noe, R. A., Moeller, N. L., & Fitzgerald, M. P. (1985). A meta-analysis of the relation of job characteristics to job satisfaction. *Journal of Applied Psychology, 70,* 280–289; Neuman et al. (1989), *supra* note 27.

68. Fried & Ferris (1987), *supra* note 66.

69. Christensen, K. (1990). Here we go into the "high flex" era. *Across the Board, 27*(7), 22–23.

70. Neuman et al. (1989), *supra* note 27.

71. Dunham, R. B., Pierce, J. L., & Casteneda, M. B. (1987). Alternate work schedules: Two field quasi-experiments. *Personnel Psychology, 40,* 215–242; Newman et al. (1989), *supra* note 27; Pierce, J. L., Newstron, J. W., Dunham, R. B., & Barber, A. E. (1989). *Alternative work schedules.* Boston: Allyn & Bacon.

72. Bond, J., Galinsky, E., & Swanberg, J. (1998). *The 1997 national study of the changing workforce.* New York: Families and Work Institute.

73. Pierce et al. (1989), *supra* note 71.

74. Nicholas (1982), *supra* note 20; Guzzo et al. (1985), *supra* note 28; Neuman et al. (1989), *supra* note 27.

75. Guzzo et al. (1985), *supra* note 28.

76. *Ibid.*

77. Neuman et al. (1989), *supra* note 27.

78. *Ibid.*

79. Nicholas (1982), *supra* note 20.

80. Neuman et al. (1989), *supra* note 27, p. 480.

81. Fagenson, E. A., & Burke, W. W. (1990). The activities of organization-development practitioners at the turn of the decade of the 1990s — A study of their predictions. *Group & Organization Studies, 15*(4), December, 366–380; Guzzo et al. (1985), *supra* note 28; Neuman et al. (1989), *supra* note 27.

82. Fox, W. M. (1995). Sociotechnical system principles and guidelines: Past and present. *Journal of Applied Behavioral Science, 31*(1), 91–105.

83. Guzzo, R. A., & Dickson, M. W. (1996). Teams in organizations: Recent research on performance and effectiveness. *Annual Review Psychology, 47,* 307–338.

84. Guzzo et al. (1985), *supra* note 28.

85. Steel, R. P., & Lloyd, R. F. (1988). Cognitive, affective, and behavioral outcomes of participation in quality circles: Conceptual and empirical findings. *Journal of Applied Behavioral Sciences, 24,* 1–17.

86. Park, S. (1991). Estimating success rates of quality circle programs: Public and private experiences. *Public Administration Quarterly, 15*(1), 133–146.

87. Botch, K., & Spangle, R. (1990). The effects of quality circles on performance and promotions. *Human Relations, 43,* 573–582.

88. Verney, T., Ackelsberg, R., & Holoviak, S. J. (1989). Participation and worker satisfaction. *Journal for Quality & Participation, 12*(3), 74–77; Townsend, T. M. (1990). Let employees carry the ball. *Personnel Journal, 69*(10), 30–36; Adam, E. E. (1991). Quality circle performance. *Journal of Management, 17,* 25–39.

89. Clark, S. G., & McGee, W. (1988). Evaluation: A method of transition — Our program is great...isn't it? *Journal for Quality & Participation, 11* (4), 50–54; Piczak, M. W. (1988). Quality circles come home. *Quality Progress, 21*(12), 37–39; Honeycutt, A. (1989). The key to effective quality circles. *Training and Development Journal, 43*(5), 81–84; Berman, S. J., & Hellweg, S. A. (1989). Perceived supervisor communication competence and supervisor satisfaction as a function of quality circle participation. *Journal of Business Communication, 26*(2) 103–122; Lansing, R. L. (1989). The power of teams. *Supervisory Management, 34*(2), 39–43; Tang, T. L., Tollison, P. S., & Whiteside, H. D. (1989). Quality circle productivity as related to upper-management, attendance, circle initiation, and collar color. *Journal of Management, 15,* 101–113; Steel, R. P., Jennings, K. R., & Lindsey, J. T. (1990). Quality circle problem solving and common cents: Evaluation study findings from a United States federal mint. *Journal of Applied Behavioral Science, 26,* 365–381.

90. Schonberger, R. J. (1992). Total quality management cuts a broad swath through manufacturing and beyond. *Organizational Dynamics, 20*(4), 16–28, p. 17.

91. Hale, R. L. (1989). Tennant Company: Instilling quality from top to bottom. *Management Review, 78*(2), 65.

92. Salemme, T. (1991). Lessons learned from employees about quality improvement efforts. *Tapping the Network Journal, 2*(2), 2–6.

93. McCormack, S. P. (1992). TQM: Getting it right the first time. *Training & Development, 46*(6), 43–46.

94. *Ibid.*

95. Ferketish, B. J., & Hayden, J. W. (1992). HRD & quality: The chicken or the egg? *Training & Development, 46*(1), 38–42; Hackman, J. R., & Wageman, R. (1995). Total quality management: Empirical, conceptual, and practical issues. *Administrative Science Quarterly, 40,* 309–342.

96. Bowen, D. E., & Lawler, E. E., III. (1992). Total quality-oriented human resources management. *Organizational Dynamics, 20*(4), 29–41; Tollison, P. (1992). Assessing TQM training needs. *Journal for Quality & Participation, 15*(1), 50–54.

97. Hackman & Wageman (1995), *supra* note 95.

98. Schonberger (1992), *supra* note 90.

99. Bowen & Lawler (1992), *supra* note 96, p. 38.

100. Axland, S. (1991). Two awarded NASA's prize trophy. *Quality Progress, 24*(12), 51–52.

101. Johnson, J. G. (1991). The culture clock: TQM and doing the right thing right at the right time. *Journal for Quality & Participation, 14*(6), 1–14.

102. Altany, D. (1992). Cinderella with a drawl. *Industry Week, 241*(1), 49–51.

103. Reynolds, L. (1992). The Feds join the quality movement. *Management Review, 81*(4), 39–42.

104. Sensenbrenner, J. (1991). Quality for cities. *Nation's Business, 79*(10), 60, 62.

105. McCarthy, G. J. (1991). TQM is key to improving services but it's not for every hospital. *Health Care Strategic Management, 9*(11), 18–20.

106. McWilliams, G. (1991, October 25). The public sector: A new lesson plan for college. *Business Week,* 144–145.

107. Velocci, A. L., Jr. (1991). TQM makes Rockwell tougher competitor. *Aviation Week & Space Technology, 135*(23), 68–69.

108. Spector, B., & Beer, M. (1994). Beyond TQM programmes. *Journal of Organizational Change Management, 7*(2), 63–70.

109. Hodgetts, R., Luthans, F., & Lee, S. M. (Winter 1994). New paradigm organizations: From total quality to learning to world-class. *Organizational Dynamics, 22*(3), 5–19.

110. Choi, T. Y., & Behling, O. G. (1997). Top managers and TQM success: One more look. *The Academy of Management Executive, 11*(1), 37–47; Hackman & Wageman (1995), *supra* note 95.

111. Beer, M. & Eisenstat, R. A. (1996). Developing an organization capable of implementing strategy and learning. *Human Relations, 49*(5), 597–619.

112. Hackman & Wageman (1995), *supra* note 95; Collins, L. K., & Hill, F. M. (1998) Leveraging organizational transformation through incremental and radical approaches to change: Three case studies. *Total Quality Management, 9*(4/5), S30–S34; Martin, T. N., & Huq, Z. (2002). A

hospital case study supporting workforce culture re-engineering. *Total Quality Management, 13*(4), 523–536.

113. *Ibid.*

114. Yusof, S. M., & Aspinwall, E. (2000). Total quality management implementation frameworks: Comparison and review. *Total Quality Management, 11*(3), May, 281–294.

115. Cohen, S. G. & Ledford, G. E. Jr., (1994). The effectiveness of self-managing teams: A quasi-experiment. *Human Relations, 47,* 13–43.

116. Wall, T. D., Kemp, N. J., Jackson, P. R., & Clegg, C. W. (1986). Outcomes of autonomous workgroups: A long-term field experiment. *Academy of Management Journal, 29,* 280–304; Goodman, P. S., Devadas, R., & Hughson, T. L. (1988). Groups and productivity: Analyzing the effectiveness of self-managing teams. In J. P. Campbell & R. J. Campbell (Eds.), *Productivity in organizations* (pp. 295–325). San Francisco: Jossey-Bass; Schilder, J. (1992). Work teams boost productivity. *Personnel Journal, 71*(2), 67–71; Cohen, S. G., Ledford, G. E., Jr., & Spreitzer, G. M., (1996). A predictive model of self-managing work teams effectiveness. *Human Relations, 49,* 643–676; Industry Report. (1996). Who's learning what? *Training, 33*(10), 55–66.

117. Buck, J. T. (1995). The rocky road to team-based management. *Training & Development, 49*(4), 35–38.

118. Guzzo & Dickson (1996), *supra* note 83.

119. Gephart, M. A., Marsick, V. J., Van Buren, M. E. & Spiro, M. S. (1996). Learning organizations come alive. *Training & Development, 50*(12), 35–45.

120. Schilder (1992), *supra* note 116; Cohen et al. (1996), *supra* note 116; Stewart, G. L. & Manz, C. C. (1995). Leadership for self-managing work teams: A typology and integrative model. *Human Relations, 48,* 747–770.

121. Versteeg, A. (1990). Self-directed work teams yield long-term benefits. *Journal of Business Strategy, 11*(6), 9–12.

122. Schilder (1992), *supra* note 116.

123. Brokaw, L., & Hartman, C. (1990). Managing the journey. *Inc., 12*(11), November, 44–50; Johnsonville Sausage, Biography: Ralph C. Stayer. (2004). Retrieved November 20, 2004, from http://www.johnsonville.com/JVF/MediaCenter.nsf/User_AJ?openview

124. Musselwhite, E., & Moran, L. (1990). On the road to self-direction. *Journal of Quality & Participation,* 58–63.

125. Beekun, R. I. (1989). Assessing the effectiveness of sociotechnical interventions: Antidote or fad? *Human Relations, 42,* 877–897.

126. Cohen & Ledford (1994), *supra* note 115.

127. Wall et al. (1986), *supra* note 116.

128. Stewart, G. L. & Manz, C. C. (1995). Leadership for self-managing work teams: A typology and integrative model. *Human Relations, 48,* 747–770.

129. Kanter (1983), *supra* note 46, p. 258.

130. Geertz, C. (1973). *The interpretation of culture.* New York: Basic Books; Ott, J. S. (1989). *The organizational culture perspective.* Pacific Grove, CA: Brooks/Cole.

131. Gade, P. J., & Perry, E. L. (2003). Changing the newsroom culture: A four-year case study of organizational development at the St. Louis Post-Dispatch. *Journalism & Mass Communication Quarterly, 80*(2), 327–347.

132. Ledford, G. E., Mohrman, S. A., Mohrman, A. M., & Lawler, E. E. (1989). The phenomenon of large scale organizational change. In A. M. Mohrman, S. A. Mohrman, G. E. Ledford, T. G. Cummings, & E. E. Lawler (Eds.), *Large scale organizational change* (pp. 1–32). San Francisco: Jossey-Bass.

133. Mohrman, S. A., & Mohrman, A. M. (1989). In A. M. Mohrman, S. A. Mohrman, G. E. Ledford, T. G. Cummings, & E. E. Lawler (Eds), *Large scale organizational change* (pp. 35–47). San Francisco: Jossey-Bass.

134. Lawrence, P. R. (1989). Why organizations change. In A. M. Mohrman, S. A. Mohrman, G. E. Ledford, T. G. Cummings, & E. E. Lawler (Eds.), *Large scale organizational change* (pp. 48–61). San Francisco: Jossey-Bass.

135. Hodgkinson, G. P., & Wright, G. (2002) Confronting strategic inertia in a top management team: Learning from failure. *Organization Studies, 23*(6), 949–977.

136. *Ibid.*

137. Galosy, J. R. (1990). The human factor in mergers and acquisitions. *Training and Development Journal, 44*(4), 90–95.

138. Daft, R. L. (1997). *Management* (4th ed., p. 751). Mason, OH: Thomson/South-Western.

139. Nevis, E. C., DiBella, A. J., & Gould, J. M. (1995). Understanding organizations as learning systems. *Sloan Management Review, 36*(2), 73–85; Hodgetts et al. (1994), *supra* note 109.

140. Argyris, C. (1994). The future of workplace learning and performance. *Training & Development, 48*(5), S36–S47; Senge, P. M. (1990). *The fifth discipline: The art & practice of the learning organization.* New York: Doubleday.

141. Cummings, T. G., & Worley, C. G. (1997). *Organization development & change* (6th ed). Mason, OH: Thomson/South-Western.

142. Argyris, C. (1991). Teaching smart people how to learn. *Harvard Business Review,* May–June, 5–15, cited in Abernathy, D. J. (1999). *Training & Development, 53*(5), May, 80–84.

143. Senge (1990), *supra* note 140.

144. Gephart et al. (1996), *supra* note 119.

145. Burden, P., MacIntosh, M., & Srikantaiah, T. K. (2000). *Knowledge management: The bibliography.* Medford, NJ: Information Today Inc.; Hicks, S. (2000). Are you ready for knowledge management? *Training & Development, 54*(9), September, 71–72.

146. Senge (1990), *supra* note 140.

147. Gephart et al. (1996), *supra* note 119.

148. Cummings & Worley (1997), *supra* note 141.

149. Gephart et al. (1996), *supra* note 119.

150. *Ibid.*

151. Senge, P. M. (1996). Leading learning organizations. *Training & Development, 50*(12), 36–37.

152. Hodgetts et al. (1994), *supra* note 109.

153. Yang, B., Watkins, K. E., & Marsick, V. J. (2004). The construct of the learning organization: Dimensions, measurement, and validation. *Human Resource Development Quarterly, 15*(1), 31–55.

154. Gephart, M. A. (1995). The road to high performance. *Training & Development, 49*(6), 35–38, p. 30.

155. *Ibid*, p. 38.

156. Van Buren, M. E., & Werner, J. M. (1996). High performance work systems. *Business & Economic Review, 43*(1), October–December, 15–23.

157. Gephart, M. A., & Van Buren, M. E. (1996). Building synergy: The power of high performance work systems. *Training & Development, 50*(10), 21–32.

158. Gephart (1995), *supra* note 154.

159. Varma, A., Beatty, R. W., Schneier, C. E., & Ulrich, D. O. (1999). High performance work systems: Exciting discovery or passing fad? *Human Resource Planning, 22*(1), 26–37.

160. Pfeffer, J. (1998). *The human equation: Building profits by putting people first.* Boston: Harvard Business School Press.

161. Lawler, E. E., III, Mohrman, S. A., & Ledford, G. E., Jr. (1995). *Creating high performance organizations: Practices and results of employee involvement and quality management in Fortune 1000 companies.* San Francisco: Jossey-Bass.

162. Vandenberg, R. J., Richardson, H. A., & Eastman, L. J. (1999). The impact of high involvement work processes on organizational effectiveness: A second-order latent variable approach. *Group & Organization Management, 24*(3), 300–339.

163. Appelbaum, E., Bailey, T., Berg, P., & Kalleberg, A. L. (2000). *Manufacturing advantage: Why high performance work systems pay off.* Ithaca and London: Cornell University Press.

164. Lipton, M. (1996). Demystifying the development of organizational vision. *Sloan Management Review, 37*(4), 83–92.

165. Trahant, B., & Burke, W. W. (1996). Traveling through transitions. *Training & Development, 50*(2), 37–41, p. 41.

166. Belasen, A. T., Benke, M., Di Podova, L. N., & Fortunato, M. V. (1996). Downsizing and the hyper-effective manager: The shifting importance of managerial roles during organizational transformation. *Human Resource Management, 35*(1), 87–117.

167. Gill, S. J. (1995). Shifting gears for high performance. *Training & Development, 49*(5), 25–31.

168. Coutu, D. (2002). The anxiety of learning. *Harvard Business Review, 80*(3), 100–107.

169. *Ibid,* p. 100.

170. Gall, A. L. (1986). What is the role of HRD in a merger? *Training and Development Journal, 40*(4), 18–23.

171. Gill (1995), *supra* note 167.

172. Farias & Johnson (2000), *supra* note 43.

173. Worren et al. (1999), *supra* note 42.

174. Rogers, G. C., & Beer, M. (1996). TRW's information services division: Strategic human resource management. Boston: Harvard Business School Press, Case #9-496–003.

175. Worren et al. (1999), *supra* note 42.

176. Burke, W. W. (1997). The new agenda for organization development. *Organizational Dynamics, 25*, 7–21; the same point is made for the field of human resource development in general by Grieves, J. (2003). *Strategic human resource development.* London: Sage.

177. Hornstein, H. (2001). Organizational development and change management: Don't throw the baby out with the bath water. *Journal of Applied Behavioral Science, 37*(2), 223–226.

178. For example, Hartley, D. E. (2004). OD wired. *T&D, 58*(8), 20–22; Church, A. H., Gilbert, M., Oliver, D. H., Paquet, K., & Surface, C. (2002). The role of technology in organization development and change. *Advances in Developing Human Resources, 4*(4), 493–511.

179. Thomas, J. (1985). Force field analysis: A new way to evaluate your strategy. *Long Range Planning, 18*(6), 54–59; Gross, D. (2004). Are profits too high? *Slate-Moneybox,* November 12. Retrieved November 20, 2004, from http://slate.msn.com/id/2109617/

180. Grieves (2003), *supra* note 176.

181. Adapted from Aquila (2004). *supra* note 47.

# 15

# HRD AND DIVERSITY: DIVERSITY TRAINING AND BEYOND

## Learning Objectives:

*After reading this chapter, you should be able to:*

1. Understand how the changing demographics of the labor market are changing the cultural fabric of organizations.

2. Describe how organizational culture is being affected by having a greater percentage of women and minorities in the workforce.

3. Describe how diversity issues are impacting organizations, as well as HRD.

4. Become familiar with different forms of discrimination, and how HRD programs and processes can help to reduce these effects.

5. Describe the ways organizations attempt to integrate women and minorities into the organization, and the relative success of these efforts.

6. Understand the purpose and methods of cross-cultural training.

■

## OPENING CASE

R. R. Donnelley & Sons Co. is the largest printing company in North America. It prints magazines such as *TV Guide* and *Sports Illustrated*, and about a third of the textbooks used in the United States.[1] Until 1996, Donnelley had primarily emphasized one-time diversity awareness training that focused on stereotypes and prejudices in the workplace.[2] However, the company felt that it needed a broader approach than this, and gave this assignment to its diversity manager.

*Questions: What might be some drawbacks of a one-time only diversity training* program? *If you were the diversity manager, what types of things would you recommend that Donnelley do to change or expand its efforts at diversity training? What would be important to you if you were to go through such a training program? Why?*

[1]Hoover's Online (2004). R. R. Donnelley & Sons Company — Overview. Retrieved on December 10, 2004 from: http://proquest.umi.com/

[2]Flynn, G. (1998). The harsh reality of diversity programs. *Workforce* 77(12), 26–33.

## INTRODUCTION

In this chapter, we will address some of the following questions:

- *What is the current status of women and people of color in the U.S. workforce?*
- *Is there a "glass ceiling" that limits the advancement of women and people of color in U.S. organizations?*
- *What is the difference between equal employment opportunity, affirmative action, and managing diversity?*
- *How effective are diversity training programs employed by organizations?*
- *What can organizations do to better prepare their employees to deal with cross-cultural issues, especially if they are sent to work in another country?*

■ *What types of HRD programs can organizations use to develop and promote a culturally diverse workforce?*

In order for organizations to compete successfully in a global economy, they must be able to attract and retain the best employees possible. For most organizations, this means recruiting and hiring a more diverse workforce (especially women and minorities, or "people of color") for roles that they have less typically held — such as management positions. As we have noted before, there has been a gradual increase in the number of women and racial and ethnic minorities (e.g., blacks, Hispanics, and Asians) entering the workforce. This trend is expected to continue at least through the year 2020.[1]

In this chapter, we will emphasize race and gender issues, as these are the most researched forms of diversity to date. However, it is important to consider other forms of diversity as well. For example, Kossek and Lobel suggest that attention also be given to diversity in nationality, language, ability (and disability), religion, lifestyle (including family structure and sexual orientation), and work function and tenure.[2]

This chapter will focus on the changing labor market and how it is influencing organizations to make changes. First, we will briefly review organizational culture and labor market trends. Next, we will review the different forms of discrimination in the workplace, their impact on women and minorities, and how organizations can eliminate or minimize discrimination. We will then discuss some ways in which organizations have attempted to increase diversity in the workforce, the relative success or failure of these efforts, as well as how they can be improved. Lastly, we will discuss some specific HRD programs and processes used to increase diversity in the workforce or prepare employees for overseas assignments, including orientation, career development, mentoring, sexual harassment training, and cross-cultural training. We will discuss diversity training, but discuss much more than this as well.

## ORGANIZATIONAL CULTURE

Every person exists within a sociopolitical culture. **Culture** can be defined as a set of shared values, beliefs, norms, and artifacts that are used to interpret the environment and as a guide for all kinds of behavior. Each culture is distinguished by a unique set of attributes, which are described in Table 15-1. These attributes help people to differentiate one culture from another. For example, when these attributes are used to describe a nationality (e.g., American), the primary descriptors would be geographic origin, language, and political institutions. These attributes can also describe groupings or subcultures within a larger culture. When describing a subset of the American culture, the descriptors might include race, food preference, religion, employment practices, migratory status, and internal/external distinctness. A visitor to the United States, for example, would notice stark cultural differences between residents of Brainerd, Minnesota; New Orleans, Louisiana; Boston, Massachusetts; and Provo, Utah.

*Organizational culture* was defined in Chapter 14 as a set of shared values, beliefs, norms, artifacts, and patterns of behavior that are used as a frame of reference for

**TABLE 15-1**

## COMMON CULTURAL CHARACTERISTICS

1. Common geographic origin
2. Migratory status
3. Race
4. Language or dialect
5. Religious faith
6. Ties that transcend kinship, neighborhood, and community boundaries
7. Shared traditions, values, and symbols
8. Literature, folklore, music
9. Food preferences
10. Settlement and employment patterns
11. Special interests in regard to politics
12. Institutions that specifically serve and maintain the group
13. An internal perception of distinctness
14. An external perception of distinctness

SOURCE: From Thernstrom, S., Orlov, A., & Handlin, O. (Eds.). (1980). *Harvard Encyclopedia of American Ethnic Groups.* Cambridge, MA: Harvard University Press.

the way one looks at, attempts to understand, and works within any organization.[3] Organizations are subsets of larger sociopolitical cultures. Relationships between the larger sociopolitical culture and organizational cultures are referred to as "cultural 'paradigms' that tie together the basic assumptions about humankind, nature, and activities."[4] These assumptions are the building blocks or the roots of an organizational culture. They are often unseen and can be inferred only through artifacts and patterns of behavior.

*Artifacts* are "material and nonmaterial objects and patterns that intentionally or unintentionally communicate information about the organization's technology, beliefs, values, assumptions, and ways of doing things."[5] Material artifacts include documents, physical layout, furnishings, patterns of dress, and so on. Nonmaterial artifacts include organizational stories, ceremonies, and leadership styles. In organizations, leadership style can be influenced by assumptions about gender and race. For example, if a male manager assumes that it is women's nature or role to give family issues priority over work issues, he might be less likely to promote women to higher levels of responsibility. These kinds of beliefs have been prevalent in our society and will be discussed later in this chapter.

*Patterns of behavior* help to reinforce an organization's assumptions, beliefs, and ways of doing things through staff meetings, training programs, filing forms, and other normal organizational practices.[6] For example, if an organization initiates a sexual harassment policy by scheduling a mandatory training program for all employees, it is communicating a high level of importance and value to this responsibility. Conversely, an organization that fails to provide adequate training to curb incidences of sexual harassment — even if it talks about the importance of reaching that goal — will be communicating that it places the issue at a much lower level of importance. Thus, patterns of behavior help to reinforce important assumptions, beliefs, and values.

Both artifacts and patterns of behavior play an important role in the socialization process. As discussed in Chapter 8, socialization is the process whereby new members learn how to function (e.g., learn norms) in a group or organization. In the absence of a prescribed code of conduct, new members typically learn how to behave by observing the artifacts and patterns of behavior in an organization.

The match between the people in an organization and the organizational culture is very important. If an organization employs individuals who make similar assumptions about people and have similar values and beliefs, then there is greater likelihood that they will demonstrate loyalty and commitment to organizational goals. Conversely, organizations that employ people from diverse cultures or subcultures, where there may be divergent assumptions, values, and beliefs, may have different experiences. These experiences, however, are not necessarily bad. In fact, there is a growing recognition that cultural diversity can have many positive outcomes.[7] This diversity, among other things, can bring a richness of perspectives to an organization.

## LABOR-MARKET CHANGES AND DISCRIMINATION

The demographic shifts that are occurring in the U.S. population will continue to impact the workforce in the future. As we have discussed in previous chapters, this includes increasing numbers of immigrants, women, and ethnic and racial minorities in the workforce. Unfortunately, discrimination remains a concern in today's workplace.

### DISCRIMINATION

Discrimination can occur in various ways. For example, **access discrimination** occurs when an organization places limits on job availability through such things as restricting advertisement and recruitment, rejecting applicants, or offering a lower starting salary.[8] **Treatment discrimination** occurs after a person is hired and takes the form of limiting opportunities (e.g., training, promotion, rewards) or harassing certain individuals because of who they are (e.g., women, members of a racial or ethnic minority). Both types of discrimination are covered under equal employment opportunity laws.

*TREATMENT DISCRIMINATION AGAINST WOMEN IN ORGANIZATIONS.* Over the past century, women have experienced substantial changes in the rights available to them in the workplace. Table 15-2 presents the results of three Catalyst studies. This depicts the limited numbers of women in top positions, as well as the advancements women have made, at least in terms of Fortune 500 companies. More broadly,

**TABLE 15-2**

## CHANGES IN THE NUMBER OF WOMEN AT THE TOP OF FORTUNE 500 COMPANIES, 1995–2003

| | 1995 | 2000 | 2003 |
|---|---|---|---|
| Percent of board of directors who are female: | 9.5% | 11.7% | 13.6% |
| Percent of all corporate officers who are female: | 8.7% | 12.5% | 15.7% |
| Percent of top officers who are female: | 1.2% | 4.1% | 7.9% |
| Number of companies where at least 25% of all corporate officers are female: | 25 | 50 | 54 |
| Number of CEOs who are female: | 1 | 2 | 8 |

SOURCES: *2003 Catalyst census of women board directors* (2003). New York: Catalyst; *2000 Catalyst census of women corporate officers and top earners* (2000). New York: Catalyst; Baue, W. (2003, December 11). Women sit in less than a seventh of Fortune 500 board of director seats. SocialFunds.com. Retrieved November 24, 2004, from http://www.socialfunds.com/news/article.cgi/article1292.html

women have made considerable progress moving into formerly male-dominated occupations such as medicine, law, management, advertising, and engineering.[9] In 2002, women made up 47.5 percent of the private-sector workforce of U.S. organizations with 100 employees or more (who reported employment data to the Equal Employment Opportunity Commission or EEOC). In these organizations, women held a majority (53.2 percent) of all jobs classified as "professional." For the category of "officials and managers," women held 34.7 percent of these jobs.[10] Despite such changes, many concerns over sex-based discrimination remain. For example, in fiscal year 2003, the EEOC received over 24,000 formal charges of alleged sex-based discrimination.[11] This number has remained fairly steady since 1993.

Historically, women have faced discrimination in terms of promotion (particularly into management), pay, and sexual harassment. Some inroads have been made in terms of *promotion*. While Table 15-2 shows that more women are holding top positions in large companies, women are still extremely underrepresented among senior management positions.[12] In 2004, the female CEOs of Fortune 500 companies were Carly Fiorina (Hewlett-Packard), Marce Fuller (Mirant), Andrea Jung (Avon), Anne Mulcahy (Xerox), Pat Russo (Lucent), Marry Sammons (Rite Aid), Marion Sandler (Golden West), and Eileen Scott (Pathmark).[13]

While progress has been made, there is still evidence of *pay* disparity between men and women across most occupational categories.[14] Disparities persist despite the passage of the Equal Pay Act in 1963. Data from the Current Population Survey compared the median annual earnings for wage and salary earners between the ages of twenty-five and thirty-four. For all workers with a bachelor's degree or higher, the pay disparity has decreased over the past twenty-five years, but has not disappeared. For example, in 1977, males in this category earned 60 percent more than females. In 1987, males earned 38 percent more than females, and in 1997, males earned 22 percent more than females.[15]

**Sexual harassment** is another form of treatment discrimination that occurs most often against women in the workplace. There are many forms of sexual harassment, from unwanted off-color jokes and comments, to outright unwanted sexual proposi-tions and touching, to offers of job rewards in exchange for sexual favors. If an em-ployee's subjection to or rejection of the sexual conduct is used as a basis for an em-ployment decision, this is referred to as *quid pro quo* sexual harassment.[16] However, even if the harassment is not linked directly to an employment decision (such as a cut in pay or loss of a promotion), it can still be illegal harassment if the behavior is found to have created a *hostile work environment*. The Supreme Court held that sex-ual harassment could occur even when there is no tangible job detriment such as a shift to a less desirable job or the denial of a promotion.[17] Some employees choose to endure this kind of treatment for a variety of reasons, including that they need the job, feel powerless to do anything about it, or are not sure of the intent of the per-petrator. However, the impact of this can be devastating. Some people suffer serious psychological and emotional trauma that can affect their ability to work effectively. Organizations that allow this kind of treatment to go unchecked are essentially send-ing a message that some of their employees are not valued and are expendable.

Several high-profile scandals and incidents have raised awareness concerning sexual harassment. In 1991, the U.S. Navy Tailhook scandal involved the harass-ment of both female enlisted personnel and officers at a social gathering. In 1996, the EEOC brought suit against Mitsubishi Motors for widespread sexual harassment at its plant in Normal, Illinois. In 1998, Mitsubishi agreed to pay $34 million to the victims of sexual harassment at the plant, which is the largest settlement ever reached in a sexual harassment case.[18] Incidents such as these have raised publicity and awareness levels about the pervasiveness of the problem. Among other things, organizations and individuals have become more aware of sexual harassment and are beginning to take steps to confront the problem in the workplace. In addition, the passage of the Civil Rights Act of 1991 (which will be discussed later) now al-lows victims of sexual harassment to sue for compensatory damages for pain and suffering in cases where the "employer acts with malice or reckless indifference to the rights of the individual."[19] One measure of the scope of the problem can be seen in the number of discrimination complaints filed with the EEOC. There were 13,566 charges of sexual harassment filed with the EEOC in fiscal year 2003.[20] Further, women filed 85.3 percent of all charges.

*TREATMENT DISCRIMINATION AGAINST MINORITIES IN ORGANIZATIONS.* Treat-ment discrimination against minorities in the workplace is seen primarily in the lack of promotional opportunities and incidents of racial harassment. Similar to the situ-ation for women, the number of formal charges of race discrimination remains high. For example, in fiscal year 2003, the EEOC received over 28,000 charges of race-based discrimination. From 1992 to 2003, the number of charges ranged from 26,000 to over 31,000 per year.[21] In terms of *promotional opportunities,* probably the most publicized was the case at Texaco Oil Company. In 1994, a group of Texaco executives were audiotaped by one of the executives discussing a pending civil rights lawsuit by 1,400 black professionals and managers who charged that they were denied promotion because of their race. During this taped conversation, the executives were heard making disparaging racial remarks and innuendos that the black employees belonged at the bottom of the organizational ladder. When the tape was made public, Texaco was forced to take action against the offending executives.

Texaco management had to publicly apologize to the black employees and offer them a $176 million out-of-court settlement.[22] Peter Bijur, Texaco's chairman and CEO, stressed in his public comments that bigotry and corporate prejudice are widespread throughout our society.[23] The potential for this kind of public embarrassment may be the best deterrent to acts of discrimination that go on within organizations.

Like women, minorities have had difficulty moving into key executive and policymaking positions. In 2002, blacks made up 13.9 percent of the workforce of organizations reporting employment data to the EEOC. However, blacks constituted only 6.6 percent of the officials and managers and 7.0 percent of the professionals in these organizations.[24] Similarly, Hispanics made up 10.9 percent of the workforce at these organizations, yet held 4.8 percent of the officials and managers positions and 4.0 percent of the professional positions. In a survey of 400 of the Fortune 1000 companies, fewer than 9 percent of all managers were minorities, including those who were black, Asian, and Hispanic.[25] Powell and Butterfield investigated the effect of race on promotions to top management in a federal agency and found that race did not directly affect promotion decisions, but that other factors (composition of the selection panel and whether panel members had job experience in the hiring department) did have an effect.[26] This suggests that if the hiring panel is composed of all white individuals, a nonwhite candidate may have less chance of being promoted.

In addition, differences have been found in career options for white and black employees.[27] Specifically, black employees have "received less favorable assessments of promotability from their supervisors, were likely to have plateaued in their careers, and were more dissatisfied with their careers than whites."[28] Further, the factors affecting the evaluation and development of minorities in organizations have been examined, including bias effects, lost opportunities, and self-limiting behaviors.[29] In terms of development, minorities are affected by such things "as absence of mentors, less interesting or challenging work as a result of being in the outgroup, and being left out of the informal social network."[30] This suggests that if organizations are going to attract and retain qualified minorities, they must remove barriers and address the developmental needs of those groups.

**Racial harassment** on the job can take many forms. The more obvious form of racial harassment occurs when a coworker verbally (face-to-face or in writing) or physically attacks a person of color because of racial differences. For example, in 2000, the EEOC obtained a $700,000 settlement from Direct Marketing Services of Arizona. Black employees at the telemarketing firm alleged that they were racially harassed, denied promotions, and paid unequal wages.[31] A more subtle form of racial harassment is when coworkers ostracize an individual by withholding important information and other resources needed to perform the job. The effects of these types of discrimination include the creation of a hostile environment and interference with the targeted person's ability to do his or her job.

## EQUAL EMPLOYMENT OPPORTUNITY

Since the 1960s, the U.S. government and individual states have established many laws and regulations that are intended to protect the civil rights of citizens. One important group of civil rights laws are those mandating **equal employment**

**opportunity (EEO).** EEO is defined as the right to obtain jobs and earn rewards in them regardless of nonjob-related factors. Title VII of the Civil Rights Act of 1964 (the main federal EEO law) and the amendments and legislation that have followed it make it unlawful for employers to make employment decisions on the basis of race, color, sex, religion, national origin, age, mental or physical handicap, Vietnam-era or disabled veteran status, and pregnancy, unless these factors can be shown to be job related. These laws are directed primarily at employment practices, including access to HRD programs, that have an unfair exclusionary impact on any of the groups specified in the legislation. Essentially, EEO legislation is intended to address illegal discrimination in the workplace, and promote a workplace that is race blind, gender blind, and so on. As such, EEO laws cover all races and both genders. This means that whites and males can allege discrimination under EEO laws in the same manner that minorities and women do, that is, they must argue that they have been discriminated against because of their race or gender. Through Title VII, the U.S. Congress also established the Equal Employment Opportunity Commission (EEOC), which is the federal agency primarily responsible for administering and enforcing EEO laws. Its role is to seek compliance wherever possible and to pursue remedies in civil court only as a last resort.

## THE GLASS CEILING

The rise of women and minorities to management positions, particularly upper-level executive and policymaking positions, has been slow. To many, it has appeared as if an invisible but impenetrable boundary prevented them from advancing to senior management levels. This barrier has been described as the **glass ceiling.** The glass ceiling is defined as subtle attitudes and prejudices that block women and minorities from upward mobility, particularly into management jobs.[32] More specifically, the glass ceiling symbolizes prevailing attitudes about different cultural groups and their general abilities, or the lack thereof, to perform some role or occupation.

The U.S. Department of Labor (DOL) established the Glass Ceiling Commission, which initiated a study of the effects of the glass ceiling on upward mobility. The goals of the initiative were:

1. to promote a high quality, inclusive, and diverse workforce capable of meeting the challenge of global competition
2. to promote good corporate conduct through an emphasis on corrective and cooperative problem solving
3. to promote equal opportunity, not mandated results
4. to establish a blueprint of procedures to guide the department in conducting future reviews of all management levels of the corporate workforce[33]

The study investigated several companies to determine the extent to which an organization's promotion patterns showed a glass ceiling pattern. Some of the findings were as follows:

1. Neither women nor minorities tended to advance as far as their white male counterparts, although women advanced further than minorities.

2. While most organizations made a concerted effort to identify and develop key (white male) employees, few organizations had taken any ownership for equal employment opportunity and access.

3. The few women and minorities who held executive jobs were in staff positions (e.g., human resources, research, and administration) that were considered outside the corporate mainstream for promotions to senior-level positions.

4. While most of these organizations held federal government contracts, most had inadequate equal employment and affirmative action record keeping.

The report also identified potential barriers to upward mobility. In addition to recruitment practices, the report cited the "lack of opportunity to contribute and participate in corporate developmental experiences."[34] This suggests that organizations should formalize the career development process in order to eliminate glass ceiling effects. A sole reliance on informal mentoring is insufficient to ensure that every qualified person is given an opportunity for advancement. Several recent articles have noted (1) some "cracks" in the glass ceiling for women,[35] (2) differences in glass ceiling effects for women than for blacks (fewer promotions for blacks than for women),[36] and (3) differences in effects across managerial level in the United States, Sweden, and Australia.[37] This suggests that further research and corporate change efforts are still needed in this area.[38]

## IMPACT OF RECENT IMMIGRATION PATTERNS

One reason for the growth in the number of minority workers has been the large influx of immigrants since the 1960s. In 2002, the U.S. foreign-born population exceeded 33 million. An estimated 52 percent of these individuals are from Latin America (especially Mexico), 27 percent are from Asia, and 15 percent are from Europe.[39] Differences based on culture, religion, and other variables must be considered as these individuals are assimilated into U.S. society and work settings.

## ADAPTING TO DEMOGRAPHIC CHANGES

Most organizations have recognized the demographic changes that have occurred in the workforce over the past forty years. In response to the civil rights and feminist movements, as well as the equal employment legislation that began in the 1960s, many organizations established programs to facilitate the recruitment and retention of qualified women and minorities. The inclusion of women, minorities, and other underrepresented groups has made organizations more culturally diverse.

**Cultural diversity** is defined as the existence of two or more persons from different cultural groups in any single group or organization. Most organizations are culturally diverse because their employees are from different cultural subgroups (whether gender, race, ethnic origin, etc.). But even if an organization is culturally diverse, it may not be aware of or acknowledge this diversity.

In this section, we will discuss three common approaches to creating a working environment in which all organization members can contribute fully — affirmative action, valuing differences, and managing diversity. In different ways, each approach seeks to extend beyond the legal mandates required by the equal opportunity (EEO) laws discussed earlier.

## AFFIRMATIVE ACTION PROGRAMS

One approach that goes beyond the obligations specified in EEO legislation is **affirmative action.** While organizations that are covered by Title VII are encouraged to practice affirmative action to increase the numbers of women and minorities in their organizations, they are not legally required to do so under Title VII. The purpose of affirmative action programs is "to bring members of underrepresented groups, usually groups that have suffered discrimination, into a higher degree of participation in some beneficial program."[40] The concept of affirmative action was written into law in 1965 as part of Executive Order 11246 (as amended by Order 11375), which was issued by President Johnson. This order requires that certain government agencies and employers (and their subcontractors) who hold federal contracts in excess of $10,000 undertake affirmative action processes to ensure equal employment opportunity. It also established the Office of Federal Contract Compliance Programs (OFCCP), which has the responsibility of overseeing the affirmative action process. According to OFCCP guidelines, organizations should take the following steps to meet affirmative action requirements:

1. Prepare a written policy statement on equal employment opportunity/ affirmative action (EEO/AA).
2. Designate an affirmative action officer.
3. Publicize an EEO/AA policy statement.
4. Conduct an analysis of the surrounding labor market to determine if its current labor force is representative.
5. If a protected group is underrepresented in any area within the organization (by department, occupation, etc.), develop goals and timetables to achieve parity with the external labor market.
6. Develop specific programs and activities to achieve these goals and timetables.
7. Establish an internal auditing and reporting system of its programs and activities.
8. Develop support for affirmative action, both inside and outside the company.

In essence, affirmative action can sometimes require actions such as preferential recruiting and hiring or placement of certain groups when those groups are underrepresented in an occupation within an organization. This is a very different premise from that used for equal employment opportunity legislation. That is, with EEO, the employer seeks to ignore race and gender as much as possible when making employment decisions. Under affirmative action, the employer is asked to explicitly consider race and gender in such decisions, if women and minorities are not adequately represented in a particular job or job category (compared to their availability in the labor market). The affirmative actions that an employer may engage in often involve HRD programs.

Affirmative action remains a volatile topic in the United States. Supporters of affirmative action believe that it is necessary for correcting patterns of discrimination, particularly when an affirmative action plan (AAP) has been ordered by the courts in cases where an organization has been found guilty of long-standing discrimination. A second justification for affirmative action is the belief that, because of institutional racism, minorities have been subjected to inferior conditions (e.g., lack of good education) and that they have thus been inhibited in their ability to compete against better-prepared whites. Therefore, preferential treatment can be one way to equalize their chances. This was the reasoning supported in the case of *Weber v. Kaiser Aluminum and Chemicals* (1976).[41] This decision allowed a temporary preference for admitting qualified members of underrepresented groups to jobs and training opportunities when a company could show imbalances in its workforce. In this case, Kaiser had previously negotiated exclusionary terms with a union that barred blacks from accessing the in-house training programs that were required for promotion.[42]

While affirmative action has resulted in employment gains for women and minorities, particularly in the professional ranks, it has vocal opponents and has created several problems. Critics argue that affirmative action goes beyond providing equal employment opportunity by allowing employers to give preference to members of protected groups at the expense of majority-group members. They claim that this preference leads to so-called reverse discrimination against such individuals. Second, it is argued that AAPs have created feelings of animosity toward the individuals and groups that have been perceived to benefit from them. A third problem with AAPs is that they can *stigmatize* qualified minorities and women who have been hired or promoted based on their achievements. When an AAP is present, some employees may feel that the successes of *all* minority and women candidates are the result of affirmative action alone. This can undermine the self-esteem of people who have worked hard to educate themselves and develop the necessary skills to be successful.

Numerous court challenges and legislation on the state level have created uncertainty about the future of affirmative action. The State of California moved to eliminate race- and gender-based affirmative action from decisions regarding public employment, education, and contracting. The initial step was a decision by the University of California Board of Regents to abolish racial preferences in favor of merit-based admissions and hiring criteria. This was followed by voter approval of Proposition 209 in the 1996 election, which eliminated race- and gender-based affirmative action in decisions regarding public education, contracting, and employment. Civil rights advocates won a temporary restraining order prohibiting the law's implementation in early 1997, but this restraining order was lifted, and a subsequent request to the U.S. Supreme Court to grant an emergency restraining order was denied. The University of Texas Law School's affirmative action program was declared illegal in 1996, resulting in a significant reduction of minority candidates being admitted to the school in the fall of 1997. Currently, affirmative action has largely been overturned at public universities in Texas, California, and Florida.[43] Taken together, the changes brought about by actions such as these will significantly affect the legality and scope of affirmative action in the current decade.

Advocates of affirmative action have responded to the criticisms leveled at it. For example, R. Roosevelt Thomas, executive director of the American Institute of Managing Diversity, stated that "affirmative action gets blamed for failing to do things it could never do . . . so long as racial and gender equality is something we grant to minorities and women there will be no racial and gender equality."[44] The growing challenge to affirmative action has led some civil rights advocates to propose modifying it as a way to retain what they see as its beneficial effects, while addressing the charges of critics. For example, Deval Patrick, former assistant U.S. attorney general for civil rights, advocated replacing affirmative action with what he calls affirmative consideration, an approach that supports merit, emphasizes qualifications, and embodies flexibility and the aspirations of an integrated workplace.[45] In summary, the status of affirmative action remains uncertain. As we move into the twenty-first century, race and gender discrimination remain troubling issues in American society. Government, employers, and citizens are still struggling to find ways to address the basic concerns that these issues raise.

## VALUING DIFFERENCES AND DIVERSITY TRAINING

Barbara Walker, former manager of the International Diversity Program at Digital Equipment Corporation, is credited with coining the phrase **valuing differences** in the 1980s. Her approach was to create an environment in which each person's cultural differences are respected. Valuing differences soon became popularized as **diversity training.** The diversity training movement gained momentum when the Hudson Institute published a report in 1987 that predicted that women and minorities would represent 85 percent of all net new entrants in the labor force by the year 2000.[46] This prediction led to a sense of urgency by employers who felt they were ill prepared to handle this kind of change. It also resulted in the proliferation of diversity consultants and programs (e.g., cultural sensitivity training), many of which came with a large price tag.[47]

It is estimated that 72 percent of organizations conducted diversity training in 2003.[48] Diversity training programs vary in scope and length. At one extreme are one- to three-day programs for managers that are designed to transform them into culturally sensitive people. Most of these are one-shot programs that have no follow-up to reinforce the issues raised in training. For example, US WEST developed a diversity program that includes two kinds of training: (1) a three-day program called Managing a Diverse Workforce for managers and union stewards and (2) a one-day version called The Value of Human Diversity for the remaining 65,000 employees.[49] Other organizations have used a different approach that includes a strategy to foster long-term cultural change. For example, Pacific Gas & Electric created a program based on the assumption that a cadre of internal trainers is needed to cultivate a multicultural organization. Employees are selected to attend a six-day certification ("train-the-trainer") diversity awareness program and, upon graduation, are expected to champion diversity in their day-to-day interactions with others.[50]

*EFFECTIVENESS OF DIVERSITY TRAINING PROGRAMS.* There is some anecdotal evidence suggesting that diversity training can at least make individuals aware of cultural distinctions. Three examples illustrate this evidence:

1. A survey of employees who attended diversity training found that 62 percent felt the training was worthwhile in raising awareness of racial and gender differences; however, most of the respondents (87 percent of whites and 52 percent of blacks) felt that race relations were good or better in their own organization *before* the training.[51]

2. An organizational evaluation of a diversity-training program at the Federal Aviation Administration (FAA) found that training made a significant difference in raising awareness.[52]

3. The results of a custom-designed diversity training program at Wisconsin Power and Light Company indicated that employees had been receptive and that the training had improved how they behaved toward others, both internally and externally.[53]

The FAA and Wisconsin Power and Light programs benefited from top management's strong commitment not only to make the program work, but also to conduct follow-up activities that would reinforce the changes.

There has been considerable criticism concerning the value of diversity training. An element of many programs is to highlight ways in which participants are different from each other. A common misgiving about emphasizing differences is that it fails to recognize that people identify with each other because of shared interests, values, goals, and experiences.[54] Another criticism deals with the lack of tangible goals, standards, and outcomes in many programs.[55] Also, the merit of the activities used in some diversity training programs has been questioned. For example, some participants complain about white male bashing, so-called political correctness, and punishment for insensitivity, and some participants say the workshops are a pointless waste of time.[56] An ironic twist is that the Texaco executives on the tape accused of racist comments used the metaphor "black jelly bean," which came directly from a managing diversity workshop in which the colors of jelly beans were used to identify people, rather than as racial or ethnic labels.[57]

The costs of doing diversity training have also been questioned. It is reported that diversity consultants bill an average cost of $2,000 per day (with some demanding four times that amount), and a service such as a "cultural audit" costs as much as $100,000.[58] Flynn estimates that companies spend between $200–$300 million per year on diversity training yet, as noted earlier, lawsuits by women and minorities remain at very high levels.[59] Table 15-3 summarizes some of the potential problems with diversity training.

In a recent review, Ivancevich and Gilbert wrote, "We have not found a single reported program that conducts a rigorous evaluation of diversity training effectiveness" (p. 84).[60] Therefore, more vigorous evaluation of diversity programs is clearly necessary to assess their effectiveness in light of the mounting criticism and the costs. For example, a survey of the factors that lead to diversity program success concluded that success is associated with top-management support, a high strategic priority to diversity relative to other objectives, the presence of positive management

**TABLE 15-3**

## POTENTIAL PROBLEMS WITH DIVERSITY TRAINING

**When trainers . . .**

- Use their own psychological issues (e.g., trust or group affiliation) as template for training
- Have their political agenda
- Do not model the philosophy or skills associated with valuing diversity
- Are chosen because they represent or advocate for a minority group
- Are not competent at facilitation and presenting, have poor credibility with trainees, or are known to be insensitive
- Force people to reveal their feelings about other people
- Do not respect individual styles of trainees
- Pressure only one group to change
- Cover too few issues and do not engage participants individually

**When the training program . . .**

- Is not integrated into the organization's overall approach to diversity
- Is too brief, too late, or reactive
- Is presented as remedial and trainees as people with problems
- Does not distinguish the meanings of valuing diversity, EEO, AA, and managing across cultures
- Does not make a link between stereotyping behavior and personal and organizational effectiveness
- Is based on a philosophy of political correctness
- Is too shallow or too deep
- Resource materials are outdated
- Curriculum is not adapted to trainees' needs or not matched with the skills and experience of the trainer
- Discussion of certain issues (e.g., reverse discrimination) is not allowed

SOURCE: Copyright © December 1992 from *Training & Development Journal* by Mobley, M. & Payne, T. Reprinted with permission of American Society for Training & Development.

beliefs about diversity, large organizations, and presence of a diversity manager.[61] Another criticism of the valuing differences approach is that its primary emphasis is on improving interpersonal relations and not on providing the *skills* needed for working with diverse cultural groups.[62] To learn these skills, a managing diversity approach may be needed.

### MANAGING DIVERSITY

Thomas defines **managing diversity** as "a comprehensive managerial process for developing an environment (organizational culture) that works for all employees."[63] This approach goes beyond both affirmative action and valuing diversity because it focuses on building a positive environment for everyone and on full utilization of the total workforce. It does not exclude women or minorities, nor does it exclude whites or males. It is an attempt to create a level playing field for all employees without regard to cultural distinction. Coming to agreement on the definition of diversity can be a very difficult thing, as many experienced trainers will attest.[64] However, one recent article defined it as "the commitment on the part of organizations to recruit, retain, reward, and promote a heterogeneous mix of productive, motivated, and committed workers including people of color, whites, females, and the physically challenged."[65] To do this, the managing diversity approach requires (1) a long-term commitment to change; (2) substantive changes in organizational culture; (3) a modified definition of leadership and management roles; (4) both individual and organizational adaptation; and (5) structural changes.[66]

The *long-term commitment to change,* particularly from top management, is necessary to allow sufficient time and resources to bring about a change in organizational culture. For example, Pillsbury has created the following managing diversity three-year objectives for its division heads:

1. To develop and implement strategic plans for creating more culturally diverse organizations

2. To increase leaders' and managers' knowledge and skills in managing a culturally diverse workplace

3. To attract, motivate, and retain women and people of color[67]

To achieve these objectives, managers must be totally committed to the program. Commitment from key organizational members (top managers, union leaders, etc.) is an important part of managing diversity. How to gain their commitment will be discussed later in this chapter.

A *substantive change in culture* is necessary if an organization expects to change the underlying assumptions, values, and beliefs that have fostered sexist and racist attitudes. Employees must learn to be more understanding of language and cultural differences and be able to identify and reject cultural stereotypes. Most organizations that have developed managing diversity programs rely on education and training programs, much as the valuing differences approach does. For example, organizations like Avon, Apple Computer, and Xerox have made diversity education the cornerstone of their managing diversity programs.

*Modified definitions of leadership and management roles* are needed to accommodate the changes in organizational culture. Not only is it important that management roles be redefined during the change process, they may also be redefined as part of the managing diversity program. For example, managers may be required to serve as formal mentors to one or more of the women and minorities in their organization. Other organizations may require managers to lead a diversity core group. To ensure that these roles are institutionalized, some organizations have created a new corporate office for managing diversity. This office gives the program high visibility, and ensures that all activities are coordinated.

Managing diversity requires *both individual and organizational adaptation,* because as the organizational culture undergoes a redefinition and begins to take on new characteristics, employees must be able to adapt to these changes. How well the organization and its employees adapt is highly dependent on the management and leadership of the change process. Sufficient support systems must be available for people who are not sure about what is expected of them and how to adapt to these new expectations. For example, some employees may feel this program is affirmative action under a new name. Managers must be able to reinforce the point that a managing diversity program favors no subgroup.

*Structural changes* are necessary to accommodate the changes in management and leadership roles and changes in individual expectations. For example, several structural changes within the HRD function may need to be made. These include (1) developing new policies that support the management diversity initiative; (2) changing formal orientation programs to place more emphasis on diversity issues; (3) developing formal career development programs; (4) adding a diversity component to some of the ongoing training programs, particularly management and supervisory training; and (5) developing a diversity resource library for all types of ongoing diversity programs.

*EXAMPLE OF A MANAGEMENT DIVERSITY PROGRAM.* As noted, managing diversity involves the development of a long-term change strategy, including both structural and cultural changes.

Table 15-4 describes Pillsbury's managing diversity strategy, which has six stages.[68] Stages 1 and 2 are used for developing the context in which the change will take place. The activities include awareness sessions with senior management who need to understand their role in the change process and how to manage diversity. These briefing sessions are followed by team sessions that focus on educating employees about some of the issues that underlie cultural diversity. If necessary, the change agent or agents may review cultural data to illustrate important aspects of the organization's culture (e.g., certain employees feel isolated). The desired outcome of these first two stages is that everyone will feel a shared need to change.

Stages 3 through 5 involve more in-depth education about how diversity can bring added value to the organization. These three-day sessions explore the underlying assumptions that lead to racist and sexist attitudes. The goal is to expand each participant's understanding of cultural differences, the value each person places on cultural differences, and the ways that including a diverse workforce will enhance the organization. The last stage, Stage 6, involves integrating the cultural strategy into the organization's business plan. Because the philosophy of managing diversity is predicated on how well managers and other members of an organization view the utilization of people from all cultures, it is essential that the long-term strategy of the organization reflect this philosophy. This strategy also includes any changes in human resource management policies that will be necessary for achieving the long-term strategy, including strengthening the recruitment, hiring, and retention of a diverse workforce.

*EFFECTIVENESS OF MANAGING DIVERSITY PROGRAMS.* There is growing awareness of the need to address diversity issues. Many organizations have achieved success with such programs (e.g., Enterprise Rent-A-Car, Fifth-Third Bank, Kraft, PepsiCo, Pitney Bowes, Procter & Gamble, United Parcel Services, and Wells Fargo were recently featured for their effective diversity practices by the National Urban League).[69] However, a problem with managing diversity is the resistance of long-held attitudes to change. Even when organizations bolster their change strategy with diversity education and training programs, there is no guarantee that all employees will place the same value on learning about their own attitudes and about

## TABLE 15-4     PILLSBURY'S PROGRAM FOR MANAGING DIVERSITY

| Stage | Objectives |
|---|---|
| I. Briefing session, half day–2 days | a. Review organization's cultural assessment data. |
| | b. Learn basic concepts regarding high performing, culturally diverse organizations. |
| | c. Review organization's diversity plan. |
| II. Team session, 2 days | a. Build team skills necessary for addressing cultural diversity. |
| | b. Clarify business rationale for cultural diversity. |
| | c. Understand differences in business style. |
| | d. Understand differences in interpersonal style. |
| III. Added value (race), 3 days | a. Enhance racial interactions and communications. |
| | b. Identify stereotyping (racist) behaviors. |
| | c. Identify and address organizational barriers to contributions of racial minorities. |
| | d. Develop strategies for greater inclusion of racial minorities. |
| IV. Added value (gender), 3 days | a. Enhance gender interactions and communications. |
| | b. Identify stereotyping (sexist) behaviors. |
| | c. Identify and address organizational barriers to women's successful contributions. |
| | d. Develop strategies for greater inclusion of women. |
| V. Added value (style), 3 days | a. Identify the value that differences in style, ethnic/race, gender, and culture bring to the workplace. |
| | b. Practice teamwork that enhances the contribution of each member. |
| VI. Strategic planning, 1–2 days | a. Integrate cultural diversity into the business plan. |
| | b. Develop plans to (1) expand educational process to the total organization, (2) enhance the human resource system, and (3) strengthen recruitment and retention. |

SOURCE: From Greenslade, M. (1991). Managing diversity: Lessons from the United States. *Personnel Management* (United Kingdom), *23*(12), 30.

other cultures, particularly if they feel they have nothing in common with members of those cultures. The fact remains that people tend to feel most comfortable among those with whom they have things in common (e.g., common cultural attributes).

Furthermore, there is a concern about backlash among whites, particularly white males. The following reactions to diversity education and training programs have been reported:

1. Deep-seated biases and prejudices that are emerging as a reaction to fast-paced social change

2. A perceived competition for jobs and resources, creating what some people see as a threatening environment

3. Race and gender issues used increasingly as a political football in the workplace

4. The tendency of some people to see the political correctness movement as a direct threat to the First Amendment — which has created a legal and social minefield

5. Confusion about such terms as *political correctness, diversity, multiculturalism, pluralism, equal opportunity,* and *affirmative action*[70]

This perceived backlash should not be ignored in a process of forced change.[71] As discussed in Chapter 14, resistance to change is rooted in personal values, beliefs, and attitudes. To overcome this resistance, we feel that organizations should consider introducing multiculturalism through a planned change strategy. This would entail making use of theories and interventions such as those discussed in the last chapter. Further, there is a growing body of work that provides guidance concerning how organizations can manage diversity in a way that is strategic, proactive, and more grounded in solid empirical and theoretical research than has typically been true to date. We refer the reader to a number of these writings.[72] As one example, Ivancevich and Gilbert outlined a number of differences between affirmative action and diversity management.[73] These are presented in Table 15-5. Others have also noted the value of a diversity management perspective for the development of self-directed work teams.[74] Finally, in the National Urban League survey of over 5,500 U.S. workers mentioned earlier, there was considerable agreement concerning what employees viewed as effective diversity practices. These are listed in Table 15-6.

## CROSS-CULTURAL EDUCATION AND TRAINING PROGRAMS

Globalization is increasingly being linked to diversity management efforts.[75] The argument is that a multicultural perspective is needed for organizations to successfully compete in the global marketplace. Globalization has also resulted in more U.S. citizens being given expatriate assignments. According to the National Trade Council (NTC), more than 250,000 U.S. citizens are working overseas.[76] To prepare these individuals for their assignments, many organizations are providing **cross-cultural**

**TABLE 15-5**

## SOME COMPARISONS OF AFFIRMATIVE ACTION AND DIVERSITY MANAGEMENT

| Affirmative Action | Diversity Management |
| --- | --- |
| 1. Reactive and based on law and moral imperative | Proactive |
| 2. Not linked in any formal manner to team building | Emphasizes building diverse teams |
| 3. Focuses primarily on women and people of color | Inclusive — race ethnicity, age, religion, sexual orientation, and physical limitations all generally considered |
| 4. Emphasis is primarily on employees and not external constituents | Considers diversity in the recruitment pool, in employees, and in the external constituency |

SOURCE: From Ivancevich, J. M., & Gilbert, J. A. (2000). Diversity management: Time for a new approach. *Public Personnel Management, 29*(1), 89.

**TABLE 15-6**

## U.S. EMPLOYEE RANKINGS OF THE MOST IMPORTANT DIVERSITY PRACTICES

| Effective Diversity Practices Theme | Importance Rank |
| --- | --- |
| Marketing to diverse customers and consumers | 1 |
| Retaining diverse talent | 2 |
| Recruiting diverse talent | 3 |
| Leadership commitment and involvement | 4 |
| Inclusive culture and values | 5 |
| Diversity education and training | 6 |
| Community involvement | 7 |
| Advancing diverse talent | 8 |
| Career development for diverse talent | 9 |
| Diversity employee communications | 10 |
| Employee involvement | 11 |
| Supplier diversity | 12 |
| Performance accountability and measurement | 13 |

SOURCE: Diversity practices that work (2004). National Urban League (p. 20). Retrieved November 29, 2004, from http://www.nul.org/pdf/ERAC-NUL.pdf

PART 3: HUMAN RESOURCE DEVELOPMENT APPLICATIONS

**training.** Most cross-cultural awareness training programs deal with at least four elements:

1. Raising the awareness of cultural differences
2. Focusing on ways attitudes are shaped
3. Providing factual information about each culture
4. Building skills in the areas of language, nonverbal communication, cultural stress management, and adjustment adaptation skills[77]

To *raise the awareness of cultural differences,* some questions that generate discussion need to be asked. Table 15-7 presents some sample questions. The discussion should focus on understanding the assumptions, beliefs, and values people have about other cultures. Without first developing insight into these elements, it will be difficult for people to value cultural differences. For example, people from Japan and some other Asian countries may have difficulty assimilating with the aggressiveness that is common in many U.S. workplaces.[78] Without understanding these differences, Americans may misinterpret the motive of a Japanese manager who is unwilling to confront an American worker who has been overly aggressive toward him.

Programs that *focus on how attitudes are shaped* help people to understand how cultural stereotypes are formed and the destructiveness of cultural bias. Even

### TABLE 15-7   QUESTIONS FOR CULTURAL AWARENESS TRAINING

| Question | Potential Areas of Discussion | Examples |
|---|---|---|
| What are some key dissimilarities between people from different cultures? | 1. Physical traits<br>2. System of values<br>3. Language or dialect<br>4. Religion<br>5. Institutions | 1. Sex, age, race<br>2. Work ethic<br>3. Hispanic<br>4. Judaism<br>5. Economic |
| How do these differences come about? | 1. Custom<br>2. Lifestyle<br>3. Shared norms<br>4. Shared experiences<br>5. Communication patterns | 1. Clothing<br>2. Food<br>3. Conforming<br>4. War veteran<br>5. Nonverbal symbols |
| What are the implications when different cultures interact? | 1. Conflict<br><br>2. Stereotyping or ethnocentrism<br><br>3. Sexism or racism | 1. When there is a misunderstanding<br>2. When a group refuses to accept a person from another group<br>3. Discrimination |

SOURCE: From Mason, H., & Spich, R. S. (1987). *Management: An International Perspective.* Homewood, IL: Irwin.

though people may understand cultural differences, they may not truly understand how assumptions, values, and beliefs underlie sexist and racist attitudes. For example, a male manager may take extra effort to understand gender differences and learn to value women's contributions at the workplace. However, because there are a limited number of female managers, he may assume that most women lack the desire (or ability) to become managers. This assumption may result in his not actively encouraging female subordinates to develop the skills needed to qualify for a management position. This may serve to create a glass ceiling. Without focusing on how these attitudes are developed, it will be difficult to change them.

*Providing factual information about each culture* is necessary to reinforce new assumptions, values, beliefs, and attitudes about different cultures. When people are strongly ethnocentric — that is, feeling that their culture is superior to others — training may be provided, with the goal of reinforcing that every culture has its own unique and valuable experiences, perspectives, and styles of approaching problems. There is empirical evidence suggesting that cultural diversity brings together different experiences, perspectives, and styles that can be used for approaching problems and situations resulting in increased productivity.[79] People need to know what these strengths are and how they can help individual workers and the organization to do a better job.

Programs that *build skills in the areas of language, nonverbal communication, cultural stress management, and adjustment adaptation* address critical interpersonal relations of employees both inside and outside the organization. In order for people to establish effective relations, they must learn how to communicate. Nonverbal communication, including body language (e.g., gestures and handshakes), can be particularly important. Table 15-8 describes how some common forms of body language used by Americans can be misinterpreted by other cultures. Part of the communication training effort should focus on learning to understand cultural differences in body language and other nonverbal communication when dealing with different cultural groups.

It is estimated that 62 percent of U.S. companies offer some form of cross-cultural training, although the average length of this training is less than one day.[80] Given the high cost of much cross-cultural training, it is worth asking whether such programs are effective or not. Fortunately, research on this question has been quite positive.[81] It would appear that well-done cross-cultural training can have beneficial effects on employee adjustment and their performance in international assignments.

## HUMAN RESOURCE DEVELOPMENT PROGRAMS FOR CULTURALLY DIVERSE EMPLOYEES

The changing demographics of the workforce present both opportunities and challenges to HRD professionals. One of the challenges is seeking to remove all causes of discrimination. HRD professionals can do at least two things. First, they must be willing to confront the underlying assumptions, beliefs, and attitudes that foster bigotry and stereotyping that exist within their organization. They can be advocates

**TABLE 15-8**     **BODY LANGUAGE IN CULTURES WORLDWIDE**

■ Acceptable interpersonal distance in various countries is

| | |
|---|---|
| 0 to 18 inches | Middle Eastern males, people from the eastern and southern Mediterranean, and some Hispanic cultures |
| 18 inches to 3 feet | U.S. and Western Europe |
| 3 feet or more | Asia (Japanese the farthest) and many African cultures |

■ It is inappropriate behavior to touch others on the head in most Asian countries.

■ Acceptable length of eye contact in various cultures is

| | |
|---|---|
| 0 to 1 second | Native Americans, East Indians, and Asian cultures (Least is the Cambodian culture, which believes that direct eye contact is flirtatious.). |
| 1 second | U.S. (To continue direct eye contact beyond 1 second can be considered threatening, particularly between Anglo- and African-American persons.). |
| 1 second or more | Middle Eastern, Hispanic, southern European, and French cultures generally advocate very direct eye contact. |

■ Variations of handshakes in various countries are

| | |
|---|---|
| Firm | United States, Germany |
| Moderate grasp | Hispanic countries |
| Light | France (not offered to superiors) |
| Soft | Great Britain |
| Gentle | Middle Eastern countries |
| Gentle | Asia (For some cultures, though not Koreans, shaking hands is unfamiliar and uncomfortable.) |
| Pointing | Generally poor etiquette in most countries, especially in Asian countries where it is considered rude and in poor taste. If pointing is necessary, in Hong Kong you use your middle finger, in Malaysia it is the thumb, and the rest of Asia it is the entire hand. |
| Beckoning | The American gesture of using upturned fingers, palm facing the body, is deeply offensive to the Mexicans, Filipinos, and Vietnamese. For example, this gesture in the Philippines is used to beckon prostitutes. |
| Signs of approval | The American use of the okay sign, the thumbs-up signal, and the V for "victory" are among the most offensive to other cultures. |
| Signaling no | This can be confusing. In Mexico and the Middle East, a no is indicated by a back-to-forth movement of the index finger. |
| The left hand | Gesturing or handling something with the left hand among Muslims is considered offensive because they consider this the "toilet" hand. |

■ Crossing legs is in poor taste among most Asian and Middle Eastern cultures. The Russians find it distasteful to place the ankle on the knee.

SOURCE: From Thiederman, S. (1990). *Bridging cultural barriers for corporate success* (pp. 133–141). Lexington, MA: Lexington Books.

for people who are victims of discrimination and must be willing to fight for institutional justice. Second, HRD professionals should examine their organization's practices in the areas of socialization, orientation, career development, and sexual and racial harassment.

## SOCIALIZATION AND ORIENTATION

In Chapter 8, we defined socialization as the process by which an individual becomes an insider through assimilating the roles, norms, and expectations of the organization. A new employee's initial experiences in an organization are particularly significant in influencing later decisions about career choices and whether to remain in an organization. For example, when learning experiences are designed for new employees, the following issues should be considered:

1. New employees (including women and minorities) may feel isolated when their cultural differences prevent them from obtaining the interesting and challenging work assignments that are needed to learn important job-related skills and to qualify for promotions.[82]

2. Women and minorities may experience additional stresses if they feel they must become "bicultural" in order to be accepted by coworkers in the majority group.[83]

3. Women and minorities are sometimes held to higher standards than other coworkers as they enter nontraditional occupations.[84]

Failure to consider these issues can result in the loss of talented employees.

Some organizations have recognized the influences of cultural differences on the socialization process and have taken steps to incorporate them into their orientation and socialization practices. For example, Armco Steel recognized that subtle attitudes and prejudices against women and minorities had a negative effect on their upward mobility. Armco saw how these attitudes and prejudices were manifested during the socialization process. Specifically, it looked for ways in which existing employees could serve as role models during the socialization process.[85] Having role models from one's own race and gender can make it easier for new employees to confront issues like sexism and racism without fearing reprisal from coworkers.

There is disagreement about the value of holding training and orientation programs that are targeted to a segregated audience (e.g., women or minorities only). Some organizations believe that if the goal of managing diversity is to get employees to work together, it is important *not* to segregate women or minorities at any point in their development. However, other organizations see such sessions as important in meeting the special needs of these groups. Organizations like DuPont and GTE provide additional classroom training for newly hired women, but the trend is to avoid the impression of preferential treatment.[86] Morrison and Von Glinow have argued, "Because women and minorities face special situations as tokens, they may need to perfect certain competencies such as conflict resolution."[87] While we agree that it may be beneficial for incoming women and minorities to be given special awareness and training programs to help them make the adjustment and deal with difficult cultural issues, these programs should exist within an overall plan targeted toward all employees to achieve the goal of multiculturalism.

## CAREER DEVELOPMENT

Most career development models and programs (recall Chapter 12) do not explicitly deal with the special concerns of a culturally diverse workforce. However, given the continued existence of glass ceiling issues and the failure of affirmative action to fully address inequities in the career advancement of women and minorities, more direct action should be taken in modifying career development systems.

Programs that promote valuing differences and managing diversity can be useful in creating a positive climate for career advancement. Although both of these approaches rely on education and training to change some of the underlying assumptions, values, and beliefs that sustain barriers like the glass ceiling, only the managing diversity approach attempts to integrate these efforts into the organizational strategy. For example, Jim Preston, former CEO of Avon, saw managing diversity as a significant part of his organization's business strategy, and stated that "if you are going to attract the best . . . people into your organization, you'd better have a culture; you'd better have an environment in which those people feel they can prosper and flourish."[88]

Organizations can modify or create career development policies and programs without using a managing diversity approach. However, if sexist and racist attitudes are prevalent, an organization is less likely to be successful using "traditional" career development techniques to help advance the careers of women and minority employees. A "new" career development program should include specific roles for managers (e.g., serving as mentors or advocates) and a formal role for HRD departments in monitoring the process.

## MENTORING TO PROMOTE DIVERSITY

As suggested earlier, women and minorities have had a harder time moving into higher level positions. Traditionally, many individuals who successfully reach top management have been assisted by a mentor. In Chapter 12, we defined **mentoring** as a relationship between a junior and senior member of the organization that contributes to the career development of both members. There is some evidence to suggest that women perceive barriers to mentoring because they feel that a male mentor might misconstrue their request as a romantic or sexual gesture, are concerned about how others feel about the relationship, and feel that the male mentor would reject them.[89]

In terms of minorities, a study found that the development of minorities in organizations is affected by such things as the "absence of mentors, less interesting or challenging work as a result of being in the outgroup, and being left out of the informal social network."[90] This is supported by research that has examined diversified mentoring relationships (i.e., those made up of a majority member and minority member) and homogeneous mentorship (i.e., those made up of both minority members or both majority members). The findings show the following relationships:

- Minorities in homogeneous mentoring relationships receive more psychosocial support (e.g., personal support, friendship) than those in diverse mentoring relationships.

- Mentors are also better role models in homogeneous relationships.

- Psychosocial support existed in diverse relationship when both the mentor and protégé showed the preferred strategy for dealing with (racial) differences.[91]

This research has led Ragins to propose a model that depicts the relationship between mentor functions, protégé outcome, and mentor relationship composition (see Figure 15-1).[92] The model suggests that the dynamics of diversified mentor relationships and their outcomes are different from those of homogeneous mentor relationships. HRD professionals who design and implement mentorship programs should be aware of these possibilities and attempt to construct their programs in ways that maximizes the benefits and minimizes the problems. As we discussed in Chapter 12, even though there are some inherent potential problems with mentoring, we feel that the benefits outweigh the potential pitfalls, and that mentoring should be part of the career development process.[93]

## SEXUAL AND RACIAL HARASSMENT TRAINING

Reports of sexual harassment have remained high over the past fifteen years. Organizations must take affirmative steps to deal with this problem at the workplace. Recent court decisions make it clear that the burden is on organizations to create a safe environment free from sexual demands or hostile acts.[94] Similar issues exist concerning racial and other forms of harassment as well. For example, the Civil Rights Bureau for the State of Wisconsin advocates a single organizational policy covering all forms of workplace harassment.[95]

A number of steps should be taken to implement training to reduce workplace harassment. Overall, the HRD process model discussed in Chapters 4, 5, 6, and 7 provides a framework for the issues that should be addressed in establishing this sort of program. The four steps listed next highlight some of the issues specific to developing and delivering a sexual or racial harassment training program:

1. *Preparation of a policy and complaint procedure.* Make sure the harassment policy is up-to-date and can be understood by all members of the organization. An appropriate policy should include procedures for (1) defining the scope of responsibility, (2) prompt and measured responses to claims of harassment, (3) authority to address the issue, and (4) multiple avenues for filing complaints. Some organizations have employees sign a document indicating that they have read and understood this policy.

2. *Assessment of the organizational climate.* It is important to determine if the organization is ready to accept the appropriate change, particularly if such

FIGURE 15-1

## COMPOSITION OF RELATIONSHIP, MENTOR FUNCTIONS, AND PROTÉGÉ OUTCOMES

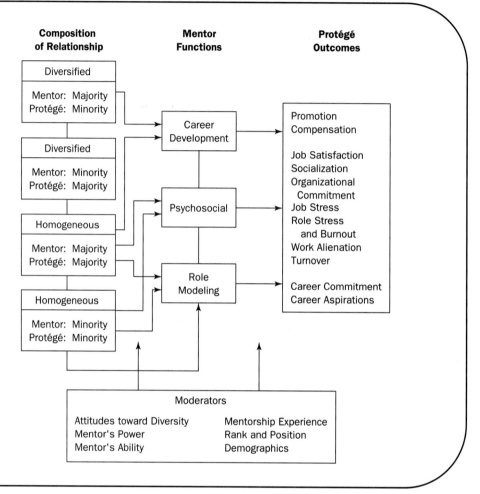

SOURCE: Academy of Management Review by B. R. Ragins, Copyright 1997 by Academy of Management. Reproduced with permission of ACAD OF MGMT in the format Textbook via Copyright Clearance Center.

training will be mandatory. Also, it is important to survey the employees to see how they feel about harassment issues.[96] The data could be helpful for determining program content. For example, if evidence shows that a number of supervisors try to discourage formal complaints, the program may need to reinforce supervisors' legal responsibilities in this area.

3. *Content of the training program.* The program should describe the current laws including interpretation of recent court decisions, review the organizational policy and procedures, communicate a set of organizational standards of conduct, outline responsibilities of supervisors, discuss methods of

counseling or referring victims, and address situations where harassment is likely to take place.

4. *Selecting the trainer or trainers.* Care must be taken in selecting a trainer who has both expert knowledge of the law and an understanding of the organizational politics. Many organizations seek an outside consultant with legal experience in this area.

In addition, the issue of whether the training should be mandatory should be assessed. As a rule, if there is sufficient evidence of widespread harassment, training should be mandatory. These steps need to be modified in situations where there is significant resistance to change. If this is the case, organizations often take a more direct approach (e.g., zero tolerance) to ensure that this kind of discrimination is eliminated or at least minimized.

Some organizations advocate zero tolerance, which suggests that policies dealing with all forms of discrimination will not be acceptable. In this situation, the policies would probably include strong sanctions against certain kinds of behavior, up to and including dismissal. Even with a strong policy, however, it is recommended that training and education be used as a vehicle for communicating the policy.

The long-term effectiveness of these kinds of interventions depends on the continued commitment of top management. As we have stated many times throughout this text, top management sets the climate and the agenda for the organization. Unfortunately, not all CEOs see discrimination, harassment, and diversity issues as a part of their agenda.[97] Perhaps incidents such as those involving Texaco, the U.S. Army, and Mitsubishi Motors, to name a few, will serve as reminders of the potential costs of not taking preventive action.

## OTHER HUMAN RESOURCE MANAGEMENT PROGRAMS AND PROCESSES

Many organizations have extended managing diversity programs beyond HRD programs and processes by changing human resource management (HRM) policies and programs to meet the special needs of the new workforce.[98] Through the development of affirmative action and "diversity recruitment" programs, many organizations have been able to develop effective recruitment methods that are more effective in attracting qualified women and minority candidates.[99] A growing number of organizations are holding managers formally accountable for diversity goals, for example, incorporating such goals into their performance evaluation process.[100] Further, the influx of women and minorities into the workforce has led organizations to modify some of their HRM practices to meet the needs of a culturally diverse workforce. For example, some organizations have devised **flexible work schedules** and child-care programs directed at the growing number of working mothers who are entering or reentering the workforce. IBM, after realizing that 30 percent of its employees had child-care needs and an equal number had elder-care responsibilities, revised its child-care program and established a program for elder care.[101]

Some organizations have responded to the problems of communicating with non-English-speaking employees. A survey of companies in southeastern New England discovered that those organizations that acknowledged problems with non-English-speaking employees identified communication as the major problem. The survey respondents said that using the services of language interpreters and multilingual supervisors was the most effective means of resolving this problem. The language interpreters can help to establish expectations, convey organizational messages, and intervene when there are problems.[102] All of these roles help to support an effective managing diversity policy and program. Hiring multilingual supervisors is probably one of the most effective means of communicating with non-English-speaking employees because they can communicate directly without an interpreter.

## CLOSING COMMENTS

We hope you have gained an appreciation for the complexity of managing a culturally diverse workforce and how HRD programs can be used to achieve this goal. Obviously, there is no guarantee that organizations that are more diverse will necessarily be more successful in the future than those that are less diverse.[103] However, we are convinced that working toward the goals of reducing discrimination and promoting diversity is fair and ethical and will ultimately lead to a climate in which all employees can thrive within an organization and contribute to its success. This requires a long-term, integrated effort.[104] Flynn points to the lack of strong positive examples of companies that can be lauded for their diversity efforts. However, companies such as Allstate Insurance have gained recognition for their efforts to "make diversity a business strategy."[105] The National Urban League study cited earlier also provides examples of exemplary corporate efforts in this regard.[106] We applaud such efforts, and hope for more. However, we close with a thought-provoking quote from Erin Kelly and Frank Dobbin:

> Will the weakened version of affirmative action found in current diversity management practices improve the prospects of women and minorities in the future? One recent study shows that diffuse diversity policies and programs are much less effective than are measures that target women and minority groups.[107] Perhaps diversity management will succeed in winning over middle managers because it embraces an economic, rather than political, rationale. But precisely because it is founded on cost-benefit analysis rather than on legal compliance, perhaps diversity management will come under the ax of budget-cutters when America faces its next recession. Because it is not required by law, diversity management is not nearly as prevalent today as were the EEO/AA programs that preceded it. But the results of diversity management will have to be examined as the programs evolve.[108]

### RETURN TO OPENING CASE

The first thing that R. R. Donnelley did was to change to an ongoing and much more intensive diversity training experience for its managers. Your instructor has additional information concerning what Donnelley did to change its diversity training efforts.

## SUMMARY

Recent demographic trends suggest that women and minorities will continue to enter the workforce in greater numbers over the next twenty years. Organizations continue to address some of the workplace issues that result from a culturally diverse workforce, with diversity initiatives extending beyond issues of race and gender. A primary concern is treatment discrimination (e.g., promotional barriers, pay, and sexual and racial harassment). Numerous laws prohibit treatment discrimination (e.g., Equal Pay Act and civil rights laws and regulations), but the law by itself is not sufficient to create a climate of fair treatment.

Historically, organizations have used four ways to integrate the workplace — equal employment opportunity, affirmative action, valuing differences and diversity training, and managing diversity. Equal employment opportunity is a commitment not to discriminate in the workplace, based on various categories protected by law (e.g., race, sex, religion, disability, age). Affirmation action is a federal regulation that places an obligation on public agencies and many other organizations that receive federal grants or contracts. Affirmative action has been highly controversial, and its effectiveness in creating a truly integrated workforce has been moderate. Valuing differences or diversity training attempts to deal with the underlying values and attitudes that manifest themselves in sexism and racism. However, because of the proliferation of diversity consultants with unproven methods, diversity training has been widely criticized. The evidence of the effectiveness of this approach is mixed to negative. Managing diversity is a long-term cultural change that seeks to level the playing field for all workers. Despite the appeal of this approach, there is not extensive evidence to date concerning the effectiveness of this approach on the long-term viability of an organization.

As organizations become more global, the need for cross-cultural training has grown. Organizations must prepare employees for overseas assignments by giving them language skills and indoctrinating them in the customs, culture, and laws of the host country.

Managing a culturally diverse workforce may include changes in various HRD and HRM programs and processes. HRD professionals must be able to adapt current socialization, orientation, and career development processes to the needs of the new workforce. HRM professionals should consider adapting other policies (e.g., benefits) in order to meet the special needs of new groups, including such things as day-care services, flextime, interpreters, and multilingual supervisors.

## KEY TERMS AND CONCEPTS

| | |
|---|---|
| access discrimination | flexible work schedules |
| affirmative action | glass ceiling |
| cross-cultural training | harassment, sexual and racial |
| culture | managing diversity |
| cultural diversity | mentoring |
| diversity training | treatment discrimination |
| equal employment opportunity (EEO) | valuing differences |

## QUESTIONS FOR DISCUSSION

1. Compare and contrast equal employment opportunity, affirmative action, and managing diversity programs. Can they occur simultaneously? Why or why not?

2. What changes, if any, have you personally experienced in the workplace? What needs to be done to ensure that all individuals, (including women and minorities) have equal opportunity all of the time?

3. Do you believe it is important to acknowledge, understand, and value differences in your organization? Explain. How are you and your friends from culturally diverse backgrounds different? How are you the same?

4. What kinds of issues would you be faced with if you were given an overseas assignment to Japan? What would you do to prepare? How would this be different if the assignment were in Canada or Mexico?

5. Describe the role of HRD professionals with respect to managing culturally diverse employees. What kinds of HRD programs support this approach?

6. In some organizations, cultural diversity efforts meet with resistance from key managers and employees. Identify at least one reason for this resistance and recommend ways it can be overcome. Support your recommendations.

## EXERCISE: VIEWS ON DIVERSITY[109]

The following statements measure attitudes toward diversity. Rate yourself on each item using the following scale: 1 = strongly disagree, 2 = disagree, 3 = neither agree nor disagree, 4 = agree, and 5 = strongly agree. After you are done, discuss diversity issues as you have experienced them in the classroom, as well as in work settings. In your view, what can be done to promote greater acceptance of diversity in both settings?

1. Everyone should learn about cultural differences.
2. Cultural diversity is a valuable resource and should be preserved.
3. Trainers should plan activities that meet the diverse needs of trainees from different cultural backgrounds.
4. I am comfortable around students whose cultural heritage is different from my own.
5. Cultural diversity is a positive force in the development of modern society.
6. Every culture has something positive to contribute to modern society.
7. Each person should feel pride in his or her own heritage.
8. I enjoy being around people who are different from me.

Visit *http://werner.swlearning.com* for links to informative websites for this chapter.

# REFERENCES

1. Judy, R. W., & D'Amico, C. (1997). *Workforce 2020: Work and workers in the 21st century.* Indianapolis, IN: Hudson Institute.

2. Kossek, E. E., & Lobel, S. A. (Eds.). (1996). *Managing diversity: Human resource strategies for transforming the workplace.* Cambridge, MA: Blackwell Publishers.

3. Ott, J. S. (1989). *The organizational culture perspective.* Pacific Grove, CA: Brooks/Cole.

4. Schein, E. H. (1987). *Process consultation* (Vol. 1, p. 264). Reading, MA: Addison-Wesley.

5. Ott (1989), *supra* note 3, p. 24.

6. *Ibid.*

7. Kossek & Lobel (1996), *supra* note 2.

8. Ilgen, D. R., & Youtz, M. A. (1986). Factors affecting the evaluation and development of minorities in organizations. *Research in Personnel and Human Resource Management, 4,* 307–337.

9. Martinez, M. (1997). Prepared for the future. *HR Magazine, 42*(4), 80–87; Chaudhuri, A., & Collins, K. (2000). The 2000 salary survey. *Working Woman, 25*(7), July/August, 58–63.

10. Equal Employment Opportunity Commission (2002). Occupational employment in private industry by race/ethnic group/sex, and by industry, United States, 2002. Retrieved November 29, 2004, from http://www.eeoc.gov/stats/jobpat/2002/us.html

11. Equal Employment Opportunity Commission (2004). Sex-based charges, FY 1992–FY 2003. Retrieved November 29, 2004, from http://www.eeoc.gov/stats/sex.html

12. Morrison, A. M., & Von Glinow, M. A. (1990). Women and minorities in management. *American Psychologist, 45,* 200–208; Hurley, A. E., & Sonnenfeld, J. A. (1995). Organizational growth and employee advancement: Tracking opportunities. In M. London (Ed.), *Employee, careers, and job creation.* San Francisco, Jossey-Bass; Blum, T. C., Fields, D. L., & Goodman, J. S. (1994). Organizational-level determinants of women in management. *Academy of Management Review, 37,* 241–268; Martinez, M. (1997). Prepared for the future: Training women for corporate leadership. *HR Magazine, 42*(4), 8087.

13 WOW! Facts 2004; U.S. multicultural and global markets (2004). Washington, DC: Business Women's Network.

14. Blau, F. D., & Kahn, L. M. (2000). Gender differences in pay. *Journal of Economic Perspectives, 14*(4), Fall, 75–99.

15. Table 12–1, Ratio of median annual earnings of all male to all female wage and salary workers ages 25–34, by educational attainment: 1970–1997. Retrieved November 29, 2004, from http://nces.ed.gov/

16. *Guidelines on discrimination because of sex,* 29 C.F.R. Sec. 1604.11(a) (1995).

17. Burlington Industries, Inc. v. Ellerth, No. 97-569 (1998).

18. Equal Employment Opportunity Commission (2000). Monitors say Mitsubishi in compliance with EEOC consent decree; sexual harassment "firmly under control" at U.S. plant. Retrieved November 29, 2004, from http://www.eeoc.gov/press/9-6-00.html

19. Zall, M. (1992). What to expect from the Civil Rights Act. *Personnel Journal, 72*(3), 46–50.

20. Equal Employment Opportunity Commission (2004). Sexual harassment charges EEOC and FEPAs combined: FY 1992-FY 2003. Retrieved November 29, 2004, from http://www.eeoc.gov/stats/harass.html

21. Equal Employment Opportunity Commission (2004). Race-based charges, FY 1992–FY 2003. Retrieved November 29, 2004, from http://www.eeoc.gov/stats/race.html

22. Leo, J. (1997). Jelly bean: The sequel. *U.S. News & World Report, 122*(5), February 10, 20.

23. Caudron, S. (1997). Don't make Texaco's $175 million mistake. *Workforce, 76*(3), 58–66.

24. EEOC (2004), *supra* note 10.

25. Morrison & Von Glinow (1990), *supra* note 12.

26. Powell, G. N., & Butterfield, D. A. (1997). Effect of race on promotions to top management in a federal department. *Academy of Management Journal, 40*, 112–128.

27. Greenhaus, J. H., Parasuraman, S., & Warmley, W. M. (1990). Effects of race on organizational experiences, job performance evaluations, and career outcomes. *Academy of Management Journal, 33*, 64–86.

28. *Ibid*, p. 80.

29. Ilgen & Youtz (1986), *supra* note 8.

30. *Ibid*, p. 326.

31. Equal Employment Opportunity Commission (2001). EEOC accomplishments report for fiscal year 2000. Retrieved November 29, 2004, from http://www.eeoc.gov/accomplishments-00.html

32. Garland, S. B. (1991, April 29). Can the Feds bust through the "glass ceiling?" *Business Week,* 33; Mize, S. (1992). Shattering the glass ceiling. *Training & Development, 46*(1), 60–62; Morrison & Von Glinow (1990), *supra* note 15; Solomon, C. M. (1990). Careers under glass. *Personnel Journal, 69*(4), 96–105.

33. U.S. Department of Labor (1991). *A report of the glass ceiling initiative* (DHHS Publication No. 1992 312–411/64761). Washington, DC: U.S. Government Printing Office, p. 3.

34. *Ibid*, p. 21.

35. Solomon, C. M. (2000). Cracks in the glass ceiling. *Workforce*, September, 86–94.

36. Maume, D. J., Jr. (1999). Glass ceilings and glass elevators. *Work & Occupations, 26*(4), 483–509.

37. Baxter, J., & Wright, E. O. (2000). The glass ceiling hypothesis. *Gender & Society, 14*(2), 275–294.

38. Meyerson, D. E., & Fletcher, J. K. (2000). A modest manifesto for shattering the glass ceiling. *Harvard Business Review, 78*(1), January/February, 126–136.

39. Longley, R. (2004). U.S. foreign-born population hits 33 million. Retrieved November 29, 2004, from http://usgovinfo.about.com/cs/censusstatistic/a/foreignborn.htm

40. Rosenfeld, M. (1991). *Affirmative action and justice* (p. 42). New Haven, CT: Yale University Press.

41. 415 F. Supp. 761 (1976).

42. Milkovich, G. T., & Boudreau, J. W. (1994). *Human resource management* (7th ed.). Burr Ridge, IL: Richard D. Irwin.

43. After affirmative action (2000, May 20). *New York Times, 149*(51394), p. A14.

44. Thomas, R. R., Jr. (1990). From affirmative action to affirming diversity. *Harvard Business Review, 68*(2), 107–117, p. 109.

45. Taylor, R. A. (1996). After Hopwood. *Black Issues in Higher Education, 13*(4), 12.

46. Judy & D'Amico (1997), *supra* note 1.

47. *Ibid.*

48. Galvin, T. (2003). 2003 Industry Report. *Training, 40*(9), 21–39.

49. Caudron, S. (1992). US WEST finds strength in diversity. *Personnel Journal, 71*(3), 40–44.

50. Johnson, R. B., & O'Mara, J. (1992). Shedding new light on diversity training. *Training & Development, 43*(5), 45–52.

51. Lynch, F. R. (1997). *The diversity machine: The drive to change the "white male workplace."* New York: The Free Press.

52. Tan, D. L., Morris, L., & Romero, J. (1996). Changes in attitude after diversity training. *Training & Development, 50*(9), 54–55.

53. Mueller, N. (1996). Wisconsin Power and Light's model diversity program. *Training & Development, 50*(3), 57–60.

54. Beekie, R. (1997). Diversity training's big lie. *Training, 34*(2), 122.

55. Paskoff, S. M. (1996). Ending the workplace diversity wars. *Training, 33*(8), 42–47.

56. Nemetz, P. L., & Christensen, S. L. (1996). The challenge of cultural diversity: Harnessing a diversity of views to understand multiculturalism. *Academy of Management Review, 21*(2), 434–462.

57. Leo (1997), *supra* note 22.

58. Judy & D'Amico (1997), *supra* note 1.

59. Flynn, G. (1998). The harsh reality of diversity programs. *Workforce, 77*(12), 26–33.

60. Ivancevich, J. M., & Gilbert, J. A. (2000). Diversity management: Time for a new approach. *Public Personnel Management, 29*(1), 75–92.

61. Rynes, S., & Rosen, B. (1995). A field survey of factors affecting the adoption and perceived success of diversity training. *Personnel Psychology, 48*, 247–271.

62. Galagan, P. A. (1991). Tapping the power of a diverse workforce. *Training and Development Journal, 45*(3), 38–44.

63. Thomas, R. R., Jr. (1991). *Beyond race and gender* (p. 10). New York: AMACOM.

64. Wellner, A. (2000). How do you spell diversity? *Training, 37*(4), April, 34–36.

65. Ivancevich & Gilbert (2000), *supra* note 60.

66. *Ibid.*

67. Greenslade, M. (1991). Managing diversity: Lessons from the United States. *Personnel Management, 23*(12), 28–33.

68. *Ibid.*

69. National Urban League (2004). Diversity practices that work. Retrieved November 29, 2004, from http://www.nul.org/pdf/ERAC-NUL.pdf

70. Mobley, M., & Payne, T. (1992). Backlash: The challenge to diversity training. *Training & Development, 43*(12), 45–52.

71. Karp, H. B., & Sammour, H. Y. (2000). Workforce diversity: Choices in diversity training programs and dealing with resistance to diversity. *College Student Journal, 34*(3), September, 451–458.

72. Jackson, S. A., & Associates (1992). *Diversity in the workplace: Human resource initiatives.* New York: Guilford Press; Kossek & Lobel (1996), *supra* note 2; Bond, M. A., & Pyle, J. L. (1998). Diversity dilemmas at work. *Journal of Management Inquiry, 7*(3), 252–269; Ferris, G. R., Arthur, M. M., Berkson, H. M., Kaplan, D. M., Harrell-Cook, G., & Frink, D. D. (1998). Toward a social context theory of the human resource management-organization effectiveness relationship. *Human Resource Management Review, 8*(3), 235–264; Dass, P., & Parker, B. (1999). Strategies for managing human resource diversity: From resistance to learning. *The Academy of Management Executive, 13*(2), 68–80; Guajardo, S. A. (1999). Workforce diversity: Monitoring employment trends in public organizations. *Public Personnel Management, 28*(1), 63–85; Gilbert, J. A., & Ivancevich, J. M. (2000). Valuing diversity: A tale of two organizations. *The Academy of Management Executive, 14*(1), 93–105; Gilbert, J. A. (2000). An empirical examination of resources in a diverse environment. *Public Personnel Management, 29*(2), 175–184.

73. Ivancevich & Gilbert (2000), *supra* note 60.

74. Hickman, G. R., & Creighton-Zollar, A. (1998). Diverse self-directed work teams: Developing strategic initiatives for 21st century organizations. *Public Personnel Management, 27*(2), 187–200.

75. Wentling, R. M., & Palma-Rivas, N. (2000). Current status of diversity initiatives in selected multinational corporations. *Human Resource Development Quarterly, 11*(1), 35–60; Weaver, V. J., & Coker, S. (2001). Globalization and diversity. *Mosaics, 7*(1), January/February, 1–5.

76. Dolanski, S. (1997). Are expats getting lost in the translation? *Workforce, 76*(2), 32–39.

77. Callahan, M. R. (1989). Preparing the new global manager. *Training & Development, 43*(3), 28–32.

78. Cox, T., Jr. (1991). The multicultural organization. *The Executive, 5*(2), 34–47.

79. Gordon, J. (1992). Rethinking diversity. *Training, 29*(1), 23–30.

80. Black, J. S., Gregersen, H. B., Mendenhall, M. E., & Stroh, L. K. (1999). *Globalizing people through international assignments.* Reading, MA: Addison-Wesley.

81. Black, J. S., & Mendenhall, M. (1990). Cross-cultural training effectiveness: A review and theoretical framework for future research. *Academy of Management Review, 15*, 113–136; Deshpande, S. P., & Viswesvaran, C. (1991). Is cross-cultural training of expatriate managers effective: A meta-analysis. Paper presented at the Academy of Management, Miami, FL; Bennett, R., Aston, A., & Colquhoun, T. (2000). Cross-cultural training: A critical step in ensuring the success of international assignments. *Human Resource Management, 39*(2/3), 239–250; Bolino, M. C., & Feldman, D. C. (2000) Increasing the skill utilization of expatriates. *Human Resource Management, 39*(4), 367–379.

82. Kanter, R. M. (1977). *Men and women of the corporation.* New York: Basic Books.

83. Cox, T. H., Lobel, S. A., & McLeod, P. L. (1991). Effects of ethnic group cultural differences on cooperative and competitive behavior on a group task. *Academy of Management Journal, 34*, 827–847.

84. Fernandez, J. P. (1988). Human resources and the extraordinary problems minorities face. In M. London & E. M. Mone (Eds.), *Career growth and human resource strategies: The role of the*

*human resource professional in employee development* (pp. 227–239). New York: Quorum Books; Solomon (1990), *supra* note 35.

85. Pickard, J. (1991). Steel partners. *Personnel Management, 23*(12), 32.

86. Morrison & Von Glinow (1990), *supra* note 12.

87. *Ibid*, p. 204.

88. Thomas (1991), *supra* note 63, p. 164.

89. Ragins, B. R., & Cotton, J. L. (1993). Gender and willingness to mentor in organizations. *Journal of Management, 19*, 97–111; Crampton, S. M., & Mishra, J. M. (1999). Women in management. *Public Personnel Management, 28*(1), 87–106.

90. Ilgen & Youtz (1986), *supra* note 8, p. 326.

91. Ragins, B. R. (1997). Diversified mentoring relationships in organizations: A power perspective. *Academy of Management Review, 22*, 482–521; Thomas, 1990, *supra* note 44; Thomas, D. A. (1993). Racial dynamics in cross-race developmental relationships. *Administrative Science Quarterly, 38*, 169–194.

92. Ragins (1997), *supra* note 91.

93. Drazga, B. M. (1998). Mentoring helps break glass ceiling. *Denver Business Journal, 49*(46), July 17, 21A–22A.

94. Segal, J. A. (1998). Sexual harassment prevention: Cement for the glass ceiling? *HR Magazine, 43*(12), November, 129–134.

95. Sample harassment policy (2004). Retrieved November 29, 2004, from http://dwd.wisconsin.gov/er/discrimination_civil_rights/publication_erd_10449_p.htm

96. Verespej, M. A. (1997). Zero tolerance. *Industry Week, 246*(1), 24–28.

97. *Ibid*.

98. Mathews, A. (1999). Diversity: A principle of human resource management. *Public Personnel Management, 27*(2), 175–185.

99. Digh, P. (1999). Getting people in the pool: Diversity recruitment that works. *HR Magazine, 44*(10), 94–98.

100. Digh, P. (1998). The next challenge: Holding people accountable. *HR Magazine, 43*(11), October, 63–68.

101. Sourentian, J. (1989). Four by four. *Training and Development Journal, 43*(11), 21–30.

102. Heskin, A. D., & Heffner, R. A. (1987). Learning about bilingual, multicultural organizing. *Journal of Applied Behavioral Science, 23*, 525–541.

103. Kuczynski, S. (1999). If diversity, then higher profits? *HR Magazine, 44*(13), December, 66–71; Suttell, S. (1998). Diversity programs a key to companies' bottom line. *Crain's Cleveland Business, 19*(26), June 29, 13–14.

104. Adams, M. (1998). Building a rainbow, one stripe at a time. *HR Magazine, 43*(9), August, 72–79; Dobbs, M. F. (1998). Managing diversity: The Department of Energy initiative. *Public Personnel Management, 27*(2), 161–175.

105. Flynn, G. (1998), *supra* note 59; Crockett, J. (1999). Diversity as a business strategy. *Management Review, 88*(5), 62.

106. Diversity practices that work (2004), *supra* note 69.

107. Konrad, A. M., & Linnehan, F. (1995). Formalized HRM structures: Coordinating equal opportunity or concealing organizational practices? *Academy of Management Journal, 38,* 787–820.

108. Kelly, E., & Dobbin, F. (1998). How affirmative action became diversity management. *American Behavioral Scientist, 41*(7), 960–984.

109. Adapted from the Pluralism and Diversity Attitude Assessment scale, Stanley, L. (1996). The development and validation of an instrument to assess attitudes toward cultural diversity and pluralism among preservice physical educators. *Education and Psychological Measurement, 56*(5), 891–897; Dee, J. R., & Henkin, A. B. (2002). Assessing dispositions toward cultural diversity among preservice teachers. *Urban Education, 37*(1), 22–40.

**360-degree performance appraisal (Chapter 4):** An approach to performance evaluation that generally uses peer, subordinate, superior, and customer feedback to obtain as complete a picture as possible of an employee's performance.

**abilities (Chapter 2):** General human capacities related to the performance of a set of tasks. Abilities develop over time through the interaction of heredity and experience, and are long-lasting. Over 100 different types of abilities have been identified, including general intelligence, verbal comprehension, numerical ability, and inductive reasoning.

**access discrimination (Chapter 15):** An example of one type of discrimination in the workplace. It occurs when an organization places limits on job availability through such things as restricting advertisement and recruitment, rejecting applicants, or offering a lower starting salary to certain types of individuals.

**action learning (Chapter 13):** A concept developed to encourage line managers to provide input to modify existing operating systems. Action learning involves having participants select an organizational problem, write a case study describing the problem, and meet with a group of other managers who face similar problems to discuss ways of dealing with the problem.

**action plan (Chapter 14):** A change intervention strategy. An action plan should specify the objective of each change activity, who will be involved, who is responsible, and when the activity must be completed. Implementation of the action plan involves carrying out each step in the intervention strategy.

**active practice (Chapter 3):** A condition of practice that suggests that learners should be given an opportunity to repeatedly perform the task or use the knowledge being learned.

**affirmative action (Chapter 15):** An organizational program or effort intended to bring members of underrepresented groups, usually groups that have suffered discrimination, into a higher degree of participation in the organization.

**alpha change (Chapter 14):** The type of change that occurs when individuals perceive a change in the levels of variables (e.g., a perceived improvement in skills) within an existing paradigm, without altering the basic configuration of the system.

**alternative work schedules (AWS) (Chapter 14):** A technostructural intervention strategy that allows employees to modify their work requirements to satisfy their personal needs.

**Americans with Disabilities Act of 1990 (ADA) (Chapter 11):** A law that prohibits employers from discriminating against individuals with disabilities and requires that employers make "reasonable accommodations" to help such employees perform their essential job functions.

**analytic needs (Chapter 4):** Needs that identify new, better ways to perform tasks.

**andragogy (Chapter 3):** A term coined by Malcolm Knowles to refer to an adult-oriented approach to learning. It assumes that compared to children, adult learners are more self-directed and more interested in immediate application.

**anticipatory socialization (Chapter 8):** The first stage of the new employee socialization process, which begins before the individual joins the organization. In this stage, the person forms an impression about what membership in an organization is like from a variety of sources, such as rumors, anecdotes, advertisements, the media, and recruiters.

**apprenticeship training (Chapters 1 and 9):** A type of training whereby an owner or a shopkeeper educates and trains his or her own workers without any vocational or technical schools. In the eighteenth century, the shopkeepers were the trainers. This is one of the origins of the HRD field.

**assessment center (Chapter 12):** A tool used in employee selection, this method can also be used to assess potential for advancement. In an assessment center, small groups of employees perform a variety of exercises while being evaluated by a group of trained assessors.

**association (Chapter 3):** A form of learning; association is the process by which two cognitions become paired together (e.g., "dozen" and "twelve items"), so that thinking

about one evokes thoughts about the other.

**ASTD (Chapter 1):** American Society for Training and Development; an organization for human resource development professionals, which also establishes standards within the training and development profession.

**attitudes (Chapter 2):** An attitude represents a person's general feeling of favorableness or unfavorableness toward some stimulus object. Attitudes are always held with respect to a particular object — whether the object is a person, place, event, or idea — and indicate one's feelings or affect toward that object. Attitudes also tend to be stable over time and are difficult to change. They are made up of beliefs, feelings, and behavioral tendencies. They affect behavior indirectly through intentions. Attitudes combine with the perception of social pressure to form intentions, which in turn directly affect behavior.

**audiovisual media (Chapter 6):** A method of classroom training that takes advantage of various media to illustrate or demonstrate the training material. Audiovisual media can bring complex events to life by showing and describing details that are often difficult to communicate in other ways.

**basic skills/literacy education (Chapter 9):** A type of training that focuses on upgrading the reading, writing, and computation skills needed to function in most any job.

**behavioral intentions model (Chapter 2):** A model that seeks to explain the relationship between attitudes and behavior. This model states that it is the combination of attitudes with perceived social pressure to behave in a given way (called subjective norms) that influences an individual's intentions. These intentions, in turn, more directly influence behavior. When attitudes and subjective norms conflict, the stronger of the two plays the dominant role in determining what the individual's intentions will be. According to the behavioral intentions model, attitudes affect behavior only to the extent that they influence one's intentions.

**behavior modeling (Chapters 2, 6, and 13):** A training method where trainees observe a model performing a target behavior correctly (usually on a film or video). This is followed by a discussion by trainees of the key components of the behavior, practicing the target behavior through role playing, and receiving feedback and reinforcement for the behavior they demonstrate. Behavior modeling is widely used for interpersonal skill training and is a common component of many management-training programs. Research has shown behavior modeling to be one of the more effective training techniques.

**behavior modification (Chapter 2):** A set of four techniques for controlling an employee's behavior. *Positive reinforcement* refers to increasing the frequency of a behavior by following the behavior with a pleasurable consequence. *Negative reinforcement* increases the frequency of a behavior by removing something aversive after the behavior is performed. *Extinction* seeks to decrease the frequency of a behavior by removing the consequence that is reinforcing it. *Punishment* seeks to decrease the frequency of a behavior by introducing an aversive consequence immediately after the behavior.

**beta change (Chapter 14):** A type of change where individuals perceive a change in the value of variables (e.g., change in work standards) within an existing paradigm without altering their basic configuration.

**blended learning (Chapter 6):** A combination of traditional (classroom-based) and technology-enhanced training.

**business games (Chapter 6):** A training method that is intended to develop or refine problem-solving and decision-making skills. This technique tends to focus primarily on business management decisions (such as maximizing profits).

**career (Chapter 12):** A pattern of work-related experiences that span the course of one's life.

**career concept (Chapter 12):** A broad idea that includes various subjective and objective components, such as a person's occupation, advancement, status, involvement and the stability of one's work-related experiences.

**career development (Chapters 1 and 12):** An ongoing process by which individuals progress through a series of stages, each of which is characterized by a relatively unique set of issues, themes, and tasks.

**career management (Chapters 1 and 12):** An ongoing process undertaken by organizations to prepare, implement, and monitor the career plans of individual employees, usually in concert with the organization's career management system.

**career motivation (Chapter 12):** A significant objective of effective career management; career motivation affects how people choose their careers, how they view their careers, how hard they work in them, and how long they stay in them.

**career path (Chapter 12):** A sequence of jobs, usually involving related tasks and experiences, that employees move through over time (typically within one organization).

**career planning (Chapters 1 and 12):** A deliberate process of (1) becoming aware of oneself, opportunities, constraints, choices, and consequences; (2) identifying career-related goals; and (3) programming work, education, and related developmental experiences to provide the direction, timing, and sequence of steps to attain a specific career goal. Viewed in this way, career planning is an activity performed by the individual to understand and attempt to control his or her work life.

**career plateau (Chapter 12):** The point in a career where the likelihood of additional hierarchical promotion is low (or is perceived to be low).

**case study method (Chapter 6):** A training method that help trainees learn analytical and problem-solving skills by presenting a story (called a case) about people in an organization who are facing a problem or a decision. Cases may be based on actual events involving real people in an organization, or they can be fictitious. Trainees should be given enough information to analyze the situation and recommend their own solutions. In solving the problem, the trainees are generally required to use a rational problem-solving process.

**causal attribution theory (Chapter 10):** A process by which people assign causes to their own and other peoples' behavior.

**certification (Chapter 9):** An outcome granted by a professional organization after a candidate completes prescribed coursework and/or passes an examination, for example, the Professional in Human Resources (PHR) certification.

**change agent (Chapter 14):** An individual who typically works with a change manager to design and implement a change strategy. Among other things, the change agent has primary responsibility for facilitating all of the activities surrounding the design and implementation of the strategy.

**change and acquisition (Chapter 8):** The last stage in the new employee socialization stage, which occurs when new employees accept the norms and values of the group or organization, master the tasks they must perform, and resolve any role conflicts and overloads.

**change manager (Chapter 14):** A person who oversees the design of the intervention strategy. This person would have overall responsibility for assessing the need for change, determining the appropriate intervention activities, implementing the strategy, and evaluating the results.

**characteristics approach (Chapter 13):** Observing the tasks managers perform and grouping them into meaningful categories.

**classroom training (Chapter 6):** Instructional methods that take place away from the normal work setting. In this sense, a classroom can be any training space that is away from the work site, such as a lecture hall, a company cafeteria, or a meeting room. It is a common instructional method.

**coaching (Chapters 1 and 10):** A process of treating employees as partners in achieving both personal and organizational goals. In the process, individuals are encouraged to accept responsibility for their actions, to address any work-related problems, and to achieve and to sustain superior performance.

**coaching analysis (Chapter 10):** An activity in coaching that involves analyzing employee performance and the conditions under which it occurs.

**coaching discussion (Chapter 10):** An activity in coaching where there is face-to-face communication between an employee and his or her supervisor. The purpose is to solve problems, as well as to enable the employee to maintain and improve effective performance.

**cognitive architecture (Chapter 3):** A foundational idea in cognitive psychology, it is defined as a fixed system of mechanisms that underlies and produces cognitive behavior.

**cognitive resource allocation theory (Chapter 3):** An attribute-treatment interaction (ATI) theory that uses an information processing perspective to explain the existence of an interaction between cognitive ability and motivation for both the acquisition and performance of moderately difficult tasks.

**cohesiveness (Chapter 2):** Cohesiveness is an important concept for teamwork. It is the members' sense of togetherness and willingness to remain as part of the group. Given team members' high level of interdependence, they must trust one another and feel a sense of cohesiveness if the team is to work together and be successful.

**communication skills (Chapter 10):** Communication skills are needed to be an effective coach. Unless a manager has the ability both to listen to employees and to get them to understand what effective performance is and how to achieve it, coaching will not succeed.

**competencies (Chapter 1):** Training and development (T&D) competencies are interpersonal skills such as coaching, group process facilitation, and problem solving. For professional employees to develop such skills, they may need to take advantage of continuing education opportunities.

**compliance needs (Chapter 4):** Needs that are mandated by law.

**component task achievement (Chapter 3):** Each component task must be fully achieved before the entire task may be performed correctly.

**compressed workweek (Chapter 14):** An alternative work schedule that involves reducing the number of workdays in a week, usually from five to four.

**computer-aided instruction (CAI) (Chapter 6):** An instructional program that uses a computer system. CAI programs can range from electronic workbooks, using the drill-and-practice approach, to compact disc read-only memory (CD-ROM) presentation of a traditional training program.

**computer-based training (CBT) (Chapters 5 and 6):** An instructional method that uses computer technology, CBT can be implemented using a computer at an employee's desk or workstation, in a company classroom, or even at an employee's home. The primary advantage of CBT is its interactivity and flexibility.

**confidentiality (Chapters 7 and 11):** A commitment not to disclose information regarding an individual's performance in training (Chapter 7), or other personal matters (Chapter 11).

**constructive confrontation (Chapter 11):** A strategy calling for supervisors to monitor their employees' job performance, confront them with evidence of their unsatisfactory performance, coach them on ways to improve it, urge them to use the counseling services of an employee assistance program if they have personal problems, and emphasize the consequences of continued poor performance. Constructive confrontation proceeds in progressive stages; at each stage, employees must choose whether to seek help from the EAP, manage their problems themselves, or suffer the consequences of their actions.

**contiguity (Chapter 3):** A basic learning theory about association that suggests that objects experienced together tend to become associated with each other.

**continuing education (Chapter 9):** A concept that promotes lifelong learning at the professional and/or personal levels.

**continuous-learning work environment (Chapter 3):** A work environment where organizational members share perceptions and expectations that learning is an important part of everyday work life.

**control group (Chapter 7):** A group of employees similar to those who receive training, yet who don't receive training at the same time as those who are trained. However, this group receives the same evaluation measures as the group that is trained, and this allows for a comparison of their scores to those who received the training.

**corporate universities (Chapter 9):** Internal learning programs that organizations develop and deliver using an academic framework.

**cost-benefit analysis (Chapter 7):** Comparing the monetary costs of training to the benefits received in nonmonetary terms, such as improvements in attitudes, safety, and health.

**cost-effectiveness analysis (Chapter 7):** The financial benefits accrued from training, such as increases in quality and profits, or reduction in waste and processing time.

**counseling (Chapters 1 and 11):** A variety of activities, from informal discussions with a supervisor to intensive one-on-one discussions with a trained professional.

**craft guilds (Chapter 1):** A network of private "franchises" built by early master craftsmen so that they could regulate such things as product quality, wages, hours, and apprentice testing procedures.

**critical incident technique (Chapter 4):** A technique used for task identification. It involves having individuals who are familiar with the job record incidents of particularly effective and ineffective behavior that they have seen on the job over a period (e.g., one year). This can be done by individuals or in groups. For each incident, the observer is asked to describe the circumstances and the specific behaviors involved, and suggest reasons why the behavior was effective or ineffective. It results in an understanding of what is considered both good and poor performance.

**cross-cultural training (Chapter 15):** Training that is typically provided to individuals who will be working in a culture other than their native culture (e.g., expatriates). It usually seeks to raise awareness of cultural differences, as well as build skills in the areas of language, nonverbal communication, stress management, and cultural adjustment.

**cultural change (Chapter 14):** A complex process of replacing an existing paradigm or way of thinking with another.

**cultural diversity (Chapter 15):** The existence of two or more persons from different cultural groups in any single group or organization. Most organizations today are culturally diverse because their employees are from different cultural subgroups.

**culture (Chapter 15):** A set of shared values, beliefs, norms, and artifacts that are used to interpret the environment and as a guide for all kinds of behavior.

**customer service training (Chapter 9):** Education that focuses on improving the interpersonal relations, problem-solving, leadership, and teamwork skills of employees who interact with customers.

**declarative knowledge (Chapter 3):** The knowledge a learner needs in order to know *what* to do, as compared to knowing how to do it (cf. procedural knowledge).

**degree of original learning (Chapter 3):** The more effectively that information is initially learned, the more likely it will be retained.

**deliberate practice (Chapter 3):** An effortful activity motivated by the goal of improving performance. It provides the best opportunity for learning and skill acquisition.

**Developmental Challenge Profile (DCP) (Chapter 13):** A ninety-six-item questionnaire based on the research investigating job features that could be developmental.

**deviant workplace behavior (Chapter 10):** A voluntary employee behavior that violates significant organizational norms, and in doing so threatens the well-being of an organization, its members, or both.

**diagnostic needs (Chapter 4):** Needs that focus on the factors that lead to effective performance and prevent performance problems, rather than emphasizing existing problems.

**discussion method (Chapter 6):** The discussion method of training involves the trainer in two-way communication with the trainees, and the trainees in communication with each other. Because active participation is encouraged, the discussion method offers trainees an opportunity for feedback, clarification, and sharing points of view.

**diversity training (Chapter 15):** Training programs designed specifically to address issues of cultural diversity in the workforce. A "valuing differences" approach to diversity training emphasizes building awareness of differences between various demographic or cultural groups, whereas a "managing diversity" approach is more likely to emphasize the skills needed to work successfully in a multicultural environment.

**downsizing (Chapters 2 and 14):** A term commonly associated with an organization's efforts to voluntarily reduce its workforce, usually in an effort to reduce cost.

**Drug-Free Workplace Act of 1988 (Chapter 11):** A law that mandated drug-free awareness programs among federal contractors and grant receivers. This includes informing employees about the availability of drug counseling, rehabilitation, and employee assistance programs.

**dynamic media (Chapter 6):** Techniques used to present dynamic sequences of events. It includes audiocassettes and compact discs (CDs), film, videotape, and videodisc.

**educational interventions (Chapter 11):** Programs designed to inform the employee about the sources of stress, what stress feels like, how stressors can be avoided, and how the individual can better cope with stress.

**ego integrity (Chapter 12):** A person's understanding and acceptance of the choices he or she has made in life.

**employee assistance program (EAP) (Chapter 11):** A job-based program operating within a work organization for the purposes of identifying troubled employees, motivating them to resolve their troubles, and providing access to counseling or treatment for those employees who need these services.

**employee counseling services (Chapter 11):** Programs that seek to ensure that employees can overcome personal and other problems (such as alcohol or substance abuse or stress) and remain effective in the workplace.

**employee orientation (Chapters 1 and 8):** A program that is designed to introduce new employees to the job, supervisor, coworkers, and the organization. Orientation programs typically begin after the newcomer has agreed to join the organization, usually on the individual's first day at work.

**employee wellness program (EWP) (Chapter 11):** Programs that promote employee behavior and organizational practices that ensure employee health and fitness.

**encounter (Chapter 8):** A step in the new employee socialization process that begins when a recruit makes a formal commitment to join the organization by either signing an employment contract or simply accepting an offer of employment or membership. At this point, an individual crosses the inclusionary boundary separating the organization from the outside environment and begins to discover what the organization is really like. During this stage, employment expectations may be confirmed or rejected.

**equal employment opportunity (EEO) (Chapter 15):** The right of applicants to be hired and employees to get promoted, paid, and treated on the basis of job-related performance, and not on the basis of legally protected factors such as race, color, religion, gender, national origin, age, disability, veteran status, or pregnancy.

**equity theory (Chapter 2):** A motivation theory that proposes that *employee perceptions* of outcomes are important determinants of behavior. Equity theory states that outcomes are evaluated by comparing them to the outcomes received by others. If employees perceive an inequity, they may change their performance or cognitions, or both, to reduce the inequity. Outcomes can also serve as a form of feedback to employees. Bonuses and recognition, for example, let employees know if they have performed appropriately and if their performance is valued by the organization.

**executive education (Chapter 13):** Educational programs that range from condensed M.B.A. programs to short courses delivered by colleges and universities, consulting firms, private institutes, and professional and industry associations.

**executive M.B.A. (E.M.B.A.) programs (Chapter 13):** An M.B.A. program that condenses or accelerates the coursework, with courses meeting once per week (typically on weekends). These programs are typically designed so that they can be completed in two years. Students tend to be older, full-time managers from a variety of organizations who have a significant amount of experience as managers.

**expectancy (Chapter 2):** A belief representing the individual's judgment about whether applying (or increasing) effort to a task will result in its successful accomplishment. People with high expectancy believe that increased effort will lead to better performance, while people with low expectancy do not believe that their efforts, no matter how great, will affect their performance. All other things being equal, people should engage in tasks for which they have high expectancy beliefs.

**expectancy theory (Chapter 2):** A motivation theory that proposes that *employee perceptions* of outcomes are important determinants of behavior. The three major components of the theory are expectancies, instrumentality, and valence. Expectancy theory states that people will perform behaviors that they perceive will bring valued outcomes. If employees fulfill certain obligations to the organization but do not receive promised outcomes (such as promotions or pay raises), they may reduce their expectations about the link between their performance and the desired outcomes and thus choose to behave differently. Further, if outcomes are not as rewarding as anticipated, the employees may revise their judgments about the value of that outcome and perform different behaviors.

**expectation (Chapter 8):** In the context of new employee socialization, an expectation is a belief about the likelihood that something will occur and can encompass behaviors, feelings, policies, and attitudes.

**expert performance (Chapter 3):** A consistently superior performance on a specified set of representative tasks for a given area or domain.

**feedback (Chapter 10):** Communication to an employee regarding work performance that is provided by a supervisor or peer.

**feedback phase (Chapter 13):** The fourth step in behavior modeling, in which each trainee receives feedback on his or her performance based on what was done well and what should be improved.

**flextime, flexible work schedules (Chapters 14 and 15):** A technique that allows employees some latitude in determining their starting and ending times in a given workday.

**force field analysis (Chapter 14):** A strategy used to analyze the driving and restraining forces of change. The value of a force field analysis is that it allows the intervention strategists to pinpoint specific support and resistance to a proposed change program.

**four-dimensional model (Chapter 13):** This model describes the managerial job and can be used to design management development efforts. Along with the integrated competency model, it provides a conceptual basis to view the role of managers within a specific organization and the competencies managers need to perform effectively.

**fundamental attribution error (Chapter 10):** An error that is the tendency to overattribute a behavior to a cause within a person (e.g., effort or ability) rather than to the situation (e.g., task difficulty or luck). A supervisor who commits this error is likely to overlook real environmental causes of poor performance and thus blame the employee for poor performance that was not under the employee's control.

**gamma change (Chapter 14):** Gamma A and gamma B are two types of change. Gamma A occurs when individuals perceive change within an existing paradigm or way of thinking. Gamma B occurs when individuals perceive a replacement of one paradigm with another paradigm that contains new variables.

**generativity (Chapter 12):** The development of a capacity to focus on the generations that will follow oneself.

**gerontology (Chapter 3):** The study of older individuals. This approach suggests that while it may take longer for older adults to learn new knowledge and skills and that they tend to make more errors during learning, older adults can and do attain performance levels equal to those achieved by younger adults.

**glass ceiling (Chapter 15):** The subtle attitudes and prejudices that block women and minorities from upward mobility, particularly into management jobs. More specifically, the glass ceiling symbolizes prevailing attitudes about different cultural groups and their general abilities, or the lack thereof, to perform some role or occupation.

**goal-setting theory (Chapters 2 and 10):** A cognitive theory of motivation that is relevant to HRD. Goal-setting theory states that performance goals play a key role in motivation. The theory proposes that the presence of performance goals can mobilize employee effort, direct their attention, increase their persistence, and affect the strategies they will use to accomplish a task. Goals influence the individual's intentions, that is, the cognitive representations of goals to which the person is committed. This commitment will continue to direct employee behavior until the goal is achieved, or until a decision is made to change or reject the goal.

**group dynamics (Chapter 2):** Group dynamics influence the way an employee may behave when interacting in a group. That is, the performance of individuals within a group can differ from their behavior alone. Groupthink and social loafing are aspects of group dynamics.

**groupthink (Chapter 2):** A group dynamic that occurs when group members are primarily concerned with unanimity, making poor decisions by failing to realistically assess alternatives.

**harassment, sexual and racial (Chapter 15):** Unsolicited, intimidating behavior, via verbal or nonverbal communication, that is directed toward an individual or a group. A hostile work environment can also be considered a form of harassment in the workplace.

**hazing (Chapter 8):** A situation where new employees are targets of practical jokes or are harassed because they lack certain information.

**health promotion program (HPP) (Chapter 11):** A program similar to employee wellness programs (EWPs) that is made up of activities that promote employee behavior and organizational practices that ensure employee health and fitness.

**high performance work system (Chapter 1):** A workplace or work system where the various parts or subsystems are aligned or fit together in a way that leads to increased productivity, quality, flexibility, and shorter cycle times, as well as increased customer and employee satisfaction and quality of work life.

**HRD evaluation (Chapter 7):** The systematic collection of descriptive and judgmental information necessary to make effective training decisions related to the selection, adoption, value, and modification of various instructional or HRD activities.

**HR strategic advisor (Chapter 1):** An individual who consults strategic decision makers on HRD issues that directly affect the articulation of organization strategies and performance goals.

**HR systems designer and developer (Chapter 1):** An individual who assists HR management in the design and development of HR systems that affect organization performance.

**human process-based interventions (Chapter 14):** A change theory that focuses on changing behaviors by modifying individual attitudes, values, problem-solving approaches, and interpersonal styles.

**human relations (Chapter 1):** A movement in the early twentieth century that advocated more humane working conditions. It was formulated as a response to the frequent abuse of unskilled workers. Among other things, the human relations movement provided a more complex and realistic understanding of workers as people, instead of merely cogs in a factory machine.

**Human Resource Certification Institute (HRCI) (Chapter 1):** An organization run in conjunction with the Society for Human Resource Management. HRCI oversees and administers the Professional in Human Resources (PHR) and Senior Professional in Human Resources (SPHR) examinations.

**human resource development (HRD) (Chapter 1):** A set of systematic and planned activities designed by an organization to provide its members with the necessary skills to meet current and future job demands.

**human resource management (HRM) (Chapter 1):** The effective utilization of employees to best achieve the goals and strategies of the organization, as well as the goals and needs of employees.

**hypertension (Chapter 11):** A blood pressure greater than 140/90 millimeters of mercury (mm Hg) over repeated measurements; high blood pressure.

**identical elements (Chapter 3):** A principle suggesting that the more similar the training and the performance situations are in terms of the stimuli present and responses required, the more likely it is that positive transfer of training will occur.

**in-basket exercise (Chapter 6):** A type of simulation used in management development programs and assessment centers that assesses the trainee's ability to establish priorities, plan, gather relevant information, and make decisions.

**individual development (Chapter 1):** The process of building an individual's skills or competencies over time. Organizations often offer career counselors to facilitate the process of individual development.

**individual development and career counselor (Chapter 1):** An individual who assists employees in assessing their competencies and goals in order to develop a realistic career plan.

**information overload (Chapter 8):** The idea that a person can absorb only so much information in a given period before learning efficiency drops and stress increases.

**informed consent (Chapter 7):** A form stating that the participants in an evaluation study have been informed of these facts and agree to participate in the study.

**instructional psychology (Chapter 3):** An academic field of study that emphasizes how the learning environment can be structured to maximize learning. It focuses on what must be done *before* learning can take place and on the acquisition of human competence.

**instructor/facilitator (Chapter 1):** An individual who presents materials and leads and facilitates structured learning experiences. Within the HRD framework, the outputs for such an individual would include the selection of appropriate instructional methods and techniques and the actual HRD program itself.

**instrumentality (Chapter 2):** The connection an individual perceives (if any) between his or her own task performance and possible outcomes.

**integrated competency model (Chapter 13):** A model that can be used to describe the managerial job and design management development efforts. Along with the four-dimensional model, it provides a conceptual basis to view the role of managers within a specific organization and the competencies managers need to perform effectively.

**intelligent computer-assisted instruction (ICAI) (Chapter 6):** An instructional program that is able to discern the learner's capability from the learner's response patterns and by analyzing the learner's errors. The goal of ICAI systems is to provide learners with an electronic teacher's assistant that can patiently offer advice to individual learners, encourage learner practice, and stimulate learners' curiosity through experimentation.

**interference (Chapter 3):** A factor that affects the extent to which learning is retained. There are two types of interference. First, material or skills learned *before* the training session can inhibit recall of the newly learned material. Second, information learned *after* a training session may also interfere with retention.

**internal validity (Appendix 7-1):** A judgment about the accuracy of the conclusions made concerning the relationship between variables in a given study. For example, it seeks to answer the question of whether changes in employee performance were due to the HRD intervention, or whether there were other causes of this change in performance.

**interpersonal skills training (Chapters 9 and 10):** Training that focuses on an individual's relationships with others, including communication and teamwork.

**intervention strategy (Chapter 14):** A framework for diagnosing, developing, and evaluating the change process in an organization.

**intranet-based training (IBT) (Chapter 6):** A training method that uses internal computer networks for training purposes. Through IBT, trainers and HRD professionals are able to communicate with learners, conduct needs assessment and other administrative tasks, transmit course materials and other training documents, and administer tests at any time and throughout the organization, whether an employee is in the United States or located overseas.

**intranets (Chapter 6):** Computer networks that use Internet and World Wide Web technology, software tools, and protocols for finding, managing, creating, and distributing information within one organization.

**ISO 9000 (Chapter 9):** A set of standards that is directed at the quality of the processes used to create a product or service.

**job analysis (Chapter 4):** A systematic study of a job to identify its major tasks or components, as well as the knowledge, skills, abilities, and other characteristics necessary to perform that job.

**job characteristics model (Chapter 14):** An approach to job enrichment. The job characteristics model is based on the premise that jobs have five core dimensions (i.e., skill variety, task identity, task significance, autonomy, and feedback).

**job description (Chapter 4):** The portion of the job analysis that focuses on the *tasks* and *duties* in a given job.

**job design/enlargement (Chapters 2 and 14):** Job design is the development and alteration of the components of a job (such as the tasks one performs, and the scope of one's responsibilities) to improve productivity and the quality of the employee's work life. Job enlargement refers to adding more tasks of a similar nature to an existing job.

**job-duty-task method (Chapter 4):** A type of task analysis method that divides a job into the following subparts: job title, job duties, and the knowledge, skills, abilities, and other characteristics required to perform each identified task.

**job enrichment (Chapters 2 and 14):** An approach to job design that emphasizes that workers can be motivated by satisfying their survival needs, and then adding motivator factors to create job satisfaction. It typically adds tasks or responsibilities that provide more variety, responsibility, or autonomy to a given job.

**job instruction training (JIT) (Chapter 6):** A set sequence of instructional procedures used by the trainer to train employees while they work in their assigned job. It is most commonly used by supervisors to train new employees in the basic elements of their job.

**job inventory questionnaire (Chapter 4):** An approach to task analysis. A questionnaire is developed to ask people familiar with the job to identify all of its tasks. This list is then given to supervisors and job incumbents to evaluate each task in terms of its importance and the time spent performing it. This method allows for input from many people and gives numerical information about each task that can be used to

compute measures that can be analyzed with statistics.

**job posting (Chapter 12):** One of the most common career development activities, job posting involves making open positions in the organization known to current employees before advertising them to outsiders.

**job rotation (Chapters 6 and 12):** A technique that is intended to develop job-related skills, which involves a series of assignments to different positions or departments for a specified period. During this assignment, the trainee is supervised by a department employee who is responsible for orienting, training, and evaluating the trainee. Throughout the training cycle, the trainee is expected to learn about how each department functions, including key roles, policies, and procedures.

**job specification (Chapter 4):** A summary of the knowledge, skills, abilities, and other characteristics (KSAOs) that are required of employees to successfully perform a job.

**Job Training and Partnership Act (JTPA) (Chapter 9):** A law that established a federal skills training program. The JTPA replaced the Comprehensive Employment and Training Act (CETA). The goal of this program was to provide training opportunities to the unemployed, displaced, and economically disadvantaged in order to help them obtain permanent jobs. Beginning July 1, 2000, the JTPA was replaced by the Workforce Investment Act.

**knowledge (Chapter 2):** An understanding of factors or

principles related to a particular subject.

**law of effect (Chapters 2 and 3):** The theory that behavior that is followed by a pleasurable consequence will occur more frequently (a process called reinforcement), and that behavior that is followed by an aversive consequence will occur less frequently.

**leadership (Chapter 2):** The use of noncoercive influence to direct and coordinate the activities of a group toward accomplishing a goal.

**learning (Chapter 3):** A relatively permanent change in behavior, cognition, or affect that occurs as a result of one's interaction with the environment.

**learning curve (Chapter 3):** A graph that shows the rates of learning. It is typically plotted on a graph, with learning proficiency indicated vertically on the y-axis and elapsed time indicated horizontally on the x-axis.

**learning organization (Chapters 1 and 14):** An organization that seeks to learn, adapt, and change in order to create fundamental or deep-level change. Learning organizations generally embrace the following five principles: systems thinking, person mastery, mental models, building shared vision, and team learning.

**learning points (Chapter 13):** In behavior modeling training, learning points highlight the key behaviors that make up an overall desired behavior that is presented during a modeling phase.

**learning program specialist (or instructional designer) (Chapter 1):** An individual who identifies needs of the learner, develops and designs appropriate learning programs, and prepares materials and other learning aids.

**learning strategy (Chapter 3):** A learning strategy represents the behavior and thoughts a learner engages in during learning. Learning strategies are the techniques learners use to rehearse, elaborate, organize, and/or comprehend new material as well as to influence self-motivation and feelings.

**learning style (Chapter 3):** A learning style represents how individual choices made during the learning process affect what information is selected and how it is processed.

**lecture method (Chapter 6):** A training method that involves the oral presentation of information by a subject matter expert to a group of listeners. It is a widely used training technique because of its efficiency in transmitting factual information to a large audience in a relatively short amount of time. When used in conjunction with visual aids, such as slides, charts, maps, and handouts, the lecture can be an effective way to facilitate the transfer of theories, concepts, procedures, and other factual material.

**lesson plan (Chapter 5):** A guide for the delivery of the content of a training program. Creating a lesson plan requires the trainer to determine in advance what is to be covered and how much time to devote to each part of the session.

**licensure (Chapter 9):** A credential granted by a governmental agency indicating that an individual is official/officially qualified.

**managed care (Chapter 11):** An arrangement where an organization, such as a health maintenance organization (HMO), insurance company, or doctor-hospital network, acts as an intermediary between a person seeking care and the physician. The general purpose of managed care is to increase the efficiency and decrease the costs of healthcare.

**management education (Chapter 13):** The acquisition of a broad range of conceptual knowledge and skills in formal classroom situations in degree-granting institutions.

**management training (Chapter 13):** A component of management development that focuses on providing specific skills or knowledge that could be immediately applied within an organization and/or to a specific position or set of positions within an organization.

**management training and development (Chapters 1 and 13):** Training programs that focus on current or future managers, and that emphasize strategic management concepts as well as developing a broader or more global perspective among managers. This broader perspective is considered essential for managing in today's highly competitive environment.

**managing diversity (Chapter 15):** A comprehensive managerial process for developing an environment (or organizational culture) that works to the benefit of all employees. This approach focuses on building an environment for everyone and on the full utilization of the total workforce. It does not exclude women or minorities, nor does it exclude whites or males. It attempts to create a level playing field for all employees without regard to cultural distinction.

**material safety data sheets (MSDS) (Chapter 9):** Sheets containing information provided by manufacturers explaining potential product hazards and safety information. This information is part of an employee's legal right to know what products are within their working environment.

**meaningfulness of material (Chapter 3):** The extent to which material is rich in associations for the individual learner.

**Mental Health Parity Act of 1996 (Chapter 11):** A law that took effect on January 1, 1998. It states that private employers with more than fifty employees who offer mental health coverage must offer annual and maximum lifetime dollar limits equal to those offered for "regular" medical benefits.

**mental practice (Chapter 3):** The cognitive rehearsal of a task in the absence of overt physical movement.

**mentoring (Chapters 12 and 15):** A relationship between a junior and senior member of an organization that contributes to the career development of both members.

**meta-analysis (Chapter 7):** A research technique where the researchers combine the results from many other studies on a given topic to look for average effects or correlations between variables. Meta-analyses can sometimes overcome the problems of small sample sizes that often are experienced by HRD evaluation studies.

**modeling phase (Chapter 13):** The first step of behavior modeling, in which trainees are usually shown a video clip in which a model performs the behavior to be learned.

**mode of learning (Chapter 3):** An individual's orientation toward gathering and processing information during learning.

**motivation (Chapter 2):** The psychological processes that cause the energizing, direction, and persistence of voluntary actions that are goal directed.

**needs (Chapter 2):** A deficiency state or imbalance, either physiological or psychological, that energizes and directs behavior.

**needs assessment (Chapter 4):** A process by which an organization's HRD needs are identified and articulated. It is the starting point of the HRD and training process.

**norms (Chapters 2 and 8):** Informal rules concerning appropriate behavior that are established within work groups. These unwritten rules often serve to control behavior within the group. At the least, norms serve as guidelines for appropriate behavior, if the employee chooses to comply. Norms send a clear message about what behavior is expected, and may lead employees to behave in ways that differ from their typical patterns.

**Occupational Safety and Health Act (OSHA) (Chapter 9):** A Congressional Act passed in 1970 that promotes safety in the workplace and created the Occupational Safety and Health Administration.

**Occupational Safety and Health Administration (OSHA) (Chapter 9):** This agency has four primary responsibilities: (1) establish safety standards, (2) conduct safety inspections, (3) grant safety variances for organizations unable to comply with standards, and (4) cite organizations where standards are violated.

**on-site safety observation (OSO) (Chapter 9):** A way for organizations to take a proactive approach to improve their safety training efforts. An OSO is a formal, structured approach for conducting a safety needs assessment.

**on-the-job experiences (Chapter 13):** Planned or unplanned opportunities for a manager to gain self-knowledge, enhance existing skills and abilities, or obtain new skills or information within the context of day-to-day activities (e.g., mentoring, coaching, or assignment to a task force).

**on-the-job training (OJT) (Chapter 6):** A training method that involves conducting training at a trainee's regular workstation (desk, machine, etc.). This is the most common form of training; most employees receive at least some training and coaching on the job. Virtually any type of one-on-one instruction between coworkers or between the employee and supervisor can be classified as OJT. On-the-job training has recently been promoted as a means for organizations to deal with the shortage of applicants who possess the skills needed to perform many current jobs.

**opportunity to perform (Chapter 3):** The extent to which a trainee is provided with or actively obtains work experiences relevant to tasks for which he or she was trained.

**organizational culture (Chapters 2 and 14):** A set of values, beliefs, norms, and patterns of behavior that are shared by organization members and that guide their behavior.

**organizational socialization (Chapter 8):** The process of adjusting to a new organization. It is a learning process whereby newcomers must learn a wide variety of information and behaviors to be accepted as an organizational insider.

**organization change agent (Chapter 1):** An individual who advises management in the design and implementation of change strategies used to transform organizations. The outputs or end results for such an individual could include more efficient work teams, quality management, and change reports.

**organization design consultant (Chapter 1):** An individual who advises management on work systems design and the efficient use of human resources.

**organization development (OD) (Chapters 1 and 14):** The process of enhancing the effectiveness of an organization and the well-being of its members through planned interventions that apply behavioral science concepts. It emphasizes both macro-level and micro-level organizational changes.

**organization transformation (OT) (Chapter 14):** A theory that views organizations as complex, human systems, each with a unique character, its own culture, and a value system, along with information and work procedures that must be continually examined, analyzed, and improved if optimum productivity and motivation are to result.

**outcome expectation (Chapter 2):** A person's belief that performing a given behavior will lead to a given outcome.

**outcomes (Chapter 2):** The results of performing a behavior in a particular way. Outcomes can be personal or organizational in nature. *Personal outcomes* are those that have value to the individual, such as pay, recognition, and emotions. *Organizational outcomes* are things valued by the organization, such as teamwork, productivity, and product quality.

**outplacement counseling (Chapter 12):** Counseling that focuses on assisting terminated employees in making the transition to a new organization.

**overlearning (Chapter 3):** An amount of practice beyond the point at which the material or task is mastered.

**participative management (Chapter 10):** An approach that requires supervisors, managers, and even executives to function primarily as coaches for those who report to them.

**pedagogy (Chapter 3):** The term traditionally used for instructional methodology. This approach has most often emphasized educating children and teenagers through high school.

**people processing strategies (Chapter 8):** Actions that organizations use when socializing newcomers.

**performance appraisal (Chapter 10):** An evaluation system that typically makes use of a standardized rating form that is used to measure various aspects of employee performance. Numerical values or ratings are generally assigned to each performance dimension.

**performance appraisal interview (Chapter 10):** A meeting between a supervisor and subordinate in which the supervisor reviews the evaluation of an employee's performance and seeks to help the employee maintain and improve performance.

**performance consultant (or coach) (Chapter 1):** An individual who advises line management on appropriate interventions designed to improve individual and group performance.

**performance management (Chapter 10):** A management tactic that goes beyond the annual appraisal ratings and interviews, and seeks to incorporate employee goal setting, feedback, coaching, rewards, and individual development. Performance management focuses on an ongoing process of performance improvement, rather than primarily emphasizing an annual performance review.

**personality (Chapter 3):** The stable set of personal characteristics that account for consistent patterns of behavior.

**person analysis (Chapter 4):** The part of the needs assessment process that reveals who needs to be trained, and what kind of training they need.

**physical fidelity (Chapter 3):** The extent to which the physical conditions of the training program, such as equipment, tasks, and surroundings, are the same as those found in the performance situation.

**poor performance (Chapter 10):** Specific, agreed-upon deviations from expected behavior.

**potential assessment (Chapter 12):** The means by which organizations ensure that they have available individuals who are qualified and ready to fill key positions when these positions become vacant. This can be done through potential ratings, assessment centers, and by succession planning.

**potential ratings (Chapter 12):** An assessment process that measures multiple dimensions and includes a summary or overall rating of the employee's potential for advancement.

**practicality (Chapter 7):** A vital issue to consider when selecting a data collection method. Practicality is concerned with how much time, money, and resources are available for the evaluation method.

**practice (Chapter 3):** A theory of learning by association that holds that repeating the events in an association will increase the strength of that association.

**preretirement counseling (Chapter 12):** Activities that help employees prepare for the transition from work to nonwork. Preretirement counseling programs typically involve discussions about financial planning, social adjustment, family issues, and preparing for leisure activities.

**pretest-posttest (Chapter 7):** A practice that should be included in research design that allows the trainer to see what has changed after the training.

**procedural knowledge (Chapter 3):** A focus on how a learner is supposed to do something, as compared to knowing what to do (cf. declarative knowledge).

**process consultation (PC) (Chapter 14):** A technique that is important to team building. It is used by change agents to facilitate meetings and encounters with the team or workgroup.

**professional association (Chapter 9):** A private group that exists to advance and protect the interests of the profession and to offer services to its members (e.g., certification, publications, educational opportunities).

**protean career (Chapter 12):** The concept that individuals drive their own careers, not organizations, and that individuals reinvent their careers over time as needed.

**psychological fidelity (Chapter 3):** The extent to which trainees attach similar meanings to both the training and performance situations. Psychological fidelity would be encouraged in a learning experience that imposes time limits on training tasks that are similar to those that exist on the job.

**quality circle (Chapter 14):** An approach of involving employees in meaningful work decisions, including solving job-related problems.

**quality training (Chapter 9):** One of the five categories of technical training programs.

**random assignment (Chapter 7):** A process in training program design and evaluation whereby the trainer randomly assigns individuals to the training and control groups. This increases the researcher's confidence that any differences between the training and the control condition were brought about by the training, and not some factor that differed between individuals in the two conditions.

**realistic job preview (RJP) (Chapter 8):** Providing recruits with complete information about the job and the organization (including both positive and negative information).

**reasonable accommodation (Chapter 11):** Under the Americans with Disabilities Act, employers must make reasonable accommodations for employees with covered disabilities, before disciplining or terminating such employees. For employees with a covered condition (such as mental illness or substance abuse), this means that the employee must be offered the opportunity for treatment and have the necessary time for the treatment to take effect before firing for poor performance is justified.

**rehearsal phase (Chapter 13):** The third step in behavior modeling, in which each trainee role plays the desired behavior with another trainee.

**reinforcement theory (Chapter 2):** A noncognitive theory of motivation that argues that behavior is a function of its consequences. Rooted in behaviorism, it attempts to explain behavior without referring to unobservable internal forces such as needs or thoughts.

**reliability (Chapter 7):** The consistency of results from a test or evaluation measure. Reliability concerns freedom from error and bias in a data collection method. A method that has little or no error or bias is highly reliable, whereas the results of a method that has significant error or bias is unreliable and cannot be trusted.

**researcher (Chapter 1):** An individual who can assess HRD practices and programs using appropriate statistical procedures to determine their overall effectiveness, and then communicate the results of this assessment to the organization or public at large. Outputs include research designs, research findings, recommendations and reports.

**research design (Chapter 7):** A plan for conducting an evaluation study.

**retention phase (Chapter 13):** The second step in behavior modeling, in which trainees perform activities to enhance the memory of what they have observed.

**return on investment (ROI) (Chapter 7):** A measure of the benefit the organization receives by conducting the training program. It is the ratio of the results divided by the training costs.

**reward structure (Chapter 2):** The types of rewards an organization uses, how rewards are distributed, and the criteria for reward distribution.

**role (Chapter 8):** A set of behaviors expected of individuals who hold a given position in a group. Roles define how a person fits into the organization and what he or she must do to perform effectively.

**role ambiguity (Chapter 8):** A situation where the employee feels his or her role is unclear. This is often the result of assuming a newly created position.

**role conflict (Chapter 8):** When an employee receives mixed messages about what is expected of him or her by others, such as a boss and coworkers.

**role orientation (Chapter 8):** The extent to which individuals are innovative in interpreting their organizational roles, versus "custodial" in maintaining what has been done in that role previously.

**role overload (Chapter 8):** A situation where the employee perceives the role as being more than he or she can reasonably do.

**role playing (Chapter 6):** A training method in which trainees are presented with an organizational situation, assigned a role or character in the situation, and asked to act out the role with one or more other trainees. The role play should offer trainees an opportunity for self-discovery and learning.

**safety training (Chapter 9):** Organizational training efforts designed to promote workplace safety.

**school-to-work programs (Chapter 9):** Efforts to prepare young people for skilled positions. Many such programs emphasize youth apprenticeships and technical preparation.

**self-assessment activities (Chapter 12):** Activities, such as self-study workbooks or career and retirement planning workshops, that focus on providing employees with a systematic way to identify capabilities and career preferences.

**self-efficacy (Chapter 2):** A person's judgments of his or her capabilities to organize and execute a course of action required to attain a designated type or level of performance. Self-efficacy is not as focused on the skills one has, but with the judgments of what one can do with whatever skills one possesses.

**self-fulfilling prophecy (Chapter 2):** The notion that expectations of performance can become reality because people strive to behave consistently with their perceptions of reality.

**self-managed teams (SMTs) (Chapter 14):** Formal groups in which the group members are interdependent and have the authority to regulate the team's activities.

**self-report data (Chapter 7):** Data provided directly by individuals involved in the training program. It is the most commonly used type of data in HRD evaluation, but also has serious weaknesses in terms of the potential value for HRD evaluation.

**self-selection (Chapter 8):** A process that an applicant goes through to evaluate whether the job and the organization match his or her individual needs. If they are incompatible, the applicant will probably not accept the position, thus keeping the organization from hiring someone who would likely be dissatisfied and quit.

**skill-acquisition interventions (Chapter 11):** Programs designed to provide employees with new ways to cope with stressors affecting their lives and performance and help keep the effects of stress in check.

**skills (Chapter 2):** A combination of abilities and capabilities that are developed as a result of training and experience.

**skills training (Chapter 1):** A training program that is typically more narrow in scope. Skill training is often used to teach a new employee a particular skill or area of knowledge. It includes ways to ensure that employees possess the specific skills (such as literacy,

technological, and interpersonal skills) that they need to perform effectively and contribute to the organization's success.

**social learning theory (Chapter 2):** A cognitive theory of motivation that holds that outcomes and self-efficacy expectations affect individual performance. It highlights the judgments that a person makes concerning what he or she can do with the skills she or he possesses. It also emphasizes that most behavior is learned through a process called modeling, that is, by observing others.

**social loafing (Chapter 2):** The tendency for group members to reduce their effort as the size of the group increases.

**sociotechnical systems (STS) interventions (Chapter 14):** A change theory that emphasizes the fit between the technological configuration and the social structure of a work unit. The relationship between social and technical systems can impact the roles, tasks, and activities in the work unit. Emphasis is often placed on developing self-maintaining, semiautonomous groups.

**static media (Chapter 6):** Fixed illustrations that use both words and images. This can include printed materials, computer slides, and overhead transparencies.

**statistical power (Appendix 7-1):** The ability to detect statistically significant differences between a group that gets trained and one that does not. There are practical limitations in many HRD interventions that limit the number of people receiving the intervention (or in the control group) to a relatively small number, thus limiting the statistical power of many HRD interventions.

**statistical process control (SPC) (Chapter 9):** A quality tool that helps to determine if a process is stable and predictable, identify common causes of variation, and clarify when employee intervention is needed. The principle underlying SPC is that most processes demonstrate variations in output and that it is important to determine whether the causes of such a variation are normal or abnormal. SPC focuses on training employees to be able to discern abnormal variations, so that adjustments can be made to the process in order to improve quality.

**stimulus-response-feedback method (Chapter 4):** A method for identifying and describing the major tasks that make up a job. The stimulus-response-feedback method breaks down each task into three components. The first component is the stimulus, or cue, that lets an employee know it is time to perform a particular behavior. The second component is the response or behavior that the employee is to perform. The third component is the feedback the employee receives about how well the behavior was performed.

**strategic change (Chapter 14):** Any fundamental change in the organizational purpose or mission requiring systemwide changes.

**strategic/organizational analysis (Chapter 4):** An aspect of needs assessment that reveals where in the organization training is needed and

under what conditions it will occur. Strategic/organizational analysis focuses on the organization's goals and its effectiveness in achieving those goals, organizational resources, the climate for training, and any environmental constraints.

**stress (Chapter 11):** A common aspect of the work experience. It is expressed most frequently as job dissatisfaction, but it is also expressed in more intense affective states — anger, frustration, hostility, and irritation. More passive responses are also common, for example, boredom and tedium, burnout, fatigue, helplessness, hopelessness, lack of vigor, and depressed mood. Job stress is related to lowered self-confidence and self-esteem. Complaints about health can be considered as psychological responses to stress, or they can be treated as indicative of some illness.

**stress management intervention (SMI) (Chapter 11):** Any activity, program, or opportunity initiated by an organization that focuses on reducing the presence of work-related stressors or on assisting individuals to minimize the negative outcomes of exposure to these stressors.

**stressor (Chapter 11):** An environmental force affecting an individual.

**subject matter expert (SME) (Chapter 5):** Individuals with particular expertise on a given topic. Many train-the-trainer programs seek to provide SMEs with the necessary knowledge and skills to design and implement a training program.

**succession planning (Chapter 12):** A way of conducting evaluations of employee potential. This process, which is done primarily for senior management positions, requires senior managers to identify employees who should be developed to replace them.

**survey feedback (Chapter 14):** The systematic feedback of survey data to groups with the intent of stimulating discussion of problem areas, generating potential solutions, and stimulating motivation for change.

**task analysis (Chapters 3 and 4):** An aspect of needs assessment that emphasizes what trainees need to be able to do to do their job or complete a process effectively.

**task identification (Chapter 4):** A step in the task analysis process. It focuses on the behaviors performed within the job, including the major tasks within the job, how each task should be performed (i.e., performance standards), and the variability of performance (how the tasks are actually performed in day-to-day operations).

**task sequencing (Chapter 3):** A principle concerning how learning can be improved. It suggests that the learning situation should be arranged so that each of the component tasks is learned in the appropriate order before the total task is attempted.

**team building (Chapters 9 and 14):** An effort to unify varied individual energies, direct these energies toward valued goals and outputs, and link these efforts to organizational results. It typically refers to a collection of techniques that are designed to build the trust, cohesiveness, and mutual sense of

responsibility that are needed for effective teamwork.

**team training (Chapter 9):** Training that emphasizes the use of teams as the basic organizational unit; it requires that workers be adaptable and able to form and re-form relationships with coworkers quickly and smoothly.

**teamwork (Chapter 2):** Emphasizes the influence of coworkers on individual behavior, and brings other interpersonal dynamics to the forefront. Two important issues for teamwork are trust and cohesiveness.

**technical training (Chapter 9):** A type of training that involves upgrading a wide range of technical skills (such as computer skills) needed by particular individuals in an organization.

**technostructural theory (Chapter 14):** A type of change intervention that is designed to (1) improve work content, work method, and the relationships among workers and (2) lower costs by replacing inefficient materials, methods, equipment, workflow designs, and unnecessary labor with more efficient technology.

**telecommunications (Chapter 6):** Methods for transmitting training programs to different locations, such as via satellite, microwave, cable (CATV), and fiber-optic networks.

**time sampling (Chapter 4):** A task identification method that involves having a trained observer watch and note the nature and frequency of an employee's activities. By observing at random intervals over a period, a clearer picture of the job is understood and recorded.

**time series design (Chapter 7):** The collection of data over time, which allows the trainer to observe patterns in individual performance.

**total quality management (TQM) (Chapter 14):** A set of concepts and tools intended to focus all employees on continuous improvement, emphasizing quality as viewed through the eyes of the customer.

**trainability (Chapter 3):** The trainee's readiness to learn. It combines the trainee's levels of ability and motivation with his or her perceptions of support in the work environment.

**training and development (T&D) (Chapter 1):** Training and development focus on changing or improving the knowledge, skills, and attitudes of individuals. *Training* typically involves providing employees the knowledge and skills needed to do a particular task or job, though attitude change may also be attempted (e.g., in sexual harassment training). *Developmental* activities, in contrast, have a longer-term focus on preparing for future responsibilities while also increasing the capacities of employees to perform in their current jobs.

**training competency (Chapter 5):** The knowledge and varied skills needed to design and implement a training program.

**training design (Chapter 3):** Adapting the learning environment to maximize learning.

**training manual (Chapter 5):** The instructional materials used for training. This can include basic instructional material, readings, exercises, and self-tests.

**training methods (Chapter 5):** Instructional approaches including both on-the-job training as well as various classroom (off-site) techniques. The selection of the appropriate technique should be guided by the specific objectives to be obtained, as well as by participant expertise.

**training program objectives (Chapter 5):** A collection of words, symbols, pictures and/or diagrams describing what you intend for trainees to achieve.

**train-the-trainer programs (Chapter 5):** A training program that identifies in-house content experts (subject matter experts) who lack training skills, and then trains them to become effective trainers.

**transfer of training (Chapter 3):** The ability to apply what is learned in training back on the job. Transfer can be viewed as ranging on a scale from positive to zero to negative. Positive transfer occurs when job performance is improved as a result of training, zero transfer when there is no change in performance, and negative transfer when performance on the job is worse as a result of training.

**transfer of training climate (Chapter 3):** Those situations and consequences that either inhibit or help to facilitate the transfer of what has been learned in training back to the job situation.

**transfer of training phase (Chapter 13):** The fifth step in behavior modeling, in which trainees are encouraged to practice the newly learned behavior on the job.

**transformational leadership (Chapter 13):** The idea that leaders are those who capture our attention, present us with a vision of what could be, inspire us to pursue the vision, and show us the way to get there.

**treatment discrimination (Chapter 15):** A type of discrimination that occurs after a person is hired and takes the form of limiting opportunities (e.g., training, promotion, rewards) or harassing certain individuals because of who they are (e.g., women, minorities).

**trust (Chapter 2):** The expectations that another person (or group of people) will act benevolently toward you.

**utility analysis (Chapter 7):** A computation that measures in dollar terms the effect of an HRD program in terms of a change in some aspect of the trainee's performance.

**valence (Chapter 2):** Valence refers to the value the person places on a particular outcome. Valence judgments range from strongly positive (for highly valued outcomes), through zero (for outcomes the person doesn't care about), to strongly negative (for outcomes the person finds aversive).

**validity (Chapter 7):** A vital issue to consider when selecting a data collection method. Validity is concerned with whether the data collection method actually measures what it is intended to measure, that is, are we hitting the right target?

**value shaping (Chapter 10):** A way to encourage continued effective performance through coaching. Value shaping begins with recruiting and orientation of new employees and is continued through training and in the manner that the manager relates to employees every day.

**valuing differences (Chapter 15):** An approach to workforce diversity that emphasizes building employee awareness of differences between members of various demographic categories.

**videoconferencing (Chapter 6):** Conducting conferences between remote locations using telecommunications technology.

**Voluntary Protection Program (Chapter 9):** An effort to help organizations meet the demands of proper safety training that has been developed by OSHA. This program encourages organizations to work in conjunction with OSHA to establish workplace safety programs.

**wellness (Chapter 11):** Condition of being mentally and physically healthy, usually as a result of an individual's diet and exercise.

**Worker Adjustment and Retraining Notification (WARN) Act (Chapter 9):** An act that requires any employer with 100 or more employees to give sixty days advance notice of a plant closure to both the employees and the unions.

# NAME INDEX

# NAME INDEX